WILLIAM SHARMAN CRAWFORD AND ULSTER RADICALISM

WILLIAM SHARMAN CRAWFORD AND ULSTER RADICALISM

Peter Gray

UNIVERSITY COLLEGE DUBLIN PRESS
PREAS CHOLÁISTE OLLSCOILE BHAILE ÁTHA CLIATH
2023

First published 2023
by University College Dublin Press
UCD Humanities Institute, Room H103,
Belfield,
Dublin 4

www.ucdpress.ie

ISBN 978-19-1-08204-38

CIP data available from the British Library

The right of Peter Gray to be identified as the author of this work has been asserted by him

Typeset in Dublin by Gough Typesetting Limited
Text design by Lyn Davies
Printed in England on acid-free paper by
CPI UK, Bumpers Farm, Chippenham, Wiltshire, SN14 6LH, UK

To Emily, with love

Contents

List of Illustrations

20. John Prescott Knight, 'William Sharman Crawford', c. 1843, oil on canvas (BELUM U.4501). Courtesy of National Museums of Northern Ireland.

21. Print of William Sharman Crawford (after T. G. Lupton and J. P. Knight) with autograph, n.d. (T1129/411). Courtesy of Public Record Office of Northern Ireland.

22. 'HB' (John Doyle), 'HB Sketches no. 822: "Dropping it like a Red-Hot Poker!"', 28 Dec. 1844, lithograph. Courtesy of National Library of Ireland.

23. 'Ejectment of Irish Tenantry', *Illustrated London News*, 16 Dec. 1848, p. 380.

24. 'Parliamentary Portraits: Mr Sharman Crawford, M.P. for Rochdale', *Illustrated London News*, 5 May 1849, p. 285.

25. 'Great Tenant-right Meeting at Kilkenny', *Illustrated London News*, 5 Oct. 1850, p. 281.

26. Handbill, 'Tenant-right and Free Trade. County of Down Election', n.d. [1852], in Crossle family scrapbook (T1689/2/66). Courtesy of Public Record Office of Northern Ireland.

27. Handbill with interim polling figures for Co. Down election, 23 July 1852 (D1252/24/5). Courtesy of Public Record Office of Northern Ireland.

28. Carte-de-visite portrait photograph of Arthur Sharman Crawford, n.d. [c. 1860-1], Coey album (BELUM.Y39038.49). Courtesy of National Museums of Northern Ireland.

29. Oliver Sarony (?), Carte-de-visite portrait photograph of William Sharman Crawford, n.d. [c. 1860-1], Coey album (BELUM.Y39038.163). Courtesy of National Museums of Northern Ireland.

30. 'The late Mr Wm Sharman Crawford, M.P. Presented gratis with "The Belfast Weekly Post". 23rd Sept. 1882' (T1129/412). Courtesy of Public Record Office of Northern Ireland.

31. The Sharman Crawford mausoleum, Kilmore graveyard, Co. Down (author's photograph, 2019).

32. The William Sharman Crawford monument, Rademon, Co. Down, 1863–5 (author's photograph, 2019).

33. Detail of the William Sharman Crawford monument, Rademon, Co. Down: the bronze medallion by S. F. Lynn, 1865 (author's photograph, 2019).

34. Anon., 'The Irish Rent Office before and since the passing of the Land Bill in 1870', *The Annals of Ulster Tenant-Right, by an Antrim Tenant-Farmer* (n.p., n.d. [Belfast, c. 1877]), pp 1–2. Courtesy of Linenhall Library.

35. 'The late Mr Ja[me]s Sharman Crawford, M.P.', n.d. (c. 1882), print (T1129/413). Courtesy of Public Record Office of Northern Ireland.

36. 'Major John Sharman Crawford, J.P., D.L. Presented gratis with "The Belfast Weekly Post". 7th Octr. 1882', print (T1129/414). Courtesy of Public Record Office of Northern Ireland.

37. 'El Kantara', frontispiece to Mabel Sharman Crawford, *Through Algeria* (London, 1863). Courtesy of National Library of Ireland.

38. 'Women's Suffrage – The National Demonstration at St James's Hall', *The Graphic*, 22 May 1880, p. 516.

39. 'Sir Edward with Lady Carson, and Lt-Gen. Sir George Richardson, talking to

Acknowledgements

As with all historical projects, this one has been dependent on the support of institutions, archives and many individuals. Research leave granted by Queen's University Belfast in 2015–16 and 2019 was essential to pursue archival research and to write, and I am thankful for the support from the staff of my academic home in the School of History, Anthropology, Philosophy and Politics, and especially its then head, Alister Miskimmon, and our Irish Studies' administrator Cathy Devlin. Financial assistance with publishing was provided by the School and the Faculty of Arts, Humanities and Social Sciences. The staff of the Public Record Office of Northern Ireland have been extremely helpful, despite all the unforeseen disruptions imposed on staff and researchers by the Covid epidemic of 2020–2. I would like to thank the Deputy Keeper of the Records, the Public Record Office of Northern Ireland, for permission to cite material and reproduce certain images in its collections, and to the Dufferin Foundation (Dufferin and Ava Papers), National Museums of Northern Ireland (Tennent Papers), M. A. A. Crawford (F.H. Crawford Diary), and the late Sir Roland T Nugent, the late Lady Nugent and the late Mrs Elizabeth Cooke (Nugent Papers). I'm also grateful to librarians and archivists at the British Library, UK National Archives Kew, Royal Irish Academy, National Archives of Ireland, National Library of Ireland, Linen Hall Library, Downpatrick Library, Manchester Archives, Rochdale Local Studies Library, Durham County Record Office and Queen's University Special Collections (amongst others), for facilitating access to their collections. Gladstone's Library in Hawarden provided a vital and inspirational writing retreat location in autumn 2019, and I am especially grateful to the then warden Peter Francis for his hospitality. In the same year Frank Boyd very kindly responded to my inquiries and gave me a tour of Rademon house and demesne and the nearby Sharman Crawford mausoleum at Kilmore. I have had stimulating conversations on the Sharman Crawfords and their contexts in recent years, and on Irish history more generally, with many historians, including my Queen's University Belfast colleagues, Ian Campbell, Marie Coleman, Elaine Farrell, Crawford Gribben, David Hayton, Liam Kennedy, Fearghal McGarry, Margaret O'Callaghan, Mary O'Dowd, Diane Urquhart, and Olwen Purdue, and in other places with Anthony Daly, Terry Dooley, Sean Farrell, Tim McMahon, Sarah Roddy and Jonathan Wright, as well as Marguerite Corporaal and members of the 'Heritages of Hunger' research network. Several papers drawn from the developing manuscript were presented at the Institute of Irish Studies QUB, at the European Social Science History Conference, the American Conference for Irish Studies, the Ulster Society for Irish Historical Studies and the Society for the Study of Nineteenth-Century Ireland, and I'd like to thank audiences at each for their questions and comments. I am particularly grateful to my colleagues Andrew Holmes and Sean Connolly for reading and commenting on sections of the text, and to two anonymous reviewers for their insights and suggestions. All errors remain of course the responsibility of the author. Above all I am indebted to Emily Mark-FitzGerald, without whose unfailing support and wisdom this book may never have come to completion.

Peter Gray
Belfast, July 2023

List of Abbreviations

AG – *Armagh Guardian*
BC – *Bolton Chronicle*
BCC – *Belfast Commercial Chronicle*
BDN – *Belfast Daily News*
BEP – *Belfast Evening Post*
BFP – *Ballymoney Free Press*
BL – British Library, London
BM – *Belfast Mercury*
BMN – *Belfast Morning News*
BNL – *Belfast News-Letter*
BO – *Bradford Observer*
BOG – Board of Guardians
BOU – *Banner of Ulster*
BPJ – *Belfast Protestant Journal*
BS – *Blackburn Standard*
BT – *Belfast Telegraph*
BV – *Belfast Vindicator*
BWN – *Belfast Weekly News*
BWT – *Belfast Weekly Telegraph*
CC – *Coleraine Chronicle*
CDS – *County Down Spectator*
CE – *Cork Examiner*
DCRO – Durham County Record Office, Durham
DEM – *Dublin Evening Mail*
DEP – *Dublin Evening Post*
DEPa – *Dublin Evening Packet*
DEPr – *Dublin Evening Press*
DIB – *Dictionary of Irish Biography*
DM – *Dublin Monitor*
DN – *Daily News*
DOC – Daniel O'Connell
DR – *Downpatrick Recorder*
EC – *Evening Chronicle*
EF – *Evening Freeman*
EM – *Evening Mail*
EN – *Evening News*
ER – *Englishwoman's Review*
ES – *Evening Standard*
FJ – *Freeman's Journal*
FLJ – *Finn's Leinster Journal*
Hans. – *Hansard's Parliamentary Debates, 3rd – 5th Series*
HJ – *Hibernian Journal*

HOP 1820–32 – D. R. Fisher (ed.), *The History of Parliament: The House of Commons 1820–1832* (Cambridge, 2009)
IHS – Irish Historical Studies
ILN – Illustrated London News
IN – Irish News
IT – Irish Times
ITL – Irish Tenant League
KJ – Kilkenny Journal
LE – Limerick Examiner
LJ – Londonderry Journal
LM – Leeds Mercury
LNRA – Loyal National Repeal Association
LS – Londonderry Standard
LT – Leeds Times
LWMA – London Working Men's Association
MA – Morning Advertiser
MC – Morning Chronicle
MCo – Manchester Courier
MG – Manchester Guardian
MP – Member of Parliament
MPo – Morning Post
MR – Morning Register
MT – Manchester Times
NAI – National Archives of Ireland, Dublin
NC – Newtownards Chronicle
NCA – National Charter Association
NCSU – National Complete Suffrage Union
NDH – North Down Herald
NE – Newry Examiner
NL – Northern Liberator
NLI – National Library of Ireland, Dublin
NMNI – National Museums of Northern Ireland
NS – Northern Star
NT – Newry Telegraph
NW – Northern Whig
ODNB – Oxford Dictionary of National Biography
PMG – Pall Mall Gazette
PRONI – Public Record Office of Northern Ireland, Belfast
RIA – Royal Irish Academy, Dublin
SC – Sharman Crawford
SI – Sheffield Independent
SNL – Saunder's News-Letter
SR – Southern Reporter
TFP – Tipperary Free Press
TNA – The National Archives, Kew
TV – Tipperary Vindicator

UAFP – Ulster American Folk Park
UCA – Ulster Constitutional Association
UE – Ulster Examiner
UI – United Irishman
UJA – Ulster Journal of Archaeology
UK – United Kingdom
UUC – Ulster Unionist Council
UUP – Ulster Unionist Party
UVF – Ulster Volunteer Force
VJ – Volunteers Journal
WI – Wexford Independent
WP – Weekly Press
WR – Weekly Register
WS – William Sharman
WSC – William Sharman Crawford
WT – Weekly Telegraph

Sharman Crawford Family Tree

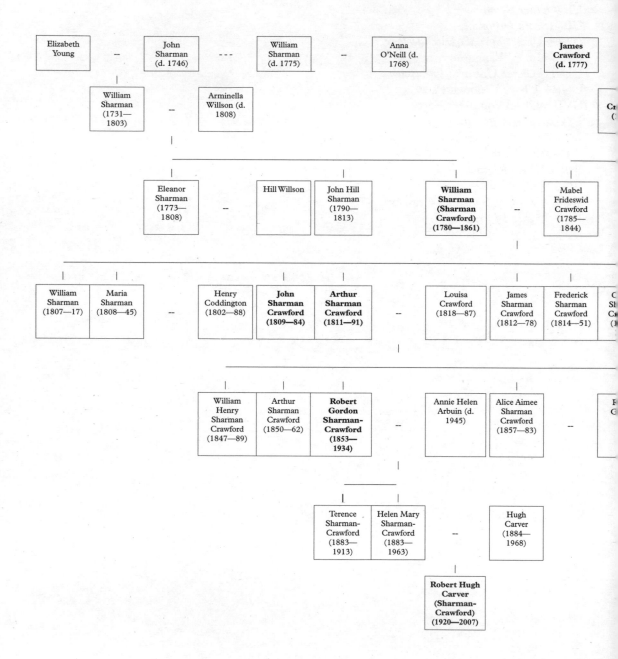

Elizabeth Young — John Sharman (d. 1746) - - - William Sharman (d. 1775) — Anna O'Neill (d. 1768) — James Crawford (d. 1777)

William Sharman (1731—1803) — Arminella Willson (d. 1808)

Cr (

Eleanor Sharman (1773—1808) — Hill Willson — John Hill Sharman (1790—1813) — William Sharman (Sharman Crawford) (1780—1861) — Mabel Frideswid Crawford (1785—1844)

William Sharman (1807—17) — Maria Sharman (1808—45) — Henry Coddington (1802—88) — John Sharman Crawford (1809—84) — Arthur Sharman Crawford (1811—91) — Louisa Crawford (1818—87) — James Sharman Crawford (1812—78) — Frederick Sharman Crawford (1814—51) — C Sh C (1

William Henry Sharman Crawford (1847—89) — Arthur Sharman Crawford (1850—62) — Robert Gordon Sharman-Crawford (1853—1934) — Annie Helen Arbuin (d. 1945) — Alice Aimee Sharman Crawford (1857—83) — F G

Terence Sharman-Crawford (1883—1913) — Helen Mary Sharman-Crawford (1883—1963) — Hugh Carver (1884—1968)

Robert Hugh Carver (Sharman-Crawford) (1920—2007)

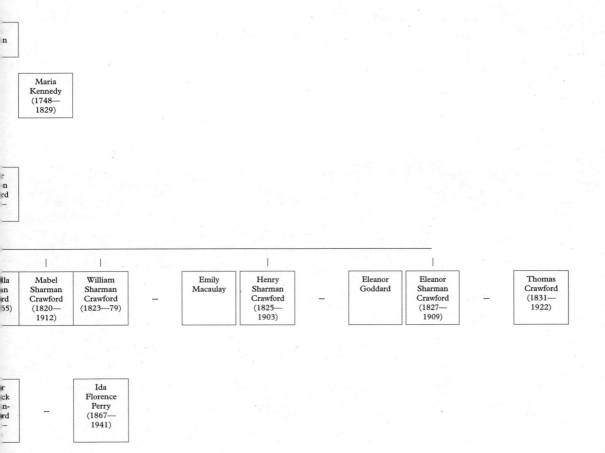

Owners of Crawfordsburn House are marked in bold.

Introduction

At the height of the devastating Great Irish Famine in 1849 William Sharman Crawford denounced his fellow Irish landlords for their heartless clearances of the rural population, which had shown 'a refinement of cruelty disgraceful to any civilized country, and which the ruling powers permit to go on with a seemingly placid assent'. Not content with accusing his own class with actions tantamount to mass murder, he then charged the members of the United Kingdom parliament with complicity:

> Will you, with reckless prejudice, be the instruments of exterminating that people over whom you hold the power, in order to carry into effect your favorite theory of consolidating the lands of Ireland for the use of capitalist farmers, and converting the Irish peasants, into the hired labourers of these monied masters? The Irish peasant, did I say? Only a very small proportion of those peasants can be employed in that manner, after you have in the same way or other rid yourselves of the surplus.[1]

These words in his pamphlet *Depopulation Not Necessary* were inflected with an indignant anger at what he saw happening to the people of his country, which informed his political response to the disaster. At first sight they appear to bear some similarity to the better-known accusation levelled by his fellow Protestant Ulsterman, the republican revolutionary John Mitchel, that 'a million and a half of men, women and children were carefully, prudently, and peacefully *slain* by the English government'.[2]

Sharman Crawford was, however, no revolutionary, but rather a man whose political life was committed to the pursuit of democratic reform, social and economic justice, and the redefinition of the relationship between Britain and Ireland through the mobilisation of non-violent popular politics. Nor, unlike Mitchel, was he a nationalist; he strongly identified with a patriotic Irishness that looked back to the enlightenment ideals of the later eighteenth century but adopted a pragmatic stance towards the constitutional polarities of the nineteenth. This book sets out to explain his political life, the reasons for his antagonism towards his own class, the origins, popularity and limitations of the strand of political radicalism he embraced and personified, which he believed deeply rooted in the soil of Ulster, and his legacies to Ulster, Irish and British politics.

To do so, we will need to explore the roots of his radicalism in the career of his father, William Sharman of Moira, who transcended the conventional Anglo-Irish gentry politics of his upbringing to emerge in the 1780s as one of the foremost 'patriotic' radical reformers associated with the Volunteer movement in Ulster. The younger William self-consciously modelled himself on his father's example and sought to render the ideals of the Volunteers' Dungannon Conventions relevant in the changed political and social landscape of the

1

nineteenth century. In exploring the impact and legacies of what became known as 'Sharman Crawfordism', we will also need also to travel beyond William Sharman Crawford's death in 1861 to review how his own children sought to maintain and enhance the radical family tradition in the 1870s-90s, as well as how that tradition became inverted in the following era of polarisation around home rule and the partition of Ireland.

At first sight William Sharman Crawford appears to embody a series of contradictions. A landed country gentleman with holdings scattered across Counties Down, Antrim and Meath, he emerged as the foremost Irish agrarian reformer of his day, becoming widely known and respected as the consistent advocate of legislation to empower the tenant farmer and curb landlordism. His own estate management consciously sought to turn his tenants from subordinates into economic partners, leading many to describe him as the ideal Irish landlord and others to attack him as a deluded and self-promoting eccentric. Looking beyond the tenant farming class, he also advocated effective welfare and employment entitlements for the labouring poor, and sought to promote this on his own estates and through active local engagement with the new Irish poor law after 1838 and in his reaction to the Famine.

Born as William Sharman into the privilege of gentry status in an acutely hierarchical society, by the late 1830s he had become a consistent advocate of democratic political reform and in 1841 was endorsed by the working-class British Chartist movement as a national spokesman for universal male suffrage. At first a sincere Anglican Protestant, he made his strongest political alliances with reformist Presbyterians, but also consistently supported Catholic emancipation and freedom of religion, and came to advocate the abolition of tithes and the disestablishment of his own church before ultimately converting to Unitarianism. An avowedly patriotic Irishman, he opposed any move towards constitutional or commercial separation from Britain, a stance which transformed an early friendship into a long-running and highly public feud with the nationalist tribune Daniel O'Connell. Yet he also consistently supported a variety of Irish self-government in the form of 'federalism', a concept which after his death would be reinvented as 'home rule'.

Based from 1827 at Crawfordsburn House in north Down, Sharman Crawford was initially focused on his home county and the adjacent industrial boom town of Belfast, but his politics soon extended beyond any Ulster sectionalism to embrace reform for the whole island. Yet he refused to take an exclusively insular viewpoint, identifying a potential for a radical democratic alliance between Irish reformers and the British working class and northern middle class, and made the industrial Lancashire town of Rochdale his adopted political home between 1841 and 1852 as the borough's MP. His interests extended beyond the domestic to opposition towards British wars of imperial expansion and fervent support for the campaigns to end slavery in the British empire and the United States. A late starter in political life – he was already 48 when he first spoke on a platform in support of Catholic emancipation in 1829 – for the remainder of his life until his death in 1861 he appeared driven by an intense and highly personal sense of radical mission which led to him rarely being far from public controversy.

Despite three decades of vigorous political exertion Sharman Crawford's career ended in apparent failure. None of his repeatedly proposed agrarian reforms were passed in his lifetime; the Irish poor law of 1838 was at best a pale and oppressive shadow of the humane welfare measure he had advocated in the 1830s; his brand of federalism faded from public debate after moments of wider interest in 1843–4 and 1848; democratic political reforms in the UK had to wait for the reluctant and gradually staged concessions by British governments from 1867 onwards. In his lifetime he was frequently mocked in both Britain and Ireland as 'crotchetty Crawford', and lambasted alternately as an 'impracticable', a 'communist' and as a conservative dressed in radical clothing. He lost three of the six electoral contests he fought, several of which generated intense emotion and outbursts of street violence. Politically thick-skinned, he manifested an extraordinary level of sheer obstinacy (in the Ulster-Scots dialect of his homeland, he could be described as 'thran') in continuing to adhere quixotically to what appeared lost causes, albeit with some reward in attaining significant levels of genuine personal popularity, especially in rural Co. Down and in industrial Belfast and Rochdale. To at least one obituarist, his fame lay not in his (elusive) successes, but in his moral adherence to what appeared the 'forlorn hope' of real change; he was:

> one of those pioneers of progress who are content to labour on in faith, and find in the working out of their own convictions, a satisfaction that ordinary politicians can only derive from the realisation of their aims. Firm as a rock in adherence to his principles, his integrity of character, modesty of demeanour, and singleness of purpose extorted the respect of all parties, despite his radical creed.[3]

Though thus thwarted during his lifetime, Sharman Crawford's achievement lay not in legislative success but in the articulation and dogged advocacy, within the UK parliament and in the wider public domain, of principles and proposals which would come to political maturity a generation or two later. William Gladstone's 1870 and 1881 Irish land acts drew on (and eventually surpassed) the measures Crawford had advanced between 1835 and 1852. The at least partly successful Irish National Land League campaign of 1879–82 built on foundations laid by the Tenant League movement of the late 1840s and early 1850s, in which Crawford played a prominent if controversial role. Although not alone, he had been one of the handful of uncompromisingly pro-democratic voices in parliament in the 1840s, ensuring that Chartist and Complete Suffrage Union outdoor agitations could not simply be ignored by the government and parliamentary opposition. He also, as we have seen, conscientiously critiqued the British government's appalling failure to respond adequately to the Great Famine in 1845–50, and, while unable to change a policy he denounced as leading to 'extermination' of the peasantry, made it clear that alternative, more humane relief and developmental policies were possible if the political will had been manifest. Later administrations were more conscious of the political dangers of repeating these policy mistakes during the hunger crises of 1879-82 and in the mid-1890s.

Sharman Crawford thus led an oppositional political life, driven by a profound personal rejection of the hierarchical claims and assumptions of his own class background, while at the same time believing his inherited educational and social privilege made incumbent on him a responsibility of leadership and popular advocacy. Despite claims made by his enemies, he was not a socialist, regarding some degree of social differentiation as inevitable and even divinely ordained. Rather, he is best understood as a radical democratic liberal, convinced that social cohesion and human progress could only be attained by ensuring equity and partnership between social classes based on democratic enfranchisement. To attain this, however, he believed the political and economic power of the landed elites had first to be curbed through legislation, and the middle classes weaned away from economic self-interest to full acceptance of legitimate working-class demands for political and welfare rights and socio-economic reform. Alienated from the modes of revolution and political violence after witnessing the catastrophic outcome and bloody repression of the United Irish rising in his youth in 1798 (a position he shared with O'Connell, who had surveyed the rebellion from the greater distance of his Kerry retreat of Derrynane), he was similarly committed to pursuing radical reform through constitutional means only, enlisting the power of mass outdoor agitation, but also recognising that reform would require an attritional long-term campaign against entrenched vested interests within the political system.

Sharman Crawford's rather obscure place in the historical literature arises in part from this difficulty of categorisation, the initial frustration of his initiatives, and his complex relationship to radical and national historical narratives. For understandable reasons, biographical studies of Ulster radicals of his era have leant heavily towards the Presbyterians drawn into the revolutionary excitement of the United Irishmen and their 1798 and 1803 rebellions. William Drennan, Henry Joy McCracken and Samuel Neilson have all deservedly received recent biographical treatment, and an overdue reassessment of the long radical life of Mary Ann McCracken is ongoing.[4] Southern Anglicans prominent in the revolutionary movement, including Theobald Wolfe Tone, Thomas Russell and Robert Emmet are also well served by biographers.[5] On the non-revolutionary side, the Dublin-based patriots Henry Grattan and Henry Flood are well covered, but northerners such as William Sharman remain largely neglected.[6]

Post-1803 Irish constitutionalist radicalism tends to be overshadowed by the protean figure of Daniel O'Connell. Studies of Belfast politics between the union and mid-century by Jonathan Wright and John Bew offer some biographical glimpses, especially of the Tennent family and their associates, while Gerald Hall's important survey of Ulster liberalism also provides some insights but treats it largely as a Presbyterian phenomenon.[7] This is true also of a more popular compendium of radical Presbyterian biography from the seventeenth to the twentieth centuries recently compiled by Roger Courtney.[8] More specifically, the widespread participation of the Ulster Presbyterian clergy in radical politics in 1800–52, including the tenant-right campaign and relations with Crawford, is addressed in Julie Nelson's as yet unpublished dissertation.[9] The middle-class romantics of Young Ireland have their biographers, most thoroughly in the case of William Smith O'Brien and Thomas Davis, while their constitutionalist rivals (arguably much more effective in the demotic world of 1840s popular politics if not in its literary afterlife) still tend to be overlooked, with the obvious exception of O'Connell himself.[10] Sharman Crawford is absent also from several recent volumes of collective biographies addressing Irish radical leadership since the early nineteenth century and Irish agrarian radicals.[11]

Life studies of a number of Irish landowners who threw themselves into popular politics of different descriptions draw attention to the model of the 'gentleman radical', a phenomenon better addressed for Britain in this period. There is of course an extensive literature on O'Connell, a lawyer drawn from the surviving Catholic small gentry of west Kerry, as the dominant Catholic political personality of the age. Both Feargus O'Connor, the Cork-born Protestant champion of Chartism in Britain, and Smith O'Brien, the Anglican Limerick landowner who joined the 1846 Young Ireland secession from the

Repeal Association and led the break-away Irish Confederation, bear certain similarities and had personal (sometimes strained, sometimes amicable) relationships with Crawford, and like him fell out spectacularly with O'Connell.[12] In a later generation, Charles Stewart Parnell and his sisters Anna and Fanny, children of a Wicklow-landed family with 'patriot' antecedents, might be seen as emerging from a similar landed radical tradition and desire to resolve the class war between landlord and tenant, albeit diverging widely in their approaches to this after 1882.[13]

Sharman Crawford's political actions and aspirations, embodied in a career that spanned the Irish Sea, locate him within the category of 'the popular politician' delineated by Simon James Morgan as a new and distinctive phenomenon of the era between 1810 and 1867. However, while the Irish-born O'Connell and O'Connor evidently shared with a number of English radical exemplars (such as Henry Hunt) the 'heroic' and 'celebrity' features Morgan sees as characteristic of this extravagant political style, Crawford fits this pattern much less well.[14] Although capable of deploying emotive rhetoric and evidently widely respected by popular audiences, he lacked the personal charisma of these popular tribunes, gave little attention to the dramatic self-fashioning they sought to perfect and preferred older models of persuasion through appeal to reason, interest and morality rather than to feeling. Crawford's growing alienation after 1835 from what later commentators might describe as O'Connell's 'cult of personality' demonstrated a personal unease with or distaste for the affective allegiance that the Irish leader consciously courted with his mass followers. The failure of his brief challenge for leadership of the Irish popular movement in 1836–7 is a reminder of his inability or reluctance to engage in such charismatic politics.

Sharman Crawford has been ill-served by historians, attracting only several exploratory articles by Brian Kennedy drawn from his unpublished 1953 doctoral dissertation, itself a pioneering piece of work but marred by lack of access at the time to his subject's manuscript archive.[15] There are also a few entries in recent biographical dictionaries.[16] It is the contention of this book that as a leading figure in the radical politics of Ulster, Ireland and Great Britain for the best part of three decades, as a distinct voice committed to exposing the injustices and oppressions of his times, as a man who spoke out to address the suffering of distressed handloom weavers of Belfast and Lancashire, of cleared Mayo peasants and of enslaved people in America, and as one who advocated a pioneering democratic vision, Crawford deserves a modern critical biography.

To place William Sharman Crawford into a broader landscape of Ulster radicalism, this study has adopted a four-generational approach to its subject. A core argument adopted here is that his politics cannot be understood in isolation from those of his father, Colonel William Sharman (1731–1803). His father's active leadership within the more radical elements of the Volunteer movement in Ulster, which saw him elected as 'patriot' MP for Lisburn in 1783, chair the Volunteer Committee of Correspondence liaising with advanced British parliamentary reformers that year, and preside over the 1791 celebrations in Belfast of the French Revolution, was almost constantly in the younger man's thought, a fact reflected prominently in the 1844 'retrospective memorandum' he wrote for his own children. This sense of an assertively radical-democratic, but non-revolutionary, inheritance was crucial both to his own self-formation and his engagement with the remnants of Ulster radicalism as these re-emerged in the aftermath of the 1798 cataclysm. Consequently, the first chapter of this book is devoted to explaining the development of

Colonel William Sharman's patriotic politics through the rise and fall of Volunteering in Down, Belfast and on the national stage, the beginnings of which roughly coincided with the birth of his son William junior in 1780. Through his marriage in 1805 with Mabel Frideswid Crawford (1785–1844), the younger William also united his father's political and economic inheritance with that of her family, which was had also been infused with radical patriotism in the 1780s–90s.

William Sharman Crawford (as he became known from 1827 on inheriting Mabel's father's estates) not only embodied a family tradition of radicalism, but sought to transmit this to his own offspring, thereby attempting to mould a political dynasty. At one point or another, most of his large family was involved in his political campaigning and activity. Three of his sons were eventually to stand for parliament, and a fourth was involved in Belfast municipal politics. This study will give particular attention to the careers of the two of his children who did most to carry their father's radical politics into the changing political and social environment of the later nineteenth century. His third (surviving) son James (1812–78) succeeded in 1874 where his father had failed twice, in being elected as MP for Down, and sought to advance his father's agrarian reformism within the context of Irish Gladstonian Liberalism before his unexpected early death in 1878. William's third daughter Mabel (1820–1912) took the family's radicalism in a novel direction, while she also sought to uphold her father's agrarian legacies, running a small estate she purchased in Co. Waterford on experimental co-operative lines between the 1860s and 1880s. Transcending her father's approach to democratic reform, which reflected the patriarchal assumptions of the early nineteenth century in concentrating on male suffrage, she adopted a pioneering role in the women's enfranchisement and feminist movements of the later decades of the century in both Ireland and Britain, after first developing her thought through travel writing on Italy and Algeria and later through journalism and pamphlets. Unlike other members of her family, she adhered firmly to Gladstonian Liberalism and home rule after the rupture of 1886, and was the last of his children to die, at the age of 92 in 1912.[17]

By that time, the locus of Ulster radicalism had moved elsewhere, principally to the labour and suffragette movements or into sections of the overlapping Irish cultural-nationalist and separatist movements, although elements of liberal-unionist agrarianism re-emerged in the form of Russellism around 1900. Crawfordsburn House was inherited in 1891 by William's grandson, Robert Gordon Sharman-Crawford (1853–1934), a career soldier with imperial experience, whose conservatism placed him in conflict with the agrarian unionism of T. W. Russell and brought him close to Edward Carson and to political volunteering of a rather different political complexion to that of his great-grandfather. He hosted Ulster Volunteer Force manoeuvres on his estate from 1913 and served as an Ulster Unionist MP and as a party delegate to the 1917–18 Irish Convention. The family tradition of radical politics thus lasted three generations before fading away into a conventional landed unionism typical of the surviving Ulster gentry families.

In the wake of Robert Gordon's death in 1934 the contents of Crawfordsburn House were auctioned and the demesne sold for public use in 1947. What survives from its contents in public repositories today are limited to two oil portraits of William Sharman (1798) and William Sharman Crawford (1843) in the collections of the Ulster Museum, and the family archives eventually deposited in the Public Record Office of Northern Ireland.[18] Frustratingly for the biographer, the personal papers are rather patchy in content, extensive for some periods (especially the mid-1830s, the federalist moment of 1843–4 and the later years of Sharman Crawford's life) but disappointingly thin in surviving correspondence for others. There is little in the collection relating to his children James or Mabel, as the archive passed with Crawfordsburn through the eldest male line from William's unmarried son John (1809–84) to his brother Arthur (1811–91) and thence to Arthur's son Robert Gordon. The estate records are more extensive, although stronger for the period after William's death in 1861. Only a small number of his manuscript letters survive scattered through other extant collections. What makes a full biography possible is the extraordinary extent to which the Sharman Crawfords lived their lives through public print. William Sharman Crawford was an almost obsessive writer of public letters to the newspapers, a medium through which he advanced his own political ideas, attacked his opponents, and promoted the movements he favoured. When combined with his frequent parliamentary speeches, and others captured by newspaper reporters at multiple public meetings and a number of important pamphlets in which he worked through his ideas at greater length, a comprehensive picture of the public man can be constructed. The same is true, if to a lesser extent, of his father William Sharman and his children James and Mabel. Connecting this to a more intimate personal and family history has proved more challenging given the limitations of the surviving sources, but I have attempted so far as it is possible, relating the private life both to his public career and the wider social and political context.

My intention has been to create what William's long-time friend and ally James McKnight looked forward to following his death in 1861. He had hoped:

> that our venerated patriot has left behind him materials for a proper history of his public and personal career; since 'The Life and Times of William Sharman Crawford' would be no merely individual biography – it must include virtually the history of his country during one of its most interesting transition periods; while an authenticated memoir of his own labours is essential as a record for the uses of futurity.[19]

The lives of William Sharman, William Sharman Crawford, and the latter's children and grandchildren ranged over a period that ran from the mid-eighteenth to the mid-twentieth centuries, and they engaged with a range of key political and social developments affecting Ulster, Ireland and Great Britain. While not a general history, the author has sought to relate the family's history to its longitudinal context of regional and national changes, ruptures and continuities, in the spirit McKnight proposed.

The text that follows is arranged along generally chronological lines. Given the centrality of Colonel William Sharman's example in shaping his son's politics, and the continuing salience of the memory of the Volunteers in Ulster radicalism for much of the following century, that movement and Sharman's role in it receive a full chapter. The text proceeds to address his son's youthful formation, marriage and inheritance of the Crawford lands and name, followed by his belated entry into reformist politics as an agent and then candidate for Co. Down in 1830 and 1831 and for Belfast in 1832, and his interest in the campaigns for slave emancipation, national education and religious equality. Chapter three traces his tumultuous relationship with Daniel O'Connell, from his conditional conversion to a 'federal' form of repeal in 1833 through his election as MP for Dundalk in 1835 to his public alienation from O'Connell from 1836 onwards over the contentious questions of tithes and an Irish poor law, and the 'Liberator's' autocratic leadership style. The chapter concludes with his abortive attempt to establish a radical reformist movement in Belfast through the Ulster Constitutional Association in 1840–1.

The fourth chapter deals principally with Sharman Crawford's engagement with Chartism, starting with his relationship with William Lovett at the time of the drafting of the *People's Charter* and addressing the circumstances that saw him elected with Chartist support as MP for Rochdale in 1841. It proceeds to discuss the breakdown (and subsequent recovery) of his relationship with Feargus O'Connor and participation with the radical Quaker Joseph Sturge in the Complete Suffrage Union campaign in 1842–4. The following sections turn to Ireland to focus on his role in the abortive federalist revivals of 1843–4 and 1848 before returning to his engagement with popular politics in Rochdale in 1845–52. Chapter five looks at the emergence of Crawford as the pre-eminent public voice of land reform in Ulster and Ireland more generally. It starts by considering his own practice as a landowner before outlining the development of his legislative approach to land reform and its theoretical justifications, initially through measures for compensation for tenant improvements and later the legal recognition of 'tenant-right' supported by rent regulation. The chapter ends with a discussion of his response to the Great Famine both as a landowner and radical MP, including a consideration of his most assertive publication, *Depopulation Not Necessary*, in 1849.

Chapter six takes a step back to review Sharman Crawford's role in the emergence of a self-conscious tenant-right movement in Ireland, initially in Munster and Ulster in 1846–8, and his relations with lay and clerical allies and with rivals for agrarian leadership, such as William Conner and James Fintan Lalor. It addresses the setbacks to the land movement posed by the failed Young Ireland rebellion of 1848 and the sectarian polarisation accompanying it, before discussing the reconstruction of the movement in 1849–50, leading to the formation of the Irish Tenant League in the latter year. Chapter seven focuses on Crawford's sometimes tense relations with the League and its alignment with his legislative proposal. It deals in detail with the confrontational Down election of 1852, in some ways the centrepiece of the whole book, in which his radical agrarianism challenged most assertively, but without success, landed dominance in the county. The chapter proceeds to trace the disintegration of the Tenant League from early 1853 and Crawford's part in this, along with his continuing commitment to tenant-right measures, even as these appeared to recede further from attainment. The eighth chapter deals more thematically with aspects of Sharman Crawford's private and public life from the 1840s: his relationship with his children, the problems of inheritance and the maintenance of a radical family tradition; his increasingly critical opinions on the British empire and militarism, and continuing adherence to democratic reformism; and his religious journey from heterodox Anglicanism to conversion to Unitarianism in his later years. The chapter ends with a discussion of his death in 1861 and early attempts to commemorate him.

The final chapter follows the Sharman Crawford tradition forward from his death; discussing in turn his posthumous contribution to Gladstonian land legislation for Ireland, the emergence of his third son James as a Liberal reformer and MP for Down in 1874–8 and of his daughter Mabel as a writer, land reformer and pioneering campaigner for women's political and legal rights. The chapter concludes with a discussion of the end of the family engagement with radicalism under his grandson Robert Gordon Sharman-Crawford, whose conservative Ulster Unionism was in turn challenged by remnants of the radical forces his grandfather had once allied with. A brief conclusion locates Sharman Crawford and his family within broader currents of radicalism in Ulster, Ireland and Britain in the later eighteenth and nineteenth centuries.

1. William Sharman and the politics of Volunteering, 1731–1803

William Sharman of Lisburn and Moira

The origins of William Sharman Crawford's radicalism can be located in his father's embrace of patriotic reform in the early 1780s. That man, William Sharman, was the eldest son of John Sharman of Aghavary, Grange of Ballyscullion, in mid-Antrim, a small landowner of around 140 acres and member of the Church of Ireland, and his wife Elizabeth, née Young.[1] William Sharman was born in 1731, and after his father's death in 1746 entered Trinity College Dublin and subsequently trained in the law at Lincoln's Inn in London. He was called to the Irish Bar in 1755 but never practised as a lawyer.[2] As a young man his prospects were greatly enhanced by coming under the patronage of his uncle and namesake Captain William Sharman of Bonnybrook, Co. Dublin, who had married Anna O'Neill of Shane's Castle in 1740 and who had no children of his own. The captain's close association through marriage with the leading branch of the O'Neills, who were one of the largest landowning families in Co. Antrim, led to him occupying a seat in the Irish parliament for their pocket borough of Randalstown in 1749–60, and subsequently becoming an active member of the Irish Linen Board, which had been created in 1711 to regulate and support the industry. He appears to have been a government supporter whilst sitting as an MP.[3]

Before his marriage Captain Sharman had himself benefitted from becoming an heir of his cousin Colonel, later Brigadier General, Richard Kane (originally O'Cahan), a professional soldier from Duneane in Co. Antrim whose family had converted to Protestantism in a previous generation. Kane served with distinction in the Williamite and subsequent wars and from 1712 was the resident British lieutenant-governor (and in 1733–6 the governor) of the Balearic island of Menorca, as well as spending several years in command at Gibraltar. His protégé Captain Sharman served for a time as deputy governor, judge advocate and as revenue collector for the island under Kane's administration, which was marked by pragmatic reformism along with religious toleration, although it was later marred by unproven allegations by local elites of intrusion on their established rights and customs.[4] Following Kane's death in 1736, Captain Sharman returned to Ireland and used his inheritance to acquire portions of land in mid-Down between Banbridge and Rathfriland in the Barony of Upper Iveagh around 1745, and a smaller estate at Stalleen near Donore in northern Co. Meath, in addition to a small north Co. Dublin demesne and country house at Bonnybrook and a city townhouse in Molesworth Street.[5] As a wealthy man of business he took an interest in political and natural history, and in advancing Protestant education in Ireland through support of the proselytising charter schools movement.[6] Captain Sharman's career was thus an ascendancy success story, and he sought to advance his nephew's prospects in a similar fashion to the way he had benefitted himself from family connections and service to the state.

It is thus likely that his uncle's political influence secured for the younger William Sharman in 1756 the post of revenue collector for the district of Lisburn in south Antrim, a position worth the respectable sum of £300 per year.[7] This was a promising appointment for an ambitious young man. The surrounding Lagan Valley had seen the enhancement of the existing small-scale linen production by French Huguenot refugees who had settled there under the leadership of Louis Crommelin from 1698 (alongside Scots and English migrants) with state and proprietorial encouragement.[8] After 1750 the trade and population of Lisburn and its hinterland expanded rapidly, with the Scotsman William Coulson establishing a damask factory in the town in 1766 and the Lagan navigation opening waterborne access to the port of Belfast from the previous year, facilitating bulk exports. With the intensification of the trade came greater class tensions within the predominantly Protestant population of the district. Reacting to the Linen Board's introduction of stricter regulations on production and against combinations, and the formation of a drapers' association to enforce these regulations and promote the interests of the linen masters, weavers assembled to protest against such 'oppressive measures' and then rioted in 1762 against their social superiors.[9] Although peace was restored after significant concessions were made to the weavers, social and political radicalism had established a lasting foothold there. As a resident, Sharman would probably have witnessed these events at first hand and his subsequent career suggests they had some impact on him. He appears to have been diligent in his office and acquired some standing locally as well as detailed knowledge of the economic and social life of the district, both of which would prove politically useful.[10] He also appears to have acted as agent for his uncle's Co. Down estates, giving him some entrée to county society and experience in land management.[11]

Captain Sharman heartily approved of his nephew's marriage in late 1772 to Arminella, daughter of Hill Willson, a landowner at Purdysburn, Co. Down, and collector of customs for Belfast. He contributed generously to their marriage settlement and named William his heir.[12] Arminella, who had previously moved in fashionable London circles, appears to have been regarded as a desirable match; an ode to her was included in a collection of romantic poems published in that city in 1773:

> *To Miss* ARMANILLA WILSON, now *Mrs SHARMAN, of Ireland,*
> Why laughs the wine with which this glass is crown'd?
> Why leaps my heart to hear this toast go round?
> It is to sense, to beauty, joy and wealth;
> It is to gentle ARMANILLA's health!
> Health to her noble father! Bless her race
> With all his virtues – with her form and face![13]

It is likely the marriage was arranged (her response to his 'repeated kind letters' in September 1772 was politely formal), but it appeared a happy relationship and she would prove an able partner for William in his subsequent political career.[14] The marriage also connected William both to Arminella's brother James, who was elected as a 'patriot' MP for Antrim in 1776, and to the influential Black family of Belfast, whose leading member in the town, George Black, had married Hill Willson's niece Arminella Campbell in 1753. Black, the scion of a wealthy merchant dynasty with family trading connections in France, Spain and the West Indies, was a member of the borough corporation with close ties to the proprietorial Donegall family, and its sovereign (mayor) on six occasions in the 1770s–80s.[15]

William Sharman was thus clearly the product of an eighteenth-century Anglo-Irish gentry world in which religious conformity, inheritance of landed property and a 'good marriage', government service at home or in the empire and (above all) patronage were crucial to getting on. But he was also open to the changing intellectual and political climate of later eighteenth-century east Ulster, and by the early 1780s began to adopt positions that would probably have shocked the conservative Captain Sharman had he still been alive. However, during William senior's lifetime their relationship appears to have been close, although this was not the case between all members of the family. The captain had also brought into his household William Sharman's youngest sister Sarah, who appears to have suffered from some sort of mental illness, and of whom William lamented that 'no Bedlamite ever was more outrageous' in her mistreatment of his elderly uncle, his wife Arminella and other family members.[16]

Captain Sharman's death in June 1775, leaving his nephew as sole inheritor of his Irish estates, allowed William and Arminella to establish themselves properly as members of the country gentry. To embody their social aspirations they had already in 1774 rented the house and demesne of Moira Castle on a 31-year lease from John Rawdon, first Earl of Moira, with whom Sharman had developed an amicable personal and political association and to whom he lent a significant amount of money in 1779.[17] Moira Castle, located eight miles southwest of Lisburn on the principal road from Belfast to the linen country of north Armagh, had been built as a mansion in the early 1690s by the Williamite soldier Sir Arthur Rawdon (see Figure 1). It became well known for its botanical and horticultural collections, initially created by Rawdon's gardener James Harlow, who imported exotic specimens from Jamaica.[18] Moira Castle was praised in 1774 for the 'tasteful and intricate dispositions of the gardens and parks' of its demesne.[19] Visiting in 1799, Gabriel Beranger, the noted Dutch watercolourist and antiquarian, described it as:

> an ancient building on the estate of the Earl of Moira which the deceased earl got modernized and made a commodious habitation; it is surrounded by a wood, which affords beautiful shady walks; a large lawn extends in front, where sheep are feeding, which is terminated by trees and a small lough eastwards; the rear contains a wood with a large opening fronting the castle, which forms a fine perspective.'[20]

For the Sharmans, this was unquestionably a desirable and prestigious address for a socially and politically aspirant couple and their family.

William Sharman was anxious to present himself as a benevolent landowner on his newly-acquired landholdings. One sympathetic Belfast publication gave his annual rental income in the 1780s as £3,000, adding that this was 'not wrung from the bowels of a pillaged tenantry', and was expended 'in relieving the distresses of the poor, and wiping the eye from the tear of misery'.[21] He was also praised in print by an anonymous Down farmer in 1787 as one of the leading agricultural improvers in the county.[22] His Upper Iveagh landholdings, comprising of all or part of ten townlands in the rolling drumlin country of the parish of Drumballyroney to the north of Rathfriland (specifically Lacken, Ballybrick,

Edenagarry and Lisnacreevy), and in the adjoining parishes of Annaclone (townlands of Ballynafoy, Cappagh and Clay), Aghaderg (Ballynaskeagh and Creevy), and Drumgooland (Ballyward) were not contiguous and lacked a suitable grand residence, but were within reasonable traveling distance from Moira, which lay 18 to 20 miles to the north. Sharman appears to have employed an agent, as in 1792 his tenants were directed to pay their rents at the house of a Mr Agnew of Dromore.[23] Incidentally, inheritance of these lands made Sharman the landlord of part of the Brunty family, whose aspirant member Patrick was christened at Drumballyroney church, and migrated to England in 1802 to study for the Anglican ministry, changing his surname to Brontë and establishing a celebrated literary family.[24] The Co. Down family remained linked to the Sharmans: a Catherine Bronte died at Lacken in 1859 and Murphy and William Brunty were recorded as Sharman Crawford's tenants on the same townland in the Griffith Valuation of the early 1860s.[25] An eccentric text by the former Presbyterian missionary Dr William Wright claimed in the 1890s that Patrick Brontë's father, Hugh, had been a tenant of the Sharmans and had introduced tenant-right theories to his landlord, but this was dismissed as fanciful by reviewers and described by William Sharman's granddaughter Mabel as unlikely, as such views were widespread among the Down peasantry of the period.[26]

William Sharman may well have adopted the model of 'improving landlord' from his friend and patron Lord Moira, who was also a member of the Linen Board and an active promoter of both flax cultivation and industrial cloth production on his estates (indeed Moira was the dedicatee of one of William Hincks' renowned 1783 series of twelve engravings on the Ulster linen trade, which was 'taken on the spot' in a Down cottage).[27] Moira had a reputation as both an improving agronomist and a paternalistic promoter of his tenants' wellbeing, education and religious observance, although his record in this respect was not unmixed as he evicted a number of tenants near Ballynahinch in contested circumstances in 1783.[28] Sharman's political development appears to have been shaped for a time by the relationship, as he followed Moira (and his own brother-in-law James Willson) in embracing the liberal 'patriot' political movement within Irish Protestant politics of the later 1770s–early 1780s, thereby placing himself in opposition to the government at Dublin Castle, despite his official employment as a revenue officer.[29] By 1784, when Sharman was removed from his official post for this political defiance, he was described as no longer needing the income, retaining it after his inheritance in 1775 only as 'an opportunity of serving his country and obliging a friend who assisted in managing the business'.[30] This may have been an overstatement aimed at boosting Sharman's 'patriotic' credentials, but did reflect his financial standing as a significant and non-indebted landowner.

The village of Moira, immediately outside the demesne gates of Moira Castle, had been laid out in the seventeenth century as a plantation settlement by the Rawdons, and by the 1770s was the hub of a fertile agricultural district containing roughly equal numbers of Anglicans, Presbyterians and Catholics.[31] There may have been some Irish spoken locally in this period, although it had disappeared by the early nineteenth century.[32] Like many parts of the north-eastern counties it was becoming heavily dependent on proto-industrial flax yarn and linen production, especially as the adjacent Lagan Valley developed as the spine of that industry. In 1780 Moira was described by one traveller as 'a thriving village, consisting of one good street, where the linen manufacture is carried on to advantage'.[33] But in the early 1770s the linen trade had been severely affected throughout the north by a serious downturn, which Captain Sharman (in common with many observers in Ulster) blamed on the British government picking a quarrel with the American colonists over taxation which disrupted the export trade, and which would lead to open war in the colonies by 1775.[34]

The recession, coming on the back of several years of bad harvests, and accompanied by changes in land management practices on some estates, brought social distress for many farmers, labourers and weavers, which in turn fuelled an outbreak of violent agrarian protests. In the vicinity of Moira these took the form of a secret society calling itself the 'Hearts of Flint', a local variant of the 'Hearts of Steel' which had previously emerged in 1769 on Lord Donegall's estates in south Antrim in protest against increased rents and fines imposed on the working farmers by Donegall and his middlemen tenants. State repression in Antrim in winter of 1770–1, after a 'Steelboy' attack on the barracks in Belfast to liberate an imprisoned colleague, decanted unrest into Down, where protest centred on rapidly rising rents, heavy county cess levies and high food prices in a time of recession in the linen trade.[35] In early 1772 unrest flared again in Down and the surrounding counties, with cattle houghing, incendiarism and intimidation becoming frequent. The actions and threats of the local insurgents led Elizabeth, Lady Moira, to write in alarm to lord lieutenant Townshend from Moira Castle in March 1772 that:

> the late outrageous behaviour was certainly not the effect of a settled plan but the consequence of a sudden rage, those that style themselves the capt[ain]s of these insurgents have slept a night or two in this town, and by all accounts I find them to be the meanest of people, and destitute of every quality capable to form a scheme, or keep up a party; of the numbers that are said to be in arms, four out of five are terrified into that appearance by the threats of having their throats cut [...] All the Protestants of Moira have been swore (by compulsion) to be true to the Hearts of Flint, and to attend to the sound of their horns.[36]

Reconsidering her panicked response to what she on reflection regarded as 'malicious' rumours, two days later she wrote again to urge the viceroy to remember the underlying social causes of the unrest, which lay not with the landowners but the government's policies, which had placed 'many hundreds of His Majesty's Protestant subjects [...] in the madness of despair'.[37] Townshend's administration swamped the district with soldiers, backed by coercive legislation, that spring, which was enough to dampen down the overt unrest, if at the price of social alienation and a renewed surge of emigration to the American colonies. One female observer (possibly again Lady Moira) wrote:

> The army are taking up the poor unfortunate wretches every day in great numbers; our roads are crowded as much as you have seen them at the time of the Maze races; but what will this end in? The north of Ireland will not recover the damage now done, these many years: our looms lie idle, and our provisions eat up by an army. A company of foot marched into Moira last night. Those that were the heads of the insurgents, went into the houses of the innocent, and took their young sons to join them, who it is now believed will share the same fate as the old offenders.[38]

The combination of repression and surging emigration was to smother this wave of rural unrest in the following years, although raising new fears for some that the 'passion for emigration' among dissenters was tending to damage permanently the Protestant interest in the country.[39] But, as James Donnelly suggests, even after economic conditions eased following the war years, Steelboyism left a persistent memory in rural east Ulster and contributed towards a decline of deference towards the landed elites.[40] It was still recalled in the mid-nineteenth century as a successful manifestation of agrarian resistance to landed intrusion on customary tenant rights.[41]

The upheavals of 1771–2 may not have been the sole reason for the Rawdons' decision to relocate from Moira Castle (which lay adjacent to the disturbed village) to their other house on the Montalto estate near Ballynahinch, and the financial inducements offered by the Sharmans as new tenants of the house and demesne were no doubt important for the heavily-indebted earl and his wife. Their son the second earl was later to mortgage the family's Down estates for £33,000 following his succession in 1794.[42] However, social unease still lingered: as late as March 1774 it was rumoured that Steelboys had set fire to Lord Moira's coach-house and carriages, although it later transpired that this was the result of an accident not arson.[43] Damage to the castle gardens by a disaffected gang from the village was only stamped out by an initiative led by the local Presbyterian minister in 1778.[44]

For the new residents of the castle from 1774, challenges arose as to how best to engage with the disruptive social forces that had sparked the outbreaks of several years before, find ways of channelling them into 'respectable' and 'patriotic' forms of expression, and rebuild bonds of sociability between the landed elite, the urban middle class and the surrounding rural population of farmers, labourers and weavers in a religiously mixed environment. The policies of the administration would also, they came to believe, need to change in response to 'popular' demands for lower taxation and the promotion of productive employment. William Sharman would rise to these tasks in the early 1780s and in doing so his politics would move in a more radical direction.

The Volunteers and Colonel Sharman

Emerging originally in 1778 as an Irish armed self-defence force against a feared French invasion, following that country's intervention in the American War of Independence, the Volunteer movement spread rapidly from its origin in Belfast across the island. Coming under the nominal command of the Duke of Leinster and Earl of Charlemont, the Volunteers had a high degree of local autonomy with individual companies retaining control of their membership and discipline. While strongly Francophobic and 'loyal' to the crown, many adherents were also sympathetic to the American colonists' claims, especially in Ulster where family and economic ties often spanned the Atlantic and resentments against the government in Dublin were widespread. As a self-conscious body of armed citizens, independent of state control, the Volunteers were open to political engagement, although this fluctuated over time and by the location and makeup of different units.[45] However the majority came to endorse the case made by the opposition 'patriot' leadership in the Irish parliament that the country's constitutional as well as commercial subordination to Great Britain, rendering it a colony in practice, should be ended, and that its legislative independence from Britain as a 'sister kingdom' under a shared crown be asserted by 'the people' in arms. Volunteer demonstrations were prominent in the campaign that led to the concession of 'free trade' (unrestricted access to British colonial markets) for Ireland in 1779–80. In February 1782 the first of a series of political conventions, attended by

250 delegates representing the 25,000 Volunteers of the Province of Ulster, assembled at Dungannon in Co. Tyrone to endorse a set of political resolutions prepared by the patriot leadership. While the meeting agreed to support their parliamentary campaign for legislative autonomy, it did so in a manner that justified the right and responsibility of the Volunteer movement to act politically as a distinct and independent body.

This combined parliamentary and 'outdoor' campaign was successful in extracting the so-called 'Constitution of 1782' from a weakened British government reeling from defeat in North America, but the limitations in reality of the new political structure were quickly apparent, and became increasingly so as a more effective and decisive British administration was formed under the premiership of William Pitt the Younger in December 1783. The politics of Volunteering after 1782 focused on two issues which were much more divisive within the movement. The first was parliamentary reform, which was loudly demanded by the middle-class and the more radical of the gentry leaders of the movement, and which had growing support from tenant farmer, artisan and labouring members in Ulster, but which also potentially threatened the control of landed magnates (including a number of Volunteer officers) over many of the parliamentary boroughs and counties that returned the 300 Irish MPs. Secondly, the revived question of Catholic emancipation sharply divided radical and reformist from conservative Protestants within the movement over the safety and legitimacy of restoring the political rights formally removed under the penal acts of the late seventeenth and early eighteenth centuries from their Catholic fellow Irishmen.

Lisburn was at the forefront of the Volunteer movement, with the first company being formed there under Captain Poyntz Stewart in June 1778.[46] It appears that Lord Moira was responsible for promoting the raising of Volunteer companies on his estates at nearby Ballynahinch and Moira in 1779.[47] Volunteering had certainly become widely established in Down by summer 1780, when 21 companies were reviewed at Downpatrick, reportedly displaying a degree of military order that impressed even previously sceptical observers.[48] The first extant reference to William Sharman's involvement comes in an advertisement for a drummer in April and then in a report of 7 July 1781, noting a meeting of the Moira corps the previous month in which he was listed as captain and thanked by his men for his 'great attention and friendship to [the] company', and for a 'generous present of 60 stand of arms and band of music'. This was an expensive outlay, and a popular one given the government's reluctance to arm Volunteer companies with working weaponry. In response the Moira company resolved that 'we will upon every occasion, use our utmost endeavours to preserve the peace and execute the laws of our country, as the most convincing proof we can give of our sincere gratitude to our worthy captain.'[49] If Sharman's election to his first command was partly due to deference towards him as the village's resident squire (albeit not its landlord), and his financial ability to equip the unit, it also owed something to the support he received from the local Presbyterian minister Rev. Andrew Craig, a Volunteer enthusiast and chaplain active in the formation of the Moira corps, who recorded that he had persuaded his friend Sharman to take on a leadership role 'contrary to the expectations, and perhaps wishes, of some of the neighbouring gentlemen, who took no part in the movement'.[50] Craig's activism was in line with that of many other Presbyterian clergymen in Ulster, who promoted Volunteering ideals and practice through a burgeoning print culture as well as through local recruitment activities and supportive sermons.[51] Although himself a practising Anglican, William Sharman's closeness to Craig, who was subsequently the minister of the First Lisburn congregation (and later also his brother-in-law), and to other Presbyterian political agents, was to remain marked throughout his Volunteering career.

By September 1781 Sharman had been elected lieutenant colonel of the newly formed Union Regiment of Volunteers, a unit title which reflected the amalgamation of the Moira, Ballynahinch, Rosevale, Aghalee and First Lisburn 'corps' or companies into one formation, which was part of a more general consolidation of Volunteer units at this time.[52] According to a later account he was offered the command of two regiments and chose the Union.[53] The regimental colonel was nominally Lord Moira, but Sharman took on executive leadership before being elected full colonel himself in April 1784, after Moira withdrew over concerns at the increased radicalism of the Volunteers on the parliamentary reform and Catholic questions.[54] In an indication of the growing strains on social deference, when Moira's son John Rawdon was proposed as the replacement lieutenant colonel, it was vehemently opposed by two officers ('one of whom remarked, he would as soon vote for *Jack Foster*'), although carried by majority vote of the officers present.[55] William Bateman of Marahinch, who appears to have also acted as an agent for Sharman's Upper Iveagh estates, replaced him as captain of the Moira company.[56]

Reflecting its quasi-democratic nature, the regiment's corps sent delegates to meet at Moira market house on 8 April 1782 to debate the resolutions passed at the Dungannon Convention of the Ulster Volunteer corps that February. They resolved, at a meeting chaired by Sharman, that, while loyal to the crown and the British connection, 'his Majesty's people of Ireland are a free people, inheritors of a free constitution, descended to them from their ancestors', and that:

> it is an undoubted right of this free people (a right which they value as their lives,) to be governed solely by their own laws. That the king, lords and commons of Ireland, are the only representatives of this crown and people; and the interposition of any other body of men with the legislature of this country, is incompatible with our fundamental laws and franchises.[57]

The meeting endorsed the Dungannon resolutions, which included a commitment to unite to use 'all constitutional means' to seek redress of grievances, and which 'rejoice[d] in the relaxation of the penal laws against our Roman Catholic fellow-subjects'.[58] In such an atmosphere of rising political expectations, increasing popular participation in political debate, and insistence on the consent of 'the people' for the legitimacy of political institutions, Sharman's position within the movement was increasingly dependent on his ability to articulate and support popular sentiment rather than solely on his social status and financial contributions.

Volunteering in Ulster became associated with challenges to traditional forms of social and political deference, especially of tenants towards their landlords' direction. In the 'linen triangle' area in particular this was enhanced, W. H. Crawford suggests, by the 'independent' social aspirations of many farmer-weavers, who were drawn to a movement that recognised their claims to citizenship and respectability.[59] The Co. Down election of 1783 saw this bear some fruit, with the Volunteer-backed 'independent' candidate Edward Ward unseating Robert Stewart, scion of the county's second largest landed family, who had failed to offer a consistent commitment to supporting parliamentary reform. The Moira Volunteers voted their thanks to Lord Moira for demonstrating his 'truly patriotic and constitutional principles' in declaring his freehold tenants free to vote as they wished in the election without fear of retribution, while a freeholders meeting at Dundonald resolved that:

> every landlord, be his rank what it may, who by threats or any unconstitutional means, attempts to intimidate his tenants from voting according to their conscience, ought to be considered as an enemy to his country, *as* America stands with outstretched arms, ready to receive the injured and oppressed sons of liberty.[60]

It is not recorded if Sharman followed Moira in giving a 'free vote' to his own tenants, but given his public position it is highly likely he did so, and this became a family political principle in subsequent elections. This was still, however, a minority stance, and most landowners continued to regard their freeholder tenants' votes as their own political property in defiance of 'public opinion'. The waters were muddied in Down by Ward's last-minute electoral alliance with the anti-reformist Lord Kilwarlin, which outraged radical opinion in Lisburn and Belfast and drew protests from some Volunteer corps in the county. The Gilford Battalion, for example, split into rival companies over protests that their colonel, Sir Richard Johnston, had shown himself 'destitute of those principles of true patriotism' in seeking to induce freeholders to vote against their conscience and for opposing reform, and similar splits occurred at Comber and Newtownards.[61]

It was the other of the county's two seats that had been the reformers' real target. The Volunteer press excoriated those members who had chosen to give their second vote to Kilwarlin, the heir to Lord Hillsborough and representative of the county's dominant Hill family interest, who topped the poll despite his open antipathy towards Volunteer objectives. Either these freeholders had failed to discern Kilwarlin's reactionary politics, it was alleged, or they had succumbed to an outdated code of servility: 'He who gives up the *first right* of a reasonable being to his landlord, there is *no other right* he will *dare* to maintain – he is a *coward* and a *slave*, and *cowards and slaves* should never tarnish the glorious lustre of the Volunteer name'.[62] Such radical sentiments posed potential threats to the authority of landlords, however popular, such as Sharman. Yet despite the absence of any record of his expressing radical political opinions before 1781, he chose not only to persevere with Volunteering as others dropped away, but now to associate himself with the more 'advanced' elements of the movement.

The Union Regiment appears to have incorporated an element of democratic principle into its own practice of internal discipline. When an officer in the regiment was accused of having signed a counter-memorial issued by the Hill interest against reform during the Down election, his fellow officers resolved to subject him to public hearings before the rank and file of each of the companies of the regiment. With only one of the five (his own, first Lisburn) accepting his defence that in signing the memorial he had acted as a freeholder and not as a Volunteer, the regiment as a whole took cognisance of the Ballynahinch company's statement that they could: '*never* [...] associate with the corps who continued in command *a man* who was doubly guilty, – of baseness to his country, and of contumacious perseverance in *ill doing*', and it demanded his expulsion, an action it deemed 'justly consonant with the spirit of the times, and with the honor of a regiment worthy of such a patriotic leader as COL. SHARMAN'. Such internal democracy had its costs – despite its high regard for Sharman, the First Lisburn Company split from the Union Regiment over this political purging of one of its officers, although this was counterweighted in 1784 by the accession of new corps from Tullylish and Donaghcloney (and later Dromore and Kilmore) to the regiment, although several of these units proved ephemeral.[63]

As Padhraig Higgins has observed, such forms of public shaming were characteristic of Volunteer units and necessary to maintain military discipline and political unity in what were voluntary bodies operating within the loose bonds of associational culture.[64] Volunteering politics were not, however, universally popular, and dissensions within the movement over reform tended to alienate more conservative members and observers. A squib, allegedly written from Moira in September 1783, cynically mocked those 'restless volunteering blades' who took their reformist ideals too seriously and who thereby challenged the established social order and potentially the British connection. The triumphant Lord Kilwarlin was urged to seek British aid to suppress their 'hellish mad parades'.[65]

Sharman's new command had initially incorporated units from the town of Lisburn and nearby Rosevale, both of which lay on the estates of the absentee Earl of Hertford. In such areas with a significant Presbyterian population alienated from the civil and ecclesiastical establishment, with relatively high literacy rates and where reading clubs existed to disseminate 'enlightened' political texts, radical consciousness was rising, reaching at least some of the working classes.[66] Radicalism was, however, by no means restricted to Presbyterians, and was manifest in Lisburn despite its local Anglican majority.[67] Political discontent had been growing in the developing linen town and its environs for some time. A satirical squib against the borough of Lisburn's two MPs, representing them as gluttonous and corrupt clients of the landlord, had appeared in 1779, and a town meeting the following year upheld patriot demands for the repeal of Poyning's Law and the Declaratory Act, which had subordinated Irish legislation to the veto of the British privy council and parliament.[68] An attempt in September 1780 by the captain of the Lisburn Volunteer Company, Poyntz Stewart, to impose a 'moderate' resolution affirming confidence in the Irish parliament and criticising those who 'from mistaken zeal would stir up jealousies', was rejected by his lieutenants and other members of the company, a reminder of its novel democratic character. Their dissentient statement asserted that 'we cannot agree to resolutions expressing a confidence in parliament which we do not feel, as we consider them in several recent instances to have forfeited that esteem which their former patriotic conduct seemed to entitle them to'.[69] Lord Hertford's public statement in 1782 that the Volunteers should be content with attaining 'free trade' and legislative independence, and that the country should put commercial development ahead of any further agitation, did not endear him to the town's radicals.[70]

Other Volunteer units formed in Lisburn, such as the True Blues and the Lisburn Fusiliers (whose captain was the future patriot MP William Todd Jones), were equally outspoken in advocating radical political reform by 1782.[71] While only one of these units, the First Lisburn Company, was associated with Sharman's Union Regiment, the assertive radicalism evident in the town would work to Sharman's benefit in 1783.[72]

While no doubt there was some rivalry between them, all these units participated together in summer manoeuvres at Belfast from 1782, bringing the local radicals of the Lagan Valley into connection with the reformist networks centred in Ulster's most populous and rapidly developing town. Around 4,000 Volunteers participated in this event in August

1782, which combined an assertion of military display with an inclusive and politicised camaraderie:

> Discipline [was] enforced without the slightest relaxation or indulgence – from the colonel to the private all dined and slept in camp, if leave was not first obtained from his superior officer. A company of wealthy independent men, bred in all the comforts of life, submitted to such restraint without repining, rather struggling who should mount the guards, and expose themselves to the [...] weather; and after being drenched with torrents of rain, wrapping their bodies in a blanket and making a wisp of straw their pillow and bed, presenting a scene that the present age may glory in [...] Such was the Belfast camp, where discipline presided, hospitality furnished the table, and through which temperance, supported by freedom, mirth and good humour, preserved an unbounded sway.[73]

Even if exaggerated for propaganda purposes, such reports suggest that these exercises helped, at least to some extent and for a time, to break down class barriers within the movement. The Belfast reviews were also accompanied by frequent balls, which allowed female participants to express their support for the movement and raised philanthropic funds for the town's poor house.[74]

The military capacity of the Volunteers as anything more than a local peacekeeping force has been disputed, even as numbers expanded to a reported peak of nearly 89,000 across the island by mid-1782. They remained highly localised and (despite attempts at 'regimentation') lacking in co-ordination.[75] Their military abilities were never put to the test as no invasion or insurrection occurred during their period in existence, although they did engage in local policing work: it was reported that the Moira Volunteers dispersed a 'riotous mob' attacking the Bishop of Dromore's property in the village in 1782.[76] To undertake anything more than this, newly elected amateur officers faced a steep military learning curve. Unlike his uncle, William Sharman had no previous military experience, and as an officer he would have been dependent on instructional guides such as the *Concise Compendium of Military Manoeuvres*, published for the Volunteers in 1781.[77] He seems to have taken his responsibilities as corps and later regimental commander seriously, and promoted military order and skills throughout his part-time soldiery, retaining significant numbers of active members within his units until their eventual demise in 1793. Despite some falling off, by 1784 the Union Regiment still numbered some 300 men and had acquired two six-pounder field guns, and in 1791 it was differentiated into 'a troop of horse, a few companies of grenadiers and light infantry, and a very fine band of music'. One English observer noted of the regiment that year, '[t]hey are in general very fine men, and are well cloathed, appointed and disciplined'.[78] It is unclear if Sharman also contributed to the cost of uniforms, but the regiment was distinguished by scarlet and blue trimming to their military tunics.[79] Music was clearly important, and a martial tune entitled 'Colonel Sharman's quickstep' was composed for regimental gatherings.[80] More seriously, Sharman sought to develop musketry skills through regular competitions for the best marksmen in each company and the regiment, with the winners being awarded silver or gold medals at his expense. The medals bore the patriotic symbol of the Irish angel-harp and crown and the motto 'For our country'.[81] These were also the emblems and motto inscribed in the belt plates and the officers' gorgets of the Moira Volunteers (see Figure 3).[82]

Whatever their objective military capabilities, the Volunteers took their status as a people's army seriously and placed great emphasis on drilling and military display. An (albeit favourably biased) account in the radical *Belfast Mercury* informed its readers that the 'mock action' of an attack and defence of a camp, carried out by the units participating in the Belfast review of July 1784, which included the Union Regiment, 'was conducted in a stile of military perfection'.[83] At the same time, Volunteer élan depended on a culture of male sociability that at least temporarily elided class differences between officers and men. Following a parade in Moira that October, the entire company repaired to the market house to dine with their 'beloved colonel', following which 'many spirited toasts were drank [sic], and the evening spent in the utmost festivity and harmony'.[84] This was a far cry from the class-related unrest of 1762 and 1772 in the district, although underlying tensions persisted. Nor was such social harmony universally the case: in places Volunteer corps were deployed to repress outbreaks of Whiteboyism and urban combinations.[85]

The Dungannon conventions and parliamentary reform

William Sharman's standing within the Volunteers appears to have risen rapidly in 1782–3, at a time when the movement was convulsed by divisions provoked by Henry Flood's campaign for a formal 'renunciation' of Britain's claim to legislate for Ireland, and the defection of some moderate officers to the newly-created government Fencible force.[86] Sharman's advancement reflected his leaning towards the 'popular' stance on these issues as well as his activist commitment to the movement and high standing in the civic life of the Lagan Valley. In July 1783 he chaired a meeting of the representatives of 45 Ulster corps at Lisburn, which resolved to requisition another provincial convention at Dungannon, this time to focus explicitly on the subject of parliamentary reform. James Kelly credits this assembly with 'signall[ing] the full commencement of a campaign for reform', with objectives well in advance of the more limited demands of the 1760s–70s.[87] Sharman was selected by this meeting to act as chair of the committee of correspondence of the Ulster Volunteers, with the key responsibility of preparing the draft resolutions of the convention and eliciting the opinions of leading reformers, which were to inform its deliberations.[88] The 'Address to the Volunteer Army of Ulster', published under his name in July 1783, strongly asserted the continuing right of the Volunteers, notwithstanding the recent end of the American war, to act as a body of armed citizens to ensure that the objectives of legislative independence were realised in practice. The case was couched in the Whiggish language of restoring the balance of an ancient constitution corrupted by venality and party interests:

> Among the many glorious effects of which a more equal representation of the people in parliament would be productive, the following are obvious: – the destruction of the party spirit whose baneful influence has at all times been injurious to the public weal – a revival of the native dignity of the crown, by imparting to each branch of the legislature its distinct and proportional weight, – and the abolition of that train of courtly mercenaries who must ever continue to prey on the vitals of public virtue, till the balance of the constitution be restored, the necessity of governing by regular systems of seduction shall no longer exist. [... parliamentary reform was] *the only measure* which can give permanency to the late renovation of our constitution or restore that virtue to the representative body, without which, though the mere forms of a free government may be preserved, its spirit must inevitably perish.

Catholic emancipation was not explicitly referenced in this document, but hinted at in the comment that by 'inculcating the glorious spirit of toleration, it [the Volunteers] has united the once distressed inhabitants of this country into an indissoluble mass'.[89] Thinking such proceedings unconstitutional, Charlemont, as national commander of the Volunteers, declined to participate in the 1783 Dungannon convention and warned against including the Catholic question in any of their deliberations, leaving Sharman and his committee to proceed at their own risk.[90] Henry Grattan agreed with Charlemont that continued outdoor agitation could be counterproductive and potentially upset the 1782 settlement.[91]

Later that month, a letter issued by the committee of correspondence observed that the representatives of 15,000 Volunteers (including those of Munster as well as Ulster) had already expressed support for the principle of parliamentary reform, and urged corps to send delegates again to Dungannon with powers to agree on a specific plan of action.[92] Letters were issued under Sharman's name to most prominent English and Irish reformers, including the Duke of Richmond, Richard Price, Major John Cartwright, John Jebb and Rev. Christopher Wyvill, which elicited supportive statements, along with differing recommendations for reform and Catholic emancipation.[93] Reading their published letters, the Belfast radical Martha McTier singled out Wyvill's and Richmond's as excellent, while she thought the Irish submissions (by Grattan, Flood and Charlemont) were insufficient and that of William Pitt (then an opposition Whig) amounted to 'nothing'.[94] Ultimately the decision on how to proceed lay with the Volunteer convention itself. As Sharman noted in his letters of acknowledgment to the English reformers, composed after the convention, 'where we find great and good men, equally zealous in the cause, differ with respect to the mode, our only choice that which seemed to us most applicable to the country we live in'.[95]

The correspondence committee's proposals to the 1783 Dungannon Convention were remarkably radical for the period and came closest to those advanced by Cartwright, Wyvill and Richmond – they included annual parliaments, vote by secret ballot and abolition of 'mean, decayed or depopulated boroughs', with transfer of these seats to unenfranchised or underrepresented towns and counties; male 40-shilling freeholders should have the vote in the counties, and householders renting properties worth £5 per annum and above in the boroughs, but no 'menial servants' unless they were a householder paying taxes. Bribery of electors would be criminalised on both sides. Crucially, the committee now also recommended the 'extension of the suffrage to such description of Roman Catholics as the national convention may deem proper objects of that great trust', a statement of support for emancipation in principle, if deferring the details of precisely who should be enfranchised at that time.[96] In line with contemporary patriarchal assumptions, the resolutions made no mention of enfranchising women, although the government press sought to undermine the reformers by mischievously asserting that they had inspired a female committee 'to assert [women's] inherent rights, and no longer patiently to be excluded from a share in the legislature of the kingdom'.[97] Even so, the reform resolutions amounted to a provocatively assertive initiative by a representative assembly that chose to ignore both the deep opposition they provoked from conservative figures in the movement and the alarm triggered in the government, which now mooted the suppression of the Volunteers.[98]

The Convention assembled in the Presbyterian meeting house on 8 September with representation from 272 corps; it thanked Sharman and the committee, welcomed the prospect of collaboration with the English reform movement, and endorsed the recommendations in general, while disagreeing on details (especially regarding Catholic emancipation). Five delegates were nominated from each county, including Sharman for Antrim, to represent them at the national convention to be held in Dublin that November.[99] This was, however, as far as the Volunteer reform project was to proceed at that time. Uneasy about the political implications of Catholic emancipation for the divided movement as well as being personally antagonistic towards it, Charlemont sought to marginalise it from the extended and rather chaotic national convention debates despite the attempts of the flamboyantly pro-Catholic Frederick Augustus Hervey, Bishop of Derry, to promote it. Henry Flood was called on to mediate and proposed his own more 'realistic' reform plan, and the terms eventually agreed by the Dublin convention now excluded Catholic emancipation completely and reined back on the Dungannon recommendations for radical parliamentary reform.[100]

Flood's appearance in the Irish commons hotfoot from the national convention at the Rotunda, still wearing his Volunteer uniform as he proposed a reform bill based on these resolutions, provoked hostility from many MPs and only half-hearted support from his former patriot ally and now political rival, Grattan. The government through lord lieutenant Northington made clear its staunch hostility to a bill he argued had emanated from an unconstitutional assembly of armed men, now openly threatening the institutions of the state, and the landed parliamentary elite showed no inclination to dilute its own power.[101] Flood's reform bill was thrown out by 158 to 49 votes in the commons, and Charlemont then directed the Volunteer convention to disperse without posing any further challenge to parliamentary authority. The *Volunteers Journal* thundered against the outcome, and published the voting list, so that 'the publick may be able to distinguish between the PROSTITUTE HACKS of Government and the REAL PATRIOTS in a certain IMMACULATE SOCIETY', but nothing could be done in the absence of manifest public support and a readiness to directly confront the government and their allied Irish magnates.[102]

If this was a major and embarrassing defeat, it did not lead to a collapse of belief in the Volunteer reform project on the part of men such as Sharman, who had now himself joined the ranks of the parliamentary patriots at the general election of summer 1783. The borough of Lisburn was a 'pot-walloper' borough with an electorate of between 350 and 400 taxpaying householders, usually kept under the tight control of Hertford's local agents.[103] Supported by the Lisburn Constitutional Club, chaired by the linen bleacher Henry Bell with the support of Sharman's old friend Rev. Andrew Craig, and which had links via the wealthy merchant Waddell Cunningham to Belfast's reforming commercial interests, Sharman and his fellow Volunteer officer William Todd Jones stood on a platform that exhorted 'independent' electors to vote with their consciences and spurn attempts to bribe or intimidate them (see Figure 4).[104] Their electoral committee assured Hertford that his tenants had no issue with him as a landlord, but that their obligation to him was met solely through the payment of rent, and asked him to 'acknowledge that we have equal privileges with yourself in the exercise of private judgment'.[105] With Volunteer enthusiasm then at its peak in the town and renewed economic distress again undermining traditional forms of deference, Sharman and Todd Jones carried the hustings for the two borough seats, placing the 'town [...] in a general blaze of rejoicing for the glorious triumph of a people over an aristocracy that formerly ruled that borough and this county with a rod of iron'.[106] The Moira and Lisburn Volunteers paraded to honour their commanders' election as they were 'chaired' through the town to popular acclaim, and reformers celebrated in Belfast under the motto 'Let fame record the glorious day, That independence gained the sway'. One aspiring epic poet extolled the episode with some hyperbole as 'Rome delivered and tyranny expelled, by Mssrs Sharman and Jones of Lisburn'.[107]

However, it seems that Sharman found participation in 'Grattan's parliament' (as it was subsequently and inaccurately labelled) frustrating. Along with other 'popular' MPs he was fined for nonattendance at parliamentary committees in the aftermath of the defeat of Flood's reform motion in 1783 (possibly intended as a tactic of disruption), although he subsequently voted regularly and presented petitions on behalf of public meetings for reform.[108] Sharman's interests extended beyond the Lagan Valley; when approached 'as so distinguished a figure in the annals of Irish virtue' by the inhabitants of Newtownards to present their petition for parliamentary reform in 1784, he expressed 'sincere satisfaction' in being able to do so.[109] He voted against the introduction of Pitt's commercial resolutions for equalising trade with Great Britain in 1785, in defence of Irish economic interests, a rare victory for the 'patriot' opposition after 1783.[110] These frustrations may well have shaped his son's later jaundiced attitude towards the much-idealised College Green parliament.

A hesitant parliamentary speaker, or as he was termed a 'silent senator', his prominence in opposition ranks, as well as his continuing Volunteer involvement, led to his dismissal from the post of collector of Lisburn in August 1784 – an event which provoked protests from the patriot press, the Constitution Club of Belfast, and one piece of political verse that lauded 'Steady Sharman, faithful to his trust / Afeared not, tho a placeman, to be just'.[111] The Builders Corps of Volunteers in Dublin, and later the Roscommon Independent Forresters, made him an honorary member to mark his public virtue in the face of ministerial 'tyranny', indicating the extension of his reputation outside Ulster.[112] One parliamentary commentator praised his character, for 'having imbibed from the best remains of antiquity that spirit of independence which formed its glory, he uniformly acts with a manly decision and a prudent zeal', while noting that an excess of diffidence and modesty had curbed his contributions to debate.[113] Parliamentary oratory was never to be a strong point of the family over the following three generations.

Sharman praised his constituents for setting 'a memorable example of reformation to the boroughs of this kingdom', and assured them that he regarded himself as their delegate to parliament, and governed by their wishes:

> If the people – who ought to be their own governors, – cannot govern their own representatives, I should very much fear lest legislation itself might be reckoned illegal. When the interests of kingdoms and generations become the subject of discussion, it is not the voice of three hundred, but that of three millions, which ought to sanctify the conclusion.[114]

Such radical opinions on popular sovereignty placed him deeply at odds with the conservative county gentry and peerage. Hillsborough complained to the lord lieutenant in 1783 that Sharman had 'distinguished himself in a very extraordinary degree in opposition to the king's government and to your excellency's administration, having continually voted against you and being determined to continue to do so, and having violently opposed me in the County Down because I am firmly attached to both'.[115]

What did patriotism mean to William Sharman? Although by no means an original thinker or writer, he left some commentary on political and economic affairs in his papers. Notes he made for an apparently undelivered speech, suggest a patriotism that was veering towards an Anglophobic economic nationalism:

> Ireland has never contained two thirds of the inhabitants she ought to contain […] It is by means such as these that there is in this kingdom perpetual scarcity and periodical famine. […] G. Britain intruded herself into this country not for the purpose of extirpation, but of subjection. The linen manufacture is the only breath that is left to an astmatick people, to keep alive a feeble existence, just sufficient to produce a crop of consumers of British manufactures – just sufficient to recruit that army, which has made, and still keeps us as a province – just sufficient to produce those taxes which are to pay it – or if not able to do that, to become a mortgage for loans for that purpose – just sufficient to produce those salaries and pensions, which make it the interest of a few to connive at the humiliation of the many[.]

Such opinions placed Sharman in alignment with the renewed anti-importation campaign promoted by Dublin 'popular' radicals such as James Napper Tandy, which was allied with the parliamentary reform movement.[116]

Sharman's constitutional thinking was never fully articulated on paper, but it is likely that it drew on 'patriotic' publications such as Rev. William Crawford's *History of Ireland* (1783), which sought to historicise Volunteering as embodying a combination of the radical Whig civic republicanism of the seventeenth century and which was only partially realised in the 'Glorious Revolution' of 1688, with the Irish patriot tradition dating back to Molyneux and Swift that identified Irish interests as separate and antithetical to those of Great Britain, and with an eirenical position that sought to separate contemporary Catholicism (which should be granted civil equality) from the now receding threat posed by political 'popery' to liberty.[117] Sharman's personal background gave no hint of the origins of his turn to political radicalism in the 1780s. Yet, caught up in the activist spirit of the Volunteer movement, and open to reformist ideas circulating in print and in the public meetings of Belfast and the Lagan Valley in particular, he appears to have become deeply committed to the political project of parliamentary reform and legislative autonomy, and open to the principle of Catholic emancipation.

A second draft manuscript surviving in Sharman's papers suggests a familiarity with Adam Smith's *Wealth of Nations* and an attempt to link its anti-mercantilism with what he saw as an immense drain of absentee rental from Ireland and the continuing restrictions on the Irish wool trade imposed by British legislation. Ultimately, however, he believed meaningful economic reform could only follow patriotic political mobilisation for constitutional change. It was for the electors to act to pursue the interest of the nation as a whole rather than that of themselves or their patrons:

> If the farmer and the manufacturer were as fond of enquiring into the causes of their own misfortunes, as they are of complaining of them, they would think the appointment of a legislator of much more serious consequence, that the eating an electioneering dinner or the shaking hands with the patron of a borough. They would begin to think that if bad laws or the want of good ones are the cause of their declension, they themselves are the first cause of it.[118]

Lisburn's electors might have shown they could do this in 1783, but Sharman opted not to give them the same opportunity to return him at the next election in 1790. Perhaps frustrated with the inaction and corruption of the Irish parliament and his own inability to make a mark in it, and aware of the costs involved in contesting the seat against a rejuvenated Hertford interest, which had 'looked with a jealous eye on the spirit of the inhabitants, and with insidious policy laboured to undermine, what it was too weak to overcome', he declined to stand again that year.[119]

Despite his election as an MP in 1783, Sharman's preference appears to have remained for participation in outdoors political agitation. The Volunteers were becoming a smaller but more decidedly radical body, focused initially on working to revive support for reform at county and borough level. At a meeting of 31 corps in Belfast that year a resolution passed to exclude any unit whose commander opposed parliamentary reform.[120] The Volunteers consequently organised a large-scale petitioning campaign for the cause.[121] The politics of Down approached fever pitch that and the following year, spurred in part by a renewed economic crisis that led one land agent to observe 'how rents will be collected amidst a starving people I know not', and to warn of organised tenant resistance to landlord exactions.[122] Although opposed to agrarian outrages, many Ulster Volunteer corps became political channels for this social unrest in this and the following years.

A county meeting attended by over 300 freeholders met at Downpatrick on 17 January 1784 to agree to petition for 'a more equal representation of the people in parliament' along the lines of the plan proposed at the Dublin convention the previous year. They resolved to 'persevere with unremitting efforts to give it its full effect', and without such reforms 'our constitution exhibits only the skeleton, and not the substance of liberty'.[123] This provoked Hillsborough to organise conservative landowners and their agents to press their tenants to sign a counterprotest, leading one agent to lament that 'we are ready to cut each other's throats about matters we neither know nor understand'.[124]

In the wake of the defeat of Flood's next reform bill in March 1784, a Lisburn assembly met in August to nominate Sharman and four others (including his fellow Volunteers, Todd Jones and Rev. William Bruce, former minister of First Lisburn and now incumbent at the newly-rebuilt First Presbyterian Church in Belfast) as delegates to a new national congress on reform. This body, which was projected by the pro-Catholic emancipation Dublin radicals, provocatively drew on American republican terminology, was shunned by many 'respectable' Volunteers and actively subverted by Charlemont and the government. The congress promptly elected Sharman its chair when it convened in William Street in Dublin in October that year. However this first meeting was poorly attended, with only 14 counties and eight towns represented, was beset by leadership conflicts between Flood and Tandy and divisions over the Catholic question, and the first session came to nothing beyond publishing its resolutions for reform and adjourning until the following year.[125] Nevertheless, the threatened prosecution of Sharman, Tandy and Sir Edward Newenham as its organisers, along with the *Volunteers' Journal* printer Mathew Carey, provoked patriotic outrage.[126] The poor attendance frustrated Sharman and spurred the young Dr William Drennan, present as a representative of the Newry Volunteers, to pen his *Letters of Orellana, an Irish Helot,* to stimulate absent northerners into belated participation. If Drennan's rhetoric was effective in provoking a more extensive Ulster Volunteer engagement with the congress's next meeting in January 1785, it did so at a price. The *Letters* combined an idealistic call for religious unity 'as a secret compact in the cause of your sinking country – for you are all Irishmen', with concessions to the more conservative Protestant view that 'the Catholics of this day are absolutely incapable of making a good use of political liberty'. If, as Drennan's most recent biographer argues, the latter reflected more the immediate needs of literary propaganda than his considered opinion on the subject, it tended to inflame further the sore of division on the Catholic question within the movement.[127]

In sharp contrast, Todd Jones had already called on Protestant reformers in a *Letter to the Electors of the Borough of Lisburn* to support full integration of Catholics into the political nation as a means of curing them of their 'habit of slavery':

> The Catholics are our brethren, and are entitled to the rights of citizenship. If we refuse them this extension, Ireland remains divided, with neither party strong enough to cope with external opponents, or to accomplish any considerable domestic reformation. Justice and affection should influence us to make them free; but if *their* dictates are not sufficiently powerful, those of policy and necessity ought – they are at present ours on terms the most moderate.

He now expressed anger at the congress's reluctance to embrace whole-heartedly a Catholic alliance to pursue reform, despite support for this from the Lisburn and Belfast contingents and a growing number of Catholic Volunteers in the movement.[128] Drennan himself had supported the formation of a Catholic company in Newry, but the tone of the *Orellana* letters had appeared to deny the entitlement of such men to participate in the political nation, a stance he would later repudiate in the wake of the French Revolution.[129]

Sharman's view on the Catholic question appears to have been similar to that of his fellow Lisburn MP, but as president of the congress he retained a neutral stance in the chair. However his comments on the congress's failure came close to despair at the falling away of public enthusiasm for reform: 'Parliament cannot speak the voice of the people, unless the people lift up their voice to the parliament'.[130] Yet he continued to adhere to a hope of eventual success, grounded on an Enlightenment confidence in the progress and eventual triumph of human reason over error and faction in politics just as had already been the case in science and religion:

> We the assembly of delegates for promoting a parliamentary reform, reflecting in the difficulties of our situation, cannot help comparing it to that of other men in all ages, who have searched for the principles of truth amidst the rubbish of error. [...] Such has been the situation of the reformers in religion – persecuted for those very heresies which become in the progress of time the establishment of empires, kingdoms and provinces. Such has been the situation of reformers in the sciences. [...] Such likewise has been the situation of reformers in politicks. The ministers of the day have ever endeavoured to cast a veil over the source of their ill gotten power; had not reformation been a principle of the constitution – it had stepped forward at this day in the barbarism of its gothick original. There has been no occasion for revolutions to bring it back to its original principles; and a long establishment of error, must have been an everlasting veto, to restoring the rights of human nature [...][131]

Resumed (and rather better attended) meetings on 20 January, 4 February and 20 April 1785 led to restatements of the congress's demands and an appeal for its members to persevere in the pursuit of reform, 'unless you would be the mockery of the world, and would have your triumph of yesterday become the reproach of today'.[132] The dangerously 'democratic' membership and aspirations of the congress drew savage attacks, in prose and verse, from pro-government prints such as the *Freeman's Journal,* which alleged that its low-bred delegates were seeking a revolution against 'church, state and king'.[133] The paper welcomed with some relief the congress's 'sinking so rapidly into oblivion' by May 1785.[134] With parliamentary resistance to reform now bolstered by Pitt's appointees to Dublin Castle, including the new viceroy the Duke of Rutland, and with Volunteer numbers falling nationally (a secret government report estimated there were only 18,649 still active in mid-1784), and the Catholic question clearly unresolved within the movement, there seemed limited grounds for hope that such reformist initiatives could succeed.[135]

Grattan now also attacked the radicalised Volunteers as 'drilling the lowest classes of the populace, by which a stain has been put on the character of the Volunteers [...] They had originally been the armed property, were they to become the armed beggary?'[136] But Sharman and his allies could not agree that the original spirit of Volunteering was dead or debased. Although another reform motion was defeated in the Irish commons on 12 May 1785, Sharman's obstinate and self-denying adherence to the cause drew praise from reformist bodies such as the Dublin Constitution Society.[137] Optimistically, the mouthpiece of northern Volunteering, the *Belfast Mercury,* reassured its readers that the congress under Sharman had consolidated the progress of opinion made since the first Dungannon convention, especially in the transcending of religious differences within the reforming campaign.[138] The government appears to have still regarded him as sufficient enough of a threat to have considered buying him off with a place on the revenue board in 1789, although this was either not followed through, or rejected by Sharman.[139]

P. D. H. Smyth, in his survey of the Volunteers and parliament, describes the northern Volunteer reviews of summer 1784 as 'the last twitchings of the corpse of political volunteering', and omits to even mention the existence of the Dublin reform congress.[140] Clearly Volunteering and its associated political bodies were losing momentum in the face of internal divisions over their objectives and legitimacy, a hostile Dublin Castle administration now backed by a strong British ministry, and contempt on the part of many Irish MPs and peers. Men such as Sharman were, however, reluctant to abandon faith in the movement. While he participated in nonmilitary bodies such as the new Dublin Reform Club and continued to support parliamentary motions for reform,[141] this did not mean – as Drennan wrongly alleged in a letter to his sister – that Sharman had lost interest in volunteering.[142] Moreover, rather than the convivial talking shop Drennan dismissed it as, the Dublin Reform Club grew to include some 500 members, and was intended by Sharman (who was one of its vice presidents) to act as an intelligence gathering body on the 'causes of national discontents' and their remedies, although it appears to have disappeared in the course of 1786.[143] Separately from the Volunteers, Sharman was also president of a local reform club at Moira, indicating a taste for associational political culture that ranged from the metropolitan elite to the village community.[144]

Sharman had meanwhile continued to promote and take a leading role in Volunteer parading in the Lagan Valley and Belfast, and to connect these to political mobilisation. This could take on elaborate and theatrical forms: in October 1784 William and Arminella Sharman entertained the entire Union Regiment in a 'Temple of Liberty' erected for the purpose on the Moira Castle demesne, after the regiment had staged a mock battle there before crowds of spectators. The description of the event in the press gives a flavour of both the local popularity of the couple and the utilisation of emblems of enlightened civic republicanism in this rural environment:

> [I]t is impossible to describe the elegance, grandeur and brilliancy of the scene that succeeded. Mrs Sharman had fitted up for the reception of the regiment, a gallery of 90 feet long, in a style that gave the most convincing proof of her generosity and taste. Over the arch at the entrance, was inscribed, in large characters '*The Temple of Liberty.*' From the floor was raised 22 arches of laurel boughs. The roof consisted of nine gothic arches composed of the same, from which hung twelve branches, which served to illuminate the building [...] Perhaps there have been few instances of such a crowd of guests entertained in so elegant and so splendid a manner. All was joy, harmony and ease. – Every one vied with his neighbour in extolling the hospitality and taste of their beloved colonel and his amiable lady. Many spirited and patriotic toasts were drunk. The night was crowned with the utmost festivity, and the whole party departed pleased and happy.[145]

The description offers a rare glimpse of Arminella Sharman as a popular political hostess, a role she shared with many Irish women drawn into active involvement with the patriotic politics of the era.[146]

The 'temple of liberty' trope itself was long associated with patriotism. A gothic temple dedicated to 'the liberty of our ancestors' had been built for Lord Cobham at Stowe in the 1740s and was associated with the English Whig 'patriot' idea of an ancient free constitution.[147] The theme was taken up in the 1780s by American patriots, who used the 'temple of liberty' as a metaphor for American civic republicanism: in 1788 a circular tempietto designed by Charles Willson Peale was built for a Philadelphia parade to celebrate the ratification of the American constitution, and the term was then applied to the plans for the neoclassical Capitol building.[148] The Sharmans' 'temple of liberty' in rural Down was a much simpler and temporary edifice, but its iconography shared something with these 'patriotic' manifestations from across the Anglophone Atlantic world.

Sharman's speech to the regiment at this occasion highlighted the Whiggish constitutional doctrines that shaped his conception of 'liberty'. He had, he assured them, only stood up 'for the rights of human nature'. These had been manifested in the contractual agreements underlying the 1688 revolutionary settlement:

> I have ever understood that the freedom of election, and the freedom of representation, are revolution covenants interwoven with the title to the crown. Every man therefore ought to maintain them, who is loyal to his king and faithful to his country. [...] If our ancestors have handed these covenants down to us loaded with encroachments, I trust the present generation is too enlightened, and too just, to entail them on a succeeding one.

It followed that their political mission was restorative, and that collective action, in arms, was required to defend such covenanted freedoms in the face of official corruption.[149]

The culture of Volunteering was diffused throughout the family's activities: the first birthday of the Sharmans' second son, John Hill, in 1791 was marked by a corps parade in Moira, celebrated in an ode that praised the Volunteers. They bore:

> Arms first assumed to guard our sacred laws
> And rescue freedom from the tyrant's paws;
> Whose pailing thunders now aloud declair,
> That all around in Sharman's joys have share.

> [...]
> See where yon distant smoak ascends*
> Enveloping a stately tower;
> There long, Oh Liberty! thy friends
> Were trampled on by lordly power:
> Til Sharman as thy genius rose
> And fixed thy standard up on high,
> With virtue arm'd opposed thy foes,
> And made the lordly tyrants fly ...
> [*Lisburn][150]

The company similarly turned out to fire three volleys to celebrate his eldest son William's birthday in 1784, an event that seems to have lived long in that child's later memory.[151] More than simply a political manifestation or tool, Volunteering for enthusiasts like the Sharmans had become a way of life.

Nor were these Moira demonstrations of the mid-1780s a swan song for the movement in the region. Sharman continued to command his Union Regiment (by this point comprised of five companies from Moira, Ballynahinch, Rosevale, Aghalee and Dromore) at annual summer reviews of the Volunteers in Belfast, Dromore and Moira in 1785–7, still anticipating a change in the wind that would propel the movement back to the forefront of reforming politics.[152] The 12 July 1787 Volunteer review at Belfast, at which Sharman commanded the left wing of the formation, saw around 2,000 men turn out on parade, and despite a very wet day thousands flocked from the town to watch them, leading one correspondent to observe that 'the spirit of Volunteering had not lost much ground in this part of Ireland', although admittedly numbers were down on previous years.[153] There were, however, more ominous storm clouds gathering. Responding to an address from the Moira Volunteers in September 1785, in which they had expressed relief that the threatened replacement of the Volunteers by a state militia had been averted that year, Sharman reminded them that Ireland's parliamentary independence was actually the child of the institution, which had a paternal duty towards it. The latest storm may have blown over, but they must be constantly on guard to render harmless the next.[154]

Belfast politics and the French Revolution

The French Revolution, beginning with the Parisian people's assault on the Bastille fortress on 14 July 1789, was to offer the rejuvenating spark that true believers in Irish Volunteering had long awaited. News reached Ireland quickly and was widely disseminated through the press, and soon began to influence both the activities and rhetoric of the Volunteers. After a review at Dromore that September, William Sharman's 300 men carried out a mock assault on the market house as the town's 'citadel', 'which afforded great pleasure to the spectators from the judicious and spirited manner in which it was conducted'. Sharman then addressed the Union Regiment and visiting Lisburn Volunteer units on the legitimacy of bearing arms in defence of liberty and the moral duty of electors to act against the 'political plunderers' of their country.[155] In their response, the Volunteers lamented that 'the present state of the country should be so unfavourable to the exertion of a virtue like yours', but observed signs of a change in the wind, hoping that 'a portion of that light, whose brilliancy at this instant illuminates a neighbouring kingdom with such distinguished lustre', would soon also fall on Ireland.[156] Dromore's market house may have taken on the imaginary contours of the Bastille to more than one observer. Indeed, the phenomenal impact of the revolution would lead to both a wider revival of political Volunteering and the resurgence of a radicalism that would initially reinspire but ultimately eclipse that of Sharman and men of his generation.

Any such radical upsurge was still building in 1790, when, despite continuing support from the Belfast Constitutional Society, Sharman stood down as MP for Lisburn. The incumbent William Todd Jones and his running mate Richard Griffith were indeed subsequently defeated at the polls and protested loudly at the widespread use of bribes by the proprietorial interest.[157] Sharman had not completely given up on electoral politics, however, and supported the re-election of his Volunteer colleagues Colonels John O'Neill and Hercules Rowley for Co. Antrim, and backed the self-declared reformer Robert Stewart (son of the newly ennobled Lord Londonderry and known as Viscount Castlereagh from 1796) in Co. Down against the openly antireform Hill interest. Stewart was successful, but only at the expense of Edward Ward, whose own reforming credentials had been tarnished by his irresolute behaviour in 1783.[158] Patriot writers, such as the poet Thomas Atkinson, continued to laud Sharman as the embodiment of civic virtue; retreating from the corruptions of parliament, he would continue to lead the citizens in arms:

> So now whilst venal arts entice,
> Ierne's sons to yield to vice,
> By Mammon bought and sold,
> The noble Sharman bids adieu,
> To Pitt's corrupted helot crew
> Who barter all for gold.
> …
> Blest man! – O rise our isle to guard,
> Yet let Ierne's voice be heard
> Dispel her anxious fears;
> Defend, defend, thy native land,
> When slav'ry threats – still head the band
> Of glorious Volunteers.[159]

The Northern Whig Club was formed in Belfast in March 1790 to promote parliamentary reform and attracted significant numbers of radical middle-class members, many also active Volunteers, alongside more conservative Whig reformers such as Charlemont. Sharman was, along with Todd Jones, amongst its first members. It soon adopted a stance in line with Sharman's views, resolving in April 1790 that 'when an unmasked and shameless system of ministerial corruption manifests an intention to sap the spirit, virtue and independence of parliament, it is time for the people to look to themselves [… or] they must soon sink into the most ignominious slavery'.[160] However the Club quickly became frustrated by the caution of the Irish Whig leadership in Dublin and deadlocked on the unavoidable and pressing issue of Catholic emancipation. A number of Presbyterian radicals, such as the linen merchant and Volunteer William Sinclair, argued that the revolution in France had proven the suitability of Catholics for democratic political rights, but Charlemont and other established leaders wanted the question quashed as inherently divisive.[161] Despite this, its members at this point remained united in regarding the outcome of proceedings in France as beneficial for Ireland, and in July 1791 organised an event at which the Volunteers and inhabitants of Belfast were invited to meet to pass approving resolutions on the French Revolution.

It was to the widely respected Volunteer figure of William Sharman that the club turned to act as chair for the public meeting and subsequent demonstration, and it was over his name that its resolutions were issued. This radical document asserted that the population of Belfast welcomed the revolution in France as men, citizens and as Volunteers, recognising it as an event of universal import, manifesting the 'resurrection of human nature'. The address's assertions on popular sovereignty pointed towards an endorsement of republicanism (albeit in a form seemingly compatible with a constitutional monarchy, as was still the case in France at that time):

> As men, therefore, we think, that government is a trust for the use of the people – the *people*, in the largest sense of that misapprehended word. We think that the public weal is the end of government, and that the forms of government are merely the mutable means for obtaining this end; means that may be changed or modelled by the real will of the public – a will supreme, paramount to all other authority.

The resolution went on to restate the political relevance of the Volunteers in quasi-revolutionary terms, declaring that 'we think the force of the people should form the guarantee of freedom, and that their freedom is the only sure guarantee of public happiness'. In Irish terms, the will of the people demanded an annihilation of 'all civil and religious intolerance', an end to political corruption, and the 'real representation of the national will' in parliament.[162] Sharman subsequently collaborated with Henry Joy (who acted as secretary and translator) as the conduit between the Belfast committee and the French National Assembly, as well as with revolutionary societies at Nantes and Bordeaux, sending to them copies of the Belfast resolutions and receiving responses from France.[163]

In addition to these proceedings, Sharman presided over the Volunteer demonstration, or what might be better described as a political pageant, that celebrated both the American and French Revolutions, as well as an incipient constitutional revolution in Poland, and connected these to the campaign against colonial slavery and to the Irish demand for parliamentary reform. The description of the order of parade in the press gives some sense of the mobilisation of French, American and Irish political symbols involved:

1. The troop.
2. The artillery of the Belfast First Company.
3. A large portrait of the venerable Dr Franklin, elevated on a poll, borne by two young Volunteers. On a scroll under the figure, the following motto, containing the doctor's own words presented itself: 'Where liberty is – there is my country.'
4. Colonel Sharman, of Moira Castle, the president for the day.
5. The First Belfast Company.
6. The Belfast Volunteer Company.
7. A portrait of Monsieur Mirabeau, borne by two young Volunteers. With the following motto, being a translation from one of his orations in favour of the rights of men: 'Can the African slave trade, though morally wrong, be politically right?'

8. Artillery of the Belfast Volunteer Company.
9. THE GREAT STANDARD, elevated on a triumphal car, drawn by four horses, with two Volunteers, as supporters; containing on one side of the canvas, eight feet and a half long by six in depth, a very animated representation of THE RELEASEMENT OF THE PRISONERS FROM THE BASTILE. The point of time chosen for its subject was that at which the first of the French guards burst into the infernal mansion of despotism. – The doors of a number of subterranean cells, and several of the unhappy victims chained to the earth in the most torturing attitudes, with skeletons of wretches that had been suffered to expire and their bodies to remain, were well and affectingly described. The soldier is represented in the act of liberating the unhappy prisoners; the principal figure among which is that of the old man who had been confined upwards of 30 years. His emaciated and debilitated figure was well calculated to promote abhorrence in the breast of every spectator. Motto at the bottom of the portrait – 'Fourteenth July, 1789 – sacred to liberty.'

   The reverse contained a large portrait of Hibernia in a reclining posture; one hand and foot in shackles: a Volunteer presenting to her a figure of liberty, supported by an artilleryman resting on a piece of ordnance. Motto – 'For a people to be free, it is sufficient that they will it'.
10. The Northern Whig Club, and a body of the citizens, amounting to a very great number, formed in pairs, closed the procession. – A green cockade, the national colour of Ireland, was worn by the whole body.[164]

After parading through the town and firing a number of 'feu de joyes', the Volunteers and leading participants dined at the White Linen Hall, presided over again by Sharman, 'whose excellent political and private virtues, stood such tests as endear him to every good mind in the kingdom'. Multiple toasts were drunk in praise of American and French revolutionary ideas and heroes, to the 'patriot King of Poland' as well as to the 'King of Ireland', to English reformers including Tom Paine, to parliamentary reform and the abolition of the popery laws, and to 'Lord Charlemont, and a perpetuity to the Volunteer army'.[165] A toast was also made to the 'society for abolishing the slave trade', already a popular cause in Belfast but rendered more so by the temporary residence in the town of Olaudah Equiano, a formerly enslaved man and campaigner for slave emancipation, who sold 1,900 copies of his memoir during his Irish visit in 1791–2.[166] Unquestionably the Bastille celebrations of 1791 were the pinnacle of William Sharman's political career, placing him (quite literally) at the centre of a demonstration of overt Belfast radicalism (see Figure 5).

However developments were already afoot that would render his political vision marginal and divide the celebrants of 1791 into opposing camps. Despite the choreographed unity of the parades, the Volunteers still publicly disagreed on the Catholic question, and a resolution for full and immediate emancipation, hastily prepared by the Dublin lawyer Theobald Wolfe Tone on behalf of the most advanced of the Belfast activists, was defeated at the public meeting. A secret committee within the Belfast Volunteers, including Samuel Neilson and Henry Joy McCracken and taking inspiration from William Drennan's scheme for 'a benevolent conspiracy – a plot of the people', had been formed in May 1791, and was not prepared to accept such cautious gradualism. The committee began working to establish a new secret society to take forward the agenda of connecting immediate and full Catholic emancipation to radical parliamentary reform.[167]

Although he had been named again as president of the parade and celebratory dinner, an attack of gout led to Sharman taking a lower profile during the Bastille Day proceedings of the following year.[168] His colleague from the Dungannon conventions John Crawford of Crawfordsburn, commander of the Bangor Volunteers and major of the Independent County Down Regiment, replaced him as reviewing general at the Belfast demonstration of 14 July 1792. The day was again marked with a parade through the town's streets, this time also involving Sharman's Union Regiment.[169] Crawford was offered command of a new Volunteer battalion to be raised in Belfast and became active in the Whig Club, while Sharman was toasted in absentia.[170] A further 'fiery and antimonarchical' address from the 'Citizens of Belfast' to the French National Assembly, penned by Drennan, was approved by acclamation at the associated public meeting, while Tone's more carefully worded resolution for Catholic emancipation was also now passed by a substantial majority, albeit with continuing opposition from more conservative figures such as Waddell Cunningham and Henry Joy, who had sought to rally the 'country corps' against it with limited success.[171] Opinion had clearly shifted in the previous 12 months, in part due to a takeover of the Catholic Committee in Dublin by a radical middle-class group led by John Keogh which appointed Tone their agent and drew up plans for a quasi-democratic convention to demand full emancipation, and also by the popular influence of Tone's 'masterful' tract *An Argument on Behalf of the Catholics of Ireland,* which was widely circulated in Belfast.[172]

Rumours that Sharman had withdrawn from the 1792 demonstration due to opposition to the allegedly 'seditious' resolutions proposed in the second address to the National Assembly were vociferously rejected by a member of the Union Volunteers in a letter to the *Northern Star,* which had been recently established by Neilson and his allies to challenge Joy's increasingly cautious *News-Letter.* The writer urged the movement to remain united in its adherence to radical reform and to spurn conspirators, and expressed total confidence in the political commitment of his regimental commander: 'The whole general tenor of the public conduct of Colonel Sharman's life, his certain illness, and the fervent expressions of his letter to the Union Regiment, is a sufficient conviction of such scandalous insinuations'.[173] Sharman himself had written to the regiment stating that 'as you are now going to commemorate a revolution, which has restored 26 million of the human race, to the dignity of human nature, from the lowest state of slavery, I make no doubt that every man of you, will feel satisfaction in rejoicing on such an occasion'.[174] The regiment maintained a consistent reputation for radicalism and support for Catholic emancipation; indeed in August 1792 Sharman vetoed the application of two newly formed companies to join it 'on the ground of their holding Peep o'Day Boy principles', that is, of association with anti-Catholic secret societies.[175] The emergence in Down of Volunteer units openly supportive of Protestant ascendancy was, however, a straw in the wind, and may have been a reaction to the outbreak of sectarian clashes in the Rathfriland district that summer as well as the potential of pro-Catholic reforms being passed through the Irish parliament as a tactical move by Pitt's administration.[176]

Sharman was fit again to review the Volunteers of his regiment and visiting contingents (now swollen to 860 men with nine new corps present) gathered at Dromore on 19 September 1792, which, unbeknownst to those present, would turn out to be the last of these events in the county. The *Northern Star* enthused that 'from the commencement of the Volunteer Institution to the present time, more genuine unaffected hospitality, or more affectionate attachment to the cause, was never displayed by any people in Ireland, than by the worthy inhabitants of Dromore'.[177] Speaking to the ranks Sharman urged them to maintain Volunteer discipline, uphold the law equally between Catholics and Protestants and against all disturbers of the peace, and continue to pursue parliamentary reform; he again welcomed the revolution in France as representing the fall of tyranny and as a harbinger of simultaneous reform across all the three kingdoms. He restated his position on the French Revolution as a symbolic moment of freedom to be celebrated and instrumentalised rather than a template to be applied to Ireland:

> Last year when I attended the celebrations of the French Revolution at Belfast, I had two motives for doing so – one was to rejoice at it – as a dissolution of one of the greatest tyrannies of the world. – The other was to rejoice at it – as a memento to the several governments of the earth – to make a timely reform of abuses – for discontents among the people may be compared to geometrical progression – in the beginning of the climax, it has the appearance of a pigmy – as it advances it becomes a giant: and where the end of it will be, is beyond the power of human calculation to determine.[178]

His continuing support for the revolution in arms in France was in line with that of the Belfast Volunteers, who paraded at the town's White Linen Hall on 30 October to express their joy at the recent military successes of the newly proclaimed French Republic, whose army had repulsed invading Austrian and Prussian forces at Valmy the previous month.[179]

In December Drennan issued an address to the Volunteers of Ireland, calling for renewed conventions to demand reform and emancipation, a call taken up by a Belfast town meeting which established an organising committee for Ulster.[180] Sharman was elected for the barony of Dunluce to the final Ulster Volunteer convention held at Dungannon in February 1793, and as such was committed to support the resolutions of the county delegates agreed at Ballymena on 14 January. Full and immediate Catholic emancipation was now unambiguously endorsed.[181] Todd Jones wrote to the *Northern Star* to assert his confidence that Catholic rights would be entrusted to the safe hands of the delegates from Antrim (of which he was also one).[182] In Down, Crawford took the lead in promoting the latest convention, reportedly winning over many with his 'spirited and rational arguments' made at a county meeting.[183] There is evidence that this position had widespread support from the localities, at least in the north-eastern counties; the Banbridge Volunteers, for example, resolved that, as 'citizen-soldiers' they were loyal to the crown and constitution, but were also firmly committed to parliamentary reform, by which they meant a 'full and fair representation of ALL the people, in the commons' house, *and without which we cannot be satisfied*'.[184]

When the delegates of five of the nine Ulster counties assembled at Dungannon on 15 February 1793, Colonel Sharman as the pre-eminent reformist senior officer was again chosen to chair the proceedings, and sat ex officio on the committee elected to draft its resolutions. The press reported favourably on the plenary meeting, one correspondent noting that 'the complexion of the meeting was highly respectable and spirited; and there is every reason to believe they will proceed with firmness and unanimity', as well as observing that the galleries were crowded with observers, including 'an elegant groupe of the fair sex'.[185] As chair, Sharman endorsed the resolutions passed as 'the sense of *the people*' for extensive parliamentary reform (including abolition of all boroughs, frequent elections and reallocation of representation based on the population and wealth of districts) and 'immediate and entire' Catholic emancipation, as well as others that rejected republicanism in Ireland and expressed adherence to the British connection through the crown.

The latter points frustrated the younger cadre of ultraradicals who had formed themselves into the secret Society of United Irishmen in October 1791.[186] Of these, Lord Edward Fitzgerald and Archibald Hamilton Rowan attended the convention from Dublin as observers, while Rev. William Steel Dickson, as a delegate from Down, took the opportunity to promote his tract *Scripture Politics*.[187] Ministerialists in Dublin affected, however, to see no distinction between the 'respectable' reformers and the republicans; in the Irish commons the law officer Edmond Stanley conflated the two and warned that if unchecked, it 'would proceed from innovation to innovation, until they introduced the worst species of all constitutions, an unbridled and unbalanced democracy'.[188]

Before breaking up on 16 February, the convention condemned the government's plans to raise an Irish militia, and vowed never to dissolve the Volunteers. Crawford voiced the dominant view that the Volunteers, if expanded, were capable of defending the country against any threatened invasion as well as of restoring the constitution to its original 'first principles'. Considerable antiwar sentiment was expressed, although the convention took the view that it should not take a formal vote on the question. Reconvening as a separate meeting of gentlemen and inhabitants of the northern counties on the same day, it recorded its concern that Ireland was 'likely to be involved in the horrors and expenses of a *foreign war;* a war by which, as a nation, we can gain nothing; but on the contrary *must* expose our commerce to depredation, and our country to unprovoked hostility'. Rounding off the business of the convention proper, Sharman was thanked both for his service as chair, and for his wider patriotic record.[189]

Although a standing committee was established under Sharman's chairmanship with powers to reconvene the provincial meeting when required and to plan a national convention to promote reform, this would turn out to be the last hurrah of the Volunteer movement, which was already under threat from parliament and was finally suppressed by executive fiat the following month. An Unlawful Assemblies Act, passed by the Irish parliament in July 1793, subsequently rendered it illegal to hold any of the description of conventions and congresses with which Sharman had been so prominently associated since 1782. So soon after its last flourish at Dungannon, it appeared the non-revolutionary campaign for reform in Ireland was now dead and radicals faced the stark choice of accepting defeat (at least for the present) or initiating a conspiracy for the violent overthrow of the status quo.

The shock of 1798

By the early 1790s the politics of Sharman and his generation of reformist Volunteer leaders were starting to look anachronistic. Approached in 1790 by Samuel Neilson about supporting the latter's plan for a standing committee to mobilise the independent electoral interest in Co. Antrim, Sharman refused to endorse any form of political organisation that required voters to pledge their allegiance to a political platform. He argued that this smacked of aristocracy and would compromise the free agency and conscience of the independent elector, which was the only guarantee of virtuous action.[190] Although both he and Neilson were active supporters of the 'independent' cause in the county, his ideal of enlightened political virtue was out of tune with the more programmatic ideas of the younger radicals, although they seemed at first reluctant to admit any rupture with the older generation.[191]

This mutual misunderstanding came to a head in the lead-up to the Volunteer parade in Belfast in July 1791, when Samuel McTier passed to Sharman a copy of his brother-in-law William Drennan's paper proposing the formation of a quasi-masonic secret radical society within the Volunteers, presumably in the hope he would join or at least not obstruct it. It is telling that, although a man of an older generation and from outside the middle-class radical clique of Belfast Presbyterians, they respected him enough to sound him out on the subject. McTier was careful as to whom the potentially seditious document was shown, excluding Dr Alexander Haliday as too close to Charlemont and as 'greatly prejudiced against the Catholics', but including Rev. William Bruce, who was however also not in favour.[192] Apparently not comprehending what was being advocated, Sharman showed the paper to his friend and relative George Black, the former sovereign of Belfast, whose son (also named George) in turn sent it via an intermediary to the authorities in Dublin Castle. Black observed it 'contained a Cataline conspiracy, that it was devilish well-written and in strong nervous language'.[193]

Sharman was thus something of a security risk to the incipient United Irishmen. Nevertheless, they still appeared reluctant to break with him completely. In August 1792, while staying with Lord Moira at Montalto, Tone and his companions Rev. Edward Berwick, the earl's private chaplain and vicar of Leixlip, and the linen merchant John Williamson of Lambeg, met with Sharman at nearby Spa and stated their case (ostensibly on behalf of the Catholic Committee) regarding cooperation with the Catholic Defender organisation in pursuit of the restoration of peace in disturbed south Down. They omitted to state that the United Irishmen had simultaneously been seeking to infiltrate the companies of his Union Regiment of Volunteers, thus far with limited success. Tone recorded in his diary:

> Mr Sharman extremely friendly and condemns the conduct of the aristocrats and their dependents; he approves extremely of the address to the Defenders which we shew him. All this very well. [...] Williamson a sharp dog: has been tampering with the Union Regiment to get addresses counter to the Belfast proceedings on the 14th of July; tried three different companies and failed in every one; obliged to give it up, yet he prates about liberality and justice.[194]

Sharman was thus understood as supporting an alliance with leaders of the Catholic popular movement to pursue jointly parliamentary reform and emancipation. But where he stopped short (unlike his younger Volunteer colleague and former fellow Lisburn MP William Todd Jones, who joined the Dublin Society of United Irishmen) was in becoming a member of any oath-bound secret society to promote this and any more radical action that might sunder the British connection.[195] As has been observed, the Volunteers' Dungannon resolutions of 1783 were more democratically advanced than the agreed position of the United Irishmen at this stage. It was not until 1793 that the United Irishmen committed to universal male suffrage and annual elections, albeit without a secret ballot. The latter's growing enthusiasm for proactive revolutionary action, if necessary pursued to the point of complete separation with Great Britain, was however, anathema to most older Volunteers, despite their lack of an alternative viable reformist strategy.[196]

What was left of the non-revolutionary Volunteer platform collapsed from February 1793 as Britain's intervention in the war with France polarised opinion, and the state's security clampdown led in March to the outlawing as a subversive organisation of the Volunteers in Ulster and the creation of a new state-controlled Irish militia raised by conscription and under harsh army discipline. Several 'military riots' in Belfast in March–May 1793, while officially discountenanced by the authorities, were clearly directed against the houses and properties of Volunteers and the *Northern Star*, and appear to have been intended by commanders to overawe the town as the Volunteers were being disbanded. Targets for the army's violence included not only random civilians in the street, but also publicly-displayed images of Mirabeau, General Dumouriez (the victor of Valmy) and even Benjamin Franklin, which were now deemed openly seditious in the context of the newly declared war with France.[197] Martha McTier attributed the absence of severe bloodshed solely to the restraint shown by the Belfast Volunteers under the influence of Henry Joy McCracken in the face of such overt provocation.[198]

Following the proclamation banning the movement on 11 March, many old Volunteers such as Sharman withdrew to their estates or professions and away from active politics, leaving more extreme radical groups to go underground. Sharman may also have felt himself compromised by the republication, by both the *Northern Star* and British radicals, of the Duke of Richmond's 1783 letter addressed to him on parliamentary reform, which in the superheated atmosphere of wartime was regarded by the government as subversive and was cited in several state trials of British radicals in 1794–5. A wave of government prosecutions of prominent Irish radicals including Drennan and Hamilton Rowan as well as the French agent Rev. William Jackson may well have reinforced this caution.[199] In the face of revolutionary plotting by the now underground United Irishmen, a number of other former Volunteers tacitly or actively came to support the counter-revolutionary Yeomanry, a voluntary corps loyal to and paid by the crown and with commissioned officers, which was raised in September 1796. Indeed, Charlemont's name was used to attract 'moderate' ex-Volunteers to this new force.[200] There is no evidence to suggest Sharman supported Yeomanry recruitment or activity in this period, although he did remain friendly with that group of moderate reformers in Belfast around Rev. William Bruce and Henry Joy who came to see the status quo as a lesser evil than a revolutionary conspiracy now tainted by the 'terror' in France after autumn 1793, and who joined the Belfast Merchants Yeomanry in 1798. Both Bruce and Joy had previously opposed the formation of the United Irishmen in 1791 and saw the execution of King Louis XVI in January 1793 and the turn in France to Jacobinism and then further military aggression as demonstrations of the dangers of republicanism and the need to pursue only moderate reform. They published their critiques of the United Irishmen and additional 'Thoughts on the British constitution' in the *News-Letter* in 1792–3 and in book form as *Belfast Politics* in 1794.[201] In contrast to their very public stance, Sharman's silence during this frenzied period meant that his posthumous identification with 'pure' Volunteering would remain unsullied by any overt association with loyalism, even if he almost certainly shared their suspicions of the direction taken by the United Irish movement.

In mid and south Ulster the political polarisation was at its most intense and heavily sectarianised; many Protestant Volunteers in Co. Armagh in particular had been strongly opposed to the political concessions to Catholics promoted by the radical leadership at the Dungannon conventions, and refused to follow the Belfast, Lisburn and some other corps in admitting Catholics to their ranks and marching to their local chapels as demonstrations of support for emancipation.[202] When sectarian conflict reignited in Armagh and neighbouring counties in the mid-1790s many former Volunteers there were thus drawn into the incipient Orange movement established at Loughgall in September 1795, and subsequently into the Yeomanry. This sectarian conflict quickly spread into west Down, where it found sympathy among those hostile to any further religious concessions. In early 1795 Dublin Castle received an anonymous letter stamped in Moira expressing alarm about alleged mass Catholic disloyalty in the area.[203] By Spring 1796 there was open warfare in parts of Down between supporters of the Orange Order and the United Irishmen and their Catholic Defender allies. Lord Downshire's agent Thomas Lane wrote to his employer in May:

> Anonymous and incendiary letters are daily found in Dromore and the Catholic families have notice to quit the place. There is a dreadful animosity apparent towards those people by others who are, I fear, without even a profession of religion. [...] Numbers of depredators from other counties, particularly Armagh, have crept among us and are too much secreted, but not a man will inform. [...] A party of horse ought to be stationed at Moira and here. Lord M[oira]'s tenants are in general bad and the infernal Northern Star and politics of Belfast disseminate too great an indifference to the calls of society and the civil power.[204]

Anxious about the intimidation and expulsion of rent-paying Catholic tenants, while wary of revolutionary subversion by the United Irishmen and distrustful of the discipline of the new militia, Lane's principal concern was for the re-establishment of social control, which he argued required military reinforcements. He subsequently reported on an incident of provocation by 'a Captain Racker for the Orange Boys [... who] headed as the tale goes a considerable body of riotously disposed fellows, etc., and with orange cockades and flags paraded round the lough swearing destruction to all papists'.[205]

In the absence of surviving correspondence it is difficult to trace Sharman's response to this growing sectarian crisis erupting around him, although there is evidence he supported attempts by magistrates to re-impose order, and he was at the head of a public meeting in Moira's market house in April 1796 at which Hugh Hamilton urged the populace to unite together against those whose 'Antichristian doctrines of *ill-will* and *persecution* – instead of that universal *love* and *charity*' were provoking many to acts of religious violence, seemingly a criticism of Orangeism.[206] The disturbances were now directly on Sharman's doorstep, for, as Lane reported, '[t]he town of Moira shelters many licentious characters and is the great inroad and resort for miscreants driven out of the counties of Armagh and Antrim'.[207] The social unity and associational amity of Volunteering was rapidly disintegrating.

Distrustful of Sharman's radical past and the overt liberalism of their landlord the second Earl of Moira (who had succeeded his father in 1793), the 'Loyalists of Moira' opted to ignore both of them in September that year, and to send a petition to the more reliably conservative Downshire. Aware of the latter's concerns over Orange disorder, the petitioners disingenuously presented themselves as 'respectable' citizens in contrast to the Defenders and Belfast radicals: 'Their enemies called them Orange Boys but certain they never acted as such, nor do they like the appellation which they never would assume except for the purpose of strengthening government and overawing conspiracies. If thought necessary they will stand forward: if not, they remain loyal and quiet'.[208]

Notwithstanding this dubious claim, Moira was among the six parishes proclaimed by lord lieutenant Camden in November 1796 and subjected to martial law. It is clear that, unlike Lord Moira's other estate at Ballynahinch, the district was already largely under loyalist control by late 1796, even before the notorious 'dragooning of Ulster' by the army and Yeomanry began under General Lake the following spring, deploying state terror in an attempt to break the United Irishmen's local organisation.[209] Although it is too simplistic to equate United Irish support in Ulster solely with Presbyterianism, a clear correlation did exist, and it may be reasonable to see the development of this hostile environment for radicalism in the 1790s as a spur to the steep demographic decline of Presbyterians (largely through high emigration) between 1776 and 1831 in Moira parish.[210]

By 1797 Belfast too was under army occupation and had been placed in a 'state of terror'; after numerous arrests the presses of the *Northern Star* were smashed by militiamen in May.[211] The French emigre traveller de La Tocnaye observed a military riot enforcing illuminations in celebration of the king's birthday in June. Fearing that a repeat of the French Revolution was imminent in Ireland he thought that the brutal tactics he witnessed while travelling south through Down and Armagh were unpleasant but necessary, for:

> [t]he poor peasant on this occasion, as in so many others, was the dupe of rogues, who put him in the front, and were very careful themselves to stay behind the curtain. The troops went through the country, burning the houses of those who were suspected of having taken the 'Union' oath, or of having arms, and on many occasions they acted with great severity.[212]

Twelfth July 1797 was marked in Belfast and Lisburn by triumphant demonstrations by Orangemen, now assembled in Yeomanry formations, under the patronage of the military commander General Lake and the civil authorities.[213] By Spring 1798, the Orange Order was also openly active in Moira, where it hosted a mass meeting of 22 lodges under the chairmanship of Grand Master Richard Owen on 27 March. The meeting restated its loyalty to the king and constitution in church and state (that is, to the Anglican establishment as well as the political status quo), and praised Camden for vigorously upholding the law and suppressing treason. The order, they claimed, had no animus against loyal Catholics, but was now actively engaged in supporting the state against rebels:

> [W]e further declare, both individually and as a body, we will, by every means in our power, assist that government that we are so warmly attached to, and that army, whose conduct, in all respects, we so highly approve, in suppressing treason and rebellion, whatever shape they may assume, whether treacherously disguised under the mask of *reform*, or more openly demeaning French anarchy; – and if the rashness of *democratic fury* shall lead an invading army to our shores, we pledge ourselves, *thus openly and most solemnly*, to oppose them with our lives and properties, and to obey, at a moment's notice, the orders of his excellency the lord lieutenant and those in authority under him for that purpose.[214]

While this claim to be ready to defend Ireland against French aggression echoed the original rationale of the Volunteers in 1778, the denunciations of 'reform' and French ideas could also be seen as a covert attack on Sharman, still resident on the neighbouring demesne, and the reformist Volunteering he had embodied. The ransacking of Lord Moira's Montalto demesne by the Yeomanry and militia a few months later following the defeat of the United Irish army of Down indicates how insecure such liberal gentlemen and their properties were.

The United Irish rebellion in Down finally broke out on 9 June 1798 at Saintfield, two days after the bloody defeat of the Antrim contingents led by McCracken at the county town.[215] Its leaders sought to rally supporters by associating the movement with resistance to landlordism, issuing a proclamation to the 'army and inhabitants of the Co. Down', '[n]ot to pay any rent to disaffected landlords, as such rent is confiscated to the use of the national liberty war'.[216] It is clear that many of those who 'turned out' in Down were also former Volunteers with some modicum of military training, and in some cases they carried emblems from their former units, such as the drum of the Rathgael Volunteers, which was said to have been displayed at the battles of Saintfield and Ballynahinch.[217] The movement had, however, been seriously weakened in Ulster by the officially-sponsored terror of the previous two years and the arrest of many of its leaders, and had delayed too long in awaiting French support and was unable to take control of the county. On 10 June the loyalist Seagoe Yeomanry, commanded by William Blacker, passed through Moira, confiscating the horses of the congregations attending Sunday services there before reinforcing the garrison at Lisburn, which strategically separated the rebels in Antrim and Down.[218] Isolated and unprepared, the United Irishmen of Down, under the ad hoc leadership of the Lisburn linen merchant and former First Lisburn Volunteers officer Henry Munro, were overwhelmed by crown forces at the Battle of Ballynahinch on 12 June 1798. Some 500 of the 7,000-strong rebel army was reported to have been killed in the fighting and subsequent rout, and widespread destruction and looting of houses by the victorious crown forces followed.[219] Witnessing Munro's subsequent execution outside his home in Lisburn, Blacker praised his personal courage, but noted that it had been folly on the part of the rebels to act separately as county contingents and fail to march together on Belfast. A few days later, Downshire was assured by his agent that the combination of executions and mass arrests was now rapidly pacifying the county:

> Information is coming in very fast from all quarters. Arms are delivering up in thousands, of all kinds, particularly pikes. Hanna of Moira, who was a recruiting sergeant for the rebels, with young Carleton, the Quaker, that went to America, is taken up, and Priest Mooney of Moira is also lodged safe.'[220]

The northern rebellion was clearly finished, with its leaders in custody, dead or fled abroad and its rank and file cowed by repression. The public execution in Belfast on 17 July 1798 of McCracken, arrested and court-martialled after several weeks on the run in the Antrim hills, publicly marked the termination of the revolt in the province.

If Sharman and his family were not directly touched by this ruthless coercion beyond their demesne walls, John Crawford was luckier to escape from state retribution. The property of one of his tenants at Crawfordsburn was burnt by the army as a reprisal and Colonel Atherton requested permission to act against 'inactive magistrates, or rather friends of the

United Irishmen', naming Crawford as one of those so suspected.[221] In 1844 the ultra-Tory Dublin *Statesman* published a letter claiming that Crawford had covered his tracks as a United Irishman and fled to England to avoid either being pressed by the Down rebels into leadership or arrested by the authorities, only returning and taking the oath of allegiance once peace was restored.[222] The paper's intention at that time was a scurrilous attack on his son-in-law, but given the circumstantial evidence, some involvement by Crawford in the movement cannot be discounted. As a friend of Drennan and the McTiers, he may well have been a member in the early years of the United Irishmen, but appears not to have been directly involved in its post-1794 revolutionary phase.

In the wake of the repression of the United Irishmen, and with continuing official endorsement of the Order through its association with the Yeomanry, Orange triumphalism was now irresistible. In 1798 the organisation claimed 28,500 members in Down, and while no doubt exaggerated, it had unquestionably grown into a mass movement, and included a number of former United Irishmen who joined either from newfound conviction or (more likely) as a survival strategy to acquire cover for their previous subversive activity.[223] Despite his antagonism towards the organisation's core doctrine of maintaining Protestant ascendancy, it appears that Sharman felt unable to decline its request to parade in the guise of Yeomanry units to the Moira demesne on 12 July 1799. At least one eyewitness regarded this manifestation as intimidatory; Gabriel Beranger (then a houseguest) recorded in his journal that at least a superficial display of orange colours was required at this time to ensure his, and presumably his hosts', personal safety:

> I spent [sic] time here in a most delightful manner until the 12th of July, anniversary of the Battle of Aughrim, when the various yeomanry of the country, divided in different bodies, each with their proper ensigns, males and females, adorned with orange lilies and ribbands, marched up the avenues. We went adorned in the same way upon the steps of the castle, to see them all pass before us; from whence they were to march to the various churches in the environs, to hear a sermon on the occasion, and then adjourn to the public houses, to spend the remainder of the day in merriment; and as all of them were strict Orangemen, and might, when in liquor, insult anyone not adorned like themselves, I was dressed out with orange lilies and ribbons [...][224]

It is difficult to read this as anything other than as an acute humiliation for the former champion of Irish reform and advocate of Catholic emancipation and his household – the event was a performative parody of the Volunteer reviews of a decade before.

Despite these multiple defeats, however, it would be inaccurate to conclude that Sharman had abandoned the political creed of his lifetime. Composing a private poem in praise of his son William Jr that year (who was then 19 years old), the elder Sharman expressed the subversive sentiment that his son would:

> Then like your ever honor'd sire
> Make stern oppression shake with fear
> And soon a spark of Gallic fire
> May light a blaze of freedom here ...[225]

Such private expressions of dissent from the now hegemonic public language of loyalism were for Sharman, as for so many others in Ulster, one of the few ways of expressing their trauma over the defeat of the radical projects of the 1780s–90s in these years.

William Sharman evidently clung to the symbolic memory of Volunteering, even as its legacies appeared to be disintegrating around him. At some point during the cataclysmic year of 1798 he found time to commission the English artist Thomas Robinson (more famous for his contemporary depiction of the Battle of Ballynahinch) to paint his portrait (Figure 6).[226] Sharman chose to be represented sitting outdoors in the Moira Castle demesne, wearing his now obsolete uniform as colonel of the Union Regiment of Volunteers, and prominently displaying his silver officer's gorget. A Volunteer review is shown as taking place at the background outside Moira Castle, and the colonel is holding a motion for reform in his left hand, and with what appears to be a copy of the Irish parliament's 1783 vote of thanks to the Volunteers under his left elbow. The demeanour of calm defiance with which Robinson depicted his face suggested the sitter's belief that despite the disasters of that year the ideals of the movement would even yet be vindicated.[227] As his poem of 1799 suggests, it was to his eldest son that he entrusted this hope.

William Sharman suffered a debilitating stroke later in 1799 and was confined to his bed for his remaining years. Thus invalided he was incapable of commenting much on the Union debates, although one pamphleteer of that year was confident that as a staunch Volunteer he would have opposed the government's bill to abolish the Irish parliament, and his friend Crawford certainly came out strongly against it.[228] Sharman died at Moira Castle in January 1803 at the age of 71 and was buried at Drumbeg.[229] An encomium by Joy in the *News-Letter* praised his patriotic endeavours as a leading Volunteer but added (echoing Joy's own controversial turn to 'moderation' after 1793) that Sharman '[s]ubsequently withdrew from public affairs in face of the licentious infatuations of the republicans'. An elegiac sonnet by 'Hafiz' (the Dromore linen-bleacher Thomas Stott) followed in the paper two weeks later, locating his death within a wintry landscape of national desolation:

> SHARMAN – lamented SHARMAN – is no more! –
> The friend of genius – to his country dear –
> A patriot prov'd – inflexible – sincere.[230]

Sharman's role in the Volunteers, along with his personal integrity, would be long remembered in Ulster political discourse. In the popular memory in Lisburn, his election headquarters in 1783 was still known as 'Liberty Hall' and was strongly associated with him and with subsequent radical politics as late as 1860.[231] As we shall see, the public memory of Volunteering and Sharman was revived in Belfast radical politics in the early nineteenth century (perhaps filling a place left vacant by the still-taboo United Irishmen, but enthusiastically recalled nonetheless). In rural Down, the memory of Volunteering also lingered. The funeral in Ballynahinch in 1837 of John Armstrong, the last surviving officer of the Union Regiment, and who had attended the 1783 Dungannon convention, was marked by the closure of all shops and an ecumenical service paying tribute to 'the memory of the venerable patriot, who regarded them all as his fellow citizens, and his fellow-Christians'.[232] Forty years later, the Presbyterian paper *The Witness* was reminding its readers of the patriotic enthusiasm surrounding that convention and quoting Sharman's 'animated address' for reform in 1783.[233]

Sharman was not entirely forgotten in England either. Penning a satirical verse on William Pitt the Younger in 1806 or slightly later, the popular London satirist Dr John

Wolcot (writing as 'Peter Pindar'), mocked the prime minister's abandonment of his early reformist leanings, and suggested this image be added to his statue:

> Upon the pedestal his worth,
> And great achievements will start forth:
> In starting capitals I mark reform,
> With Col'nel Sharman's volunteers,
> With pointed muskets, swords and spears,
> To raise for dying liberty a storm.[234]

In conclusion, what can be said about the politics of Volunteering as manifested by William Sharman, a second-rank but nevertheless highly regarded, even revered, figure within the Ulster movement? Inevitably it has been overshadowed by the separatist republicanism of the United Irishmen. The Whiggish constitutionalism of Volunteering politics was already under strain by the mid-1780s and was eclipsed by the highly polarised and febrile politics dominant from 1793 to 1803. However, the patriotic reformism of Volunteering was not without its successes, especially in 1779–82, and the Dungannon conventions articulated what in eighteenth-century terms was a radical alternative to the constitutional and confessional status quo. It is clear from the history of Sharman's Union Regiment that active volunteering continued in mid Down and the Lagan valley throughout the politically regressive years of the later 1780s before being enthused and revived by the news of the fall of the Bastille in 1789. Constitutional reformers such as Sharman welcomed (at least initially) the revolution in France and continued to regard the citizen in arms as manifested in the Volunteers as the essential lever to extracting reform from a recalcitrant and corrupt parliament, until war with France, which permitted the state to expand and mobilise its own military forces, and to repress the Volunteers as potentially seditious, undermined this position. Nevertheless, without the Volunteer mobilisations of the 1780s and early 1790s, inculcating radical and egalitarian ideas through the medium of a citizen's militia, the United Irishmen would not have been possible.[235] Volunteering's legacy was subsequently contested by both constitutional nationalists such as Daniel O'Connell and by protestant radicals such as Colonel Sharman's son, William Sharman Crawford, who sought self-consciously to transpose the politics of his father into the very different conditions of the early nineteenth century.

As Gerald Hall and Stephen Small have argued, the Volunteer movement spoke with 'a cacophony of political languages' in the late eighteenth century, some looking back to the Protestant 'public band' tradition of self-defence, others genuinely influenced by Enlightenment ideas. If Hall is right to propose that Ulster liberalism was one of the political languages that emerged from Volunteering, one significant strand worth further investigation is the non-republican but democratically-aligned radicalism that paradoxically found landed Anglican leadership over three generations of the Sharman family.[236]

2. The making of an Ulster radical: William Sharman Crawford, 1780–1832

Youth and formation

Colonel William and Arminella Sharman's eldest son, also christened William, was born at Moira Castle on 3 September 1780, around the time his father launched his public career on becoming captain of the Moira Volunteers.[1] A daughter, Eleanor, had been born some years earlier in 1773, and another son, John Hill, would follow in 1790. Reflecting on his childhood in a 'retrospective memorandum' penned in 1844, William Sharman Crawford (as the eldest son became legally known from 1827) recalled that even in his earliest years he had been moulded by his father's ideas and politics:

> I spent my infantine [sic] years in the domicile of my father at Moira Castle as his general residence but every year spending the winter in Dublin during the parliamentary session and notwithstanding my early years (being only ten years old when my father retired from parliament) I took a deep interest in all the great political questions on which I would hear him enlarging on the domestic circle of our fireside.[2]

A beloved but sickly child, restricted indoors during the winter and 'kept under constant rules of regimen to guard against stomach derangement, and much against my own will [...] made what you would call a crock and a pet', the young William was not sent to school (except possibly for a short period at a local one run by the rector of Moira), nor entrusted to a tutor, but taught directly at home by his parents.[3] Any gaps left by the colonel's pedagogy in mathematics and the classics were filled by voracious reading in the well-stocked castle library:

> I was taught by him to read and write – and also arithmetic. I was very well grounded in Latin, and read the principal school books – and was taught some Greek. This was all the education I got under the tutelage of my father, but I had a great desire for learning, and I instructed myself in history both ancient and modern, and mathematics and mechanics, geography and astronomy, etc.[4]

Books would remain central to him throughout his life; in 1843 he chose to have himself painted while reading, and the family collection was later described, just prior to its liquidation by auction in 1947, as 'one of the best libraries I have ever visited [... a] wonderful treasure house of literature'.[5]

His father's intense pride in his son's educational and social attainments, and belief that he would carry forward his political legacy, can be found in the private poetry he composed and which is preserved in the family papers.[6] Surviving documents also indicate that their mother Arminella taught the children to draw (Figure 8). William made little use of this skill beyond childhood, but his sister Eleanor became an accomplished watercolourist and appears to have later studied for a time with Gabriel Beranger.[7] Visiting Moira Castle in 1790, the English travel writer Charles Topham Bowden was charmed by the family:

> Mrs Sharman is a lady of great sentiment and humanity. All her felicity seems to be centred in the education of her children; and indeed her instructions have not been lost on Miss Sharman, for she is one of the most accomplished young ladies, of her age, in the kingdom. She has a very elegant taste for poetry and Belles Lettres. She paints inimitably well; and is a capital performer on the piano forte'.[8]

Beranger's copies of Eleanor's watercolours of Moira Castle and Greencastle in southern Co. Down have survived in the collections of the Royal Irish Academy (Figures 1 and 7).[9] There is also evidence that Eleanor assisted her father with his political correspondence, and that she composed patriotic poetry.[10] She married in 1804 a cousin, Hill, son of Captain James Willson who was Arminella's brother and had been the patriot MP for Co. Antrim in 1776–83. She appears to have died (of unknown causes) relatively young in 1808, and William remained on good terms with her widower to the 1830s.[11]

The older Sharmans withdrew from public life as the political environment deteriorated and constitutional reformism was rendered impossible from 1793, and the younger William recalled frustration at the constraints imposed on him, especially when it was resolved he would not attend college to protect him from what his parents feared would be moral as well as bodily contagion. Rare excursions were permitted when he was 17–18 years old, 'when I was allowed as a special favour to pay some visits to Belfast to old Dr McDonnell, and Mr Henry Joy at the Lodge'. The choices of who he was permitted to visit were significant: Joy, the former editor-proprietor of the *News-Letter,* a Volunteer colleague of the colonel and joint secretary of the Dungannon conventions and of the Northern Whig Club, had co-published *Belfast Politics* with Rev. William Bruce in 1794 as a refutation of republicanism and revolutionary conspiracies. He would join the Yeomanry in June 1798, and later established the Belfast Merchants Yeomanry corps in 1803 in response to Robert Emmet's rising.[12] Dr James McDonnell was cofounder of the Belfast Dispensary and Fever Hospital in 1797 and an active figure in the town's cultural and intellectual life. He had at first been on friendly terms with the United Irishmen, hosting Wolfe Tone's 1791 visit and helping Thomas Russell find employment with the Belfast Reading Society (later the Linen Hall Library). He had been a public advocate of abolition of the slave trade and linked this to the case for immediate and full Catholic emancipation in the Belfast debates of 1791–2. However he was also strongly opposed to any revolutionary conspiracy and his contribution to the reward for the apprehension of Russell after the failed 1803 rising led Martha McTier to label him 'the Brutus of Belfast'.[13] Both could thus be trusted to steer the young man safely away from any risk of involvement with the town's United Irish underworld while encouraging a liberal outlook on politics.

There is no confirmed portrait of the younger William Sharman before the several caricatures made of him in the late 1830s and works in oil of the early 1840s. However, it is likely that a painting now in the collections of the Ulster Museum, attributed to Thomas Robinson in 1798 and labelled by the museum 'Portrait of a Young Man (possibly a United

Irishman)' is actually of him (Figure 9). The facial features resemble those of the older Sharman Crawford captured in the 1840s, and it is known that Robinson was at Moira Castle in 1798 to paint his father's 'Volunteer' portrait. The auction listing of Crawfordsburn House's contents from 1947 includes an oil painting, of nearly identical dimensions to the Ulster Museum portrait, with the artist's name missing, described as 'Gentleman, seated, with atlas in hand', an unusual attribute which matches the picture in question as well as the habits of the bookish young William. Another entry in the Crawfordsburn catalogue lists an additional painting attributed to Robinson of a boy in a red suit flying a kite, which was possibly a portrait of William's younger brother John Hill, who would have been eight years old in 1798.[14]

If his father's debilitating stroke in 1799 lifted many of the previous restrictions on his freedom, it also saddled the younger William with the responsibility of managing the family's estates and caring for his ailing mother. He joined a number of Down country gentlemen in signing a petition against the Act of Union in March 1800.[15] If he engaged in any rebellion against his father's ideals it was short-lived, and was within the field of a redefined 'patriotism' in altered circumstances. In 1803 he followed Joy into the Yeomanry, and was gazetted lieutenant and then captain of the Moira Infantry, which he had raised in the wake of Emmet and Russell's attempted rebellion and the reignition of the European wars after the brief cessation of 1802–3.[16] The national complement of the Irish Yeomanry expanded from 63,000 to 80,000 in 1803 as many new corps were formed in what appeared to many a moment of national emergency.[17] By this time that force had come to be regarded as playing a more broad-based patriotic role in protecting Ireland from threatened invasion by an aggressive and militaristic Napoleonic France (a danger rendered more realistic by the small-scale French landing in Co. Mayo in 1798 and the assemblage of a large invasion force in northern France in 1803), and was accompanied by the construction of a chain of defensive Martello towers around the Irish and British coastlines. Faced with this pressing national emergency, the Yeomanry now began to recruit more Catholics. Lamenting the rise of religious polarisation in his 'retrospective memorandum', Sharman Crawford commented that 'from this time the Yeomanry ceased to bear the character of a mere party force and were generally extended over Ireland as a national defensive force'. In 1804 Captain Sharman offered the government the services of his unit for defensive purposes anywhere in the United Kingdom, but as the Napoleonic invasion scare receded and most Irish Yeomanry commanders regarded their remit as being strictly local, the offer was not taken up.[18] He was presented in May 1805 by the NCOs and rank and file of the Moira Yeomanry with a sword 'as a token of their gratitude for his unremitting attention to their discipline and good order', however by 1808 he had resigned his commission.[19]

The reason for this appears to have been his shock, as second in command at a Yeomanry review in Down at some point in 1807–8, at having his orders that the Moira unit 'brigade' together with another Yeomanry corps directly refused, with threats of violent resistance, by his own men. The visiting corps from Scarva, he recalled before a parliamentary committee in 1835, contained some Catholic recruits, and the Moira Infantry, which were comprised entirely of Orangemen except for himself and another officer, refused to co-operate with it on the sectarian grounds of inherent Catholic disloyalty. Feeling under personal threat himself, 'because it was known I was a friend to Catholic emancipation', he found he could not enforce military order at the review and later felt obliged to resign his commission, thus ending his brief flirtation with military life in disillusionment.[20] This was a far cry from the political fraternity and consensual discipline his father had enjoyed with the Moira Volunteers two decades before, and which the young William may also have aspired to when joining the new corps in 1803.[21] As Allan Blackstock has observed in his history of the Irish Yeomanry, such resistance to 'brigading' was common in Ulster at this time, and there were other incidents of threatened mutiny over the inclusion of even small numbers of Catholics or expressions of support for emancipation on the part of liberal Protestant officers.[22]

William Sharman's subsequent career, especially from 1829, suggests a continuing degree of reverence towards his father's political ideals and a desire to restore them to relevance in the changed circumstances of the 'age of reform', albeit without the restoration of an armed force such as the Volunteers, which now appeared unfeasible. His memorandum of 1844 identified the location of his father's documents in the family house, suggesting deep familiarity with his political life, as well as indicating his own close reading in the published histories of the period.[23] The 'Volunteer' portrait of the colonel by Robinson travelled to his son's new house at Crawfordsburn in 1827 and presumably was given pride of place there. In addition to his father's papers, he also became deeply familiar with the speeches and writings of the patriot leader Henry Grattan, and used them liberally in his own addresses and publications.[24] He would also pen a short history of the Irish Volunteer movement himself towards the end of his life, albeit for a contemporary political purpose.[25]

William's stance on one of the most formative political events of his lifetime – the United Irish rebellion of 1798 (and its more muted echo in 1803) – was ambivalent. Unlike the slightly older Daniel O'Connell, who managed to cover his youthful flirtation with the United Irishmen through concurrent membership of the Dublin Yeomanry and a well-timed retreat to west Kerry in 1798,[26] William has been both too young and too closely protected by his family and his father's friends to have been drawn into the revolutionary movement. Yet he had been fully conscious of the upheavals of that year, which had raged around the family home at Moira. He could not but have been aware of both the continuities between the radical political ideals of the Volunteers of east Ulster and the United Irishmen, of the atrocities carried out by the forces of the state in 1797–8 and of the sectarian triumphalism of Orangeism in its aftermath. He is almost certain to have been present at the humiliation of his family by the Orange parade to the Moira demesne in July 1799.

Like O'Connell, he referred relatively infrequently to the rebellion in his later political career, taking its principal lesson to be that non-violent popular politics must take the place of any counterproductive resort to revolutionary action, which had proved so disastrous in 1798. In his 1844 'retrospective memorandum' he placed the responsibility for the revolt principally on government repression, as:

> in the years 1792 and 1793 proclamations were issued by the government with a view of putting down all remnants of the Volunteer system. From this time the organization began to assume a private and illegal character and ultimately ended in that open manifestation of hostility to the authority of England which produced the rebellion in 1798.

He blamed the government for empowering the sectarian force of Orangeism through incorporating it into the Yeomanry from 1796, which he was at pains to show was based on totally different principles to the Volunteers (while also admitting his later participation in the latter once it had 'ceased to bear the character of a mere party force').[27] If his stress on the role of state and Orange provocation in igniting the rebellion tended to downplay the activism of United Irish idealists, it did, as Trevor McCavery suggests in his study of rebel motivation in north Down, reflect in part the complex reasons that drove many Presbyterians to 'turn out' there in 1798.[28]

Like many post-1803 Ulster radical reformers, he maintained connections with some who had been involved in the United Irish movement. His son John visited the exiled northern United Irishmen William Sampson and Andrew Bryson in New York in 1835 (sending back to his father a copy of the former's memoir), suggesting amicable relations between them. Sampson's argument that the United Irishmen had been reluctant revolutionaries provoked into action by reactionary British policy aligned with his own understanding of 1798.[29] In the following year Sharman Crawford supported a petition for clemency for Arthur O'Connor, requesting the unexpired sentence of exile imposed on him as a United Irish leader be lifted. Such an intervention may well have attracted the attention of Arthur's nephew Feargus O'Connor, who had a deep personal commitment to vindicating both his uncle and his father Roger and bitterly resented their persecution after 1798.[30] In Belfast Crawford came to work closely with some former United Irish members or sympathisers who subsequently took up reformist politics, such as Charles Hamilton Teeling and members of the Tennent family, although there is no record of direct engagement with those who endeavoured to keep the radical tradition of republicanism alive in the town, including Mary Ann McCracken and Jemmy Hope (the latter in later life an Owenite socialist who was highly critical of the limitations of tenant-right politics). Despite this, his enemies had no hesitation in associating him with the rebels of 1798 on numerous occasions.[31]

In contrast, his filial loyalty to the Volunteer tradition was evident to his enemies as well as his friends, with one hostile critic in 1830 commenting that 'it could [not] be at all wonderful, if the son of Sharman and liberty at Lisburn, or the nephew of Wilson and liberty in Antrim, should inherit some of the seeds of ambition which led those vain men to push themselves into situations, so far above either their abilities or their circumstances'.[32] In revering (if not idealising) his father's generation Sharman Crawford was far from unique and shared this stance with O'Connell. Both believed that there were lessons to be learned from the ultimate failure of that movement. Thomas MacNevin's laudatory *History of the Volunteers of 1782*, published in 1845, was in step with his own view that only with a clear commitment to Catholic emancipation and equal citizenship, and determined and non-violent leadership endorsing full parliamentary reform, could the movement have fully succeeded – and indeed these were positions he understood his father as having promoted within its ranks.[33] What made Crawford increasingly unusual was his desire to restore this radical tradition to the heart of Ulster Protestant politics, and to recentre and take further both the democratic and social equity dimensions of that inheritance.

Marriage and inheritance

On 5 December 1805 William Sharman married Mabel Frideswid Crawford. There is no record of where and when the couple met, although hints about a romantic attachment can be found in a poem by his father praising his son's dancing at a ball in 1799 also attended by the Crawfords, which suggests a possible relationship from around this time, although Mabel at that point was only fourteen.[34] The Sharman and Crawford families had long been closely associated, with Mabel's father John serving as a Volunteer officer and delegate to the Dungannon conventions and the Reform Congress. Crawford continued to be politically active in Down politics after 1798, strongly criticising the Act of Union as likely to 'hazard the existence of that connection it intended to perpetuate', and becoming antagonistic to the Stewart interest and its leader, Lord Castlereagh, who was after 1798 widely regarded as a turncoat by northern reformers.[35] He remained active in the affairs of Belfast, taking a leading role, for example, in an 1822 town meeting to raise a charitable subscription for the famine-hit southern counties.[36] Mabel's mother, formerly Maria Kennedy of Cultra, who according to Martha McTier was 'the only woman [John Crawford] ever loved', was also from a Volunteer family.[37]

If the match was politically and personally harmonious it did not at first greatly advance William Sharman materially, as Mabel's younger brother Arthur Johnston Crawford was the heir to the family's properties. Piecing together the relationship between William and Mabel is difficult given the absence of much extant personal correspondence between them. They were to have 12 children together, born between 1807 and 1827 (their eldest child, christened William, died in childhood in February 1817 and was buried at Waringstown), and he was distraught when she died, aged 59, in 1844.[38] She seems to have shared his political vision, and in one of her few surviving letters expresses 'exultation' that her and her husband's conduct should meet her father's approbation, and looked forward to a visit they would make together to Crawfordsburn in 1817.[39] Mabel certainly took a close interest in William's political affairs from 1830, acted as a political hostess, and encouraged her children to participate in his campaigns.[40] Sharman's relationship with his own mother, however, became more fractious after his father's death and his own marriage, involving disputes over money matters and care for his ill younger brother John Hill, who died of consumption a year after graduating from Trinity College, Dublin in 1812.[41] After leaving Moira Castle, Arminella Sharman took up residence in Belfast, were she was cared for by her sister's daughters, Margaret and Mary Craig (children of the Volunteer clergyman Rev. Andrew Craig); she died in the suburb of Windsor in 1808.[42]

In 1805 the Sharmans' 31-year lease on Moira Castle expired; the castle and estate were then sold by the second Earl of Moira to Thomas Bateson, and the big house was subsequently demolished after falling into ruin.[43] For the next two decades the young married couple and their expanding family led a peripatetic life. They were resident for some time at Farm Hill House near Waringstown, Co. Down, five miles south-west of Moira, and then leased the larger Windsor Lodge in Waringstown village after purchasing the fee-farm of the demesne from Richard Magenis in 1807 (who in turn held it from Rev. Holt Waring of Waringstown House). The arrangement proved profitable: Sharman cut and sold £2,000 worth of timber from this property before the lease was transferred to John Brown in 1820.[44] This period of residence in a village dominated by a major cambric factory may have introduced Sharman to the forms of industrial production to which he would continue to pay close attention; he later considered establishing a water-powered flax spinning establishment at Crawfordsburn, but did not pursue this.[45]

By the end of 1819 the family were living at 11 Fitzwilliam Square East in Dublin, with some periods also spent at Stalleen House on their Co. Meath estate.[46] While the Sharmans were at the latter, their eldest daughter Maria (born 1808) met Henry Coddington, heir to the neighbouring Oldbridge House estate on the Boyne. They married in 1827, and she was to die in childbirth in 1845 leaving eight surviving children.[47] William Sharman had been appointed by his landowning peers to the grand jury for Down in the same year as his father's death in 1803, and he appears to have been a regular participant in the county governance exercised by this oligarchic body from then onwards (including during his years of residence elsewhere as an absentee). Although his still relatively limited means made him at best a minor player in county political affairs before 1827, his period of residence in Dublin in the 1820s allowed him to observe the mobilisation of the Catholic Association under O'Connell at close hand, and it appears to have been this model of non-violent reformist agitation that influenced his future political career.

The family's prospects were transformed by two deaths within five months, in what William was later to describe as 'an unexpected dispensation of Providence'.[48] The first was that of Mabel's brother Arthur on 13 October 1826. Arthur had been ambitious, serving as high sheriff for Down in 1818–9 and as major of the North Down Militia, and took advantage of his wealthy cousin Lord Caledon's patronage to secure return to parliament for the notorious rotten borough of Old Sarum in 1818–20.[49] His time in the commons was not successful, and his love life was equally blighted: in 1812 he had been rejected as a suitor to Lady Emily Stewart, sister of Lord Castlereagh. He died a disappointed man, unmarried and childless, reportedly the victim of the accident of 'falling out of his gig'.[50] Within a few months in February 1827 John Crawford followed his son to the grave, after amending his will to make his daughter's husband his sole heir without entail, on the condition that the latter adopt the Crawford family name along with his own.

William was happy to comply, noting that his father-in-law had expressed 'feelings of unlimited confidence in me – perhaps beyond what prudence might justify'. He was quick to ensure a generous settlement to John's widow Maria, who was to live for another two years. He wrote to her:

> Your comfort for remainder of your life was the first object of his heart. [...] he could not leave you Crawfordsburn as it was strictly entailed on his children – but if you wish to retain it as your residence and be mistress of the establishment there I hope you will consider the house and its contents as your own for life, in addition to provisions for you in his will, and I will make every arrangement necessary for support of the establishment – in this I express your daughter's wishes equally with my own. But if you do not wish this, your continued residence with myself and family would give me the greatest possible gratification, by giving us all the opportunity of at least endeavouring to discharge those duties which affection, gratitude and every good feeling of the heart demands from us [...]

He went onto apologise for any brusqueness of manner he may have previously displayed, having noted, 'a natural backwardness of manner which I never have been able to overcome & not any want of proper affections in the heart'.[51] In March 1827 he received a royal warrant to add his wife's family name and arms to that of his own, and was known subsequently as William Sharman Crawford.[52] The family motto would prove particularly apt: 'Durum Patientia Frango', or 'through patience I overcome difficulty'. Although Mabel's mother died at Crawfordsburn in 1829, the two families remained close; his second surviving son Arthur married in 1846 Louisa Alicia, daughter of Mabel's uncle William Crawford, who had moved to Cork in 1779 and cofounded in 1792 what became the highly successful Beamish and Crawford Brewery in the city. William's youngest daughter Eleanor would also marry in 1863 her second cousin Thomas Crawford of Belfast. By 1827 William, Mabel and their large family (there were 11 surviving children by that year, of whom only Maria had her own household) were living at Crawfordsburn, with their children being educated at home by tutors.[53]

The inheritance of 1827 brought William two significant estates in Down, the principal one being at Crawfordsburn, located on the coast between Holywood and Bangor in the north of the county, and which had been the Crawford family's seat since around 1670, when several townlands had been purchased from Lord Clanbrassil by William Crafford or Crawford, previously a sitting tenant and a descendant of Scottish settlers. By 1740 a land register had recorded the estate name of Crawfordsburn.[54] Adjoining the much more extensive Clandeboye estate of Lord Dufferin, the Crawfordsburn estate was relatively modest in extent, covering some 430 acres (89 of which were laid out in demesne gardens and parkland) divided between several townlands, and part of the estate village of Crawfordsburn and a nearby corn mill. The major draw was Crawfordsburn House, standing on an elevated site overlooking Belfast Lough, which had been built in three stages in the seventeenth, eighteenth and early nineteenth centuries. The old whitewashed house, 'a large, square, plain, commodious building', had long been a landmark for ships approaching Belfast, and was functional rather than ornate, which suited its new owner's unostentatious tastes.[55] Joseph Molloy's view of the house, etched and published by E. K. Proctor in 1832, depicts it from the shoreline of the lough at a perspective of some distance, appearing rather closer to the water than it actually was (Figure 10).[56] The demesne's attractive seashore and wooded glen and waterfall became a popular excursion site for the surrounding urban populations under William's ownership (and with his permission).

The second estate, 20 miles to the south at Rademon near Crossgar, had been acquired by John Crawford in consequence of his father's marriage in 1740 to Mabel, daughter of Hugh Johnston, MP for Killyleagh; it came to him after the death without heirs of her brother Arthur Johnston in 1814. It contained another substantial seventeenth-century house sitting within a larger 323-acre demesne. With Rademon came the good-quality agricultural land of nearby Creevycarnonan and Drumgiven townlands in Kilmore parish, and the non-contiguous townlands of Ballywillin (or Ballywoollen) in the parish of Killyleagh and Dunbeg Upper in Magherahamlet parish on the eastern slopes of Slieve Croob, which contained a larger number of smallholding tenants of mixed religious affiliations.[57] When these were added to the existing Sharman patrimony in the barony of Upper Iveagh, the family now held some 5,748 statute acres in Down, in addition to the 754 acres at Stalleen in Donore parish in Meath (along with a profitable limestone quarry at nearby Sheephouse, that supplied the building needs of the town of Drogheda), the 27 acres around his great-uncle's former house at Bonnybrook near Dublin, and his grandfather John Sharman's original small property at Aghavary in Antrim.[58] This consolidation lifted the Sharman Crawfords into the ranks of the middling Down gentry, although still falling well below the county's top ten landowners with estates larger than 10,000 acres, and minuscule in comparison to the aristocratic magnates the marquesses of Downshire and Londonderry, who owned some 64,000 and 24,000 acres respectively in Down by the 1870s, in addition to major holdings elsewhere in Ireland and in Great Britain. The new estates ensured Sharman Crawford a substantial income, despite setting lower than usual rents – the family's Down estate was valued at nearly £6,000 per annum in the mid-1870s – and made possible an 'independent' political career that had until then appeared beyond his reach.[59]

Like his father and John Crawford before him, the younger William maintained an interest in the cultural and political affairs of the town of Belfast. In 1813 he was named as a patron of the town's musical festival, held to raise money for the Belfast Charitable Society and its poorhouse.[60] He was also a subscriber to the Belfast Academical Institution, founded in 1810 following a campaign by radical and reformist Presbyterians to bring higher learning to the town, and opened with a patriotic address by William Drennan in 1814. A supporter of its non-denominational ethos, Sharman Crawford himself was elected vice president of 'Inst' in 1831 and was active in the role.[61] His principal public activities prior to 1827 were, however, those of a country gentleman and showed limited evidence as yet of his inherited radicalism. He appears to have served on the grand jury in most years, chairing a meeting as high sheriff in 1812 in which his father-in-law unsuccessfully attempted to persuade it to support retaining the long-standing county MP Francis Savage without a contest. Although silent on this occasion as chair, in light of his subsequent politics William may well have sympathised with the impassioned argument of the radical Belfast merchant Eldred Pottinger that the freeholders of the county, and not its leading landed families, should decide on their own representation.[62] He retained his family's long-standing support for Catholic emancipation, being one of 24 Protestant gentlemen who signed a petition in its favour at the county town of Downpatrick in 1812.[63] He developed good relations with the Catholic clergy of the county and was present as a collector at the opening ceremony of the new chapel (subsequently the cathedral) in Newry in 1829.[64] Active participation in county local government made him critical of its elitism and led him to criticise its modes of operations and to lobby the Whig government in 1831, and later administrations, for reform of the Irish grand jury laws. His apparent indifference towards other common modes of gentry sociability – such as gentlemen's clubs and the turf – also tended to mark him out from his county peers and enhance a reputation for asceticism. He did later join the Down Hunt Club in 1830, but, unlike his sons, appears to have been an infrequent participant.[65]

In 1808 Sharman had been made a justice of the peace for Down.[66] His role as a magistrate frequently brought him into contact with cases of agrarian violence, beginning in 1808 with an outbreak of attacks seeking to prevent the sale of land to outside bidders at Bleary, near his then residence at Waringstown, that led to at least one death and a subsequent inquest.[67] His stint as high sheriff in 1811–2 also gave him responsibility for enforcing legal actions for distraint of goods for rent, and also evictions.[68] Although the principal responsibility of the magistrate was to investigate and punish rather than to ameliorate, his extensive experience as a member of the county bench of magistrates from that year would have made him very familiar with the grievances of the rural poor and the triggers of agrarian unrest in landlord practices, knowledge he later put to political use.

Unavoidably, his role as a magistrate also brought him face to face with the sectarian violence stirred up again by the campaign for Catholic emancipation and the loyalist counter-agitation. Crawford found himself dealing with manifestations of this in 1830, as the Orange Order reasserted its claimed right to parade despite a government prohibition. The village of Crossgar, adjacent to his newly acquired Rademon estate, had been disturbed by clashes between Orange and Catholic factions since the start of the year.[69] A 12th of July march threatened to descend into open rioting in the context of tensions raised by previous sectarian incidents as well as national politics, to be triggered when 'a number of those bodies marched from distant parts, say ten miles and more, from Protestant districts into a district where there was a Catholic population'. Having sought and received a warrant from Dublin Castle to act on his own initiative, he called on military reinforcements from Downpatrick for his small police detachment, had several Orange marches dismantled, faced down the Orange leaders who insisted they had authority to march from the Duke of Cumberland, made some judicious arrests and prevented an outbreak of rioting. With assistance from the Catholic bishop of Down and Connor Dr William Crolly, with whom he became friendly, he subsequently negotiating a 'treaty of mutual forbearance' between the opposing sectarian parties that saw no marches on either 17 March or 12 July the following year.[70] Other towns, such as Newry and Belfast, were less fortunate that summer and witnessed serious riots. In 1831 he sought guidance from Dublin Castle on how best to take pre-emptive action against any provocative Orange 'party processions' in the Crossgar district on St Patrick's Day.[71] This proactive stance is unlikely to have made him popular with the significant Orange membership in the county, which staged large and aggressive demonstrations elsewhere, including one near Banbridge on 12 July that led to violence in which four died. Despite his efforts, sectarianism continued to provoke antagonism in the district; Crawford's 'truce' broke down in February 1832, when a riot in Crossgar left one Catholic dead, and in 1833 the local Catholic priest opposed the establishment of a permanent police post there unless one half of the stationed constables were Catholics.[72]

The Crossgar district appeared, however, to be somewhat exceptional in the Sharman Crawford estates in the level of religious animosity that was manifested there. In the 1830s the Upper Iveagh lands seemed to be much less disturbed. Fr McArdle of Aghaderg (a parish which contained two Sharman Crawford townlands) informed the visiting antiquarian John O'Donovan in 1834:

> that every denomination of Christians in the neighbourhood lent their assistance in completing [the new chapel at Loughbrickland]. Indeed the inhabitants of this part of the country seem to agree very well notwithstanding their differences in religious opinion, and I was much gratified to find the Presbyterian clergyman, Mr Little, walk in to this priest with an appearance of the most friendly and intimate sociability.[73]

Indeed, after spending some time in the area while researching the Irish origins of local place names, and consulting with the Catholic and Protestant clergy, O'Donovan was favourably impressed by the 'civility, kindness and hospitality' he had met with, which belied the reputation of the county for conflict.[74] Crawford would subsequently seek to promote and build his political career in Ulster on just such foundations of Catholic-Protestant co-operation, especially on the shared agendas of land reform and opposition to tithes, albeit with mixed success in the face of renewed 'dissentions'.

Political initiation: the Down Election of 1830

Looking back from 15 years later, Sharman Crawford recalled his first steps into active political life in 1828–9:

> I did not for many years take any prominent part in politics, whilst at the same I adhered firmly to the opinions I had received from my father's example and instruction – but when the agitation of the relief of the Roman Catholics from their disabilities assumed an active form, I joined the ranks of those, who contended for the removal of these oppressive laws, which was finally carried by the exertions of Daniel O'Connell in the year 1829.[75]

The climax of the Catholic emancipation campaign in 1828–9 was highly polarising in the northern counties. The Orange Order had been temporarily suppressed by the lord lieutenant in 1825, but the sectarian energies it embodied found other outlets seeking to defend the 'Protestant constitution', especially in the form of the Brunswick Clubs. Given limited support from the county elite, these appear to have been less active in Down than in south Ulster, but there were nevertheless assertive Protestant demonstrations against emancipation at Rathfriland, Waringstown and other locations, supported by landowners and clergy. A popular petition against emancipation had been got up in Bangor parish in 1826 to which John Crawford had been 'decidedly hostile', and feelings continued to run high locally. The legal revival of the Orange Order from autumn 1828 added to tensions.[76]

In the first of what would eventually be hundreds of excursions into the letters columns of the press, William Sharman Crawford wrote in May 1828 in support of his brother-in-law Hill Willson, refuting a published claim that that the latter had subscribed to the branch of the New Reformation Society established in Belfast, and stating that he had explicitly declined to do when it became clear that its purpose was 'to put down the papists'. Willson, he asserted, was no friend of Catholicism, but believed it pointless to seek conversions so long as the Catholics were politically oppressed.[77] So heated was this exchange that a duel was agreed between John Bell of the Reformation Society and Willson, with Crawford to act as the latter's second, although this was prevented by the temporary detention of Willson and Crawford near Belfast.[78]

Moving beyond the local to the national sphere, Crawford was on the platform of meetings of the Friends of Civil and Religious Freedom at the Rotunda in Dublin on 20 January 1829, joining liberal Protestants such as Lords Cloncurry, Rossmore and Leinster, the Catholic Whigs Thomas Wyse and Lord Killeen, and the Protestant O'Connellite Tom Steele. This organisation had emerged following O'Connell's appeal to Cloncurry to mobilise liberal-Protestant opinion in reaction to the rise of the Brunswick Clubs, and it was promoted by the patriotic salonniere and novelist Lady Morgan. It had drawn up a lengthy petition linking Ireland's economic and social advancement to full Catholic emancipation, which was ultimately signed by some 2,000 gentlemen, 52 MPs and 69 peers and baronets, and delivered to the prime minister, the Duke of Wellington (who gave it a frosty welcome), on 12 January.[79] Although he did not himself speak at the Rotunda except briefly to second a motion expressing support for the ousted pro-Catholic viceroy Lord Anglesey, Crawford is likely to have been struck by the effort made by the elderly Whig MP for Waterford city Sir John Newport, himself a veteran of the 1783 Rotunda Convention, to connect the current crisis to the legacy of the Volunteers: 'Had the rights the Volunteers then established for themselves, been demanded by them equally for their Catholic countrymen, Ireland would have been spared many of the unfortunate events which have since happened'.[80]

By the time this meeting took place the government had already privately conceded the necessity of some form of emancipation in the wake of O'Connell's electoral victory in Co. Clare in July 1828, resulting from the electoral revolt of the county's Catholic 40-shilling freeholders, and was striving to convince the king that there was no alternative. However the Rotunda rally may have had an effect in demonstrating the strength of opinion held by a significant segment of Irish Protestant notables. Only on 28 January 1829 did George IV reluctantly permit his ministry to proceed with the Catholic Relief Act, along with its associated 'securities' aimed to curb the danger of further political revolts in Ireland.

Crawford made his first recorded platform speech at Newry in February 1829, at a county meeting held in support of Catholic emancipation chaired by the Catholic landowner Captain Nicholas Whyte of Loughbrickland and which included Bishop Crolly and the former Downpatrick MP Edward Ruthven on the platform. After emphasising the centrality of a union of Catholics and Protestants for the success of the movement, Crawford articulated his own reasons for supporting it:

> The conduct of the Catholic body has been such as to give reason why their claims should be conceded. I feel you are doubly entitled to my support as a Protestant as the safety of the church to which I belong depends not for this support on oppressing others but on the exercise of those charities which are taught to us in the records from which our religion is derived. At the present moment no man ought to remain neutral; every good man should be assisting his king in effecting the objects which his majesty has in view for the pacification and advancement of our country. As a Protestant, I now stand forward to assist by all constitutional means my Catholic countrymen in claiming for them a full participation in the benefits of the constitution.[81]

He would retain a lifetime attachment to the idea that persecution and coercion would always remain both immoral and counterproductive, and that religious unity was essential for social progress.

With success now assured in parliament, the Catholic Association launched a testimonial for O'Connell in April 1829, raising sums from all over the island to compensate him for his efforts in leading the campaign and recoup his lost legal earnings as a barrister. Offering to contribute, Crawford reiterated his position on emancipation. As a 'liberal Protestant' he could only agree that the successful outcome was due chiefly to O'Connell's 'persevering exertions, in concentrating the national energy and national power, through the medium of that association, of which he was the originator and sustainer'. His admiration was not uncritical, but he felt that anything said or done that he disagreed with might be pardoned given the 'great good' achieved and the provocations under which O'Connell had to work.[82] If O'Connell was not yet aware of his northern admirer, he was soon to become so. For his part, Crawford paid close attention to the example of O'Connell's apparent success in forcing reform on a recalcitrant British administration through mass peaceful agitation and alliance building, while retaining reservations about aspects of the newly acclaimed 'Liberator's' dictatorial style and wider policy objectives.

As a significant landowner, active magistrate and grand juryman, Crawford was now a player, albeit a novice one, in county elections. Before the 40-shilling freeholders were disenfranchised by the legislation of 1829, Down had one of the largest county electorates, with 14,623 qualified freeholders recorded in 1812. Numbers were much smaller after the 1829 cull, with only 1,825 remaining in 1830 and 2,215 in 1841, a tiny fraction of the county population of some 350,000 in 1831, and limiting the rural vote mostly to the larger 'strong tenant' farmers renting over 30 acres by lease.

After expensive feuding in the decades preceding and following the union of 1801, the dominant Downshire (Hill) and Londonderry (Stewart) landed interests had, from 1812, established a pragmatic 'junction', dividing the two county seats between their family members or nominees and suborning most of the smaller gentry families into supporting them. Both interests were well versed in electoral registration and management of their own tenant freeholders and those of their gentry allies, and in directing the patronage of the county to their mutual advantage. 'Independents' struggled to counter the electoral weight of these two voting blocs, which between them accounted for around 36 per cent of county electors in 1830 (with just under a quarter of all registered voters resident on the Downshire estates), and were thus obliged to adopt more popular platforms in the hope of winning voters, or at least the second votes of those whose first was already pledged to their landlords' choice (voters had two votes, which could be split between candidates or 'plumped' together for one).[83] Temperamentally drawn to the 'independent' camp, Crawford had limited personal weight – a list of freeholders for 1830 included only 44 registered voters residing on his properties in the county – but was increasingly politically active.[84]

The 'independent' candidate for the county in 1830 was Colonel Matthew Forde of Seaforde, who had previously been elected an MP with the support of the 'junction' in 1821, on the understanding that he would step down once Lord Castlereagh's nephew Frederick Stewart came of age. Reluctant to do so in 1826, Forde eventually withdrew under pressure before the poll. He complained about the 'junction between the two marquesses to crush me, and through me the independence of the county', and, convinced that this 'ought and must raise a spirit that will show them they cannot ride over the county in the manner they could wish', indicated his intention to stand again at the next election, which came following the king's death in 1830.[85] Forde was by no means a radical – he was a reluctant convert to Catholic emancipation in 1825 and had a mixed record of voting on 'popular' issues – but he nevertheless presented himself as a strong reformer in the lead-up to the 1830 poll, endorsing shorter parliaments, abolition of 'rotten boroughs' and transfer of their seats to unrepresented large towns, and the reduction of sinecures.[86] His campaign hoped also to capitalise on widespread antagonism towards the threatened increase in corn spirit duties and stamp duties, which had been proposed by the outgoing chancellor of the exchequer Henry Goulburn, and which would have impacted negatively on the county's agricultural interest if implemented.[87] Against a coalition of two scions of the dominant houses, Frederick Stewart, now styled Lord Castlereagh following his uncle's suicide and his father's accession to the marquessate in 1822, and who was a lord of the admiralty in Wellington's administration of 1828–30, and Lord Arthur Hill, brother of the third Marquess of Downshire and sitting as a moderate Whig, he faced what were regarded by observers as 'immense odds'.[88]

Entering the county's political arena in 1830, Crawford vigorously backed Forde's candidacy and joined the County Down Independent Freeholder's Club that acted as his main electoral vehicle. First established in 1826, by 1830 the Club had, according to Crawford, a membership of 80–100 and branches in six other towns in addition to its Downpatrick headquarters.[89] From 1829 it was under the leadership of Edward Ruthven and Edward Wolstenholme, who described themselves as 'liberals', and who encouraged Forde and his neighbouring landlord General Meade (the latter unsuccessfully) to stand as their candidates.[90] Unlike most of his peers in the county gentry, Crawford publicly refused to instruct his own tenants on how they should cast either of their votes, preferring to act through example and persuasion, for while he 'admit[ted] that a reasonable deference on the part of the tenant both to the wishes and opinions of his landlord is desirable [...] it ought be the result of affection and not coercion, of persuasion and not command'.[91] This was a principle he had adopted as early as 1805 on his newly inherited Upper Iveagh lands, when he had declared his wary support for Castlereagh (whose conduct he had often disagreed with) as a counterweight against Downshire control of the county at that year's by-election, but had determined not to influence his own tenants' electoral choice on the matter.[92] While this position seems to have had some support, on that occasion the weight of the Hill interest, albeit dressed up by its propagandists as a freeholders' revolt against the venal, power-hungry and unpatriotic Castlereagh, carried the day.[93] In 1805 the young William Sharman appears to have escaped the attention of the writers of political squibs, but his future father-in-law, mocked as 'Hampden Crawford – *a quondam patriot*' was less fortunate. John Crawford was made to deny the revival of the United Irishmen (in which it was implied he was implicated) to Castlereagh, stating instead that 'there is a junction of property and real independence against you, that is IRRESISTABLE'.[94]

In 1830 William Sharman Crawford welcomed the fact that Arthur Hill was canvassing for his own tenants' votes (a practice other landowners refused to permit), but advised them that, although claiming to be a reformer, Hill was working as part of a coalition calculated to destroy the independence of the county. While Forde's record had not been spotless, he was still the candidate most deserving of popular support, as '[h]e alone has now given you a distinct pledge as to his future conduct'. [95] He reassured his Upper Iveagh tenants in a public letter that no action would be taken against anyone voting otherwise, as it was their constitutional right to vote as they wished and a matter of public virtue to decide what was in their own best interests.[96] The resolutions passed by the Independent Freeholders Club on 7 August under his chairmanship essentially restated Crawford's arguments to his tenants: that free exercise of the franchise was a civil right, essential to prevent oppression and overtaxation by parliament, and that:

> the corrupt exercise of this right, or the wilful application of it in any manner inconsistent with the public good, is a breach of trust, and a crime against society of the most extensive magnitude, because it affects the interests, not of a few individuals, but of nations, and of generations yet unborn.

Indeed, the reduction in the county electorate had rendered this more important, by making the choices of individuals of even greater significance. The coalition now seeking to monopolise the county's representation had no real interest in promoting parliamentary reform or in the retrenchment of taxation that was so necessary to the country's welfare.[97]

Crawford's idealism quickly came into conflict with the reality of what turned out to be an acrimonious and violent contest. In a series of polemical partisan letters, later published bound together with the election squibs and satires, a 'Down Elector' (understood to be the rector of Newtownards, Rev. Mark Cassidy) accused him of foolishly associating with a self-interested and cynical 'junta' of malcontents in 'the Club'.[98] Chief amongst these was Ruthven, aspirant radical MP for the borough of Downpatrick and hero, it was alleged, of the town's corrupt 'potwalloper' electors, who had their own pecuniary interests in seeing a contested county election. The 'Elector' declared Crawford a hypocrite for having indicated to his tenants his preference before proclaiming freedom of election, and (with more justification) for turning a blind eye to the overt electoral management adopted by Forde himself on his Lecale estates, and by his allies Lords Bangor and Annesley and William Hamilton of Greyabbey, whose tenants had been instructed to 'plump' for the colonel.[99] The latter point was difficult to refute, although an anonymous response to the 'Down Elector' in the press (possibly by Crawford himself) reasserted the case that it was the 'duty of the elector to shake off his chains, and to show to his *superiors* in rank that they are his *inferiors* in virtue'.[100]

Some optimism for the Forde interest was provided by the adherence of Rev. Holt Waring, dean of Dromore, an outspoken Orangeman and Brunswick Club member, and 'very proud of his Cromwellian dynasty', who nominated him on the rather eccentric grounds that the 'junction' candidates would support Wellington in his intention of establishing a military dictatorship to quash Protestant liberties. All three candidates had in fact supported the 1829 Catholic Relief Bill and had heterogeneous religious support, and despite Waring's involvement sectarian issues appear to have played a limited role in 1830. Both Downshire and Londonderry had been cautiously in favour of emancipation, although neither was prepared to associate with the 'liberal Protestants' of the Friends of Civil and Religious Freedom in 1829.[101] The association of such 'Brunswick parsons' as Waring with Forde may, as the *Newry Examiner* alleged, have led some Catholic priests in the county to urge their congregants not to vote for him.[102]

Speaking in support of Forde's nomination, Crawford advocated a number of reform measures which fell within the Whiggish demands then being advanced by the parliamentary opposition: a reduction in the number of close boroughs and transfer of seats to unenfranchised large towns, the removal of sinecurists and the end of oligarchal control in parliament. His emotive advocacy of 'freedom of representation' on the part of the electors suggested the more radical democratic path he would take in the future, but for the moment he was constrained by the political limits of the 'independent' coalition formed for the purpose of overturning the 'junction' in the county.[103]

On nomination day Forde swept the hustings in the Downpatrick courthouse packed with his own supporters by a show of hands, but found winning the formal poll more challenging.[104] After seven days of polling in the county town, where all county electors then had to vote, Castlereagh and Hill triumphed with 930 and 837 votes respectively, with Forde trailing on 765. There had been sporadic rioting over the course of the week, which was blamed by the 'Down Elector' on the mobilisation of the (implicitly Catholic) Downpatrick mob and their rural allies from Lecale and Loughinisland by Ruthven and the Independent Club seeking to intimidate pro-junction voters. It is clear from his own account however that contingents of 'security men' accompanied the £10 freeholders from the Hill and Stewart estates, and that these gave as good as they got on the town streets.[105]

While an outlet for popular unenfranchised politics, these street affrays did little to influence the outcome. Jupp's analysis of the 1830 poll book indicates that if there were 'independent' voters in the county, they were not (with the possible exception of Crawford's and few others) the tenant farmers; 96 per cent of the Hill and Stewart tenant freeholders voted for the 'junction', while 93 per cent of Forde's tenants plumped for him. Support from the tenants of most of the other major landowners for the 'junction' candidates had been similarly solid. While efforts made by the Hill-Stewart interest to assert the integrity of their candidates in promoting the real interests of the county and its economy may have assuaged some dubious voters, there is no question that it was traditional forms of landed influence, and effective management of it, that determined the result.[106] The *Northern Whig*, convinced that the fear of coercion lay at the root of the result, complained that the voters were 'so long habituated to the dictation of their enslavers, that, like the Spartan Helots, the very sight of their masters has been sufficient to terrify them into submission', and it endorsed the secret ballot as the only way to break their chains.[107]

The triumphalist *Narrative,* which appeared in print later in the year, also included a number of crude visual satires drawn by the author of the 'Down Elector' letters (and a self-portrait as a florid and well-fed country gentleman). The principal sketch, a folding sheet entitled 'See-Forde! & Lecale Anti-tax-Cart!' is of interest here as containing the first representation of Sharman Crawford in political caricature. In the rather crude satire, representing the procession of Forde's supporters into Downpatrick on the first day of polling, Forde is shown arriving in his open carriage at his election headquarters at Denvir's Hotel (or 'Hot-Hell'), drawn by his supporters including Ruthven and Bangor as horses. The carriage is surrounded by disreputable allies, including the butcher Ranagan, leader of the town mob, and the eccentric and shirtless pedlar 'Tantarabarbus' (William Scott), whose drunken endorsement embarrassed the candidate and provided ammunition to the caricaturist. Driving Forde's barouche is Wolstenholme, who is shown seated on the buttermilk churn he used as a contractor to supply the county gaol; behind him was Holt Waring, 'with a broken orange lilly hanging out of his pocket'. Bringing up the rear, in the subordinate place of footman, is 'SHEERMAN' (a deliberate misspelling of Sharman, and suggesting a lowly agricultural occupation), described in the 'explanation' as 'in the place nature intended for him, with his speech on independence sticking out of his pocket' (Figure 11).[108] He carries the 'club' of the Independent Freeholders Club surmounted by a parrot labelled 'Pretty Poll'. Crawford's angular thinness and susceptibility to illness (he was later mocked as 'A very spare man, with a very spare purse, / And a drop at his nose that would water a horse')[109] would, as here, become a common theme for satirists. Even if his friends could not deny his 'meagre and feeble-looking' appearance, they also observed the keenness of his eyes and his physical determination to overcome such limitations, which would contribute to his political longevity.[110]

If there was little pretty about the Down poll of 1830, the bruising defeat seems to have whetted Crawford's appetite for politics rather than suppressed it. In a tetchy exchange of correspondence with Hill, he defended the political activity of the Independent Club and committed himself to supporting its activities to register electors in advance of any future contest.[111] Although the 'Down Elector' sneered that not a single gentleman of the county attended the consolatory dinner given to Forde by the Club on 16 September, in fact Crawford spoke 'amidst loud cheers' at what the *News-Letter* described as a convivial event. For him the election was less about Forde personally, as he acknowledged that 'many who voted against him did so independently and conscientiously', but the establishment in the public realm of the constitutional principle of the political independence of electors, especially the tenant farmers. The editors of two liberal papers, the *Northern Whig* and *Newry Examiner,* were present at the dinner, along with a number of Belfast reformers, including the banker and future MP John McCance; Crawford's star was on the rise even as Forde, who left the dinner early, was finished in political life.[112]

Crawford's prominent role in the Down election certainly drew O'Connell's attention. He wrote to Cloncurry that he hoped the 'hereditary patriotism' of Sharman Crawford might now be recruited to the incipient Repeal movement.[113] In the meantime, the collapse of Wellington's Tory administration, and its replacement by a Whig government headed by Earl Grey on 22 November 1830, opened the prospect of a parliamentary reform bill that both O'Connell and Crawford could endorse, even if both thought it (and more especially the subsequent Irish reform bill) insufficiently radical in its provisions.

Down again: the Election of 1831

It was no surprise, then, that Sharman Crawford decided to stand himself for Down in the general election precipitated by the Reform Bill crisis the following year. On 19 April the Whig government was defeated on a 'wrecking amendment' to its bill and asked King William IV to dissolve parliament, which he did on 22 April, so they could go to the country on the sole issue of the Reform Bill. Forde had been a compromised candidate in 1830 and Crawford saw himself as free from those encumbrances, and at the same time able to deploy his own enhanced income to support a contest. In the intervening months, his politics had moved in a more radical direction, at least in part in reaction to the witnessing the harsh realities of county electioneering in 1830 and in response to the growing political excitement over the politics of parliamentary reform. He informed the Belfast reform dinner on 30 December 1830 that he was now convinced that only the secret ballot (which was excluded from the government's bill) could guarantee freedom of election and ensure the full benefits of any further parliamentary reforms.[114] In January 1831 he pressed the high sheriff of Down to summon a county meeting to debate and vote on resolutions supportive of reform.[115] The ensuing meeting agreed on triennial parliaments, against corruption and that the commons be elected by the 'free, uninfluenced and uncontrolled voice of the people', although Crawford warned against the dangers of the violent agitation for reform as seen in parts of Great Britain, which simply offered the authorities opportunities for repression. The case for the secret ballot had been made at a previous county meeting in Armagh, but at this time he agreed it be kept off the Down meeting agenda so as to avoid 'disunion' between reformers, not least given the opposition of the sitting 'reform' MP Lord Arthur Hill.[116]

While the Down Independent Club was to be deployed again to promote his campaign, the 1831 challenge in Down was much more closely co-ordinated with the Belfast radicals. The campaign was launched at a meeting in the Commercial Buildings of that town on 30 April. The seat targeted was that of Castlereagh, as a Tory who was formally pledged against the Reform Bill. His opposition was evidently unpopular in the county: at Banbridge his effigy was burnt on one of numerous bonfires lit to celebrate the second reading of the bill.[117] In Belfast the merchant and prominent seceder Presbyterian John Barnett declared that he was delighted that Crawford would stand on the 'enlightened principles' of reform, 'but it would be strange, indeed, if the son of William Sharman, and the relative of John Crawford, of Crawford'sburn, held contrary opinions'. Castlereagh, on the other hand, had 'proved himself well inclined to tread on the people, and crush them in the dust'.[118] Unable to influence the election in their own borough (which was still in 1831 a closed corporation whose MPs were in effect nominated by Lord Donegall), but anxious to ensure that the Reform Bill would indeed presage the destruction of 'old corruption' and the Anglican privileges they associated with them, the leading Belfast Presbyterian reformers established a co-ordinating committee chaired by the merchant and former United Irishman John Sinclair and raised finance to support Crawford's election.[119]

A petition prepared by the Independent Freeholders Club in early 1831 had attracted the signatures of over 1,300 county freeholders for a range of measures, including a reduction of taxation and adoption of a graduated property tax, and abolition of the tithes paid to support the established church along with sinecures and pensions.[120] This seemed to suggest a groundswell of support for an electoral challenge to the dominant landed families. Another meeting of freeholders at Downpatrick in early May resolved to endorse Crawford and (less enthusiastically) Lord Arthur Hill as supporters of the Reform Bill that had been 'demanded by the voice of the nation, and absolutely necessary to avert a national convulsion'. It also resolved to send delegates to other parts of the county to promote local branches of the Club to aid with canvassing, although Crawford insisted that only tenants and not landlords be canvassed.[121] However, despite his personal preferences, Crawford pitched his election address in terms similar to Forde's in 1830, avoiding mention of the ballot for the moment and endorsing the government's bill as a rallying point for reformers of all stripes:

> It has been imputed to this county, that its representation was reduced to the state of a closed and hereditary borough. I confidently hope that the result of this election will prove that the freeholders have a knowledge of their rights, and a determination to enforce them. The success of our common cause depends on your energy and zeal. And if you are pleased to honour me with your voluntary, uncontrolled and unpurchased suffrages, I trust I shall not be found false to my professions, or inattentive to your instructions.[122]

At a boisterous hustings that followed, he was pressed by Castlereagh on whether his personal views exceeded the terms of the Whig measure, and Crawford now confirmed his support for triennial parliaments and, if it could be shown that the free expression of the public voice could not be secured by open voting, for the secret ballot. He praised Downshire for announcing his permission for his tenants the exercise of their second votes as they desired (in an apparent break with the 'junction' of the previous two decades), but complained that this right was denied to their tenants by Londonderry and his allies in the county gentry, and that he had been refused access to canvass some estates, such as that of Roger Hall at Narrow Water.[123]

Hall, in common with many of the Tory landed gentlemen, regarded Crawford's stance as unforgivable treason to his class and was ready to drop his previous antipathy towards the Stewarts to oppose him; he confided to Andrew Nugent:

> This morning's Belfast paper, The Guardian, has in it the resolutions passed at the last meeting of the Independent Club, as also Crawford's address to the county, both of which have caused my blood to boil, when we consider who and what he is to aspire to such an honour. The resolutions I think are not only revolutionary, but dictating to a degree, and carrying on the same system of endeavouring to cry down the aristocracy and lower the gentlemen of the county in the opinion of the humbler classes. My feeling is that this horrid club has gone already too far, and that those who do not belong to it or subscribe to its doctrines, ought to come forward and support the candidate who is opposed to it.[124]

Nicholas Price shared the alarm that Crawford's campaign was threatening a general insurgency against the landed order, writing that 'there is such a cry throughout the county for reform, that I really do think the landlords will almost lose their influence with their tenantry' and warning of parallels with 1798.[125]

As it was known that a number of Londonderry's tenants, as well as Nugent's at Portaferry, had signed pro-reform petitions, there was initially optimism in the Crawford camp.[126] The Stewart interest responded by representing their man as also in fact a moderate reformer, while at the same time sounding a dog-whistle appeal to Orange anxieties: franchise reform in Ireland, Castlereagh stated, would be 'less favourable to Protestant interests than would be desirable to those who would wish to maintain them'.[127] There followed a propaganda campaign, including a flurry of squibs against Crawford and the alleged interference of the 'disloyal' Belfast middle classes in the affairs of the county. Voters were warned that the Reform Bill would lead to clearances of £10 freeholders, and 'overturn the Protestant religion in Ireland'. Castlereagh himself claimed that the reform agitation could only promote the adherents of 'revolution and confusion', most particularly O'Connell and his Repealers, who sought to undermine '[o]ur most revered establishments of *monarchy* and *religion*'.[128] This was in line with the antireform public stance adopted by the Grand Orange Lodge of Ireland in April, although this was contested by some plebeian Orangemen.[129] Holt Waring was now absent from the 'Independent' camp and indeed would come out vehemently against reform at an Orange meeting later in the year.[130] Crawford was potentially vulnerable on the repeal question given his previous public support for O'Connell and the latter's public assertion in early 1831 that he might prove a 'patriotic' convert to the campaign, and consequently he felt obliged to make known his opposition to repeal as likely to provoke unrest and to undermine the British-Irish connection.[131]

Appeals were made to paternalism as well as sectarianism. Crawford was mocked in verse as a brazen upstart without the means to maintain a place in the representation of the county and hence not a true gentleman.[132] Rumours were also spread (plausible given the previous year's contest) that Downshire's declaration of free choice in his tenants' use of their second ballot was for show only, and that a vote for Castlereagh alongside Hill was expected by him and his agents. This obliged Crawford's committee to resort to counter-propaganda; they issued a poster insisting that Downshire's tenants 'were at perfect liberty to give their second votes to whom they pleased!', and urged voters that, as Down was no longer a 'CLOSE Borough', they should act 'with the spirit of freemen; or be content to remain forever in slavery and disgrace'.[133] Further posters exhorted electors to support Crawford and Hill to defeat the 'Boroughmongers' and ensue reform and retrenchment, although more ominously another hinted at retribution against those who broke their oath to support reform:

> If you are so lost to the interests of yourselves and your children, as to belie your former professions, and now vote for LORD CASTLEREAGH good care shall be taken to hold up your names in the public prints, as unworthy of liberty, confidence, or trust. The names of all the voters will be published in a black list, who, upon this trying occasion shall, like Esau, sell their birthright for a mess of pottage.[134]

As was usual, the highly charged election was marked by tumult in Downpatrick. Uproar broke out in the courthouse when the Lancastrian schoolmaster Maurice Cross, who was secretary to Crawford's Belfast committee, attempted to address the hustings, leading to 'as fine a specimen of savage ferocity, and of the confusion and anarchy of a political pandemonium, as one need ever expect to witness'.[135] After a standoff with the sheriff, Cross was allowed to speak the following day on the necessity of radical reform and the perfidy of Castlereagh in playing the Orange card.[136] Although the first day of polling had gone well for Crawford, with more votes cast for him than for Castlereagh, there were ominous signs that not enough of the crucial second votes were coming his way, and a placard was displayed outside the polling booths by his supporters aimed at the Downshire tenantry, calling on 'every freeholder, who is a reformer, [to] vote for BOTH reformers, or be silent, and thereby prove himself a consistent man'.[137] As the election proceeded, the reform squibs became increasingly desperate as Crawford's early lead slipped away, one threatened the revived publication of 'black and red lists' to shame those who had pledged to vote for reform, but now backed 'THE UNBLUSHING TORY, CASTLEREAGH'.[138]

The result announced at close of polling on 16 May 1831, must have come as a huge disappointment: Hill had topped the poll as expected with 1,671, but Castlereagh had polled 1,067 to Sharman Crawford's 917. In victory, Castlereagh's propagandists hailed the 'Glorious defeat of the Belfast Radical Club' and circulated scurrilous verse associating the radicals with the United Irishmen, revolution and infidelity with the 'Sale by auction, at Downpatrick [...] of the Belfast branch of the RADICAL STUD, of WILLIAM CARMAN SHAWFORD, Esq.'. These were serious accusations and their inclusion of this item gave rise to legal action against the publisher by John Barnett.[139]

Crawford himself was mocked as poor 'Shear-man' for the crushing losses he had sustained in the unsuccessful challenge to the county establishment.[140] In fact, Crawford spent at least £1,808 of his own money on the contest, the largest block of which (£708) had gone on 'council, agents and attorneys'. While this was not sufficient, as the squib-writers claimed, to beggar him, it was a substantial outlay for a middling landowner (at least a quarter of his annual rental), and even with supplements from his Belfast backers, was dwarfed by the resources available to the county magnates. In the hotly contested election of 1805 it was estimated that Lady Downshire had spent £30,000 and Lord Castlereagh had expected to lay out £40,000, and sums expended from Hillsborough and Mount Stewart in 1830 and 1831 may well have been similar, although expenditure by candidates for county seats in this period was more frequently in the range of £3–5,000.[141] In a political environment where lavish expenditure was expected by voters and 'corruption' commonplace, Crawford's idealistic abstemiousness was likely to have been a real barrier to success.[142]

In defeat, Crawford refused to accept that the result reflected the 'free and uncontrolled opinion of the electors of the County of Down', producing documents to demonstrate that Downshire's agent John Reilly and his brother had intervened to express at the minimum 'implied hostility' towards him, while other landowners had been brazen in instructing their tenants to vote against him, including those who had 'expressed their warmest wishes for my success, and their desire to support me'.[143] Following this up in a public letter he accused the Hill interest of underhandedly reviving the 'junction' duopoly and Castlereagh of being responsible for having 'the dying embers of religious discord rekindled, and the obsolete claims of feudal domination maintained and asserted [...] and a portion of the aristocracy lending themselves to rivet the chains of subjection, on both their own body and that of the people'.[144]

Specific claims he made about individual landlord behaviour, such as that of Price at Saintfield, brought some rebuttals. Crawford alleged that at least one of Price's tenants who had promised his vote to him had subsequently withdrawn it on the threat of being turned out of his house, but Henry Simpson then claimed that the Saintfield tenants had voted for Castlereagh out of deference to their landlord, not from threatened coercion. Price appears to have taken the issue to law, leading to sworn statements being taken from tenants that they had expressed support for Crawford only to get rid of him during his canvass, and that Price had not threatened coercion. There is a suggestion that Nugent of Portaferry, who was also furious over the canvassing of his own tenants, may have challenged Crawford to a duel over the allegations, as William wrote to him; 'I shall never refuse to meet you on any occasion that you ask it. I shall therefore be at Newtownards at the time mentioned'. Despite this no duel appears to have occurred, and neither are there any later references to Crawford engaging in such 'affairs of honour', although at this stage of his life he seems to have had no objection to a principle still at the heart of the gentry code of male behaviour.[145]

How accurate was the charge of coercive vote-management? It seems that Crawford and the reformers had underestimated the residual appeal of popular deference to the representative of a resident, wealthy and relatively generous landlord (and his allies), not least when lavish amounts of spending were available both for electoral purposes and the 'treating' of residents in the whiskey-fuelled illuminations that followed on the Londonderry estates.[146] For many social deference was grounded in the material support a resident landlord and the 'estate charities' he funded could offer to insecure tenants in return for their compliance.[147] The reformers had also underestimated the residual strength of the 'junction' of family interests, despite their ostensible division on the partisan issue of reform. While not discounting incidents of landlord retribution in Down elections, Jupp's analysis suggests that overt punishment for electoral misdemeanours was rare, and that deference based on paternalism and habit remained a real force in this period.[148]

This is plausible, although it does not entirely account for the failure of the evident public enthusiasm for reform of early 1831 to translate into greater support for the most whole-heartedly reformist candidate, and the overt deployment of the sectarian card in what was still a highly charged post-emancipation context is likely to have had some sway, and was clearly seen by the Stewart camp as necessary in 1831 (when it had evidently not been against Forde in 1830). Crawford's dalliance with O'Connell had laid him open to charges calculated to arouse the fears of voters influenced by Orange calls for pan-Protestant unity in the face of continuing Catholic agitation. The high-profile support of the Belfast reform committee also opened Crawford's campaign up to sustained allegations from his enemies that he was backed by the old revolutionaries of 1798.[149] His antagonist Rev. Mark Cassidy contributed to these and also threatened tenants on the Londonderry estates that signing any pro-reform petition would lead to 'their names [being] annexed to documents which neither they nor their *best friends* approve of'.[150] There were some well-publicised cases of landlords following up on threats by taking retribution against tenants who had voted for Crawford, such as the case of Peter Johnston of Newtownards who was evicted without compensation from his farm on the Londonderry estate.[151] Crawford later charged Lord Dufferin with having issued overt warnings of the material consequences that would follow from any of his tenants disregarding their landlord's 'advice', and his neighbour had made it clear that he would counter the 'agitation' of his tenants with warnings of what would follow from 'interrupting the ties' between tenant and landlord.[152]

In any case, the prohibitive costs of challenging the county duopoly and the electoral failure of 1831 cast a long shadow for Crawford. The seat would remain in the uncontested possession of the Hill-Stewart 'junction' for another two decades until he and the 'independent' Conservative David Ker challenged them (and each other) under very different circumstances in 1852. The outcome in Down was replicated in the other Ulster counties, where after a flurry of contests in 1830–1, a pattern of what Suzanne Kingon describes as 'easy aristocratic control' was reasserted, virtually monopolising representation in the Conservative interest.[153]

What was as issue in the Down election was, amongst other things, a clash of ideas about what should constitute the landlord-tenant relationship in its political and social aspects. For Crawford and his Belfast allies in the committee and the *Northern Whig*, deference should never be an inherited right attached to proprietorship, but must be earned by the example and practice of the landlord and even then could never be absolute. It followed that tenants must have a reciprocal (if not equal) relationship with their landlord, able to make rational and unfettered choices about their own best interests and subject only to landlord persuasion if the case made merited their support.[154] Crawford praised those who had demonstrated a 'steady and determined character' in 1831 in the face of the cynical deployment of landed power, and drew comfort from the fact that his campaign had encouraged a substantial increase over Forde's vote in 1830.[155] This is a position he would seek to advance through supporting both economic and electoral reform thereafter, moving well beyond the constraints set by the need to support the Whig reform measure of 1831–2.

The Belfast Election of 1832

Relations between Daniel O'Connell and the northern reformers deteriorated sharply as he pivoted his mass following towards an explicitly nationalist objective from 1830. Sharman Crawford had signed the Leinster declaration against repeal of the union in January 1831 along with many other liberal Protestants, and during the Down election campaign publicly rejected repeal as likely to stir up religious discord and damage Ireland's economic interests. Despite this, O'Connell was aware of Crawford's support for Catholic emancipation and endorsement of radical political reform and had noted in a letter in April 1831 to his ally Lord Duncannon, the Irish Whig political 'fixer', that 'Sharman Crawford is the man for Down' and was one of the most suitable men in Ireland for election to parliament.[156]

At the same time, in the wake of the Down defeat Crawford was beginning to explore southern political avenues. As a Meath landowner he was present and spoke at that county's meeting in support of the Reform Bill in October 1831, at which there was a significant O'Connellite presence.[157] Shortly after he wrote to O'Connell's new body the National Political Union (NPU) in Dublin, stating his reasons for opposing a simple repeal that would create two rival sovereign parliaments, while remaining open to the desirability of a subordinate 'local legislature' for Ireland, and expressing hope for a juncture with O'Connell (for whom he continued to express admiration) on the reform question if repeal could be put aside for the moment. Welcoming the approach, O'Connell made a garbled allusion to Crawford's Volunteer heritage and long-windedly rebutted his objections to repeal, but instructed the secretary to respond that differences on this question were no obstacle to membership as 'any conscientious reformer' was welcome to join the NPU.[158] The exchange would later be recalled as Crawford's first articulation of 'federalism', and would begin an extended and fractious relationship between the two men marked over the next 16 years more by acrimony than by this initial show of mutual conciliation.[159]

For the moment the pursuit of Dublin-oriented politics was postponed. Crawford's enthusiastic collaboration with the Belfast radicals, and creditable performance against weighty odds in the Down contest of 1831, placed him in a strong position in the town. A Belfast Reform Society meeting in May 1832, called to express support for the Whig ministers who had temporarily resigned in the face of house of lords' opposition to their Bill, warmly welcomed his support for the 'cause of the people' with cheers and 'shouts of "Colonel Sharman, of Moira" and "John Crawford, of Crawfordsburn!"'. Under the Irish Reform Bill that followed the passage of the English one, the closed borough of Belfast would be opened to a middle-class franchise of £10 householders, and the Society envisaged Crawford as a desirable candidate for the first post-reform election. On his part he urged collaboration with the NPU, expressing regret that many Protestants had been misled into opposing reform and were mistakenly setting their interests against those of the whole country: 'He must admit, though a Protestant, that his Catholic fellow-countrymen had taken the lead, in the advocacy of the rights of the people; but, he hoped, this would not long be the case'.[160]

With the reform bills safely passed in May 1832, to public celebrations in Belfast and Bangor, the Society formally invited Crawford to stand as one of its two candidates for the borough, with the other requisition going to the young lawyer Robert James Tennent, nephew and political heir of the former Volunteer officer, United Irishman and Presbyterian radical leader, William Tennent. They would stand on a joint platform demanding further reform of the franchise and of the grand jury laws, the abolition of slavery, the East India Company's monopoly and Irish tithes, with the appropriation of the surplus wealth of the established church going to public uses.[161] The Tennent family's claim that they were among the 'natural leaders' of the mercantile town was, however, to provoke something of a popular backlash, especially as they made little effort to hide their United Irish past.[162]

As was expected, the Chichester family sought to defend its proprietorial interests by running its own candidate, Lord Arthur, the 24-year-old fourth son of the second Marquess of Donegall, who represented himself as a moderate Whiggish reformer. More problematically for the Belfast Reform Society, controversy quickly arose over its selection of candidates. James Emerson Tennent, a cousin by marriage of R. J. Tennent, felt that he had been unfairly passed over by the Society given his well-attested reformist credentials, and (after at first claiming a reluctance to heed calls that he should stand against those he agreed with on policy) established his own election committee in alliance with the Chichesters and the borough corporation.[163] His charge that the Reform Society had acted in the same manner as the Donegalls in selecting its candidates in camera without putting it to a public meeting gained some traction, although it soon became evident that he was prepared to construct a much more conservative electoral coalition to pursue his personal ambitions. Refusing to accept his accusation of favouritism, the Reform Society's leadership claimed he had been put up by a 'few pretended friends who wished to divide the party', and R. J. Tennent's candidacy was subsequently approved by a show of hands at a public meeting of electors. But the damage had now been done and it was clear that Emerson Tennent would attract significant personal support in the town, especially among more conservative Presbyterians who looked to the stridently anti-Catholic Rev. Henry Cooke for spiritual leadership and who feared O'Connell's mobilisation of the Catholic masses. A number of prominent electors, declaring themselves strongly opposed to repeal, signed a requisition on 8 September calling on him to stand, and he declared his intention some days later.[164]

Emerson Tennent quickly acquired the support of the *News-Letter* and its editor James McKnight, who had trained in orthodox Presbyterian theology but opted for journalism over the ministry, in opposition to the more radical *Northern Whig*, which was edited by the Non-subscribing Presbyterian James Simms. What may have begun as a personal rivalry (with religious undertones) arising from damaged *amour-propre*, quickly escalated as the two groups began to throw political and religious barbs at each other.[165] McKnight, a man of wide intellectual interests and a 'zealot of Protestantism', was personally open-minded in his outlook and had developed a friendship with Rev. Fletcher Blakely, the non-subscribing minister of Moneyreagh, with whom he would collaborate in the later tenant-right movement along with Sharman Crawford.[166] In 1831 his paper had come out in favour of the Reform Bill, blaming the passage of Catholic emancipation on the corruption of the 'old' parliamentary system.[167] In 1832, however, he also felt himself personally slighted by the 'natural leaders' of Belfast liberalism and despite his personal support of further reform and the abolition of tithes, he threw his paper whole-heartedly into partisan warfare in the joint Chichester and Emerson Tennent interest, presumably with the support of the paper's Scottish-born proprietor Alexander Mackay.[168]

Crawford was anxious not to be drawn too deeply into the internecine disputes of the Belfast Presbyterian bourgeoisie, and insisted on maintaining his own election committee with its own budget to avoid giving the impression of being too closely in 'coalition' with R. J. Tennent. He subsequently complained about his name being drawn into the 'odium' of the Tennents' personal political squabbles with their municipal rivals, which he believed had politically damaged himself.[169] However in September he agreed to the addition of a 'general committee' drawn from the Reform Society members and chaired by the industrialist Robert Grimshaw, which promoted their joint interest in returning two full-blooded 'independent' radical reformers to parliament. As with the previous year's Down election, he gave a personal oath that his campaign would never resort to any manipulation of voter registration or corrupt practices in pursuit of votes and confirmed that he remained supportive of the secret ballot.[170] The reform campaign's abstemiousness was mocked by the *News-Letter* for expecting the public to stand in pouring rain to hear 'the "fairy music" of independent eloquence', without the reward of the expected supply of whiskey, 'or even the milder substitute of a keg of coffee at the Temperance Hotel'.[171] Indeed Crawford was mocked in satirical song for providing no beer to the electors and expecting Grimshaw's committee to meet all the election costs.[172]

Issuing his first electoral address on 24 August, Crawford made clear his belief that the 1832 reform acts had not gone far enough in either Ireland or England. The 'restoration' of triennial parliaments was essential, and Ireland remained underrepresented in the commons as it had benefitted less than Scotland in the 1832 redistribution in being given only an additional five seats. On the principle that there should be neither class legislation nor 'taxation without representation', tithes and vestry assessments, 'by which the religion of one sect is sustained and exalted at the expense of all others', should be abolished, and the unrepresentative county grand juries reformed. Government corruption and sinecures had still to be curbed, and colonial slavery must be ended (albeit with some form of compensation to slaveholders). A subsequent query to all candidates from the Belfast Anti-Slavery Society led to a statement by Crawford that the 'tyrannical and unjustifiable assumption of authority of man over his fellow creature' must be terminated immediately. Judicial reform, and an end to 'taxes on knowledge' were also in his opinion desirable. R. J. Tennent's published address was virtually identical to Crawford's in its pledges.[173] In a later speech, Crawford noted that it was 49 years since his father had come forward 'in obedience to a like call from the electors of the borough of Lisburn' to aid them in 'asserting their rights, and throwing off the unjust pressure of aristocratic control', and that he was proud to be embodying the same principles in Belfast.[174]

Early in the campaign it became obvious that the Reform Society's opponents would seek to raise the repeal question as a stick to beat their rivals. The *News-Letter* pressed for an anti-repeal pledge from candidates, leading Maurice Cross to urge that this subject be kept out of view for the present.[175] This attempt to sidestep the issue was unsuccessful, especially given O'Connell's overt campaign behind candidates pledged to repeal in other parts of Ireland. The masters of the Orange lodges of Belfast condemned one of their members who had come out for Crawford as the 'popular candidate' against Emerson Tennent, and made explicit that they were 'directly opposed to the sentiments' he had expressed.[176] The popular balladeers were quick to follow this lead. One song composed in Ulster-Scots dialect urged loyalists to reject the middle-class reforming clique and back Emerson and Chichester as supporters of the 'good cause' of political Protestantism:

> We want nae squire frae Crawfordsburn,
> To spoil the church and crown;
> We'll ha'e nae pack o' radicals,
> To rule this loyal town:
> But we'll gi'e one vote to Chichester,
> Because we love the blue,

And another to brave Emerson,
For he's baith leal and true.
For there'll be nae luck about the 'house,'
There's be nae luck ava;
There'll be little justice in the house
If our good cause should fa'.[177]

Another comic squib mocked Sharman Crawford's lanky physique and pretensions to advance his personal ambitions at the expense of the town:

The Laird o' C—burn he's narrow an strait,
Yet his head is ta'en up wi' the affairs o' the great;
He wanted a 'seat,' the braw biggin to keep,
But favours like that are no bought just so cheap.

His political unreliability was flagged by suggesting he'd be as happy at College Green (i.e. a post-repeal Irish parliament) as at Westminster. His canvassing of the 'Smithfield hotels' with John Barnett indicated the pursuit of voters in that predominantly Catholic slum district, to the outrage of his 'loyal' critics.[178] Behind the facade of reform, the Orange satirists insisted, lay a plot 'prepared in the Council of Rome: / Her polluted adherents she chose, / For to execute her design'; it followed that true defenders of Protestantism must reject the 'vain upstart of Crawfordsburn' and rally to Emerson Tennent and 'great Donegall'.[179]

This attack on reformers came in the context of heightened sectarian tensions in the town in the preceding years, with several murders in April and serious rioting in May 1832. The latter was spurred by restoration of the Whig government and triumph of the Reform Bill, which was celebrated by a mob attacking the antireform *Guardian* newspaper office and a nearby 'Orange' pub, leading to retaliatory gunfire with one fatality.[180] While both Orangeism and its Catholic Ribbonite counterpart remained minority movements in the town, and concentrated mostly among lower-class migrants from the countryside (few of whom were voters) in districts such as Sandy Row and the Pound they still played an active role in the street politics of the election. Orangeism clearly already had some middle-class adherents, and its 'respectability' would be bolstered by the arrival in 1833 of Rev. Thomas Drew as incumbent of Christ Church in College Square.

Pressed to state his position on the contentious corn laws of 1815, a potential stumbling block for a landlord standing in a mercantile and industrial constituency, Crawford made clear his opposition, in principle, to the current UK corn law as 'unjust, and unfavourable, in its operation, to all classes; and especially oppressive to the labourer and mechanic', while at this time favouring gradual rather than immediate abolition to give agriculture some temporary protection against unfair foreign competition and hence allow it time to adjust. Duties on the articles consumed by the poor should, he argued, be reduced at once, and replaced by some form of inheritance levy on landed property (a tax, he noted, which already existed in France).[181] His private views, which echoed reforming Whig thinking on the corn laws at this time while being well in advance of them on taxation, mirrored this public statement.[182]

As the Belfast contest progressed, he began to distance himself more from the Reform Society committee and Tennent's campaign. He was embarrassed by the report in September of Grimshaw's abortive approach to Lord Templemore to use his influence with his Ballymacarrett tenants in the more rural part of the constituency east of the River Lagan to support the reformers. Templemore opted instead to throw in his lot with his Chichester relatives, and Crawford insisted that he was in coalition with no other candidate and that he disclaimed any attempt to solicit a landlord for his votes.[183] By November the rift had been patched up somewhat by the Reform Society's secretary Edward Getty, and Crawford had undertaken to focus his attention on 'break[ing] into the ranks of our common enemy', leaving the joint committee to manage the existing pro-reform voters.[184] As part of this, he pointed to evidence of a coalition between Chichester and Emerson Tennent's supporters in seeking to exclude likely radical electors at the registry, a practice which had led to complaints to the chief secretary from some disgruntled Belfast citizens.[185] However underlying tensions clearly remained between the radical candidates.

In autumn 1831 the Belfast trades unions and co-operative societies had been instrumental in the formation of the Reform Society and manifested their support for parliamentary reform through public demonstrations involving several thousands.[186] Campaigning in the town in 1832 first brought Crawford into engagement with such 'respectable' manifestations of working-class political activism and he opted to ally himself with them in a turn which would have long-term consequences for his political outlook. Appealing to the manufacturing population of the town in November 1832, he projected himself as the 'poor man's friend', albeit from a liberal position that promoting their interests would not fundamentally damage those of any other class. He was no leveller, he said, for '[i]t is ordained by Providence, that gradations will for ever exist in society'. Still, the mass of the people should be rendered comfortable and happy by ensuring employment at wages proportionate to the prices of necessities. To attain this, free trade should be moved towards, with a view to attaining fair prices for farmers and manufacturers and ensuring that demand for labour was maintained. Taxation should be more equitably distributed with cuts to the consumption levies on the poor man's necessities. Civil and religious liberty was the right of all, requiring an end to religious discrimination or privilege. Religious discord was, he asserted, being whipped up in the borough and used to obscure the population's real interests:

> Be upon your guard, take care that the workings of religious fanaticism be not brought to aid in securing on you the fetters of political corruption; and the tottering fabric of monopoly and undue influence be not propped up on the basis of religious intolerance, and be again elevated into proud pre-eminence over your rights and interests. – If it be so, it cannot be said you had no warning voice to guard you against the catastrophe.[187]

Social progress depended, he concluded, on both Catholic and Protestant and on cross-class co-operation on the basis of equity.

Not all reformist electoral messages were phrased in such polished a manner as this. Both sides deployed writers of popular songs and squibs to make their arguments more accessible to a less literate audience, including the non-electors. Grimshaw's committee was urged to pay for and distribute the work of an anonymous writer who had previously produced material for Crawford's campaign in 1831.[188] One of his pieces, 'New Song to an Old Tune', praised Crawford for his honesty and readiness to pay his bills (a barbed comment on the Chichesters' notorious indebtedness). [189]

Emerson Tennent was mocked in these rhymes as a turncoat of no principle and a 'toadie to a lord', seeking to present himself as all things to all parties while pursuing his own self-interest, but who would if returned aid Chichester in upholding tithes and the privileged Anglican interest. [190] One song contrasted his dishonesty and two-facedness with the moral virtues embodied by the reform candidates:

> Poor Sharman and Bobby in vain
> May rely on their honesty steady:
> They can talk but in *single speech plain,*
> Whilst I have the *double tongue ready.* [191]

Despite such raucous expressions of optimism, by late November it was becoming evident to Crawford and the Reform Society committee that the election was starting to slip away from them as it appeared that the Belfast middle classes were less radical than had initially been assumed. The withdrawal of one of the two radical candidates to concentrate their votes was mooted. Crawford thought that if necessary this should be done immediately, but was reluctant to step down himself given that his name had been given precedence in selection by the Reform Society and stated he would do so only if those who had signed the requisition to him explicitly urged him to do so. [192] For his part, Tennent, while acknowledging Crawford's seniority, insisted that his own candidacy was vital in bringing out the radical Presbyterian vote without which neither would succeed, as it was 'vain to deny, that my interest in my native town is stronger than yours'. [193] In the end no agreement could be found and both proceeded to the poll, with Crawford stating that to step aside at such a late stage would be dishonourable to himself, his supporters and his country. [194]

With all political arguments fully rehearsed by the end of the long campaign, a public dinner of Belfast electors, held in the newly opened gymnasium on 4 December, was more about symbolism than policy. With the cost of admission set low at 2s. 6d. to admit the 'humblest elector', around 750 were present while others were turned away when the hall was full. The hangings celebrated the recent victory of the Reform Bill alongside portraits of the king and the government ministers Lords Grey and Brougham, and Lord John Russell. A Union Jack was balanced by 'a large flag with a harp, etc., being the sail makers' flag', along with flags of some of the other craft guilds and trades and the flag of the Belfast Reform Society. At the centre was displayed 'an old Volunteer flag, of '82, [...] which attracted much attention'. Continuing the patriotic theme, at the other end of the room was 'a very handsome representation of Erin, appearing disconsolate, with one hand on her harp, and a staff and cap of liberty in the other; motto – "The victim of misrule."' Transparencies relating to reform and freedom of election hung on either side. If the symbolism of the United Irishmen was too raw and problematic to display, that of the Volunteers was deemed by Belfast radicals to offer a historical legitimacy further embodied by Crawford's person.

As the principal speaker, Crawford sought further to historicise the reforming moment of 1832 with reference to the town's and his own family's past, recalling a tradition of mutual co-operation for liberty and the national good, and eliding the more problematic intervening history of 1798. Proof of the possibility of such collaboration was:

> brought to my mind by the flag which is before me (Mr Crawford here pointed to the Volunteer flag.) Look to the period of the Volunteers; then the aristocracy, the gentry and the people, were all united in the common cause of their country's good; and you know the noble results of that union, and you know the after results of their separation. [...] I think I can assert, without fear of contradiction, that the town of Belfast has, for a long period of time, been the steady and consistent supporter of civil liberty. If I wanted proof of this, I have only again to look up to the flag which is suspended before me. I ask, where did the Volunteer institution originate? Was it not in the town of Belfast? Where was it continued and supported? Let us recollect the Belfast reviews: these recollections alone, give acknowledged and pre-eminent claims to Belfast, in the records of Ireland[.]

Belfast now could not show itself unworthy of this glorious past. Perhaps looking beyond the upcoming poll, he concluded that while he regarded himself as a suitable man to represent the town, he would respect the views of those who thought otherwise, and continue to hold out the hand of friendship to all.[195] Radical reformers needed to take the long view regarding both the past and future.

Given the recent canvassing, the defeat of the radicals in December may not have been entirely surprising to them or their supporters. Chichester, who had done little but appeal for deferential recognition to the Donegall interest (and its continuing patronage) and vague support for the sitting government, topped the poll with 834 votes. Emerson Tennent's efforts to mobilise conservative (and indeed sectarian-minded) Presbyterian voters paid off with a second-place result of 723, leaving the radicals R. J. Tennent and Crawford to bring up the rear with 625 and 616 respectively. Personal popularity had again failed to secure Crawford a parliamentary seat. For one conservative squib writer, this was a triumph for the Chichesters against the 'arbitrary party who have dared to insult and degrade Lord Donegall' and for Emerson and the 'respectability of the town' against the 'mob' which had allegedly been courted by Crawford.[196] Another crowed that the 'Repealers and rebels' had been defeated and the 'pride of the radicals' humbled by Emerson Tennent, while one of the latter's supporters announced that 'the Protestants had gained this victory, and that they would continue to maintain their ascendancy: they had trodden down their enemies and they would keep them down'.[197] The chairing of the successful candidates was taken as an excuse by the town's Orangemen to parade down the Catholic-majority Hercules Street, provoking a riot that led to four deaths and the deployment of troops of dragoons in support of the civil authorities.[198]

What lay behind the radicals' failure in 1832? Orangeism remained a minority, if growing, force in the town, but had evidently rallied to Chichester and Emerson Tennent, although probably not bringing many votes for them given its still predominantly lower-class character. It is however possible that (as in other places), threats of exclusive dealing by Orangemen may have had some impact: Hoppen's analysis of the 1832 Belfast vote by occupation indicates the anti-radical candidates had a clear majority among the town's shopkeepers, while trailing the radicals in support from the merchants, manufacturers and artisans.[199] However withdrawal of patronage by the town's elite could also have an impact: one shopkeeper who voted for the radicals in 1832 complained two years later that his upper-class customers had never returned and he now sought aid in finding new employment.[200] It appears that Crawford and Tennent had won the bulk of the Catholic vote, but if Catholics made up around a third of the town's population by the early 1830s, their share of the middle-class £10 ratepayer voters was much lower, and they subsequently protested that legal barriers had been placed in the way of their registration in the shape of a municipal anti-Catholic qualification oath.[201] An attempt to break this alliance by claiming spuriously that Crawford was concealing private religious bigotry behind public beneficence was refuted by the Catholic former United Irishman (and member of the Reform Society committee) Charles Hamilton Teeling, who reported that Crawford employed four Catholic servants at Crawfordsburn, and had cared for one who was sick at significant personal expense.[202]

Significant sections of the town's majority Presbyterian bourgeois electorate had evidently opted for Emerson Tennent, possibly, as Hall suggests, following the orthodox Presbyterians Cooke and McKnight in regarding the supposedly 'new light' Tennents and their allies as religiously suspect in the wake of the 1829 schism in the church, and as unrepentant heirs of the revolutionary 1790s and hence as inherently suspect in the face of the perceived O'Connellite threat to pan-Protestant interests.[203] Crawford may well have suffered collateral damage by association with the Tennents and their allies, while the town's Anglican vote went principally to Chichester. In addition, class anxieties were also never far from the surface; the registered electorate in 1832 was only 1,658 men out of an expanding population assessed the previous year at over 53,000, leaving the vast majority unenfranchised and rendering Crawford's self-conscious appeals to the town's lower classes politically counterproductive as middle-class voters began to worry about plebeian unrest as the wider reformist coalition of 1831–2 unravelled.[204]

The Donegall interest had, after antagonising Presbyterian reformers for much of the period since 1800 by maintaining a tight grip on the town's local government structures in the pursuit of its own self-interest, tacked by 1831 to supporting the 'moderate' reform belatedly embraced by parliament, and adopted 'graceful surrender' as a tactic to retain their position in the face of unavoidable change. For those middle-class electors who felt some residual deference to the resident local dynasty, the 'moderate' position taken by the Chichesters, and by Emerson Tennent in alliance with them, made them a less risky option than the 'ultra-radical' Crawford and R. J. Tennent. In bitter disappointment, the *Northern Whig* lamented the 'old professed reformers' and 'liberals of 98' who had voted for one or both of the conservative 'reformers' in 1832, however the poll book demonstrates a high degree of partisan polarisation, with 86 per cent of electors voting along 'party' lines and only 9 per cent dividing their votes between Chichester and one of the radicals.[205] Emerson Tennent would later align himself with the moderate Conservatism of Robert Peel, and there was evidently a significant bourgeois constituency for such 'Tamworth' liberal-conservative politics in the town. At the same time, the election had also seen the emergence of the solicitor John Bates as a key electoral organiser and strategist; his skilful manipulation of registration lists was already evident and would lie behind Conservative party successes in the parliamentary elections that followed and its hegemonic control of the elected town council from 1842 after the implementation of the Irish municipal reform act.[206] The 1832 Irish Reform Act had retained the rather chaotic Irish voter registration system established in 1727, which in the hands of capable political agents such as Bates, could be and was used to exclude opposing voters for failing to meet a range of often arbitrary criteria and to enhance their party's electoral chances through facilitating impersonation and sharp practice. Hoppen notes that the 'real' electorate of Belfast in 1840 was still around 1,900 as opposed to a 'nominal' one of 6,000, at a time when's the town's population had increased to around 70,000.[207]

Only when it was too late did the radicals realise their mistake in running two candidates against such well-organised and funded opposition; a last-minute placard issued on the second day of polling by Tennent's supporters calling for remaining voters to plump for him as the stronger candidate infuriated Crawford and led to a recriminatory exchange of letters in the wake of defeat over who should have had 'precedence'.[208] A proud man who had now been electorally humiliated twice in two years, Crawford complained that he felt '*my* interests were dishonorably betrayed to serve *his*', but ultimately accepted Tennent's explanation that he had not personally approved the offending placard. He continued to deny that he was evidently the 'weaker' candidate or to accept any personal responsibility for the defeat, while repeating that he would have stood down had the joint committee and Tennent formally requested him to do so.[209] In the wake of this falling out he never entirely trusted the Belfast radical leadership clique again, although relations had been patched up somewhat by the mid-1830s and he was, as we shall see, to make another bid for leadership of reformism in the town in 1840.

Although a serious setback, the 1832 defeat was not wholly fatal for the reforming or Whig-liberal interest in Belfast, and the Chichester stratagem only briefly delayed the eclipse of proprietorial politics. Following Emerson Tennent's and Chichester's formal defection from the Whigs in the wake of Lord Stanley and Sir James Graham's departure for the newly minted Conservative party led by Peel in 1834–5, John McCance (Crawford's reformist ally in the 1831 Down election) was returned in the place of Chichester, although he died several months after his election in 1835. Two Whig-liberals were returned in 1837, only for parliament to overturn their election in 1838 on a petition claiming electoral irregularities and seat their Conservative rivals instead; in 1842 the pro-reform David Robert Ross took one of the seats (alongside Emerson Tennent) after parliament overturned the apparent Conservative clean sweep of 1841 on another petition and ordered a by-election. R. J. Tennent himself finally served as Whig-liberal MP for the borough in 1847–52, more than a decade after he had been defeated again in an 1835 by-election. 1832 was however, Crawford's last attempt to contest Belfast. He would now look elsewhere to other allies and opportunities to pursue his political career as a radical.

Sharman Crawford's radicalism

Following his 1831 and 1832 electoral defeats, Crawford worked to widen and deepen his radical credentials in a variety of ways. Already a declared opponent of chattel slavery in the British empire, calls from the Belfast Anti-Slavery Society during the Belfast election had led to him clarifying his position to endorse immediate and full abolition, albeit with some form of compensation (in the absence of which it was unlikely to pass parliament). Attempts by Conservative squib-writers to claim that he had trimmed to Belfast radical opinion on the matter were unconvincing and they dismissively tagged him as 'Sharman Negro'.[210] The Slavery Abolition Act passed by parliament in 1833 fell short of these demands, instead establishing a staged system of 'apprenticeships' for enslaved people in the West Indian colonies which essentially allowed for the continuation of forced plantation labour until 1840 (later shortened to 1838). This, and the unexpectedly huge scale of the payments to slaveholders – totalling 20 million pounds to be funded by a long-term public loan – combined with the continuing existence of slavery in the United States, the Spanish empire, Brazil and other territories which were supplied by illegal slave trading, kept the British anti-slavery campaign alive. In 1837 the Belfast Society resolved that anything less than universal, immediate and total abolition would abet the 'moral crime' of slavery and that the apprenticeship system had continued injustice in British territories.[211]

Anti-slavery appears to have been a family concern at Crawfordsburn. Writing to his mother Mabel from Baltimore, Maryland, in 1836, her eldest son John expressed shocked indignation at witnessing it in practice: 'If you hate slavery my dear mother, not having seen the effects of it, whether on the wretches themselves, on the country, and above all its demoralising effects on their masters, the whites, how much more if you had seen it as I have'. John was not sure that immediate abolition there was practicable, but was certain the American south could not progress while it continued to exist.[212] His sisters Eleanor and Mabel would later become actively involved in anti-slavery activity in Belfast focussed on American abolition. This position however may have created tensions within the family as their daughter Maria's husband Henry Coddington of Oldbridge House claimed unsuccessfully for compensation for the enslaved people on the Creighton Hall plantation in St David, Jamaica, as an owner-in-fee after 1833.[213]

William continued to attend and speak at meetings of the Belfast Anti-Slavery Society and later also the British and Foreign Anti-Slavery Society in London. At an 1838 Belfast meeting he denounced the 'subserviency' of Irish MPs in supporting the government's 'swindle' of 1833 that threw the inflated costs of emancipation on the public and failed to deliver complete freedom.[214] In January 1846 he presided and made the speech of welcome at a public breakfast in Belfast to Frederick Douglass, the great African-American emancipist and 'fugitive slave', who had arrived in Ireland the previous August at the invitation of the Quaker Richard Webb of Cork to promote the Irish edition of his autobiography *The Narrative of the Life of Frederick Douglass, an American Slave*, and to revive flagging overseas support for the abolitionist cause in America.[215] Douglass gave a series of well-attended public lectures on American slavery at the invitation of the Belfast Anti-Slavery Society, which led to some controversy following his attacks on denominations (especially the Scottish Free Kirk) which retained links with and received funds from slaveholding churches in the US. Introducing him at the reception, Crawford welcomed the fact that slavery was no longer legal under the British constitution, and praised Douglass's campaign to end it completely and universally. Its existence was, Crawford stated, doubly pernicious in the United States, which:

> professed to have a constitution founded on the rights of the people – which professed the principles of democracy, and yet kept up a system of slavery, by which a great portion of their fellow-creatures were deprived of all civil and religious rights whatever (loud cheers). It was sufficiently bad, in those states that were governed by arbitrary authority, to maintain the system of slavery; but it was doubly bad – it was tenfold worse – in a state professing democratic principles.

American claims to liberty and justice would thus ring hollow so long as slavery was allowed to continue there. Moreover, any clergy who sought to justify or benefit from it were, he agreed, transgressing the fundamental truths of Christianity:

> He would ask, how any clergyman, could go into the pulpit and read the doctrines of Christ, and avoid denouncing, as an iniquity, the institution of slavery. [...] Could it be maintained, that the blacks were a race not entitled to the favour of the almighty? Would they maintain that the almighty made distinctions between the black race and the white? Surely such a principle could not be maintained by any who professed to be guided by the principles of Christianity.

If any doubted the equality of blacks to whites they had, he continued, only to consider the person of Frederick Douglass himself, who manifested the falsehood of such racial slurs and demonstrated that, if their energies were unleashed, black people could show themselves not only to be equal but even morally superior to whites.[216]

Crawford went on to chair another anti-slavery meeting at First Bangor Presbyterian Church on 13 July 1846, at which Douglass again spoke to denounce those who maintained religious fellowship with slaveholders. If Crawford's assertive anti-slavery stance, like that of Daniel O'Connell, was unlikely to win many friends in large parts of the United States, it did create common ground with some of the leading evangelical Irish Presbyterian opponents of the system, such as Isaac Nelson, even if the stridency of attacks on the Free Kirk may have alienated others.[217] He spoke again on a platform with Douglass and the English Quaker anti-slavery stalwart and 'moral radical' Joseph Sturge at the British and Foreign Society's general meeting later that year in London, urging that body to assert its moral power in pursuit of the extirpation of the evil of slavery and oppose racial discrimination.[218] Douglass later returned the compliment; in 1848 his New York paper *The North Star* expressed support for Crawford's pursuit of democratic reform, and lectured British Chartists that physical force was illegitimate so long as such men remained in parliament.[219]

State education was another subject that Crawford took up in the early 1830s, sparking a local fracas with a neighbouring landlord. In 1831 the Whig government had introduced a national education commission for Ireland, with responsibility to support the construction and maintenance of non-denominational schools from Treasury funds. Despite the inclusion in the national board of representatives of all the main denominations (under the chairmanship of Richard Whately, Anglican archbishop of Dublin), the proposal drew strong objections from those with vested interests in church-controlled education. Protestant opposition centred on the designation of separate periods for religious instruction and the use of biblical extracts rather than the bible in full in the classroom, and fears that the Catholic church would wield de facto control over the new system. Crawford had previously taken an interest in the work of the Kildare Place Society, but accepted its defunding by the state and now supported the government's scheme on ecumenical grounds, although he believed better education alone to be no social panacea and likely merely to increase discontent if not tied to measures to promote welfare and political freedom.[220]

In February 1832 Lord Dufferin, as the principal proprietor of the parish of Bangor, called a public meeting at the town's market house on the new act. The wording of Dufferin's requisition made clear his purpose: 'Let every inhabitant of this parish, who loves *The Bible,* who wishes the rising generation to be instructed from it, and who seeks the moral renovation and well-being of his country, be present at the meeting'. This formed part of a wider movement across the province in which Tories rallied to the defence of bible-based education as a stick to beat the Whig government and as a site on which conservative Anglicans and Presbyterian followers of Dr Henry Cooke might find common political ground.[221]

In Bangor, those opposed to Dufferin's proposal to insist on a system of 'scriptural education' in place of the government scheme looked to Crawford for leadership. It was soon clear that they formed a majority at the meeting; they insisted on a debate and then voted down Dufferin's proposals. In their place were proposed a series of resolutions against tithes, for 'separate' religious education within the new non-denominational national system, and for it to be given a fair trial. Dufferin and his allies felt obliged to retreat in angry disgust at this insurgency in a meeting they had called and sought to suspend proceedings.[222] For the *Northern Whig,* which reported the pointed exchanges between Dufferin and Crawford verbatim, these events amounted to a 'defeat of the enemies of education' and a victory for 'true Protestantism' over incendiary bigotry.[223]

Crawford seized the opportunity in a follow-up pamphlet (the first to appear under his own name) to upbraid Dufferin and his ilk for seeking to stir up religious discord against a pragmatic measure of social improvement:

> the state of a large district of this county, at the present moment, proclaims, in characters of blood, that my apprehensions are not unfounded. [...] To what cause is this attributable, but that excitation produced by the misrepresentations and inflammatory harangues uttered at meetings, such as that you have been lately countenancing in the parish of Bangor; at which meetings, peers of the realm, clergy of the establishment, clergy of other Protestant denominations, and magistrates of the county, proclaim to the people, that their religion is to be subverted, their bibles taken from them, as popery (as they call it) to be elevated, to the destruction of Protestantism; that these measures are to emanate from the government of the country; that the king spurns from him his Protestant subjects; and, in addition to all these, a call made on the people, to arm themselves? This, my lord, exceeds, beyond all measure, any speeches or efforts of the great agitator, whom I have so often heard you condemn; and whose indiscretion, or occasional intemperance, I do not advocate; but at the same time, my lord, he has had real grievances to complain of, on the part of the Irish nation, which ought to be a just palliation of some intemperance; but if it be a crime to agitate, how immensely is that crime increased, if not only agitation but false misrepresentation proceeds from those who hold the highest honours.

Religion, he concluded, was not the real motivation of such sectarian agitation, rather it was an attempt to protect existing monopolies of power and emolument. Such deceptions could last only so long, even for those whose perspective had been distorted by Orange ideology, for 'the time will come [...] when the eyes of the people will be opened, and they will discern who are their true friends'.

He went on to elaborate on his own religious philosophy, which he said informed his politics. A true reading of the scriptures would reveal not only the means of attaining eternal salvation, but the requirements of moral living: for the wealthy these required taking action to reduce the unfair burdens of the poor, which deprived them of even the 'reasonable comforts of food and clothing'. On the other hand, the bible ensured to the poor man freedom of thought and action, elevating him in independence of mind and body; but any attempt to force it on him would be counterproductive without good moral example.[224] While drawing such spiritual conclusions, Crawford was at the same time not slow to press his political advantage: an address containing the pro-national education resolutions agreed at a second meeting in Bangor was dispatched to and welcomed by the prime minister and presented to the commons.[225]

A local squib-writer commented on the Bangor education fracas in less elevated terms. The setback for Dufferin had, he asserted, been a defeat for local Toryism and high Anglicanism, and a personal triumph for Crawford: "'O woe is me,' said Dufferin, "not because I fly the foe – / But it most sorely grieveth me, / That Crawford sees me go.'".[226] Dufferin's allies did not concede defeat, however, and a 'Protestant of Bangor' retaliated by claiming that Crawford, a man allegedly of servile ancestry and 'almost a stranger to the parish' was compensating for his ignominious defeat in Down through the noisy agitation of resolutions 'drafted for the occasion from a squad of Jacobins in Belfast'.[227] Dufferin wrote angrily to Crawford to express his sense of betrayal, only to receive the response that, while he held him in personal regard, Crawford stood over his charges and would not compromise his 'independence'.[228] The neighbours remained on poor terms until Dufferin's death in 1836.

Local tensions over educational provision would continue: by 1837 the village of Crawfordsburn had an endowed (Church of Ireland) school founded by Dufferin in 1834 as well as a national school supported by Crawford, who paid over 40 per cent of the master's salary, and which educated both Protestant and Catholic children.[229] His support for the latter school gave rise to an electoral slur in 1832 that it featured a sign reading 'No bible read here', which Crawford felt obliged to refute by insisting that the rules of the national board on 'separate' religious education were followed to the letter at Crawfordsburn.[230] He would continue to uphold the principle of non-denominational education once in parliament, arguing it had been 'decidedly successful' in educating Presbyterians and Catholics in the north, and hoping (over-optimistically) that it would eventually be instrumental in allaying animosities and bringing together future generations in greater amity.[231] In similar vein, he later supported the non-denominational (to its critics, 'godless') Queen's Colleges Act in 1845 which established higher education institutions in Belfast, Cork and Galway, and remained an advocate of state-supported 'mixed education' to the end of his life, in England as well as Ireland.[232]

Crawford assiduously courted all strands of Presbyterians through his patronage of congregations on or adjacent to his estates. While this was politically astute, it also reflected his genuine Protestant ecumenism, which would ultimately see him accede to unitarianism late in life. He was a financial supporter of the Rademon Non-Subscribing Presbyterian congregation at Kilmore, where in 1832 the assembled ministers of the Armagh Presbytery (including Rev. William Bruce and Rev. John Mitchel, father of the future Young Irelander), met at the installation of a new minister. Afterwards they toasted 'the best of landlords; may his talents and virtues soon be exercised in a field worthy of their usefulness and excellence'.[233] Less than a year later Crawford was present at the opening of the new orthodox Presbyterian meeting house at Kilmore, where the sermon was delivered by Dr Henry Cooke.[234] In the same month he wrote personally to Dr Thomas Chalmers, the celebrated Scottish evangelical preacher, asking him to speak at the opening of the newly rebuilt First Presbyterian Church in Bangor (where though not a member, he was a 'seat holder and subscriber'), expressing his conviction that Chalmers' words would have a good effect on anyone 'who was not irrecoverably tainted with the poison of sectarian hostility'.

Having heard Chalmers preach before, possibly when the latter had spoken in Belfast in 1827 in support of reconciliation between Presbyterians of antagonistic theological opinions. He was certain the effect of his words would be irenic, softening that 'spirit of religious dissension, emanating originally from political dissension [which] has taken possession of the mind of the great body of the people, and obliterated what ought to be the great object of all religion – love towards God, and good will towards man'.[235] Chalmers declined this invitation on the grounds that he no longer itinerated to preach, although he did return to Belfast in 1842, when Crawford was present to hear him.[236]

It followed that Crawford would be an active supporter of Presbyterian demands for religious equality, and he would endorse the demands for the full legal recognition of Presbyterian marriages that the government was reluctant to concede until 1844.[237] Indeed he put himself forward as a parliamentary advocate of their interests in contrast to the mostly Anglican Tory MPs for Ulster constituencies.[238] However, political and theological disputes within the extended Presbyterian family left him in a more difficult position. His anti-Erastianism would have rendered him sympathetic to the widespread Irish Presbyterian support for Chalmers and the breakaway Free Presbyterian Church in Scotland in 1843 in its opposition to lay and state patronage and the constraints on religious freedom this implied. But the antagonistic disputes between the orthodox and unitarian wings of the Irish Presbyterians over ownership of church property in the wake of their 1830 split was more troubling, especially when the Remonstrant Synod leader Dr Henry Montgomery actively lobbied the Peel government for its support in 1844. Crawford opted to endorse the government's 1844 Dissenters' Chapels Bill, which recognised the property rights of existing congregations, on the grounds that this best protected religious freedoms.[239] However neither this stance nor his consistent opposition to the regium donum payments to ministers seem to have greatly damaged his relations with the orthodox Presbyterian clergy, many of whom were to participate in his later agrarian campaigns, tentatively from the mid-1830s and more whole-heartedly by 1847.

Despite his often-strained relations with the political leaders of Irish Catholicism (especially from 1836), Crawford also maintained good relations with many Catholic clergy over his lifetime, not only the parochial clergy on and around his estates, but leaders of the church in Ulster such as Archbishop Crolly and Bishops Denvir and Maginn. His collaboration with the radical Dublin cleric Fr Thaddeus O'Malley would play an important role in the development of his thinking on both poor relief and federalism as a solution to the Irish constitutional question. He was a frequent attender at fund-raising events for Catholic churches, such as the consecration of the new chapel at Banbridge in June 1841, at which the temperance campaigner Fr Theobald Mathew gave the sermon.[240] Non-sectarian collaboration behind democratic and political reforms remained central to his political vision, and such public engagements appeared central to pursuing that.

The elections of 1830–2 in Down and Belfast had confirmed Sharman Crawford as a leading figure within Ulster radicalism. They had also demonstrated his limitations. Looking back to the heyday of Volunteering in the 1780s, his constitutional thought was still principally concerned with the right of freeholders and ratepayers to fair and uncorrupted representation in a mixed constitution. Although well in advance of Whig moderates, especially on the questions of the secret ballot and triennial parliaments, he was not at first fully a self-identified democrat, still publicly holding back from universal male suffrage in 1832 on the grounds that the principle of the constitution linked suffrage to property.[241] The string of defeats, growing disillusionment with the limited achievements of the reformed parliament elected that year and of Whig governments to achieve substantive reforms in Ireland or Britain, would lead him towards a more advanced radicalism and a reconsideration of Ireland's relationship with Great Britain over the next half decade. He would also begin to sketch out the land reform proposals that would become so closely associated with his name and seek to turn these into legislation from 1835. All these ideas would be developed through dialectic relations with both O'Connell and the new voices of British and Irish political radicalism of the 1830s.

3. O'Connell, repeal and the national question, 1832–41

Approaching repeal, 1833–4

In the wake of his Belfast defeat Sharman Crawford turned to developing his ideas on Ireland's constitutional relations with Britain in pamphlet form. Originally written during the Belfast campaign, but held back on the advice of his election committee, *A Review of Circumstances Connected with the Past and Present State of the Protestant and Catholic Interests in Ireland* appeared in mid-February 1833, jointly published in Belfast and Dublin and (as with most of his pamphlets) also serialised in the press.[1] He was fully conscious that most reformist northern Protestants were anxious about the threat they perceived from Catholic majoritarianism under O'Connell's strident leadership and the political costs of appearing too close to it, and was also aware that most Protestants regarded the union as economically beneficial. Nevertheless, Crawford urged them to engage constructively in dialogue with the repeal movement and to consider a potential compromise solution.

Crawford began with a justification of the stance taken by liberal Protestants in rejecting the politics of Protestant ascendancy and advocating the redress of the historic grievances of the majority Catholic community on the island. He answered the question of whether Irish Protestants and the government had followed Catholic emancipation with necessary further concessions by, 'like an Irishman', asking another (rhetorical) question: would Protestants be content if they continued to be subject to the galling discrimination and humiliations that Catholics still endured? These grievances were multiple, and included the levying of tithes and church rates to support exclusively the minority established church, the monopolisation of policing and the legal possession of arms by Protestants, and discrimination in the formation of juries and appointments to the magistracy and judicial bench. If Protestants had been subjected to such penalties imposed and maintained under a legislative union, surely they too would have resisted and sought its repeal? Moreover, any justification of minority supremacy under the 'law of conquest' could only be self-destructive as it constantly stimulated the Catholics towards rebellion against those who held monopoly power without democratic legitimacy. Without denying the bloodshed incurred in past risings, it was, he thought, fair to say that the Catholics always had the excuse of provocation as the victims of oppression. This was a vicious cycle that needed to be broken, in the shared interest of all communities on the island.

The renunciation of Protestant ascendancy did not in his view require any personal relinquishing of genuinely held faith, for the 'arrogant assumption of political power and wealth is opposed to the principles of Christianity and to the precepts of Christ'.[2]

Crawford was moving towards the doctrine that voluntarism in religion was not only politically desirable, but essential for the spiritual truths of Protestantism to prevail through persuasion and example, and would soon pursue this to its natural conclusion of seeking the disestablishment of all churches and full separation of church and state. Those who insisted on resisting Catholic demands to render emancipation real in fact and not just in name were, he argued, the real separatists; it was they who would be to blame if the union failed after Catholics had been driven to extreme modes of redress.

But this outcome was not inevitable. The desirability of some form of union had, he continued, been demonstrated by the constant and damaging disputes between the two parliaments over trade policy from 1785, and the military and financial stresses of war from 1793. The confusion that arose had hurt the smaller and weaker country more than the stronger, thereby stimulating communal antagonisms within Ireland. On the other hand, it was clear that the benefits promised to Ireland from Pitt's Act of Union had not been realised. Grattan had thus been right to warn that a partial union – one of parliaments, not of nations – would lead to the neglect or subordination of Irish interests, to greater absenteeism and an inequitable drain of taxation. Grattan's argument that the policies adopted by the Irish parliament after 1779 had done more to promote the economic wellbeing of the country than anything enacted since 1801 could not, Crawford believed, be refuted.

Nor was any great change now evident. The Whig administration formed in 1830 had failed in its promises and continued to short-change Ireland: there had been only a minimal increase in Irish representation in parliament to 105 (Crawford believed it was due at least 165, or 183 seats if population ratios alone were considered).[3] Ireland had also been treated with contempt in being left behind England in terms of the franchise and registration law reform. If, as English interests argued, Ireland should remain under-represented because it was poor and thus made a smaller contribution to the national treasury, the cause of this lay in England's subordination of Ireland's economic interests and its unfair fiscal extractions – under-representation was thus part of a vicious circle copper-fastened by the current union.

Rather than abolish the hated tithes levied to support the established church, the Whig government had merely tinkered, while imposing collection with 'unprecedented harshness and severity'. He condemned the coercion deployed in a vain attempt to curb the angry popular reaction then manifest in the 'Tithe War'.[4] With nearly the whole of the English liberal party voting with the Whig government on these measures, it was, he thought, no wonder that the majority of people in Ireland saw no hope of justice except through restoring a parliament of their own. Ireland had, he summed up, obtained through the union only '[t]he evils of British connexion, without the advantages, – the name of the British constitution, without the reality, – the exaltation of the minority of her population, at the expense of the majority'.[5]

If the British connection was to survive at all, Crawford concluded, a complete change of policy was required, putting new foundations in place of the corruption and lack of consent that had been laid during the constitutional reframing of 1800–1. If the government really did intend to maintain Protestant ascendancy it should then administer Ireland as a conquered country, tear up all forms of representation and rule by the sword alone. If this was too much to stomach (as he believed it was for majority British opinion), it must seek instead to govern by giving equal rights, privileges and profits to all classes. But Crawford was coming to believe that a simple change of heart by British government would not be enough. While retaining his scepticism about the workability and stability of having two sovereign parliaments within the same political entity, he now suggested an 'intermediate course', which would 'secure, in some degree, the benefits of local legislation, without throwing off the beneficial control of an imperial legislature in imperial concerns'. He proceeded to sketch the preliminary outlines of what would later be termed 'federalism', giving Ireland a representative assembly with tax-raising powers and defined 'local' responsibilities, and replacing the grand juries. This body would take on the vital tasks of improving and maintaining the transport, public works and judicial infrastructure of the country with the aim of strategic development; it should develop an appropriate Irish poor law system, and take on other policy areas where Irish distinctiveness needed recognition. Its location in Dublin would, moreover, revive that city's fading fortunes.

In answer to Protestant fears of a loss of control under such a representative assembly, Crawford asserted that addressing just Catholic claims was likely to end religious enmity, and observed that Catholics had supported the abolition of the test acts against Protestant dissenters and other measures to promote the civil and religious liberties of all. But if this turned out not the case, any bid for Catholic ascendancy under a federal constitution would draw the intervention of England and Scotland in defence of genuine Irish Protestant civil rights. O'Connell's power in Ireland was indeed real, but rested on his monopoly of the leadership of the campaign for legitimate civil rights granted to him by others. Under other circumstances this would change: 'Let others do their duty [...] let them aid O'Connell when he is in the right, and then they will acquire the power of opposing him if he should be wrong'.[6] Similarly, the alleged political power of the Catholic priests was simply a reflection of the dissatisfaction of the people they served (and who paid them), and was at least deployed in the national interest, in contrast to the self-interest displayed by many of the established church clergy.

With this pamphlet, Crawford was attempting to place himself as an interlocutor between Ulster Protestant liberalism and the Catholic mass movement. This was a difficult balancing act, and eventually would prove unworkable. In the moment of 1833 however, with O'Connell seeking Protestant allies and northern liberal Protestantism lacking alternative political leadership, it appeared to have potential. The pamphlet received wide circulation. Praising the author as having 'a mind deeply conversant with the causes of our misery, and well fitted to point out the means of our regeneration', the *Northern Whig* printed extensive extracts on its front page.[7] In Dublin the moderate O'Connellite *Freeman's Journal* praised Crawford's reforming record and antecedents, and welcomed his 'very useful and clever pamphlet'. It believed he represented the 'feelings of the intelligent portion of the Protestant community' and that his views were fully deserving of respect. However it opted only to print extracts critical of Protestant ascendancy and government policy, and did not reflect on his preference for a subordinate parliament over 'simple repeal'.[8]

The *Freeman* was sufficiently taken with Crawford to agree to publish from September 1833 a series of letters on 'The expediency and necessity of a local legislative body for Ireland', which would be later pulled together into a second pamphlet published in November. The paper was now convinced that he had made 'the question of Irish nationality

[...] a Protestant question', and his leadership would help restore Ulster Presbyterians to the forefront of the patriotic struggle.[9] The pamphlet was published by and also serialised in the *Newry Examiner*, a paper that was owned by Charles Teeling, and served a Catholic and liberal Protestant readership in south Down and north Louth.[10] In *The Expediency and Necessity* Crawford elaborated on themes raised in the earlier publication and offered a critical commentary on the parliamentary session of 1833. Claiming to be non-partisan and unprejudiced, he attacked Whig defenders of the government for excusing its inaction and deafness to popular demands. He asserted that the Orange or ascendancy party had acted hypocritically in not breaking with the administration and campaigning for outright authoritarianism, while liberal Protestants had proved too indecisive and passive. For their part, Repealers needed to be more explicit about their objectives and how they would manage the predictable constitutional and economic problems that would arise in the future British-Irish relationship.

Crawford responded to the Irish ministerial Whig Thomas Spring Rice's disparagement of the achievements of 'Grattan's parliament' in his recent *Edinburgh Review* article, by drawing a rigid distinction between the period when that parliament had been obliged to heed the wishes of the public through the pressure of the Volunteers, and its later years when it had not and thus had lapsed wholly into corruption. By then it had comprised merely 'representatives of a sect – the corrupt agents of English power' and had not served Ireland's real interests.[11] When population growth was factored in, Spring Rice's boasted figures for post-union economic growth looked unconvincing, especially compared with the evidence of rapid development in the 1780s. Claims of British generosity to Ireland after 1801 paled when the drain of some £3 million per annum in absentee rentals was taken into account, along with the excessive rate of 'imperial' taxation set in 1800 and not revised after the post-war crash. Rather than indicating growing prosperity, he argued, the statistics for agricultural exports since the union hid the advancing immiseration of the rural population:

> let these questions be answered by those who have witnessed the daily feeding of the Irish labourer, the mechanic, or even the farmer; and who knows that potatoes, in different forms, constitute nearly their whole subsistence; that the only addition consists of a portion of oaten meal with water to drink; and that if buttermilk (or that which is the refuse of the churn, after the butter is extracted,) can be substituted for water, it is a luxury; that wheaten bread, or the produce of wheat in any form, seldom or ever enters their lips.[12]

The recently announced royal commission into the condition of the Irish poor would, he was sure, bear out this evidence of social stagnation or regression, and that Ireland simply could not afford to export its agricultural produce on the scale recorded; the country's enormous export of migrant labour further proved this point. Agrarian disorder, which had disappeared during the Volunteers' heyday, had returned in the 1790s and remained widespread through to the present as a proxy for misery and despair.

Reviewing the session of 1833, Crawford concluded that the Irish coercion act merely compounded the ministry's failure to deal with the underlying problem of tithes and popular resistance to their extraction. No effective relief had followed – tithes and taxes remained as heavy as ever, without any assistance to the poor; the former 40-shilling freeholder voters remained subject to eviction now they were no longer of political value to the landowners and seen as a mere encumbrance on the land. O'Connell's support in Ireland remained as strong as before. In such circumstances it could come as no surprise that the peasantry should turn to the desperate violence of secret societies, and all the new coercion act had succeeded in doing was to increase anger at the government and determination to resist tithes and support O'Connell and the repeal of the union.

It had turned out, he concluded, that the British-Irish reformist alliance of 1831–2 (of which he had been part) had been constructed on false premises, for:

> sad experience now proves to Ireland, as on former occasions, that England's freedom is Ireland's slavery – that England's prosperity only dooms Ireland to a more depressed state of misery and political degradation [...] and what renders the case still more hopeless, is the general apathy and indifference of the British nation, and worse than indifference of the Scotch, towards matters connected with Irish policy.[13]

The 1833 government measures on Irish church temporalities and tithes were grossly inadequate to address the underlying problems. As an Anglican layman himself, he took the view that Catholic emancipation and the repeal of the test acts had rendered the principle of an established church redundant, and that instead the Church of Ireland should place 'the regulation of its discipline and government in a body, constituted solely of its own members', and abandon any claim to revenues beyond those derived from its own landholdings; the alternative was for it to become openly 'a mere state machine to answer political purposes', lacking any claim to religious freedom.[14] If the state really wanted to uphold the interests of the Protestant church, it would look to the precedent set by the compensation payments issued to facilitate slave emancipation that year, as the 'tithes are *there* the badges of slavery, imposed by British power: British wealth should be called on (at least to assist), in redeeming the consequences of British injustice'.[15]

All of this mismanagement proved, he argued, the need for a local legislature, as did the sheer scale of local Irish legislation transacted (poorly and expensively) at Westminster. Ireland's social and economic distinctiveness, manifest in the high levels of social unrest, rendered a common system of legislation across the UK impracticable. Thus, the alternative of a complete assimilation of law and taxation between the two countries could not work in Ireland's interest. This was a pragmatic rather than a nationalist argument for limited self-government aimed squarely at wavering Protestants.

Crawford next took some steps towards articulating what his 'local legislature' might look like. The union could not be repealed without creating new terms for the connection with Great Britain, setting out both the powers and limitations of the new Irish legislative body. There must be no return to either the legal or the virtual dependency of the old unreformed Irish parliament before and after 1782. While details had still to be worked out, these should take account of the just claims of both countries, and the need to maintain a mutually beneficial connection between them, especially in terms of trade. England's own legislative independence needed to be respected, along with its control over its colonies (except to the proportionate extent granted by Ireland's contribution to 'imperial' revenues). Who would adjudicate in the division of local and imperial powers? He sidestepped both this and the issue of whether the superior legislature should be a British or an 'imperial' (i.e. cognate with the American federal) body, focusing instead on the benefits to Ireland of having a local legislature with control over internal tax-raising powers, its own military and civil establishments, and the enactment of all measures of local operation.[16] In return for granting Ireland this boon, England would gain from no longer having to spend money and political capital in maintaining the divisive and unstable union, and gain Irish friendship in the promotion of its global interests. Crawford was here advocating what would later be described as a devolutionary settlement; it was left unclear at this time as to whether this would also be or become truly federal, a term he did not himself employ until 1843–4.

Crawford was not the only figure exploring such ideas at the time. It is unclear if he was yet aware of the self-defined 'federalist' thinking of the radical Catholic priest Fr Thaddeus O'Malley, who had brought out a series of letters on the subject in 1831 that had been influenced by the classic American *Federalist* texts by Hamilton, Madison and Jay of the 1780s. O'Malley, an independent thinker who often found himself in conflict with episcopal authority, and who also vehemently supported the separation of church and state, was to become a significant voice in the Irish radical politics of the 1830–40s and an ally of Crawford on several campaigns in defiance of O'Connell's authority.[17]

In rejecting Grey's government's claim to be acting in Ireland's interests, Crawford was placing himself outside the partisan alignment of most Irish liberal Protestants who supported the Whig-liberal party with a degree of tribal loyalty. He had, he commented, become convinced that with respect to Ireland the Whigs and Tories shared the same object – the subjugation of Ireland to English interests. The difference between them was thus one of style rather than substance:

> [T]he Whigs were equally desirous to effect the same object; but they fondle on their victim – they pet and caress her with their lips – they offer her the sweetened cake, whilst they withhold the substantial nourishment; and thus, by pampering and tantalizing, lead her into that state of disobedience, which renders correction, as it were, a kindness, and exertion of authority a duty.[18]

Ireland's hope lay, he continued, in the dissension and feuding between these two English factions, which would allow a third, Irish, party to emerge and exploit all constitutional opportunities to assert the country's rights. In claiming this, Crawford was now aligning himself with the strategy of O'Connell's Repeal Party, formed in the aftermath of the 1832 general election, which was seeking to wield a balance of power between the British parties. Crawford's aims were to draw liberal Protestants away from Whiggery and to participate in this alternative project, and to shape the constitutional objects of the Irish party to what he regarded as something more practicable and sustainable than the populist nationalism of the O'Connellite platforms. Neither Orangemen nor Whigs in Ireland should trust British governments to defend a policy that England was coming to see as contrary to its own strategic interest – that of upholding an outdated and destabilising Protestant ascendancy. Instead, Protestants should ally with the majority, and look to their own property, education and intelligence to assure they maintained a leading place in the country; the alternative was, in the long term, certain defeat, marginalisation and permanent insecurity.[19]

The second pamphlet drew admiring commentary from the *Freeman*, which combined enthusiasm for his advocacy with a mild rebuke to his reluctance to countenance 'unconditional repeal'.[20] His hopes of bringing at least a section of Ulster liberal Protestantism along with him received a major setback however, when the *Northern Whig*, previously a strong supporter, published its commentary in early 1834. Alongside a lengthy extract, the editor expressed puzzlement as to whether Crawford was actually now a repealer or not. His proposal seemed to amount to something like a 'national grand jury', falling far short of the autonomous parliament that O'Connell demanded. To his credit, it conceded that Crawford's argument was clearly and ably stated, and avoided the romanticised eulogies to the old Irish parliament so common in O'Connellite discourse. But, the editorialist argued, his statistical review had badly miscalculated the growth in Irish exports and real wealth since the union, and seemed to be adopting a position inimical to free trade. Taking a line that would become typical of Belfast liberal unionism, the *Whig* claimed that the principal flaw with Crawford's scheme was that it would deny Ireland any say in the trade policy of the UK, which would remain beyond the purview of the local legislature.[21]

Responding to this criticism, Crawford insisted that his previous opposition to repeal had been conditional, but that after a fair trial the failings of the reformed parliament had convinced him that some form of Irish self-government, alongside a rejuvenated British connection, was essential. His statistics were accurate, and he could stand over his argument for falling living standards since 1801. His purpose had been to stimulate unprejudiced discussion on the subject, which he hoped the paper would support rather than seek to shut down. The *Whig* reacted by doubling down on Crawford's alleged errors of political economy.[22] The dispute rumbled on into February 1834, with two more letters from Crawford, in which he pointedly asked what alternative the paper offered to what it had previously acknowledged to be the coerced subordination of Ireland, eliciting support from the *Newry Examiner* and the Belfast *Northern Herald*.[23] If the extended and intemperate exchange reflected the prestige Crawford held among Belfast liberals as a man whose opinions mattered, it also signalled a rift that was only likely to widen.

Dundalk politics, 1834–6

O'Connell saw Crawford's demarche of 1833 as an opportunity to be seized, in line with his 'leading object' at the time of obtaining high-profile Protestant support for repeal of the union.[24] He announced to his followers that Crawford's publications presaged a breakthrough for the movement in Ulster:

> Believe me, that when men of his rank, fortune, talents and high character take the lead in seeking for 'the repeal,' the national restoration of Ireland is at hand, and we shall achieve national independence, as a portion only of the Irish nation achieved Catholic emancipation – that is – without violence or crime, without causing one tear to flow, and without incurring the possibility of shedding one drop of blood.[25]

It was not in the Liberator's interest to draw attention to the nuances of Crawford's position. Rather, in dedicating an 'Address to the Protestants of Ireland' to him in January 1834, O'Connell highlighted the apparently whole-hearted accession of the northern radical and joked that he would be happy to be 'one of *your tail*'.[26] In parliament he boasted that Crawford 'was now an avowed and determined, a staunch and uncompromising, repealer', and predicted that many in Ulster would follow suit.[27]

Seeking to maintain his independence, while paying tribute to the Liberator's achievements and potential to do good for Ireland, Crawford responded by pressing O'Connell on how his 'simple repeal' would deal with the likely clashes between two sovereign parliaments over commercial policy, and ensure the retention of what he regarded as the non-negotiable boon of free trade between the islands. Ulster Protestants could, he insisted, only be persuaded to convert to repeal once these core issues were candidly debated and resolved.[28] In the absence of clear statements on these heads, he added, his own allegiance to the movement could only ever be conditional. Nevertheless, Crawford was mobbed by supporters at a mass repeal and anti-tithe meeting at Navan, Co. Meath, and his speech there met with 'repeated acclamation'.[29]

In late April 1834 the commons finally debated O'Connell's motion for repeal of the union, only to throw it out by the massive majority of 523 to 38. The leading speaker opposing the motion was the same Spring Rice whose statistical arguments Crawford had sought to undermine in his 1833 pamphlet. Writing from Westminster, the (then Repeal) MP Richard Lalor Sheil thanked Crawford for his role in exciting public support for the cause in Meath, and mocked Spring Rice's performance, adding that the defeat was but the opening salvo in a long campaign.[30] O'Connell's biographer Oliver MacDonagh also notes the Liberator's good humour in the wake of what might have been seen as a humiliating setback, suggesting that it freed him to pursue a tactical campaign of extracting concessions from Whig governments while maintaining lip-service to repeal, which was more congenial to his own pragmatic brand of politics.[31] While this shift indeed presaged improving relations between O'Connell and the British Whigs, it would ultimately strain his relations with more intransigent Irish and British radical figures, such as Crawford.

In a public letter to O'Connell in June, Crawford endorsed the party line that '*the repeal question is not dead, but sleeps*', but that it should continue to be substantially agitated. His principal concern now, however, was to ensure the total abolition of the tithe system. He couched this in terms of his growing personal adherence to religious voluntarism, extending beyond the campaign for total abolition of the tithes which made his own church 'an extortioner of the property of the nation, by the power of the sword', to the removal of all state subsidies to churches. This must also include the Presbyterians' regium donum, which had, in his view, rendered that church 'a mendicant accepting alms from the purse of the nation, dispensed as the benevolence of the crown shall think the clergy worthy of its favour'.[32] This critique echoed those of radical Presbyterians including William Drennan, who regarded the government's restructuring of the grant in 1799–1803 as rendering it a tool of political control.[33] A subsequent public letter by Crawford welcomed O'Connell's endorsement of his arguments, and reiterated his conviction that the only hope for retaining Protestant property and position in Ireland was to abandon sectarian hostility to the demands of the majority and make common cause with the Catholics for the mutual benefit of all.[34]

While he fully supported Crawford's position on tithe abolition in his public letters, O'Connell was more circumspect in his private correspondence. It would be difficult, he wrote, to prevent landlords gaining from any reform of tithes, and some compromise with the Whigs could smooth the path for repeal by leading to the replacement of reactionary judicial and civil officials in Ireland with those more conducive to political progress. He wrote to Crawford:

> You are one of the few who appreciate the crisis at which we are arrived. The times we live in are those in which a transition ought to be made from the factious misrule of centuries to the

sway of a paternal and protective government [...] A government which leaving to the people the free and protected choice of local magistracies will remove at one blow nine tenths of the causes of oppression – a government which will render law clear and simple in its enactments and justice cheap and expeditious. These are the objects of our ambition and I believe they are attainable. The virulence of sectarian animosity is certainly our greatest obstacle [...] The Orange faction [must be] rendered impotent by the loss of governmental and ecclesiastical patronage [...] If that faction became powerless the course would be free to canvass and obtain all the advantages of a local legislature – a measure which it is my first and deepest object to attain and one to which I unremittingly tend whether in the bustle of active agitation or in the calm of that [discussion?] which makes me leave at this moment a clear field for exhibition of the follies and vices of the hereditary enemies of Ireland.[35]

In public he reassured his 'excellent friend' that they were in total agreement on the mode to bring tranquillity, and with it prosperity, to Ireland – the redress of grievances and, above all, the end of the tithe system: 'Until the TITHE SYSTEM IS ABOLISHED – totally abolished, not IN NAME only, but in ESSENCE and in PRACTICAL REALITY – Ireland cannot experience tranquility'.[36]

O'Connell was anxious to integrate Crawford into the repeal movement by finding him a parliamentary seat, and by March 1834 it was resolved that he would be invited to represent Dundalk.[37] The Irish Reform Act had turned that constituency from a closed corporation borough controlled by the earls of Roden into a £10 ratepayer constituency with initially 318 registered electors, the great majority of whom were middle-class Catholics. Following the Reform Act the previous Roden nominee James Edward Gordon, evangelical founder of the Protestant Reformation Society, was replaced by the Catholic reformer William O'Reilly.[38] The Repeal movement was, however, strong in Dundalk and was prepared to oust O'Reilly (a divisive figure and whose vote against the repeal motion in April sealed his fate) to make way for O'Connell's new favourite.[39] While his acceptance paved an easy path to parliament at the next general election, he was to discover that it left him highly vulnerable to the dictates of the party machine.

The next general election came unexpectedly, after parliament was dissolved in December 1834 at the instigation of the minority Conservative government formed the previous month under Sir Robert Peel and the Duke of Wellington. Crawford now received a formal and unanimous invitation from the Dundalk Liberal Club and was pleased to note that there would be no Conservative challenger. A requisition, signed by 146 electors, ensuring victory, was received and accepted in person by Crawford amid scenes of some enthusiasm.[40] This was important to a man whose personal finances had been strained by the contests of 1831 and 1832. He wrote to his son John that the absence of a contest left him 'no apology for refusing'.[41]

O'Connell's new policy of promoting an electoral alliance with Whig-liberals under the aegis of an 'Anti-Tory Association' posed certain problems for the new convert, who had so recently denounced the two British parties as pursuing essentially the same policies in Ireland. The answer he posited in a public letter was that the alliance was a resting stage made necessary by the slow process of winning over 'the liberal portion of the Protestant community of Ireland', which could only be done 'by perseverance and moderation, and by the desire to yield such securities as may be deemed necessary to protect Protestant rights, and to maintain the connexion with England in the same state and under the same crown'. Repeal remained O'Connell's ultimate objective, but in the short term he saw maximising the number of pro-reform MPs as a more broadly-based Irish party would create the greatest leverage. He believed that candidates should give a pledge to accept recall by their constituencies if they disagreed with them on the subject of repeal when that subject was debated again.[42] Crawford acquiesced in the strategy and joined the Association on O'Connell's nomination: sixty-five 'Anti-Tories' were returned under the alliance in 1835, with thirty-four of these (including Crawford) being self-declared 'Repealers' of varying levels of commitment.[43]

Crawford's uncontested return was welcomed by the *Newry Examiner* as a glorious triumph for 'one of the purest patriots and most exalted public men of whom any country can boast'.[44] At the electoral proceedings he thanked the Catholic electorate for demonstrating their non-sectarianism in returning a Protestant and gave them a Whiggish lecture on the legacy of the 1688 'glorious revolution' in establishing the principle that all power and laws emanated from the people and should be used for their benefit. He continued that while the constitution had been until now a dead letter in Ireland, it would be no longer. He would seek to restore the Protestant church in Ireland to true Christian principles by removing the powers of provocation that had led to the recent bloodshed over tithe collection at Rathcormac, and work to ensure equal treatment to all denominations and classes (while also promoting the town's specific local needs). His speech was rapturously received in Dundalk.[45] At a celebratory dinner some weeks later he returned to the subject of Rathcormac, where on 18 December 1834 between twelve and twenty protesters had been killed by soldiers enforcing the collection of tithes, condemning the government for ignoring the inquest verdict of murder, for praising the army's conduct and for then deploying it unconstitutionally during the elections. All this, he concluded, was reminiscent of the state terror of 1798, and was proof of Britain's unfitness to rule Ireland.[46]

Although returned for a Leinster constituency, the election served as an excuse for supporters in Down to give him the triumphant chairing he had previously been denied. On returning home:

> [e]very exertion was made by the people of Crawfordsburn, Bangor, and the surrounding neighbourhoods, to give him a joyous reception. As soon as the evening closed in, bonfires and tar-barrels blazed on the hills; the houses along the road he was to pass were brilliantly illuminated, and the village of Crawfordsburn was strikingly beautiful, every window presenting a blaze of light – triumphal arches were erected: one very tastefully decorated was opposite the national school-house. After he passed through Holywood, the roads were thronged with people, who evinced their joy and satisfaction, by the most enthusiastic plaudits. A regular procession of the people of Bangor, Crawfordsburn, and the surrounding country, met him a mile from the village, and drew him to his hospitable mansion, amidst the loudest acclamations [… later the people] dispersed, some to their own houses, some to the village, where they were regaled by a plentiful supply of 'Johnston's Brown Stout'.[47]

The *Whig* noted his personal popularity even with those of differing political opinions, and Crawford himself expressed thanks that he had few personal enemies and that even his opponents had congratulated him on his election.[48]

His first session in parliament (of what eventually would be thirteen) is unusually well documented, with correspondence with his son John detailing his parliamentary observations and experience surviving in his papers. Arriving at Westminster in March 1835 he found the opposition divided and fractured, while Peel's minority administration had been buoyed up by the defection of Stanley and his allies (including Emerson Tennent) from the Whigs. His initial feeling was that Ireland would continue to be marginalised and demonised in press and parliament:

> The Tory papers are doing all they possibly can to increase [their advantage] by exciting the jealousy of the English members and English people against the Irish members – they say that the late victory was obtained by the power of the latter <u>against the sense of the people of England</u> – and they endeavour to implicate the Whigs of England with the political principles of O'Connell – and I can assure you their labour is not going for nothing – because there are already considerable symptoms among the Whigs at their meetings of a desire to cast off the Irish.[49]

He still trusted O'Connell, he told John, to lead the Irish party on a temperate course to maximise their advantage. This again meant acquiescing in the Irish party's participation in the Whig-liberal party meetings at Lichfield House, and O'Connell's negotiation of an unwritten 'compact' with the more sympathetic 'Foxite' Whig faction led by Lord John Russell and Lord Duncannon. The agreement would commit his followers to backing a new Whig government in return for commitments on Irish tithe, parliamentary and municipal corporations reforms, and patronage concessions.[50] If Crawford felt unease at this deal, as seems likely given his later actions, he at first concealed it.

His first intervention in the commons, on 12 March 1835, was to speak in support of a petition he presented from Drumbo in Down, signed by 1,396 people (mostly Presbyterian) for the total abolition of tithes and the regium donum. His assertion that this was the general opinion of the county drew a riposte from his old adversary Lord Castlereagh, now a household official in Peel's administration.[51] A further petition to the same end with 4,756 signatures from nineteen Down and Antrim parishes was sent to Crawford and the Belfast MP John McCance several weeks later. Despite representing a Leinster, and later an English, constituency, he became the preferred conduit for radical petitions from north-east Ulster, and also soon developed a reputation as an assiduous attender and speaker on a range of parliamentary topics that drew his interest. Despite his previous coolness towards R. J. Tennent after their joint defeat, by 1836 he was co-operating freely with him in preparing and presenting petitions from Belfast for amendments to the municipal corporations bill and in countering Emerson Tennent's responses.[52] Indeed after praising him several months later at a dinner in Belfast, R. J. Tennent angrily denied the claim in a Tory newspaper that 'in his heart, he hates [Crawford], and has hated [him] since the election of 1832'.[53]

Crawford claimed to have been present at every division 'on any matter of the smallest public importance' in the 1835 session.[54] One parliamentary observer dismissed his parliamentary talents as no more than 'mediocre', but praised his industry and commitment:

> The active part he takes, both in and out of the house, in every thing that relates to Ireland, joined to the extreme honesty of his character and liberality of his opinions, makes him deservedly respected both in his native country and in the house. He is a man of great modesty. He wants confidence in himself [...] The expression of his countenance is pensive, with a tinge of melancholy about it. He is one of the most humane men in the house.[55]

Crawford set down his intentions to advance proactively his own legislation on landlord-tenant relations and reform of the grand jury laws.[56] Like Feargus O'Connor (who has lost his Cork seat in 1835 as a consequence of being found unable to meet the property qualification for membership), he clearly regarded his interventions to be consumed by an 'outdoors' public via the press rather than simply as parliamentary exercises.[57]

Speaking in the house committee on the state of the Irish church he re-iterated his views that Protestantism enjoined the necessity of protesting against any violation of the rights of conscience. For the time being he followed the Irish party line in stating that he preferred that the united parliament should now give justice on this matter, with a resort to repeal being made only if this was not delivered.[58] However he evidently saw himself as speaking both to and for those in Ireland who bitterly opposed the tithe system.

Within a few weeks of the opening of the session it was evident that, despite the opposition's divisions, Peel did not have enough support for his own policy on the Irish church, and that there was an majority in the commons for the principle of appropriating the 'surplus revenues' of that church to other public purposes.[59] This would become the touchstone of the session, and soon the ministry was reeling from a series of defeats before it finally collapsed in April.[60] The new ministry, headed by Lord Melbourne, with O'Connell's allies Russell and Duncannon in prominent cabinet roles, and the sympathetic Lords Mulgrave and Morpeth sent to Dublin Castle as lord lieutenant and chief secretary, was much more to O'Connell's taste. Legal and civil appointments of Catholics and liberal Protestants, a number nominated by O'Connell himself, followed. Despite finding himself on the same side as Morpeth in parliamentary debates on tithes, and his personal friendship with Mulgrave, Crawford's underlying suspicion of Whig intentions continued and would become clearer as their own Irish tithes bill, now containing the appropriation clause, took shape. For the time being, however, he maintained what he thought was 'prudent' course of seeking its amendment and hoped he was 'gaining the good opinion of the house'.[61] He had a low view however of most of his fellow Irish MPs, who he thought lacked his own high levels of motivation.[62]

While remaining alert to the need to retain the support of his constituents in Dundalk – he made a personal donation of £50 to the building of a new Catholic chapel there, consulted the town merchants on their wants and lobbied successfully for the Treasury to make it a bonding port for tobacco imports[63] – he also continued to take a close interest in the development of Belfast. In 1835 he managed as chair of the committee the parliamentary proceedings on the private bill for the Belfast and Cavehill Railway.[64] This initiative, which was unsuccessfully 'fought every inch' by Emerson Tennent and his Conservative allies for what Crawford thought were self-interested reasons, was intended to open up the quarrying of limestone on Cavehill north of the town for construction and export, and began his lifelong interest in promoting railways as a mode of economic development.[65]

One area where Crawford and O'Connell were fully in agreement, and which was also in line with the new Whig administration's priorities, was on the Orange Order. O'Connell repeatedly made the case that the short-lived Peel administration had legitimised the revival of Orangeism as a mass movement, and encouraged the tendency of conservative local and judicial authorities to tolerate or surreptitiously promote acts of sectarian violence or intimidation. In contrast, Mulgrave's administration in Dublin Castle was prompt to act against Orange activity in Ireland.[66]

As we have seen, Crawford's animus against the order was long-standing, and was revived by the equanimity with which the former Whig Lord Downshire allied with Down Orangemen in the 'great Protestant demonstration' against Whig church policies he hosted at Hillsborough on 30 October 1834. At Lord Roden's insistence the symbolic trappings of Orangeism were omitted so as not to embarrass the more moderate gentry present (such as the 1830 'independent' candidate Forde), but the desire of the county landed elite to enlist plebeian political Protestantism in an anti-government front was evident.[67] In the absence of any support from his peers, Crawford gave up his initial intention to attend the meeting to move a hostile amendment against Protestant ascendancy, and settled instead for circulating a declaration protesting at the restricted nature of this so-called 'county meeting'. This was ultimately signed by only 122 men, many of them from the lower classes, a number dwarfed by the estimated 30,000 or more who were reported as attending the rally.[68] He was attacked in absentia at the Hillsborough meeting as a repealer.

In the press, Crawford warned Downshire that thus associating with a body whose activities were often illegal and potentially seditious would place him and other magistrates in an impossible situation regarding upholding justice.[69] He also opposed the appointment of Orangemen who had attended the meeting to the constabulary.[70] The Presbyterian evangelical Dr Henry Cooke's much lauded proclamation at the meeting of the 'banns of marriage' between Presbyterians and Anglicans had, Crawford later asserted in parliament, been repudiated by the Presbyterians, who mostly supported tithe reform and had signed petitions in large numbers to demonstrate this.[71] The subsequent disruption by an 'armed mob' of Orangemen of a mostly Presbyterian parochial meeting to draw up a petition against tithes and the regium donum at Ballykelly in Co. Londonderry, also drew his ire. Yet despite the evidence of a renewed mass Conservative movement in Ulster in 1834–5, it seems not all Orangemen opposed reform; a petition from Drumbo for corporation and tithe reform was signed by 1,650 persons, of whom 'over one hundred' were reported as being Orangemen.[72]

Although they had been uneasy and distrustful allies out of political convenience in 1831, Crawford's rift with the powerful Downshire interest was now open following its alliance with Orangeism and would remain so for the remainder of his political career. The former MP General John Meade thought him the only person of property in the county openly opposed to the Hill interest by 1836.[73] The following year Downshire joined Roden in Dublin at a meeting to protest in 'pithy but respectable language the damage these cursed papists have done', and his heir assured Peel in 1837 that attempts by Crawford and the Belfast radicals to arouse Down against them would be met with counter-meetings.[74]

In July 1835 Crawford gave evidence to a commons select committee into the Orange Order. Recalling his previous encounters with Orange unrest, he concluded that all party processions tended to create religious dissension. The Order was, he testified, inherently a disruptive force in Irish society.[75] At a time when much of the national focus on Orangeism was coalescing around an alleged 'plot' by the king's reactionary brother the Duke of Cumberland to mobilise the order for his own dynastic ambitions, Crawford was pleased that extracts from his evidence relating to Orangemen citing the authority of the duke for illegal marching in 1830 received wide press coverage.[76] The *Northern Whig* was sure that the aim of the Orange conspiracy was to replace the king's niece, Princess Victoria, with Cumberland as heir to the throne, and that it must be 'vigorously dealt with'.[77] The evidence was taken up by the radical Joseph Hume in his parliamentary motion against the order, and Crawford was part of the majority that voted for Hume's motions condemnatory of alleged Orange infiltration of the army.[78]

When Hume resumed his attack on the order early in the 1836 session, Crawford insisted that it was not the rank-and-file, who suffered as much from 'bad government' as 'their Catholic bretheren', but their self-interested leaders and the government who were at fault. The institution should, he concluded, be made illegal and ordinary Orangemen brought back to obedience to law, but an example needed to be made of those who had instigated the impressionable to violence.[79] Several weeks later he wrote to R. J. Tennent welcoming (somewhat prematurely) that parliament had now given the 'death blow' to the order, while regretting that the house's impatience had precluded him giving another speech on the subject.[80] Updating her son John on his father's activities, Mabel wrote in March 1836 that 'the [Orange] leaders, Cumberland, Shaw, Lefroy etc., have recommended the poor dupes to acquiesce – it remains to be seen whether they will or not. I much doubt it but the leaders are detached and it is a desperate game now with them.'[81] Seeking to pre-empt official suppression, the Grand Orange Lodge in London dissolved itself and called on other lodges to follow suit. The Grand Lodge of Ireland did so, despite strong internal opposition, on 14 April, although organisation continued at local level in a lower key over much of Ireland.[82]

Crawford's own intended legislative initiatives of 1835 did not get far. His grand jury measure was put to one side, and his draft landlord-tenant bill did not reach the commons floor until 2 July, when leave to bring it in was finally granted. The *News-Letter* published the bill in full with approving commentary; it had evidently piqued the interest of its editor James McKnight, an antagonist in 1832 but whose growing interest in land reform would eventually make the two men political allies. The landlord-tenant bill, in its many iterations, would dominate the remainder of his political life, and forms the focus of chapters five to seven below.[83]

Two issues grew in importance late in the session and in the following months that opened up rifts in his relationship with O'Connell. The first, predictably, was the tithe question. On this, Crawford became certain that O'Connell was too ready to accept a compromised and inadequate measure. He wrote privately in July 1835: 'I dislike this bill beyond measure and unless it should be much altered I will never give a vote <u>for it</u>. [...] I think the tithe bill a mass of absurdity. There is no possibility of mending it – and my utter astonishment is how O'Connell can support it'.[84] He expressed uncertainty about his future relationship with O'Connell in another letter to his son:

> <u>between ourselves</u> I have great doubts whether he really wishes such [practical] measures to be passed. He is externally kind and civil towards me when we meet but has never shown the smallest desire to have any communication on our mutual views on public questions – of course I never intrude mine. I think the government are led much by his opinion (as undoubtedly they ought to be), and having that with them they give themselves no trouble about any other person. I think he has agreed to this tithe bill. If he had insisted a different sort of measure would have been produced – but time will show. I can not admire his conduct.[85]

On 12 August 1835 Crawford went public with his opposition to the government's tithe bill, proposing an amendment to abolish tithe completely and replace it with a tax on rentals to compensate the life-interests of incumbent clergy but which would eventually also be appropriated to educational and poor relief purposes as these interests expired.[86]

By this point he was certain that criticism of him in the O'Connellite *Pilot* was intended as a warning for straying off-message on key measures.[87] Although largely kept under wraps during the 1835 session, Crawford would expand on his objections to the bill in a series of public letters to his Dundalk constituents during the recess, which were published in pamphlet form in October as *Observations on the Irish Tithe Bill*. While the bill might vary the amount levied and mode of collection, in his opinion appropriation of the surpluses proposed would still leave the establishment bloated out of proportion to its communicant numbers and would prove a dead letter in improving social or educational provisions, while the offensive principle of ascendancy would remain intact.[88] Rapacious landlords would simply add the commuted tithe charge to the rents of tenants at will, in what would be an unholy compromise of the just demands of the people. The result would be further stimulus to agrarian conflict, without removing the established church from the hostility of the majority. His objection was not, he repeated, to the Irish government under Mulgrave, which had indeed shown a disposition 'to promote a kindly and more equitable distribution of the powers of the country', but to a cabinet policy which would fail to produce the religious freedom Ireland had demanded and which the Church of Ireland needed to fulfil its spiritual mission.[89] As an Anglican he also objected to the increased temporal power the bill would give the state over the church. His position on this was cognate with the anti-Erastianism of the high churchmen of the Oxford Movement, although his vision was of a Protestant church freed from the entanglements of establishment and reliant on the contributions of its own members and property holdings. His outbursts attracted supportive notice from elements of the British radical press, even as they infringed the discipline of the O'Connellite party.[90]

If there could still be any doubts on his position, they were answered by a public letter in December. Crawford quoted back to O'Connell his multiple commitments to total abolition of tithes as a fundamental principle. Russell's bill could not be accepted as an 'instalment' as it upheld the principle of tithes; neither did it really treat them as 'national property'. If maintenance of good relationships with a reforming government was desirable, that government should be persuaded to drop a measure so at odds with justice to Ireland; if it did not, the 'experiment' of postponing repeal to try reform should come to an end.[91] Reflecting on the letter, he thought it had been expressed:

> with respect and civility – but certainly the case is put very strongly and by implication rather conveys a charge of inconsistency. The letter has attracted public attention more than anything I ever published and I think it will be highly important in increasing my influence in Ulster because it will be clearly manifest that I am not a joint of the tail of the great man'.[92]

Something of the sting was taken out of the issue by the defeat of the 1835 tithe bill in the house of lords followed by a delay in reintroducing it in the 1836 session. In the meantime, O'Connell made an effort to conciliate Crawford, as he was still at this time reluctant to repudiate a useful ally. For his part, Crawford participated actively in O'Connell's Reform Registry Association set up in early 1836.[93] Writing to John on 5 April he remained optimistic that he had swung the argument on tithes to his position:

By the way O'C[onnell] and I are on the best terms. When he met me in London he came up in the most cordial manner. I met him in the same manner – and so we have continued since that time. I have the honour of being the first of the party who ever expressed a different opinion from O'Connell without being pounced upon.

With petitions still coming in backing abolition, he was confident that the government could be checked, and even if this failed, 'still it will give the cause of religious liberty a lift to have the question debated and a respectable division on it – for I must have all the Irish and English radicals with me whether they like it or not'.[94] As late as June 1836 the truce held, with O'Connell making concessions in response to Crawford's pressure for amendment of the Irish municipal corporations bill; Crawford noted that 'notwithstanding all this he and I are the best friends. He has never shown a symptom of feeling against me in any way'.[95] This hubris was soon to be punctured when O'Connell backed the revived government tithe bill in July while Crawford denounced it as impinging on 'the right of conscience against the tyranny of establishments' and stamping Catholics 'with the name of slave in the land of their birth'.[96] When O'Connell failed to back his demand that sixteen Irish corporations be added to the twelve the government had retained within the municipal corporations bill as sent back by the lords, he wrote to his Dundalk constituents criticising the 'compromising policy adopted [...] by the distinguished leader of the Catholic body', to which he would not submit.[97] Their relationship was evidently splintering, and would be further strained by their divisions over an Irish poor law.

An Irish poor law, 1833–8

Sharman Crawford first engaged in substance with the question of a poor relief measure for Ireland in a long letter to the *Northern Whig* in late 1833. This was provoked by what he saw as the narrowly Anglocentric proposal modelled on the existing English law being pressed by the radical English political economist George Poulett Scrope, on the grounds that the absence of such legislation was giving unfair advantages to Irish farmers in swamping the British market with cheaper imported food. Crawford upbraided him for ignoring the subjection and impoverishment of the majority of Irish peasants in what appeared a protectionist desire to defend English interests and for failing to make the case for the wide range of social and political reforms essential for Irish regeneration. While rejecting what he saw as Scrope's simplistic desire to impose the 'old' English law on Ireland as a form of regressive taxation, and warning of replicating the abuses of that system in Ireland, he admitted the urgent necessity of some levy on landed incomes to provide useful and remunerative employment to all the labouring poor who required it, alongside generous provision for the 'helpless' and sick poor from a compulsory rate.[98] Scrope took Crawford's criticisms on board; within a few years the two men would be working co-operatively to pursue an agreed measure that they believed would serve Irish as well as English interests.

Having previously flagged the desirability of some kind of suitable poor law, it was no surprise that Crawford returned to this issue once elected in 1835. However the escalating western subsistence crisis of that year, and O'Connell's personal antagonism to any such measure, upped the political odds and made it a flash-point of contention between the two men over the following years. Crawford had by now become convinced that a generous poor law, modelled on Scrope's conception of the 'old' English poor law but funded exclusively by a levy on Irish landowners, was essential for social equity in Ireland.

Unlike England and Scotland, Ireland had no national poor law and welfare provision was restricted to an uneven hodgepodge of dispensaries, municipal and county charitable institutions and voluntary relief bodies. Pressured by public opinion in both Ireland and Britain to take some initiative on the undeniable problem of extensive and growing Irish poverty, Grey's government had in 1833 instituted a royal commission of inquiry under Archbishop Richard Whately of Dublin. This did not issue its third and summative report (which itself proved highly contentious) until 1836. In the meantime, a partial potato failure and subsistence crisis in 1834–5 had placed immense stress on many western districts.[99]

Although this crisis had very limited impact on the relatively prosperous agricultural districts of Down or on Dundalk and its hinterland, Crawford regarded it as his duty as an Irish MP to take a leading role in investigation and response. By the summer of 1835 reports of distress in Connacht were attracting attention, and the French social commentators Alexis de Tocqueville and Gustave de Beaumont visited Newport in Mayo at the invitation of the parish priest, Fr Hughes, to investigate for themselves. Crawford himself tabled petitions from this district in July claiming that 5,000 out of a district population of 14,000 were starving.[100] He drew parliament's attention to petitions which charged the local landlords with treating the people 'not as human beings but as inferior creatures', and read from the parish priest's letter in the commons:

> The great bulk of the people are crushed to death with the weight of their misery. Even while I write the cries of starvation pierce my ear and my heart, knowing my utter inability to relieve it. Our streets are crowded by thousands of famished creatures pressing in from the country. Famine has made them well nigh desperate. Some of them say, that they will no longer respect the laws of society or the rights of property, as their dire distress is not attended to by those whose duty it is to relieve it; and they threaten that they will not die of hunger while they have strength left to take the means of satisfying it from those in whose possession they are. They are at the very height of misery; and I shudder to contemplate the results, if speedy relief be not afforded them.[101]

Crawford presented corroborating evidence from police and magistrates, and demanded immediate government interference to relieve the starving and prevent the indefinite recurrence of famine through the peasantry being forced to consume their remaining seed potatoes. Immediate relief was vital, but the underlying causes of the crisis in social injustice also needed to be addressed:

> the distress now prevailing in the county of Mayo was not the result of improvidence; on the contrary, its immediate cause was the entire and total failure of the potato crops in that district. Though that was the immediate cause, the distress had several causes, some of which, from operating at all times, might be said to be more influential than the failure of one crop. The first of these was the enormous rents which were demanded and promised in Ireland. That excess might be imagined, when he stated, that in many parts of Ireland the rents reserved exceeded the whole amount of the produce of the land. Next came the evils of an absentee landed proprietary. Again, another cause of distress was to be found in the expulsion of the small tenantry from the lands heretofore in their occupation.[102]

While the Irish government took Crawford's evidence and similar reports seriously and initiated a crisis response through relief works and food depots in the west, the wider remedial measures he suggested remained for the time being in limbo.[103]

Irish MPs met in London in late June to discuss the situation, reviewing a proposal by Sir Robert Sydney for a system of public works funded by a national lottery. Crawford approved of this as an emergency measure, although it could only be a stopgap for a proper poor law system.[104] A poor law bill had been introduced to the commons that session by Sir Richard Musgrave, the Whig MP for Co. Waterford, which Crawford supported despite believing that it failed to go far enough.[105] He expressed frustration at the hostility towards it expressed by O'Connell and Spring Rice (now chancellor of the exchequer), and what he saw as Musgrave's craven capitulation when the bill was lost.[106]

Crawford was ready to confront the government by moving its proposed new coercion bill be limited to a few months and tied to a vote on a poor law bill early the next session. The lines for a new clash with O'Connell had been clearly drawn; with an eye to his northern support base, Crawford thought this no bad thing. He told his son John in August:

> It is quite plain O'Connell and I are getting into collision more or less – on this question particularly – I want some principle of assessment on rents for the poor. I do not want that it should be distributed on the English system – but I want to get the money at any rate and then the grand difficulty will be over [...] It will be a great sport to our northern friends if we should be on opposite sides – I have no objection at all that they should perceive I am not one of the tail.[107]

In November 1835 he made his first recorded visit to the west to inspect personally the social conditions in Mayo, but he also took the opportunity to address a political meeting at Castlebar. A better harvest had now reduced the immediate threat of mass starvation, he observed, but he remained convinced that a permanent solution to extreme poverty was imperative.[108]

Writing to the magistrate George Howell in April 1836 to express thanks for pro-poor law resolutions passed at a Dublin meeting and agreeing to present its petition, Crawford set out his own position on what an Irish law should encompass. Nothing less than a recognition of the principle of the '43rd of Elizabeth' (i.e. the old English poor law) would do. By this he meant not the specific terms of that act (which had been radically altered by the English Poor Law Amendment Act in 1834), but its original premise: 'that it is the duty of the state to provide that no individual shall be in such destitution as to want the means of existence, unless from the *wilful* refusal to exercise his own power to attain them'. This would, he stated, place him and the Dublin resolutions at odds with the recently published Whately report, 'which describes the poor law system as a poison', and which rejected the principle that 'the poor man shall not starve in the land of his birth while means can be found for his relief'.[109] This stance placed him on a collision path with the party leader, who privately dismissed the 'foolish' Dublin resolutions for demanding 'that most destructive of all experiments, employment for the able bodied out of the poor rates!!!', and undertook to curb anything more than was offered under the 1834 English act.[110]

For different reasons, the government also decided to reject Whately's incoherent bundle of recommendations and establish its own fast-track inquiry undertaken by the English poor law commissioner George Nicholls, with the view to bringing in a modified version of the new English poor law the following session. Protesting against this further delay, Crawford called on O'Connell to clarify his comments on the subject. He read extracts from his own research in Mayo, but insisted that the evidence demonstrated a compulsory poor rate was required for the east as much as the west, and was a more important question even than tithes. He proceeded to recite an extract from the commission's evidence concerning a case in Dundalk, where a large number of persons expelled by a neighbouring landlord took refuge in the town in utter destitution. The landlord was applied to for a subscription to aid their relief, but refused, saying it was a matter of indifference to him what became of the tenantry ejected from his estate. Such cases showed the absolute necessity of a compulsory enactment which would render the landed proprietors responsible for the poverty they had created.[111]

Crawford complained privately that O'Connell was still attempting to 'slip through our fingers' on a firm poor law commitment.[112] But O'Connell had tactical reasons for tacking backwards and forwards on the question, as well as an underlying ideological antagonism to legislative intervention by the state between what he idealised as the paternalist resident landlord and his dependents among the rural poor. His preference was for voluntary charitable activity, which he followed in his personal practice and defended through an endorsement of Thomas Chalmers' moralistic stance against all poor laws as enemies of Christian charity.[113] However, in the context of widespread public alarm about hunger in 1835 and frustration over the government's postponement of legislation, expressed in 'a great cry in Ireland', O'Connell had swung back towards appearing to support a poor law as a means to curb evictions.[114] Until late 1836 both his private and public utterances indicated he would accede reluctantly to any government measure that did not revive the 'evils' of the '43d of Elizabeth'.[115] In November at a speech to the Trades Political Union in Dublin, however, he ruled out supporting anything beyond an absentee tax; he now thought the 1834 English act had done good as 'it was a kind of repeal of the poor law', but was could not be replicated in a country with '2,300,000 beggars' where it would destroy domestic charity, increase vice and pauperism, and depress wages. This might, he admitted, be an unpopular stance with sections of the Catholic clergy and public, but he was convinced he was in the right and in line with Catholic moral dogma.[116]

Although known for his personal generosity on his own estates, Crawford explicitly rejected O'Connell's case for landed paternalism as an alternative to a law-based welfare system. Responding to an appeal from Nicholas Whyte in 1837 for landlord contributions to tackle poverty in the Co. Down parish of Aghaderg, Crawford argued that such random charity should be replaced by a legal assessment on land, which all who really cared for the poor advocated. He would personally aid any voluntary subscriptions from tenants on his townlands for their own poor, but would not bail out those neighbouring landlords who refused to put their hands in their own pockets. Only the passage of an effective poor law would provide an equitable solution to this problem of landed irresponsibility.[117]

When the government finally introduced its Irish poor law measure in early 1837, based on Nicholl's recommendations for a limited workhouse-based system of indoor relief only, funded by rates on landed property, it rapidly polarised Irish opinion. O'Connell and Crawford now reversed the positions they had adopted on the tithe bill, with the latter giving a cautious welcome to what he regarded as a flawed but amendable poor law, while O'Connell quickly took on a stance of fundamental hostility. Opposing the bill's second reading, he claimed the proposed system was unaffordable, placing too great a burden on the ratepaying tenantry while offering only inhumane and minimalist relief to the destitute.[118] O'Connell had clearly identified the central weakness of the government bill in terms of Irish opinion – the harshness of any system based on a workhouse test – but this was a superstructure erected on his deeper opposition to a poor law of any description. Along with William Smith O'Brien and other Irish supporters of the poor law principle, Crawford now had to defend the idea of a taxation-based welfare system while seeking to soften and extend the practical form it would take. Poor laws were, he insisted, essential instruments of social justice which taxed wealth to meet the needs of poverty; what Ireland needed, however, was a mechanism that would tackle the seasonal distress of small landholders without requiring workhouse incarceration or the grant of 'despotic powers' to poor law commissioners.[119] He was part of the minority of fifty who backed Smith O'Brien's amendment to allow guardians to permit other modes of relief outside the workhouse.[120] The government bill was lost on the king's death in June 1837, and by the time it was re-introduced and passed in the 1838 session, Crawford was no longer an MP.

What is likely to have hardened O'Connell's stance on this issue was his perception that radicals within his political organisation, including Crawford, John Lawless (who had challenged him for control of the Catholic Association in 1825) and Fr Thaddeus O'Malley, were seeking to wrest public support away from him on the question. In 1836 he had also had to cope with the acrimonious defection of Feargus O'Connor, who also alleged that O'Connell had subverted his own efforts to carry a generous Irish poor law and denounced him as a 'whimsical dictator'.[121] In July that year O'Connell established the General Association of Ireland to raise funds and keep Irish opinion focused behind him on supporting tithe and municipal corporations reform, but which became increasingly used by his rivals as a platform to challenge him on poor laws.[122] Crawford's demand in a public letter of 2 August that the Association now give the poor law question top priority was a direct challenge to O'Connell's control over strategy.[123]

Merging opposition to the government tithe bill with his own scheme for a generous poor law, on 14 December 1836 O'Malley moved, to 'loud cheering' in the General Association, the full appropriation of tithe for relief of the able-bodied poor. Crawford and O'Connell clashed very publicly on the poor law question the following day. Speaking in support of O'Malley's motion, and praising his Christian concern for the poor, Crawford forcefully dismissed O'Connell's historical and political-economic objections to poor laws. Good poor laws were everywhere (including the United States), he asserted, responsible for reducing pauperism.[124] A good poor law was one that recognised the moral entitlement of the distressed poor to assistance, and placed the cost of relief on the landowner:

> For my part, I consider every man has a right, in the first instance, to relief; and next I consider that the proprietor is bound to afford it to those who cultivate the land and produce all the wealth (cheers). How did the people of England obtain poor laws? Because they would not lie down and die of starvation as the Irish had done.

There were many causes of Irish poverty, but 'the most effectual remedy was a poor law', based on compulsory taxation and which penalised rack-renting and callous eviction. This drew an angry response from O'Connell, who accused him of setting himself up as the 'state physician' intent on imposing the expensive 'quack medicine' of poor laws on the country.[125] Previous disputes between them had been mostly about political tactics, but this was an ideological divide on social entitlement and welfare, and it would only become more heated. The exchanges drew the attention of the London-based Irish radical James Bronterre O'Brien, who urged support of O'Malley's scheme and damned O'Connell's social conservatism.[126]

Crawford's public letters to the General Association on poor laws in early 1837 further raised the emotional temperature around the issue.[127] Catholic and nationalist opinion in Ireland was deeply divided, but with evidence of majority clerical support for the O'Malley-Crawford position.[128] But already a 'sub-movement' was afoot, and it was more difficult to sustain the case for a poor law in the aftermath of the introduction of the government's highly regressive bill, and the string of defeats on amendments sponsored by Smith O'Brien, Crawford and others in the commons further weakened their public support.[129] During the Easter recess of 1837 O'Connell directly attacked O'Malley in the General Association for undermining the 'fountains of benevolence' and moral bonds of society, thereby shifting the ground against his internal rivals.[130] Crawford followed O'Connell's hostile speech on the second reading of the government's poor law bill in April with an acerbic rebuttal: O'Connell himself, he argued, had offered no meaningful remedies to the crisis of pauperism. At the same time, he admitted the government's solution was also deeply flawed and required heavy amendment:

> The great mass of poor persons in Ireland were the small holders [...] of land. If they were to compel the poor man to go from his holding into the workhouse, how could he ever make any exertions to improve his circumstances? His small farm must go into a state of desolation; and he could never after look to any means of advancement in the world. Such would be the result of having a poor-law in Ireland without a law of settlement, and of having the relief of the poor confined, without any kind of discretion, to a system of relief in the workhouse.

He believed Ireland could afford an effective poor law and that landlords needed the fiscal stimulus of poor-rates to force them to employ the poor and to moderate their excessive demands for rent.[131] He threatened to withhold his vote from the third reading if concessions were not made, but he and his allies had little leverage against British majorities for each of the bill's clauses and they could not shift O'Connell from non-cooperation. With Lawless now suffering from collapsing mental health and Crawford on the receiving end of barrages of criticism from the O'Connellite press, the case for a generous poor law was being lost, although O'Malley continued to support the government bill as an instalment, and retained some support for this position within the clergy.[132]

The 1838 session saw a convergence of energetic O'Connellite and Irish Tory public campaigns against the renewed poor law bill, and the defection of a number of previously sympathetic Irish Whig-liberals. This posed problems for the government, although it could ultimately rely on British Whig-liberal and moderate Conservative votes to get its measure through both houses.[133] For Crawford the outcome of this confrontation was a massive setback to his hopes of tapping popular Catholic politics for his reformist projects. Out of parliament from mid-1837 he continued to use public letters to criticise O'Connell's fundamentalist resistance to all poor laws and alleged betrayal of his proclaimed political principles, and attacked him for failing to use his political authority to 'extort' the necessary amendments to the government's bill. Had O'Connell put his weight behind the crucial concessions required – granting a statutory right to relief, allowing a law of settlement by electoral division, removing a clause to fund emigration, giving guardians power to grant outdoor relief, and adding a rating clause to impose a surcharge on rackrenting landlords – a popular and effective measure might well, in Crawford's opinion, have been achieved. But the government was only concerned, he argued, with calculating 'how a certain (vaguely computed) number of paupers are to be imprisoned and fed in these prisons', losing sight of how a proper poor law would make landlords responsible for poverty on their estates and impose stimuli to curb rackrenting, evictions and neglect.[134] By Spring 1838 this was a lonely position to maintain; at a Down petitioning meeting presided over by his son John as county high sheriff he found his case for lobbying for a heavily amended compulsory measure rejected in favour of a call for a local opt-out.[135] Despite all this, like O'Malley he continued to regard the act passed in 1838 as a necessary first stepping stone to the more advanced and generous measure that Ireland deserved, and he would campaign for this in subsequent years.[136]

On the implementation of the act in the north in 1840, he welcomed even the restricted poor law as embodying the redistributive principle of social justice.[137] Following the formation of the Newtownards poor law union in 1841, he joined as an ex-officio magistrate guardian and was elected chairman of the board, even though he was a comparatively minor landowner in the district. He would hold the post for most of the next twenty years and seek to render the limited poor law as humane and generous as was legally possible in the union.[138] While by no means free from the moralistic attitudes towards the 'undeserving poor' common at the time – he believed that mothers of illegitimate children should be kept separate from other women in the workhouse to prevent moral contamination, and that 'sturdy beggars' should be penalised – at the same time he advocated a system that treated the poor fairly. Men who abandoned their illegitimate children should, he argued, be made financially responsible through the extension of the bastardy laws to Ireland; persons vagrant out of necessity should not be prosecuted but assisted; those confined in the workhouse should be properly fed and clothed; and above all the poor law should allow outdoor relief to those suffering from life-cycle poverty and those destitute from sickness or accident.[139] These issues would return to the forefront when the Great Famine threw the already vulnerable poor law into crisis after 1845.

Opening the feud with O'Connell, 1836–7

While important policy divisions had been emerging between Crawford and O'Connell for some time, open warfare broke out between them only from summer 1836. Within a year Crawford would lose his parliamentary seat and be expelled from the Repeal movement amid great public bitterness. This would have wider and lasting ramifications for the relationship between northern liberal/radical Protestantism and popular Catholic nationalism on the island, that would prove difficult to reconcile. While much of this was due to O'Connell's authoritarian style of leadership and the underlying sectarian attitudes of some of his adherents, Crawford's own moralistic obstinacy and refusal to compromise his political principles also played their part.

Crawford's accusation that O'Connell was surrendering the rights of his country to answer the purposes of a British party was published in a series of public letters starting in

July 1836, with appeared in the Dublin, Belfast and London press. O'Connell's first great compromise, in accepting the disfranchisement of the forty-shilling freeholders in 1829, had, he argued, now come home to roost with the clearance of those former voters creating widespread peasant misery. The poor man's interest, both political and agrarian, needed protection which O'Connell was now failing to offer.[140] The next day Crawford publicly dissented from a resolution in the General Association which expressed approval of the Whig government's legislative measures for Ireland.[141] In public letters to his Dundalk constituents he defended his actions as derived from 'an imperative sense of my duty', and blamed the reintroduction of the unacceptable tithe bill principally on the people's leader for failing to use his influence to veto it. If (as he thought was inevitable) a clash over popular rights had to come with the anti-democratic house of lords, it should be on a matter of real principle and not on some miserable compromise such as the tithe bill.[142] A further letter damned O'Connell for pursuing the interests of property at the expense of the poor, through his endorsement of the Irish coercion act of 1835.[143] His letters, and his abstention on the tithe bill vote in parliament in July 1836, drew fire from the O'Connellite press, which warned about the need for party unity and decried Crawford's lack of prudence: by agreeing to postpone repeal while seeking reforms through the British parliament, had Crawford not adopted just the same practical policy that he now attacked O'Connell for?[144]

O'Connell's initial reaction to this onslaught was measured. In the General Association he defended his consistency and called Crawford's first letter 'ungenerous and uncalled for'; if Crawford could forgive himself for writing it, O'Connell would, he declared in patronising tones, also forgive him.[145] Goaded into a more robust response by further public letters, O'Connell now claimed that Crawford's multiple and repeated misrepresentations of him must be based on ignorance, not least about the nature of the coercion act. Crawford's words, he asserted, could only empower Tory efforts to undermine both O'Connell and the Whig government, and thereby the future stability of Ireland by unleashing 'the Orange virulence at present pent up and restrained'. O'Connell was seeking to play his own 'Orange card': if Crawford's recalcitrance encouraged others in rebelling against Whig measures and collapsing the ministry, he would bear moral responsibility for the catastrophe to follow.[146]

Rather than back down in the face of this criticism, Crawford escalated with a line-by-line refutation of O'Connell's charges that he had misinterpreted the coercion act.[147] Grasping the political dangers of the situation, the veteran Protestant radical Lord Cloncurry sought to intervene, writing to Crawford that he himself had disagreed with O'Connell on occasion and endorsing Crawford's menu of necessary reforms, while stressing the obligation of unity in the face of their common political enemies.[148] Crawford denied any desire to break up the movement, but highlighted what he regarded as a democratic deficit at the heart of the Irish party's practice. O'Connell's tactics were, he was convinced, profoundly mistaken and not based on the popular will, and must therefore be abandoned:

> I wish to have the principles of action decided on by the voice of the nation. To that voice I am willing to yield; but I hold it, that no system of action can have weight or respect which is founded solely on the dictation of any one individual, however distinguished; or on the adhesion of a party for party objects; or on such a line of conduct as can give pretext to our opponents to impute to us such motives.[149]

He did not specify how exactly that public voice should be captured, although implicitly it was through bodies such as the General Association, which he and his allies now saw a counterweight to the dictatorial leadership wielded by O'Connell within the movement.

Worryingly for O'Connell, it was evident that Crawford had a supportive constituency within the body. A speech to the General Association (at which O'Connell was absent) on 27 October was greeted with 'long continued cheers', even though it repeated a number of his charges. The Association was 'the only means of representation which the people have just at the moment' and was the medium 'through which their wrongs are to be made known' – in effect it was a repeal parliament in embryo.[150] When the two antagonists faced each other in another crowded meeting of the Association on 17 November there was evidently support for both, and unease on the part of many others about a split. Crawford reiterated his position on complete and immediate tithe abolition and defended himself against Orange as well as O'Connellite charges of treason. He would stand by the real 'Protestant principle' that 'no man should be compelled to worship God in any manner but that which his conscience dictates'.

O'Connell insisted he did not seek a triumph over Crawford, but that the assembly had to accept the political reality that progress must come through gradual instalments, and urged him not to emulate the English radical Henry Hunt, who had obstinately opposed the 1832 Reform Bill on the grounds it did not deliver all of his aims at once. Sensing the meeting's mood for at least a temporary truce, Crawford responded with an olive branch by reminding O'Connell of their friendship in the joint struggle for Ireland's interests. While not withdrawing his resolutions for total abolition, he did not at this point contest O'Connell's motion to refer them to a standing committee, which appeared to offer a pathway to collective policy-making.[151]

This offered only a short breathing space. 'Unexpectedly', according to one commentator,[152] the resolutions came back with the unanimous endorsement of the committee and were tabled again at an open meeting on 24 November. Making of the best of this, O'Connell proclaimed himself a committed voluntarist and as fully in agreement with Crawford on principles, but also drew attention to his own resolution of support for Mulgrave's Irish administration. For Crawford this seemed like a victory. He clarified that he was not personally against Mulgrave, nor against accepting instalments towards justice to Ireland, so long as these did not concede the fundamental principle concerned, and thereby make further instalments more difficult to obtain – something which he was convinced the Whig tithe bill was bound to do. Typically, he added that his father's generation had made the mistake of accepting such an instalment in 1782 and had thus failed to sustain freedom against a counter-reaction:

> I must confess I have a most unconquerable dread and hatred of receiving instalments of rights. My dread of this practice is very great, and I have drawn it from a consideration of the history of my country. In that period of her greatest glory since she was united to England, 1782, when the principle of her independence was wrested from England by the Volunteers, there was one great error committed – they were contented with an instalment. If they had insisted upon the rights of Catholics to vote and to be elected we would never have had the Union. By this one error the independence of parliament was rendered useless […]

Taking lessons from history, he made clear that he himself would never speak or act contrary to what he considered right for the country.[153]

Given its heavy coverage in the British press, it was inevitable that this public confrontation in the General Association would attract the attention of the journalistic satirists.[154] It was however the Irish Catholic emigre caricaturist John Doyle who created the most effective satire on the split. Doyle, who had since 1829 drawn his series of political sketches anonymously under the initials 'HB', was unquestionably the leading London-based graphic satirist of the post-1832 period. He had long attacked O'Connell as a dangerous but hypocritical figure, pursuing his own self-interest at the expense of Ireland and England alike. In December 1836 he for the first time added Crawford to his gallery in his print 'A scene from Hudibras', thereby acknowledging his recognition by the metropolitan political class as a significant 'player' (Figure 13). As was his common practice, Doyle parodied a literary text for political effect, in this case Samuel Butler's late seventeenth-century mock-heroic epic poem *Hudibras,* which itself had mocked the radical religious sects of the English Civil War and Interregnum. In the pictured scene, which appears to draw loosely on William Hogarth's 1725 print 'Hudibras in tribulation', the conceited and anti-heroic knight Hudibras and his squire, the puritanical Ralpho, find themselves locked together in the stocks and were, in the accompanying couplet: 'in hot dispute / Within an ace of falling out'. The 'knight', in Doyle's depiction an overfed and well attired O'Connell, complains of Ralpho's 'cuckoo's tone', while beside him Crawford appears as a gaunt ascetic, garbed in puritan hat and cloak, responding that 'none that see how here we sit / Will judge us overgrown with wit'. Neither of these two squabbling figures were to be taken too seriously as threats to the established order, as the 'Church wardens', the Tory Lords Wellington and Lyndhurst, had them, according to a notice pinned above, well contained in the village stocks (implicitly by blocking radical tithe reform in the house of lords).[155] Although the *Morning Post* criticised the likenesses of the political figures, other Conservative journals welcomed the satires with relish – the *Kerry Evening Post* praised the presentation of 'Popery and Puritanism in hot dispute', and recommended the latest HB series to its conservative readers in O'Connell's home county.[156]

Despite such satirical sideswipes Crawford ended 1836 in the ascendant, albeit still facing hostile criticism in the O'Connellite press as an 'impracticable'.[157] With his allies John ('Honest Jack') Lawless and Fr O'Malley he would continue to seek to use the General Association in defiance of O'Connell to promote their agenda for an Irish poor law and total abolition of tithes over the following months, although, as we have seen, the first was to founder on the rocks of their reluctant support for the regressive Whig poor law bill of 1837–8.[158] Wounded by the public criticism at the heart of his political domain, and perhaps anxious about a leadership challenge, O'Connell was also planning a counter-offensive that would see Crawford expelled from the movement and lose his seat within a year.

Expulsion from Dundalk, 1837

Crawford began the new year with an appeal to his northern base to follow him in adopting an independent rather than uncritically supportive stance towards the Whig government. At a dinner held in his honour in Belfast on 5 January 1837, attended by the liberal civic and economic elite of the town and presided over by his former running-mate R. J. Tennent, he now spoke against repeal unless it was demonstrated to be essential by the failure of the government to pass the necessary Irish reforms. He outlined his political philosophy: the 'aristocratic' Whigs, while preferable to the 'tyrannical' Tories, could not be expected to take the initiative on meaningful reforms, unless pressurised and led by 'the propelling power of the national voice', a *'moral* force of public opinion', that would prove stronger than resistance to change in parliament. Even if such a manifestation threatened to unseat the current administration, it would ultimately strengthen the party's popular appeal and hence its eventual triumph: reformist direct action should thus be put before parliamentary tactics. To achieve the desired ends, alliances with British reformers who shared a common interest in 'justice to Ireland' were essential and must not be impeded by any short-sighted Irish particularism. Perhaps with an eye to the Catholic Bishop of Down and Connor Dr Cornelius Denvir, who spoke afterwards to endorse him, Crawford then went out of his way to praise O'Connell for attaining emancipation through moral-force mobilisation, thereby setting an example for all subsequent radical reformers, while implicitly criticising his current quietism. A supportive letter from the primate, Dr Crolly, was also read, suggesting a desire to create a non-sectarian 'Ulster' reformist bloc as a counterweight to O'Connell.

The speech was well received, and would form the basis for Crawford's later excursion into an attempted Belfast-based radical movement, even if many of the town's liberals were evidently hesitant in following him into any confrontation with Melbourne's administration.[159] His speech drew approving comments in the anti-ministerialist English radical press, which praised it for demonstrating a pan-British radical patriotism. To the *Weekly True Sun,* it tended 'to bind us all together in the common cause of the people, who, whether Irish, Scotch, or English, have but one common interest. That is the true union of reformers.'[160] That the Irish dispute was being closely followed across the Irish Sea would later redound to Crawford's benefit.

Any chance of reconciliation with O'Connell did not last long. On 13 January O'Connell announced in the General Association that his patience was exhausted now that Crawford had confirmed he would actively oppose the reintroduced Whig tithe bill; 'any further steps to conciliate this gentleman are at an end'.[161] Crawford, it seemed, had reneged on what he regarded as his commitment to support the government in November 1836, and thus was now little better than a Tory. Pre-empting Crawford's intention to speak in his own defence at the next scheduled meeting of the Association, O'Connell wrote directly to him, stating that hostility to the Dublin Castle administration was 'in my humble opinion tantamount to hostility to the people of Ireland'.[162] He moved resolutions at the next meeting stating that, if total abolition of tithe proved impracticable, it would be the 'bounden and sacred duty of our representatives to fall back upon the next best measure, the abolition of part, provided the same be accompanied by the appropriation clause'. Countering Crawford, he claimed Catholic emancipation had in fact also been attained in instalments, through the pre-1800 relief acts that had paved the way for the 1829 measure. Crawford, he inferred, now belonged with the anti-Irish radicals of England, led by the renegade Feargus O'Connor, or to the mock liberals and Orangemen of the north.

In his rebuttal, Crawford defended his own political independence and consistency. He concluded by vindicating the spirit of liberty he saw rising in Ulster, which O'Connell appeared to despise as it was outside his personal control. Nor would he tolerate any slander against his own and his family's patriotism: 'There is no recreant blood in my veins; I did not derive any from my father; none came to me from Colonel Sharman; the blood that circulates in my heart is pure; or if I become corrupt in my own body, I hope it will not descend to my son.' While he would not divide the General Association on O'Connell's resolutions, he repeated that he could not in conscience support them.[163]

Insisting on carrying the resolutions against him, O'Connell resorted to accusing Crawford of northern prejudice: 'I have been battling all my life against the bigotry of the north', he expostulated, 'and I am sorry to see that the enlightenment that has now come upon us as to its political horizon, now consists merely in the knocking down of friends and letting the enemy in upon us'.[164] The loyal *Pilot* followed up with a lengthy editorial echoing this prejudicial line of assault: 'CROTCHETTY CRAWFORD' of 'THE BLACK NORTH' was its target.[165] When the *Newry Examiner* dared to express support for Crawford, it was lambasted as having been 'bitten with *Sharman Crawfordism*'.[166] This onslaught must have taken a personal toll on Crawford; after a private meeting with him, the lord lieutenant commented that he was certain of his underlying support for the government and couldn't 'help pitying' him for the attacks he was being subjected to.[167] For their part, Tory commentators expressed *schadenfreude*. A mock heroic 'epitaph' in the *Newry Telegraph* smirked with false pathos:

> Loud let the nation utter forth her grief,
> Poor SHARMAN'S dead!
> Alas! He faded like a withered leaf –
> Why should his life of brilliancy be brief?
> Where shall we look for comfort or relief?
> His spirit's fled!
> [...]
> He would no longer be a chained and slavish log
> To DANIEL's 'tail;'
> He would no longer cringe before the demagogue,
> And died a martyr, floundering in a bog.
> His sole distemper one called 'go the hog' –
> Let empires wail.[168]

On the other hand, Crawford's 'most honourable and most praiseworthy' conduct was admired by other voices in the north. The reformist large farmer Guy Stone noted in his diary that 'O'Connell by this action of his[,] for all may be traced to him[,] has in my opinion completely destroyed the confidence of all liberal Protestants in him'.[169]

Crawford had made some effort to try to keep his Dundalk constituents on side. On 28 September 1836 a gala dinner given to him by the electors of the town, patronised by Archbishop Crolly, had given no cause for alarm. Crawford gave 'an eloquent and powerful speech', lasting nearly two hours, which was received with 'reiterated and rapturous cheering'. The local paper reported that 'almost every one of the whole electoral body of the town' who were of sound political feelings had attended and honoured him enthusiastically. The *Newry Examiner* saw the constituency and its member as perfectly matched.[170] Believing himself strongly supported locally, Crawford had offered to vacate the seat if called on 'by a respectable number of those who elected me'.[171] What seemed implausible in September 1836 had by early 1837 become a real threat. Dundalk was an O'Connellite town and the pressure on its MP became intolerable following his open conflict with the Liberator.

On 28 January the *Morning Register* reported, 'with regret', that Crawford had tendered his resignation to the electors. His request for a public meeting in the town had been refused, and instead he had been informed that the electors would require their representative to support a reintroduced government tithe bill. Angry at not having had the opportunity to defend his position, the MP angrily announced his resignation and left town. The paper thought the electors had committed an error of judgment in forcing his hand and urged Crawford to retain his seat, at least for the coming session.[172] Nationalist opinion was divided – the *Freeman's Journal* hoped an amicable settlement could still be found, as Ireland could not easily dispense with his services, while the *Pilot* blamed Crawford for picking a quarrel with his constituents on 'crotchetty' grounds, and thought the departure of this insolent 'tool of Toryism' no loss.[173]

For Crawford, the fundamental issue was not so much the tithe bill itself, and certainly not the maintenance of the government, but dictatorial control of the Irish movement by its leader. He wrote to the electors:

> the real meaning of your instructions might have been expressed in two words – *obey O'Connell*. If I would abandon principles so often declared and enforced, and thus make myself the lowest and most degraded joint in *his* tail, I would then be the worthy guardian of your liberties, and assessor of your rights. If I refuse to take this course, you indirectly claim from me *the alternative*, without the manliness to demand it in plain terms.

He had consistently reported his political stance to them since 1835 without complaint, but was now, it appeared, to be condemned by a private conclave and without the opportunity of a public defence. They were, he concluded, simply doing the bidding of their master in expecting him to 'be dragged through the mire, at the chariot-wheel of the conqueror'.[174]

With the start of the new session imminent, however, he resolved that his resignation would not be instantaneous, and he travelled to London at the end of the month.[175] Justifying this, he wrote that he would remain in his post until the Dundalk electors nominated a successor, but without taking the pledge they had demanded from him.[176] The Dundalk electors were prevailed on to meet again on 7 February and withdraw their attempt to curb their MP 'in the free exercise of his judgment on the church question.' Previously alerted to their intentions, Crawford had returned to the town and now also publicly withdrew his resignation. The rift was temporarily patched up in the interests of political expediency, but the underlying chasm was widening.[177]

An uneasy truce held so long as the tithe bill was not at the forefront of parliamentary business, but this could not last long, and in early May Crawford indicated he would take the lead in promoting hostile amendments to it.[178] Dividing the house on his own motion for its total abolition, he mustered only eight supporters against 128 (including O'Connell) for the government.[179] His return to public prominence led Doyle to follow up his previous satire with 'Another scene from Hudibras' on 10 February, in which Hudibras/O'Connell and Ralpho/Crawford are now released from the stocks that had previously held them, only to come directly to blows in a ridiculous 'just quarrel'. Both were depicted as being equally at fault and clearly neither deserved the public's sympathy (Figure 14).[180]

Disgusted at what he saw as the cravenness of the Irish party, and the backlash from the O'Connellite press, Crawford wrote with some anger to his son John:

> If the Catholics give way on this point they and I part for ever. [...] Of course the Dundalk people will stick by O'Connell (because I now will throw away the scabbard as respects him) and I will not stand again for that place or any Catholic constituency or any constituency at all while this miserable, perfidious, disquieting policy is to be proceeded with. No honest man can be of the least use – all that I care about now is to preserve my own honour and character and while I am in parliament steadily and boldly to maintain my own principles by my votes or otherwise.[181]

A public letter followed the same day, explaining his frustration. The 1837 tithe bill would be worse than its predecessors, as it had now dropped the appropriation clause and incorporated some lords' amendments and would give Ireland no real benefit in return for the abandonment of religious liberty.[182] He wrote to his own tenants warning them that if passed this 'bill of oppression' would oblige him to increase rents and suggesting they protest against it before it was too late.[183] Further published letters 'to the people of Ireland' kept his by now well-trailed opinions before the reading public.[184]

Despite evidence of widespread Catholic clerical and lay unease about the weakness of the government's tithe bill – Archbishop MacHale warned O'Connell of the 'deep and general discontent' it had aroused – ultimately Catholic opinion rallied behind 'the Liberator'.[185] This seems to have sparked in Crawford an underlying fear of 'political Catholicism' shared with most other Ulster Protestant radicals and dampened, if temporarily, his enthusiasm for all-Ireland political action. O'Connell's continuing political hegemony up to his death in 1847 would impose restraints on him.

O'Connell's alarm that Crawford's vote against the tithe bill's second reading might overturn the Melbourne administration in the crucial period of a royal succession seems exaggerated in retrospect but was genuinely held. O'Connell denounced his stance as 'insanity'.[186] In fact Crawford's motion was symbolic only and was lost by 215 votes, but this did not stop the repeal papers reopening a barrage against his 'Quixotism'.[187] The *Morning Register* advised constituencies to take immediate action against the eight Irish liberals who had voted with him in the minority so as to safeguard the third reading, although its reporter observed that Crawford's much-repeated points were now boring the house, which 'scarcely paid them the least attention' and with chatter drowning out much of what he had to say.[188]

By now convinced that his parliamentary career was all but over, Crawford told his son that his remaining objective was to thwart O'Connell:

> Your mother is apprehensive of O'Connell flooring me – but what can he do to me – he can not impugn my character or principles – he may turn the Catholics against me but what do I care for that. I am fully determined to leave parliament. I care not one straw about popularity if I can not found it on the basis of honest principle. Then I have nothing to fear when I act uprightly. If I can upset O'Connell's machinations I am doing the greatest good that man can do. And if he has the power to sink me still I am sure as that I hold the pen in my hand that the day is approaching when my principles and conduct will receive their due value from the public.

He believed he still had some allies in the parliamentary group – including the Co. Galway

MPs and O'Connell's brother-in-law W. F. Finn – and he would not shrink from seeing his course through whatever the outcome.[189] This self-assured obstinacy, at times amounting to bloody-mindedness, was a hallmark of his character that would continue to inform and also to undermine his subsequent political career.

The anticipated parliamentary showdown was not to come. On 20 June 1837 King William IV died, leading to a suspension of the session and a dissolution pending fresh elections. Within a few days Crawford confirmed what was by then inevitable, that he would not seek re-nomination for Dundalk.[190] As if to add insult to injury, the electors then chose Thomas Redington, a Catholic landowner and ministerial Whig, and later the under-secretary for Ireland in 1846–52, to replace him. Crawford's ally Edward Ruthven also protested that he had been purged and replaced by a Catholic ministerialist in Kildare.[191] Rather than go quietly however, Crawford took the opportunity of his 'unshackling' to lambaste his opponents in print. Nationally, he asserted, he had been isolated by those who had worked to subordinate the country's interests to those of a governing faction, thereby 'annihilating' public opinion. The people could only attain their liberty through asserting their rights against the governing elites, but of that there appeared no sign at present.[192]

An extended series of public epistles from Crawfordsburn followed in the months after the elections, which the nationalist press continued to carry, recognising Crawford's continuing standing and the opportunities these offered for good copy. The letters featured a swingeing assault on both the strategy and the political morality of the Irish leader and represent a profound alienation from the conversion to O'Connellism that Crawford had undergone in 1833. He now pulled no punches. Ireland had been betrayed by O'Connell, who had promised the Irish people freedom, only to sell his allegiance to the Whigs in return for a dole of patronage, which in turn had been used to enhance his own position. Crawford now projected himself as the defender of democratic values against such grubby dealing.

Not only was O'Connell a drag-chain on meaningful change, but his venality had brought the Irish cause into contempt with much of the British people and thereby gave succour to the Tory attempts to revive their 'no-popery' campaign. Only an honest policy and an abandonment of 'Machiavellian' trimming could rescue the situation. O'Connell's recent flattery of the new queen, Victoria and subservience to the now openly anti-reformist Whigs was unworthy and demeaning to a democrat. In contrast, he concluded, he himself had renounced political ambition and now sought only to speak the truth to power: 'I am shunned by all parties as an *impracticable;* but I have the satisfaction of observing that the views I entertain are creeping into the public mind; and if these views be correct, a seed is sown which may yet ripen into fruit.'[193]

While ministers thought Crawford's letters a failure and unlikely to do mischief, they continued to appear through September 1837.[194] He denounced the Whigs' failure to reform the corrupt and partisan magistracy, except through the addition of stipendiary magistrates who merely added to government patronage as state agents. The 1836 police reform had, in his opinion, created a centralised armed force in the Irish Constabulary, rather than placing policing under the control of a democratised local government. With coercive legislation still on the statute book, this amounted to an increase in arbitrary state power in Ireland. Crawford's alternative recipe for Irish pacification was to link a politics of 'civil rights' (in Britain and Canada as well as in Ireland) with that of social security and education.[195] While Mulgrave may have been sincere, there was another, more influential, faction in London who were intent on 'riveting, by legislative enactments, the chains of arbitrary power upon the limbs of my unfortunate countrymen'.[196]

The nationalist press responded to this escalating assault with a combination of laments at his indiscretion and fury at his 'foul libel to a man and foul mischief to a cause'.[197] Crawford was charged by leader writers and correspondents with spiteful jealousy against the Liberator, with aiding and abetting the Tory enemies of liberty.[198] The *Pilot* discerned not only the ravings of a 'Crotchety curmudgeon', but more ominously those of an anti-Catholic; the letters embodied 'that insolent condescension of Protestants, when deigning to patronise long-suffering Catholicity'.[199] However the letters were welcomed enthusiastically by some British radical voices, which denounced O'Connell as a mere tool of the middle-class 'Catholic shopocrats' and praised Crawford for exposing the truth of his deception of the Irish masses.[200]

O'Connell's 'Letter to the people of Ireland', written from Derrynane on 2 September 1837, avoided mentioning Crawford by name, although complaining he was the 'chosen object of variegated and petulant calumny from what ought to be an unexpected quarter'. His letter was effusive in defending his own strategy – pronouncing Ireland's loyalty to the new queen and the Whig ministry at length and placing the maintenance of the ministry first before the menu of 'justice to Ireland' reforms that were still required, as only through keeping the Tories out could anything useful be attained. Repeal had now been comprehensively subordinated by O'Connell to the experiment of gradualist reform.[201]

Crawford ended this series of letters against O'Connell after the sixth, having thoroughly aired his grievances in the public arena, but without, as it first appeared, having made any political converts or forced a reconsideration within the nationalist camp. For the O'Connellite press, the series had been a miserable failure and placed Crawford permanently outside their political combination as an 'impracticable' and an over-ambitious hypocrite.[202] O'Connell's mocking dismissal of the letters in a speech to the Trades Political Union, followed by an ironic letter questioning Crawford's motives in producing his 'melancholy superabundance of words', provoked a further exchange late in the year.[203] Crawford now added the further charge that O'Connell had dissolved the General Association at the behest of the government to muzzle precisely the sort of dissent within Ireland that he affected to find risible.[204]

These vituperative exchanges would continue between the two men and their supporters over the following years, and made any future co-operation next to impossible. O'Connell's dismissal of Crawford in November 1837 had a ring of patronising finality:

> I prepare to take my leave of you forever. Write one thousand and one letters against me, you have dispensed me with answering or even reading them. Write away. But before we part allow me to bestow on you my unlimited compassion and generous forgiveness. Let me superadd one parting word of advice [...] Never again make an atrocious charge against any man, though he be a friend, without knowing something of the matter, or of having some proof.[205]

This would turn out to be a little premature, as Crawford refused to be silenced in his campaign to prove O'Connell 'a gratuitous traitor to the cause of civil and religious freedom'.[206] As he had anticipated, the confrontation did him no harm with his Ulster radical-Protestant base, and, as O'Connell's star dimmed for British radical reformers, would open up new political pathways for his political project across the Irish Sea.[207] Remarkably, he also managed to retain some grudging respect for his personal integrity and the 'abstract' correctness of his opinions from some moderate O'Connellites such as the future Cork mayor and Repeal MP William Fagan.[208] As we will see in a later chapter, Crawford's developing profile as the champion of landlord-tenant reform would also make it difficult for Catholic Irish political opinion to exclude him permanently from its purview.[209]

'Precursors' and 'Crawfordites', 1838–40

Now lacking a parliamentary seat, Crawford continued to resort to his favoured instrument of lengthy public letters to newspapers to pursue his campaigns in 1838–9. As the principal arguments had been worked out in the previous two years, these tended towards repetition, albeit enlivened by denunciations of further concessions as the poor law and tithe bills were amended on their course through parliament in the 1838 session, and by critiques of O'Connell's own public missives. As before, he held O'Connell's pusillanimity towards the government and failure to live up to his previous commitments to the people to lie at the root of the absence of equitable and just measures.[210] These exchanges attracted international attention and proved something of an embarrassment to the Irish leader.[211]

A letter from Fr James Hughes, the parish priest of Newport, Co. Mayo, provoked Crawford to offer a review of his own political strategy in May 1838. He agreed with Hughes that it appeared the people of England were determined not to do Ireland justice but added that recent experience had led him to exclude the inhabitants of the northern industrial counties from this condemnation: 'the people in that district seemed to me desirous to hold out to Ireland the hand of friendship in a common struggle for the liberties of the whole people'. But nothing could change until the people of Ireland themselves mobilised (as they had in 1828–9) to gain the respect of England and compel it to grant justice from a sense of its best interests and well as its duty. Crawford doubted the utility of Hughes' alternative plan of an Irish home-consumption campaign (an echo of the Volunteer initiatives of the eighteenth century), which could alienate those putative allies in the British industrial belt. Instead, Ireland should agitate uncompromisingly for core reforms: abolition or the total appropriation of tithe for poor relief, a corporation bill on the same terms as that for England, repeal of the 1835 coercion act, and a fair increase in representation. Once roused, they should then build an alliance with the British left, while keeping repeal as a reserve position:

> Let her next appeal be to the British people – let her offer to join them in all legal means for the enforcement of their rights, provided they reciprocally join in pressing the rights of Ireland. If they do so (and I prognosticate they will do so, *because it is their interest to take* that course) Ireland, in common with even the liberal party in Britain, *must succeed*. If Britain refuse the hand of fellowship to Irishmen, then Ireland must contend for herself, single handed [...] and then, above all, Ireland would be in a position to demand (and I will say *to enforce*) the principle of self-government.[212]

In another letter he reaffirmed his conviction of the need for an Irish legislative body, 'in connexion with, but not subverting, the imperial representation', but asserted that Ireland must first prove itself worthy by throwing off O'Connell's delusive and dishonest agitation, and reject humiliating subservience to Whig government.[213]

The logic of Crawford's position required him to continue his bearding of O'Connell in the hope of either shaming him into an about-face, or weaning away his mass support. The fact that he himself lacked sufficient political capital with Irish Catholics, or the necessary levels of personal charisma, to have much chance of bettering the Liberator at his own game appears to have caused him no self-doubt. Following another barrage of public letters that mixed close reasoning with moralistic anger, Crawford travelled to the Corn Exchange in Dublin to attend a meeting of O'Connell's constituents on 18 August 1838, assembled there to establish a new body to replace the General Association. This 'Precursor Society' would ostensibly seek to promote Irish reforms, while reviving the threat of repeal agitation if these were not advanced by the end of the 1839 session. It was in this agonistic environment, with the great majority of the crowd evidently hostile to Crawford, that he now confronted his former ally in person. This required some personal courage and a thick political skin. Rising immediately after O'Connell had set out the aims of the body, Crawford reiterated his charges, persevering despite interruptions, catcalls, hisses and general 'confusion' in the assembly. He rearticulated his case that, as it was agreed now was not the time to press for repeal, an alliance with the advanced British radicals rather than the Whigs was the only way forward, and that O'Connellite attacks on them had been counterproductive:

> With what chance of success can they approach a body, which has been insulted with the epithet of being enemies to the Irish people, and of having united with the Tories, in perpetuating injustice to this country? (Hisses.) I stand up here on the part of the English radicals – (groans and hisses.) – and I boldly say, that that body are anxious for justice to Ireland – (oh! oh!) – but they are equally anxious, that principle should be sustained. (A voice in the crowd – You are always spouting about principle.) – Let the English people be appealed to, on that ground, and he was confident, that they would support Ireland.

Thus baited in front of his core supporters, O'Connell's riposte mixed acid sarcasm about Crawford's unfashionable dress sense, with an appeal to the authority of his own charismatic leadership and achievements. Crawford, he sneered:

> does not act for the country, I do so. (Hear, hear, hear.) He agrees in every principle otherwise and there is his speech for you. Why, if I were to tell him, that I know, as well as if I was under that white waistcoat he wears, the feelings that actuate the hon. gentleman's breast, I would be only telling him the truth; and by the way, let me tell the gentleman, white waistcoats are not at present at all in fashion in London. (Laughter.) He has been writing letters, during the last winter, for the newspapers, assailing us, and trying, by every means in his power, to distract us in the pursuit of our claims; but heaven help the readers, what a quantity of space has been lavished on them! [...] Let him now come forward and say, what has he ever done for Ireland? Did he ever do anything of the slightest possible utility for the country? What have I done? Will he say he has done as much?

O'Connell concluded by telling Crawford to his face that he was now his enemy, and an enemy to repeal, leading to the latter's response that he still held personal respect for O'Connell despite objecting to his 'humbug agitation', being hooted down by the crowd in the hall.[214]

The inaugural Precursor Society meeting was thus ostensibly a humiliating defeat for Crawford, and O'Connell's mocking ditty, 'What brought you here, Sharman my jewel, – / What are you after, Crawford, my man?', would be taken up by a chorus of loyal supporters in meetings and the nationalist press.[215] Nevertheless, extensive newspaper coverage of the encounter in the British as well as Irish press may have redounded to his advantage. Even those at odds with his politics expressed admiration for his courage in having 'braved the lion in his den'.[216] The Chartist *Northern Liberator* praised his attempts to 'grapple with that worst and most formidable foe to liberty that now exists in these islands, namely, Mr Daniel O'Connell'.[217] Crawford's example led Christian Isobel Johnstone, the radical feminist editor of *Tait's Edinburgh Magazine,* to announce it was dropping support for O'Connell and to publish instead a long letter by Crawford on 'Observations on Irish policy' in September 1838, which called for the unity of radical forces to create an irresistible moral power for change.[218] This demarche drew support from many northern Irish reformers, and more surprisingly from a few Catholic voices, including Father Patrick Davern of Bruff in Co. Limerick, who wrote to the press in support of Crawford's critique of O'Connell's compromises.[219] Nor did the setback silence him: he continued to pump out public letters damning O'Connell's 'apostasy' on tithes and condemning the Precursor agitation.[220]

There is some evidence that this reaction initially placed O'Connell on the back foot. He wrote to his confidante P. V. FitzPatrick in October that he had been despondent in the face of such attacks, but that Crawford had now overreached himself and 'written himself into trouble'.[221] The letter in question was Crawford's second on 'religious liberty', which accused O'Connell of seeking to either have the Catholic church established in Ireland, or else have its clergy paid through a form of the regium donum. While the Catholic church might not wish either outcome, the payment of their clergy was, he believed, a logical extension of Whig religious policy and O'Connell, having accepted the principle of tithe and religious establishments in the 1838 Act, could not be relied on to oppose it, while the Catholic people seemed incapable of refusing 'the *dictum* of this despotic leader'.[222] With this statement, Crawford appeared to have crossed the line into denying the sincere desire for religious and political liberty of Irish Catholics – a position that distanced potential Catholic friends and gave plentiful ammunition to his enemies.[223] His former ally the Belfast Catholic lawyer (and from 1838 editor of the *Newry Examiner)* Thomas O'Hagan turned on him, writing to the press anonymously as 'Ulsterman' in condemnation of this apparent anti-Catholic stance.[224] The O'Connellite loyalist Tom Steele accused him of 'mistaking his noisome drivel for sulphuric acid' and deliberately provoking discord.[225] At open air public meetings on tithes, such as those at that at Kiltolla, Co. Galway, Crawford and his presumed associate Fr Davern were now jeered and 'groaned'.[226] O'Connell took advantage of this turning tide of opinion to 'hurl defiance' at him and accuse him of inflaming the 'ulcerous sore' of Ulster Protestant bigotry.[227]

Although not without some support in Dublin, especially in the shape of the newly established *Dublin Monitor,*[228] these attacks led Crawford to fall back further on his core constituency in the north. A letter attacking O'Connell's inconsistency on whether he sought 'equalisation' for Irish Catholicism with the religious structures of England and Scotland, was addressed to 'The friends of religious liberty in Ulster'. In this he discountenanced any religious antagonism towards Catholicism but complained of the political behaviour of the Catholic community, which was determined 'by their too humble submission to the dictation of their leader'. [229]

What was Crawford's constituency? The *Northern Whig* remained for the moment a supporter of his position (so long as repeal remained off the table). The orthodox Presbyterian *Londonderry Standard* was critical of his 'radical and republican' core supporters, whose 'nucleus [was] among the radical Unitarians of Ulster, and are more widely recognised under the ridiculous appellation of *Liberal Protestants*'. But although suspicious of their record, the paper expressed admiration for Crawford's personal political stance, and attempt to 'din the northern "twang" into [O'Connell's] ears'.[230] It would later also become a strong supporter of his tenant-right campaigns. Crawford had always been careful to maintain his political presence in the north, and it was to what this paper termed 'the *radicals* of Ulster – the *Crawfordites*' that he would return.[231]

After the previous tempestuous years, 1839 was, for the most part, one of reflection and personal development for Crawford, before he returned the political forefront again in 1840. Part of the reason for this was his withdrawal to Crawfordsburn to focus on refining and focusing his agrarian thinking, a process that would lead to the serialisation in the press of his articles in 'Defence of the small farmers of Ireland', which would subsequently appear in book form that December.[232] This publication would enhance his reputation as one of the leading agrarian reformers on the island, and make it difficult for O'Connell and his southern supporters to completely sever all political relations with him given the popularity of land reform.

The other major development in his politics in 1839 was a wholehearted commitment to the immediate abolition of the corn laws. On 19 March the *Northern Whig* published and endorsed his long letter on the subject, in which Crawford demurred from the resolution of Co. Down landlords to petition parliament to uphold the laws and sought to integrate his personal hostility to agricultural protection with his broader agrarian and welfare thought. He was coruscating in his critique of the class-interests of his 'own' order: there were now, he thought, no grounds for any compensation to the landed interest (barring the abolition of the new tithe rent charge) as it had for decades profited immorally from the high grain prices produced by the corn laws' restrictions on imports. Rather than, as landowners alleged, promoting Irish agricultural development, the laws had perverted the evolution of Irish society through stimulating an export trade in grain that the working population of the country simply could not afford:

> It has arisen from the efforts of those who had no capital but their bones and sinews – whose necessities compelled them to labour to procure food for subsistence – and to procure that subsistence they were compelled to labour; also, for another purpose, namely to pay the rent of the land on which that subsistence was produced. Thus when prices fell, but rents did not fall, the cultivation increased, and the export increased; because it required a greater quantity of produce to meet the landlord's demand – and this increased quantity of produce brought to the market, was abstracted – not from the profits of the farmer, for he had none before – not from the money capital of the farmer, for he had none before – but from the means of existence, from his food, from his clothing, from his fuel, from his furniture, from his cattle; and, when nothing more could be abstracted, he has been turned out, to become a wretched wandering pauper, depending on the charity of those who were approaching to the same condition [...] Thus cultivation and production have failed to be the indications of national prosperity. The

profits have been absorbed by the owners, instead of the cultivators, of the soil – and poverty, crime and vagrancy have been the necessary accompaniments.

Repeal of the corn laws would be no panacea, but it would at least take away the excuse for high rents and remove the bounties 'by which those landlords are induced to create an artificial famine in the midst of plenty' by exporting as a surplus the grain that was desperately needed for home consumption. Only when the labourers and farmers had food security in their own country could such agricultural exports be morally permissible.[233]

Crawford's pathway to corn law repeal was thus quite distinct from many of its middle-class advocates in Great Britain who saw it as a mode to increase industrial profits, but he was quick to respond to an invitation to subscribe to the Anti-Corn Law League's circular when this was sent to him later in the year, and announce himself a supporter of that organisation. Yet while it was an essential measure, he believed that corn law repeal could never be insulated from other reforms, and he urged the League to take a sympathetic position on the reduction of agricultural rents as part of its campaign.[234] By early the following year he was appearing on League platforms, and spoke at its Manchester banquet in January 1840, and was present at the meeting of the 'Operative' League that followed to appeal to working-class supporters.[235] In March he was a speaker at a petitioning meeting in Dublin against the corn laws, arguing that the 'whole community' and not just the manufacturers suffered from the system.[236] This placed Crawford on a potential collision course with many of his Chartist admirers, who adopted a hostile stance towards the League as embodying a selfish bourgeois class interest. Convinced that corn law repeal and democratic reforms were compatible and that a cross-class radical alliance for both was possible, Crawford adhered to this position, and would seek to give it practical expression.

O'Connell regarded himself as being as enthusiastic a corn-law repealer and agrarian reformer as Crawford. To demonstrate this to his public, and perhaps also with an eye on what threatened to be a fatal disintegration of the Whig administration in Spring 1839, he again pursued a tactical rapprochement. To the surprise of many, speeches given at Dundalk and Newry seemed to indicate first a change of tone and then to offer an apology for any offence given to Crawford the previous year.[237] In September, with the Precursor Society now wound up, he praised Crawford's 'admirable letters in opposition to the depopulating system' to the Trades Political Union in Dublin, albeit mangling the details of his political genealogy.[238]

Given the bad blood between them, it seems surprising that Crawford's initial response to these overtures was also conciliatory, although he may have been conscious that he have previously gone too far in suggesting there was an appetite for Catholic endowment. Speaking at a county meeting in Meath, which had been called to express support in the threatened Whig ministry, he accepted the proffered olive branch , and praised the achievements of the Normanby administration in Ireland without endorsing government policy more generally.[239] This seeming rapprochement was met with rejoicing in Navan and satisfaction in the Irish liberal and nationalist press.[240] While this may have been good politics at that moment in an Irish context, it did lead to Chartist journals attacking what they saw as Crawford's 'apostasy' in realigning with O'Connell in support of a Whig government.[241]

But such a rapprochement could not last as O'Connell and his support organisations were swinging back towards a full-blooded repeal campaign. When the TPU, on O'Connell's prompting, issued a welcoming address to Crawford, he responded with a polite but robust rejection of 'simple repeal'. This was consistent with his public stance since 1833–4, but now had a harder edge. A simple restitution of a sovereign Irish parliament would, he insisted, prove unworkable, for the reasons already stated. It was important that Ireland still have a say in 'imperial' legislation, but he now added a new concern. The continuing manifestations of sectarianism in Irish society and politics, continually stirred by the 'violent extremes' of both the popular and landed parties, made it desirable that Westminster retain some sovereign oversight of the devolved legislature. The UK parliament had recently imposed autocratic suspensions of the autonomy of both the Canadian and Jamaican assemblies – but past experience had shown it could do this as easily with an 'independent' as with a 'local' legislature, whereas in the case of the latter, the continuing presence of Irish MPs at Westminster would impose some sort of check on its arbitrary action. But most importantly for Crawford, recent experience had convinced him that the interests of the British and Irish lower classes were the same, and could and should be brought into common cause 'on principles, not of *separation,* but of *identification'*.[242] Crawford was now positioning himself explicitly as a UK-wide radical politician, with (for the moment) only a residual interest in devolved government for Ireland.

This inevitably provoked a riposte from O'Connell, which reignited their feud. Crawford was, the Liberator complained, neither a repealer nor a unionist, 'but a sad and speculative combination of both'. His plan was delusive and would find no supporters, as it lacked any 'of the racy ingredients which excite the spirit-stirring, soul-moving animation for "fatherland and liberty"'.[243] The renewed quarrel gave rise to malicious rumours that Crawford was about to convert to Conservatism or 'turn Orangeman', forcing him to write to the press to refute 'so extraordinary a fabrication'.[244] As O'Connell moved steadily towards reviving the repeal agitation through establishing the 'National Association for Full and Prompt Justice or Repeal' in April 1840 (renamed in July the Loyal National Repeal Association), in the belief that it was 'the only topic that can animate the entire mass of the population', the need to refute Crawford's objections took increasing precedence over any possible co-operation on the corn law or land reform issues.[245] One of the first acts of the new Association was to establish a committee specifically to answer his critiques of simple repeal.[246] Although initially restrained by the perceived need to prop up the tottering Whig government for as long as possible, the ground was being prepared for a revived mass outdoor campaign against a new Conservative government, and no public dissent in Irish popular politics could be tolerated.

The Ulster Constitutional Association, 1840–1

Lord Stanley, now a leading Conservative, proposed an Irish Registration Bill in 1840, in a move which all Irish reformers regarded as a hostile attack on existing suffrage rights, and which many feared the Whig administration was now too weak to counter. O'Connell sought to use the threat to bolster support behind his new Repeal Association. Self-excluded from this, Crawford now moved to create a separate, Ulster-based, vehicle for resistance and for pursuing further electoral reforms. The foundation of his 1840 agitation was laid in the leadership role he took in organising the 'Down declaration' in late 1839 – a county-wide petition which denounced Lord Roden's parliamentary attack on the exercise of law and order in Ireland by the Normanby administration.[247] By January 1840 some 15,500 signatures had been collected (three times more than the rival Conservative address), although an attempt by Crawford to have the declaration acclaimed at a public meeting was stymied when an 'Orange mob' occupied the Downpatrick courthouse, allegedly with the collusion of local magistrates.[248] Crawford and his allies were successful again later that year in engineering a liberal county address to the queen, to the chagrin of the local Tories.[249] Despite his distrust of the British Whig leadership, there was clearly no antagonism between Crawford and the Dublin Castle team, and he attended the farewell dinner to Morpeth at the Theatre Royal in 1841, at which a testimonial signed by upwards of 170,000 was presented in appreciation of his services as chief secretary.[250] Indeed he observed that Morpeth and Lord Ebrington (Normanby's successor as lord lieutenant from 1839) had been sincere in their desire for Irish reforms but been overruled by London.[251]

On 10 January 1840 Crawford addressed a 'great meeting of the reformers of Ireland' in Dublin on the need to protect voting rights through easier registration of poorer electors, while upbraiding Irish MPs on their failure to pursue an equalisation of the franchise with England and other crucial reforms.[252] Dissatisfied with this body, he nevertheless developed a rapport with another speaker, David Robert Ross, a liberal Down landowner.[253] Crawford's objections to Stanley's bill, set out in a public letter, focused on its tendency to render the legal costs of registration and the risks of rejection on technicalities much higher for the poorer voter, while smoothing the way for registration of wealthy £50 freeholders and clergy. Rather than assimilating practice with England, the bill was calculated to promote the 'disenfranchisement of the *honest, independent* voter, who should desire to serve his country – unpledged to parties, uncontrolled by undue influences'.[254]

Crawford and James Simms of the *Northern Whig* were the joint secretaries for a public meeting of protest that followed in Belfast.[255] Responding to counter-charges made by his old rival Emerson Tennent, Crawford returned to the theme that the union could only be made whole if political rights were equalised:

> Feeling, as I do, that *imperial legislation* is necessary for the interests of Ireland, I claim *perfect assimilation – I claim identification – I claim equal rights, liberties, and franchises with Britain;* and I am satisfied, that all the friends of freedom in Britain, would concede that assimilation, provided we incorporate ourselves with them, in all constitutional means to advance the people's rights [...][256]

The assimilationist stress in his letter laid down a clear line of distinction from O'Connell and fudged for tactical reasons his previous advocacy of a limited form of repeal.

Seeking to capitalise on the momentum generated by the reactive public meetings of the previous months, in June 1840 Crawford and Ross set up, with the endorsement of the *Northern Whig,* the Ulster Constitutional Association.[257] The two men acted as joint secretaries, while the honorific chairmanship was offered to the Whig peer the second Earl of Charlemont, in deference to the role his father had played in leading the Volunteers.[258] Indeed, he was subsequently toasted at an association dinner to the tune 'The Volunteers' march', which a reporter noted was cheered in 'the most enthusiastic character that we ever witnessed' – another effort to legitimate contemporary reformism through appeal to late eighteenth-century memory.[259] The body was intended to be broad-based, encompassing all reformers from moderate Whigs to democrats, but had a high membership fee of one pound (later halved to ten shillings) limiting access to the middle classes; it was open to Ulster residents who were 'friends and supporters of constitutional freedom, and who accordingly recognise the just and reasonable claims of all their fellow-countrymen, without distinction of religious profession, to equal rights, to equal laws, and the blessings of imperial government'.[260] If membership of this predominantly liberal-unionist body appeared something of a regression in Crawford's politics, it later became evident that his participation involved a degree of entryism, and that he aimed to persuade its members to adopt a more advanced reformist position.

O'Connell's attempts to suborn the new northern body under his own Repeal Association attracted strong opposition and created problems for northern Catholic reformers as to where their loyalties should lie.[261] Rebuffed by Crawford and Ross, O'Connell urged northern Catholics to break with the Belfast Association, but several prominent men nevertheless still took out memberships, including Thomas O'Hagan and Charles Gavan Duffy, now editor of the *Vindicator,* recently launched with O'Connell's backing as a new voice for Belfast Catholics.[262] Ross welcomed the adherence of a number of 'papishes' headed by a Down parish priest and expected Archbishop Crolly's endorsement to bring in more.[263] When the UCA met publicly for the first time in August 1840, at the new Belfast Music Hall, free tickets were issued to non-members (probably at Crawford's instigation), and a crowd of over 700 attended, including many women in the gallery. Crawford was the lead speaker, reiterating his reasons for shunning any alliance with O'Connell, lamenting the previous failure of Irish MPs to support British reform motions, including Thomas Attwood's presentation to parliament of the first Chartist petition in 1839, and urging the 'energetic and vigorous union' of the reformers of the three countries of the UK as the only way of defeating the blockages to reform posed by the house of lords and Conservatives in the commons.[264]

Needled by this, the Repeal Association and the *Pilot* alleged that the UCA was a deliberate 'diversion against repeal', set up to prevent its successful expansion in the north, a charge that was repudiated by Crawford and his supporters.[265] The war of words with the Repealers would again rage on for the following months, with O'Connell using US political jargon for extreme democrats to mock him as a 'Locofoco' and turncoat, and as the 'wizard of the north', and Crawford asserting his political consistency and the fatal flaws of the 'constitution of 1782'.[266] His concern that O'Connellite rhetoric was inclining more towards separation and away from devolution pushed him towards a stronger defence of the British connection and rejection of the Listian protectionist nationalism beginning to appear on Repeal platforms. It was, he argued, the distortions of the corn laws and the avarice of landlords and not British colonial policy that was imposing poverty on Ireland. Rather than fantasising about 'fictitious and exploded system' of industrial and agricultural protectionism, Irish politicians should focus on supporting practical reforms and look to the example of the north:

> I ask, why should not Dublin prosper as Belfast is prospering? – why should not the elevated chimneys of manufactories be raising their heads over your city? – I shall be told there is no capital. I ask, where does Belfast find capital? Belfast is working on capital created by the

enterprise and industry of her own people. What is it produces the prosperity of the northern portion of the province of Ulster, but the same enterprise and industry in conjunction with a better system of connexion between landlord and tenant?[267]

Although he remained politically at odds with Henry Cooke, such polemics came close to the latter's 1841 defiance to O'Connell: 'look on Belfast and be a Repealer – if you can'.[268] To O'Connell it appeared self-evident that the 'Crawfordites' were seeking to separate Ulster from the rest of Ireland, and Crawford was certainly playing to a sense of Ulster particularism at this moment.[269]

The UCA's public meetings initially proved popular with Belfast liberal gentry and middle classes. In addition to its original stated purposes of opposing Stanley's bill and working to maximise the registration of potential liberal voters in Belfast, it adopted a series of reformist resolutions, albeit ones that were rather short on detail.[270] Ireland, it resolved, should have 'equal rights, privileges and franchises with Britain', and the Irish Reform Act of 1832 should be amended to bring it into closer line with its original principles, including greater protection to voters, and 'the right of voting founded on a more uniform, simple and comprehensive test of qualification'. Any such reforms needed to be attained by 'moral power' alone, be agreed through consensus among reformers, and be uniform throughout the UK. These vague aspirations were a far cry from the stark and simple democratic demands of Chartism, and from the commitments that Crawford was simultaneously making in England, and led, as we shall see, to a brief spat with Feargus O'Connor.

Fully conscious of this apparent inconsistency, Crawford addressed it in a speech to the UCA in October. After a preface claiming continuities between the association and the reforming agenda of the Volunteers in 1783 in their common pursuit of political liberty, he admitted that he would 'go farther in the extension of the franchise than a great many of those around me', and that while never renouncing these principles, he would not press them at present for the sake of maintaining unity behind the campaign. At the same time he insisted that alliance with the 'rational reformers of Britain' was essential, with the implicit understanding that franchise equality between the two countries would deliver in Ireland whatever the more advanced movement in Britain could achieve. Aware of the drain of Ulster Catholic support from the movement, he urged Protestants to remember the discrimination and provocations under which Catholics still laboured, and to forgive and forget any harsh words spoken in haste – religious unity remained essential for the attainment of liberty in Ireland, even if O'Connellite repeal was a distraction.[271]

However, becoming impatient, Crawford tried to nudge the UCA into supporting a specific franchise reform plan in December 1840. His resolution was for a form of household suffrage, enfranchising settled and 'industrious, labouring and operative' male heads of households in Irish towns and counties. This fell some way short of the Charter's 'universal suffrage', as it would explicitly exclude any 'paupers and vagrants' whom Crawford stated might be open to exploitation by unscrupulous electoral interests, as well as adult men living with a ratepaying father, and all women (who were also absent from the Charter).[272] Such a measure, he argued, would bring the Ulster Association into line with the resolutions of the Leeds Parliamentary Reform Association (LPRA) by enfranchising the majority of the adult male population, and should be accompanied by resolutions for the secret ballot, redistribution to create equal voting districts, shortening parliamentary terms to a maximum of three years, and abolishing property qualifications for MPs. A decision on the plan of reform had become urgent, as it was 'the hinge upon which the utility of the association must turn. It will decide the question whether we are to expect any co-operation from British reformers or not'.[273]

Limited as the proposal may have been for tactical reasons, household suffrage still proved too 'advanced' for the extremely cautious middle-class liberals of Belfast. Abruptly turning away from Crawford, the *Whig* feared his reform plan would distract from the priority of registration and prove divisive; it was doubtful that the public mind was prepared for it.[274] When he put it to the Association at a special general meeting on 17 December 1840 in what the *Dublin Monitor* reported as a 'speech most replete with sound argument and the most liberal views', he had support from Ross and more half-hearted endorsement from the Whig peers Charlemont and Gosford. Opposition to household franchise was led by the influential non-subscribing Presbyterian Dr Henry Montgomery, who thought it inopportune and likely to associate them with the 'wild theories' of the Chartists, a view seconded by the former Whig-liberal MP James Gibson. In a written communication R. J. Tennent declared his view that it was not a 'practically urgent' matter and should be dropped in favour of more consensual policies.[275]

Crawford's typical acerbity against class interests may well have alienated parts of his audience. Although he asserted that household suffrage would merely restore the ancient constitution and 'common law right' of England, many middle-class liberals, he asserted, feared it out of cowardice:

> many reformers of the present day seem unwilling to admit this great principle practically. They talk of the rights of the people, but they seem afraid of the people. There are many who say the franchise should be extended, but still not go beyond the bounds of the favoured class (hear, hear, hear), or to go in so small a degree beyond that class, that the power shall be kept in the same hands.

The working class had, he affirmed, as great a stake in society and its prosperity as any other, or more so given that they had nothing to fall back on if employment failed but mendicancy or poor relief. Where workers had votes, as in Norway, the democratic cantons of Switzerland or the northern American states, there had been no assault on property. Ultimately the only security for bourgeois property was to demonstrate the mutual benefits of cross-class co-operation in conditions of political equality:

> You must make friends of them by equal laws, by equal rights, by justice and kindness, by convincing them that the laws are made as well for their protection as yours; and that they have a just share in the making these laws by which they are governed. Then, if evil comes upon them by unavoidable misfortune, they submit with patience, with submission and good order, because they feel they have the means of redress in their own hands, through the medium of such improved laws as may be necessary.

By no means a socialist, Crawford envisioned such 'improved' laws as a combination of the removal of unjust burdens (repeal of the corn laws, reduced indirect taxation and cutting wasteful expenditure) and progressive measures (such as more humane poor laws, state employment schemes and landlord-tenant reform). Similarly, educational advancement would flow from the conferral of civil rights and should not be a prerequisite for the vote.

In the meantime, working men were more than capable of demonstrating virtue and sound judgment in choosing their own representatives (who like most 'gentlemanly radicals' he anticipated would be men of better education and social standing), especially once they were protected from undue influences by the ballot. The remaining checks and balances of the constitution would prevent any risk of democratic excesses, but unless democracy was given its due place in the constitution and its just grievances were redressed, it would spill out into violence or reckless agitation, as with the 'physical force' Chartists in Britain or the Repealers in Ireland. Irish history offered proof that trust could be placed in the working people of the country without the risk of social revolution:

> These were the principles of the Volunteers, and these are the principles for which I am contending (cheers). I conceive I would be a recreant to the blood which flows in my veins, if I did not support the rights of the working classes (great cheering). Were not the Volunteers themselves almost wholly composed of the working classes; and had not these men arms in their hands, subject to no control but the willing obedience to the higher classes? Of whom their leaders were composed (hear, hear, and loud cheers)? They did honor to the confidence reposed in them – they were the uniform supporters of the rights of property.[276]

Crawford's rhetoric may have enthused his supporters in the hall (many of whom were probably again non-members in receipt of free tickets) but was not enough to win over his many middle-class and gentry opponents who remained, despite his reassurances, anxious about their property given the recent upsurge of labour unrest. The Association opted to postpone a decision on his motion to avoid giving the impression of a public split.

This deliberate stalling, and the open hostility of the *Whig* to any reopening of debate on his proposals, led Crawford to express public frustration about this 'retarding policy'. If indeed the UCA did not agree with his views, he argued, it was essential they adopt a fully reasoned alternative after open and full discussion of all the options. He had, he wrote, already stepped back from his 'full demand' in proposing only a household suffrage as 'a bond of union on which the bolder and more timid reformers could rest', an indirect reminder that he had already signed the People's Charter for universal male suffrage in 1838. The preference of the moderates for a mere reduction of the borough franchise to £6 and county franchise to £10 ratepayers was unacceptable as continuing the exclusion of the working class, thereby compromising the Association's founding principles.[277] Writing to Samuel Smiles of the LPRA (who had attended a meeting in Belfast earlier in the year), he expressed optimism that the UCA would still endorse household suffrage, as it had already done for his other reform points.[278] Ross, however, was pessimistic, admitting that opposition had been much stronger than they had anticipated and fearing the consequences of driving off a third of the membership if they pressed forward.[279]

The reason for this reluctance of Belfast's liberal middle-class elite to embrace enfranchisement of working-class men is not difficult to discern. The town's population had nearly doubled to 73,000 over the twenty years to 1841, driven principally by the exponential growth of linen manufacturing and associated trades. Visiting in 1843, the German travel-writer Johann Georg Kohl was impressed by the sheer scale of capital investment, production and marketing in the industry, but also alarmed by the resulting social distress and class conflict:

> Within the last forty years many cotton spinning and weaving factories have also been added; and on the whole Belfast now numbers twenty-one great 'cotton and linen-yarn factories,' some of which are so vast as to employ 2,000 persons, and some of them rise to the imposing height of eight stories. A very considerable quantity of linen, I believe much more than one-half, is still made in the country by hand-looms; yet 'power-weaving' [...] is increasing every day. The melancholy and much-felt battle between the hand-loom and the power-loom, which in some towns in England has been decided in favour of the latter, is going on in Belfast.[280]

Crawford was more than aware of both the plight of the handloom weavers and the tensions in labour relations in the new factories and was appealed to by representatives of the workers to act as an honest broker and advocate for their interests. In doing so he put himself at odds with his erstwhile bourgeois allies in the linenocracy, who had no desire to see their employees politically empowered.

Crawford's stance on the franchise drew belated support from Duffy's *Vindicator*, which welcomed the threatened secession of Montgomery and his 'Dunmurry coterie' of conservative reformers from the UCA.[281] It also signalled an unlikely truce with O'Connell, who had praised the Belfast household suffrage resolutions in the Repeal Association, and whose son John corresponded privately with Crawford with a view to preventing 'injurious divisions' between them on the franchise question.[282]

If the O'Connells' tactical objective was to neutralise Crawford's opposition to the Liberator's forthcoming visit to Belfast, it was only partly successful. He politely declined to attend a 'reform' dinner to O'Connell on 18 January 1841 on the grounds of maintaining his political consistency, for 'if repeal be the leading object, then, in my opinion, no agitation for any minor object of reform can be advantageously entertained at the same time'. His own support for a local legislative body was not, he maintained, consistent with O'Connell's campaign for 'full legislative independence', which would inhibit the union of the combined moral power of the people of Britain and Ireland in favour of democratic reform.[283]

Crawford thus sat out on the sidelines O'Connell's disastrous visit to Belfast, but it is certain that his reformist cause was damaged by the sectarian polarisation and rioting that ensued, stirred up in large part by Cooke's determination to confront what he represented as a nationalist incursion into 'Protestant' Belfast.[284] O'Connell's rally had to be abandoned, and he was quickly escorted out of town by the police following attacks on the Royal Hotel where he was staying, and on the houses and properties of Belfast Catholics (see Figure 15).[285] Cooke, at this time backed by McKnight's *News-Letter*, stirred up opposition to any further parliamentary reform on the grounds that it would prove a stepping stone to Rome rule by enfranchising more Irish Catholics.[286]

When Crawford's household suffrage motion finally came before the general committee of the UCA, now chaired by R. J. Tennent, in early January 1841, it was defeated by a large majority, and he was quick to disclaim any responsibility for the committee's preferred £6 and £10 rating franchise that would restrict the vote to the middle classes and only the best-paid artisans.[287] Although Crawford and Ross, along with Charlemont and Montgomery, represented the UCA at an aggregate meeting of Irish reformers in Dublin later in the month,[288] his interest in an organisation which had so publicly failed to follow his radical lead began to wane. In the face of some Repeal heckling in Dublin, but with a statement of support from O'Connell, he re-iterated his argument that household suffrage was as far as he was prepared to compromise from his preferred option of universal suffrage and was the least that would satisfy the working people, who would no longer tolerate being a 'slave class', and thus allow an alliance with British democratic reformers.[289]

The *Whig* blamed Crawford for the torpor of the UCA in the face of the re-introduction of Stanley's registration bill that session, and its inaction in contesting the Belfast borough registration in early 1841.[290] To the delight of the Tory press the paper declared it could no longer work with such a self-proclaimed Chartist, who lacked any real support in Ireland.[291] Despite this threat, Crawford did not break immediately with the UCA – at its next general meeting on 25 February he acknowledged that the body had voted to postpone indefinitely his motion, and as joint secretary he advanced the consensus position on opposing Stanley's bill and supporting Morpeth's alternative measure for a registration based on a £5 ratepayer franchise, albeit in a rather subdued tone.[292] In the event, the dissolution of parliament in May 1841 swept away both bills, and the attention of Belfast's liberals returned to the borough election, and they selected a 'balanced ticket' of the presumed radical Ross with the moderate Whig Earl of Belfast (the heir of the Marquess of Donegall). With Belfast's Catholics now distanced from the Protestant liberals, Ross and Belfast were defeated, and only after the election was overturned on petition and with the liberals opting to run a single candidate at the following by-election did Ross finally obtain a seat in 1842.[293] Once elected his politics skewed in a more conventionally liberal direction and he clashed with Crawford in parliament on several occasions before giving way with poor grace to R. J. Tennent as liberal candidate in 1847.[294]

By the end the Ulster Constitutional Association limited itself to petitioning for commercial reform and supporting the liberal candidates in the May 1841 election. While Crawford took the opportunity to use it as a platform to denounce the corn laws, and attacked Russell for suppressing Morpeth's registration bill, it was now clear he would need to look beyond Belfast if he was to advance the rest of his radical agenda, and he formally washed his hands of the disintegrating body in October that year.[295] He had already committed to standing as a democratic radical in an English constituency, and this is now where his energy was directed.

4. Chartism, federalism and Rochdale politics, 1837–52

The People's Charter, 1837–8

On 31 May 1837, Sharman Crawford attended, along with eight other British and Irish MPs, a meeting at the British Coffee House in Cockspur Street, London. They came at the invitation of William Lovett, secretary of the London Working Men's Association, to discuss support for a bill based on the LWMA's petition for universal male suffrage, which Lovett had already entrusted to the radical MP for Bath, John Arthur Roebuck. Lovett noted later his disappointment with the stances taken by most of the MPs at this and a follow-up meeting a week later; their nominal support for universal suffrage had been tempered by considerations of parliamentary practicalities and a preference for incrementalism, or they had expressed opposition to the linked demand for annual parliamentary elections. Crawford he regarded as an exception, as he 'agreed most fully with the principles of our petition and differed from the other hon. members as regards their fears of impracticability; he thought the way to make these principles practicable was by agitation and enquiry'.[1]

Whatever his reservations about these potential allies, most of whom he believed cared more about retaining their seats than promoting advanced electoral reform, Lovett thought six of them useful enough to ask them to sit on the committee that would prepare a draft bill, which the LWMA would then promote to other working-class radical bodies in pamphlet form. Lovett's candour in criticising his guests to their faces drew fire from O'Connell, who sought to gain control of the meeting in a fashion with which Crawford would have been all too familiar. Lovett recalled: '[O'Connell] began a very warm and elegant philippic against me, commencing by saying that the gentleman who has just addressed you has spoken with all the impassioned eloquence of *impracticability*, and not very likely to be attended with any beneficial results. And then he continued in a strain calculated to crush me, by the mere power of words, had we been addressing an Irish audience'.[2] O'Connell's takeover bid was checked by Lovett's comrades in the LWMA, but they were reluctant to break with him completely given his parliamentary muscle, and in 1837 O'Connell was not yet ready to openly spurn the English radicals. Consequently, O'Connell, Crawford, Roebuck and three others were invited to join the drafting committee, along with six members of the LWMA. In the event Crawford and Roebuck lost their seats in the ensuing election, and O'Connell, who was now closely allied to the administration, proved of little practical value: Lovett consequently wrote the pamphlet himself with minimal assistance from others. It was published belatedly on 8 May 1838 as *The People's Charter:With the Address to the Radical Reformers of Great Britain and Ireland* (Figure 16).

This set out six inter-related demands for radical parliamentary reform: annually elected parliaments, universal male suffrage, equal voting districts, no property qualifications for candidates, voting by secret ballot, and payment of salaries to MPs. The pamphlet also acknowledged the 'reasonable proposition' of female enfranchisement but suggested this be postponed until the initial six points had been attained. None of these was new, and indeed its introduction drew attention to their long gestation on British radical reforming platforms, emphasising the continuity of a tradition which represented itself as seeking to restore popular constitutional rights long usurped by corrupt political elites. Perhaps to honour Crawford's supportive role, Lovett quoted at length from the Duke of Richmond's 'celebrated letter to Colonel Sharman' of 1783, in which he thought 'more and more that the RESTORING *the right of voting to every man universally, who is not incapacitated by nature for want of reason, or by law for the commission of crimes, together with annual elections, is the only reform that can be effectual and permanent'.*[3] Lovett concluded that only when the six points of the charter were enacted in law and self-government returned to the people, would the political and social evils created by '*corrupt* and *exclusive legislation*' be put to an end and the 'enlightenment of the people' hitherto hindered by the 'selfish government of the few' be attained.[4]

The LWMA was but one of a myriad of radical bodies that emerged as popular disillusionment with the limitations of the 1832 Reform Act became widespread, and in opposition to a Whig government imposing what was widely regarded as class legislation, most notoriously in the form of the 1834 Poor Law Amendment Act. Of these organisations, the LWMA was one of the smallest and most 'elite' in composition, drawing membership mostly from skilled artisans and 'distressed' members of the lower-middle class. As Malcolm Chase observes in his history of Chartism, while Lovett was a tireless organiser and writer, he lacked the charismatic leadership skills to build and direct a mass political movement harnessing working-class frustration. His *People's Charter* would become the foundational text of the Chartist movement, but the LWMA and its successors would play only a limited role in its diverse and fissiparous organisation, with Lovett himself ending up embittered and marginalised. Already by 1837 he had clashed bitterly with Feargus O'Connor, who had accused the LWMA of downplaying working-class concerns such as the persecution of the Glasgow cotton spinners that year for 'conspiracy' in taking industrial action, in their pursuit of bourgeois reforming allies.[5] In reaction to such attacks, the 1848 London edition of the *People's Charter* was prefaced by a lament against those who 'by their mischievous conduct, [are still] trying to keep those asunder who ought to be united against the common enemy.[6] Lovett's memoir was also largely given over to score settling with his rivals, especially O'Connor.

Feargus O'Connor had broken acrimoniously with O'Connell and devoted himself to rebuilding a political career as the tribune of working-class radicalism in Great Britain. His candidacy for Oldham in 1835 had been unsuccessful, but introduced him to northern English industrial conditions and politics. His subsequent campaigning was modelled both on O'Connell's success in creating and using mass movements for political leverage, and on the recently deceased Henry Hunt's oratorical power over popular radicalism. In 1837 he founded in Leeds his own weekly newspaper, the *Northern Star* (the name was deliberately chosen to echo its United Irish predecessor), which soon acquired an enormous readership and gave O'Connor a national platform to supplement his frequent speaking tours.[7] A highly charismatic orator and direct and emotive communicator through his weekly letters in the *Star*, O'Connor rapidly became the dominant personality in the burgeoning Chartist movement. Like Crawford he was a scion of the Irish minor landed gentry, with radical antecedents; he was the son of the romantic patriot Roger O'Connor and nephew of United Irish leader Arthur O'Connor. From a Protestant family that idealised its descent from the Gaelic high kings of Ireland, he inherited a small estate in Cork in 1820, but was saddled with heavy debts. O'Connor never lost interest in Irish politics, but after 1837 concentrated on moulding British Chartism around his own assertive and often intolerant personal leadership. This quickly led to open hostilities with Lovett and later with the Irish-born socialist James Bronterre O'Brien. Run-ins with O'Connor would also frequently compromise Crawford's engagement with British radicalism after 1837.

Daniel O'Connell's attacks on trade unionism on both islands and ever closer alliance with the Whig government in 1837–8 alienated British working-class radicals, a process amplified by O'Connor's relentless attacks on his former chief.[8] In this context, Crawford's sustained and public criticism of O'Connell helped raise his stock in Great Britain. His comments against the monopolising of political power by landowners had also attracted attention on the radical left: a pamphlet entitled *What is Property*, published by John Temple on behalf of a London-based 'Society for the Diffusion of Political Knowledge' in 1836, quoted as its epigram Crawford's statement that 'if there be any true definition of property, it is that which defines it as the thing which man creates by his own labour', before proceeding to demand the restoration of the franchise to artisans and labourers.[9] In August 1837 Crawford 'exposed' an alleged plot by O'Connell and the 'philosophical radical' Joseph Hume to collude with the government in maintaining Whig MPs for radical constituencies such as Dunfermline in return for a quid pro quo, thereby denying these constituencies 'freedom of election'.[10] His denunciation of the bourgeois radicals for this betrayal was well received by working-class leaders such as Lovett: 'The radicals *now*', Crawford wrote, 'instead of boldly standing on their own principles, and *on these alone*, combine themselves in this degrading union, and adulate a government which have proved themselves the most injurious enemies of the extension of popular liberty'.[11] His stance also drew encomiums from anti-government middle-class radicals such as Samuel Smiles, editor of the *Leeds Times*, who became a public admirer.[12]

Crawford's reputation and appeal was extending beyond London. In October 1837 he responded at length to a supportive address from the Working-Men's Associations of Tyneside. It was 'no small encouragement to a man struggling in the path of duty', he wrote, to receive such an endorsement from the working classes there, and he hoped that his example would help promote a 'moral revolution', unleashing the power of public opinion to make great changes in society (as indeed O'Connell had once done) and undermining monopolies. He added, with some bitterness, that he had no desire to return to parliament as presently constituted, as it had no respect for plain speaking of the truth.[13]

An address from the Edinburgh Radical Association praised his refusal to be carried away by the 'delusive' cry of justice for Ireland, spurning this 'mere political toy' for a determination to 'give justice to every British subject'.[14] Crawford's answer contained a statement of his personal definition of radicalism, utilising the horticultural metaphor:

> By radicalism I mean the striking at the root of our evils and of the abuses of the state – I

mean the taking out the canker at the root, and to give the whole tree new vigour and life, and thus causing the sap to circulate equally through all its branches and buds, diffusing genial nourishment and vigour alike to the trunk and extremities. I do not mean, by radicalism, the application of palliatives to the sores which show themselves here and there, plastering up the canker at one place, to cause it to break out with more violence in another; and thus, while a temporary and superficial remedy is applied, allowing the whole frame to become irretrievably diseased – and then no remedy can be found but total extirpation of the whole tree, and the planting of another in its place.

The British constitution could yet be saved, he believed, but only by bringing it into line with the progress of the people; it followed that the radicals seeking to root out corruptions and deformities within it were the true conservatives. If a violent revolution was to happen, it would be the fault of the 'destructives' in the old elites, not the reformers. Any franchise system based on property owning or holding was a feudal remnant; every man who paid taxes (including the universal indirect ones on consumption of necessities) was entitled to a share in determining how these should be levied and spent.[15]

In early 1838 Crawford, accompanied by his son Charles, toured the north of England as an invited speaker at radical meetings at Leeds and Stalybridge, at both of which O'Connor was also present. At the former he endorsed universal suffrage and the ballot and stated (in a criticism of the new poor law) his conviction that 'the poor should be sustained at the cost of those who were more fortunate'. At Stalybridge he condemned the corn laws, the new poor law (with its Irish imitator) and unjust and excessive taxation.[16] At Leeds Crawford, 'like our friend O'Connor' was hailed as bringing together the true shared interests of the people of Ireland and England. His presence, which was seen at this time as that of a visitor not a potential rival, drew the support of the *Northern Star,* which commented that: 'the speeches of Sharman Crawford are such as reflect the highest honor on the man, the statesman, and the patriot, by whom they were uttered'.[17] However, a run-in at Leeds with Augustus Beaumont, editor of the *Northern Liberator,* who attacked him for refusing to endorse physical force methods, suggested future troubles.[18]

At a radical meeting the following week in the Lancashire industrial town of Rochdale, cheers were given for Crawford and O'Connor (neither of whom were present), while the Whig MP for the borough, John Fenton, was roughly quizzed on his attitude to the core demands of universal suffrage, the ballot, annual parliaments and no property qualifications.[19] Fenton, a banker and industrialist, was unpopular due to his support for the new poor law, and was expected to retire from parliament before the next election, creating a potential vacancy for a more advanced reformer. While the 1838 tour raised popular consciousness of Crawford in industrial England, he did not as yet give any indication of relocating his political career there. However, the O'Connellite press growled that he had now joined the ranks of the English 'mob orators', and was turning a deaf ear to the threats of class violence frequently heard on such platforms.[20]

Despite these forays to Britain – he also visited Manchester in June for an 'ultra-radical' dinner to Oldham MP John Fielden – Crawford's political focus in 1838 remained resolutely in Ireland.[21] He declined an offer to stand for Glasgow, suggesting instead that the radicals invite Roebuck, and turned down a number of offers to speak, including one from Lovett to endorse the Charter on a LWMA platform in Westminster in September. The reason, he declared, was because lacking an Irish constituency, he could currently only speak for himself.[22] He also declined an invitation to co-chair the mass Chartist demonstration at Hartshead Moor in the West Riding of Yorkshire in October.[23] But he had not changed his mind on radical reform. On receiving a copy of Lovett's LWMA address to the Irish people, which called on them to unite with Britain in creating 'free and equal institutions', he assured Lovett that he joined him 'on the general principles on which the "People's Charter" is founded', and on the universality of franchise, although this did not mean (as he was sure Lovett agreed) that 'every individual, male and female, and every pauper, vagrant and criminal' should have the vote. He would support all peaceable and constitutional means to attain this.[24] In absentia, Crawford remained a popular figure in British radical circles, being toasted at a Barnsley radical dinner held in memory of Hunt in November 1838 as 'the real friend of the Irish poor'.[25] In December the LWMA would also come to his defence in his public dispute with O'Connell over religious voluntarism.[26] However, it would take the frustration of his Ulster Constitutional Association project of 1840–1 to push Crawford decisively towards a British political pathway.

Rochdale politics, 1838–41

The borough of Rochdale would become Sharman Crawford's political base for the next decade and more. First approached to stand by the radical association of the town in June 1840, by the time of the 1841 general election he was the agreed joint candidate of both the radicals and liberals for the single-member constituency created in 1832 and had been endorsed by the local and national Chartist leaderships. How did an Irish landowner come to stand and win in the contested seat, how did he engage with the politics of the borough, and to what degree can he be regarded as a Chartist MP?

Rochdale, located ten miles north-east of Manchester, had developed as one of the first industrialised towns in England. The population of the district had grown enormously, from around 36,000 in 1800 to the 86,481 enumerated by the 1841 census. Of these, around sixty-five per cent were employed in manufacturing, predominantly in the textile mills (producing both cottons and woollens) that dominated the town and its outlying villages, or in related trades.[27] Patrick Joyce observes that in Rochdale these factories were smaller than in many other industrial areas at the time (in 1841 employing on average fifty-three 'hands' in woollen and 119 in cotton mills), which tended to produce a more autonomous and politically active working class, but also promoted a more intimate relationship with the middle-class employers.[28] Such small-scale production tended, some argued, to promote distress and unrest. A fatal riot in the town in 1829, in which female flannel-workers appear to have been at the forefront, was blamed by a local nonconformist clergyman not solely on moral failings, but on the smallest producers undercutting 'regular manufacturers' and thus forcing down the rate of wages to misery levels.[29]

The leadership of radicalism in late-1830s Rochdale was shared by James Taylor, a local hat manufacturer and Methodist lay-preacher, and Thomas Livsey, son of a blacksmith and later a corn-dealer and brass-foundry partner, who was to play a central role in borough politics for decades. Like Crawford, Livsey was an Anglican who favoured disestablishment (while supporting what he saw as the rightful interests of the church), who had a 'consuming passion for politics', and saw himself as a disciple of 'Billy Cobbett'.[30] The local radical association they founded in 1838 rapidly adopted the six points of the Charter, but eschewed physical force as a means to attain them, while remaining open to shows of working-class strength. In November 1838 they welcomed O'Connor to the town in a torchlight rally involving some 3,000 participants.[31] Government warnings soon led to the suspension of this particular tactic, but other mass meetings followed in the district, attracting police and magisterial surveillance, and in which Livsey was prominent in urging moral force and defusing potential clashes between the people and the authorities.[32] In November 1839 the Rochdale Chartists again marched through the town by torchlight and were addressed by Livsey and O'Connor; at this event the latter and Rev. Joseph Stephens urged the workers to arm themselves, but Rochdale escaped the violence seen at Newport that winter and suffered relatively few arrests in consequence. Livsey presided over the petitioning meeting in February the following year that called for the release of the 'Newport rising' prisoners, and for the formation of a ministry that would support manhood suffrage.[33] He was elected a poor law guardian (and subsequently chair of the board) in 1840, an office he sought to use to subvert the workings of the hated poor law amendment act.

At first sight Rochdale might appear difficult electoral territory for a radical reformer given the restricted franchise. Electoral contests attracted popular excitement and were usually accompanied by disturbances, but at first were dominated by the established political parties. James Taylor stood for election as a radical in the first contest for the parliamentary borough in 1832, only to be well beaten into third place behind the Whig and Tory candidates.[34] In 1835 the Whig John Fenton lost narrowly to the Conservative John Entwistle, but retook the seat in an 1837 by-election, in part thanks to the organisational energy and skills of the young John Bright. The son of a local Quaker millowner, Bright had joined the Rochdale Reform Association in 1834 and was involved in temperance, parliamentary reform and anti-church rates agitation before being drawn towards the cause of free trade. By 1839 he was managing his father's cotton spinning factory near the town and was active in the recently formed Anti-Corn Law League. He had visited Belfast and Dublin in 1832 and may have been aware of Crawford as a consequence of observing the Belfast contest that year.[35] By 1837 he was also a vocal public critic of the 'unholy deeds' of the Irish church establishment.[36] Crawford's candidacy was, however, due principally to the vision of Livsey in recognising an opportunity when Fenton formally announced his intention to stand down in 1840, and his skill in building a radical coalition attuned to the developing micropolitics of Rochdale.

Rochdale witnessed a remarkably high degree of partisan polarisation at municipal level, closely aligned to religious divisions within the middle class.[37] The town had one of the highest proportions of nonconformists in England (at seventy-one per cent of recorded Sunday attendance in 1851),[38] and antagonism to the payment of compulsory church rates there had been heightened by the aggressive insistence on their legal rights by the vicars, Rev. William Hay and his successor Rev. John Molesworth. Both were highly combative characters. Hay had been rewarded with the wealthy living of Rochdale as a reward for his political services as a magistrate during the Peterloo massacre in Manchester in 1819 and was loathed by northern radicals as a reactionary political parson. Molesworth was a high-church religious controversialist appointed to Rochdale from Canterbury in December 1839.[39] In August 1839 hundreds of Chartists had crowded into the parish church, some 'in their working dress', to disrupt the Sunday services. Subsequent parish vestry meetings (open to all ratepayers and held in the churchyard, and attracting crowds of 8–12,000 in 1840) voted on several occasions against setting church rates, heard rousing voluntarist speeches made by Livsey and Bright, and elected a number of nonconformist churchwardens and sidesmen (who were sometimes also Chartists), with the anti-church party decisively gaining the upper hand by 1843.[40] Molesworth complained bitterly about nonconformist tactics used to gain control of the vestry elections and the slighting of the establishment.[41] In reality, Livsey had brokered an alliance between the Chartists and middle-class nonconformists of the town which agreed on setting a 'voluntary' church rate, and it was Molesworth and his allies who had rejected any compromise and turned to retributive tactics against ratepayers who voted against the church's asserted rights, a stance which 'inflamed the working classes almost to a state of madness'.[42] The *Manchester Guardian* opined in 1840 that it was the hostility of the vicar that had driven the Chartists of Rochdale to seek a liberal alliance.[43]

Crawford's outspoken religious voluntarism, as well as his support for the principles of the Charter, hostility towards coercion and readiness to take on established interests including the Melbourne administration, certainly recommended him to Livsey. According to William Robertson's 1880s history of town, it was Livsey personally who proposed Crawford as a candidate to the Rochdale Radical Association, and subsequently persuaded Bright and the bourgeois Reform Association that they should back him as a joint candidate instead of the latter's preferred option of the free-trade convert Milner Gibson, and despite the reservations of some of its wealthier members.[44] For Bright, Crawford's outspoken support for corn law repeal by this point may also have been crucial.

Crawford had again turned down a request to stand as a radical against the Whig T.B. Macaulay at Edinburgh in 1839.[45] But in the context of his attempts to build alliances between British and Irish radicalism and setbacks in Belfast the Rochdale offer no doubt appeared more attractive. A visit to the town hosted by the Radical Association in June 1840, at which he spoke to a gathering in which the 'old radicals and new Chartists' formed a majority, appears to have persuaded both sides that the fit was right, and the *Northern Star* was optimistic that the seat was winnable if the local Whigs complied.[46] Fenton's decision to sign the requisition to Crawford settled the latter point; he offered to resign immediately to provoke a by-election, but it was decided that a delay to give time to revise the registration lists was preferable.[47] On 24 July 1840 some 300 electors met in the town to sign the requisition, and while this was well short of the nominal 900 voters of the borough, it offered a strong base for a potentially successful campaign should an election be called.[48] Although the meeting was unanimous on the invitation and on establishing an election committee, it was temporarily marred by the overspilling of Irish politics. The *Manchester Guardian* reported that:

> By some means or other an Orangeman, who said his name was James Maginn, from Bolton, got into the room, and began to address the meeting on the extreme opinions entertained by Mr Crawford, but the chairman stopped him, and gave him to understand, as he was not an elector, he would be allowed to leave the room, which he accordingly did.[49]

By November the requisition's signatories had increased to 389, a probable majority given the revision downwards of the electors as non-ratepayers were struck off the list.[50]

The emerging radical-liberal alliance in Rochdale was, for all Livsey's efforts, susceptible to wider Chartist politics, and had to weather a serious crisis in October 1840. Crawford made no secret of his personal support for Smiles' Leeds Parliamentary Reform Association (which was sarcastically dubbed the 'Fox and Goose Club' by the *Northern Star*) as a vehicle for bringing about the British-Irish radical conjunction he so desired (see Figure 18). Smiles had attended meetings of the UCA in Belfast, and Crawford wrote to him early that month pledging its support.[51] For O'Connor the LPRA's platform of household suffrage and triennial parliaments was a dilution of the principles now embodied in the recently established National Charter Association, and Smiles' alliance with the Anti-Corn Law Leaguers highly suspect. Imprisoned for sedition for fifteen months in York gaol in 1840–1 and able to communicate via his paper only after a noisy public campaign, O'Connor was in no mood to make concessions to anyone who appeared open to alliance with the 'tyrannical' Whig government or diluting the working-class purity of the movement.[52] Initially supportive of the Rochdale invitation to Crawford, on 17 October his *Northern Star* exploded against the 'Ulser Association' [sic], accusing him of having betrayed his principles of five years in appearing to endorse a Whig government. As was typical of O'Connor's prose, the assault on Crawford was highly personal:

> His besetting sin is a pride that apes humility. He is a diffuse writer, a mumbling speaker, a loose and egotistical reasoner, a crude thinker, a bilious digester, and has a costive delivery; while, with all the appearance of an open and frank bearing, he has now proved that jealousy, selfishness and vanity have been the propelling powers of his every action. He has not the brains to lead – he has not the fortitude to follow; and therefore he has assumed the position of an engine placed behind a heavy baggage train to shove it up the hill.[53]

A follow-up editorial the next week accused Crawford of idealising the Volunteers of 1782 and embracing the 'hackneyed nonsense' of an extension of the franchise by instalments. In a garbled historical vein, he claimed Crawford was really just another Irish Whig:

> We arraign Mr Crawford upon the unsoundness of his principles; upon the variety of his principles; and upon his utter ignorance of all political principles. Mr Crawford declares that he will never rest content so long as Ireland remains in a state of inferiority to England. [...] He then goes on to say that they [...] are there that day to demand the same thing that the glorious Volunteers demanded in 1782 [...] but when the reformers of 1832, and the Volunteer Protestant officers of 1782, had got their own share, they allowed the soldiers to fish for themselves [...] Now fume as the Irish Protestant patriots may, there is no getting over that one startling fact, that the Irish Protestant officers raised the price of their own borough property, by the valour the courage and the union of the Catholic soldiers, and then laughed at them when they asked for their share of the scramble. [...] Does not Mr Crawford know, that the English people had power in 1832, as the Irish people had in 1782, to carry universal suffrage – and that they only appeared satisfied because they imagined they had carried it [... A] most monstrous declaration for any Irishman; but still more monstrous for one who was a Repealer, an unconditional Repealer, and one who was there to act the part of the Volunteers of 1782, who would have held such doctrine as high treason to the Irish people![54]

Given O'Connor's supremacy over British Chartism by this time, such attacks could easily have terminated Crawford's Rochdale political career before it had even begun. He had, however, no intention of being thus intimidated. In late November Crawford again visited Rochdale to receive the requisition and spoke to a crowd of 5,000, stating that he would struggle for household suffrage as a step towards giving 'every industrious man and good member of society' the vote, along with the ballot, short parliaments, repeal of the corn laws and extensive amendment of the poor laws.[55] Defying O'Connor, he went on to Leeds to speak on a LPRA platform with Smiles. On this occasion it was O'Connor who backed down, claiming now that he had been misled by deliberate misreporting of Crawford's speeches in the Whig papers, and thanking him for 'making amends'. Reversing its previous rhetoric, the *Northern Star* now praised his courage for standing up to O'Connell, 'in a white waistcoat too', and for seeking genuine unity between Irish and English radicals. Choosing to ignore the dalliance with Smiles, the paper made a full recantation, at least for the time being:

> we can assure Mr Crawford that we have many times heard Mr O'Connor declare that to Mr Crawford he looked for the restoration of the public mind in Ireland, from the abyss of misconception and ignorance into which Mr O'Connell has cast it; and we think we may say for him further, that no one circumstance could afford him greater pleasure than to be able to retain that high opinion that we believe he entertains of Mr Crawford. [...] What a triumph will now be that of the electors of Rochdale, when they shall have returned a man too honest to be a slave, and not too proud to defend himself before the people! [...] Yes! We shall now hear the real state of Ireland in the house of commons; and be it remembered that Mr Crawford has long since declared himself an advocate for, and supporter of, Mr O'Connor's five-acre plan. [...] Hurrah! then, for Crawford and Rochdale [...][56]

Despite their other differences, a mutual antipathy to O'Connell, a shared interest in agrarian reform, and Crawford's cordial relations with Livsey and the Rochdale Chartists, would ensure that they remained on reasonable terms until after the 1841 election.

The *Northern Star* now became convinced that O'Connell was plotting to undermine Crawford's candidacy at Rochdale, either by offering a delusive friendship, or by manipulating immigrant Irish voters against him. There was, it claimed in January 1841, a 'desperate attempt to assassinate Sharman Crawford', by destroying him with 'blarney'. He was warned to watch out for any poisoned cup offered him in apparent conciliation and thus become another of O'Connell's victims.[57] The paper chose to turn a blind eye to Crawford's presence at the LPRA's 'Reform Festival' that month, despite O'Connor's determination to disrupt it and destroy Smiles as a rival.[58] Crawford's attempts to square the circle of reaffirming his commitment to the principles of the Charter, while maintaining the acceptability in the short term of a household suffrage that would include lodgers and well as householders, was lost in the uproar, but it does not seem to have damaged him in Rochdale.[59] O'Connor's lieutenant in undermining the Leeds meeting, Lawrence Pitkethly, exempted Crawford from his diatribe against the false middle-class reformers on the LPRA's platform; as 'one of the most generous and humane of men, and consequently, a Chartist', he asserted, Crawford could only have been misled by others.[60]

O'Connor's forbearance concerning Crawford's ecumenical leanings at this time may have been tactical. As Matthew Roberts has argued, Chartism and the Repeal movement had overlapping reform agendas but by 1841 they were coming into sharp competition for the allegiance both of Irish migrants in Great Britain, and, with the development of Chartist bodies, in Ireland itself. In September 1841 the Repeal Association banned Chartists from membership, a move, which while not entirely successful in practice, reflected unease about the rival appeal of 'O'Connorism'. This provoked O'Connor into retaliation.[61] In this context, bringing one of Ireland's most prominent anti-O'Connellites into the Chartist orbit appeared, at least for the present, sound policy.

Crawford's personal popularity, at least in his newly adopted political home, was also evident. Attending a mass meeting called by the ACLL at Heywood in January 1841, at which Bright and other local corn-law repealers were heckled by Chartists, Crawford was instead cheered for insisting that suffrage reform and corn law repeal were mutually compatible. The *Northern Star's* reporter noted the positive responses to his speech from Chartists in the otherwise unruly crowd: 'A person in the meeting, "That's the most honest chap that's got up to-neet."', and 'A shout of "may you get in", amidst cheers that lasted for some time'.[62] His identification as a 'gentleman reformer' free from associations with industry appears to have enhanced his standing with working-class radicals. At the same time Crawford felt obliged to beg the Chartists not to disrupt such anti-protectionist meetings, which he felt smacked of physical force rather than the power of persuasion and could only prove counterproductive.[63]

Although by no means a supporter of physical-force Chartism, Crawford wrote and spoke in support of the campaign to grant a pardon for the three leaders of the 1839 Newport rising, whose capital conviction had been commuted to transportation to Van Diemen's Land. While he could not condone the resort to political violence as had broken out in the town, he believed it had been 'created chiefly by the conjoint oppression of the corn laws and the new poor laws', and by the betrayal of the hopes of the people by the Whig ministers. Any such vindictive punishment for political offences thus provoked should, he argued, be abandoned.[64] He repeated these principles in his electoral address, criticising the continuance of judicial coercion against political offenders, and the 'despotic power' created by the raising of county police forces.[65] This was a popular line to take with all Chartists, for whom the 'martyrdom' of the Newport leaders as well as other Chartist prisoners, and hostility towards state coercion of the popular movement, were key points.

Still confident that they could wrest back the seat and benefit from the rising tide of Conservative fortunes under Sir Robert Peel, the Rochdale Tories expressed indignation at what they saw as the imposition of an Irishman on the borough, and, no doubt with an eye to weaning away moderates, selected as their candidate James Fenton, brother of the outgoing Whig member.[66] Fenton was an Anglican landowner and co-owner with his brother of a cotton mill, but a staunch opponent of repealing the corn laws. He got off to a bad start by offending the local nonconformists by posting his electoral placards on the Sabbath.[67] In contrast to the popular excitement associated with the Crawford campaign, Fenton was described as carrying out an unostentatious but successful canvass, and the Conservatives were still hopeful of success (as they were in other northern boroughs in 1841).[68] But Tory tactics also involved seeking to sow mutual suspicion between Rochdale's Whigs and Chartists, and to greenwash Crawford as a disreputable Irish interloper who would betray all English patriots by reviving the disloyalty of 1798. The Tory *Manchester Courier* attempted to stir up jingoism, insisting that:

> The recreant Whigs of Rochdale have hoisted the same *green rebel flag, under which the enemies of England stood when they evoked the aid of France to join Ireland in invading our shores;* – they have joined the ranks of England's deadliest enemies, and are prepared to march to the attack under the leadership of MR. SHARMAN CRAWFORD [...] It is true that SHARMAN

CRAWFORD has declared himself in favour of their 'charter,' but MR CRAWFORD's Irish blood warms, instinctively as it were, towards his own countrymen.[69]

With tensions between Lancashire Chartists and immigrant O'Connellite Irishmen high in spring 1841 following a series of violent incidents in Manchester, Crawford would have to tread carefully, notwithstanding his well-known antagonisms towards the Irish leader. Moreover, like other Lancashire mill towns, Rochdale had a tradition of popular Orange organisation which was undergoing a revival in the early 1840s; the attempt to identify Crawford with Irish rebellion may have been calculated to stir such sentiments.[70] However, the Irish-Chartist antagonisms seen in Manchester were exceptional, and the movement enjoyed widespread support from Irish immigrants across the country, many of whom would have welcomed rather than been alienated by attempts to associate the popular candidate with the memory of 1798.[71] Rochdale had a significant Catholic minority, with a chapel established in 1829 and served by priests of Irish heritage.[72]

At a mass meeting of the non-electors of the town on 3 June, a resolution was carried unanimously to support Crawford.[73] Although denied the vote, non-electors would play an active role in the campaign and make a significant contribution to his victory. This was evident from the day of Crawford's arrival in town, when, after staying at Bright's house, he 'was escorted into the town [...] by two bands of music, electors, and other inhabitants, six abreast, and several gentlemen on horseback'. Stopping in the yard of an iron foundry, he addressed the crowd on his pledges to remain independent of all parties and governments, to seek 'a just extension of the suffrage', the ballot, the abolition of church rates, and his desire 'to establish commercial liberty by repealing all duties imposed for the protection of class interests'. He was then processed through the streets of the town and back to Bright's.[74] Crawford welcomed both the support of the non-electors and the scale of the procession as evidence of popular adherence to 'that great cause which we jointly support [...] the abatement of monopolies, political, religious and commercial.'[75] Despite this show of unity, the crowd was certainly not under liberal control and was capable of autonomous action. Several days later, this time without Crawford and the 'gentlemen', the town band and several thousand non-electors 'promenaded' to an assembly point to hear Taylor denounce the recent coercion of Chartists by Irish Repealers in the pay of the Whigs of Manchester, to cheer O'Connor, Frost and the Charter, and to burn an effigy of O'Connell.[76]

Given previous experience, it was unlikely that the election would pass off without some violence. The Conservatives had their own lower-class supporters, including Orangemen and miners from outside the town, and supporters of the two candidates clashed in the week before polling:

> On Wednesday evening the blues (Mr James Fenton's supporters), reinforced by a party of colliers from Smallbridge, paraded the town with a band of music. They were met in Yorkshire-street by a numerous body of electors in Mr Sharman Crawford's interest, when a skirmish took place, the result of which the seizing of a drum belonging to the blues, and breaking it into pieces. Some blows were exchanged, but the reformers maintained possession of the field and were complete victors.[77]

Following the nomination meeting on 30 June, which took place before a crowd of up to 10,000, with many female supporters wearing party colours observing in the surrounding buildings, the liberal press reported that 'all was quiet, with the exception of a skirmish about some flags (occasioned by the collision of the two processions), in which a few heads were broken'. The hostile *Courier* insisted that the 'reds' (the reformers) had started a riot and that their 'Irish ruffians produced their bludgeons, using them in the most savage manner'.[78] A popular history of the town, published many years later, suggests a more sustained conflict, in which attempts by the blues to storm the reformers' headquarters of Tweedale's Hotel, aiming to 'carry off' a number of timid liberal voters who had been 'bottled' there until the time for them to vote arrived. According to this account this provoked a counter-attack by Crawford's supporters, which included a number of his fellow-countrymen:

> The Irish, considerably augmented by harvesters, swarmed the hotel and its passages, being armed with their favourite 'springs of shillalah.' About eleven o'clock of night a formidable body of Tories, weaponed with rods of iron, made a very determined attempt to carry off some of the fugitive voters. A frightful encounter ensued and raged for about ten minutes ending by the Irish and their liberal friends driving away in all directions the courageous attacking party. Many on both sides were seriously injured, and the place was strewn with shillalahs and iron rods, and with hats, caps and other articles.[79]

If this was a far cry from Livsey and Crawford's calls for 'moral force', it suggested that in Rochdale at least, voteless Irish migrant labourers (industrial workers as well as seasonal agricultural *spailíni*) were prepared to join forces with local Chartists to promote their favoured 'Irish' candidate's success through robust street politics, an alignment quite different from that at nearby Manchester. Two Irishmen and an Englishman were later charged with assaulting a Tory voter and fined forty shillings each – fines which were paid by 'Sharman Crawford's Whig and Chartist friends'.[80]

At the nomination meeting, Livsey interrogated Fenton on his positions on the Charter and other radical demands, with almost universally negative responses; Crawford, wearing in his hat a red cockade with strawberry flowers and green leaves, gave a speech which made his commitments on these points clear and stressed the essential unity of Irish and English reforming objectives. The cockade combined the traditional liberal colour red with radical green elements; strawberries were symbolically associated with the Chartist land plan.[81] The following day's proceedings saw Crawford triumph with a poll of 399 votes to Fenton's 335, with no further public disturbances.[82] Disappointed Tories blamed their defeat on the 'strangely compounded gang of political partizans composed of Whigs, Radicals and Chartists', who had prevailed, according to the *Bolton Chronicle*, by 'intimidated by threats of personal attack, exclusive dealing, and other equally despicable proceedings'.[83] An analysis of the published poll-book indicates certain occupational patterns in voting – Fenton had clear majorities among 'gentlemen', bankers, lawyers and publicans, while Crawford dominated among those involved in the textile trades, including drapers, manufacturers, weavers and wool-staplers. Occupations that might have been susceptible to working-class 'exclusive dealing' pressures, such as boot and shoemakers, cloggers, grocers and shopkeepers, also tended to favour him, while all the town's confectioners voted for Fenton.[84] Crawford's election was widely celebrated in the town, and O'Connor was quick to assert that Crawford, along with John Fielden and General William Johnson at Oldham, had not been elected, as some papers had reported, as Whig-liberals; rather, he wrote in the *Northern Star,* 'we claim them as Chartists'.[85]

Universal suffrage, 1841–2

Sharman Crawford's election for Rochdale resulted in his return to the commons after a gap of four years. While he maintained a determination to pursue his personal agenda of Irish reforms, he also took his responsibilities to his Rochdale constituents and British democratic radicalism seriously. Unlike many other MPs who adopted a purely instrumental attitude towards those who returned them, Crawford reiterated his doctrine that, as the borough's representative, he would report annually to the people on his parliamentary performance and resign his seat if they were dissatisfied. This was similar to his father's stance as MP for Lisburn in the 1780s. He was also prepared to put questions to the town and tailor his votes accordingly, a pledge he kept in March 1842 by appearing at a public meeting organised by Livsey and Bright at which he defended his votes and undertook to advance popular opposition to the corn laws and income tax and in favour of the Charter.[86] Although by no means the most accomplished parliamentary orator, he was again an assiduous participant in debates; an *Economist* survey in 1843 found him to be the fourth most regular attendee of the twenty-six Lancashire members, voting in 120 of the 220 divisions that session.[87] He was described in 1850 as second only to Hume in his attention to the business of the house, and proven in 'his devotion, not only to the rights of his constituents, but to the rights of justice and reason, the rights of honesty and the dictates of conscience'.[88]

Well known as a practitioner and advocate of agricultural co-operation and equity between landlords and tenants, he had also previously taken a close interest in industrial conditions and living standards. In February 1838 he had chaired a committee of arbitration involving Belfast's magistrates, textile masters and representatives of the handloom weavers, to work out an agreed legislative instrument to regulate industrial relations in the town in place of employers' proposals that had sparked labour unrest. The weavers and magistrates had reached consensus, with Crawford regarded as an honest broker, only for the linen masters and their representative, Emerson Tennent, to later break the agreement and push for a much more punitive measure in 1839.[89] After his 1841 election, the Belfast handloom weavers presented Crawford was an address, 'expressive of their esteem for him as a landlord, a magistrate, as a politician' and noting that he had proved a 'friend and advocate of the working classes'. In their view the people were now coming to 'think for themselves' and were conscious that the distressed conditions suffered by weaving families arose from the high food prices and lack of demand for cloth caused by the corn laws, from the dissolution of the Linen Board, and from the disenfranchisement and swamping of the forty-shilling freeholders. They would celebrate his Rochdale election victory as their own:

> Rejoice, ye sons of the loom, rejoice!
> To tyrants never bend the knee;
> But join, with heart, and soul, and voice,
> For Sharman Crawford and liberty!

In response, Crawford welcomed the address from representatives of a labour movement that was non-violent and free from sectarianism, and he undertook to promote working-class interests, seek the abolition of the corn laws and advocate the allocation of garden plots to labourers, in addition to pursuing their enfranchisement.[90] If this represented an ameliorative strategy generally consonant with a flexible interpretation of liberal political economy, it was one the town's handloom weavers were still at this point prepared to engage with.

This positive relationship with the Belfast labour movement persisted: in 1844 it was to him and not the hostile borough MPs that the town's mill operatives sent their petition, signed by up to 10,000 workers, in support of the ten hours bill to reduce the hours of labour. In presenting their petition, Crawford observed that if the workers were properly represented in parliament, legislation shortening working hours would be passed; this placed him into conflict with his former colleague David Ross, who now felt obliged to defend the interests of Belfast's linenocrats as an MP for the borough.[91] Crawford later became a patron of the Belfast Working Classes Association, a philanthropic body set up in 1846 by the campaigning doctor A. G. Malcolm to lobby for improvements to the sanitary and working conditions of the poor, and which survived to 1875 until replaced by the more autonomous Working Men's Institute.[92]

Returning to Rochdale in summer 1841 Crawford spent some days visiting the working poor of the town in their own homes, talking to the labouring families about their 'wants and necessities', and making notes on social conditions.[93] His prioritisation of this drew admiration from the Operative Board of Trade in Dublin, which wished that all MPs, including their own, should show such interest in the lives of their poorer constituents.[94] Personal knowledge and experience of the conditions of the working classes in both industrial towns of Belfast and Rochdale would inform Crawford's parliamentary contributions in the coming sessions. His exposure of the appalling social misery in Rochdale was later cited as a stimulus to the formation in the town in 1844 of the pioneering Co-operative Society that would be emulated across the country as a mode of delivering cheap and unadulterated food to the working poor; Livsey was an active supporter of the new movement of the 'Rochdale pioneers' and for a time its treasurer.[95]

Crawford's participation in the commons as a 'Chartist' MP, in the abbreviated second session of 1841, began well. He took advantage of the debate on the new parliament's address to the crown to condemn the Opium War with China as unjust and murderous, and to reject Robert Peel's proposal for a sliding scale corn duty as wholly inadequate to the needs of the country. The popular demands for franchise reform, the ballot and shorter parliaments, and for amendment of the oppressive English poor law, had, he complained, been ignored.[96] Several days later he moved an amendment to the loyal address that reflected the Chartist position:

> the distress which your majesty deplores is mainly attributable to the circumstance of your whole people not being fully and fairly represented in this house; and that we feel it will be our duty to consider the means of so extending and regulating the suffrage, and of adopting such improvements in the system of voting, as will confer on the working classes that just weight in the representative body which is necessary to secure a due consideration of their interests, and which their present patient endurance of suffering gives them the strongest title to claim.

It was the exclusion of the great majority of the population that had, in his view, distorted

139

economic and fiscal policy, giving rise to 'what was properly denominated, class legislation, and that it had been productive of gross monopolies', of which the corn laws were just the most objectionable and oppressive. Predictably, however, given the newly-returned Conservative majority and amid signs of what the *Hansard* reporter noted as 'the house being very impatient', his amendment was lost by thirty-nine to 283 votes.[97] Ominously, the existing middle-class radical leadership of Roebuck, H.G. Ward and John Leader attacked him vehemently for not consulting them on his motion and walked out of the chamber in protest, but he drew vocal support from other radicals including the newly-elected Richard Cobden, who later observed with approval that the motion had stirred up working-class support for anti-corn law meetings.[98] Cobden briefly considered Crawford as a potential rival to O'Connor for British working-class leadership, observing to the Manchester League organiser Edward Watkin that in partnership with himself a reformist union of classes might then be possible.[99] There is no evidence this went beyond private musings, but O'Connor may have developed similar concerns that Crawford was being touted as a potential rival.

Despite the heavy defeat of the amendment, O'Connor was initially delighted by Crawford's readiness to sideline the old guard and force radical reform to the forefront of parliamentary attention. In his view, the Roebuck and Ward had exposed their shallowness and '[a]ll honour [was due] to Sharman Crawford the honest and true advocate of the people's right'.[100] Crawford's assertiveness also proved popular with provincial Chartist bodies, and with their newly-formed sister organisation in Dublin the Irish Universal Suffrage Association, whose anti-O'Connellite secretary, the woollen merchant Patrick O'Higgins, expressed praise for his fellow Irishman. Indeed, it was reported that the IUSA offered Crawford their presidency in 1841; although he declined, he appears to have maintained good relations with the Dublin body.[101] Like most Irish Chartists a supporter of 'simple repeal' and allied to O'Connor, O'Higgins nevertheless continued to hold Crawford in high personal regard and was attracted to his tenant-right campaign, publishing a short tract in support of it in 1845 that was denounced by O'Connell as incendiary and threatened with prosecution by the government.[102]

Shortly after Crawford made good on his promise to pursue the reform of the new English poor law, making use of information he had gleaned from observing conditions in Rochdale. Credible information had reached him, he told the prime minister, that:

> there were 136 persons living on 6d. per week, 290 on 10d., 508 on 1s., 855 on 1s. 6d. and 1,500 on 1s. 10d. per week. Of these five-sixths had scarcely a blanket among them; eighty-five families had no blanket, and forty-six families had only chaff beds, without any covering at all. When such a statement had been placed in his hands, he could not in duty to his constituents remain silent at his post. He was compelled to plead in their behalf for some measure of immediate relief.[103]

It was later reported that the government had hired a man to investigate Crawford's statistics, but no refutation was made public, and the *Times* declared his figures 'distressing'.[104] His principal target was the determination of the English Poor Law Commissioners to press ahead with the elimination of out-door relief, following their strict interpretation of the 1834 act. This was based, he argued, on a false understanding of poverty as arising from the profligacy of the poor themselves and hence requiring punishment. Social reality was different: the distress of many arose from economic circumstances outside their control. From this it followed that the punitive regime of the workhouses, which terrorised many of the deserving poor from seeking relief or subjected them to association with the vicious and destroyed their family ties, was immoral. After citing a long litany of cases of abuse of workhouse inmates (which he observed were now spreading to Ireland from England), he pleaded with the government to suspend urgently the indoor relief order in the face of unquestionable distress in the country. Aware that his motions were bound to fail in the face of majority Conservative and Whig support for the new poor law dogma of 'less eligibility', he nevertheless explained his philosophy for forcing divisions on such issues: only when 'the people saw there were men in the house ready to support their rights by advocating their measures' would effective out-of-doors pressure be aroused.[105] He would continue to make the case for radical reform of both the English and Irish poor laws in the following session. In Ireland, he observed, where a million pounds had been squandered on workhouses, the poor remained without effective assistance and were starving; the 1838 act was a failed experiment that needed fundamental rewriting.[106]

Crawford, in line with the few other pro-Charter MPs in the 1841 parliament, faced a dilemma on how practically to advance universal suffrage and its associated reforms. One option, favoured by O'Connor and the radical MP for Finsbury Thomas Duncombe, was to fall back on another mass petition to parliament for the Charter, backed up by threats of a national strike and civil unrest should it be ignored. While popular, this strategy had already failed once in 1839 and led to the debacle of the Newport rising and alienation of non-violent supporters of democratic reform. While not eschewing petitioning, Crawford's alternative was two-fold: to disrupt parliamentary business by filibustering on votes of supply while simultaneously calling up mass demonstrations of 'moral force' behind the Charter, and at the same time building (on the local Rochdale model) an alliance with middle-class radicals on the twin objectives of universal suffrage and repeal of the corn laws. With O'Connor proving strongly opposed to any such pact, and many working-class radicals deeply suspicious of what they saw as the bourgeois self-interest behind the League, this was to prove deeply divisive. Crawford, ever focused on the practical goal of getting reform legislation through parliament, lost sight of the autonomy of working-class political organisation through the National Charter Association (NCA) and its branches that was prioritised by O'Connor and his allies.

His partner in the new initiative was the Birmingham-based Quaker merchant and philanthropist Joseph Sturge, whom he appears to have met through the Anti-Corn Law League in 1839.[107] Sturge was a revered figure in the anti-slavery movement and one of the founding members of the League, but a late convert to universal suffrage. Previously a Benthamite 'rational reformer' and still an economic liberal, he told a fringe meeting of the League in November 1841 that he had been persuaded of the wisdom and necessity of universal suffrage by a recent visit to the United States, and now believed working-class enfranchisement essential for pursuing the moral reform of the country.[108] Sturge drew on support from the new weekly *Nonconformist* newspaper, edited by the former Congregationalist minister Edward Miall, who connected 'universal suffrage' with the campaigns for the abolition of church rates and ultimate disestablishment of the Church of England. The paper welcomed the League's acceptance of Sturge's motion as 'the first blush of dawn after a long political night [...] a courteous, manly, noble move [...] towards reconciliation with the labouring classes'.[109]

Crawford's participation in the planning of the new movement was at first impeded by an attack of typhus fever, apparently caught from a child sitting on his knee, which left him recuperating at Crawfordsburn in December 1841. Although in January some Tories 'industriously circulated a report' that he was dead, his illness was temporary.[110] Sturge pressed ahead with drawing up a declaration and circulating it for signatures, but the central premise was one already publicly stated by Crawford – that 'no subject of England can be constrained to pay aids or taxes even for the defence of the realm or support of the government, but such as are imposed by his own consent, or that of his representative in parliament'. The document, promoted by the northern 'moderate' reforming press, quickly started attracting signatures from supporters of the League, even if Cobden himself remained sceptical of its value.[111] If there was any doubt about Crawford's adherence it was scotched by his appearance at a meeting called by Sturge in London to promote 'the union of the middle and working classes' in February 1842. In an appeal to democratic liberalism Crawford insisted that their real class interests were shared:

> he rejoiced to think that there was a probability of obtaining what was so essential to the interests of the whole community – a complete union between the employing and the working classes or this country. It was essential to the prosperity of this country, that there should be unity and friendly feeling between them; and it was to be regretted that it had ever been interrupted. He hoped the time was coming when ill feeling would no longer exist. He considered that all their evils arose from class legislation – (hear, hear) – and that they never would be obviated till the whole people were fully and fairly represented in the house of commons – (cheers.) He considered that the corn law agitation and the agitation for an extended suffrage ought to go hand in hand together, and aid one another. Without that degree of union they could not expect to carry a repeal of the corn laws, nor could they expect any good legislation of any description. From the house of commons, constituted as it now is, they could expect no good measure, not till the people had the full power of electing their representatives (hear.)[112]

With Universal Suffrage Societies formed in Birmingham and Manchester, numbers of subscribers rising rapidly, and old Chartists such as Lovett, John Collins and Henry Vincent expressing interest, Sturge and Crawford felt there were grounds for optimism.[113] James Taylor, while a member of the NCA, wrote in support of the initiative as a sign of 'better times'.[114] The new movement attracted some popular press support: Joseph Livesey's weekly *The Struggle*, founded in late 1841 in Preston to promote corn-law repeal and temperance reform, and with a circulation estimated at 15,000, endorsed Sturge's new movement in terms aimed at a 'respectable' working-class readership (see Figure 19).[115] However, it was one matter to acquire for the declaration, as Sturge reported, 'a cordial concurrence [...] on the part of the middle classes, and especially of philanthropic and religious individuals', and another to pursue the 'general signature by the adult male population of this empire', which was likely to be regarded by many Chartists as infringing on their hard-won territory and potentially a capitulation to the capitalist masters of industry many held responsible for driving down urban living conditions.[116] If John Belchem's critique of the complete suffrage movement as embodying the 'unthinking arrogance' of middle-class reformers in assuming the right of leadership and control of democratic agitation has some validity, it perhaps overstates the gulf between Chartist and 'Complete Suffrage' political cultures, especially in places such as Rochdale where these still appeared to be compatible.[117]

Crawford's relationship with O'Connor had already become strained by November 1841 following another press war between Crawford and the Irish Repealers. Although he shared a deep antipathy towards O'Connell, the Chartist leader retained a firm adherence to the idea of simple repeal for Ireland, and sought to incorporate this into the NCA platform. He still esteemed Crawford as 'a personal friend, and political ally', but could not countenance his seeming apostasy on Irish self-government.[118] Nor was he prepared to offer any olive branch to 'complete suffrage', which he associated with the now defunct LPRA. Writing in the *Northern Star* on 18 December, he painted the incipient movement as a middle-class Whig plot to undermine the integrity of the Charter. Nothing coming out of the ACLL, and associated with what he depicted as its anti-democratic supporters, could benefit the working class: 'they would seduce us with individuals, using for that purpose the names of the best, such as Sharman Crawford, Mr Sturge, and Colonel Thompson'.[119] Bronterre O'Brien agreed that the League were 'as slippery as eels' and urged non-co-operation 'until they yield to the Charter suffrage'.[120]

Nevertheless, O'Brien, along with Lovett, Collins and Vincent, agreed to come to a conference convened by Sturge in Birmingham to work out a definitive 'complete suffrage' platform in April 1842.[121] After some protest over the body's reluctance to refer explicitly to the 'People's Charter', Lovett, on behalf of the working-class delegates, eventually endorsed the formation of the new National Complete Suffrage Union (NCSU) with Sturge as president, which took as its programme the six points of the original Charter, despite some middle-class misgivings about annual parliaments and payment of MPs in particular.[122] Bright's amendment for triennial elections was defeated, but Lovett reluctantly agreed that the name of the 'People's Charter' be omitted from the final resolutions.[123] Crawford (who attended along with his son Charles) undertook to act as the parliamentary voice of the NCSU, and sympathetic electors were urged to write to their MPs to request they support his forthcoming motion.[124] The adoption of a platform virtually indistinguishable from that of the NCA caused problems for O'Connor. Crawford had been careful to keep the Rochdale Chartists (whom Livsey had brought out strongly against the corn laws) appraised of his intentions and used them as a back-channel to the NCA's national convention.[125] O'Connor was even initially minded at that convention in April to move a vote of thanks to Crawford and the Rochdale men, but withdrew the former under criticism from more hardline members and adopted a harsher tone.[126] For his part, Bronterre O'Brien, while not prepared to follow Lovett and others into the NCSU, was defensive about his own readiness to engage in dialogue with 'the honest middle-class man' and prickly about O'Connor's criticism of him for doing so.[127]

Despite O'Connor's initial hesitation, the two movements now appeared on a collision course as the NCSU proceeded to create its own national network. The Chartist convention's efforts were focused on its national petition, already circulating for signatures since the previous November in the provinces, and which it planned to present to parliament on 3 May 1842. On Duncombe's advice a delegation was sent to seek to persuade Crawford to postpone his complete suffrage motion until after the petition had been submitted and debated. Meeting them at Westminster, Crawford at first assured the delegation that he was 'exceedingly anxious' to avoid any conflict and would communicate with the NCSU committee on how best to proceed. Almost immediately however, any potential compromise unravelled. On returning home he read a copy of the national petition, presumably given him by the delegates. It touched on two raw nerves; both the extraneous matter attached to the Charter and the tone of the petition deeply disturbed him. In line with O'Connor's preoccupations and a desire to win over Irish support, repeal of the Irish union had been added to the petition's demands, an accretion that Crawford believed undermined the UK-wide scope of the Charter, especially as affecting an equal redistribution of seats.[128] Secondly, he objected to the tone of the petition, which implied support for 'the physical-force system'. While he meant no offence to the convention, he believed them wrong in their tactics and would therefore not postpone his own motion.[129] While Crawford retained some friends within the mainstream Chartist body, this obstinate challenge to O'Connor's authority angered many others.

Consequently, on 24 April he brought forward as planned his own commons motion for reform of parliamentary representation. In what his supporters described as a 'very temperate, lucid, argumentative and eloquent' speech, he drew attention to numerous petitions already received by the house calling for universal suffrage, often alongside repeal of the corn laws, as well as the resolutions of the NCSU's Birmingham conference. The 1832 Reform Act had, he argued, woefully failed to end corruption, bribery and landed control of parliament; the consequence had been the betrayal of promises to bring peace, retrenchment and other reforms. Class legislation in taxation, the poor laws and the mistreatment of Ireland had continued unabated. Aware of his audience, he repeated the argument that universal male suffrage (excluding paupers, vagrants and the insane) would unite the industry of the country with its property to their mutual advantage and safety, depriving agitators of their power by doing justice to the working man. At the same time, the approach taken by the NCSU was a more acceptable one from what had gone before:

> I am fully aware that a weapon has been placed in the hands of the adversaries of reform by the injudicious proceedings which have been adopted at a former period by the out-of-door advocates of the principles which I have now brought before the house. The attempt to carry these measures by the action of violence and tumult threw back, very far indeed, the cause of reform, but I am not the organ of those who would act in that way [...] The first resolution of the conference of delegates declares that their object is to obtain a full, fair, and free representation of the people by Christian means alone, and this declaration was cordially joined in by all the delegates of the Chartist body who attended.

He followed with a jab against the 'extravagance of the demands' made in the forthcoming national petition. At the same time, the people could not be blamed for expressing justified anger while suffering under blatant class legislation, and any further refusal of just demands would invite further disturbances.[130]

His motion was strongly supported by the parliamentary radicals and O'Connell, and predictably was dismissed as a constitutional threat by government ministers, although a number of Whigs indicated they would support his motion with the intention of later cherry-picking the elements they thought safe to enact. Still, the minority of sixty-seven in favour was larger than expected (even in the absence of many Irish MPs), although still overcome by a majority of 226.[131] This meant that the national press took the motion seriously, even if most papers gave multiple reasons for declining to support it. For the

Morning Chronicle, Crawford's arguments about class legislation were irrefutable, although it doubted the safety of enfranchising the working class, which might swamp the 'intelligence' and damage the economy of the country: Britain should beware taking such a 'leap in the dark'.[132] The *Times* similarly admitted Crawford's case that the 1832 Reform Act had maintained many elements of the old aristocratic constitution and that arguments for its 'finality' were indeed untenable, but the paper argued that giving the vote to the ignorant and unpropertied would only make things much worse, and pointed out the inconsistency of not also seeking the vote for women.[133] Even the *Dublin Monitor*, previously a cheerleader for Crawford, now came out vocally against universal suffrage. True to its name, the *Northern Whig* seconded the London liberal press's criticisms and attacked Crawford for bringing forward the 'wholly impracticable' demands of the Charter.[134]

With Crawford's motion thus stymied, attention now shifted to the national petition, which was paraded through the streets of London and ceremoniously presented on behalf of the Chartist convention by Duncombe on 2 May and debated in the commons the following day. The petition claimed to bear 3,315,752 signatures (including 19,600 from Rochdale and 2,000 from Belfast), two and a half times more than the previous Chartist petition of 1839, and evidence, Duncombe asserted, of the 'manifold grievances and distresses' endured by the working classes.[135] Analysis of the petition suggests that, despite some anomalies, it was signed by upwards of a third of the adult population of Great Britain.[136] Crawford did not speak in the debate (for which he was criticised in the Chartist press), but did vote for Duncombe's motion for a full debate on the Charter – which was lost by forty-nine votes to 287.[137] Thus both parliamentary initiatives for democratic reform in 1842 were checked by conservative vested interests backed by the organs of liberal middle-class opinion, expressing class anxieties about the democratic demands of the lower classes.

Petitions and obstruction, 1842–4

The responses of the NCSU and NCA to these twin setbacks of Spring 1842 were different, although initially complementary and pragmatic. Despite their evident differences, O'Connor opted to place Chartist muscle behind Sturge's candidacy at the Nottingham by-election in August. After a heated contest that saw O'Connor active in street disturbances, Sturge won overwhelmingly a show of hands on the hustings, but lost narrowly at the poll to the Conservative proprietor of the *Times*, John Walter (who had taken a populist stance against the new poor law, and was later unseated for extensive bribery).[138] The collaboration evident at Nottingham was not to last, however, and later fell victim to O'Connor's erratic leadership. For Crawford, parliamentary logic now dictated preparing a legislative campaign with the NCSU's full support that he hoped would come to fruition in the next session (while in the meantime using debates on other issues such as the income tax to keep the suffrage question fresh and potentially win over converts).[139] This approach did not exclude peaceful agitation, and Crawford advised the NCSU that 'a greater impulse out of doors must first be obtained before our power in the house of commons can be increased in any great degree'.[140] By the end of the year, its 'missionaries' had established ninety branches, often with local nonconformist or temperance support, with particular strength in Scotland, the south-west, Yorkshire and the Midlands.[141]

The NCA resolved to keep its own agitation separate from that of the NSCU, and in a number of places its activists pressed for direct action through industrial sabotage and threats of violence. Although O'Connor did little to directly promote this campaign, political frustration and the social pressures arising from the harsh economic depression and consequent high unemployment and immiseration of 1842 led many workers to engage in politically-infused industrial action and confrontational street protests. In the Staffordshire collieries, anger provoked by lay-offs, wage cuts and the payment of wages through the exploitative 'truck system' (in kind), led to plugs being pulled from the boilers of steam engines, rendering them inoperable. As this form of industrial sabotage spread to other areas, it belatedly attracted support from the *Northern Star*. Across swathes of the industrial north of England and lowland Scotland in particular, class conflict between factory workers and their employers was exacerbated and confrontations with the police and military followed, with Chartist activists pressing home the message that economic grievances were bound up with the absence of political rights. O'Connor and the NCA still neglected to endorse calls for a political general strike, but arrests of local activists created more bitterness, which was often directed against the middle-class led NCSU and ACLL.[142] In turn this wave of industrial militancy further spooked potential supporters of democratic reform among the middle classes, thereby undermining the raison d'etre of the NCSU.[143]

In Rochdale, Crawford worked with his local allies to minimise the fall-out between the rival universal suffrage movements that was happening at the national level. Livsey had been threatened with prosecution for allegedly promoting a visit of the 'plug-drawers' to the town that had triggered a serious food riot and had been advised to leave under an alias by a friendly radical magistrate, but he soon returned. Benefitting from some favourable comments from Bronterre O'Brien, and the continuing confidence of the Dublin Chartists, Crawford also returned to the borough in August 1842 to present his report on the session to an open-air public meeting chaired by Livsey, followed by a dinner with the town's middle-class liberals.[144]

Crawford and Sturge then proceeded to tour lowland Scotland to stir up support for complete suffrage, addressing large and appreciative crowds.[145] At Edinburgh, Crawford denounced the city's Whig MP T.B. Macaulay for impeding democratic reform and invoking a military despotism to protect property should the suffrage be extended, and quoted Richmond's 1783 letter to his father in defence of the consistency of radical reformers.[146] In the distressed cotton town of Paisley, free membership tickets for a NCSU branch were issued to unemployed workers following addresses by Crawford, Collins and Vincent.[147] Joseph Hume privately expressed support for the campaign, telling Crawford that '[i]f the Chartists would show a little more charity towards those who desire to effect the extension of suffrage (which they also desire) in their own way we might expect ere long to make that impression on the existing electors that would secure the extension of popular power in the house of commons.'[148] Not all went smoothly, however – at Dumfries supporters of O'Connor shouted down the NCSU speakers, and *Northern Star's* correspondent trusted this would be 'the last attempt of the vampires to seduce the good and true men of Dumfries from their duty'.[149] Nevertheless, the local press claimed that Crawford's presence had done much to 'heal the breaches' there between the middle and working classes.[150] At Dundee, however, Crawford's attempts to promote reforming unity were followed by acrimonious clashes between Chartists and Complete Suffragists during the ensuing municipal elections.[151]

Undeterred, Crawford put together a cheap pamphlet combining his public statements on the suffrage question for the NCSU, reiterating his case that the exclusion of the working classes from parliament was fundamentally unconstitutional. He was at pains to minimise the counter-argument that Chartist 'excesses' had rendered the case for radical reform illegitimate. While he continued to condemn violence and those who led the people towards it, he asked his readers to consider the underlying causes of unrest – the betrayal of the people by middle-class liberals in 1832 after using them to obtain their own ends, and the abnegation of leadership when popular social and economic grievances against monopolism were voiced. While he admitted that he thought some of the wording of the national petition impolitic, he affirmed that the reasons that so many had signed it were clear and justified. Even the disruption of League's meetings, while unwise, was understandable so long as middle-class activists kept aloof from franchise reform.[152]

How was complete suffrage to be attained given that fewer than ten MPs supported the Charter's principles in full? As things were, Crawford observed, the working-class movement stood alone in demanding their rights, aided only by a few individuals from the other classes with the moral courage to support them. However, the requisite mobilisation of moral power needed cross-class collaboration and this in turn would depend on persuasion and conversion. While the Charter remained the foundation document of reform, Crawford concluded that the name 'Chartist' was, in the eyes of those who needed to be won over, tainted with the outbreaks of violence; rallying around the banner of 'complete suffrage' thus offered a tactical alternative that was more likely to attain the same end.[153]

Crawford was absent from the disastrous second conference of the NCSU which Sturge summoned at Birmingham in the last week of 1842, arguing that as an MP he should not impinge on its debates but perhaps also thinking that it was poorly timed and planned.[154] The conference was intended to restore the spirit of collaboration evident the previous April and at the Nottingham election, but it was swamped by avowed Chartists, who were elected en masse by the local representative meetings that they dominated, despite the NCSU's attempts to reserve some places for the nominees of parliamentary electors. It was not, however, the openly hostile O'Connor who gave the conference its death blow, but the previously supportive Lovett, in a move described by the *Times* as 'a complete stunner'. Rejecting the proposal of a 'bill of rights' recommended by the council of the NCSU that would incorporate the six points but avoid using the name, Lovett moved an amendment insisting the bill be based explicitly on the People's Charter. Strongly supported by O'Connor his motion was carried by a large majority. Over the protests of the 'Sturgeites' the NCSU had suddenly been severed from its purpose and the 'Brummagem parliament' broke up in defeat after Sturge and his allies walked out.[155]

O'Connor followed up this victory by seeking to disrupt the local Rochdale radical alliance. Speaking there before a large and raucous crowd in January 1843, he, in what the *Manchester Guardian* described as a 'wild speech', damned the League and threatened violence if its aims were pursued to success. Rochdale, he proclaimed, would no longer be safe territory for its activities.[156] However, Crawford's local popularity proved more resilient than O'Connor hoped, as did agitation there against the corn laws. Its MP was to present a petition signed by more than 10,000 residents for their repeal later that year.[157] The attacks may themselves have been an attempt to distract attention from the disintegration and infighting that then plagued the NCA, and which led to the dismissal of the *Northern Star's* editor, William Hill, in July.[158] Meanwhile, the NCSU attempted to revive itself with public 'soirees' in Leeds and Bradford in the spring, although the *Northern Star* sneered about low attendances at these.[159] It discussed fielding thirty to fifty candidates at any future election to emulate O'Connell's tactic of pursuing the parliamentary balance of power, although with its limited popular support this seems a rather far-fetched ambition.[160] In Birmingham its supporters sought to initiate an 'electors league' to commit voters to support only candidates pledged to supporting Crawford's universal suffrage motion, but with limited success.[161]

The fall-out from the Birmingham convention did not end Crawford's attempts to enact the central tenets of the Charter. His first attempt to raise the suffrage question in the 1843 session was stymied by parliamentary manoeuvring to 'count out' the house, and which he blamed more on the Whigs than the government.[162] Nevertheless, he proceeded to undermine Charles Buller's motion to relieve distress through the 'systematic colonization' overseas of the UK's alleged 'excess population', with what one paper described as a 'Chartist' amendment. Crawford moved:

> That the resources derivable from the lands, manufactures, and commerce of the United Kingdom, if fully brought into action, are adequate to afford the means of giving employment and supplying food to the whole population; and that, therefore, before any measures be adopted for removing to foreign lands any portion of that population, it is the first duty of this house to take into consideration the measures necessary for the better application of these resources to the employment and support of the people.

For Crawford, opposition to the Malthusian projects of the emigrationists was intimately connected to the need to give the working classes a voice in parliament.[163] This intervention drew praise from Chartists in both Rochdale and Dublin.[164]

He moved his parliamentary reform motion again in May 1843, justifying 'complete suffrage' on historicist grounds as a restoration of the ancient constitution of England.[165] While supported by some other radicals, the debate was marred by a direct attack on the motion by his former Belfast confederate, David Ross, who alleged that he had heard speakers at northern English suffrage rallies call for the destruction of the factories and an end to 'all the follies of monarchy'. Crawford and Duncombe scrambled to deny that such words had been used at meetings they had attended, but the damage had been done, and the motion was lost by thirty-two to 101 votes.[166] A bill he proposed for triennial parliaments was also lost in the commons in June.[167] His efforts at least regained him some renewed Chartist support – at a meeting at the People's Hall in Wednesbury in Staffordshire in June he was loudly cheered and praised for his disinterested patriotism, and Vincent's lectures in support of the NCSU and Crawford's strategy were reportedly well-received in Liverpool.[168] Meanwhile, Rochdale Chartists continued to regard their 'excellent member' as the obvious conduit for their memorial in support of the political prisoners incarcerated after the summer 1842 strikes.[169]

At the same time, the lukewarm (at best) support of the Anti-Corn Law Leaguers for franchise reform undermined the strategy. Despite assuring Sturge that he would back the discussion of Crawford's first 1843 suffrage motion, Cobden was silent during the debate and failed to vote; he observed that he was 'sorry that circumstances forced the whole of the points of the Charter upon you – especially as it has not had the effect of conciliating the Chartists, or rendering them a tittle more friendly to the complete suffragists than if you had taken your ground upon manhood suffrage only'. The fault lay in his view with the 'old Chartist party', who had 'completely alienated the middle class who are of course the electors'.[170] Cobden was also at odds with Sturge at the time over whether differential duties should be maintained against slave-produced sugar from Cuba and Brazil, while the O'Connellites were distracted by the Repeal 'monster meetings', leaving Crawford fatally isolated in his parliamentary campaign.[171]

Although increasingly preoccupied by Irish business in 1843–4, Crawford remained loyal to the principles of complete suffrage, and was working out a new line of attack for the next session. Experience of having been at the receiving end of procedural manipulation had shown him that the only effective way to put pressure on the government would be to target the vote of supplies for state expenditure with delaying amendments to draw attention to popular petitions for reform. This was, he now argued, the only constitutional pathway still open, as 'the people should have the power to close their purse-strings till their grievances are redressed, and the forms of the house give them the means of doing so'. In essence he was proposing, thirty years before the adoption of the tactic by Charles Stewart Parnell and his allies, a campaign of parliamentary obstruction to force reform on to the legislative agenda. But this tactic would only work if mass public opinion could be mobilised in its support, with sufficient petitions bearing numerous signatures coming in and if enough sympathetic MPs were ready to show sufficient moral courage in the face of the 'obloquy and reproach' of their peers and join him in taking such obstructive action.[172] A further letter offered some elaboration – while an indefinite suspension of supplies might not be feasible, radicals should engage in a 'war of reduction' on chosen items, especially cutting wasteful spending on the standing army through forcing divisions on each line of its budget.[173] Seeking to garner support for this approach, Sturge called with O'Connell in Dublin (who was now briefly aligned with Crawford on 'federalism' as an alternative to repeal) before travelling north to Crawfordsburn.[174] Sturge also brought the remnants of the NCSU national committee into line with Crawford's new strategy, and provincial committees, including the one in Rochdale, followed suit.[175]

Crawford's suggestion of a national convention of reformers from Britain and Ireland to meet in parallel with parliament met with support from sections of the press.[176] Even in the absence of such backing, he was prepared to take his stand against the raising of extra revenue to pay for the coercion of Ireland.[177] Most reforming MPs were sceptical, while O'Connor continued to criticise 'Crawfordism' as a deviation from true Chartism, but Crawford's supporters found grounds for optimism behind what appeared the 'forlorn hope' of his plan in reports of enthusiastic support from meetings in the midlands, north and Scotland.[178] At Rochdale, a public meeting endorsing his interruption of supplies strategy was seconded by 'a working man, who made a very excellent speech, which was repeatedly cheered by the whole assembly'.[179]

Still unsure of the extent of popular support, he proceeded to implement his campaign as soon as the 1844 session opened. At the 'request of his constituency at Rochdale', he moved first an amendment to the government's self-congratulatory address in answer to the Queen's speech for an inquiry into the people's grievances. Criticised by the prime minister for seeking to undermine the conventional forms of parliament, the amendment was lost by twenty-nine votes to 285.[180] The debate was followed by meetings in London organised by Sturge and intended to provide Crawford with the support he insisted was essential for the success of obstructionism. But like the Birmingham conference, the last of these was deliberately sabotaged and ended in fiasco:

> The proceedings were violently interrupted, and at last abruptly brought to a conclusion by the interference of Mr O'Connor and the Chartists, who said they were determined not only to have the charter, but the very name if it! The scene is said by the reporters to have been indescribable. Mr Crawford then, of course, dissolved the meeting.[181]

To the *Leeds Times*, O'Connor was guilty of 'blackguardism'.[182] The sympathetic *Bradford Observer* similarly lamented the consequences of the Chartist insistence on their '*shibboleth*' and undermining of any popular manifestations behind Crawford. The consequence would be inevitable defeat, albeit not without some moral compensations:

> It requires the nerve of a martyr to contemplate the task of opposing this huge iniquity in the house; and it requires an almost superhuman love to humanity, and an almost superhuman amount of pity for its woes, and patience with its follies, to be able to persevere in serving it, in the face of such suicidal madness as has been exhibited at the meetings referred to.[183]

At a follow-up meeting in London, Bronterre O'Brien and Lovett agreed to support Crawford's efforts to stop the supplies, but only if this was done explicitly in the name of the People's Charter.[184]

It was against the troubled background of this stand-off that he proceeded with his attempt to impede the vote of supplies on 6 February 1844. Accusing the house of supporting class legislation, he insisted that an inquiry be established into reform of the representation, which must accede to the will of the people made through petitioning. Refusal would lead to the radicals raising repeated amendments against the votes for supply, until the house saw sense.[185] The motion was lost by twenty-two to 130, with one paper echoing Peel's criticism that it appeared to impeach the whole frame of society and seek a social as well as a political revolution.[186] Few Irish MPs were present to support Crawford, with more following Smith O'Brien's call to boycott parliament in protest against the state trial of O'Connell than were ready to listen to the Catholic Bishop of Galway's plea that they support the supplies campaign.[187]

This defeat seemed emphatic, but the motion was intended solely as the opening salvo of a campaign; a series of other divisions on the army and navy supplies followed, but with diminishing minorities. Radical hostility towards aggressive British imperialism in Sindh and the Punjab, encouraged by Crawford's speeches criticising 'the bloody, unjust, and unnecessary wars that had taken place in India', gave some impetus to public meetings in the north and Scotland held to gather petitions, while at the same time antagonising British imperialist feeling. An Edinburgh petition endorsing Crawford was reported to have 15,000 names on it.[188] His supporters remained confident that the public would eventually rally behind his 'noble' campaign.[189]

However, Chartist antagonism against the NCSU again erupted in a number of places and frustrated further attempts a coalition-building. In Rochdale, the formation of a branch supporting him was interrupted by Samuel Kydd, a Chartist 'missionary' from Glasgow, insisting that the Charter was the only legitimate foundation for popular reform. Amidst the uproar that followed, Livsey struggled to calm fratricidal tempers, but feared that 'the working men had damned their own cause by their division that night'. [190] Although temporarily successful in soothing the situation, a second meeting broke down as Kydd and his supporters attacked the 'Sturgeites' amid chaotic scenes. The *Manchester Guardian* reported that 'the greater part of the Chartists appeared to be lads from thirteen to eighteen years of age' (although there had also been a group of young female Chartists who sang a hymn about the Newport martyrs); for the *Northern Star,* this amounted to a famous victory over the town's 'Shoy-Hoy' faction.[191] Similar interventions upset NCSU rallies in Leeds and Finsbury, leading the *Nonconformist* to denounce O'Connor as a demagogic agent of Toryism.[192]

Crawford attempted to rescue the deteriorating situation by publishing in March a public letter 'to the unenfranchised people of Great Britain and Ireland', in which he lamented that parliamentary sympathy for his amendments on the supply votes was ebbing in the face of insufficient demonstrations of outdoor support. His argument was tinged with despair, for although 'most honourable efforts have been made in some localities to give me an effective support, the great mass of the nonrepresented have made no move [and] till such a move be made any attempt to stem the power of class-legislation is futile'.[193] While the *Nonconformist* asserted that he had mapped the pathway for a future obstructionist campaign, the *Northern Star* blamed him for his own failure; in seeking to 'pull down the Chartist flag' and seeking to set up his own party he had brought failure upon himself. He should now confess his error and fall back into the Chartist ranks.[194]

Faced with the 'utter failure' of his 1844 campaign, and with his wife now dangerously ill, Crawford withdrew from parliament for a period and travelled back to Crawfordsburn.[195] Given his obstinate temperament, however, this pause did not last long, and he returned to the commons in May to propose another ill-fated bill to extend the parliamentary suffrage to all adult men. Under questioning, he was now ready to admit that 'although he did not include women in this measure he was not prepared to say that women should not in some cases possess the suffrage' – an advanced position for the time, albeit latent in nature.[196] Although checked in all his moves, and with none of the promised O'Connellite support, he admitted to Sturge that he remained reluctant to abandon a cause to which he had committed himself.[197] But with the movement for democratic reform deeply divided and in the doldrums, and middle-class indifference painfully displayed by Sturge's humiliating third place in the 1844 Birmingham by-election, he opted not to raise the question in the subsequent sessions, apart from a symbolic amendment to Lord John Russell's motion on the state of the country in May 1845 to 'give immediate attention to the claims so repeatedly urged in the petitions of the people for an extension of the parliamentary suffrage'.[198]

Sturge's memoirs later reflected on the causes of their joint failure:

> The great bulk of the working classes, with the glamour of delusion still before their eyes, had committed themselves to other guidance. The middle classes, whose patriotism is seldom very adventurous, studious of their own ease and profits, morbidly sensitive to ridicule, and scared by the fear of political disturbances, regarded the question with increasing apathy, the more especially as they saw in the growing strength of the Anti-Corn Law League the prospect of another speedy remedy for the grievances which pressed most heavily upon themselves.[199]

With attendances at meetings falling, Sturge stepped back from national campaigning, and Crawford was distracted by domestic concerns and then largely turned his legislative energies elsewhere.[200]

Although stymied in his campaigns for democratic reform, Crawford never abandoned his belief that radical change was possible and indeed could only be effectively carried through parliament. This confidence to some extent reflected his own class background: as a landed gentleman (however heterodox in his opinions) he was at ease among the London social elite. Reflecting this, in 1843 he commissioned a full-size portrait from the established society artist John Prescott Knight (Figure 20).[201]

Knight's portrait, which was exhibited at the Royal Academy before travelling to Crawfordsburn, captures the political intensity of Sharman Crawford as an MP in his early sixties. Pictured seated informally, he looks towards the viewer intently, while at the same time appearing impatient to return to reading a volume he has bookmarked with one finger, presumably a text being consulted for preparation of a speech or public letter. The image parallels a description of his appearance written by a sympathetic contemporary, who also noted his 'comprehensive' preparations for his regular parliamentary interventions:

> His personal appearance has something about it commanding, although nothing strikingly prepossessing. In stature he is decidedly over the middle height and tolerably erect in his figure; his form is slender in the extreme, and he is generally habited in a black frock-coat, buttoned up very closely over the chest up to the neck. His forehead is rather lofty but not particularly indicative of great intellect, while his head is covered with a profusion of jet black hair, which is well arranged, and looks remarkably well over his marble-like brow. His eyes, of a dark hue, are rather large and expressive, his nose is prominent, and his mouth strongly defined. The form of his face, which is particularly pale and slightly pitted with small-pox, is somewhat thin and angular. There is generally a very pensive expression hanging about his features, and there seems an air of melancholy in the cast of his eyes. He does not, from all appearance, possess very good health, although he is generally very regular in his attendance at the house.

Continuing his commentary, John Evans reflected on the weaknesses of his parliamentary performances, which tended to undermine his intentions and which contrasted with his much more effective engagement with supportive mass meetings:

> When Sharman Crawford rises to address the house, his modesty and lack of confidence appears a great barrier to his making any decided impression upon the minds of his hearers. He is neither energetic nor animated, and the slow, quiet tones of his voice scarcely fill the place. His action too, is cold and monotonous, a feeble up-and-down swing of the right arm, and an occasional movement of his head, composing his principal movements from the beginning to the end of his oration. His voice is tolerably clear, but neither musical nor sonorous. He generally, however, commands the attention of the honourable members, and is heard throughout his speech, which usually occupies some half or three-quarters of an hour, with respect, and all the silence that the house of commons can maintain.

Despite these limitations, he could not be challenged on his mastery of the details of his areas of expertise, and his patience and equanimity in the face of setbacks was admirable:

> he always preserves his temper, and [...] he never allows his feelings to get the better of his judgment, or show any personal animosity to an opponent. [...] The equanimity of Mr Crawford's temper certainly often gives him a great advantage over his opponents, and with

his natural modesty and humanity of disposition, there is no man incurs less of the ire of honourable members.[202]

Although created ostensibly as a private family artefact, by autumn 1844 Knight's image of Crawford was circulating more widely in the public realm, thanks to a mezzotint engraving of it produced by Thomas Goff Lupton, copies of which were offered for sale in Belfast at fifteen shillings apiece.[203] A cruder and cheaper autograph woodcut print of Lupton's image was subsequently produced for sale to his less well-heeled admirers (Figure 21).[204] There was clearly some market for Crawfordiana and what it epitomised, even if this was geographically and socially limited.

Federalism and the Irish question, 1843–8

In the wake of the Whig defeat at the 1841 general election, O'Connell had again turned his attention to 'outdoor' agitation in Ireland for repeal of the union. Initially his focus lay on maximising the advantage to his movement of the belated passage of the Irish Municipal Reform Act of 1840, through securing control of the reformed urban corporations, especially that of Dublin, which he was to represent as lord mayor in 1841–2. Having achieved this, he renewed the Loyal National Repeal Association and its local auxiliaries in preparation for a new popular campaign that he intended to equal or excel that for Catholic emancipation in the 1820s. In early September 1842 he instructed his personal secretary, William O'Neill Daunt, to start making 'arrangments [sic] for opening the campaign of agitation', drawing on the support of the Catholic clergy and a newly appointed network of parochial 'Repeal wardens'.[205] By the time of his Mansion House speech of 28 February 1843, proclaiming a new crusade for 'simple repeal' to be attained during that 'Repeal year', fresh ground had been laid for a national mobilisation.[206]

Crawford had previously criticised O'Connell for hypocritically soft-pedalling repeal while seeking government patronage, a charge he reiterated in October 1841 along with warnings of the counterproductive dangers of its agitation. O'Connell was alleged to have described Crawford as an 'Anglo-Saxon rat' in his response, and Tom Steele whipped up '*bitter contemptuous resolutions*' on his conduct from the London Repealers.[207] However the charge was clearly no longer valid by spring 1843. The renewed repeal campaign posed particular problems for Crawford: he could not endorse it and remain consistent with his previous politics, but to oppose it completely would associate him with an intransigent unionism that was clearly at odds with majority opinion in Ireland and which he had previously condemned in 1833–5. He retained an allied constituency in Dublin in the shape of the Irish Universal Suffrage Association, who were bitterly opposed to O'Connell for his past betrayals on democratic reforms while at the same time also highly sensitive to charges of unionism, while the northern Protestant radicals were deeply alarmed at O'Connell's unleashing of Catholic majoritarianism.[208] At the same time, there appeared some scope for rebuilding bridges, as his proposals for a practical fixity of tenure for tenant farmers were proving popular on repeal platforms, as was his consistent opposition in parliament (from which most Repealers were absent in 1843) to any coercion or repression of the Repeal movement.[209] One Repeal versifier going by the name of John Lennon urged that:

> The sweet voices of Erin our Crawford conjure,
> Hope lives in affection eternally pure –
> Love, truth and experience on him, will prevail,
> To abandon the Saxon for Grania-Uaile.[210]

There was little real chance of Crawford being so conjured to join the Repeal Association, notwithstanding O'Connell's renewed invitation issued in summer 1843.[211] But he felt the need to offer some constructive alternative in the face of the mass participation in the 'monster meetings' and what he believed to be the inherent threats arising from them of violent outbreaks and state repression. The passage of the Irish Arms Bill, which introduced arbitrary search powers for the constabulary and draconian punishments for possession of illegal weapons, pushed him into action, as he stated that 'he would not be a party to a charter of slavery against his country'. Such coercive measures would also, he feared, embolden clearing landowners to pursue further mass evictions against a defenceless peasantry. He told the commons that a union maintained by such means ought not to be, and could not be, continued.[212] Exasperated by the government's assertion that concession was at an end and O'Connellism must be put down, he stated with some emotion at a Whig party meeting on 17 July:

> Let the consequences be what they might he would join his countrymen in whatever constitutional movements they might make to obtain its [the union's] dissolution. Hitherto he had looked upon the advocacy of repeal as a wrong course; but in the existing state of affairs in Ireland he would not say that his countrymen should not withdraw their minds for a season from such engrossing topics and direct their undivided energies to securing a repeal of the union.[213]

However, he opted not to join the Repeal Association, but to return to the alternative ideas he had articulated at length a decade previously.

Crawford's answer to the dilemma thus lay in 'federalism', a term he first articulated in a letter to the *Dublin Monitor* in July 1843 in response to an article advocating it. He stressed that this position was in continuity with the proposals for a 'local legislative body' combined with continuing 'imperial' representation that he had maintained since 1833, but he now emphasised the high degree of autonomy a local legislature should have in making Irish laws, with no British law having validity there unless confirmed by it. Unlike O'Connell's rash 'simple repeal' scheme, such a measured proposal would, he hoped, receive support from 'all real friends of freedom in the United Kingdom', while meeting the just grievances of Repealers without the risks that might lead to full separation.[214]

O'Connell's initial response to this letter was conciliatory, but with a continued insistence that Crawford join the Association as a first step towards finding common ground, as had Catholic federalists such as Thomas O'Hagan and Bishop Kennedy of Killaloe.[215] Perhaps surprisingly, this stance was echoed by the *Nation*, the weekly mouthpiece of the 'Young Ireland' group of advanced nationalists, who praised Crawford and stated that the federalists had 'principles identical with those professed by the Repealers, and that [they] will, eventually, and of [their] own free consent, merge with the great national confederation'.[216] Thomas Davis, the paper's chief leader writer, had previously considered federalist ideas himself, at least as a transitional step to full repeal, and regarded the federalists as 'a body of educated men who wish us well'; he later met with Crawford and his Belfast associates in October 1844 in the hope of negotiating with them a workable joint plan.[217]

In his answer to O'Connell's latest invitation, Crawford put aside the acerbic tone of previous exchanges, and, while declining to join a body whose principles were not his own, left open the space for further dialogue. What he sought, he told O'Connell, was a sustainable system of self-government, based on a principle which would later be termed that of 'subsidiarity':

> The principle of self-government by representation should be carried out through every institution of the state; and local taxation, whether into parish, a county, or a town, should be imposed, and managed, by the bye-laws affecting that locality enacted by a body representing the locality which that taxation or those laws affect, and the whole kept under the control and regulation by the central power of imperial representation. This, in my judgment, is the principle of the British constitution – it is the principle of the corporate system. It is the only true foundation of all representative government.[218]

Any immediate opportunity to debate this concept this was squeezed out by the demands on O'Connell of the outdoor repeal campaign until after the government's proclamation of the Clontarf monster meeting planned for 7 October 1843 and its subsequent initiation of legal proceedings against him for sedition. Rather than risk a potentially violent confrontation with the state, which it was now clear would not bow to popular pressure as it had in 1829, O'Connell suspended the campaign and began exploring alternatives, leaving open a possible compromise.[219] When the next session opened Crawford urged the government to drop its anti-repeal statement from the Queen's speech and rejected its case that the notices calling on people to assemble in 'military array' at Clontarf contained anything illegal.[220]

An Irish federalist group began to cohere in the hope of offering an alternative to the stark alternatives of unionism and full independence and produced a 'remonstrance' to draw attention to itself in August 1843.[221] The federalists now including a number of liberal Ulster Protestants previously active in the UCA, such as David Ross and Charlemont's son Henry Caulfeild, who cited Crawford as having persuading them of its viability.[222] From within the Repeal Association, Fr Thaddeus O'Malley insisted in December 1843 that it was an 'open question' and one that he still wholeheartedly supported:

> My impression is, that the disrelish for federalism, so far as it has shown itself, is mainly attributable to a misconception of it – to a vague notion of its implying an admission of inferiority to England; whereas as Mr Crawford himself shows [...] it implies no such thing. I, for my own part, will do what I can to remove that misconception, for I have a profound conviction that federalism is the position we should take up, as being at once the most attractive of friends and the most terrible against enemies [...][223]

A number of pro-repeal writers, including the Catholic journalist and repeal warden Miles Keon, also published views sympathetic to Crawford's arguments for a 'third course'.[224] The federalist position attracted the strong support of the *Dublin Monitor*, although the *Northern Whig* remained sceptical about Crawford's schemes for 'paper parliaments'.[225]

With O'Connell at least temporarily softening his statements on federalism in later 1843, as suited his political tactics in the wake of the Clontarf debacle, an opportunity for collaboration seemed to present itself.[226] Having been burned by previous experience, Crawford and his northern allies still refused to join the LNRA.[227] Rather, they turned to refining what federalism actually meant (especially on the crucial definition of 'local' legislation) and to attracting supporters in both Ireland and Great Britain. Crawford was fully aware that to succeed he would need to persuade not just the O'Connellites but elements of the British political establishment and Irish Whigs; as he noted in a draft speech, liberals should support it, especially those 'who say the people are the source of all legitimate power'. [228]

He was also aware of the need to at least attempt to win over Irish unionists. In an open letter in January 1844 he restated his argument that, whatever its intentions, the union had failed to give Ireland equal rights within the UK, instead imposing on it subordinating and biased legislation which had been pushed through by ignorant English majorities. It was this misgovernment which had forced the Irish people into becoming repealers; the solution lay not in seeking the chimera of 'identification' or full integration into the UK (as Ireland's unique circumstances he now saw made this impossible), but in implementing the safest mode of repeal – that was, through a federal constitution maintaining the British connection through Irish participation in an 'imperial' legislature as well as through the joint crown.[229]

Initial responses to this appeal were not promising. Presaging the arguments later rehearsed in the home rule debates from the 1870s, the *News-Letter* identified what it saw as the crucial weaknesses in any federal scheme: it would prove impossible to limit the powers claimed by an Irish parliament, and there was no independent tribunal to adjudicate in cases of dispute between it and Westminster; any constitutional concession would merely encourage Irish separatists; there was no more sense (and much more danger) in devolving local powers to a Dublin 'parliament' than allocating them to enhanced county grand juries. It went on to argue that, in the case of the 'reserved' power of going to war, the imperial parliament must also have supreme control over taxation if Ireland was not to have the ability to undermine the crown's ability to wage it.[230]

Federalist answers to these and other objections were deferred in the early months of 1844 while Crawford pursued his ill-fated 'stopping the supplies' campaign in pursuit of democratic reform in parliament, and Ireland was fixated with the drama of O'Connell's state trial and brief imprisonment in Dublin's Richmond Bridewell for seditious conspiracy.[231] Crawford declined to attend the banquet held to celebrate O'Connell's release after his successful appeal in September, but he expressed sympathy with his victimisation at the hands of an unconstitutional and biased legal system, and hoped that in future they could work together 'in a common struggle for national regeneration'.[232]

O'Connell responded directly in his speech at the banquet, assuring him again that not only were there federalists in the Association, but that he himself was now prepared to adopt such an option:

> We prefer – most of us – prefer the simple repeal of the Act of Union; but there is not one of us that would not be content to repeal the Act of Union, and substitute a federal parliament (hear, hear.) Not one. I don't think federalism to be the best; but I was never one of those who had such an overweening opinion of the infallibility of my own judgment, not readily to yield to argument, and co-operate with any man that thinks better. I am ready to join with the

federalists to repeal the Act of Union, and obtain, in the words of Mr Sharman Crawford, the power for Irishmen to make laws to bind Ireland.

He proposed Grey Porter, a young Fermanagh Protestant landowner and self-declared federalist who had joined the LNRA, and who had previously published a rather rambling book promoting a 'local legislature', to take a lead in negotiations.[233] Porter was preparing a new pamphlet on federalism, although this turned out to be lacking in precise details and was rather derivative, and he appears to have taken little part in what followed.[234] In taking this policy departure, O'Connell may have been recognising the need to rebuild bridges with patriotically-minded liberals after the polarising rhetoric and implicit threat of violence in the monster meetings had led to an unstable dead end, a point pressed on him by some correspondents.[235] Tory critics, meanwhile, dismissed his lionising of the insignificant Porter and adoption of the 'humbug' of federalism as merely an expedient ruse to ensure the continuing flow of the 'Repeal rent' due in November.[236]

Privately, O'Connell took a more cautious view of the federalist option, at least until its precise content was clear. He wrote to Smith O'Brien, who had recently joined the Repeal Association:

> The first step, will be for the federalists to display themselves. The second to appoint a committee of arrangement at which you and my son John should attend to secure us all from any compromise tending to render precarious the right of Ireland to 'legislative self-protection'. I do believe the men who are *about* to be prominent and sincere and inclined to go the full necessary length with us. Of course our duty is to avoid every delusion. And as to any compromise, *that* is not to be thought of.[237]

Subsequent criticism of the idea of federalism in the *Morning Chronicle* had the effect of rallying much of Irish repeal opinion behind O'Connell in this initiative, and the *Freeman's Journal* expressed optimism that northern Presbyterians might now follow the Anglicans Sharman Crawford and Grey Porter into the repeal camp.[238] Well informed observers believed that the federalists were a substantial and potentially influential group. Davis noted optimistically that 'the wealthiest citizens of Dublin, Cork and Belfast, many of the leading Whig gentry and barristers, and not a few Conservatives of rank, hold federalist opinions. They include Episcopalians, and Roman Catholics, Repealers and Anti-Repealers'; he acquired a list of eighteen Irish peers and numerous MPs and other influential men who were believed to support it.[239] The Catholic Whig Thomas Wyse was confident that seventeen MPs (including himself) would back a federalist settlement.[240]

In a long letter from Derrynane on 2 October, O'Connell set out what he believed the federalist position to be – essentially identical to the 'simple repeal' platform except on the specific powers granted to the Irish parliament and continuing Irish participation in a 'congressional or federative parliament' in London. He declared himself open to discussing details with the federalists on both these heads.[241] At the same time, as he told FitzPatrick, it was essential to avoid committing to any potentially divisive details until it was clear the movement would accept the principles of federalism.[242] Still impatiently awaiting the federalists' response, on 12 October he publicly declared in his 'Derrynane manifesto' his new-found 'preference for the federative plan, as tending more to the utility of Ireland and to the maintenance of the connection with England than the mode of simple repeal', noting the areas of 'imperial' concern in which Ireland would have 'her fair share and proportion of representation and power'.[243] This was taking a calculated risk give the uneasiness within the movement's ranks on the subject, even if he still reserved the right to reject any specific scheme once this was tabled, but he hoped a successful rapprochement with the liberal federalists might win over some 'great Whig leaders' and force the government's hand in coming to terms on self-government.[244]

O'Connell finally received privately the first draft of the federalists' plan on 20 October and wrote to Smith O'Brien to give his views on it. Although the public face of the movement, he noted, Crawford was only one of a group of associates behind the paper, who were led in Dublin by the Catholic merchant William Murphy of Smithfield, the 'principal "brains carrier" of the Irish Whigs', and the wealthy Presbyterian coach-builder Thomas Hutton (brother of the former Whig MP for the city).[245] The northerners would host the next federalist meeting on 26 October, including Crawford, Caulfeild and Ross as well as O'Hagan, who O'Connell regarded as his confidential agent in the matter. He admitted he saw promise in the paper, but it was a 'skeleton' that required detail to give it 'nerve and sinew and flesh', and he promised not to commit to anything publicly without O'Brien's consent.[246]

While the O'Connellite provincial press mostly fell into line with his letters on federalism, accepting the Liberator's authority on the matter, it was clear that not everyone within the movement was happy.[247] The editor of the *Nation*, Charles Gavan Duffy, gave voice to this unease on 11 October, when he warned O'Connell in a public letter that, while dialogue was welcome, '[t]he federalists are useful allies, but most unsafe leaders', and that the membership would not tolerate any concession of the reality for the 'mere shadow of repeal'. Moreover, he asserted that O'Connell was acting unconstitutionally in seeking to change policy on this crucial issue without full debate and agreement within the Repeal Association.[248] Duffy later recalled that his opposition arose not from any personal animosity with the federalists, but from a conviction that any such attempt at political juncture between them engineered by O'Connell would end in disaster. His letter, an open challenge to O'Connell's leadership, caught both the Liberator and some of his own Young Ireland colleagues off-guard, but was supported by many repeal activists.[249] O'Neill Daunt (who had sparred with Crawford in 1841 on this very issue) also expressed muted dissent from O'Connell's new official line in giving 'preference' to federalism but would not openly oppose his leader.[250]

O'Connell, who was acutely aware of such restiveness, expressed impatience at the delay in news from the Belfast meeting, suspecting 'it has gone off upon some crotchet of Sharman Crawford', or that it had 'been quashed by the Whigs in the Murphy line, and by the Tories and *crotchets* in the Protestant and radical sections'.[251] He instructed O'Neill Daunt to stall on the subject until he arrived in Dublin and the federalists had reported, reassuring him that even if his experiment in drawing them out failed, the Repeal movement would gain from being seen to offer conciliation.[252] The *Northern Whig* reported on 5 November that a 'federal declaration' prepared by Crawford, Caulfeild and others had in fact been sent to the Dublin committee, where it had run into difficulties over divisions on the extent of powers proposed. It appears likely that Crawford was pushing for a more robust form of federalism than others thought expedient. Word came to O'Connell that he was 'most active, sincere and hopeful as regards federalism'.[253] At the same time, it appears that Ross and others in the Belfast group were dispirited on finding little support for their scheme in the town, where the industrial middle classes were benefitting from a trade boom which made them 'distrustful of experiments of a political nature', and where strong hostility to 'simple repeal' had been manifest in the street politics of 1841.[254] The Dublin group was now also dragging its heels; Ross wrote to Davis that Crawford and he were 'both surprised and vexed at the hesitation of parties who, till lately, seemed all eagerness to take the initiative in a federal movement'.[255]

As nothing seemed to be coming out of this negotiation, and time was becoming short, Crawford now took it on himself to propose a definitive federalist plan, which was publishing in four public letters issued between 7 and 12 November 1844.[256] His prefacing remarks expressed some frustration with his associates:

> [the question] is misunderstood by many, and misrepresented by others, whilst its friends leave it in the hands of its opponents to be tortured and twisted at their will and pleasure, without seeming to have the moral courage to avow their faith or defend its truth. I am of the opinion that those who hold that Ireland requires the application of this principle are doing deep injustice to their country by shirking at this period from its advocacy.

Rather than bear the stigma of deserting a cause he had long adhered to, he now insisted on bringing his own plan into the public domain in response to O'Connell's invitation.[257]

In doing so, he remained acutely suspicious of O'Connell's motives, believing him capable of any political contortion that would best serve his immediate interests. In November he wrote to Smith O'Brien, a fellow Protestant 'gentlemanly radical' with whom he felt some personal affinity, what was later described as a 'confidential and affectionate letter' expressing his acute suspicions about O'Connell:

> He wants to take the same undignified course, humbugging both repealers and federalists; trying to make the repealers believe they are federalists and the federalists that they are repealers, and keeping a delusive joint agitation, knowing right well that whenever particulars come to be discussed they would split up like a rope of sand. I conceive that the principles of '82 and those of a federal constitution are so essentially different that it is impossible for the supporters of each to work together, unless one gives way to the other.[258]

He also expressed 'disgust' at his fellow federalists' lack of drive or direction. O'Brien had himself come out publicly in late October in favour of 'simple repeal' as more conducive to the interests of Ireland, while stressing his view that the federalists were true 'friends of Ireland' and deserving of attention. In 1844 persuasion and conversion, rather than fudging their differences, seemed to both men the only way forward.

Crawford's working out of his federalist scheme can be found in a series of draft memoranda preserved in his manuscripts for 1844 on which his public letters were based. Although he was well informed on American and European models of federal government,[259] he preferred to reference as a constitutional model and precedent the 1840 Canada Act, which he saw as establishing something that resembled a federal relationship between the UK and the newly united colony, although unlike the later 1867 British North America Act, the 1840 Act did not allow for internal confederation between provinces within Canada. While the Act did not give Canada representation in the 'imperial' parliament (which Crawford thought would be desirable for all the colonies in the long run), it did establish internal self-government and sought to distinguish between 'local' and 'imperial' powers, and he used the bill as a template for preparing his Irish proposals. To protect the religious minority, the Canadian model of giving Westminster a veto on 'any act which shall in any manner relate to or affect the enjoyment of or exercise of any form or mode of religious worship' should be included, and 'all laws or acts for the regulation of commerce or navigation' should be UK-wide and thus reserved powers, ensuring the continuation of free trade between the countries. Laws relating to crown succession and to foreign treaties should also be 'imperial'. Ireland should have a separate exchequer, which should receive all local and the Irish proportion of 'imperial' revenues, from which it should pay a fixed quota for naval and military costs but no other imperial expenditure, with the Irish parliament retaining the right to increase this in case of war should it think fit. Ireland would also take on a fixed share of the existing national debt. Beyond these restrictions, Ireland should have full legislative autonomy over its internal affairs.[260]

Crawford's preference was for 'federalism all round', but pending such a demand for local legislatures in Scotland and England, he drafted what should be proceeded with regarding the more urgent case of Ireland. In the absence of a complete revision of constitutional relations across the archipelago, this rendered Crawford's plan more devolutionary than truly federal in practice, although he adhered to the latter description. In his view Ireland's constitution should be bicameral, with an elected assembly and hereditary legislative council, with powers to make laws with the assent of the monarch (or a governor acting in her stead). Weighted majorities of each house would be required for any internal constitutional or electoral amendments. He expressed his views on the principle of a house of lords elsewhere: while it had an entitlement to protect the interests of property, as an unelected chamber it should 'possess no greater power than is necessary to retard hasty legislation' and hence lack any veto power.[261] The proposed Irish assembly would in turn elect a number of their members to attend the imperial parliament (and the legislative council would nominate representative peers), where they would debate and vote only on UK-wide reserved matters and on any Irish bills specifically referred to it. To make this work, the speaker at Westminster would need to designate such business and set aside time at the start of the session for it.[262]

In separate 'Notes for a speech on federalism' he sought to define the slippery term:

> by *federalism* I mean a construction of the connection between any two or more countries which establishes local legislative bodies with local powers, subject in certain matters, which may be termed imperial, to the superior control of an imperial legislature [...] but there are various shades and degrees of difference in the mode of constituting such a connection from the pure federalism of the American states, in which each state has a local legislature and an imperial representation, to the imperfect specimens supplied by the nature of the constitution of our colonial legislatures which are in combination with, and subject to an imperial legislature in which they are not represented – but in which I conceive they ought to be represented.

While this might appear a revolution in British constitutionalism, it was, he argued, the minimum required to provide the remedy demanded by the specific Irish situation: a 'perfect federal system' would have to wait until public opinion caught up in Scotland, England and other parts of the empire, while an interim practical solution for Ireland was urgently required. Local legislative bodies were no innovation in the British empire (even the tiny Isle of Man had one), and given the manifest failure of the existing union and impossibility of real assimilation due to the extent of socio-economic difference, Ireland's autonomy must be revived:

> There can hardly be any two countries in any manner connected together, which exhibit more marked differences in the most important points of their condition and social relations than England and Ireland. The former country is at the height of prosperity as regards commerce and manufacture, and abounding in wealth and disposable capital – the latter country is wanting all these, and her population in the lowest state of agricultural poverty [...] and then is it possible that the same laws and institutions can be applied without variation to this widely dissimilar condition of things. [...] it might as well be said that the same nutrient would be fit for the adult and the infant; the food that would be fit for the man would kill the child. So Ireland will continue in her depression, and become politically dead, if she is treated under the same laws and institutions which are suitable to the matured wealth and prosperity of England.

The proposed a federal relationship would give Ireland sufficient fiscal and policy independence to tackle its own problems effectively.[263]

These ideas were restated and published in his public letters. While he dropped the idea that Ireland should contribute to the national debt (a concession due as compensation for past misgovernment), he stressed that the continuing 'imperial' contribution to military expenditure entitled Irish participation in the 'imperial' parliament, on the grounds that such taxation carried with it the concomitant of representation. His case for federalism was essentially a pragmatic one (with a trace of residual patriotism) and he was aware it would not satisfy separatist nationalist ideologues:

> These propositions will not meet the views of those who claim for Ireland a separate national existence – they will allege that my propositions will place her rather in the position of a colony rather than a nation. I cannot help this; I repeat what I have often before stated – that I can conceive no means of separate national existence, except by a separation of the crown as well as the parliament. By this I mean a perfectly independent condition, and I think this condition cannot be obtained; and if temporarily obtained, would not be preserved.[264]

In other words, the prevailing geopolitical conditions rendered full Irish independence impossible in a world dominated by predatory empires. Choosing not to mix up his 'complete suffrage' agenda with federalism, he also left the details of the franchise and electoral arrangements of the Irish assembly to future deliberation, so long as this was based on a 'full, fair and free representation of the people'.[265]

However, by the time the last of Crawford's letters appeared in print, the federalist window had already been firmly shut. O'Connell wrote to the LNRA from Derrynane on 8 November, impatiently upbraiding the federalists for not as yet producing any definitive plan. His tone was much cooler and he now declared 'that it is much better to limit our exertions to simple repeal, and confine our efforts to the restoration of the Irish parliament without seeking anything further'. There were three main reasons for the *volte face*. The first was alluded to in the letter: British Whig hostility. If O'Connell had at one point hoped that party's leadership might take up federalism as a conciliatory alternative to repeal, this was now clearly exploded. Indeed, he stated he believed Whig pressure to lie behind the federalists' continuing silence.[266] This had not previously been so clear: in January 1844 the party ideologue Nassau Senior had appeared open to the idea of rotatory parliaments, and in early September even the Conservative home secretary, James Graham, had expected the opposition to come to an arrangement with O'Connell on federalism. However the party leader Russell reasserted an unwavering unionism in a letter sent to the Duke of Leinster on 13 September.[267] The response of the *Morning Chronicle*, warning that federalism was as likely as simple repeal to provoke a civil war, confirmed the party line.[268] This clear rejection evidently came as a relief to some Irish Whigs; the landed Catholic Francis Wyse (brother of Thomas) issued a pamphlet in October mocking Grey Porter and denouncing federalism as both impracticable and dangerous, not least because it gave encouragement to the campaign of tenant insubordination against their landlords.[269]

Secondly, federalism had failed to gain much discernible support from northern Protestant liberals; the *Northern Whig* remained hostile, and the *Banner of Ulster*, representing reformist orthodox Presbyterian opinion, also now came out against Crawford's constitutional proposals.[270] The final and more immediately pressing cause was growing hostility towards federalism within the Repeal movement itself, coalescing around the Young Irelanders, who were already restive after O'Connell's seeming capitulation at Clontarf. The Repeal Association meeting on 11 November, from which O'Connell had been absent, was interrupted by cries of 'we won't have federalism' and 'no federalism – we must have repeal'.[271] Duffy's *Nation* sustained a highly negative editorial line towards it, claiming that it would simply 'effect *another union* disastrous to the interests of Ireland', only this time with the unwilling consent of the people, and pressing O'Connell to adhere to the standard of 'simple repeal' and let the federalists go their own way.[272] Duffy was careful, however, to avoid any direct criticism of O'Connell's leadership.[273] If there was any doubt about how O'Connell would now move, it was removed by a letter of 16 November to the Repeal Association, which threw red meat to his more advanced nationalist supporters; Crawford's third letter did not, he stated:

> contain one single principle, or matter of detail, which ought or could be adopted by the Irish people in their noble struggle for the restoration of Irish nationality. [...] Mr Crawford's plan seems to me to be an elaborate scheme to make matters *worse* than they are at present, and to reduce Ireland from a nominal equality with England to a real and vexatious provincial degradation.[274]

His federalist plan would be referred to a LNRA committee, but it was clear it was already dead in the water.

In a subsequent speech at Cork O'Connell sought to lay a smokescreen by implausibly claiming he had meant something totally different by 'federalism' – a new partnership relationship with Britain to be negotiated only after the full restoration of Ireland's 'constitution of 1782'. The only detail he divulged is that he thought Ireland must retain control of its own customs duties, which was in clear opposition to Crawford's plan.[275] Back in the Repeal Association on 26 November he was happy to amuse his supporters by mocking the federalists, telling his audience the 'secret' that 'federalism is not worth that (snapping his fingers)', and that 'they are none of my children, I have nothing to do with them'. He singled out Crawford from the charge of indolence only to accuse him of 'humbugging us' with a plan that was not federalism at all.[276] For all the Liberator's bluster, it was clear to observers that the climb-down from his 12 October letter was a clear triumph for the Young Ireland faction. Davis was scathing about O'Connell's claims: 'O'Connell's federalism is self-contradictory. Two supreme parliaments! Bah! – that is not federalism, or Porterism, not anything but an apology for a guilty blunder'.[277] Duffy acknowledged his short-term victory, but much later acknowledged that O'Connell's abrupt switch from hot to cold had permanently alienated the northern federalists who might otherwise have promoted the cause of nationality in their own way, underplaying his own active role in this outcome.[278] Even so, he and Davis had been keen not to create a total rupture with the federalists, and Davis even urged R. J. Tennent to stand for Belfast in 1845, pledging support for him as a federalist.[279] Young Ireland's tactical coup would prove short-lived, however, as O'Connell was already turning toward back-channel negotiations on a new reformist Whig alliance on the Lichfield House model, the outcome of which would lead to the secession of both the Young Irelanders and Smith O'Brien from the Repeal Association in July 1846, ostensibly over 'peace resolutions' renouncing physical force.[280]

For the moment, though, satirists enjoyed O'Connell's embarrassment on the issue. John Doyle returned once more to the O'Connell-Sharman Crawford antagonism in a new political sketch, 'Dropping it like a red-hot poker!', published in December 1844 (Figure 22). Crawford now appeared as an old man infirmly leaning on a stick and addressing O'Connell, depicted as an obese clown, his pockets stuffed with 'tribute' and wearing the 'Milesian cap' of Repeal on his head. O'Connell wails about burning his fingers from picking up a red-hot poker labelled 'federalism', while Crawford tells him it was 'All your own fault. Why did you take it up at the wrong end?'. The answer lies behind O'Connell, where a young masked figure wearing a hat labelled 'Nation' has been beating him with the wooden sword of 'Young Ireland'.[281] Doyle was deploying loosely the figures of the Commedia dell'arte tradition, most familiar to British Victorians through the 'Harlequinade' sequences in pantomime, with O'Connell the buffoonish clown as garishly reimagined for the London stage by Joseph Grimaldi and Crawford as the elderly and foolish miser Pantaloon. 'Young Ireland' is here treated relatively benignly as the cunning servant Harlequin, perhaps reflecting the (still unthreatening) novelty to metropolitan readers of this group of internal critics of O'Connell within his movement. One London newspaper took the opportunity to reinforce a now entrenched trope about Crawford's miserliness: 'the face and figure in the sketch have all the delicate attenuation proper to a gentleman who, to the possession of some thousands a-year, is said to add so remarkable a degree of caution that for fear of fire he will not allow even smoke to be seen issuing from his kitchen-chimney'.[282] It was clear however, that the hypocritical O'Connell rather than Crawford was the principal target of the sketch.

If the collapse of his federalist plan dispirited Crawford, he left no record of it. His belated development of the scheme and muted response to its rejection may have been due to the acute illness of his wife Mabel, who was to die at Crawfordsburn on 21 December 1844. His plan had received little public support – the other federalists had melted away and few Irish papers other than the small-circulation *Dublin Monitor* had endorsed it.[283] His English allies Sturge and Miall had offered some encouragement, although this was counterbalanced by fervent denunciations by O'Connor in the *Northern Star*.[284] But alongside the sneers from the Tory press about his delusional ambitions of constitution making, the episode did produce some grudging admiration for him. Almost alone of the federalists he had been prepared in complete sincerity to put his plans on the subject before the public, and single-handedly take the resultant flak from all sides.[285] Although at odds on any limitation to national autonomy, Davis evidently valued his opinions and integrity and agreed with the need to ensure the protection of Protestant religious freedom in any future Ireland. He wrote to O'Brien from Belfast in late October 1844, that 'federalism is not and cannot be a final settlement though it deserves a fair trial and perfect toleration', suggesting that he and Duffy were not fully in agreement in their response.[286]

Federalism lay fallow for some years after 1844, but Crawford was prompted to return to it after O'Connell's death in 1847 by the plan formed by leading Young Irelanders to visit to Belfast. Crawford wrote privately to Smith O'Brien, to whom he was 'very sincerely attached', to invite him to Crawfordsburn and discuss his opinions. He had not changed his own view that, for an Irish parliament to be re-established, it must be either on the federal or the colonial (that is, the Canadian) model. Objections to this based on *'nationality'* were fine-sounding, he informed O'Brien, but would cut no ice with either Britain or northern Protestants, who would weigh all proposals on the scales of whether they would threaten or enhance their material prospects, and for whom free-trade was non-negotiable. Any proposal which did not meet these practical issues head-on, and preferably debate them on Irish platforms and in parliament, was doomed to fail. Nevertheless, he believed the prospects for some form of federal repeal were now improving: the British public was becoming restive under the costs of Irish famine relief, and the proposal to raise an income tax in Ireland would make a strong case for a representative Irish parliament to expend it.[287] O'Brien spent several days at Crawford's home, but the Young Irelanders chose to disregard Crawford's pragmatic advice and pressed ahead with their Belfast rallies. It was the violent response of an O'Connellite 'Old Ireland' mob in Belfast, rather than Protestant hostility, which put paid to their 1847 initiative without their ideas gaining much traction in the north.[288]

However, the ongoing famine crisis had something of a radicalising effect on Crawford himself, and he returned to the repeal question in 1848. Responding in May that year to a letter from Bishop Maginn of Derry, he assured him that 'I should feel it the proudest day of my life, if I could lead on the Protestant population of Ulster in an effort for the restoration of a domestic parliament' and stated that he would give his support to the incipient Protestant Repeal Association (PRA) then being formed in Dublin. He felt that a joint Protestant-Catholic agitation on this subject now could alone stave off a civil war along sectarian lines.[289] There were some hints of support for this position in Ulster – the Lurgan Tenant Right Association for example expressed its frustration with the blocking of land reform legislation, and told him that, while loyal to the crown, they agreed that 'Ireland will alone be regenerated through the instrumentality of a native parliament'.[290] However, with few prominent adherents apart from the poet and antiquarian Samuel Ferguson, the PRA struggled to fulfil the excitement with which it was greeted in the nationalist press.[291] A stir was created by the appearance at its meeting in Dublin on 12 July 1848 of a group of Orangemen in full regalia, but the bulk of that organisation was pursuing a different strategy of assuring the government of its militant loyalty in the face of a threatened Young Ireland rebellion, and received surreptitious official endorsement.[292] Any members who joined the PRA were quickly purged.[293]

Crawford nonetheless wrote to promote the opening of a branch in Belfast, warning that the British strategy of divide and rule might lure Orangemen into seeking to maintain a nominal (and ultimately delusive) Protestant ascendancy. Instead, 'a *real* ascendancy, [could be] founded on the only stable basis [...] that of the honorable performance of public services', and Protestant leadership would benefit the whole national community through participation in a 'federative' Irish parliament. Seeking again to stir deep Protestant patriotic memory, he urged the restoration of 'the principle of legislative independence, as acknowledged by the constitution of 1782, subject to such modifications as would be best suited to guard against collision on matters of imperial interest, affecting the connection of the two countries under an imperial crown'.[294] O'Neill Daunt later claimed that Crawford had thereby 'recanted his imperialism, and declared his assent to the principles of 1782', but clearly he had not abandoned a preference for federalism.[295] There was some constituency for such an organisation in Belfast in 1848, as well as some sympathy for the cross-sectarian ideals, if not for revolutionary methods. However, as Frank Wright has argued, Protestant support for repeal was predicated, paradoxically, on the demise with O'Connell of the threat of pan-Catholic mass mobilisation, while at the same time it lacked the sheer weight of numbers that O'Connell had commanded, and which might alone have leveraged a constitutional concession from British government.[296]

The PRA faded quickly from sight in the wake of the abortive Ballingarry rising, which was led by the vacillating Smith O'Brien on 29 July 1848 and rapidly quashed by crown forces backed by coercive legislation. As the brief federalist revival receded, Crawford fell back on an adapted version of Lord William Fitzgerald's idea of annual sittings of members of the imperial parliament in Dublin to deal with Irish matters (in effect acting as a self-selecting grand committee on Ireland which would be dominated in practice by Irish MPs), to be held before the full UK parliament convened at Westminster. Along with several other former federalists, he joined Fitzgerald's society to promote this in 1848.[297] However liberal unionists were wary of his appropriation of this 'moveable parliaments' scheme as a covert stepping stone to repeal, and as likely to revive nationalist agitation.[298] Crawford continued to advocate this scheme in public meetings, the press and parliament, but it foundered in the 1850s due to a combination of Irish nationalist opposition and British indifference.[299] This was another setback, but he continued also to oppose any move towards the 'centralisation' of Irish governance, such as the proposed abolition of the lord lieutenancy in 1850.[300] He subsequently adhered to some form of 'rotating parliament' scheme to address the multiple failings of the existing system, but by 1855 had become convinced that repeal of any sort would never be conceded, as 'the union is a measure now so intimately connected with the imperial government of the UK, that it must be held as an irreversible law, which cannot be superseded without a violent rupture of the connexion of the two countries'.[301]

Rather than manifesting inconsistency or confusion, as one commentator suggests, his position on Irish home government was seriously considered and offered as a mode of resolving the competing demands of Irish and British nationalisms on Irish governance. Crawford was himself no nationalist of either the Irish or British variety, but a pragmatist with an underlying 'patriotic' belief that Ireland was eminently capable of governing itself and that this would best promote its people's distinct interests, while recognising what were then the stark geopolitical realities of British suzerainty and the commercial advantages to Ireland of remaining within with the UK single market. Ulster Protestants were for him unquestionably part of the Irish national community and would be most likely to acknowledge this when given guarantees of protection of their religious liberties and unfettered access to the British trading block ensured by a federal relationship. His plan failed to acquire traction in the 1830s–40s due to adverse circumstances (including O'Connell's loss of nerve on federalism in 1844, the pursuit of ideological purity by Duffy and his associates, and British and Ulster Whig-liberal myopia) and a failure to mobilise mass support behind the idea rather than due to any internal incoherence.[302] But what had been dismissed so readily by nationalists in 1844 would return to the heart of Irish politics in the early 1870s in the form of Isaac Butt's plan for 'home rule' (essentially for Butt a revived federalist project), belatedly attract British Liberal support with W. E. Gladstone's 'conversion' to Irish self-government of 1885–6, and remain prominent for the following half century until swept away amidst the cataclysm of world war, a republican rebellion and its revolutionary aftermath.[303] Indeed Crawford was claimed retrospectively as an early 'Home Ruler' in 1874.[304]

Rochdale politics, 1845–52

Despite the bitter conflict over complete suffrage and his distraction into the Irish constitutional debate in 1843–4, Crawford was able to maintain his local political coalition at Rochdale, secure an uncontested re-election there in 1847 and hold the seat until 1852. Several factors made this possible. Firstly, the micropolitics of dissent and the church in the town that had paved the way for his invitation to stand in 1841 continued to prevail, and he was consistent in promoting reforms popular with both the working and much of the middle classes of the town. Also, although Chartism declined as a national force in these years, the Rochdale radical leadership of Livsey and Taylor remained intact and allied to Crawford, while Feargus O'Connor's enthusiastic turn towards land reform as the new central issue in Chartist activity created some common ground with Crawford and allowed for some patching up of the relationships strained to breaking point in previous years.

The vicar of Rochdale, John Molesworth, had refused to accept his previous defeats on levying church rates, and published (according to a hostile source in 1843) 'a monthly pamphlet which he calls "Common Sense," in which he raves against Dissent and slanders in turn every party who refuses to submit to mother church'.[305] He also published an angry pamphlet appealing to the government against the town's chief magistrate Clement Royds for passing over himself and other leading Tories for appointments to the bench.[306] Molesworth's noisy protests not only kept the town's nonconformists on their mettle, but alienated moderate Anglicans. This is the context in which a petition was drawn up in Rochdale, signed by 2,000 people, stating that if public executions were to continue 'under the sanction of the religion of the state', they should be performed as a religious ceremony and carried out by the clergy of the state church. This was intended as a mocking slight to the their pretensions, and was duly presented to the commons by Crawford (himself an opponent of capital punishment) on 11 March 1844.[307] Whatever the intention, this sparked a storm of fury in the Irish and English Tory press against the 'vulgar infidelity' of his alleged plan, apparently proposed on behalf of 'the scum of stagnant Chartism and socialism', to turn the clergy into 'common hangmen'.[308]

Crawford's participation in this stunt would be long remembered with anger by conservative Anglicans and by Molesworth in particular. However it is unlikely to have done him any harm with nonconformists, and may have enhanced his standing within the Anti-State Church Association (ASCA), of which he was now a member, as did his call at its 1844 conference for complete disestablishment throughout the UK.[309] In a predominantly nonconformist borough such as Rochdale (which was to elect Miall, the voluntarist editor of the *Nonconformist* as his successor in 1852) these associations were politically advantageous, and the local branch of the ASCA endorsed his return in 1847.[310]

Crawford's intense voluntarism placed him in a difficult position in 1845, when he felt obliged to oppose the government's Maynooth bill to greatly enhance the state's subvention of the seminary, not, he was quick to point out, from any hostility to Catholic education, but because it would open the door to complete state endowment of that church at the expense of its independence and religious freedom. His amendment against the bill attracted only two votes in addition to the tellers, but a point had been made. With full consistency, he also spoke and voted against the annual grant of the regium donum to the Irish dissenting clergy.[311] Given the general unhappiness about the Maynooth grant in many British constituencies (albeit for different reasons) this stance was unlikely to have been unpopular in Rochdale, even if it did little for his standing with Irish Catholics, who in general welcomed the 1845 grant even with suspicion of Peel's motives.[312] Indeed, despite some complaints made by an Irish Chartist about his criticisms of O'Connell, a public meeting held at Rochdale to hear his sessional report in 1845 voted unanimously to endorse his actions during that session.[313]

Any doubts about his sympathy towards Catholicism's right to practice freely and organise its internal affairs in the UK as it saw fit was dispelled by the firm stance he took against the Whig government's Ecclesiastical Titles Bill. In a public letter to Livsey in December 1850, Crawford lamented some of the language used by Pope Pius IX in the alleged 'papal aggression' of that year relating to the re-establishment of a Catholic territorial hierarchy in England and Wales but defended the church's right to create and name its own sees. Rather than stoking religious alarmism against Rome, the Church of England should, he argued, follow the 'true Protestant position' of ending the corrupting influence of the state establishment.[314]

In the face of mockery from Belfast Protestant voices, he made it clear he would vote against Russell's attempt to ban Catholic use of territorial titles throughout the UK, and followed through on this when parliament reassembled in 1851.[315] His opposition, he asserted, was one of principle, as 'the bill was in effect really to establish the arrogant claim of superiority of the established church over voluntary churches'. His amendment to exclude Ireland from the bill was lost, but restored some of his popularity with the country's Catholic MPs, many of whom were now acting collectively as the 'Catholic Defence Association'.[316] His stance also sparked a further round in the war of words in the press with Molesworth over the meaning of true Protestantism.[317] Commenting on the published exchange of letters, the conservative *Manchester Courier* admitted that Crawford was 'every inch, a gentleman, though his politics are detestable'.[318]

Nonconformity and voluntarism cut across class lines, but Crawford also remained strongly associated with specifically working-class social grievances. Principal among these was the campaign for a legally limited working day associated with Lord Ashley's Ten Hours Bill, an issue which tended to divide employers from workers sharply. A noisy public meeting in Rochdale in April 1844 resolved on a petition in support of such a provision to be added to the government's new factory bill, and to ask Crawford to present it.[319] Doing so before the debate on the government's bill, which would have permitted some restrictions for children, but only limited ones for women and young people aged thirteen to eighteen of twelve hours daily and nine on Saturdays, he proceeded to challenge the laissez-faire assumptions voiced by both the government and by those middle-class radicals who opposed any restrictions for adult men and limited ones for other categories of workers:

> The working classes were not free agents; they were obliged to obey the commands of their masters to work as many hours as they were told; they were not in a condition to say they would work so many hours and no more (hear, hear). Such was the condition of the men and women of the manufacturing districts, and the legislature, therefore, was bound to step in and protect them against oppression[.]

The new poor law had, he argued, forced many previously relieved out of doors into the overcrowded labour markets, forcing down both wages and working conditions, and reducing some men to working seventeen or eighteen-hour days. This was both immoral and economically unnecessary, and, he asserted, deeply resented by the industrial workers of both Belfast and Rochdale.[320] However, the ten-hour clause amendment was defeated that year and the government's limited restrictions were passed in its place.

When Ashley again proposed his ten hours clause to limit all working men and women's hours to this maximum in 1846, Crawford endorsed it, arguing that this was the will of the people of Rochdale.[321] As in 1844, he was also chosen to submit a parallel Belfast petition, this time signed by 17,000 operatives and other residents.[322] Excessive working hours, he argued, were contributing to a public health catastrophe – government inquiries had shown the average lifespan in industrial towns was ten years shorter than in the rest of England, and had fallen sharply since the previous century. Pressure on women to work long hours had also produced an epidemic of drugging children with opiates to keep them sedated while their mothers laboured out of sheer necessity. Fierce competition between manufacturers made it impossible for fair-minded individuals to lessen such exploitation without loss: hence only state regulation could make the difference to the worker, who 'might be said to be in a state of absolute slavery to his employers; for he had no alternative but to do what they wanted, or to starve, or to enter the workhouse'.[323] The 1846 measure, which the Oldham MP John Fielden had introduced as an eleven-hour bill with an option to reduce the working day to ten hours, was again lost, albeit by a relatively small margin of ten votes. Crawford and Ashley shared a platform in Rochdale in February 1847 to support its reintroduction, at which strong female as well as male enthusiasm was demonstrated, despite opposition from a 'comparatively small' minority of those present.[324] Although generally liberal in his political economy, Crawford envisaged effective state-imposed limits to the operation of free markets where these could be demonstrated to create social inequity, as was clearly the case both with industrial labour markets and landlord-tenant relations.

Crawford strongly supported Fielden's 1847 Factory Bill (which restricted the hours of women and young workers to ten hours but not yet those of adult men) against attempts by middle-class radicals such as Hume, Bright (now MP for Durham) and Ross to stymie it. However, with the support of the Whig leadership this bill now finally passed into law.[325] While they were unenthusiastic, the act was tolerated by middle-class nonconformists in

Rochdale on moral grounds.[326] Passage of the act did not, however, end the 'short time' movement in the north, as meetings to protest against evasion by millowners continued, and an amending bill was required in 1850. In that year Crawford supported Ashley's narrowly defeated amendment to ban all night-time working for children.[327]

He also continued to support resistance to the full implementation of the new poor law in Rochdale and other northern industrial districts. In 1843–4 he had again attacked in parliament the principle of the English law as deliberately imposing cruelty and suffering on the working poor, and in 1844 lobbied for the abolition of the bastardy clauses of the act. In 1845 he also opposed the new Scottish poor law on the grounds it would do nothing to curb or alleviate the clearances then devastating Sutherland and other highland districts.[328] Later in 1844 he appealed directly to the home secretary not to permit the poor law commissioners to prohibit outdoor relief in Rochdale, in the wake of large and angry public meetings there. In response, Graham loftily declared that it was a 'statute of general operation' that he had no dispensive power to modify.[329]

Notwithstanding protests and petitions from the town and the local poor law guardians chaired by Livsey since 1840, the commissioners proceeded with Whitehall backing to attempt to put the new regulations into practice in November.[330] That month, Crawford spoke on an anti-poor law platform in the town with Livsey and Fielden, which endorsed a delegation to approach Graham personally, only for this to be turned away from the home office without redress.[331] He could only continue to protest against this 'unconstitutional' slighting of local democracy, forcing a debate on the treatment of Rochdale in March 1845, in which he restated his view that generous poor relief was derived from both the social contract and scripture: 'The working man of England had a right either to have work or a subsistence'.[332]

The rearguard campaign against the implementation of the new poor law had some local success, as the guardians continued to refuse to impose the workhouse and universal labour tests and retained autonomy for the local 'almshouses' to give relief without 'degradation'.[333] Crawford's prominence in this campaign further bolstered his popular support in the borough, as Livsey continued to mobilise working-class antagonism towards attempts to suppress local independence and to maintain traditional welfare entitlements.[334] As economic conditions deteriorated in Lancashire in spring 1847, now augmented by the mass migration of famine refugees from Ireland bringing with them the typhus epidemic, Livsey and Crawford jointly approached the Whig home secretary, Sir George Grey, for external assistance to the Rochdale Union, but with limited success.[335]

Irish issues briefly threatened to upset his relationship with Livsey in 1847. In September that year a Dublin inquest jury found the Rochdale guardians responsible for the death of an immigrant Irish boy, Michael Duignan, in the process of him being 'removed' from the parish on a Dublin-bound steamship. This practice was widespread in Lancashire during the Famine and provoked much anger in the Irish ports where such 'paupers' were habitually discarded after their repatriation. Responding to letters from Livsey, Crawford insisted on a full official inquiry into the death as essential to satisfying the 'public mind' in Ireland. In the end, the Rochdale inquiry pointed to suffocation on board the overcrowded ship rather than any neglect by the poor law authorities as the real cause of the tragedy and Livsey insisted that Rochdale and other parishes would continue to treat Irish migrant paupers 'with humanity and consideration', while insisting on the legitimacy of the policy of removal of those without 'settlement' rights.[336] Crawford appears to have accepted this, but the episode is a reminder of the potential risks as well as advantages of representing a 'popular' English constituency. A recapitulation by the Rochdale board of its entitlement to use the policy of pauper 'removal' was later referred to by the radical Young Irelander Michael Doheny as a 'declaration of war' against the Irish people requiring retaliation. The choice of Rochdale (one among many making similar statements) was probably no accident given the next item on the agenda was Crawford's tenant right proposals.[337]

After the sustained antagonisms between the Complete Suffrage and Chartist movements in 1842–4, relations gradually improved between the wings of the democratic movement. Tory papers drew no distinction between the factions and continued to regard Crawford as 'the parliamentary organ of the Chartists'.[338] While O'Connor was loath to abandon his bitterness against Sturge and others he believed had damaged the cause by challenging his leadership, with the divisive corn law question finally removed by the Peel administration in 1846, and the NCSU now inactive, there were fewer occasions for overt clashes between them.[339] In Rochdale the repeal of the corn laws was marked by a large and exuberant parade, organised by the town's manufacturers but with apparently enthusiastic working-class participation (although Molesworth refused to allow the church bells to be rung in celebration).[340] In the context of a war scare with the United States early that year, the *Northern Star* expressed its 'delight' at Crawford's letter to his constituents in support of the 'no vote, no musket' agitation against any compulsory militia enlistment in England in the absence of parliamentary reform.[341]

O'Connor's efforts to reorientate Chartism towards his ambitious land reform programme from 1843 also opened new grounds for collaboration. The Chartist land plan drew on ideas of popular agrarianism long extant in British radicalism associated especially with William Cobbett (although it kept its distance from rival schemes linked with Robert Owen's 'socialist' co-operativism as advocated by G. J. Holyoake and others). These were in line with Crawford's 1839 defence of small farms and anti-Malthusian opposition to mass emigration.[342] O'Connor's 1843 tract *A Practical Work on the Management of Small Farms* echoed his case for the moral and economic efficiency of small family farms and applied this to the liberation of the British industrial proletariat. He argued that a successful experiment demonstrating the viability of the scheme by establishing 5,000 working-class families on smallholdings through collective effort would pave the way for a much larger programme once the attainment of the Charter opened up government to popular demands. Although this drew the fire of socialists such as Bronterre O'Brien as a distraction, it was nevertheless popular with his core followers at a time when enthusiasm for the Charter was waning.[343] The Chartist Co-operative Land Society, established in 1845 with the aim of resettling subscribers (to be chosen by ballot in the first instance) on small plots carved out of the estates it would purchase, attracted at one point over 70,000 paying members. The settlement of the first estate, at 'O'Connorville' in Hertfordshire, was celebrated with a 'National Chartist Jubilee' in August 1846, and several others followed.[344] But in the face of major legal obstacles, and with O'Connor's personal finances intertwined with that of the Society in a complicated and problematic fashion, it had difficulty establishing and sustaining the model 'back to the land' communities of transplanted industrial workers that it originally envisaged.[345]

Struggling to place the scheme on a sounder footing, O'Connor asked Crawford to give it his imprimatur by serving as one of the trustees of the New Chartist Land Company in 1847, along with Duncombe and Fielden.[346] Despite the open hostility towards the scheme of his erstwhile allies in the League and *Nonconformist,* Crawford agreed. They subsequently toured the Chartist land settlements together in early 1848, and the Chartist leader was pleased by his reaction:

> I started for Gloucester to convey your esteemed and valued friend, Mr Sharman Crawford, to Snig's End, to witness the pleasurable spectacle of eighty families, heretofore slaves, and living in underground cellars, taking possession of their own castles and their own labour fields. This good man was excited and delighted with what he saw […] it is an extraordinary thing to find Mr Sharman Crawford, one of the largest landed proprietors in Ireland, declaring in the house of commons, that the cultivator of the soil and the proprietor of the soil are co-partners in the soil; it was, upon that account, delightful to me to be able to illustrate that grand principle to that good and generous man.[347]

Crawford was also named a member of the commons select committee that investigated the Company's financial affairs in 1848. Although its report exonerated O'Connor personally from any financial wrongdoing, it drew attention to mismanagement and the over-optimistic assumptions lying behind the scheme and the fact that it had contravened the law on friendly societies.[348] Fully aware of this, but also conscious that O'Connor had renounced all support for physical force agitation in preference for his land project, Crawford continued to give it the personal support that O'Connor craved, touring the Chartist settlements again with him in late 1849, and hence helping to keep the scheme afloat as popular interest began to fade and O'Connor's debts accumulated.[349] Indeed, Crawford endorsed efforts to establish a similar Freehold Land Society in Rochdale.[350] O'Connor's attempted intervention in the incipient tenant-right campaign in Ireland in 1849–50 was not welcomed by Gavan Duffy, but his argument that Irish peasants and British industrial workers shared common political ground chimed with Crawford's politics.[351] In 1851 O'Connor again praised Crawford's honesty and agreed with the old Irish Chartist Patrick O'Higgins' opinion that recent republican attacks on O'Connor drew on the playbook of O'Connell's attempts to undermine Crawford.[352] He endorsed the objects of the Tenant League and Crawford's leadership role within it.[353]

This improved relationship helped pave the way to Crawford's uncontested re-election at Rochdale in the general election of summer 1847. Locally, his annual appearance to justify his votes before mass meetings of electors and non-electors alike had helped maintain a popular rapport. A Lancashire dialect address by 'O Rachda Felley' produced by the Printers Trade Union to celebrate the repeal of the corn laws the previous year had commented 'Aw gess we shol av elekshun soon; we shol send Sharman ogen, fur noboddi elze ul stond no chans whatsumevvur'.[354] Nationally, Chartist preparations for the elections were patchy, and the election of O'Connor himself at Nottingham was largely fortuitous. In Rochdale, however, they worked in tandem with a professional and well-financed Liberal Reform Association, effectively preparing the ground in the registration courts.[355] At the same time, Crawford's standing amongst the nonconformist middle-classes of Rochdale remained extremely high. In the view of the local monthly, the *Pilot,* his record proved him 'a friend of the people'.[356]

In the light of this, the local Conservatives at first concluded that their prospects were 'hopeless' so long as Crawford was standing and declined to field a candidate.[357] In response to a formal requisition signed by a majority of electors, he agreed to let his name go forward again.[358] A last-minute candidacy by George Fyler, a lawyer and London-based anti-poor law Tory, was headed off at a public meeting by an intervention by Livsey, who 'very coolly cautioned the electors, and non-electors, against being deluded by strangers, assuring them that their old friend and late member would arrive in Rochdale on the following day'. Next day Livsey nominated Crawford before a supportive crowd of 4,000, and Fyler withdrew; Crawford was formally returned on 30 July it what was something of an anticlimax.[359]

Preoccupied with Irish issues as the famine continued to rage and his land reform proposals began to attract outdoors support, Crawford was less prominent in pursuit of democratic reforms after 1847. Nevertheless, he offered his support to the 1848 national Chartist petition, remained opposed to any government resort to coercion and continued to advocate the release of political prisoners. He kept his distance from the Kennington Common mass meeting in London on 10 April that had been intended to marshal outdoors support for the presentation of the third Chartist petition to parliament that day and which collapsed in disarray in the face of a government ban on processions and middle-class mobilisation against Chartist 'disorder'. He voted with O'Connor in the minority against the government's Crown and Government Security Bill on the day the Chartists met at Kennington.[360]

Crawford continued to believe that a class alliance must be pursued to attain democratic reforms, a position O'Connor himself was now reluctantly (if inconsistently) conceding. That month he was listed as one of the MPs who supported the 'new movement' promoted by veteran Chartist R. J. Richardson to mobilise middle-class support for household suffrage and triennial parliaments.[361] In July 1849 he seconded and spoke in support of O'Connor's motion to have the People's Charter again debated in the commons. While he was open to a staged enactment of its points, he stated that he continued to adhere to the document he had signed personally back in 1838 and endorsed O'Connor's justification for its passage using the doctrine of popular sovereignty, for 'the people were the source of all legitimate power; and how, he would ask, could there be legitimate power that was not conferred by the people through their representatives?'.[362]

Crawford had kept himself well clear of the alliance established in 1847–8 between O'Connor and the increasingly militant Irish Confederation and its club network in both countries. While the conversion of the Young Ireland leaders to universal suffrage was belated and in some cases superficial, the French Revolution of February 1848 had a radicalising effect on them and the Confederates sought to extend their relationship with the British working-class movement.[363] Even so, in March 1848 John Mitchel expressed frustration at the Irish Chartist leader Patrick O'Higgins' continuing adherence to 'moral force' and was personally sceptical about such elements of the Chartist platform as the secret ballot and annual parliaments. Confederate attempts to resuscitate 'physical force' Chartist conspiracies in northern England later that year (including in Rochdale) fizzled out with limited support.[364] While clearly sympathetic to the radical repealers seeking Irish independence, O'Connor was no revolutionary and showed no desire to return to the polarising divisions within the British democratic movement or to encourage incipient republicanism in either country; after Kennington he was moving away from the tactics of the radical 'mass platform' and towards a broader politics of labour reformism.[365] By May of that year he was praising both Crawford and Sturge as 'honest men', and urging collaboration between the parliamentary reformers and outdoor agitation, and in 1849 he recommended Crawford's 'right and honest course' in proposing to move again for universal suffrage and shorter parliaments.[366]

This position had support in Rochdale, where Livsey co-operated with Bright and the middle-class radicals in May 1848 in hosting a meeting calling for franchise reform, reduced taxation and retrenchment.[367] However, ultra-radicals within the movement disagreed with O'Connor's newfound irenicism, and in that month a crowd of Chartists led by Ernest Jones barracked a London meeting of the 'People's League' (a new pro-universal suffrage body established by that perennial organiser William Lovett) at which Crawford, Sturge and Miall were among the speakers again urging working and middle-class collaboration behind democratic reform.[368] Factionalism and infighting thus continued to dog the movement, while Crawford was to criticise the middle-class parliamentary radicals for losing interest in the cause of reform by 1851.[369] As the Chartist movement broke apart, O'Connor became an increasingly marginalised figure, whose increasingly eccentric public behaviour gave way to mental collapse in 1852.[370]

In his annual report at Rochdale in November 1848, Crawford explained his preoccupation with Ireland (whose conditions were also a question for England), while lamenting what he now saw a the 'forlorn hope' of political reform, undermined that year both by the defection of soi-disant radical MPs, and the failure of the people to demonstrate the 'public virtue' necessary to prove their claims. His mood was one of depression exacerbated by bouts of ill-health, tempered by a sense of duty to continue as a public representative and support democratic and social reforms when possible, but already by 1849 he was reported to be considering resignation before the next election.[371] However, he retained his seat until the dissolution of 1852 and continued to consult and report annually to his constituents there, and remained popular in the town.[372] He retained a leading role in promoting reformist causes, including state education through acting as vice-president of the Lancashire Public Schools Association.[373] The radical weekly *The Leader* summed up the popular mood when it was clear in late 1851 that the MP would finally step down:

> Rochdale is happy in having a representative like Mr Sharman Crawford, happy also in knowing how to appreciate him for his consistent integrity and unfaltering devotion to the cause of the people. Rochdale elects its member free of expense, sends him to parliament an independent man, requires of him very properly an account of his doings there, and handsomely acknowledges his services. On Thursday week Mr Crawford gave in his account, and obtained a receipt in full with more than honourable mention; and on Friday, to celebrate the event, his constituents invited him to a public dinner. [… He] is respected and esteemed by all radicals, by the generous among his opponents, and […] beloved by his tenantry in County Down.[374]

Although his formal association with the borough ended in 1852, he would return on a number of occasions and continued until his death in 1861 to participate in person or through print in its political life, still advocating manhood suffrage, the ballot and redistribution of seats. In 1855 he was presented by Livsey with silver candelabra worth one hundred guineas, raised by a testimonial subscription in the town; at the reception he wore the red cockade first sported at the 1841 election.[375] In 1859 his 1843 speech to the non-electors of Rochdale on democratic reform was republished in the town as part of a revival of the campaign for political reform. He assured his Lancashire readers that (unlike others) there was no danger of him drifting towards Toryism as he got older and that his reformist aspirations were as ardent as ever. The objective remained the same as that twenty years before: the old body of the constitution needed invigorating by infusion of the new blood of the working classes – and this was the only way by which the lengthened stability and prosperity of the British empire could be secured.[376]

5. Landlordism, agrarian reform and Irish famine, 1827–50

Agrarian practice and theory

William Sharman Crawford's inheritance in 1827 of John Crawford's estates of Crawfordsburn and Rademon greatly enhanced his holdings scattered across counties Down, Meath and Antrim. Under the terms of his father-in-law's will he received the new lands unentailed, on the condition that they would not be sold, divided or encumbered, giving him significantly more freedom of action as landlord here than on the strictly entailed lands inherited from his father in 1803.[1] He chose to live at Crawfordsburn, not the largest estate, but located close to the political hub of Belfast and the site of a substantial house. Resident agents at first managed his other estates, including the long-serving and popular Robert Johnstone of Ballywoollen at Rademon, and the 'respectable farmer' William Bellew at Stalleen, until his elder sons were capable of taking over their management.[2] By 1836 his third surviving son James was already being dispatched to Meath to collect the Stalleen rents and would later take over management at Rademon.[3]

Sharman Crawford followed John Crawford and his predecessors' established practice of acting as a liberal landlord of the Rademon estate. This proved popular; the leading tenants there presented him with a supportive address and testimonial of silver plate in 1835. In response, he assured them that he would continue to act in line with his predecessors' maxim:

> of 'live and let live,' [which] I have endeavoured to abide by; feeling that the true interest of the landlord, can only be sustained, by securing the prosperity of his tenants: – *his* interest and *theirs*, are, in my opinion, inseparable, – and the landlord who extorts an immoderate rent, will experience, at no distant period, that injury to *his own* interest, which he has previously inflicted on theirs, and, to a certain degree, on the whole community, of which they constitute a portion.[4]

Indeed, at some point he had erected at Kilmore an engraved panel praising Arthur Johnston (who died in 1814) as a model landlord and pledging himself and his successors to maintaining his example. Such 'improving' rhetoric was commonplace with landowners, but Crawford determined to embody it in practice. His favoured form of management involved close personal inspection of his properties, and making equitable agreements where possible directly with his tenants.[5] For example, in 1835 he visited a parcel of land on the Rademon estate which had recently fallen out of lease:

> He went from house to house, and from field to field; and, after having viewed all, he said, that from the neat and commodious houses, together with the high state of improved cultivation in which the land then was, it was evident that considerable money had been laid out in the houses and land, – but added that it was not his money that had done it; therefore, he said, he had no right to make the tenant pay any additional rent for those improvements [...] also, that he did not wish to let his land at a higher rent than it could pay in a natural state.[6]

He followed the Johnstons and Crawfords also in becoming an active patron of local agricultural societies with many tenant farmer members, such as the Bangor branch of the North Eastern Farming Society and the Bangor Ploughing Society.[7] He and his sons would continue to play a leading role in these local bodies for decades, building up the family's prestige with Down farmers beyond his own holdings. Following a ploughing match at Killyleagh in 1841 organised by the local farming society, he was toasted as 'the best of landlords and most benevolent of men'.[8] However, he disapproved of societies that promoted livestock farming to the exclusion of tillage as not being in the interests of small farmers, and opposed the formation of such a body in the Newtownards union in 1860.[9]

On his own estates, Crawford appears to have favoured granting thirty-one year leases to larger tenants, although in evidence to the Devon Commission in 1844 he stated that he thought that the length of tenancies should vary according to the quality of land and the ability and resources of the tenant, and that many of his smaller tenants held at will. Indeed he was concerned that fluctuations of prices and uncertainty over the corn laws made it virtually impossible to set a fair rent over an extended period of lease. He disapproved of long leases (some of which he had inherited at very low rents from his predecessors), which he believed provided little stimulus to improvement by the sub-letting middlemen who previously held them.[10] However, at least one twenty acre farm on the Rademon estate was advertised in 1837 as still under the old system of a lease for three lives (all still in being) at the low rent of 10s 6d per acre, but with, the seller of its tenant-right affirmed, several hundred pounds of improvements having been made over the previous decade. Such leases for lives often lasted for longer than fifty years and tended to depress the incomes of landowners as prices rose, and frequently triggered tenurial crises when they fell in.[11] Another fifty-six acre plot at Creevy was also in the hands of a middleman with six under-tenants as late as 1859, although this phenomenon appears to have been more uncommon than on other Ulster estates in the period.[12] Reluctant to offer any fixed proportion of output value that would constitute a 'fair rent' given the many variables involved (he believed 'very superior' land, especially when put to grass, should pay more), Crawford was confident that this could be ascertained for any holding by a fair and impartial valuation, and stated that a 'moderate rate' on his estates in 1844 was around 25 shillings per (Cunningham) acre annual rent, which was based on such a measure.[13]

He acquired relatively early a reputation for equitable treatment of tenants, including in setting and adjusting rents at significantly lower levels than those of neighbouring landlords. One correspondent to the *Northern Whig* asserted in 1833 that Lord Dufferin's Killyleagh estate was leased at twice or three times the rent per acre as Crawford's nearby land at Rademon.[14] In their testimony to the Poor Inquiry Commission in 1835, tenants in the barony of Upper Iveagh gave evidence in open session at Rathfriland that while other local landlords had been raising rents, Crawford had pegged his to £1 5s (25 shillings) per acre, which was half of what was now charged on the adjoining estates belonging to

Downshire and others.[15] This may have been exaggerated – W. A. Maguire has calculated Downshire's average rents on new leases granted on the Kilwarlin estate in the 1830s at 35 shillings per Irish acre (also determined by valuation rather than competition) – but it does suggest that Crawford was charging well below the odds.[16] Crawford himself informed the Devon inquiry that in the parish of Bangor one large landowner had reduced rent only by one third from the very high pre-1815 wartime levels, whereas the value of produce had fallen by two-thirds, rendering the old tenants insolvent and draining the capital of their successors.[17]

He also demonstrated that he was prepared to forego rent to promote improvements; taking personal control of a portion of land at Lacken on the Iveagh estate in 1838 on the termination of a middleman's lease, he held the rents of the subtenants at the previous low rate, and required the direct payment of only one third of what was due to him for the first year, permitting the tenants to invest the remaining two thirds in bona fide improvements (including of their dwellings).[18] It appears that he resisted any temptation to consolidate the smallholdings in this townland – with the exception of one large farm of seventy acres held by the Kennedy family, the remainder was still in the hands of thirty-four small tenants holding between one and twenty-four acres when it was surveyed for the Griffiths Valuation in 1863, shortly after his death.[19] While setting a personal example of this sort was important, its limitations were evident to him and he maintained it would require state intervention to bring redress on a larger scale to tenants on the estates of less scrupulous rent-extractors.

He was also prepared to intervene directly in disputes between tenants and within tenant families to ensure equity, taking advice from local clergy, such as Fr John Keenan of Annaclone, where this was deemed appropriate. Although in general he discouraged subdivision, in 1838 he made an agreement with a small tenant named Patrick Greenan at Lacken, to allow him an acre of land on which to erect a cottage, while his wife, who had been 'most unkindly treated by her husband and also [...] by other members of the family' was to retain the family cottage and the bulk of the family's land. If Greenan abandoned or ill-treated her again, he was to lose his cabin and acre in punishment.[20] For his part, Fr Keenan held Crawford in very high regard as a landlord, accompanying him on his visitations and remarking from the altar of his chapel that '[t]here is not a tenant on his estates who holds from him that is not in comfort and independence'.[21] The family's approach to estate management was meticulous, if invariably sympathetic to those who made an effort at self-improvement; in 1844 detailed accounts of individual arrears of the smallholders in Lacken were recorded, along with their plans for paying these off.[22]

Crawford endorsed the operation of the 'Ulster custom' of tenant right on his estates, defining it succinctly as 'the selling by the occupier of his interest in the occupation' and noting in 1844 that this was usually valued at £20 to £30 per acre on estates where the tenants had full confidence in their landlord and rents were moderate. His role in this transaction was solely to approve the incoming tenant.[23] If such tenant-right values were indeed seen on his estates, this would have equated to between sixteen and twenty-four years purchase on his average rents, far outstripping the four to six years' purchase more common in Ulster before the Famine, and higher than on nearby estates.[24] The assistant commissioner taking evidence for the poor inquiry in Upper Iveagh in 1835 was astonished by the size of 'tenant right' payments given for farms of all sizes there, with the full consent of the proprietors; he observed that the purchase money was raised through savings accrued from working as small dealers in the linen trade or other occupations, and by borrowing from neighbours.[25] The system of 'free sale' of tenant right appears to have operated on Crawford's Meath as well as his Ulster estates.[26]

In practice the 'Ulster custom' of tenant right varied considerably in its operation both regionally and between individual estates, but was widely regarded by tenants in the province as a form of disposable property grounded in their landholdings. Crawford's understanding of it was based on the long-established forms common in the north-eastern counties and especially that of Down (although even here it was restricted to greater or lesser degrees on some estates).[27] In embracing the custom in its most extensive form on his own holdings, Crawford allied himself with the emerging Ulster tenant-right movement and sought to give this leadership through his attempts to codify and attain legal recognition of the custom. However, this posed certain problems: while he clearly recognised that in practice the custom acknowledged the sale of the outgoing tenant's 'goodwill' – an entitlement to 'the peaceable enjoyment of the farm' for the purchaser – political logic led him to emphasise instead the centrality of inherited, purchased or completed improvements to the farm as the basis for its legal recognition. The difference between these points of emphasis could be blurred (as they frequently were in the custom itself), but were later to give rise to political tensions.

The Sharman Crawfords took a hands-on interest in agricultural matters, with William's wife Mabel managing the home farm on the Crawfordsburn demesne during his frequent absences. She wrote to her son John in 1835 to inform him about the marketing and butchering of the family's pigs and the worrying condition of their potato crop.[28] In that year their home farm also supported a herd of forty-eight cattle.[29] Even when absent on parliamentary business in London, William also took a close interest in the demesne farm. Horticultural specimens raised in the walled gardens at Crawfordsburn (especially fruit and vegetables) were of high quality and regularly won prizes at local exhibitions.[30] Over time the family would also experiment with producing flax seed, a vital ingredient for the extensive linen industry, but much of which had to be imported from abroad as a raw material. He promoted home production of flax seed as import substitution to the Belfast Flax Society in 1842, and followed this up in practice on his farm.[31] Crawford also encouraged such trials nationally through his membership of the Royal Flax Improvement Society, founded in 1841 with the object of advancing domestic flax and flax-seed cultivation as part of a 'judicious rotation' of crops that would not harm food production.[32]

This was part of a long-standing engagement with agricultural societies that began as early as 1829, when he chaired a meeting of the 'Society for the Improvement of Ireland' in Dublin which considered the model of Dutch 'pauper colonies' and arterial drainage schemes for Ireland.[33] He later sought to promote an 'improved' agriculture through active involvement from 1841 with the Royal Agricultural Improvement Society of Ireland, and to which he subscribed £25 that year. Typical of his 'hands-on' approach, he took a place on its sub-committee on husbandry and practical agriculture.[34] In 1846 he promoted to it the work of the Irish Waste Land Improvement Company in persuading tenants to engage in crop rotation on reclaimed lands.[35] He later also joined the Chemico-Agricultural Society of Ulster, and served as its president (as did his son John), an organisation which promoted 'high farming' innovations.[36] Always eager to advance agricultural science and its public dissemination, he promoted the career of the former farmer and secretary of the Bangor Agricultural Society Thomas Skilling, who was appointed first manager of the national school board's model farm at Glasnevin in 1838, later worked as agent to the co-operative idealist Lord Wallscourt in Co. Galway, and became the inaugural professor of agriculture at Queen's College Galway in 1849.[37]

Unlike many other 'improving' landlords, however, Crawford was adamant that, given the right stimulus and security for returns, and effective agricultural education and landed patronage, more advanced farming could and should be carried out on small family farms for mutual benefit. Stressing the duties incumbent on a resident landlord to attend to his tenants' and labourers' interests, he told the Bangor Farming Society in 1844 that its work was 'calculated to improve the conditions respectively of the large and small farmer, and by the proper and judicious arrangement of the division and sub-division of land, the poorer classes will be attended to.'[38] To advance these ends, he sponsored and judged a number of agricultural prizes offered through the local farming societies.[39] He also took a close interest in the conditions of the labourers on his and adjoining estates, reporting on this to the poor inquiry in December 1833.[40] His genuine interest in improving the quality of agriculture on behalf of the tenant and labourer through promoting agricultural societies and prizes was contrasted in 1851 with what some saw as the more cynical concerns of other landlords:

> Sharman Crawford does not cower stealthily behind agricultural shows and societies, that he may rush upon the tenant and plunder him of the fruits of his industry. If he encourages 'those excellent incentives to competition and agricultural skill,' it is that the tenant may reap the reward. Not so, however, with others of his order to whom the district society is nothing better than a fattening process – a sort of decoy […] to tempt the landholders to put out their capital in the land for landlords to gobble it up in the shape of increased rent.[41]

While it is unclear how much impact such societies had, there is evidence of rising productivity arising from a grain-based rotation on the small farms that made up much of his Co. Down holdings.[42]

Crawford's personal philosophy of landlordism was set out in a response made to an address from his Rademon tenants congratulating him on his recovery from serious illness in 1842. His treatment of them as his friends and not subordinates was, he asserted, grounded in a conviction that the role of landlord was one divinely intended not to be one of mastery but rather of responsible trusteeship and leadership by example:

> property in land is not conferred for the aggrandizement of the individual, but to discharge in return those duties, to the community, which the possession of that property gives him the leisure and means to perform. The landed proprietor is not placed over his fellow-men, to act the part of an arrogant and unfeeling superior, but to deal with him in that manner, in all cases which the duties of the friend would require. And the bounties he has received from a kind providence, imposes upon the possessor of them, the more stringent obligations to fulfil the will of that providence, by promoting the happiness and well-being of his creatures.[43]

What distinguished Crawford from others using similar rhetoric was his readiness to abide by the logic of his position to the extent of making considerable rent sacrifices with a concomitant reduction in personal income, and a to push for legislative means to impose similar restraints on his recalcitrant fellow landlords.

Frustrated by the delay in seeing his personal tenurial practices rendered into law, in the 1840s Crawford sought to regularise his long-established modes of estate management by drawing up formal agreements with his own tenantry on recognising compensation for improvements and establishing a mechanism to determine fair rents. During the Great Famine, in the context of an upsurge in evictions for default in payments of rent across the country, he drafted an agreement that he hoped would serve as a model to be emulated by other landowners. This document was based on the principle that 'it is just and necessary that improving tenants holding from year to year or at will by determinable tenures, should receive compensation for all permanent improvements, made at the cost of the tenant which are attached to the soil and surrendered to the landlord at the termination of their tenancies', and that it was the duty of landlords to formally acknowledge this in a society where such improvements were usually made by the occupier and not the proprietor. He prepared tables of improvements that would enhance the productivity of the land, and a series of rules for establishing their value (adjusted for depreciation over time) and ensuring this was paid over to any removed tenant where he had invested his capital and labour in making them. Tenants voluntarily surrendering their holdings should instead be given full freedom to sell their tenant right at market rates, with the value of any improvements they had made being transferred thereby to the incoming tenant. In cases of dispute, arbitrators should be appointed, with eviction suspended until the process was concluded and the costs of any unreasonable arbitration falling on the responsible party. Suitable 'improvements' for compensation would include building or repair of farm dwelling houses, farm offices and roads, drainage, clearing rocks, and making fences, gates and piers.[44]

The final version of the agreement, completed on Christmas Day 1846 and issued in printed form to the tenants, added further detail and rationale. 'Tenant right' was now more clearly defined as follows:

> 1st. That in case of ejectment or surrender of the premises at the requirement of the landlord, the tenant, being qualified according to the terms herein stated, shall be entitled to claim and receive from such landlord, or by agreement from the incoming tenant, the value of his right of occupancy including the value of all buildings and improvements then existing on the premises made at the cost of the tenant or by his predecessors in the tenancy of whom the claimant shall be the legal representative by inheritance, purchase or otherwise. 2nd. That the tenant shall have liberty at any time to sell his interest or right of occupancy in the premises, he finding in his place a solvent tenant to the satisfaction of the landlord.

Any claim to tenant right under these regulations would be strictly limited to cases where the tenant was resident, could demonstrate exertion had been made to increase productivity, and where the tenant had offered to stay on his holding at a 'fair rent' (determined by the poor law valuation minus the rateable value of any houses built by the tenant or predecessors for which no compensation had already been given). Subdivision or granting of cottier plots to labourers without the landlord's permission would invalidate any claim. Leaseholders could avail of the same terms at the end of their leases, and in all cases, rent arrears and fines for mismanagement could be deducted from any compensation sums payable. In setting the level of compensation in cases of eviction, the arbitrators should take into consideration the market value of the tenant right, the principal aim being to provide a major disincentive for landlords to evict where a tenant was willing and able to continue on their holding at a 'fair rent'. Evicted tenants should retain their right freely to sell their tenant right or 'good-will', with arbitration only coming into play if the landlord attempted to prevent this.

Summing up, Crawford recommended his plan to his tenants as just and equitable to all parties, and assured sceptical observers that its constraints on landlord powers were in line with a both natural justice and historical precedents:

> It will be said by some that this restraint is a violation of the rights of property. I say not. Property in land is not absolute ownership. The state both holds and proclaims the right of resumption, but the state in that case pays the value. The most haughty aristocrat has no higher title from the state than a tenure determinable on that condition. I leave to the landlord the same power of resumption by paying the value of the tenant's interest and improvements. I do not violate the landlord's rights. I place them on a just and useful, and consequently more stable, foundation. I am not introducing any new principle. I am only reducing to practical rules the unwritten law of 'tenant right', founded on the long established custom of this part of Ireland by which its superior prosperity has been permanently established.[45]

In addition to issuing it to his tenants, he forwarded a copy to the former prime minister Sir Robert Peel, to demonstrate both his bona fides on the subject and in the hope (not realised) that Peel would place his weight behind any future legislation based on it.[46] Following up his letter to his tenants several weeks later with another concerning rents, Crawford noted that his were already lower than those on neighbouring estates and that he had 'uniformly conceded' customary tenant right, and that consequently he would not grant formal rent abatements. But given the crisis brought on by the potato failure (then in its second year), there would be no compulsion of payment but instead a reliance on the honesty and good-feeling of the tenantry, and full allowances made for any industrious tenant in genuine difficulties to pay what proportion of rent they could manage. Any shortfall of rent made by neglectful tenants would, however, be charged against their tenant right. It was through such landlord-tenant collaboration, 'by conjoint efforts and mutual good feeling [that] my tenants and I will be enabled to pass through the ordeal of this great calamity, without permanent injury to their interests or mine'.[47] As Guinnane and Miller have argued, supported by econometric analysis, such recognition of tenant-right was indeed very much in the landowner's economic self-interest, as it acted as a guarantor of tenant exertion and transferred the costs and difficulties of ejectment to deductions from tenant right payments.[48] However, even within Ulster, where the custom was widely acknowledged by landowners, both the extent of Crawford's adherence to 'fair rents', and insistence that the custom be legally enforced and extended to all provinces, was regarded by his peers as setting dangerous precedents.

In practice, ejectments from the Crawford estates appear to have been rare, even during the later famine years when much of Ireland witnessed an orgy of landlord clearances. Even with hopelessly improvident tenants, generosity was more common. In early 1850 Thomas Barron, holder of a forty-one acre farm at Stalleen, was assisted to emigrate with his family to America, despite Barron's default on the eight and half years' arrears owed on the expiry of his lease in November 1849, due in significant part to his living beyond his means for years. Calculating the 'goodwill' on his farm (including all improvements) at £10 per acre barely covered the arrears due. Writing to the tenant, William's son Arthur commented that he thought his father had been too lenient in making him a payment for further improvements of £113 to cover his family's emigration, after making all allowances for the potato failure and low agricultural prices.[49] This would not be the only time a member of the next generation of Sharman Crawfords would question their father's 'lenient' practice of tenurial management.

By 1849 Crawford was aware that the reliability of the pre-Famine poor law valuation as a basis for 'fair rents' was being undermined by rapid fluctuations in the prices of agricultural produce, the impact of the repeal of the corn laws (phased in between 1846 and 1849), and a developing agricultural recession coming on the back of the famine crisis. In correspondence with his son James (now based at Rademon and responsible for managing it and the Iveagh estates) it became evident that complaints were now starting to be made about the rent levels, especially in the Banbridge district.[50] James was still learning the trade of land management, and still needing guidance. His father advised him not to stick mechanically to a calculation of twenty per cent of the value of produce as a fair level for rent, to discuss rent reductions on classes of land rather than individual holdings, and to wait until the average prices of the year were available rather than using those of any fixed day as a guide.[51] At the end of 1849 William produced another document to be conveyed to the tenants, setting out new arrangements for calculating rents. This would reduce rents for the following three years (1850–52), in line with falling agricultural prices, to be followed by a further adjustment based on an average for the previous year. He insisted that the costs of corn law repeal should not be borne solely or even mainly by the tenantry, and that recovery was likely in the near future so long as the chimera of a revived protectionism was shunned.

Some problems had arisen due to a valuation carried out by a professional agriculturalist in 1847, when grain prices had been artificially high due to famine; replacement by a system based on a three-year average would thus be fairer and allow for some reductions where these were found to be necessary. Such a mechanism would also remove the element of subjectivity from the calculation of rent that gave rise to suspicions against landlords and hence held back innovation, and it would form a model for legislation. 'I wish to see', he insisted, 'my tenants holding an equal position of independence with myself – each equally entitled, by law, to his just claims from the products of the soil, and each having equal powers to enforce his claims'.[52]

A detailed schedule agreed by Crawford and twenty-six tenants from the Upper Iveagh townlands was attached. It identified the published Belfast market prices for wheat, oats, bacon and butter (the last double weighted, demonstrating the growing commercial importance of this commodity), averaged for four quarterly price points, as the basis of the future calculation of rent.[53] This plan was published in the press, with the *Banner of Ulster* praising it as a 'judicious, equitable and really philosophical disquisition on rent' in contrast with the erratic or self-interested behaviour of other Ulster landlords, while to the *Freeman's Journal* the agreement was an 'act of justice not benevolence'.[54] On the basis of this new agreement, William advised James in early 1850 that reductions on the Banbridge district rents of around a quarter would be fair.[55]

His initiative appears to have been understandably popular with his tenants; a delegation with representatives from all three Down estates presented him with an address in April, thanking him for his exertions in mitigating the calamity of the famine. In contrast to other landlords, Crawford had always striven to make his tenants independent and happy, and 'we may emphatically designate [him] the best of landlords'.[56] The *Banner* proposed the address be printed in golden letters to recognise the 'fundamental charter' Crawford had established with his tenants.[57] The Presbyterian minister of Annaclone observed that Crawford had reduced rents by around one fifth and had negligible arrears on his lands, in contrast to the 'feudal tyranny' practiced on the Downshire properties.[58]

Similar practices were extended to his other properties; in March 1850 it was noted that his tenants on his small Aghavary estate were paying the lowest rents in mid-Antrim.[59] A travel writer interviewing a tenant farmer on the Rademon estate in summer 1850 found that Crawford had reduced his rents there from around 20 shillings to 14 shillings per Cunningham acre (or 10s 6d per statute acre), which had made him yet more popular:

> I congratulated the old man on having such a landlord. 'Oh sir,' said the farmer, 'he is a *good man*, and his son James, who acts as his agent, is a *good man*.' I was delighted to hear from the lips of an aged tenant such an emphatic confirmation of my own opinion of this worthy patriarch and his family. What a striking contrast there is in the rents he charges for his land compared to that charged by some of the largest landholders in Down and Antrim. Why, on the Hertford estate, land of equal quality would be nearly double the rent quoted.[60]

More remarkably, Crawford chose to forego raising his rents in the wake of the surge in agricultural prices from the early 1850s, even though this caused some tensions within his own family.[61] In early 1852 he issued another circular setting out the principles of his triennial rent review; although butter prices had risen markedly, he noted that wheat (which had been left out of the 1849 revision at the desire of the tenants) remained depressed and the price of most other products was largely unchanged, and consequently he would peg his rents at roughly the same level for another three years. If any tenant was dissatisfied with the new rent he would put it to independent valuation, and in return he would expect all tenants to pay their 'fair' rents promptly.[62] He took the latter requirement seriously, visiting the Banbridge estate with James in March 1852 to negotiate the payment of reasonable arrears with individual farmers and insisting on at least one year's rent arrears due before November 1851 with a threat of legal action for non-compliance.[63] The *Ulster Gazette* praised his rental policy as 'wise because [it is] the honest, the just policy. Mr Sharman Crawford is beloved by his tenantry', while the *Whig* saw it as a model for the rest of the country.[64] However, in a period of rising prices, the renewed rent pegging of 1852–5 also gave rise to some negative commentary. The 'sacrifice of several thousand pounds of rent' over several years drew criticisms of 'vanity' and 'puffery' from his critics.[65] Crawford was certainly not alone amongst landowners in allowing rents to fall below price rises in the post-Famine years, but his adoption of a mechanism that excluded any arbitrary or erratic changes gave a welcome degree of security to tenants.[66] This relationship of landlord-tenant collaboration and mutual support appears to have been genuinely popular and established the foundation of Crawford's national standing as the spokesman for the tenant interest.[67]

Although clearly no rack-renter, Sharman Crawford appears to have generated sufficient rental from his estates to maintain himself and his large family in sufficient comfort (if by no means in ostentation compared with many other landowners), and free from debt. Despite his rent reductions, he emerged from the Famine sufficiently solvent to purchase through the encumbered estates court in early 1851 the small Woodfort House demesne and nearby tenanted land (some 374 acres in total) from the estate of Benjamin Hosford near Bandon in Co. Cork, at a cost of £1,875.[68] It is unclear how long this land was in the Sharman Crawfords' possession, and it may have been bought with a view to supporting his son Arthur's recent marriage into the Cork branch of the Crawford family.[69] As will be seen, his daughter Mabel was also later to purchase land in Co. Waterford through the land courts on which to carry further her father's tenurial experiments. The model of landlord-tenant relations in Ulster was one the family believed exportable to other parts of the island.

The development of the tenant-right bill, 1835–7

From his first entry to parliament in 1835, Crawford demonstrated a fixed determination to have his agrarian doctrines translated into legislation, and thereby to render what he regarded as the best practice in landlord-tenant relations on his own estates universal across Ireland. His announcement in April that year that he would introduce a motion for a bill to amend the law of landlord and tenant in Ireland was welcomed by the *Northern Whig*, as 'we do not think there is another man, in the house of commons, who understands [this subject] better'.[70] His intention drew support from a radical Presbyterian lawyer from Co. Londonderry, Samuel McCurdy Greer, who would become one of his most long-standing allies in the Ulster tenant right movement, and who directed attention to the operation of the existing law against the interests of both landlords and tenants, as it 'punishes a man for being industrious and public-spirited, – placing him often in a worse situation than the idle and improvident'.[71]

It was not until 2 July 1835 that Crawford's first Irish landlord-tenant bill was presented, seconded by Belfast MP John McCance, although by this late stage in the session his object was, he admitted, mainly to get it printed for further discussion.[72] Although significantly modified and elaborated on in later years, the 1835 text would provide the foundation of what would be known, through to the late 1850s, as 'Sharman Crawford's Bill'. Its aim was to promote improvement of land and farm buildings by the occupying tenants where landowners generally did not undertake such works themselves. Under its terms, tenants would be entitled to claim compensation from their landlord at the end of their lease or termination of tenure for the value of the improvements they had made or inherited, subject to deductions for deterioration over time, with independent arbitration if the landlord rejected the claim. Each party would nominate an arbitrator, with a third selected by mutual agreement, with a determination by any two of them forming a final settlement of any claim. Refusal by landlords to co-operate would leave them open to a legal suit by the tenant in the county assistant barrister's court, with the risk of a levy of treble the legal fees on the proprietor if the tenant's claim was upheld. Only improvements and buildings that increased the rental value of the holding and which were suitable for farming could be considered for compensation, with an upper limit (yet to be determined) set on the amount. Landlord consent would be required for future improvements, except those essential to drainage and buildings for dwellings. Compensation payments could be avoided in whole or part by the award of a new lease 'at a rent not greater than the fair value of the land', to be determined by the arbitrators. No ejectments or 'distresses' (seizure of crops or livestock in lieu of rent) could take place during the period of arbitration or legal proceedings, with landlords subject to fines if they attempted this, and tenants also open to fines if they overheld their tenure without good claims. These provisions would also apply to subtenants under middlemen, giving this highly vulnerable group the right to claim compensation against the head landlord if the intermediary one defaulted on his rent.[73]

Crawford was sanguine about his bill proceeding no further than its first reading in 1835, telling his son that he would implement fully its provisions on his own estates anyway, and he would promote the dissemination of the text in the press.[74] Hostile responses from Irish and English Tories such as Frederick Shaw, Henry Goulburn and Charles Wynn indicated it would be stoutly resisted, but the non-committal stance of ministers and support from both Smith O'Brien and R. L. Sheil and even from the unlikely source of the *Times* for the principle held out some grounds for optimism.[75] However, with few exceptions, his fellow Ulster proprietors strongly opposed his initiative and regarded him as a renegade. Landownership in the province was highly concentrated: ninety-five individuals held over 10,000 acres each (totalling thirty-eight percent of the area), possessed the significant political power that came with such property, while another 1,230 owned between 500 and 10,000 acres (a further forty-six percent of land area). In east Ulster in particular these gentry families were more likely than elsewhere in Ireland to be resident and politically active in their localities and would demonstrate their determination to resist by whatever means available to them what became labelled 'Sharman Crawfordism'.[76]

In September 1835 Crawford flagged his intention to reintroduce the bill in the next session.[77] James McKnight welcomed his initiative in the *News-Letter*, republishing the text in full and asking for comments from correspondents on improving its details.[78] McKnight later noted that one motivation for his support of Crawford's proposal was an awareness that many landlords were then conspiring to curb or abolish the Ulster custom of tenant right, and that a constitutional movement was required to offer an alternative to the reactive violence of secret societies. He dated the first widespread encroachments on the custom to the mid-1830s, as many landowners began to pursue consolidation of farms to take advantage of rising livestock prices and obtain the higher rents they would support.[79]

Crawford's strategy from 1835 was an attempt to square the circle of the conflicting forces of reactionary landlordism and reactive agrarian social violence. His bill aimed to give concrete form to peasant demands for tenurial security in the form of legal recognition of a 'tenant right' linked to improvements that he believed would offer a 'practical fixity' to all but the most dissolute, while rationalising this to sceptical British legislators as a utilitarian mechanism to stimulate tenant exertion and hence the agricultural improvement that would benefit all.[80] Given the overwhelming weight of proprietarian vested interests in parliament this would be an almost insurmountable challenge, but, perhaps inspired by the eventual success of both the Catholic emancipation and parliamentary reform campaigns, he looked to a combination of attritional persuasion, mobilisation of popular support in Ireland, and exploitation of any weakness in British administrations to eventually carry the measure.

In the lead-in to the 1836 session Crawford responded at length to criticisms made of his first bill in the press, taking the opportunity to expostulate further on its principles and answer objections.[81] He also promoted it to Irish audiences in person, speaking at a meeting in Bangor in October 1835, where he stressed its universal applicability to the whole island. State intervention was, he argued, essential to ensure social justice to the poor occupier, who was not, *pace* the doctrines of orthodox political economy and the ignorant claims of English and Scottish MPs, a free agent:

> Under present circumstances, he must either take his land at the dictation of his landlord, or have no shelter under the canopy of heaven. [...] The want of employment for labour forces the poor man to look to the possession of land for subsistence; the competition raises the rent above the real value. When he gets the land he must have a shelter [...] The almighty did not intend, that man should lie, like a brute, under the shelter of a tree; and that he should eat the grass produced by the spontaneous bounty of providence. It was decreed that man should exist by his labour. The tenants of Ireland must either be capable of existing in the manner I have described, or they must spend a portion of their labour and capital in improvement, however small that may be. Is it not then, an object of national interest to secure justice to the tenants of Ireland, – to protect them from actual robbery?

Confiscation of the tenant's property in his improvements was the cause of his impoverishment, and consequently of agrarian violence and unemployment. The better off emigrated, while the poorest were reduced to the desperation of starvation. Crawford cited the evidence recently published by the poor inquiry commissioners as proof of the social consequences of the system in the Irish west (where improvable waste land was plentiful). While his bill would offer a remedy, he anticipated there would be opposition, because it would 'powerfully tend, to remove that slavish control to which the tenant is, at present, subject', and which landlords were loath to surrender. But only peaceful mass agitation and petitioning of parliament, and persuasion of landowners that reform was in their true interests, could counter such obstruction.[82]

These early meetings attracted relatively small numbers, but included some who would later become important organisers in the tenant-right movement. These included the liberal large farmer Guy Stone of Comber.[83] Believing it necessary to spread this message beyond his north Down base and adopted seat at Dundalk, Crawford travelled to Castlebar in Co. Mayo, where he proposed a combination of tithe abolition, the introduction of an equitable poor law, and his landlord-tenant measure as the solutions to the crushing poverty and threatened famine he witnessed there. His speech there was acclaimed by the Catholic archbishop of Tuam, John MacHale.[84]

Persuading a Westminster parliament composed predominantly of landowners and rentiers, and in which many of the middle-class members were adherents of the doctrines of laissez-faire, to adopt a measure of state inference in landlord-tenant relations that would curb unbridled property rights, was a tall order in the 1830s. Nevertheless, Crawford observed in 1836 that 'British parties are so balanced in the house of commons that the representatives of Ireland can turn the scale' if the people were prepared to recognise their inherent power and agitate for their rights out of doors.[85]

Fortified by a number of petitions of support for the bill from public meetings (including one from Dungannon that was forty yards long and signed by 11,140 persons),[86] Crawford returned to the fray in the next session. In March 1836 he reintroduced his bill, with some changes from the previous year's version: yearly tenants-at-will were now explicitly included, prospective improvements should be recorded in a parochial registry and, where the landlord objected, compensation should be granted only up to a fixed limit (three-fifths of the increased rent compounded at twenty-years purchase, or a maximum of £100) and then for what were deemed necessary improvements only. Landowners, especially those holding under entail, would also have greater powers to undertake improvements themselves and obtain compensation for damage to their land or subletting to a 'pauper tenancy'. The bill, he asserted, would address the crisis of poverty by curbing rack-renting and giving tenants the security to undertake the reclamation of waste lands and create, ultimately, the kind of community of feeling that explained Ulster's greater rural prosperity.[87] If the modifications in the 1836 bill were intended to assuage landed opposition, they proved of limited effectiveness. After a short debate marked by hostile pronouncements from Tory landowners, and a statement of general support for discussing the topic further from the emollient Whig chief secretary for Ireland, Lord Morpeth, the bill proceeded without a division.[88]

Crawford's bill attracted some support in parts of the British press, including a highly favourable report in the *Morning Advertiser*, the widely-read mouthpiece of the Licensed Victuallers' Society.[89] It also drew endorsement from the O'Connellite *Morning Register* as offering a valuable check to the 'feudal degradation' of Irish tenants, although it was deemed not to go far enough in the absence of a strong poor law.[90] Reports of extensive and heartless evictions, including one of twenty-nine families on the Vandeleur estate in west Clare, which had been drawn to Crawford's attention by the curate of Kilrush, inclined the liberal *Dublin Evening Post* to support his proposals.[91] However, without a manifestation of mass outdoor support, and with Crawford increasingly distracted by his disputes with O'Connell, the 1836 bill was deferred several times and never made it to a second reading.

Despite these political setbacks, Crawford retained solid political support for his proposals amongst the Presbyterian tenantry and townsmen of north Down. A public reform meeting held at Newtownards, a market town six miles south of Crawfordsburn, saw large and enthusiastic participation and support expressed for his political agenda, despite attempts by the Anglican parson, Lord Londonderry's agent and local Orange activists to subvert it. Speakers at a dinner included not only his three eldest sons, but a number of Presbyterian clergymen along with R. J. Tennent, Thomas O'Hagan and the editor of the *Northern Whig*. Crawford explained that his bill had been 'turned about' by objections in parliament, but that he would move a committee of inquiry to see if any of these could propose a better plan (which he doubted). He assured his audience that landlord-tenant legislation was not dead.[92] However, it got no further in 1837. Replying to an inquiry, Crawford explained why his backbench initiative had again been frustrated. His proposal for a select committee of inquiry had been rejected by the government, while in the face of Tory opposition and Whig indifference he could not prevent his bill being shunted to the back of the parliamentary agenda, with only post-midnight slots made available when it would be impossible to get a proper discussion. King William IV's death and the subsequent dissolution of parliament had finally killed off all chances, and the only hope for the future now lay in getting the 'general voice of the country' raised behind a new bill.[93] Thus the first phase of his agrarian reform measure in parliament ended in defeat and frustration.

At the same time, he was clearly tapping into a rich seam of popular feeling in the northern counties. One Belfast-published anonymous pamphlet of 1836, possibly by a

Presbyterian clerical author, was dedicated to him in the assurance that he would sanction the 'great principle' argued therein of the 'natural right' of the peasant to have a joint-ownership of the land with the proprietor. Crawford's public actions had, the author observed, demonstrated him 'fearlessly grappl[ing] with *absolute ownership* – that monster which has long devastated society, and rendered it one scene of desolation and misery; and I am proud that it is in my power, even by this slight testimony, to mark my deep sense of your *well-directed* and *uncalculating* patriotism.' The text went on to argue both scriptural and rational grounds for the rejection of absolute ownership of land (from which all social and political corruptions arose), to praise the reformist legacy of the Volunteers and more ambiguously the United Irishmen, to laud the lesson of moral-force mobilisation proffered by the Catholic agitation, and note that any advantages Ulster tenants had over other Irish peasants arose from their historic resistance to absolute landlordism. Although less clear on the specific remedies to be adopted (despite sympathetic references to the campaign of 'Tommy Downshire's Boys' in pressing for lower rents through collective action in 1830–1), the sentiments expressed in this pamphlet were widely shared and constituted a base for Crawford to seek to build on in future.[94] Widespread activism by both Presbyterian and Catholic clergy would in future prove central to a revived tenant-right movement.

A Defence of the Small Farmers of Ireland, 1837–45

Out of parliament in 1837, Sharman Crawford pulled together his thoughts on land reform in two pamphlets. *Observations on the Necessity of an Amendment in the Laws of Landlord and Tenant, in Conjunction with a Total Repeal of the Duties on Foreign Corn,* was directed to the commercial, manufacturing and agricultural classes of Great Britain and Ireland and urged an alliance between tenant-righters and free-traders in both countries.[95] Lengthy extracts were published in the *Northern Whig.*[96] He couched his economic thinking in a religious framework: the fundamental social problem in Ireland arose, he claimed, from human attempts to frustrate divine benevolence through the imposition of monopolies. Claims to absolute ownership of landed property by the landlord were thus immoral and impolitic and were asserted in defiance of providence. Landlords were thus impious as well as misguided in claiming absolute proprietarian rights, as 'whatever human laws may say, I maintain, *the land is not his own, – cannot be his own, – except subject to the great ordinance of the almighty'.*[97] No contracts could be freely made when there was such a huge imbalance in social power; tenants were unfairly subordinated in tenurial relations just as they were in the exercise of the franchise and the landlords could extract extortionate rents through the threat of eviction. This ran against what he described as the 'natural right of man to the soil'.

It was to introduce the necessary restrictions on landed avarice and ensure social equity that he had introduced his bills, although these had failed due to lack of public support. A precedent for such intervention had been set in the 1833 Irish Church Temporalities Act's treatment of tenants of church lands; what he sought was, he asserted, simply the extension of that principle to cover all tenants on privately owned estates.[98] Legal checks on landlord powers of eviction and setting extortionate rents would benefit all classes, especially in the context of the anticipated abandonment of the corn laws, which had stimulated artificially high food prices benefitting only landowners and corn merchants. Such checks should include not only a valuation for fair rent and compensation for improvements made in case of eviction, but also recognition of what Crawford described as '*the value of that equitable (vested) interest which the landlord desires to deprive him of*', in other words, his customary tenant right.[99] He was prepared for a long and potentially unrewarding struggle to attain this; for while (echoing the Volunteer slogan of 1791), '*Nothing which is morally wrong can be politically right*', the public duty of pursuing this would impose 'a kind of martyrdom of the individual who discharges it'.[100] While he was prepared to take this on himself, ultimately it would be up to the people themselves to insist on reforms in their own interest.

Observing a rash of 'extermination' by clearing landlords reported in other parts of Ireland in later 1837, he urged the papers to take up his measure as the only effective curb on such behaviour, and to promote an agitation behind it. He pressed the editor of the *Wexford Independent* to support him in pursuing this non-sectarian 'practical object' of a constitutional agitation against 'extermination' in the south-east.[101] While that paper and others responded sympathetically to his call,[102] its coincidence with the nadir of Crawford's breakdown in relations with O'Connell continued to impede the development of any such national movement.

When he returned to focus on land reform in print again in a second pamphlet in 1839 the political situation had shifted significantly. An Irish poor law (however inadequate) had been passed, along with what he regarded as the fatally compromised tithe act. A sustained agricultural and commercial depression, threatening regional famine in the west by summer 1839, and which continued to deteriorate through to the crisis year of 1842–3, was then underway. With more time to review the nature of the agrarian problem in Ireland and the utility of legislation, Crawford produced his most considered statement on the matter in instalments carried by a number of Irish newspapers from September, and then as a 130-page tract entitled *A Defence of the Small Farmers of Ireland* in December.[103]

The immediate stimulus for this composition was the renewed prominence given to the idea that the solution of Ireland's social problems lay in 'colonization' or mass assisted emigration, an idea which had been floated in the Whately commission's third report in 1836 and which was revived with the launch of the South Australian Colonization Society in 1839. This scheme had some support in both Ireland and the colony, which was seeking an influx of white 'free labour' to develop its economy on land appropriated from the indigenous peoples, but clashed with Crawford's insistence that Ireland needed development not clearance.[104] Although not opposed to voluntary or even some small-scale assisted emigration to the antipodes, Crawford reacted to what he (correctly) identified as the Malthusian underpinnings of the colonisation scheme as advocated by the political economist Robert Torrens.[105] His first objective was to refute the Malthusian doctrine, which he feared was widely held as a 'fashionable mania' by Irish landlords, that Ireland was fatally overpopulated relative to the means of subsistence, that this was at the root of the country's agricultural malaise or retrogression. If Torrens' premise was accepted, it followed that only a major reduction of population would permit an agrarian restructuring into large farms managed by capitalist farmers and worked by proletarianised landless wage-labourers orthodox economics held necessary for future prosperity. In rejecting the theoretical underpinnings of the Irish overpopulation thesis, and the concomitant of what he believed must be a coercive depopulation strategy favoured by landlords and potentially the state, Crawford was in line with the refutations offered by other anti-Malthusians such as George Poulett Scrope, John Revans, formerly secretary to the Irish poor inquiry commission, and Fr Thaddeus O'Malley, all of whom published tracts on Irish poverty and development in the 1830s.[106] What he added to the mix was a defence of the economic rationale and potential of small-farm agriculture drawn from the existing social model of north-east Ulster with which he was personally familiar.

Crawford's core argument was that the small-scale, intensive farming of high population density counties such as Down and Armagh, in the context of socio-economic conventions that tended to reduce the threat of predatory landlordism there, was demonstrably as or more productive than the extensive capitalist farming that characterised England and lowland Scotland, and which was promoted as a universal model for Ireland by orthodox liberal political economists such as Nassau Senior.[107] Torrens' figures purporting to demonstrate the gulf between Irish and English farming productivity were, he argued, based on fallacious assumptions, and masked a serious underproduction problem in both countries. Moreover, the absence of available capital in Ireland in the hands of either farmers or landowners rendered redundant any social solution not based on harnessing the productive potential of small-scale and labour-intensive husbandry applied to advanced crop rotations and stall-feeding of cattle.[108]

The social landscape of Down, he argued, while not perfect, represented a model that was not only morally and economically superior to both the pauperised expanses of the Irish west and the consolidated and depopulated vision of Ireland favoured by the Malthusians. The Down model was moreover exportable to the rest of the island. At the heart of this was a mixed farming pattern of small family farms rarely extending beyond sixty acres, along with a cottier-labourer class who were themselves typically landholders of plots of around five-six acres. Crucially, the latter arrangement, permitting labouring families to raise their subsistence on their own fields while freeing them also to earn wages in either agricultural or industrial occupations, led to less cutthroat competition for employment, higher wages, and much lower demand for formal or informal poor relief than elsewhere, where a more exploitative 'conacre' system of subletting to labourers was in force. Small landholding labourers were, Crawford insisted, not only less economically vulnerable but more productive, with a consequence that rural society was both more stable and more prosperous. Rather than the demoralising indoor relief offered to the destitute under the 1838 Irish poor law, this model offered underemployed labourers the potential to better their conditions and utilise any seasonal downturns in agricultural or industrial employment by turning to their own resources: self-help, underpinned by access to land at reasonable rates and some developmental work funded by the state and landowners, was the only real solution to the crisis of rural poverty. Paradoxically, given his stark opposition to that author's Irish workhouse plan, he was able to draw on George Nicholls's third report on Irish poor laws, which lauded the social conditions created by small farm agriculture in Belgium, to argue that the principle manifest in the social constitution of Down was a universal one.[109]

Crawford admitted that the particularities of north-east Ulster were related to the availability of cottage industry opportunities in linen manufacture, but argued that these had declined with the mechanisation of flax spinning since the 1820s without any dislocation of rural society in this part of Ireland. This may have been something of a blind spot; while not anti-industrial, he clearly held a somewhat nostalgic attraction for the mixed industrial-agricultural society that characterised the proto-industrial phase of industrial development, and did not dwell on the devastating consequences of the collapse of cottage industrial employment in many parts of south Ulster and north Leinster and Connacht in the 1830s and the loss of bargaining power by rural handloom weavers over much of Ulster.[110]

This defence of the productive potential of small farms posed an obvious problem: why was it that extensive subdivision and cottier landholding in Connacht had produced misery not prosperity in that province? His answer, which he insisted drew on personal inspection of the pauperised western districts as well as the evidence from the recent social inquiries, pointed not to overpopulation or any cultural consequences of Catholicism but rather to the distorting influence of landlord-tenant relations there. Exploitation by middlemen and agents of absentee proprietors was rife, the institution of rundale or joint tenancy strangled individual enterprise, and neither the small farmer nor labourer were offered any inducement to self-exertion or improvement beyond the bare minimum required for family survival.

The solution, viewed from Crawfordsburn, was to export to the west and south the essence of that social institution that had provided the social security necessary for northeast Ulster's historical divergence from the rest of the island: tenant-right.[111] He rationalised this divergence as originating from the Ulster plantation, a historicised interpretation that was later elaborated on by McKnight.[112] Although simplistic and exaggerated, the 'plantation' argument was intended not to assert Ulster's irreconcilable difference from the rest of Ireland, but to assert a long historical precedent for state regulation of landlord-tenant relations and to suggest that at specific historical moments – such as in the present 'reformist' conjuncture between Britain and Ireland – new social institutions might be introduced with beneficial and lasting consequences. Modern research has suggested that the Ulster custom emerged instead in the eighteenth century from the sale of the residue of a lease by an outgoing tenant, and from the practice of giving preference to sitting tenants when a lease terminated, which survived in customary form after leases became less common, but McKnight's interpretation was widely believed at the time.[113]

Social recovery and the extinction of agrarian violence in the west would, Crawford maintained, require state action in the form of the introduction of agricultural education and schemes of waste-land reclamation for resettlement of part of the population. But the measure 'of importance incomparably beyond all others' would be the legal and compulsory extension of tenant right. In this radical-utilitarian vision, the stimulus to acquire security against eviction through creating 'improvements' would bring forth the natural industrial tendencies of the Irish peasant, while at the same time benefitting the suspicious landowners by boosting the productivity and long-term profitability of their land. A virtuous circle could be created if only the landowners and their political representatives would abandon their proprietarian attachment to the untrammelled 'rights of property' and Malthusian delusions and accept the principle of compensation for improvement.

The letters and subsequent pamphlet drew protests from Torrens and praise from Lord Cloncurry.[114] Perhaps more significantly, his arguments were well received in the Whig *Morning Chronicle*, which noted that 'the relations of landlords and tenant in Ireland are absolutely a blot on the national character'.[115] This raised a hope, vain as it turned out, that Crawford's sustained advocacy was at last bearing political fruit at Westminster.

Returning to parliament as MP for Rochdale in 1841 Crawford noted that 'as an English representative I did not give up my advocacy of the Irish tenant rights question'.[116] There was already evidence of some rapprochement with the repeal movement on his land reform proposals, which, the *Morning Register* observed, 'proved [him] the uncompromising enemy of oppression, and the poor man's disinterested friend'.[117] O'Connell had in March 1841 declared himself a convert to the principles of fixity of tenure and compensation for tenant improvements, and credited these ideas to Crawford.[118] A series of letters restating the arguments of the latter's 1837 and 1839 pamphlets were, at O'Connell's behest, read into the minutes of the LNRA in April 1841, a conciliatory move which Crawford welcomed.[119] He announced that he intended to bring in a modified version of his tenant compensation bill in 1842, again receiving supportive comments from O'Connell.[120] In the end this bill was squeezed out due to pressure of other parliamentary business that session.[121] Meanwhile, the deteriorating economic conditions in both countries associated with the severe agricultural and industrial crises of 1839–43 intensified concern about landlord-tenant relations. These years saw an upsurge in well-publicised cases of eviction and reactive violence and pressure for the inclusion of demands for some form of 'fixity of tenure' in the O'Connellite repeal platform.[122]

In April 1843 O'Connell raised for discussion in the Repeal Association the rival agrarian programmes of the south Leinster-based agitator William Conner and that of Sharman Crawford.[123] Perhaps aware of the growing national appeal of the latter and suspicious of rival public meetings, O'Connell opted to reject Conner's plan of 'dual ownership' based on 'a valuation and a perpetuity' as infringing on the 'just rights' of responsible landlords and because he believed it would deepen antagonisms between tenant farmers and labourers.[124] Adhering to the ideal of cross-class collaboration, albeit under the stimulus of corrective legislation, O'Connell endorsed Crawford's tenant compensation bill, alongside his own preferences for compulsory twenty-one year leases and penalties on absentee landlords, and incorporated these into his 'monster meeting' platform speeches.[125] If personal relations between Crawford and O'Connell remained tense at best, the endorsement of elements of his programme by the mass movement gave it renewed momentum. It also permitted a revival of open displays of popularity for Crawford in areas where his anti-O'Connellism had previously rendered him persona non grata: at Bellewstown in Meath in April 1843 a repeal demonstration toasted 'William Sharman Crawford and fixity of tenure', to the accompaniment of Robert Burns' radical song 'A man's a man for a' that'.[126]

Conner appealed rhetorically to Crawford to support what he argued was his own more radical and direct solution to agrarian demands.[127] Expressing something like envious frustration at Crawford's access to the press and playing up the sacrifices he had made personally in promoting land reform through local meetings, Conner nonetheless found something to praise in Crawford's published critiques of landlordism. The problem, he argued, lay in Crawford's reluctance to embrace direct rent controls and absolute fixity, which he argued amounted to a betrayal of the tenants' cause.[128] Conner's tendency towards self-promotion and apparent inability to co-operate with others (he would later clash publicly with his protege James Fintan Lalor) would rule out any such combination, if it was genuinely intended, with Crawford. He was briefly imprisoned in 1842 for using inflammatory language, and expelled from the Repeal Association in September 1843 for promoting a rent and rates strike in defiance of O'Connell. Patrick Maume comments, with some justification, that Conner 'believed his theories were demonstrable as a mathematical proposition; this certitude, and his tendencies towards egotism and self-dramatisation, brought about an intransigence which limited his political effectiveness'.[129] Crawford appears not to have responded directly to a man he may well have regarded as a loose cannon: his own belief at this time was that practical security and fair rents were more likely to be attained indirectly through a measure to enforce retrospective compensation for improvements, which was likely to prove the first and not final step in attaining full justice for the tenant.

In 1843 Crawford was one of a number of Irish reformers, including Wyse and Smith O'Brien, pushing the government and parliament to adopt land reform as a non-coercive means of responding to the challenge posed by O'Connell's resurgent movement. He argued vociferously that social distress provoked by a landlord campaign of 'extermination' and acute poverty unalleviated by an effective poor law was fuelling both the repeal movement and agrarian outrages.[130] In the commons he cited a figure of 70,000 persons suffering from ejectments over the previous five years, and reiterated that his own support for the union was conditional on the redress of the just grievances of Ireland.[131] In moving his motion for an inquiry into the condition of Ireland in July, O'Brien endorsed the general principles of Crawford's scheme, while others lobbied the opposition Whig leadership to take up the issue.[132] McKnight in the *News-Letter* urged Irish landlords to back Crawford's bill as a means of undermining O'Connell's allegedly separatist appeal, although this had limited impact and other Conservative papers denounced Crawford as an agent of an 'anti-landlord war'.[133] After demanding a full inquiry into the land question, Crawford re-introduced his compensation bill in August that year, after appealing privately to Peel not to oppose such a 'practical' measure and to allow it proper time for debate. Aware there was little time left that session, he stated he would bring it back it the following year.[134] O'Connellite opinion, while sceptical that parliament would ever pass such a bill, was generally supportive of it as a foundational measure for tenant rights, although doubts were expressed as to parts of the mechanism for determining the value of compensation.[135]

Although non-committal on legislation, and insistent that he would not infringe on the rights of property, Peel had an eye on Irish Catholic public opinion and was careful not to dismiss Crawford's proposal outright. Admitting that there were real problems in the agrarian condition of Ireland, he undertook to investigate this further, a commitment that Crawford accepted as sufficient grounds to drop his own bill that session.[136] The prime minister in return offered the concession of a full public inquiry, to be chaired by the Earl of Devon, a figure close to Peel and himself an 'improving' Irish landowner, into Irish land tenure.[137] While he may not have entirely trusted Peel, Crawford was prepared to give the inquiry the benefit of the doubt, and was amongst the first to give evidence when it finally convened early the following year. This appearance allowed him to elaborate on the intentions of his bill – which was not to provide the vague 'fixity of tenure' advocated by some agitators, but rather to offer the tenant the opportunity to 'acquire a practical fixity' through his own exertions when his past and present improvements were legally valued as tenant right. His thinking had, he admitted, moved on somewhat from the first versions of the bill in the mid-1830s, and he now also believed a fair rent, determined using the new machinery of the poor law valuation, and revised regularly in line with price movements, should be mandated by removing the legal power of recovering rent by the process of 'distress' from landlords who set rents above the valuation level. Although proposing to work through financial penalties rather than prohibitions, Crawford's thought by this point was evolving to embrace a version of the '3Fs' of fair rent, fixity of tenure and freedom of sale of tenant right, later central to the tenant movement from the 1850s to the Land League era. He also deployed statistics to demonstrate that Ireland was not overpopulated, and that the labouring poor could be comfortably settled on small lots of two acres if secure and fairly rented and seasonal labour was also available from farmers at fair wages.[138]

Although the appointment of the Devon Commission was rightly regarded as a victory by Crawford, hopes that his parliamentary persistence and argument would prevail were frustrated by its merely permissive and minimalist recommendations on tenant compensation in 1845, and its clear preference for the landlord undertaking such works of 'improvement'. More worryingly for Crawford and his allies, the commission reported that the 'Ulster custom' was acceptable only where proprietors had succeeded in imposing limitations on the amounts paid for 'sale of goodwill' and rejected any move towards its legalisation.[139] This reflected the arguments of some large Ulster proprietors, such as Downshire, that unrestrained competition was an obstacle to the consolidation of holdings that he regarded as essential on his estates, which led to action to curb 'free sale'.[140] The Devon report provoked protest meetings in various parts of Ulster, including one at Crossgar where Crawford himself lectured his tenants on the disjuncture between the evidence collected and the feeble remedies proposed.[141]

Crawford may also have been led to reconsider the sufficiency of his previous emphasis on compensation for existing improvements by the publication in 1845 of William Neilson Hancock's *The Tenant-Right of Ulster, Considered Economically*. In other respects an orthodox liberal economist, Hancock was incensed by what he saw as the Devon Commission's assault on the Ulster custom, and constructed his defence of it around a commentary on his brother John's evidence to it, which was based on his experience as a land agent in Co. Armagh. The pamphlet criticised Crawford's previous proposals as defective in denying the tenant's claim if ejected for non-payment of rent, and for not making provision for transmission of the claim for compensation to his successors, as well as in its mode of calculating compensation.[142] Hancock's publication came to be regarded as a cornerstone of the economic case for custom-based tenant right, and Crawford was careful in later iterations of his measure to emphasise the primacy of the 'Ulster custom' and the need for regular valuation to determine 'fair' rent. He felt obliged to reassure the *Banner,* which had taken up Hancock's critique, that his intention had always been to give greater practical security to the custom through legislation and never to usurp it.[143]

Peel's government followed up the Devon report in 1845 with what would be a the first of a series of government bills for compensation for tenant improvements, which the *Morning Chronicle* dismissed as merely 'a modification or fragment of an old bill of Sharman Crawford'.[144] To the *Banner,* however, Stanley's compensation bill of 1845 was in fact its antithesis, as intended to ignore retrospective improvements and hence destroy the tenant right of Ulster, while the *Freeman* also concluded that it was intended solely to kill off Crawford's much better bill.[145] The *Vindicator* claimed it was an unscrupulous attempt to rob two and half million people of sixty million pounds worth of their property in the form of unexhausted improvements to the soil.[146]

Frustrated by this manoeuvre, Crawford informed the prime minister that he would revise and reintroduce his own bill in July 1845.[147] When printed it drew some criticism from ultra-nationalists as not being radical enough, but had support from Ulster farmers' meetings.[148] Neither bill proceeded that year, but Crawford reflected publicly towards the end of the year on the progress attained. Stanley's bill while 'objectionable and delusive' in content, had conceded the principle 'that an ejected tenant is entitled to demand by the rule of justice, and should be secured by the sanction of the laws, a fair compensation for all unremunerated improvements'. His 'ten year's struggle' had, he believed, at last begun to bear fruit, although more extensive agitation would be essential to ultimate success.[149] That campaign would be transformed by the impact of the Great Famine, which was taking shape in the wake of the first potato failure that autumn.

Response to the Famine, 1845–9

The behaviour of Ireland's political representatives during the Great Famine has attracted significant and largely deserved criticism from historians. Brian Walker has drawn attention to the apparent paucity of serious discussion of the famine crisis on the platforms of candidates contesting Irish constituencies in the general election of summer 1847.[150] This may be somewhat overstated, as there is some evidence that the eviction-related issue of tenant right was forcing itself on to some hustings. But with the collapse of the O'Connellite political machine into self-serving factions and the still under-developed state of the Tenant League, not to mention the priority of survival preoccupying many of those who had previously participated in mass political activity (especially as non-voters), electoral politics indeed failed to reflect the urgency and scale of the crisis devastating the island.

Class and partisan interests – and the perceived antagonism of British public opinion – threw the majority of Irish peers and the large Conservative block of Irish MPs on to the defensive, utilising familial and ideological affinities with British Conservatives to seek to minimise damage to the landed and Protestant interest in Ireland. With a few exceptions, such as Lord Monteagle, most Irish Whig-liberals rallied to Lord John Russell's government from its formation in summer 1846, being rewarded (as in the cases of the Catholic Whigs Thomas Redington, Richard Lalor Sheil and Thomas Wyse) with government posts or patronage. Despite unease with that government's policy, overt opposition from most Catholic MPs was rare before the ecclesiastical titles bill crisis in 1850–1. Following the collapse of O'Connell's health in early 1847 and his death in May, the mantle of Repeal party leadership passed to his uncharismatic and politically inept son John, who struggled to maintain his father's legacy despite the residual authority the name still conveyed and the continuing loyalty of most of the clergy. Given these centrifugal forces, it was hardly surprising that an attempt to construct a non-partisan 'Irish party' speaking for the country's interests foundered in early 1847 in the face of insuperable obstacles of different class, religious and personal allegiances.[151]

This is not to say that critical Irish voices independent of the partisan blocs were wholly absent in the famine years. A small number of individuals offered relatively coherent resistance to the dominant lines of policy and articulated alternative programmes for relief and reconstruction, while remaining antagonistic to landlord strategies of clearance and pursuing subsidies. One of these, before his withdrawal from parliament and reluctant adoption of physical-force separatism in 1848, was William Smith O'Brien, with whom Crawford sought to co-operate in resisting the imposition of coercion and extracting more humane relief measures in 1845–7.[152] A handful of English radicals challenged the government consensus on Irish policy, the most prominent of whom was Poulett Scrope, joined by Feargus O'Connor after he became MP for Nottingham in 1847. Arguably the most active and consistent radical parliamentary critic of government policy was, however, William Sharman Crawford. This was picked up by the *Spectator* – not generally a supporter of his brand of politics – in early 1847: 'The […] subject [of a remedy for the destitute state of the Irish poor] was very scantily handled by the Irish members', it observed, 'Mr Sharman Crawford, himself Irish though representing an English constituency, was a striking exception'.[153] More forthrightly, the *Freeman's Journal* contrasted his activism in countering the self-interested scheming of Irish landlords in parliament with the miserable failure of the 'Irish Party' to establish itself.[154] Although sympathetic to some of its aspirations, Crawford kept his distance from that body as it opted to keep its deliberations out of the view of the press, in contrast to his own ethic of political transparency.[155]

Crawford's interventions during the Famine were not restricted to words, but also involved direct action on his own estates. Following his established practice of activist landlordism, he undertook responsibility for famine relief, either acting personally during the parliamentary recess, or via his elder sons John, Arthur and James, who had management responsibilities for the separate parts of the estates. William himself chaired the Newtownards Union board of guardians when he was able to, and during his absences in London the post was often filled by the vice-chair, his ally Guy Stone, who also appealed to the Dublin authorities for more assistance and the extension of the poor law with the support of the board.[156] Crawford's younger son Frederick also sat on the Newtownards board, was a very regular attender and occasionally acted as chair. Crawford was also active on the baronial presentment sessions for public works and urged county landowners to follow his example in offering work at good wages on his estates to those who needed it. The usually antipathetic *Downpatrick Recorder* expressed frustration that more Down landowners ignored his call to prompt action in autumn 1846 and was concerned about free riding by other less scrupulous proprietors.[157]

James Sharman Crawford sat on the Downpatrick board of guardians and later also the union's soup kitchen finance committee; he argued in vain for early collective action under the poor law but also ensured employment for the labourers on the family's Rademon estate on through drainage works affecting some fifty tenements. He also paid for relief out of his own pocket 'like a good Samaritan' for individuals on neighbouring estates who fell through the official poor law net, and organised the distribution of charitable funds, including money sent from Guernsey for the poor of Crossgar.[158] William's fifth son, Charles, was appointed an assistant poor law commissioner in February 1847 with responsibility for inspecting the south-western unions, and acquired a reputation for professionalism and fairness in this role.[159] William's unmarried daughters, Arminella, Eleanor and the future travel writer and suffragist Mabel, took an active role in female philanthropic activity in Belfast, for example serving as patronesses or supporters of charitable bazaars for the relief of Connacht on behalf of the Belfast Ladies' Relief Association in 1846, 1848 and 1850.[160] On the Sharman Crawford estates rents were pegged at valuation level (and as we have seen, reduced through an elaborate mechanism in 1849 in response to the falling prices), while rent arrears were often waived.[161] More immediately, at Crawfordsburn in early 1847 William was reported as dispensing meal to his tenants at half the market rate, and giving bread and broth to his own labourers at dinner with the option also to purchase meal at subsidised prices.[162]

Although Crawford's locus of operations in Down was very far from the most acute zones of famine in western and south-western Ireland (a point he was later to highlight and perhaps overstate for rhetorical purposes), its impact and the suffering of the rural poor there was real enough, as he pointed out in parliament as early as January 1846. His estates lay in the 'oatmeal zone' of northern counties less exclusively dependent on potato subsistence, but in the Upper Iveagh barony potato conacre was still widespread and provided a large share of the food of the labouring poor, especially given the decline of textile employment. One resident observed in 1835 that both cottiers and labourers there were highly vulnerable.[163] With more than half the potato crop lost in the region in 1845, Crawford observed that oatmeal prices had already risen by fifty per cent and numbers in the Newtownards workhouse were close to double the previous peak of 200.[164] A few days later he urged that the state provide outdoor relief in food where required.[165] Even in the normally prosperous union of Downpatrick, he noted in May 1846, the unusually high price of potatoes was causing distress, rendering vital access to food imports which would be cheapened by the abolition of the corn laws.[166] These statements drew criticism the local Conservative press, which accused him of exaggeration of the situation in support of 'the traitor Peel' in the latter's decision to move against the corn laws, but subsequent developments were to bear Crawford out.[167]

The situation would escalate in Down from this point, especially after the catastrophic potato failure of summer 1846, which was declared to be 'total' in the Newtownards union.[168] The 1851 census revealed a population decline for the county overall of 10.5 per cent since 1841 – well below the 24 per cent national shortfall, but still an unprecedented (at least since the 1740s) decadal reduction in numbers. If much of this fall can be attributed to emigration, a long-established practice in response to distress in Down, famine-related deaths evidently occurred too. One estimate puts excess mortality for the county at seven per cent of the population, and if this was weighted towards the poorer upland districts mostly covered by the Banbridge, Kilkeel and Newry poor law unions, it also had an impact in the east and north of the county. There is evidence that, at least in the year 1847, the impact of potato blight combined with other factors to produce acute distress throughout much of county, leading to famine-related deaths and provoking concern over its effects and in some cases political conflict over relief and agrarian rights. A crisis in the linen weaving industry, beginning in the urban centres of Belfast and its eastern suburb of Ballymacarrett in late 1846 and escalating through the following year in response to a credit crunch that peaked in October 1847, along with the collapse of consumer demand, threw many smallholding families reliant on part-time industrial earnings with into crisis and led to high unemployment in both urban and rural areas dependent on linen weaving. In his study of the Famine in the county, James Grant suggests that, even in this most favoured region, destitution and fever may have threatened the lives of around twenty per cent of the county's population at its peak in 1847.[169]

Attending, along with his son James, a baronial presentments session for Upper Iveagh in January 1847, Crawford urged the 'instantaneous relief' of real distress, despite his doubts as to the efficacy of the government relief works. Other landowners, including Downshire, were still reluctant to admit the scale of the crisis in the district, and tried to talk it down, but were challenged by the report of the inspector of public works, the assertions of the local Catholic clergy, and the unrest of a hungry and impatient crowd gathered outside Castlewellan courthouse. Captain Brereton, the inspector, estimated 1,800–2,000 families were in distress in the half-barony and at least £3,000 was required for relief that month. Under pressure, the gathered landowners felt obliged to cede ground and follow Crawford in voting for the necessary public works alongside a relief subscription.

With the intensification of the blight and collapse of the potato economy on which so many depended, there was real distress in Upper Iveagh which was met temporarily by these public works, but as the government rapidly scaled these back from March 1847, the poor law unions, ratepayers and landed proprietors were expected to shoulder the burden. On 9 February the Banbridge union guardians informed the Dublin commissioners that the workhouse was already full.[170] The tenants of the Ballybrick electoral division (one partly-owned by Crawford) raised a charitable subscription for the district's poor, and appealed successfully to the local landlords for equivalent subscriptions.[171] Some short-term assistance was granted under the 'soup kitchen' or temporary relief act when finally implemented in summer 1847, with over 4,400 daily rations being issued in the Banbridge Union in late July, but this had been phased out by September that year.[172]

Evidence from the census suggests the Sharman Crawfords had mixed success in maintaining the populations on their scattered land holdings. On some of their Upper Iveagh townlands (such as Lackan, Ballybrick and Ballyward), numbers of both population and houses remained stable between 1841 and 1851, as was also the case at Rademon (where the number of houses increased from thirty-five to thirty-seven) and in Crawfordsburn village. However there were population falls of between twenty and thirty per cent on some of the other townlands that Crawford had part ownership of, and a massive reduction of forty-three per cent (and thirty per cent of houses) on the poor Slieve Croob townland of Dunbeg Upper, only partly offset by an eleven per cent recovery of population by 1861 at it seems some people moved back after the potato and the agricultural economy revived.[173] It is likely that the disappearing houses were mostly in the lowest or 'fourth' class; in the county as a whole these fell from nearly 14,000 in 1841 to 2,114 by 1851, while houses in better classes all increased in number. Given the family's refusal to countenance clearances, it appears likely that migration of labourers and their families (in some cases temporarily) accounted for the bulk of the population drain, along with the waves of epidemic fever.

The Crawford family's direct efforts were not restricted to their Down properties. Visiting Stalleen in November 1846, Crawford made clear his intention to recognise the operation of tenant right there on the same terms as in the north, with an entitlement of free sale of interest to himself or to any solvent incoming tenant should a farmer wish to sell up their holding. His own resources would be used to fund drainage works through low-interest loans to tenants, while a portion of his rents would be remitted to a district relief committee chaired by the parish priest in support of local donations. His own land currently under pasture would be ploughed up to provide employment in tillage. The *Drogheda Argus* was impressed at his commitment to maintaining the livelihoods of the sixty small tenant families on the estate, noting his policy 'shuts out famine and pestilence from his tenantry, and secures their future comfort', and urged other Leinster landowners to emulate him.[174] Cottier-labourers fared less well, although the estate offered the sum of £5 each to a number of cottiers to give up their plots and cabins and emigrate.[175] The population of the townland fell twenty-five per cent to 322 between 1841 and 1851, and the number of houses by fourteen per cent to fifty-nine.[176]

In north Down the unfolding famine crisis led to confrontation between Crawford and the dominant magnate in the area. Writing in January 1847 to his employer, Lord Londonderry, the land agent John Andrews warned that 'the distress of the poor has been fearfully increasing', and stated in the following month that the voluntary charitable soup-kitchen set up in Newtownards was in heavy demand, and 'the poor and destitute are pressing on the workhouse beyond its powers of reception'.[177] Andrews' principal concern related to the ability of tenants on the extensive Londonderry estates to pay their rents at a time when major improvements were being made to the demesne at Mount Stewart, leading his employer to agree to some rent abatements and payments to the voluntary relief subscriptions in the district. However, the landowner's seeming reluctance to contribute to an extent commensurate with his enormous means (he had acquired extensive coal revenues in Co. Durham following his second marriage in 1819), and Andrews' enthusiasm for making use of the crisis to weed out 'weaker' tenants, drew criticism from the radical press and his political opponents.[178] Both the *Banner* and *Londonderry Standard* attacked Londonderry personally for his apparent indifference to widespread suffering.[179]

As gross overcrowding increased in the workhouses, a town meeting called for the granting of outdoor relief to at least some classes of destitute poor, but was resisted by Andrews and the Dublin commissioners. By February 1847 the workhouse was twenty-five per cent over capacity and more destitute people were flooding in.[180] However, the majority of guardians on both the Newtownards and Downpatrick boards repeatedly rejected any resort to outdoor relief even when this was legalised under the poor law amendment act of June 1847 and approved for at least the elderly and disabled by the commission in the autumn.[181] As Wright has observed, the resort to state-sanctioned outdoor relief (and the bureaucratic interventions involved) appeared to many landowners as likely to discredit their local authority and undermine tenant deference, and its absence in much of east Ulster is thus no reliable indicator of local conditions.[182]

Crawford had been calling for just such an intervention since the start of the year, when he told the commons:

> The union-house of Newtownards had 800 inmates; the female children were lying seven in two beds; the adult women were sleeping three in two narrow beds placed together; sickness prevailed to a great extent, from the crowded state of the house; the board had asked leave to give the poor one meal a day out of the house, but no assent was given to it. In the workhouse of Downpatrick the smallpox had broken out, yet the poor must be relieved in it. Was it not inhuman to send them to such an infectious place? He called on the government to give a discretionary power to guardians to give outdoor relief. On the part of the board of Newtownards, he could say they wanted no assistance from the government; if they had the power of giving out-door relief, they could supply the poor themselves; the property of the locality could support the poor if they were not restricted in the power of doing so.[183]

By the autumn the legal power to give outdoor relief had finally been granted, but was now being frustrated by local landed resistance, and he lodged formal protests in the minutes in July and September against the board's majority decisions against permitting outdoor relief or appointing relieving officers.[184] This refusal provoked appeals from others in the town, on grounds of Christian charity, to turn 'the tide of public opinion in favour of out-door relief', and criticisms were made of Londonderry's obstructionism.[185] The failure of this campaign to reverse the harsh policy provoked Crawford's resignation as chair of the Newtownards guardians in September, followed by Stone as vice-chairman and Robert Nicholson as deputy-vice-chairman.[186] They continued to protest at the number of deaths in the town's workhouse (seventy-four between August and November), the extent of overcrowding, and the 'unjust, uncharitable and unchristian' stance of Londonderry and Andrews in refusing to countenance outdoor relief funded from the poor rates.[187] For his part, Andrews expressed contempt for the poor and anger at the commission for continuing to press the matter: outdoor relief would pander to those 'whose great aim is to attain the means of enjoying petty luxuries in their own filthy cabins but who are unwilling to submit to the discipline and even dislike the cleanliness of the workhouse'. The commission, he concluded, must not be allowed to force Newtownards into the same category as Skibbereen.[188]

Crawford had upheld the principle of outdoor relief since the mid-1830s and his inability to see it implemented locally in 1847 was thus a cause of great personal frustration. Nevertheless, he was re-elected chair of the board of guardians in April 1848 after the majority had given way to legal threats and appointed relieving officers in January, and he continued to serve despite his grave concerns about local policy to impede outdoor relief.[189] Yet the underlying problem remained unresolved: in 1848–9 only thirty-seven persons received outdoor relief in the union, compared to 2,033 inmates of the workhouse and its auxiliaries.[190] His son James similarly proposed the appointment of relieving officers at Downpatrick as a step towards granting outdoor relief, which was also voted down by the landed interest on that board. In contrast, in Banbridge Union outdoor relief was permitted (after some delays) by the guardians once the workhouse again became full.[191]

Although preserved from the sheer scale of humanitarian catastrophe overwhelming the west, tenants in county Down were aware of the very visible distress manifested locally in 1847 which affected the labourers and small farmers most acutely, but saw indebtedness threaten even some better off farmers. Most felt acutely vulnerable in the context of sustained economic crisis in the later 1840s and early 1850s to a perceived landed assault on the tenant 'property' embodied in the 'Ulster custom' of tenant right. As we will see in the next chapter, this gave rise to widespread agrarian agitation, focused on Crawford's reform proposals. Thus the famine may have been experienced differently in Down from the west, but it still caused a number of excess deaths, stimulated an upsurge in emigration and provoked agrarian and political confrontations with established authorities. The regressive policies adopted by Londonderry would be remembered with some bitterness by small tenants and Presbyterian clergy, while Crawford's behaviour was regarded as exemplary.

Crawford's national policy interventions during the Famine years were shaped by his pre-existing economic ideas, his experience and observation of distress in Down, and by his empathy with the peasantry in less favoured parts of Ireland. While a dedicated free trader, believing repeal of the corn laws would benefit the working classes in Ireland as well as Britain by promoting cheaper grain imports, he supported a memorial from Belfast for restrictions on distilling alongside the immediate opening of the ports to food imports in November 1845.[192] He strongly backed another December 1846 petition originating in a town meeting for the suspension of brewing and distilling to maximise the grain available for human consumption – a proposal rejected on doctrinaire grounds by both the Peel and Russell administrations (as well as by the *Northern Whig* as an infringement on the principle of laissez-faire).[193] He had long been on record as a stern critic of the scale of export of Irish grain to Britain as a cause of potato dependency and domestic hunger, but his principal concerns in 1846–7 were not so much with exports (which that year had already fallen to below half the pre-famine rate due to higher home consumption and a poor harvest), but with the provision of cheap imported food, of productive public works, and of generous poor law and medical relief throughout Ireland.[194] In a small victory he persuaded the Peel administration in 1846 to amend its medical relief bill to permit the provision in hospitals of 'nutriment, if necessary for their cure, in the cases where the poor persons are destitute'.[195] Any sympathy he may have had for Peel's more pragmatic government was, however, destroyed by its resort to a new coercion bill that spring. This would, in his opinion, address only the symptoms and not the social causes of agrarian unrest.[196] Consequently he felt obliged to cast his vote against the bill, even when the government made it a confidence measure and resigned when it was defeated.[197]

The more economically doctrinaire Whig-liberal administration formed in summer 1846 proved even more resistant to his appeals. A lengthy public letter he sent to the prime minister Lord John Russell, published in the *Times* on 14 December 1846, demanded in place of the government's already failing public works relief programme a proper 'labour rate act', drawn up in the spirit of the old English poor law, imposing rates on landowners to employ the destitute on useful public works, with exemptions for those (like himself) who were already giving sufficient private employment on their estates. His own class must bear the principal burden for their previous actions, as 'if we, the landlords of the present day, have by inheritance the estates of our forefathers [...] can we throw off the responsibility attached to their misdeeds? In justice we cannot.' But the state was also responsible, through misgovernment or inaction in the face of the evidence of Irish underdevelopment and sustained distress, and must shoulder its fair share of the costs, especially through subvention of 'distressed' unions. In parallel with Smith O'Brien, Crawford insisted that public works must be reproductive – that is, improving the permanent productive capacity of the country to raise foodstuffs – and that in return for landowners being given greater powers to mobilise their resources through abolition of restrictions of entail and covenants, tenants too must be given security for their exertions through the enactment of tenant right.[198] The *Times* welcomed the letter as 'a powerful reply to the petty and dishonest arguments by which Irish landlords have so long fought off the discharge of their obligations', although it was much less enthusiastic about the outlay of British taxpayers' money.[199] The liberal *Daily News*, while acknowledging Crawford's 'benevolence, honesty and candour', denounced any poor law without a workhouse test as confiscation, and urged instead legislation to encourage English capitalists to purchase Irish land and liberate its productive potential.[200]

The problem for Crawford was, that while the Whig government and many of its middle-class British liberal allies agreed with his conviction that the behaviour of the Irish landlord class was the proximate cause of the famine crisis, they denied both the legitimacy of state-funded reproductive relief works, and, beyond a limited advance of state loans for land improvement to solvent proprietors, the fiscal responsibility of the state to assist them.

Despite some support for the 'Irish' case from within the Dublin Castle administration (the lord lieutenant until May 1847, O'Connell's former ally Lord Bessborough, was himself an 'improving' Irish landowner), the Treasury in London insisted that public works relief be penal – imposing disincentives on the labourers through piece work payments and wage rates deliberately deflated below the already abysmally low private wages, and on the landowners through the denial of funding to works of permanent utility. In both cases the rationale, articulated through the correspondence of assistant secretary Charles Trevelyan, lay in addressing a perceived moral hazard: both the labourers and proprietors must be forced away from allegedly 'demoralising' state-funded relief towards privately initiated work projects and employment if Ireland was ever to be regenerated. But with private works restricted to a small minority of landowners (like Crawford) with the will, legal power and resources to invest, the consequences in spring 1847 of paying relief wages below starvation level were, as Crawford was only too aware, catastrophic. Hundreds of thousands were to perish across the country as the government's public works schemes proved expensive failures and the destitute could not, as he protested in parliament, earn enough to match the escalating food prices and hence their families fell below the line of subsistence into starvation and susceptibility to famine fever.[201] In April 1847 he seconded O'Brien's bill to reconstitute public works around 'reproductive' projects, but this went nowhere in the face of government and press hostility.[202] Crawford also appealed in vain for state assistance for food importation by releasing Royal Naval vessels to bring grain from America, and urged the extension of income tax to Ireland as a quid pro quo for further British financial assistance, a measure which was not adopted until W. E. Gladstone's 1853 budget, too late to do anything except dissolve the remaining famine debt.[203]

Consistent with his conviction that landlords must be made to bear the costs of the destitution they had created, Crawford strongly supported the government's poor law amendment bill as it passed through the commons in spring 1847, while insisting (unsuccessfully) that the rate burden fall exclusively on the proprietors in the first instance rather than being partly paid by tenant farmers, and that a generous and humane regime of outdoor relief be introduced for all when the workhouses were full and immediately for widows with children.[204] He opposed the proposed increase in the number of ex-officio magistrate (usually landowning) guardians, arguing instead that the elected guardians should have discretion in determining forms of relief, and that relief by loan might be more appropriate for smallholders.[205]

His frustration with the final form of the extended poor law, which was put into operation as the principal relief mechanism from September 1847, lay less in the measure in principle than with the way it was administered and the failure to accompany it with appropriate remedial measures. He did, however, denounce as class legislation the 'quarter acre' or Gregory clause, tacked on to the bill to appease Irish Conservatives and hence ease its passage through the lords, which denied poor law relief to any tenant or cottier holding more than a quarter acre of land (that is, more than a garden plot). Demanding in vain its repeal in March 1848, he observed that 'if a poor man, having more than a quarter of an acre of land, was so unfortunate as to be in destitution, he was absolutely doomed by that clause to starvation'. His bill to abolish the clause was lost by twenty-one votes to 114, but he would continue to denounce the operation of the clause as 'fatal to the prosperity of Ireland'.[206] As the session progressed his alienation from the government, which he now believed had deliberately sabotaged his tenant right bill as well as betraying its August 1846 commitment to Irish relief and reconstruction, grew markedly.[207]

In July 1848 Crawford made an impassioned speech to the commons, summing up what he regarded as the abject failure of the government's Irish policy in that session. The attack was aimed to hit Russell, who had publicly identified himself with Irish reforms since the early 1820s and worked in alliance with O'Connell under the Lichfield House compact in the 1830s, where it would hurt most. In the place of the raft of remedial measures promised at the start of each session since 1846, Crawford pointed out that there was now exclusively a reliance on military force to hold Ireland in thrall, which risked provoking a 'servile war'. The landed campaign of estate clearance which had begun in earnest in 1847, had, he insisted, thrown the country into just such a class conflict, aggravating and extending famine through the deliberate denial of housing and livelihood on top of the loss of sustenance. The British government was as guilty as the landowners of the consequences:

> When the land was confiscated, [the landlords] were set over the people as tyrants over slaves, and taught habits of oppression by the law; and if they were acting tyrannically, the conduct of the governments of England had been in great fault for it. Parliament ought to set about the correction of the evil by good and fair laws as between landlord and tenant, with a view to restore confidence and kind feeling.[208]

In a public letter he condemned claims that the famine had been largely averted by the exertions of voluntary charity, with its implication that Ireland should demonstrate gratitude. This was an argument promoted in Trevelyan's government-approved tract *The Irish Crisis*, published early in 1848, and was constantly reiterated in the British press.[209] Charity was, Crawford asserted, being evoked to cover up the government's abject failure to respond effectively and to bring Ireland's own resources to bear on the crisis. He objected to a circulated address he had been asked to sign which lauded the 'noble generosity of England' while ignoring the 'misrule, injustice, and oppression of British governments' which had caused Irish degradation. He would not be any party to the self-satisfied and evasive British narrative of the Famine being constructed by government apologists on behalf of the state.[210]

If Crawford had any residual hopes that shaming Russell might induce the prime minister to reconsider his priorities and assert authority over his unruly ministers and the recalcitrant Treasury, and revive the abandoned menu of remedial measures, he was to be bitterly disappointed. The 1849 session saw only the passage of an Encumbered Estates Act to facilitate sale of indebted estates (which Crawford did not oppose but thought would do nothing for the Irish destitute in the short term) and the highly controversial Rate-in-Aid Act. Like the Tory lawyer Isaac Butt and many commentators in Ulster, he denounced the latter as a fundamental undermining of the principle of the Act of Union and an evasion of British state responsibility for by throwing the costs of supplementary assistance to the 'distressed unions' of the west exclusively on to the recovering eastern and northern poor law unions of Ireland. He spoke on platforms with Conservatives who opposed the Rate-in-Aid on Ulster particularist grounds, but Crawford's argument was that the immense drain of capital from Ireland since the union entitled it to a just share of the Treasury's funds.[211] However his parliamentary motion that 'it is unconstitutional and unjust to impose on Ireland separate national taxation for the wants of particular localities, so long as the public general revenue of Ireland is paid into an imperial treasury, and placed at the disposal of an imperial legislature for the general purposes of the United Kingdom' was thrown out by 139 to fifteen votes.[212] A small-scale extension in 1849 of the government's land improvement and drainage act he dismissed as grossly inadequate, while attempts to pass a more generous poor employment bill, which he promoted along with Poulett Scrope, went nowhere.[213] He continued to insist that 'the wretched condition of the peasantry in the west of Ireland was to be attributed to the conduct of the Irish landlords – to their exaction of large rents, which had reduced the peasantry to the lowest description of food, and that in the smallest quantities', but saw no real efforts being made to ameliorate this.[214] Deeply frustrated with this, and with the ministry's lack of interest in his suggestion of a 'discriminating rate' or smaller taxation areas to ease the burden on employing landowners, he turned now to a public appeal in print.[215]

Depopulation Not Necessary, 1849–50

In producing a comprehensive review of the state of Ireland and the reforms it required in October 1849, Crawford chose to communicate directly to British opinion through the pamphlet press. Bluntly titled *Depopulation Not Necessary: An Appeal to the British Members of the Imperial Parliament Against the Extermination of the Irish People*, this was his first major excursion into print since 1839 and his most impassioned publication. It combined a coruscating moral critique of British mismanagement of famine and of Irish landlord ruthlessness, with a programmatic outline of the reconstructive measures he believed essential for his country's recovery. His priority was to counter the demographic and economic doctrines being used to justify the escalating campaigns of estate clearance and consolidation of holdings – the 'depopulation' of his title.

To challenge again the 'the detestable doctrine of the Malthusian economists', he offered a contrasting analysis of the social state of the north-eastern Ulster counties, which he observed had significantly higher population densities, with the distressed western districts still ravaged by starvation and fever.[216] His 'home' poor law union of Newtownards had, he alleged, survived the Famine relatively unscathed by hunger-mortality, despite being nearly twice as densely settled as was the average for unions in Connacht:

> No public money was ever asked or received in the union of Newtownards. Through all the distressed times, the poor were sustained solely by the funds of the union; and we have no beggars going about belonging to the union. No out-door relief has been given or found necessary, with the exception of small sums allowed for contingencies arising from sickness or accident, certified by the relieving officer. No able-bodied men have received relief, (unless temporarily from some particular cause) there being generally sufficient employment for all industrious men who seek it.[217]

The reason for this regional divergence lay not in racial or religious differences, nor even in the greater industrial development in the north-east, but, he argued, in the social dynamics of the Ulster countryside, underpinned by the social security offered by the recognition of tenant right. He followed McKnight in tracing the historical roots of this custom to the partnership established between landlord and tenant that was necessary for the success of the plantation of Ulster, in contrast to the oppressive tenurial regime derived

1. Gabriel Beranger, 'Moira Castle', watercolour copy of a sketch by Eleanor Sharman, 1799 (RIA, 3C 30/82). Courtesy of Royal Irish Academy

2. James Carey, 'The Lisburn and Lambeg Volunteers firing a "Feu de Joie" in honour of the Dungannon Convention, 1782', coloured print, 1890s. Courtesy of Irish Linen Centre and Lisburn Museum

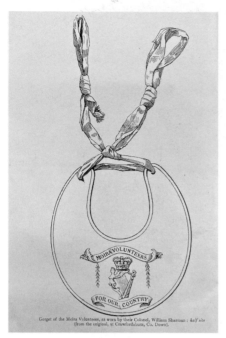

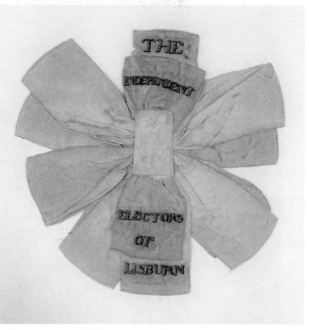

3. 'Gorget of the Moira Volunteers, as worn by their colonel, William Sharman', *Ulster Journal of Archaeology*, 16:1&2 (1910), p. 6

4. Rosette worn by William Sharman at the Lisburn election of 1783 (D856/F/9). Courtesy of Public Record Office of Northern Ireland

5. John Carey, 'Volunteers Parading up High Street [Belfast] at the Commemoration of the Storming of the Bastille, 14 July 1791 or 1792', drawing, 1893 (BELUM.Y.W.10.21.18). Courtesy of National Museums of Northern Ireland

6. Thomas Robinson, 'Colonel William Sharman', 1798, oil on canvas (BELUM.U141). Courtesy of National Museums of Northern Ireland

7. Gabriel Beranger, 'Moira Castle, second view', watercolour copy of a sketch by Eleanor Sharman, 1799 (RIA, 3C 30/82). Courtesy of Royal Irish Academy

8. Sketch of a man and a boy, possibly by William Sharman, junior (c.1785–90) (D856/F/4). Courtesy of Public Record Office of Northern Ireland

9. Thomas Robinson, 'Portrait of a Young Man (possibly a United Irishman)', 1798, oil on canvas (BELUM.U136). This painting is probably of William Sharman, junior. Courtesy of National Museums of Northern Ireland

10. 'Crawford's Burn', engraving, in Joseph Molloy and E. K. Proctor, *Belfast Scenery* (Belfast, 1832)

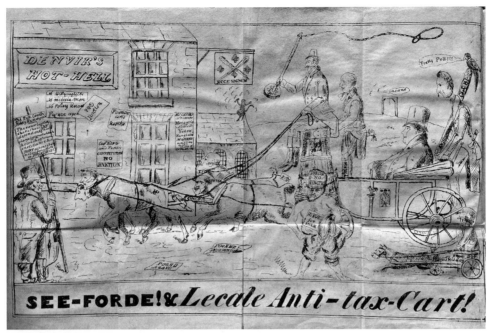

11. 'SEE-FORDE! & Lecale Anti-tax-cart!', folding print, in Anon., *Narrative of the Proceedings of the Contested Election for the County of Down* (Belfast, 1830). Courtesy of Linenhall Library

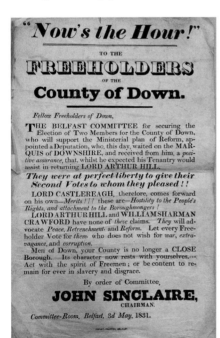

12. Election poster from County Down election, 'Now's the Hour!', 3 May 1831 (D1748/G/780/3). Courtesy of Public Record Office of Northern Ireland

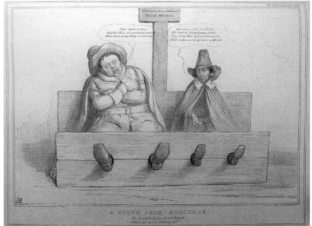

13. 'HB' (John Doyle), 'HB Sketches no. 458: "A Scene from Hudibras"', 1 Dec. 1836, lithograph. Courtesy of National Library of Ireland

14. 'HB' (John Doyle), 'HB Sketches no. 466: "Another Scene from Hudibras"', 10 Feb. 1837, lithograph. Courtesy of National Library of Ireland

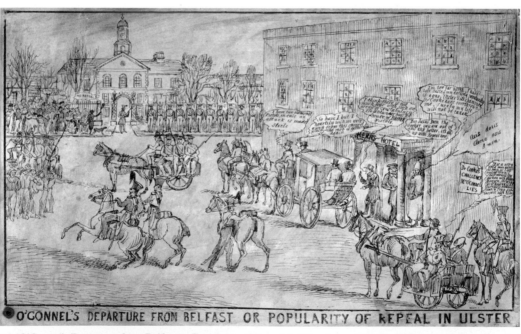

15. 'O'Connel's Departure from Belfast or Popularity of Repeal in Ulster', engraving in Anon., *The Repealer Repulsed* (Belfast, 1841) (BELUM P4.2005). Courtesy of National Museums of Northern Ireland

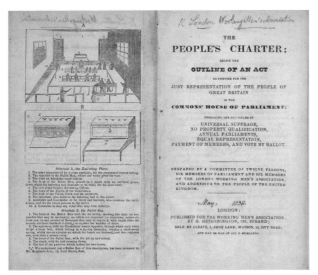

16. London Working Men's Association, *The People's Charter* (London, 1838), p. 1

17. William Sharman Crawford's cockade worn at the Rochdale election, 1 Jul. 1841 (D856/D/61). Courtesy of Public Record Office of Northern Ireland

18. 'The Goose Show', *Northern Star*, 23 Jan. 1841

19. 'Storming the Castle of Monopoly', *The Struggle*, No. 23 (*c.*Jun. 1842), p. 1. Courtesy of Touchstones Rochdale

20. John Prescott Knight, 'William Sharman Crawford', *c.*1843, oil on canvas (BELUM U.4501). Courtesy of National Museums of Northern Ireland

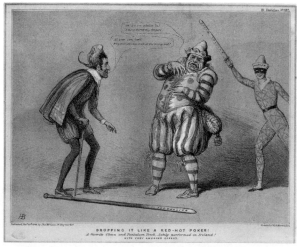

21. Print of William Sharman Crawford (after T. G. Lupton and J. P. Knight) with autograph, n.d. (T1129/411). Courtesy of Public Record Office of Northern Ireland

22. 'HB' (John Doyle), 'HB Sketches no. 822: "Dropping it like a Red-Hot Poker!"', 28 Dec. 1844, lithograph. Courtesy of National Library of Ireland

23. 'Ejectment of Irish Tenantry', *Illustrated London News,* 16 Dec. 1848, p. 380

MR. SHARMAN CRAWFORD, M.P. FOR ROCHDALE.

24. 'Parliamentary Portraits: Mr Sharman Crawford, M.P. for Rochdale',
Illustrated London News, 5 May 1849, p. 285

25. 'Great Tenant-right Meeting at Kilkenny', *Illustrated London News*, 5 Oct. 1850, p. 281

26. Handbill, 'Tenant-right and Free Trade. County of Down Election', n.d. [1852], in Crossle family scrapbook (T1689/2/66). Courtesy of Public Record Office of Northern Ireland

27. Handbill with interim polling figures for Co. Down election, 23 Jul. 1852 (D1252/24/5). Courtesy of Public Record Office of Northern Ireland

28. Carte-de-visite portrait photograph of Arthur Sharman Crawford, n.d. [*c.*1860-1], Coey album (BELUM.Y39038.49). Courtesy of National Museums of Northern Ireland

29. Oliver Sarony (?), Carte-de-visite portrait photograph of William Sharman Crawford, n.d. [*c.*1860–1], Coey album (BELUM. Y39038.163). Courtesy of National Museums of Northern Ireland

30. 'The late Mr Wm Sharman Crawford, M.P. Presented gratis with "The Belfast Weekly Post". 23rd Sept. 1882' (T1129/412). Courtesy of Public Record Office of Northern Ireland

31. The Sharman Crawford mausoleum, Kilmore graveyard, Co. Down (author's photograph, 2019)

32. The William Sharman Crawford monument, Rademon, Co. Down, 1863–5 (author's photograph, 2019)

33. Detail of the William Sharman Crawford monument, Rademon, Co. Down: the bronze medallion by S. F. Lynn, 1865 (author's photograph, 2019)

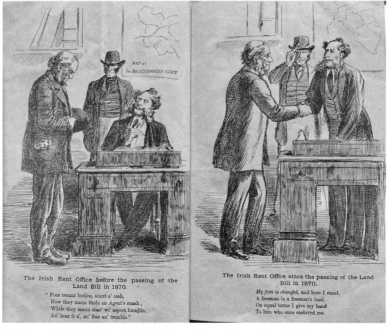

The Irish Rent Office before the passing of the Land Bill in 1870.

"Poor tenants bodies, scant o' cash,
How they maun thole an Agent's smash;
While they maun stan' wi' aspect humble,
An' hear it s', an' fear an' tremble."

The Irish Rent Office since the passing of the Land Bill in 1870.

My fate is changed, and here I stand,
A freeman in a freeman's hand.
On equal terms I give my hand
To him who once enslaved me.

34. Anon., 'The Irish Rent Office before and since the passing of the Land Bill in 1870', *The Annals of Ulster Tenant-Right, by an Antrim Tenant-Farmer* (n.p., n.d. [Belfast, *c.*1877]), pp 1–2. Courtesy of Linenhall Library

THE LATE Mᴿ Jᴬˢ SHARMAN CRAWFORD, M.P.

35. 'The late Mr Ja[me]s Sharman Crawford, M.P.',
n.d. (*c.*1882), print (T1129/413). Courtesy of Public
Record Office of Northern Ireland

MAJOR JOHN SHARMAN CRAWFORD, J.P., D.L.

PRESENTED GRATIS WITH "THE BELFAST WEEKLY POST"
7ᵀᴴ Ocᵀ. 1882

36. 'Major John Sharman Crawford, J.P., D.L.
Presented gratis with "The Belfast Weekly Post". 7th
Octr. 1882', print (T1129/414). Courtesy of Public
Record Office of Northern Ireland

37. 'El Kantara', frontispiece to Mabel Sharman Crawford, *Through Algeria* (London, 1863). Courtesy of National Library of Ireland

38. 'Women's Suffrage – The National Demonstration at St James's Hall', *The Graphic*, 22 May 1880, p. 516

39. 'Sir Edward with Lady Carson, and Lt-Gen. Sir George Richardson, talking to (mounted) Col. Sharman-Crawford', photograph, n.d. (*c.*1914) (INF/7/A/2/65). Courtesy of Public Record Office of Northern Ireland

40. Robert Welch, 'Crawfordsburn House', photograph, *c.*1888 (D2460). Courtesy of Public Record Office of Northern Ireland

from colonial conquest evident elsewhere in the country.[218] Unfettered exploitation had debased the western peasantry materially and morally – they were 'free labour on the land of those imperious slavemasters' the landlords, who had 'perverted the nature of the people [… and] made them fraudulent and dishonest'. Amid outbreaks of agrarian violence (a 'defensive civil war' waged by the peasantry) and tenants absconding without paying rents, the landowners were now simply 'reaping the fruit of the seeds you have yourselves sown'.[219]

Making this polemical point about the gulf between north-east Ulster and Connacht led him to understate the extent to which the Famine had impacted on even relatively favoured districts such as north Down in 1847 (and to neglect to mention his own resignation as chair of Newtownards board over the outdoor relief question).[220] But the point had some substance – mortality had been relatively low in the union and by later 1849 it was recovering from the famine shock with under one per cent of the population still receiving relief. It appeared undeniable that population density and small landholdings in themselves did not explain the mass mortality that had characterised the west.[221] Rather, acute impoverishment arising from extreme social inequality and exploitation had rendered that region much more vulnerable to the shock of the potato failure. This explained the continuation of appalling levels of destitution in the west: Connacht as a whole had eleven per cent of its population (based on 1841 figures) in a state of 'pauperisation' in 1849, with many unions over fifteen per cent and Clifden at an extraordinary thirty-seven per cent.[222]

The 'merciless' landlord campaign of clearance, whether by ejectments or 'voluntary surrender' under the Gregory clause, was now he argued the principal driver of famine suffering. Legislation passed in 1848 to regulate evictions was being openly flouted with official sanction. He quoted from a report on western conditions recently published by the emigre Polish philanthropist Paul Strzelecki, previously the agent of the British Relief Association and who had returned on his own initiative in summer 1849 to distribute more charitable funds he had raised in England. The picture painted was appalling:

> Mercy is talked of – even an act of the legislature passes – but no mercy is practised. The act of the legislature proclaims that mercy, while the executive powers of the state are employed to aid the landlords in committing the widespread desolation which Count Strzelecki describes. 90,000 holders of land – emaciated, sick, and naked – have been turned out without a place to cover their heads, in the face of an act of parliament 'to protect and relieve the destitute evicted poor.' Is this the way to improve the morality of the people? – to teach them truth and honour and honest dealing?

He regretted that even the benevolent Strzelecki had been unable to free himself from the pernicious 'consolidation theory' in making his report.[223] Crawford may have been somewhat unfair to the Pole, who testified to a house of lords committee in 1849 that while he did think some consolidation necessary, relief must always take priority over restructuring, as '[t]he very first thing which it is the duty of the public to look to is, that the immediate distress should be relieved, and that people in the British empire, so long as the empire possesses any means, should not be allowed to die from starvation […] You cannot reason in an abstract way when you see men dying in the streets'.[224] Whatever their differences on the land system, however, the evidence of continuing suffering that Strzelecki had exposed was undeniable.

What then was the solution to the continuing crisis of the south and west? Not surprisingly, given his consistent advocacy of legislative intervention under this head since the mid-1830s, the legal recognition or extension of the Ulster model of tenant-right throughout the country, accompanied by the setting of rents by independent valuation linked to average prices (as he was then introducing on his own estates), was a sine qua non. Such an intervention would, he argued, create effective co-ownership: as 'every tenant holding under this custom may be considered as a peasant-proprietor; and from hence it appears to me arises that same prosperity in this portion of Ireland, which is found to exist in other countries where the occupier of the soil has all those advantages which the interest of ownership creates'.[225] Rack-renting, which was alongside rundale tenancy the curse of the west, would be eliminated. Supplementary measures would see a land court established with powers to compel the buying-out of middlemen, the facilitation of leases, the suspension of distraint for overdue rents and the enforcement of compensation for improvements made in cases of eviction. But this would not be enough given the urgency of the situation.

Who was, or should be, a tenant farmer? He insisted on both the viability and desirability of small farms in Ireland worked largely by family labour, drawing on his Down experience, as well as the recent writings of the heterodox economists W. T. Thornton and John Stuart Mill (who Crawford rather clumsily misnamed throughout his pamphlet as 'Mills'), and the travel writers Samuel Laing and Charles Le Quesne, who all lauded the small-farm systems of continental Europe (especially Belgium, Norway and Tuscany) and the Channel Islands and believed this system applicable to Ireland.[226] Previously in 1845 he had cited Laing's defence of small-holding peasantries in Europe, along with Nicholls' report on agriculture in Holland and Belgium, in defence of small farms and against the seizure and consolidation of common lands.[227] This heterodox position stood in contrast with the hegemonic 'English' doctrine of agrarian economics associated with Nassau Senior and Torrens, which he accused the Irish landlords of implementing at immense social cost, and of consolidating cleared land into large holdings to be let to 'capitalist' tenant farmers employing wage-labour.

But what of the labouring mass of the Irish population, whose tiny cottier potato-holdings or conacre plots fell below any viable bar for self-sufficiency and comfort, and who the blight had rendered redundant and subject to appalling levels of mortality? This was the class whose lives were now, he argued, being 'sacrificed' in the name of the 'English theory of consolidation'.[228] He acknowledged that tenant right could do little for the hundreds of thousands clinging to such rack-rented microplots, while the 'official' alternative of their proletarianisation into landless labourers on consolidated capitalist farms could employ only a fraction of their numbers and would face violent resistance from agrarian secret societies. If, as Crawford continued to contend, mass assisted emigration was a counter-productive and impractically expensive mode of reducing their numbers, some alternative must therefore be offered to the current wave of cottier 'extermination'.[229]

His answer – although he was by no means the first or only writer to put this forward during the Famine years – was 'home colonisation', that is, the resettlement of 'surplus' labourers on 'waste lands' within Ireland. Crawford had co-sponsored and enthusiastically supported Poulett Scrope's 1846 parliamentary motion for a waste land reclamation scheme as an alternative to emigration, on the grounds that 'by having the waste lands in their possession, the government would be able to provide allotments where there was an overflow of population, while, by introducing an improved and proper system of farming, they would be enabled to advance the agricultural education of the people', and as 'one of the most essential modes of removing the horrors of the clearance system'.[230] Scrope had drawn on figures prepared by the Devon Commission to argue that there was sufficient reclaimable land to create 'a *class of yeomanry* – so wanted in Ireland, *cultivating their own lands for their sole profit'*.[231] In 1848 Crawford had supported the Roscommon MP Fitzstephen French's motion for a major land reclamation scheme.[232] In 1849 he now returned to this theme. To be workable on the scale required, this would require the compulsory purchase by the state of hundreds of thousands of acres currently lying unproductive in bog and mountain side, public employment of the relocated labouring families on drainage and infrastructural works, and ultimately the allocation of agrarian plots of eight to ten acres to these families as state tenants with tenant-right based leases. A relocation of upwards of 200,000 labouring families to the waste lands would, he calculated, free up enough land to enlarge the remaining cottiers' holdings to viability with a grain-based farming rotation and would be well within the capacity of the wastes as calculated by the Devon Commission at over 3.7 million acres. While private enterprise and landowners had no interest in reclaiming this land, self-interest and family labour would motivate relocated peasants to produce small but reasonable profits.

Crawford's waste-land settlement scheme may have seemed visionary, even with the intellectual authority it now derived from the peasant-proprietor economic theory articulated by John Stuart Mill in his *Principles of Political Economy* (and previously sketched out in a series of *Morning Chronicle* articles on Ireland in the winter of 1846–7). Crawford would not have agreed with the neo-Malthusian case made by Thornton and Mill against an extension of the Irish poor law, nor with Mill's view that tenant-right legislation was premature (even if he acknowledged its economic utility), given the 'danger of tampering in times of political and moral change, with the salutary prepossessions by which property is protected against spoliation'. But Mill's heavyweight endorsement of both the viability of small-scale peasant production and moral superiority of the relocation of cottiers as proprietors on waste lands over mass clearances was welcome.[233] Moreover, the idea had received an official imprimatur through the one million pound waste-land reclamation plan that had been briefly taken up by the prime minister himself in late 1846, only to be abandoned several months later in the face of cabinet and parliamentary laissez-faire resistance and the fiscal retrenchment associated with the banking crash of 1847.[234]

By late 1849 Crawford evidently believed it was worth reminding the public that this abortive scheme was still relevant and linked it more directly to the principle of peasant proprietorship. This required framing it within a moral broadside against British legislators and public opinion for rendering it the only humane policy option left. Would the landlords, he asked rhetorically, 'be the instruments of exterminating that people' through their ideological pursuit of the proletarianisation of the peasant?[235] If the Irish landlord class as a whole was guilty of such self-interested barbarity, ultimate responsibility for mass mortality must lie with Britain as the sovereign power and more specifically with its ruling political class. Further inaction would leave MPs fully answerable for the lives they would sacrifice and, he implied, justify the rejection of British rule espoused by Irish separatists: 'What a stain on the British name is the record of such proceedings! And still more so, when the undeniable truth is recollected, that the foundation of all this aggravated misery has been the maltreatment, the injustice, and the neglects of British rule'. With emigration affordable only by a limited number, upholding the 'rights of property' thus meant active complicity with an 'extermination' that amounted to mass murder.[236]

Although Crawford's primary objective was still the provision of security through the legalisation of tenant right with its concomitants of indirect fixity of tenure and fair rents, which he equated with co-ownership, his support for the 'home colonisation' project advocated by Scrope, Thornton and Mill points towards an acceptance of the logic of full peasant proprietorship, where this could be attained by a partial nationalisation of 'waste' land without full expropriation of landowners.[237] As state tenants, his waste-land settlers would still be required to pay a low ground rent and be subject to some form of oversight by state officials, but would have practical fixity and be wholly free from landlordism. The legalisation of tenant right here and elsewhere would give tenants the benefits of ownership, as 'the act of sale is a proprietory act'.[238] Any wider scheme of state facilitation of land transfer through Treasury advances was at this point far in the future and the idea of revolutionary confiscation for 'nationalisation' of tenanted land was restricted to a small number of social republicans such as James Fintan Lalor, but Crawford's acceptance of the principle of peasant proprietorship, at least in theory, seems evident by 1849. If his position on full-scale land transfer was undeveloped by the time of his death in 1861, it would be contested by land reformers in later decades and supported by his daughter in the 1880s.

Depopulation not Necessary attracted some immediate attention and was reprinted in early 1850 to meet 'great popular demand' in Ireland.[239] Crawford made sure it was circulated to British newspapers as well as leading political figures and commentators.[240] Polite responses came from opposition parliamentarians such as Peel and Graham, who praised his patriotism and benevolence of purpose, but were not followed by any policy change. This may have been a disappointment, given Peel's brief floating of the idea of a developmental commission for Connacht earlier in the year. The prime minister, chancellor of the exchequer and lord lieutenant made no comments on the pamphlet beyond acknowledging receipt, while the home secretary assured him he would read it as he was aware that Crawford 'possesses so much information and entertains such benevolent views […] with regard to the Irish people'.[241] Cobden appeared interested only in the renewed protectionist threat to free trade that Crawford had flagged in the text.[242] It was generally well received by much of the Irish press – the *Freeman's Journal* called on readers to join Crawford's war against extermination, while Duffy in the revived *Nation* welcomed it as 'one of the clearest and most conclusive arguments ever made for the destruction of a nefarious system', and even the *Downpatrick Recorder* conceded it agreed with his main arguments – but with a few mildly supportive exceptions such as the *Leeds Mercury* and *Northern Star* the British press largely ignored it.[243] In line with British public opinion's and government's indifference towards Irish suffering and prioritisation of their own economic interests, 'natural causes' would be left to play themselves out in Ireland.[244]

Beyond his local relief activities in Down and Meath (and even partly there, as we have seen), Crawford's initiatives during the Famine thus ended in failure. His parliamentary oratory, lobbying and back-bench bill-making were no more successful in shifting the policy juggernaut than his excursions into public print. He expressed his frustration with British indifference to Irish affairs more generally in the 1849 pamphlet:

It is melancholy to me to reflect how many members act as legislators for our unfortunate country, who are in total ignorance of the circumstances connected with that country; who have imbibed certain dogmas and prejudices, on which they legislate, without ever seeking any real information, or even attending to that with which the debates of the house might supply them. I reflect with pain how often I have witnessed a debate on Irish questions, more especially the landlord and tenant question, carried on with empty benches, which have been vacated by British members at its commencement; and when the division bell announced its termination, the return of the same members to give their votes, as prejudice or party guided them, without having heard an explanation of the question on which they were about to vote, or an argument for or against it.[245]

Perhaps he should not be judged too harshly for his reluctance to abandon the constitutional pathway, despite such setbacks. The alternative of mass outdoor agitation was equally problematic in these years, as the primacy of survival tended to crowd out participation for many of the lower classes. O'Connor's revived Chartist campaign in Britain ran out of steam at the Kennington Common mass meeting in 1848, and ineffective revolutionary posturing of John Mitchel and the shambolic fiasco of Smith O'Brien's adventurism at Ballingarry in Ireland in the same year proved deeply counterproductive in terms of addressing the issues of famine (if more attractive to subsequent nationalist mythmakers). But as well will see in the following chapters, it was in outdoor mobilisation where Crawford's energies in the latter years of the Famine were increasingly concentrated.

The importance of his interventions on Famine policy lies in offering an articulated challenge to the dominant orthodoxies in parliament and a potential alternative to the depopulating forces of hunger and clearance. How sustainable the 'home colonisation' scheme could have been had it been enacted is a moot point. Turning so much of Ireland's bog and uplands to arable would have massively altered the landscape of the countryside, potentially at some cost to biodiversity (even with a 'natural' crop rotation system). However, the 1849 plan offered both infrastructural investment and some security to the peasant in place of the previous ad hoc arrangements of reclamation by squatters. Following Mill and Thornton, Crawford was convinced the 'magic of property' inherent in the semi-proprietorial terms of settlement would work to restrain subdivision and rampant population growth from placing excessive extractive demands on these holdings, as was widely believed to be the case with monoculture cottier plots. However it also required a degree of active state intervention that would not be seen in rural Ireland until the formation of the Congested Districts Board in 1891.

Even if had been implemented and operated, it is probable that such an arrangement would only have been transitional – with rising living standards, the commercial pressures towards pastoralism, and the higher demands of maintaining production on less favoured land, it is likely the pull of cheaper fares, remittances from relatives and employment opportunities in the new world would have led to a population outflow from the Irish countryside anyway in the second half of the century. Perhaps only one thing is evident. Had Crawford's proposals been attempted, the British political establishment might have bought time and saved itself some of the obloquy it attracted at the time and since for abandoning the poor of Ireland to 'extermination'.

6. The emergence of the Tenant League, 1846–50

The origins of agrarian politics, 1846–7

If the onset of the Famine threatened the survival of millions of labourers, smallholding tenant farmers and their families, its impact on Ireland varied by region and over time. The poorest half of the population, already at or near the line of subsistence before 1845, were rendered destitute and subject to death by hunger or infectious disease by repeated potato failures, the inadequacy of state aid and landlord indifference or oppression. For those farmers with access to more land and resources, especially in the less extensively ravaged regions of east and north Ulster, much of Leinster and east Munster, death by hunger was less of an immediate threat (although the risks of contracting a contagious fever remained real). However, in the calamitous economic situation prevailing amid a developing agricultural depression, an inability to meet the demand for rent and escalating poor rates made eviction and consequent destitution a real and evident danger for middling and 'family' farmers. Added to this, the market value of tenant-right in Ulster plummeted due to falling prices, low demand for tenancies and a glut of holdings offered for sale by farming families anxious to escape Ireland via the emigrant ship. This loss of security further imperilled farmers in regions where custom had offered some form of guarantee for the capital invested in purchasing 'goodwill' and making improvements to the land.

Thus while Famine disrupted and undermined the forms of mass outdoor politics developed by O'Connell in the 1820s–40s, as personal survival replaced agitation as the priority for many of those involved in the great 1843 campaign for repeal, for the less severely distressed but still vulnerable sections of the agricultural population collective action against landlordism continued to appear essential. In regions with a tradition of violent agrarian secret societies, distress and fear provoked an upsurge in 'outrages' in 1845–6 and again in the winter of 1847–8, which were met by harsh state repression. In other areas, especially those with a more highly developed commercial agriculture and literacy in English, collective action took on a more constitutionalist colouration, drawing in places on the modes of the now largely defunct O'Connellite movement, but acquiring new leadership and a more urgent and specific focus on land reform. Sporadic and regionalised in form in the later 1840s, this movement would take a national shape as the Tenant League in 1850, briefly unite the non-violent agrarian agitation of Ulster with that of the rest of Ireland, but then break apart under the pressures of its own political contradictions amid the recovering agricultural situation of the mid-1850s.

Sharman Crawford had long held that just such a mass movement was essential to the success of any land reform legislation for Ireland, as only this could put the required social and political pressure on both Irish elites and the British parliament. His early hopes had been largely frustrated by his public alienation from O'Connell from 1836, but were revived as the Famine sparked widespread tenant unrest and O'Connell's death opened up new opportunities. Crawford's complex and controversial role in the rise and fall of the mass land agitation of 1847–57 is the subject of this and the next chapter.

When Peel's last chief secretary, Lord Lincoln, introduced a tenant compensation bill in June 1846 similar to Stanley's of the previous year, Crawford again welcomed the concession of the principle of intervention, but insisted it needed to be retrospective in scope and have no upper limit on the value of improvements.[1] Disappointed by the extreme cautiousness of the Conservative proposals and distrustful of the intentions of the incoming Whig government in summer 1846, Crawford issued a series of public letters addressed to the occupying tenants of Ulster reiterating the urgency of land agitation. The first, written on 8 July, made it clear that the previously limited scope of his own parliamentary bills for compensation had been tactical and did not encompass fully what he envisaged as 'justice' to the tenant farmer. In the wake of the government's admission of the need for some remedial legislation on compensation, and the growing rural crisis in Ireland, he now argued that something stronger should be demanded: 'these bills are not to be taken the true index my own views, or comprehending the full extent of your just claims, but rather an attempt, on my part, to get the greatest amount of benefit for the tenant class which circumstances would admit of'. Compensation for improvements, while essential, was insufficient in itself and he now feared might be used as a pretext to undermine the practice of the 'Ulster custom' of tenant-right where it existed. Legislation was thus required to affirm the tenant's claim to his 'beneficial interest' in his holding, which he summarised as a mixture of the value of his capital expended on the holding, and the 'value of the future means of subsistence which the continuation of occupation would afford', the amount of which should continue to be determined 'by the custom of the district'.

Now was the time to raise the ante of the campaign, as:

> times are changed, and, as in all cases wherein just reform is withheld, a greater measure of reform is claimed and obtained. So with your case. You have now the great moral power of public opinion, both in England and Ireland, in your favour. You stand on high ground, from which you cannot be driven, except by your own fault. You ought to demand, and accept nothing short of, the full and simple measure of justice [...] Your custom of 'tenant-right' is as well established as any custom in England. Why, then, should it not be made equally valid in law, as it confessedly is in justice? *Demand, then, that your custom be made law.*

Only when this right was thus acknowledged could the necessary partnership between landlord and tenant be fully realised.[2]

Crawford's intervention drew praise in the Repeal Association from the ailing Daniel O'Connell, although the latter's decision to seek a new Whig alliance and the secession of Smith O'Brien and the Young Irelanders rendered it of little value as the platform for a land reform campaign.[3] A more promising straw in the wind was the enthusiastic tenant-right meeting held at Comber, Co. Down, at which Crawford's letter was read by the non-subscribing Presbyterian minister, Rev. Fletcher Blakely. While careful to praise the local landowner Lord Londonderry for recognising tenant right on his estates, the meeting agreed to support Crawford's call for legislation. Indeed, one of his own tenants, James

Bingham of Rademon, called on 'the tenant farmers of Ulster, and of Ireland, to rally round Mr Crawford, as the English people did around Mr Cobden, and success is certain'.[4]

While such an assembly in north Down was most likely to be open to Crawford's proposals, what is striking is the extent to which his strategy proved attractive beyond that region and saw off alternatives to become the basis of the national programme of the Tenant League. Even by 1846 there were some signs of this. The *Tipperary Vindicator* and other regional papers carried in August a letter by 'Marcus' urging the farmers of that county to follow the 'sagacious and sturdy Northerns' in supporting Crawford's initiative and attain for themselves what the Ulstermen were seeking to protect. For this (anonymous) voice, an all-Ireland agitation was essential. The common cause should, the writer asserted, be pursued at first through petitioning meetings, but with a 'readiness, if necessary, to form with them "a Tenant Right League"' for mutual protection.[5] Both the *Tipperary Vindicator* and the *Kilkenny Journal* strongly endorsed the letter, the latter insisting that 'ours must be a moral warfare: petition and argument are the only weapons which we must use', and confidently asserting that 'if all Ireland calls for the tenant right, it must be conceded', just as the corn laws had fallen earlier that year to a mass campaign. The Belfast *Vindicator* added that recent bloody uprising of Polish peasants against their nobles had demonstrated the futility of an agrarian civil war: only mass peaceful agitation by the farmers in their 'righteous and holy cause' could and would succeed.[6]

A second letter from Crawford on 7 August expanded on the essential point of how a 'fair rent' might be determined. 'Tenant right' could never, he argued, be an excuse for a tenant's idleness or neglect; giving legal security would promote improvement by removing obstacles to self-exertion, but the law should also include provisions to allow the landlord to take legal action for recompense in any cases of damage or deterioration of a holding, with the value determinable in court and deductible from the tenant right payment. The law would only come into operation when a landlord refused the renewal of a tenancy offered at a 'fair rent'. Determining this required an enhanced form of periodic public valuation by trained valuators. If a landlord refused to let at the valuation rent thus calculated, the evicted tenant could then claim the value of his 'beneficial interest' under tenant right. Rents could rise over time, but only if they remained pegged proportionally to the valuation of the land and the tenant was guaranteed a just return on his labour and invested capital.[7] As he explained in a later letter, the valuation was not intended to establish a judicial 'fair rent' for all tenancies and would not prevent an incoming tenant offering more, but would 'have an indirect power, of great weight' over letting rates by establishing a pecuniary incentive to landlords not to exceed what was reasonable.[8] Best practice on Ulster estates would not be affected by such an intervention, as free sale of tenant right to the incoming tenant would continue, but only the justice attainable through civil action under such legislation would end the resort to illegal combinations in the countryside to protect peasant interests in places where the custom was not recognised in full.[9]

A third letter referenced the now evident calamity of the second, and nearly total, potato failure of August 1846, and made clear that the landlords of Ireland had brought the crisis on themselves and must be made to share the consequent losses to a degree that reflected the illegitimacy of their previous behaviour:

It is indeed likely to prove an awful retribution for past injustice and neglect – and what brought them to this condition? The people were forced to live upon potatoes (and not even enough of potatoes); the corn was abstracted. [...] No means were taken to instruct the people in a better system of agriculture; none to give employment in any form; none to give them any security for their own labour expended on their tenements; the people were allowed to waste their time in indolence, and every vice which indolence produces. If the people are indolent, blame not them but those who forced them into this condition. Now this cobweb state of existence is suddenly rent asunder and a mass of desolation is the result – wholly arising from the unjust and disorganized system of the relation of landlord and tenant.[10]

A final letter in the series dealt with the technicalities of the valuation, which he argued should be under a dedicated commissioner, must improve on the methodologies of the existing Griffiths and poor law valuations, and ensure equity between the competing parties.[11]

Response to the letters in the liberal and nationalist Irish press was generally positive. To the *Londonderry Journal,* the third letter stood out as addressing the philosophical root of the matter – that as merely 'trustees' for the public, the landowners must be subject to legislative regulation of the letting of land. Crawford had effectively answered those misrepresenting him as a 'democratic leveller', and the letters had provoked an 'immense sensation amongst all classes of tenant farmers', evidenced in the correspondence the paper had received.[12] Although the *Cork Examiner* did not carry the series, a 'tenant farmer' wrote to the paper recommending them with enthusiasm.[13] This endorsement appears to have had an impact on O'Connellites – the Drogheda poor law guardians passed a motion in support of the enactment of tenant-right legislation, claiming Crawford's approval of such actions (and over the protests of his son-in-law Henry Coddington, who was an ex-officio guardian).[14] Smith O'Brien also cited Crawford with approval in putting forward his own ideas on land reform in the *Nation,* with the aim of presenting these to a meeting of Irish landlords.[15] Although they agreed on tenant right they disagreed on some matters: O'Brien adhered to the longstanding nationalist preoccupation with absentee landowners, whereas Crawford regarded any levy on them as a distraction, noting correctly that absentee estates could be well managed and resident landlords were often more oppressive.[16]

As yet there were limited signs of popular mobilisation taking shape on the issue, but this would come in the following year. The first major and sustained tenant organisation emerged not in the north, but in Cork in early 1847. Leadership for this initiative came from John Francis Maguire, the owner-editor of the *Cork Examiner,* and William Trenwith, a Protestant large tenant farmer at Ballycurreen and a merchant and pawnbroker in Cork city.[17] Maguire had responded positively to a suggestion in an English paper that a 'Tenant League' be formed to emulate the success of the Anti-Corn Law League and promoted Trenwith's letters, written under the pseudonym 'a tenant farmer', applying that logic to Ireland.[18] Trenwith then published in the *Examiner* on 4 January 1847 an appeal to farmers to form a 'Tenant League' to advance their own interests independently of the landowners, who had reportedly quashed a planned county meeting out of fear of criticism of their harsh exactions. He included a call to action: 'HURRAH FOR THE TENANT LEAGUE!!! Tenant farmers I told you before "that your reliance must be upon yourselves alone." Your landlords, in place of being your "natural protectors", have become your unnatural persecutors and slanderers.'[19] One of Trenwith's earlier letters (which were circulated in pamphlet form) had quoted Crawford's third letter approvingly.[20]

The first meeting of the Cork League on 9 January 1847 was praised by the *Examiner* as involving 'a most respectable and substantial class of men, who, in every state, for the bone and sinew of the public weal', with Trenwith taking the post of secretary. The arguments made were, it reported, cautious and prudent, accepting the legitimacy of the rights of property, but demanding the legal protection of their own class's rights and 'safety in a season of peril'. Demands were made for rent abatements, assistance for small farmers and compensation for any improvements made in case of eviction.[21]

A public meeting later that month drew attendance from tenants from the rural hinterlands of the city, along with a number of Catholic priests.[22] Protestant clerical support was less forthcoming, but any examples of it, as with one cleric writing from Naas, Co. Kildare, were eagerly welcomed by the *Examiner*.[23] Amidst the range of famine-related grievances raised at the meeting of 26 January, Maguire himself proposed they rally behind support for a more programmatic approach to land reform. His resolution advocated 'the necessity of fixity of tenure, compensation for improvements, and the general extension of the tenant right of Ulster'. In Maguire's view, the tenants needed not only to place the pressure of public opinion on their landlords to abate rents and curb ejectments, but to seek 'wholesome and radical' reforms through parliament.[24] Having agreed on its aims, the Cork organisation proceeded to raise subscriptions, draw up its regulations and promote the development of sister bodies in neighbouring counties, with the hope of building a national movement that would be non-sectarian and non-partisan in character.[25] Membership was set at a shilling a year, with a subscription of ten shillings entitling a member to stand for election to its council, in practice restricting this to more substantial farmers.

Although the Cork agitation at first made little direct reference to Sharman Crawford, the inclusion of the demand for the extension of the Ulster custom by law to the south reflected his promotion of this idea. Moreover, the commitment to a parliamentary strategy drew attention back to him as the foremost advocate of land reform at Westminster. This was recognised by the *Freeman's Journal*, which welcomed the emergence of the Cork movement while at the same time flagging Crawford's upcoming parliamentary motion on tenant right in February 1847 as the most important issue affecting Ireland.[26] Also expressing support for the Cork Tenant League, the *Nation* connected the campaign to the efforts of 'the honest and excellent Sharman Crawford, who of all public men has been the most persevering and energetic, in demanding that the tenant-right shall be legalised in Ulster, and extended to Munster, Connaught and Leinster'. The paper was certain, however, that no 'English' parliament would ever concede tenant right and that the land movement should therefore direct its attention towards national independence.[27] While it regarded his bill as 'an imperfect half-measure', it nonetheless upbraided the 'Irish Party' for failing to support it and that it deserved the backing by the incipient Tenant League movement.[28]

Crawford's motion on the law of landlord and tenant in Ireland, proposed to the commons on 11 February 1847, restated his now well-known position on land reform, and was widely reported in Ireland. Widespread starvation, now evident to all through press reports, he argued rendered land reform ever more urgent, especially given the recent resolutions of landlord bodies against even limited outdoor relief, and the continued export of food. Even good landlords were responsible for the delinquencies of their ancestors in mismanaging the land, and he would take his own share of the blame and accept a curb on his legal powers. Unless legislative action was taken to 'give the improving tenant in occupation a sufficient permanency of tenure, or else establish the tenant's right to claim by law full compensation for all benefits created by the expenditure of his labour and capital' all other 'remedial' Irish measures would prove futile.[29]

This appears to have been an attempt by Crawford to capitalise on the growing antagonism towards Irish landlords in British public opinion to leverage the Whig government towards either letting his own bill pass or introducing a substantive measure themselves. The chief secretary, Henry Labouchere, prevaricated that a government bill would soon be brought forward and Crawford did not force his motion to a division, but his centrality to any parliamentary strategy for reform had been reinforced. In early 1847 there was support from some surprising places. Londonderry wrote to Crawford to express his 'extreme gratification at your most excellent speech', endorsing his arguments regarding the beneficial effects of the Ulster custom, and assuring him that the motion had planted 'the *good root* that [...] must sooner or later arrive at maturity'.[30] He added that he regretted the opposition to the motion voiced by his son Lord Castlereagh, which had in turn been excoriated by the *Londonderry Standard*. The paper likened parliamentary obstruction of tenant-right legislation to resistance to slave emancipation and argued both that 'aggressions' against the custom in the north (where tenant right was of greater antiquity than many landowners' claims) and the necessity of its exportation to the south made it essential that tenants form 'an *active*, as well as an *immediate* organization' in support of Crawford.[31] James McKnight, still at the *Belfast News-Letter*, but soon to move to the *Standard* and take a more direct role in the Ulster agitation, also expressed support for Crawford's proposed legislation.[32]

Welcoming the Drogheda board of guardians' petition, Crawford repeated his conviction that the government would not act without public pressure, for 'there never was a time when it was more necessary for the people to declare their opinions on this matter [...] unless the voice of the nation be strongly raised there is every reason to fear that the case will be indefinitely postponed'.[33] Writing to the *Standard* he urged the north to exert pressure behind his reintroduced tenant right bill. The burdens of famine relief must not be imposed on the tenants without compensation.[34] A supporting editorial explicitly praised the Cork Tenant League and urged Ulster tenants to follow suit.[35] Others agreed: the *Kilkenny Journal* thought nothing more needed to be added to Crawford's letters on the substance of the tenants' claims, but that every county must 'exert themselves to facilitate and secure that extension' following the 'glorious example' of Cork and in rivalry to 'the landlord coalition, the "Irish Party"' then meeting in Dublin.[36] Maguire continued to promote the movement through his paper, observing in February the collapse of the rotten structure of rural society, the deaths of at least one hundred thousand and the consequent necessity of popular mobilisation for mutual self-preservation through the power of collective action. What he envisaged was not a social revolution by force but reviving the O'Connellite tactic of using numbers to influence elections.[37]

Trenwith and his allies in Cork were intent on doing just this. In February they issued an 'Address to the tenant farmers of Ireland' calling on them to form a 'vast confederacy to ensure the redress of grievances'.[38] A series of 'Tenant League papers' by Trenwith followed, distributing the arguments and objectives of the movement nationally, pronouncing that the '*Tenant League* will never cease to labour until every man is *secured* in the enjoyment of the fruits of his own labour', and asserting the common interest of the tenant farmer and the labourer in the face of landlord greed.[39] Direct communications were opened with potentially influential tenant leaders elsewhere to encourage the formation of branches in other counties.[40] Welcoming the formation of a branch at Cove (Cobh) in April, Trenwith urged members to petition against hostile amendments to the Irish poor law, including both Lord George Bentinck's rating clause and William Gregory's quarter acre clause.[41] A branch at Gorey in Wexford had also come into existence in March.[42]

Crawford's most recent series of letters had also made an impact in Ulster, with one Antrim farmer writing to the *Whig* to praise his arguments and to warn that any attempt to curb tenant right risked sparking a revival of the 'Hearts of Steel'.[43] Other writers urged tenants to resist landed incursions and for the Presbyterian clergy to assert their leadership of their community.[44] Attention to the relationship between rents and the 'Ulster custom' had been focused there by the widely-reported case of William Berwick, a substantial tenant of Lord Downshire whose rent had arbitrarily been tripled on the expiry of his lease (allegedly in punishment for organising petitioning against tithes and church-cess), leading to the collapse of value of his tenant-right, which he was obliged to sell at a great loss.[45]

One biographical sketch of McKnight credits him with establishing a tenant-right association in the north in summer 1846, assisted by Samuel McCurdy Greer and several Presbyterian ministers, although this seems unlikely.[46] It was not until spring 1847 that northern organisation started to acquire a public profile. Reporting on a tenant-right meeting in Coleraine in Co. Londonderry in March, the *Freeman's Journal* praised the unselfishness of the 'northerns' in seeking the extension of their custom across the island by law and welcomed the creation of a 'solemn league and covenant' for tenant right.[47] The meeting was organised by Greer but also included a number of local landowners who voiced support for the custom.[48] In early April the *Londonderry Standard* obtained the rules and publications of the Cork league and proposed the immediate formation of a northern league on the same model, starting in Derry city, a move welcomed in turn by the *Examiner*.[49] The *Standard*, reassured by the respectability of the Cork organisers, urged its readers to overcome any reluctance to join as their fate depended on countering the existing landlord combination. In the *Nation*, Duffy excitedly welcomed this incipient union of 'the several movements of north and south into one irresistible league'.[50] The foundations of a unified Irish Tenant League were now being laid, even if its progress would prove far from smooth.

Central to the tenant-right mobilisation in the north was the leading role played by Presbyterian clergy. Andrew Holmes has characterised this a part of a wider manifestation of 'Covenanter politics' within the denomination that combined evangelical religious conviction with stress on a 'social gospel' that sought redress of economic injustice. For the many Presbyterian clergy drawn from tenant families, sympathy with the plight of that class came naturally, but even those without such ties tended to equate landlordism with the evils of 'prelacy' and see it as complicit in the social subordination of Presbyterians. The intensity with which such views were held was no doubt enhanced by the social and spiritual crisis of the Famine.[51] To reinforce this equation, McKnight brought out a *Catechism of Tenant-Right* in 1850, which used scriptural extracts to argue that the question was one 'of LIFE, MORALS and RELIGION', and it is clear many clerics agreed, and were at least temporarily prepared to subordinate deep suspicions of Catholicism to engage in collaboration with the priests on this head.[52] Issuing a second, expanded, edition of his pamphlet later that year, McKnight reiterated that it was important that poor tenants unable to afford newspapers had access to such a simple catechistical text, to 'answer the sophisms of landlords, agents and their hirelings'; Crawford was quoted approvingly therein.[53]

If the northern movement was promoted principally by Presbyterian lay and clerical agents, it received a significant cross-denominational boost in May 1847 with the adherence of the Catholic bishop of Derry, Edward Maginn. The bishop wrote to Trenwith (who had sent him the League's address) offering his full support and stating his opinion that attainment of tenant right was now more important than repeal of the union. He drew analogies between Irish landlords and American slaveowners:

> *The cotton-grower of Lancaster, South Carolina, has as much right to claim, without compensation, the calicoes of Manchester, Glasgow, or Paisley, because he supplied to the manufacturer the raw material, as the landlord has to the tenant's improvements, because he let him the land.* To thrust men out on the world who reclaimed the bleak and barren mountain side or deep morass [...] may have a sanction in law, but has none from justice [...]

He was delighted to see the tenants of Ulster stirring in their own defence thorough a strictly peaceful and constitutional agitation and was certain they would now join with the Cork organisation. The League's leadership had set the best example for Ulster, as its committee was comprised of many of every creed, united in brotherhood to work for the common good. Maginn praised Crawford for his full recognition of tenant right.[54] An assembly of tenant farmers meeting in Derry city on 26 May resolved to insist on attaining security of tenure and '*universal* recognition and *application* of this great principle of justice, namely, that the *rights* of the tenant shall be guaranteed by law as well as the rights of the *landlord*' by means of a tenant-right act. Gratitude was due particularly to Crawford 'for the persevering and zealous manner in which he has, during many years, and in the face of multiplied discouragements, advocated our rights as a class'.[55]

Attention was again directed to Westminster, where Crawford had already announced his intention to bring in his own tenant right bill (the sixth version of his measure) that session.[56] This he did in April, following Russell's explanation that Bessborough's (ultimately fatal) illness had held up preparation of any ministerial measure.[57] The new version for the first time incorporated the legalisation of tenant-right customs wherever these existed in Ireland, alongside the extension of compensation for past improvements elsewhere (until such time as the Ulster custom could be extended nation-wide), and a clause to provide for the continuation of a tenancy at a 'fair rent' which would be set by valuation. Predictably, the government dragged its feet by fielding no ministers at the second reading debate on 28 April and discussion was adjourned, with the *Freeman* concluding that it had been sabotaged by both the ministry and 'Irish Party'.[58] The paper excoriated the apparent indifference of Irish MPs to the bill and warned that the new tenant movement would punish this: 'The sturdy yeomen of Ulster – the men of Down, and Antrim, and Londonderry, harmonized with the Tenant League of Munster, which, though still in its infancy, has formed a centre for the collection and expression of southern opinion' would hold them responsible at the polls.[59] Such threats, and Crawford's reiterated appeal that tenant security would stimulate profitable employment of the labourers in a time of famine, were not enough to prevent the defeat of his bill on 16 June by a margin of 112 to twenty-five. Popular radicals such as Poulett Scrope rallied behind him, as well as the Cork MPs and (more surprisingly given his previous opposition) Lord Castlereagh, but the government was loyally supported by many Irish liberals, including Crawford's erstwhile ally David Ross, as well as most Tories.[60]

The 1847 elections, Holy Cross and after

The loss of Sharman Crawford's 1847 tenant-right bill was not unexpected and was treated by its supporters as a setback and a spur to more intensive tenant mobilisation before he reintroduced in next session.[61] In the meantime two opportunities presented themselves. Firstly, the government announced its intention to dissolve the 1841 parliament and hold national elections in August. This would allow the new tenant-right movement a first chance to test its strength at the polls. Secondly, with the social crisis of the Famine temporarily blunted by the relatively effective soup kitchen relief system that summer, and a reasonable grain harvest giving larger tenant farmers (if not the potato-dependent labourers and cottiers) some breathing space at least before the next rent gale in November, the possibility of a resort to public meetings and petitioning in support of tenant-right opened up, at least in the east, north-east and parts of the south. The turn to outdoor agitation was accompanied by certain risks to the movement's initiators, and would open the floor to more radical voices and public arguments about what the ultimate aims and methods of tenant mobilisation should be, which came to a head at the Holy Cross meeting in Tipperary that autumn.

In the wake of his commons defeat, Crawford wrote to Trenwith to thank him and the Cork Tenant League for their support. He was sure the setback was temporary and that it had the desirable outcome of exposing the delusion of the promised Whig legislation and of stimulating popular attention to the question.[62] The Cork League had an early opportunity of flexing its electoral muscle in late June, when in the wake of O'Connell's death a county by-election was held; it promptly pressed the candidates to declare their support for tenant right. The Catholic magistrate Maurice Power was always the favourite as a Repealer but moved to secure his election by committing to support Crawford's bill and getting the League's endorsement.[63] This outcome was replicated in the general election with followed in August. Both the Cork city MPs attended meetings of the League and voiced their support for its aims. Endorsed by that body, they and the two sitting county MPs were all returned, the latter without a contest.[64]

In a public letter Crawford called for the use of similar tactics in other constituencies. Only fourteen Irish MPs had voted for his 1847 bill, he noted, with similar numbers against and the great majority absent. He accused the Russell government (in contrast to Peel's) of acting dishonestly, and charged the Irish MPs supporting it with a share of the guilt, while most British MPs remained wilfully ignorant of Irish realities. The solution continued to lie in popular action to change the parliamentary calculus:

> Although you have difficulties to contend against, no question was ever in a more certain position to insure success, if supported with energy by a constitutional agitation, and peaceful

organization, backed up by an honest exercise of the elective franchise at the ensuing elections. [...] I have said this question may be thus made a test of British legislation; but it will be no less a test of *yourselves*. It will prove whether the electors and people of Ireland have the public spirit and honesty to do their duty, and whether Protestants and Catholics can be brought together in a united effort for the *public* interests. You – the tenant class of Ireland – are now in the condition of serfs. [...] You are slaves, and so you deserve to be, if you do not use those means which are legally within your power to rescue yourselves from so degrading a position.

The roadmap to victory appeared to involve the securing of a pro-tenant-right majority of Irish MPs, who would then act independently of government and oblige the ministry to give their 'reluctant consent' to his measure through exerting parliamentary pressure.[65]

While such calls no doubt helped stimulate the spread of the League idea, few places were as advanced as Cork in terms of organisation and membership after the ravages of the previous months. In late June a committee was established to draw up regulations for a Tenant League of Ulster based in Derry, and the *Londonderry Journal* urged it to take action against the county members (one of whom had voted against Crawford's bill while the other abstained) and the borough's Whig MP Sir R. A. Ferguson, who had also opposed it.[66] The *Armagh Guardian* carried an address to independent electors of that county calling on them to vote only for candidates pledged to support the bill of 'your zealous, honest, independent, and incorruptible friend, Mr Sharman Crawford', which alone could bring about the regeneration of Ireland.[67] In Enniscorthy a meeting of farmers resolved to support no candidate in Wexford who would not vote for the principles of Crawford's bill, while in Meath the 'popular' candidates, Corbally and Grattan, appeared at a county meeting at Navan to endorse the bill and the principal of extending the Ulster custom to the south, and lauded the need to unite north and south. A Meath Tenant League was formed, with Catholic clerical support.[68]

In the boroughs of Dundalk and Drogheda the Whigs William Somerville (now chief secretary) and Torrens McCullagh (his private secretary) were returned only after verbally endorsing 'tenant right' under pressure from the local popular press. Somerville, a Meath landowner, later distanced himself from the impression that he was 'impregnated with all the nonsense which is daily put forward by a hundred writers with reference to it', while acknowledging that something must be done to assuage public opinion. McCullagh, who was only seated after a petition, had stated that 'on the question of tenant-right he perfectly coincided with Mr Sharman Crawford', and would prove a more sincere convert.'[69] The city of Dublin election saw the Repealer John Reynolds unexpectedly take a seat from the divided Conservatives, on the back of a populist manifesto that included tenant right.[70]

The outcome of all this activity was mixed, especially in the north where existing political interests were heavily entrenched. R. J. Tennent was finally able to take one of the Belfast seats in place of Ross by mobilising a Presbyterian-Catholic coalition of voters around a platform that included tenant right alongside Presbyterian representation and free trade.[71] In Co. Londonderry the sitting Conservatives were in the end returned unopposed, and it was not until 1852 that Greer was able to initiate a 'radical' challenge at the polls. The 1847 elections, taking place during famine conditions when political funds were scarce, the Repeal party in abeyance and the tenant movement still coalescing, was in many ways premature for a full-scale electoral challenge. Nevertheless, the *Northern Whig* was sanguine that progress had been made, if only in shifting political discourse around land reform, which 'was made a topic for examination at the hustings; and it would be difficult for any Irish member to be popular who would declare himself adverse to tenant right'. [72] There was no contest in Down that year, but Crawford, having been already re-elected at Rochdale, presented himself at the formal hustings at Downpatrick, and amid 'great confusion', directly challenged Lord Edwin Hill (who had succeeded his brother Lord Hillsborough in the seat in 1845 on his succession to the marquessate) to explain his 'disappearance' from the division of 16 June.[73] The gauntlet had been thrown down for a full-scale assault on the Downshire interest in the county when parliament was next dissolved.

Although the pre-eminent voice in the debate on tenant right in 1847, Crawford's strategy and objectives for land reform were never hegemonic in Ireland. As we have already seen, he had clashed in the early 1840s with William Conner, who had restated his theories in an 1846 pamphlet and whose loyal followers continued to rally behind his slogan of 'a valuation and a perpetuity'.[74] In April 1847 the *Cork Examiner* received and published a letter from 'a plain speaker' sharply criticising Crawford for being too timid and wayward in his proposals and recommending Conner's more straightforward plan for tenant fixity with 'fair rents' based on valuation, and with facilities for tenants to purchase their holdings.[75] Positions to the left of Conner's were now also being articulated in the press. For its part the Cork Tenant League had remained open on the details of any solution to the tenant question, and the policy of any national movement was still up for contestation. Aware of this, Crawford's advocates stressed the tactically adroit and progressive nature of his approach. Neither his 1847 bill nor its previous iterations had, the *Standard* pointed out, ever been regarded by him as a final solution, but only as an attainable first step, 'a mere *instalment* of justice'. While it was true that his bill contained no direct guarantee of 'fixity of tenure', this did not mean that he would stop once the principle of state intervention in Irish landlord-tenant relations had been legally enacted.[76]

Such a gradualist argument cut no ice with those who rejected the utility of any parliamentary strategy. One new voice emerging in 1847 taking this line was that of James Fintan Lalor. At first a follower of Conner (whose estate at Inch was close to his father the middleman farmer Patrick Lalor's property at Tinnekill), the younger Lalor's political and social thought had become radicalised after 1843, rejecting his father's O'Connellism for republican separatism and moving towards an agrarian philosophy which ultimately looked towards land nationalisation to be attained through social revolution. Gavan Duffy had given Lalor space in the *Nation* in spring 1847 to develop his ideas in print. However the paper also continued to print letters supportive of Crawford's position that compensation must be linked to industry and for amelioration of the landlord-tenant relationship through legislation, even while it expressed scepticism as to whether this was possible.[77] Lalor's freedom of manoeuvre in that paper was somewhat hampered by the Irish Confederation's preferred strategy of seeking a patriotic alliance with disillusioned Irish landowners against the British government, but his writing seethed with anger against that very class and the exploitative land system of which the proprietors formed the pinnacle.[78]

In his first major piece of political journalism, published on 24 April 1847, Lalor set out his personal interpretation of the Famine and what the correct response to it should be. He argued that providence had now dissolved Irish society; the potato failure had done 'the work of ages in a day [...] it has unsettled society to its foundation; deranged every interest, every class, every household [...] it has come as if commissioned to produce, at length and not too soon, a dissolution of that state and order of existence in which we have heretofore been living.' While not hesitant to direct blame to both landed self-interest and British hostility towards the Irish people for what followed, ultimately Lalor attributed the moving agency in this social dissolution to divine providence: the disasters of famine had revealed that 'it is God's will that society should stand dissolved, and assume another shape and action; and he works his will by human hands and natural agencies.'

Whereas both Trevelyan and many Irish liberals welcomed the proletarianisation of the smallholding tenant and cottier as a divinely intended prerequisite for the new tripartite rural social order on which a progressive capitalist agriculture must be built, to Lalor this threatened not just immediate suffering, but the destruction of the independent class that constituted the true 'people' of Ireland. Rather than be the passive victims of dispossession and extermination, Lalor asserted, it was now this class's historical mission to assert itself and place itself at the centre of a new social constitution; landowners must either abandon their privileges and collaborate with the agrarian movement, or themselves face confiscation and expulsion as the enemies of 'the people'. The responsibility of agency, however, lay with the tenant farmers and their leaders, and any failure to grasp the opportunity for social revolution would amount to national suicide. The language Lalor employed to convey this idea was both provocative and apocalyptic in tone, but his sense of personal mission, as Marta Ramon points out in her edition of his writings, was more practical, at least at this point.[79] Social and political action, rather than pietistic resignation or nihilistic posturing, was, he appeared to believe in 1847, the necessary response.

Lalor's problem was that there was a disconnect between his ultra-radical agrarian vision, which increasingly stressed the necessity of 'repealing the conquest', or returning sovereignty over the land of Ireland to its people – an agenda which would necessitate a social insurrection to create an occupier proprietory or full-scale land nationalisation – with the political means open to him.[80] Most Young Ireland leaders were at best lukewarm towards his insistence on the primacy of agrarian action, and even John Mitchel adopted only elements of Lalor's arguments against landlordism and tended towards a catastrophist vision of a republican revolution erupting from the nadir of absolute misery rather than Lalor's preference for national independence and social revolution being attained simultaneously.[81] Mitchel's insistence on an all-out rent and rates strike to provoke a peasant rebellion was denounced as suicidal by other Young Irelanders sympathetic to agrarian reforms such as Michael Doheny and T. F. Meagher and led to his resignation from the Confederation Council and the *Nation* in February 1848.[82]

Lalor's bid for leadership of the tenant movement began and ended in 1847, when he approached Trenwith to jointly organise a demonstration in Tipperary that would lead to the establishment of a Tenant League there.[83] The county had a history of agrarian unrest, and by September there were reports of widespread and in places violent resistance to the collection of rent. The *Cork Examiner* expressed sympathy with the unrest while doubting that Crawford's bill would be sufficient to meet the raised expectations of the people.[84] The moment for a more revolutionary tenant movement may have appeared imminent; Lalor's letter announcing a meeting at Holy Cross near Thurles on 19 September warned tenants and labourers that renewed famine and landlord extermination faced them if they did not act now to settle the land question once and for all.[85] However, as Lalor's fiery print rhetoric began to attract attention from the conservative press, more moderate reformers such as Maguire and Trenwith started to back away. On 17 September the *Examiner* felt obliged to stress that the meeting would be a strictly constitutionalist affair and only in the fevered imagination of the *Times* would it form the stimulus to a 'servile war'.[86] In the face of a Catholic clerical boycott of the meeting the paper distanced itself from what in the end turned out to be an embarrassing fiasco.

The Holy Cross meeting on the 19th had been, the *Examiner* reported the following day, a thin and unimportant affair attended by only between 1,000 and 2,000 people (only a dozen of whom were farmers, it claimed), and had been ill-considered, badly organised and likely to set back the tenant cause. The resolutions proposed were less extreme than expected given Lalor's articles, calling only for the extension of the Ulster tenant-right to Munster and for a 'fair rent' calculated by valuation, and deprecating any rent strikes, while the speeches made by Lalor and Doheny were less exuberant and provocative than had been anticipated. A later report in the *Dublin Evening Post* offers some hint as to the discrepancy between Lalor's previous print rhetoric and the relative moderation of the platform resolutions: the local organising committee had been deeply divided over whether to prepare 'resolutions subversive of all forms of law' or to stay in line with the position adopted by the Cork tenant-right movement. In the end the 'frieze-coated' farmers had prevailed in drawing up the resolutions, and although they had not then taken places on the platform, this had obliged the reluctant radical orators to back their more moderate positions.[87]

The meeting collapsed into acrimony for quite different reasons when Lalor's erstwhile mentor, William Conner (misnamed by the *Examiner* as O'Connor, suggesting he was little known in Munster), arrived on the platform, and in the face of a largely hostile crowd proceeded to lecture them on his own claims to primacy as a campaigner and to 'teach them their rights, knowing which and understanding they would be the better prepared to defend them by every peaceful, legal and constitutional means'. The proceedings degenerated into a slanging match with Conner charging Lalor with being a neophyte and his father a rackrenter, and Lalor responding that his adversary was an incendiary and traitor to repeal. After insults were exchanged, chaos ensued:

> Mr Lalor here rushed across the platform, and having gripped Mr O'Connor with both hands, by the coat collar, endeavoured to hurl him from the platform, amid deafening shouts of encouragement from the crowd, who rushed furiously forward to the platform, upsetting the reporters and overturning all before them. [... Lalor] then left the platform accompanied by the chairman and one or two gentlemen, and Mr O'Connor being now left in sole possession of the hustings, proceeded to address the meeting on the question of tenant right, amid mingled hooting, cheering, with cries of 'hear him,' 'go on,' 'speak out,' 'no, no,' and great uproar. The gentleman had not been in possession of the attention of the meeting (if attention to a speaker could be said to exist in a scene somewhat resembling the preparation for a faction fight) – when a tremendous onslaught was made on the hustings, the props of which being demolished, the whole fabric came to the ground; and in the terrific uproar and tumult that followed the reporters were forced to decamp with all possible speed, leaving the assemblage to conduct the sequel of the proceedings as they best thought proper.[88]

The Holy Cross shambles ended both Lalor's and Conner's careers as agrarian agitators and provided much ammunition to the movement's enemies. Even the more sympathetic

Tipperary Vindicator believed the debacle had seriously set back the tenant movement in the county, although it hoped not decisively.[89]

In the aftermath of Holy Cross, there were calls for the Cork Tenant League to distance itself from the 'hot-brained, filmy-eyed theorists of Tipperary', but also to take advantage of the surge of British interest in the subject to push on with its objectives.[90] It was evident to many that Catholic clerical support, so evidently absent on 19 September, was essential to success, and the accession that month of the influential Carlow priest Rev. James Maher, a leading controversialist and uncle to Paul Cullen, who was then rector of the Irish College in Rome, was a welcome boost. Crawford also travelled to Munster in late September, officially on a fact-gathering mission about social conditions in the company of his son Charles, the poor law inspector for the region, but also with a view to boosting the league movement and promoting national co-ordination.[91] No admirer of Lalor, he had nevertheless seen the Holy Cross meeting as potentially having propaganda value by alerting landlords to the seriousness of the situation in the countryside:

> The same measure which would once have been accepted, would now be received with dissatisfaction; claims of a more extended nature are put forward, which it may be difficult to compromise by any limited adjustment, and dangerous to refuse. [...] I admit it is most undesirable to have assemblages of great masses of people collected together to call for the redress of grievances. But who is in fault if excess be committed? Those landlords who refuse the remedy of an admitted evil – those governments who have neglected or refused to redress that which even their own commissioners have declared to be an intolerable grievance. You call on the government to stop the Tipperary meeting. Suppose that is done, will it stifle the feelings which produce the call for that meeting?[92]

Crawford was invited to speak at a tenant rally at Thurles, Co. Tipperary, on 26 September, but thought it politic to postpone this 'until all the disappointment and excitement of the Holycross meeting was cooled down'. He assured James Ryan (who was glad to learn had not been involved with Lalor's meeting) that he would be happy to address the new Tipperary Central Tenant League the following month as part of his object 'to create a temperate national movement in support of just principles'.[93] The *Examiner* interviewed him and reiterated its commitment to supporting Crawford's conception of tenant right as a means of concentrating public opinion on a given point, and reported on the public dinner to be thrown for him by the Cork Tenant League.[94]

In the event pressing business at Crawfordsburn drew him north earlier than anticipated, leading him to apologise to Trenwith for missing the dinner and disappointing his friends in the city.[95] Consequently he was absent from both the rescheduled meeting at Thurles (at which speakers loudly distanced themselves from Lalor), and the very large rally held at Kilmacthomas, Co. Waterford, on 21 October, which involved nearly 100 priests and was addressed by John O'Connell, and which greatly boosted the morale of the movement in Munster after the setback.[96] The younger O'Connell, seeking to revive his father's movement in the wake of the Young Ireland schism, clearly saw a political opportunity in the tenant movement, but at the same time was careful to credit Crawford. He told the Repeal Association that he thought 'Mr Sharman Crawford's conduct on this occasion was most praiseworthy. He carried all these theories into practice'.[97] Also on the platform at

Kilmacthomas was the landowning Whig Sir Thomas Barron, who had lost his Waterford city seat in 1847 would regain it at a by-election in March 1848.

As the movement spread nationally, the Cork League declined in importance. Part of this was due to the resignation of its founding figure and driving force, Trenwith, as secretary for personal reasons in October 1847 (his wife had died several months previously, but this was probably due more to the financial embarrassments that saw him briefly imprisoned for debt in 1848).[98] Trenwith was later to play a subordinate role in the revived Tenant League movement in the county.[99]

Returning to Ulster, Crawford was lauded for his tenant-right work, and the newly formed Ulster Tenant League announced a dinner in his honour in Derry on 27 October. In a major coup, the general assembly of the Presbyterian church agreed a resolution in support of tenant right (despite the opposition of Henry Cooke) and lobbied the new lord lieutenant, Lord Clarendon, in favour of Crawford's bill, reflecting the sympathy of the majority of its clergy for the plight of their tenant communicants.[100] Both the Presbyterian and Catholic clergy were well represented at the Derry celebration, and Bishop Maginn sent an enthusiastic letter of support. It was the lord lieutenant's dismissive response to the resolution of the general assembly, however, that formed the focus of Crawford's speech. Clarendon had fallen back on the proprietarian assumption that any legalisation of tenant right would endanger the sanctity of property rights. Crawford responded by denying this and re-articulating his alternative philosophy of property – one that drew both on labour theory of value ideas and the conception of property as a trust, dependent on the demonstration of communal utility and hence subject to regulation in the national interest:

> The sacred rights of property! He would put it to them whether the rights of property could be regarded as sacred, if the rights of labour were not looked on as sacred too? What had been the origin of all property except labour? What, except labour, created property of every description? [...] Labour, he contended, was the first basis of all property; and he denied that the latter could be regarded as free from danger so long as the rights of labour were left without protection[.]

Parliament had conceded the principle of protecting labour rights in manufacturing through the ten hours act; why should the poor occupying tenants of Ireland be denied the same? Give the tenants throughout the country the security they demanded, he argued, provide agricultural education and encouragement, and remove bankrupt landlords through an encumbered estates act, and Ireland would soon be able to produce enough grain to feed all its population and provide a surplus.[101]

Crawford's speech was well received, not only in the usual sources, but in sections of the Ulster Tory press such as the *Newry Telegraph*, which contrasted his pragmatic and practical approach to the 'shallow and noisy demagogues' of Holy Cross, and in the *Belfast Protestant Journal*, which took the *News-Letter* and *Northern Whig* to task for bourgeois liberalism and failing to recognise and endorse Crawford's critique of absolute property rights.[102] The Derry banquet appears to have been a successful public event and was commemorated in at least one popular song, which concluded:

> Then true to each other, as brother to brother,
> With Crawford our eloquent pleader,

We for tenant-right will together unite,
With him our invincible leader![103]

Crawford was not the only one present seeking to promote an all-island alliance to promote radical social reform while sidelining the 'national question'. McKnight, who as the new editor of the *Londonderry Standard* had been central to organising the event, had opened his own line of communication with Gavan Duffy. While continuing to eschew repeal, McKnight (an Irish speaker who had promoted language revival in the pages of the *News-Letter*) welcomed the non-sectarian ideals behind Young Ireland and praised Duffy's work in promoting the movement in the south, while warning him that the Confederates' strategy of conciliating the landowning class was folly. Joint action on the land question was, he wrote to Duffy, the key to progress:

> I am most anxious to unite together *Irishmen of all classes* and of *all religious denominations* in the tenant-right movement. This is my great object in the meantime, and if I can succeed in it, so far as Ulster is concerned, an important *national* good will be achieved. The electoral constituencies, both in boroughs and counties, will be *emancipated* from aristocratic *dictation* by the concession of a *proper* tenant-right, and an *improper* or *useless* one, we are determined to *reject*. When the constituencies are rendered practically *independent*, and the people are legally *secured* in regard to their *just rights*, and have the *means* of being comfortable in their social circumstances, if they are *dissatisfied* with the *political* condition, it will then be fully in their power to give *effect* to the *national will*, without having recourse to any other than the agencies of *peace*.

The Ulstermen were ready to fight 'the battle of Tipperary' to pursue their common national interests, but would not give primacy to repeal, as that could lead merely to the 'uncontrolled despotism of a *landlord's parliament* in Dublin' without any check from Westminster. Nevertheless, he concluded, Duffy and his associates would always be welcomed as friends so long as they adhered to moral force methods.[104] Duffy's reluctance to sideline repeal in 1847 and brief flirtation with revolution in 1848 initially frustrated this olive branch, but the offer would be renewed and accepted in 1849.

In November, Crawford clashed again with the radical Young Irelanders, this time in person at a meeting of the Irish Council in Dublin. This body had been established in summer 1847 with the aim of bringing together Irish representatives and landowners of different persuasions to agree on common policies as a successor to the still-born 'Irish Party'. Seeking to restart the faltering initiative, members of the Repeal Association and Irish Confederation co-operated in hosting a public conference in Dublin, but this did little except expose further antagonisms within and well as between the rival nationalist movements.[105] During a debate on the landlord-tenant question, John Mitchel, supported by Michael Doheny, assertively challenged Crawford's position that Ulster tenant-right was based on tenant improvements, past or present, and insisted that it was thus a form of absolute property quite distinct from the principle of compensation for improvements, that it could always be sold to the highest bidder in full or in part and that it protected the tenant from arbitrary rent increases. Recognising this right across Ireland would, Mitchel insisted, give tenants 'a joint proprietorship in the fee-simple of the land' and offer a complete substitute for the 'infamous and wasteful' poor law.[106]

Crawford spoke at length in the next session, answering both Mitchel's assertions and Cloncurry's concerns that tenant-right would do nothing for the destitute labourer. While he regretted the expression of 'extreme views' by Mitchel, he understood that these arose from frustration at the failure of the landlords themselves to propose and enact any measures of justice. Having said that, he was adamant that tenant right as it currently existed, was founded on the rewards of labour and industry, which gave the tenant a permanent interest proportionate to the value thus created. What was being sold, the 'beneficial interest', was in fact his share of the profitable surplus of the holding, which was not fixed but dependent on its improved state. Indeed, he added, a recent petition from the Londonderry tenants had advocated it precisely on these grounds. While he referenced McKnight's historicist case for its origins (in response to the antiquarian Samuel Ferguson's critique of this claim), he insisted that the principal argument for it was one of present utility rather than historical precedent. What he was arguing for was not so much 'compensation for improvements', but tenant right as the perpetual property of the tenant, the value of which fluctuated according to the improvements made or inherited. As a universal 'principle of justice' rather than a regionally specific customary practice, tenant right was thus suitable for extension not just across Ireland, but Great Britain as well, with clauses to prevent abuses and bar any unauthorised subdivision. He reminded his audience that his earlier bills had been constrained by circumstances to look only for compensation for improvements, but with public opinion now behind the custom, he would be inclined to pursue its extension nationwide.[107]

Supported by Greer, Crawford's arguments proved persuasive to many, in the words of the *Freeman,* letting 'in a flood of light on the subject', and winning 'several avowed converts' including the Cork MP William Fagan to his position.[108] Mitchel backed down somewhat on his assertion that tenant right was wholly unconnected with improvement, making the two men temporary allies in arguing against a Whig-inspired motion to look to compensation only and not a tenant right based on a combination of occupancy and improvement. In the end, however, a barn-storming speech by Doheny appears to have got up the backs of the landlords present, and Mitchel's pro-tenant right amendment was narrowly defeated at the meeting.[109] The debate had opened up divisions within the Young Irelanders, with Thomas D'Arcy McGee arguing against tenant right, Smith O'Brien proving reluctant to break completely with the conservative landowners and Gavan Duffy still anxious to bring Crawford and other 'federalists' into the Confederation and attach it to the non-violent agrarian agitation he preferred. If Mitchel appeared briefly to endorse a tenant-right plan not dissimilar to Crawford's, he and his allies were increasingly drawn to the revolutionary vision of Fintan Lalor and were impatient with constitutionalist proceedings.[110]

This 'Mitchelite' preference for revolutionary action arose in part from personal sensibilities and self-promotion, and from fury at the continuing sufferings of the country in the face of government indifference or attempted social engineering, but it also reflected an impatience arising from the facts on the ground. The new Confederate Clubs movement was struggling to break out of the towns into the countryside and the vast bulk of the peasantry (if they were engaged with politics at all in the maelstrom of 1847) apparently remained loyal to the Repeal Association and its allies in the clergy. Dismissing the vote in the Irish Council against tenant right as a minor setback, the *Freeman's Journal* pointed to the continuing tenant movement in the provinces. A mass meeting was held several days later at Cashel, Co. Tipperary, with an estimated attendance of 20,000, addressed by John O'Connell and other Repeal MPs, and by several priests including Archdeacon Michael Laffan. It gave prolonged applause in absentia for Crawford and his tenant-right principles as well as deprecating the events at Holy Cross.[111] It was Laffan's speech that drew most attention, with critics, including the lord lieutenant, accusing him of stirring up agrarian unrest and demanding his behaviour be drawn to the attention of the pope, while defenders pointed to his local action against agrarian secret societies and strict adherence to peaceful protest.[112] Laffan appears to have spoken for a large section of the Catholic clergy of the province: the same month a Tipperary priest wrote to the prime minister expressing his full support of the plans of Crawford for the extension of tenant right and a valuation for 'fair rent'.[113]

A tenant-right meeting at Skibbereen in west Cork, unusually attended by the local Anglican as well as Catholic clergy, and by Dr Daniel Donovan who had done so much to publicise the mortality crisis of the district earlier in the year, was also supportive. Dr Richard Webb, the rector of Caheragh, commented that he had been converted to 'Sharman Crawford's plan, for there was nothing more misunderstood than tenant right, should be beneficial to the country'.[114] The prominent place of the Anglican clergy at Skibbereen reflected their high profile in philanthropic relief work in the district; elsewhere in Munster it was the Catholic clergy who took on much of the local organisational lead for the movement.[115] However the constitutionalist movement was not so fully united as this might suggest, and divisions were highlighted when O'Connell wrote to the press to insist on his own construction that the tenant right extended to the south must be for occupancy only as many poor tenants lacked the means to have made any improvements.[116]

The summoning of parliament for a short emergency session in November 1847 gave Crawford, as well as the Repeal leaders, a further opportunity to project themselves as popular tribunes. Although his threat to reintroduce his tenant right bill was not followed through due to the lack of time, it seemed to ruffle the government, which placed coercive measures to curb the serious outbreak of agrarian 'outrages' in Ireland at the head of their agenda but without any of the promised remedial measures.[117] Crawford took full opportunity of the debates on the government's crime and outrage bill to excoriate the behaviour of the landlords and the counterproductive folly of employing coercion to quell the violence sparked by their campaign of land clearances. Government inaction in the face of social collapse had, he argued, left it with blood on its hands:

> Were not the present government under a deep responsibility for the blood shed within the last six months? His firm belief was, that if a proper measure had been brought forward and carried through the house in the last session, we should not have had one of the murders which had disgraced the country. He would therefore put it to the present government to consider that responsibility, and no longer to trifle with this great question. What was the cause of the disorders of Ireland, but the disregard of the rights of property? We heard of the sacred rights of property; but were there no rights of poverty? Had the poor man no rights of property? But the rights of labour were not secured.

It followed that he could support no coercive measure unless it was yoked with substantial agrarian reform.[118] He justified his vote against the crime bill on the grounds that measures tackling only the symptoms and ignoring the causes of outrages were doomed to fail, and that the root cause remained the existing system of landlordism. However, in the face of significant rural violence, especially in the Munster counties of Tipperary, Limerick and Clare, the bill passed with large majorities, opposed only by the Repealers and a small smattering of British radical MPs, including Crawford and O'Connor.[119]

1847 thus closed with significant progress made, in the face of exceedingly difficult social conditions, in the development of a mass tenant movement, and general coalescence around the proposals set out by Crawford in his public writings and tenant-right bill. This had been checked to some extent by the preoccupation the British press and parliament with Irish agrarian 'outrages' in the latter months of the year, augmented with an increasing complaint of Irish 'ingratitude' for the previous outlay on famine relief (albeit mostly in the form of loans) and a belated sympathy for the landowners and agents put in fear for their lives. Sustained attempts were made by its enemies to associate the tenant right movement with the violent resistance to clearances, especially in disturbed southern counties and Ulster borderlands. Nevertheless, the *Freeman's Journal* was optimistic that the objective of legislative intervention to ensure tenant security could still be attained if the movement persevered and widened its geographical reach.[120] Success in 1848 would depend on a number of factors, including the government's response and the tenor of British public opinion, and the relationship between the constitutional and an emboldened revolutionary form of popular politics in Ireland.

Defeated revolutions, 1848–9

The Ulster tenant right movement began the new year assertively by expanding into Co. Monaghan with a mass meeting at Ballybay on 11 January 1848. This was a brave choice given the district's history of violent sectarian conflict; it was the home of the notorious publican and land agent Sam Gray, a leading Orangeman who had been accused of the murder of Catholics in 1824 and 1840, and finally convicted in 1844 after several failed prosecutions, only for the verdict to be overturned on appeal. Ballybay had also been the site of political confrontation between armed loyalists and John Lawless's Catholic supporters allegedly intent on an 'invasion of Ulster' in 1828.[121] The location seems to have been deliberately selected in an attempt to demonstrate that the tenant cause could transcend religious and partisan antagonisms and face down landlord attempts to exploit these through stirring up a 'no-popery' cry, and it drew on the local activism of Presbyterian clergy, most prominently Rev. David Bell.[122] Speaking at the rally, Crawford argued that such mass meetings offered a constructive alternative to the resort to illegal conspiracies. Unity was required to pursue the redress of class grievances, rendering religious divisions irrelevant. He wrote to the local organisers:

> The working classes, as well as the larger holders of land, have no security for the rights and profits of labour. Human nature cannot rest without seeking a remedy for such a state of things. If a legal remedy cannot be obtained, an illegal remedy will be resorted to. Then I say, in order to prevent illegal combination, the people should be encouraged, by orderly and constitutional meetings, to lay their grievances before the legislature.[123]

The nationalist press proclaimed the meeting a success, seeing 'Orangeman and Catholic casting to the winds all recollection of their former animosities' under the combined influence of the Catholic and Presbyterian clergy. The elderly Sam Gray himself attended the meeting, with one of his sons taking an active part in its organisation; indeed, Sam was observed to participate in the 'loud cheers and laughter' when a Catholic priest urged that 'their charter toast [should] be – tenant right – no rates – and NO SURRENDER'.[124] Between 2,000 and 3,000 people were present, and the meeting was reported as good natured and peaceful, and stimulated further meetings in the county.[125] Ballybay appears to have become a centre of tenant-right agitation, and Bell again proposed it as a site for a rally in 1850 both for its symbolic power in transcending its previous 'bad eminence' and because the 'landlord party' dared not disrupt meetings there.[126]

Crawford's statement at Ballybay that landlord rights could only be maintained when they acknowledged their land must be held according to the constraints of the public interest, which was in accordance with the laws of God, man and nature, was well received.[127] This meeting, with the parallel ones held the same week in Counties Cork and Kilkenny, raised the morale of supporters, but also drew attention to the absence of a central co-ordinating body. The problem with this continued to lie with the difficulty such a body would face in maintaining its distance from partisan entanglements – the *Freeman's Journal's* breezy assurance that it should work in alignment with John O'Connell's Repeal Association did not command universal agreement, not least in places such as Ballybay.[128]

Given the prominence of Crawford in the movement, his speeches were closely read and critics sought to identify inconsistencies or points of dissension to exploit. The *Northern Whig*, at this point a lukewarm supporter of tenant-right legislation, claimed to have discovered some novelty of definition in his Ballybay speech, leading him to defend his position in print and in his speech to the next Ulster rally held at Coleraine. Whether it had its roots in the plantation or not was not essential, he insisted, as the Ulster custom was established to give security for the value of labour and capital expended by the tenant in improving the productivity of his farm, and consequently *'industrial occupation'* was a requirement of the recognition of tenant right. Abuses had indeed occurred, he conceded, where the right had been claimed for land in a deteriorated state, and had been allowed due to lack of legal standing of the practice. However, such cases were rare and the value of a tenant's 'beneficial interest' reflected in most cases the accumulated worth of improvements made over time under conditions determined by the setting of a 'fair rent'. Variation of rents between estates tended above all to determine the market value of tenant right, which is why he argued his plan must be accompanied by an impartial valuation to determine a fair letting value. While he acknowledged that the current value of tenant right to rack-rented western smallholders might be negligible, the stimulus given to improvement would, he was convinced, generate a valuable tenant right for them within two years. In the meantime, a temporary bill to check arbitrary evictions would also be required.[129]

At Coleraine, where his speech was preceded by the reading of another ecumenical letter from Bishop Maginn, he summarising what he meant by tenant right in fifteen points. He also felt obliged to add a riposte to Mitchel's recent public assertion that tenant right could only be established 'by the determined opposition of *armed men*'. This was a major escalation from Holy Cross and Mitchel's own case made at the Irish Council, in effect a call to armed resistance, and as such it threatened to derail the peaceful agitation built up over the preceding six months. In response Crawford called for a restatement of the principle of adherence to strictly non-violent mass action in pursuing what he insisted was an attainable end. This did not mean he was turning a blind eye to social atrocities by the landlord class; indeed he denounced clearances and their Malthusian justification:

> There is a most unfortunate notion entertained in the minds of a great portion of the people of Ireland – and I must say of England also – that when the population becomes overcrowded, the superabundant part of the people become a nuisance, and that they must be exterminated, before the condition of society can be improved. There is a disposition evinced by some owners of the soil that this class of the poor must be exterminated – must be got rid of. [...] I firmly believe that there are in the resources of the soil of this country ample means of comfortable subsistence for all the people who live on it, if those resources could only be developed (hear, hear) – I would rather endeavour to improve the condition of the people here than to see them sent away to other countries, where we would not know how they would progress.

Where he differed from Mitchel was in his preference for measured language over the former's Swiftian 'savage indignation', and his conviction that any attempted social revolution in arms would be bloodily repressed and thus prove as counterproductive as the rising of 1798.[130]

At Downpatrick on 31 January he outlined the new tenant right bill he intended to introduce to parliament that session should the promised government measure turn out to be (as was anticipated) inadequate to the needs of the people. His speech earned praise for moderation from the *Downpatrick Recorder,* but attacks from the *Times.*[131] The principle of payment for tenant right had been already recognised, he argued, in the Land Clauses Compensation Act, under which courts had powers to allocate payments to tenants who lost land under compulsory purchase for railway construction: indeed a recent adjudication on the Londonderry estate in Down had proved this. His simple bill would retain such discretion on determining sums to the courts, but extend the tenant's right to claim to include all Irish tenants who could demonstrate an industrial occupation of land. As before, claims would be related to a 'fair rent' value, with any compensation being negated by the landlord allowing the tenant to remain in possession at such a 'fair rent' or by the free sale of the tenant right to a solvent incoming tenant. The courts would have the power to reduce or annul completely the sum due to the tenant in the case of proven neglect leading to deterioration of the value of the holding, and any future unauthorised subdivision would also annul any claim.

The proposed bill immediately attracted condemnation in Mitchel's new weekly, *The United Irishman,* which in its first issue reprinted the *Times'* attack on it as a 'quack remedy', stirring up 'the mud at the bottom of the social system'.[132] Following up in an editorial letter, Mitchel now proclaimed that immediate revolutionary action was the sole resort that could save the tenant class from annihilation:

> Now, friends, I think I hear some genteel patriot saying to you – meet, then, agitate, make your voice be constitutionally heard in parliament! Organize, educate, conciliate! Place yourself in the hands of Sharman Crawford, and he will contrive you another dreary bill; and after he has bored the house with it for half a dozen sessions, the survivors of you will see what will come of it; – but take care, the genteel patriot will say, that you do nothing to repel or *alarm* the better classes; after a while they will be flocking to your ranks for nationality' remember that without them you are but a vile 'mob,' and above all beware, beware of sedition, privy conspiracy, and rebellion!

As sweeping clearances gathered pace, it was difficult to refute Mitchel's assertion that the legal system of Ireland was heavily loaded against the peasantry, nor was it easy to answer his rhetorical question 'if agitating and petitioning a foreign parliament be useless, then what are you to do?'.[133] But apart from urging a rent and rates strike, Mitchel remained vague as to details of his alternative land plan – in March 1848 he published a series of letters from Conner denouncing Crawford as 'a most inveterate stickler for landlord domination', but failed to make any explicit reference to Lalor's more advanced agrarian ideas.[134] For his part, however, Lalor was furious with Mitchel for 'stealing his opinions and parading them as his own' and attacked in print his 'incredible policy of inciting a revolution without making any preparation for it'.[135] The outbreak of revolution in France on 22 February, quickly followed elsewhere in Europe in what at first appeared to be a bloodless 'springtime of the peoples', seemed to offer encouragement to Mitchel's revolutionary enthusiasms, and the state's resort to political coercion would in the end also push reluctant former colleagues such as Smith O'Brien and Gavan Duffy towards chancing a rising out of desperation.

For Crawford revolution was never a realistic option. From his perspective there was no evidence of either the capacity or spirit for revolutionary action in the Irish countryside, and given British resources and determination to hold Ireland by force, any attempt at such would end in a bloody catastrophe. Sporadic peasant resistance looking back to the traditional forms of secret societies, while understandable given the sheer scale of landlord provocation and injustice, also offered no real or lasting solution to the underlying problems. For all its frustrations and apparent fruitlessness, therefore, constitutional mobilisation and agitation appeared to him the only mode with any chance of success (however limited or distant) in improving the conditions of the people.

In February 1848 the government at last introduced its own tenant compensation measure, a limited measure that was to be largely prospective in nature. Responding to the chief secretary William Somerville, Crawford rejected the bill as not only inadequate, but likely inadvertently to overthrow the existing tenant-right custom of Ulster. With retrospective claims limited to tenants with rents over £10 and a low ceiling set for compensation payments, and all claims to expire within twenty-one years of the completion of the improvement, he argued the bill offered little more than Lincoln's 1846 bill, while giving landlords an excuse to abrogate the custom where it was observed. None of the security for investment and employment that Ireland urgently needed to give agricultural wages to the starving labourers, and thereby the entitlement to consume food, would be delivered.[136] The *Freeman's Journal* agreed – Somerville's bill would require cumbersome and expensive machinery beyond the reach of most tenants, and for a paltry amount that fell far short of the basic demands of the tenant movement.[137] The *Banner* urged the continuation of pressure from without to force the ministers to reconsider their grossly inadequate offer, while the bill was vigorously denounced by a wide range of clerical and lay Presbyterian voices.[138]

Agreeing that further agitation was the only adequate resort, Crawford issued a manifesto 'to the tenant farmers of Ireland, but more particularly of Ulster', urging them to reject the government bill. He offered a detailed critique of its machinery, pointing out the numerous legal opportunities whereby landlords could frustrate even the constrained compensation for improvements offered. Nothing could be salvaged from this 'mockery of concession'.[139] There was some response to his call in the countryside; at Banbridge a meeting of some 4,000 tenant farmers presided over by both Presbyterian and Catholic clergy was enlivened by repeated denunciations of the government bill as 'robbery! robbery!' and strong support was expressed for Crawford. One Presbyterian clergyman urged all Ireland to rally behind the banner 'of their patriotic and intelligent leader', and called on the 'spirited yeomanry of Ulster' to remember the 'ravaged fields and desolated farms of Skibbereen'. Somerville's bill had, he continued, been brought in at the behest of the guilty landlord class and deserved to be thrown out.

Crawford reintroduced his own previously announced tenant-right bill on 7 March, with the support of Poulett Scrope and in the anticipation of government hostility.[140] Moving the second reading, he appealed to British MPs' concerns about the costs of Irish governance and the positive effect his bill would have for taxpayers, whereas 'refusal to pass this bill on the part of that house would be construed into a declaration of war against the rights of the people of Ireland'.[141] However Hume disparaged any legislation that recognised Irish social difference and urged instead the doctrinaire free-trade alternative of an encumbered estates act. Somerville sought to tease open perceived inconsistencies in Crawford's position between compensation for occupancy and for improvements and disparaged the false hopes that tenant right could ever be 'arbitrarily' extended outside Ulster.[142] When the government succeeded in getting the debate adjourned, radicals and nationalists voiced outrage at its indifference to incidents of illegal clearances, including the case of a Galway village burned down by an evicting landlord which was denounced by Scrope and Crawford as an 'agrarian outrage', and the subsequent 'extermination' of large numbers of poor tenants on the Mahon estate in Roscommon through eviction and forced emigration.[143]

Writing to McKnight (in a letter read to a crowd of around 6,000 organised by the Lurgan Tenant Right Association), Crawford set out his analysis of the political situation, highlighting the problem of liberal adherence to laissez-faire:

> There is a most determined hostility with the imperial legislature to the recognition of the tenant-right of Ulster. There are three sections of enemies. First – the Irish landlord interest, which includes the government, who appear to me to be under the thraldom of that power. Second – the English landlord interest. Third – the free-trade economic section [...] I shall briefly tell you, that all the arguments of the free-trade section had one main feature, namely, that the consolidation principle ought to be sustained, as the only means of regenerating Ireland, that the small holder and working occupier should be dispossessed of land and thrown on wages, or else on the poor-rates – that the confirmation of institution of tenant-right would prove an obstacle to this result – and that no obstruction should be interposed to the landlord's right of dispossessment, with a view to carry out this principle. The English members who support this view have what I would call the absurd idea, that the extension of the Irish poor law had created a sufficient protection against the consequences of the extermination which this system would create.

Nevertheless, he would persevere with his bill and, with their support, seek to find a way forward. His insistence in this point sparked some tensions within the movement. McKnight suggested that the 'industrial occupancy clause' of the bill that some (including himself) had issues with, had not been of Crawford's own framing, but 'forced on him, in order to conciliate some support for his proposition'.[144] It's not clear if he had any authority from Crawford to state this, and the two men continued on good terms thereafter, but this point of friction would re-emerge in 1850–1.

Supporters continued to hope that British opinion could be brought round by economic reasoning: a *Banner of Ulster* correspondent eagerly cut open the pages of Mill's *Principles of Political Economy* in May 1848 to find in it strong support for the practical benefits of Ulster tenant-right but a reluctance to legislate to maintain and extend it, and a preference instead for the creation of peasant proprietorship through state-aided land purchase. This was disappointing, but at least it offered a 'respectable' critique of the existing system of landlordism and Mill was to become more supportive towards tenant right over time.[145] Although the Lurgan meeting showed little signs of disheartenment in the Ulster movement, it could no longer claim the support of all tenant farmers in the region: a rival movement had been started by Dr Henry Montgomery, which sought with the support of R. J. Tennent and the *Whig* to nudge the government through personal lobbying into making limited concessions on its own bill to suit Ulster farmers.[146]

Crawford's 1848 bill was in the end heavily defeated (by a margin of twenty-four to 147 votes) on 5 April, despite support voiced by John O'Connell, O'Connor, Scrope and (with reservations) Castlereagh. MPs for counties Armagh, Carlow, Cork and Tipperary also spoke in favour of his bill. Allying against it with the Whig home secretary, Sir George Grey, was Joseph Napier, MP for the University of Dublin and a figure emerging as the leading Irish Conservative spokesman on the land question. Napier admitted that the landlord-tenant relationship was moral as well as commercial in character, but rejected Crawford's bill as threatening spoliation on a principle that rested on shifting and varied definitions. He concluded that any ameliorative legislation (which must maintain established property rights) required first the suppression of subversive nationalist agitation to stand any chance of success.[147] Napier's opposition was backed up by an article in the *Dublin University Magazine* for that month by Rev. Samuel O'Sullivan, which rubbished McKnight's thesis that the Ulster custom originated in the Ulster plantation, locating it instead in the 'barbarous' Brehon laws of ancient Ireland. His article sought to connect the origins of the current land agitation to the discredited Conner, seeking thereby to undermine the 'credulous' and 'inconsistent' Crawford and McKnight.[148]

If this new parliamentary defeat led to predictable crowing in the *United Irishman*, which issued a renewed cry to resist rents and ejectments at the point of a pike, it posed serious problems for constitutionalists.[149] Writing to McKnight, Crawford lamented that the bill had been 'peremptorily rejected' by British MPs, and that only fourteen Irish MPs had voted for it to twenty-eight against (a larger number than the previous year). Ulster tenant right would now come under increased threat from predatory landlords, and would diminish in value due to falling confidence. The situation was now dire, and the Mitchelites were worsening it by goading the government into coercion:

> The violent, seditious, and indeed, I may say, treasonable, writings and speeches of individuals in Dublin, have created a pretext to the government for the proposition of a general law, imposing penalties to the extent of transportation for life, at the discretion of a judge, for words spoken, by which even the thoughts or intentions of the mind can be constructively applied to any of the several objects declared as criminal in the specifications of the bill, amongst which is included – the uttering of words which shall indicate 'a compassing, imagination, invention, device, or intention to overawe both houses or either house of parliament'. [...] it will be no

> easy task for any man, at any public meeting called for the redress of any grievance, to keep
> himself secure from the meshes of this act [...]

Still, the electoral process remained open, and Ulster tenants should continue to work to persuade their representatives of the case for tenant right or replace them if they refused.[150]

The Ulster tenant movement as a whole was clearly in no mood to surrender. Students at the Belfast Academical Institution protested noisily against the omission from the town's loyal address to the lord lieutenant of any supportive reference to Crawford's bill.[151] McKnight summoned another rally at Dungannon on 25 May, warning that the government and landlords were using Mitchel to undermine them. The choice of the venue was not accidental, as '[n]ever since the memorable Friday, the 15th of February, 1782, when the celebrated assemblage which decided the destiny of a kingdom, took place, has a meeting of equal importance been held in Dungannon'. There could, he insisted, be no compromise with the 'feudal gentry' short of full tenant right, and it was the entitlement of every free man under the British constitution to maintain his right to pursue it.[152] It was reported that 15,000 farmers attended, surrounded by a circle of 'a great number of ladies from the adjacent country'. Letters of support were read from the Presbyterian moderator of the synod of Ballymoney and Coleraine, from the Catholic Archbishop of Armagh and Bishop of Clogher, from Bishop Maginn of Derry, and from Crawford, who was attending Westminster to vote for Hume's motion for household suffrage and triennial parliaments.

Echoing McKnight's historical reference, Crawford expressed pride in his father's achievements, and pain that the reform movement he had led had been undermined by religious dissensions promoted by the establishment. The same must not be allowed to happen again, as '*United we stand – divided we fall!*' The Dungannon resolutions of 1783, insisting that freedom consisted in being governed only by laws to which the people had assented, through their freely chosen and responsible representatives, remained as relevant now as then. His letter was ecstatically received by the crowd.[153] As on previous occasions, the press drew particular attention to the extraordinary degree of religious harmony at the meeting, with the 'flags of Orange and Green planted side by side', although Orange support for the movement was loudly denied by others.[154] In its aftermath, the *Banner* was confident that the movement would triumph as English tenants were beginning to demand their own rights in emulation of Ulster, and Crawford drew the attention of parliament to the size and demands of the Ulster meetings in the hope this would get the attention of the British press.[155] For his part, McKnight sought to exploit class divisions within the Orange Order to win over tenant-farmer members to the cause, with some temporary success at Garvagh in Co. Londonderry on 12 July, but less so elsewhere.[156]

This optimism of Spring 1848 proved premature, as two interrelated phenomena combined to smother this first phase of tenant-right agitation. As Mitchel and his associates moved into openly calling for a revolution against British rule in the context of European upheavals and renewed Chartist unrest in Great Britain, the government responded with a series of security measures. The Crown and Government Security Bill, introduced in April, provoked Smith O'Brien in his last appearance in parliament to denounce British treatment of Ireland as on a par with the tyrannical oppression of Sicily and Poland by reactionary powers, and to defend the Irish Confederation's efforts to attain Irish freedom. Its aims in sending a delegation to Paris and promoting the arming of the people (on the model of the 1782 Volunteers) were, he argued, not revolutionary but defensive, and its objective remained the legislative independence of Ireland attained by Irishmen, 'if possible, without civil war'. If the government provoked violent resistance by imposing coercion, he warned, it would find its security forces and apparent alliance with the Orangemen unfit for purpose. While he denied the charges of treason levelled against him, O'Brien's uncompromising defiance was unlikely to win over many supporters.

Not all would-be revolutionaries followed Lalor and Mitchel in deprecating Crawford, despite his evident antipathy to violent action. A political fantasy published in the *Boston Pilot* in April imagined the 'second week of the Irish revolution' following the flight of the British authorities, with patriotic gentlemen playing their part and Crawford presiding over a land tenure commission.[157] Crawford had no time for such day-dreaming or for O'Brien's grandstanding. Rather, he was more concerned with the collateral damage the political crackdown would cause the tenant-right movement, with coercive legislation threatening transportation for any act of agitation. He was in the minority of thirty-seven that voted against the security bill, comprised of repealers and a smattering of British radicals that included Cobden and Bright, although not Scrope.[158]

With Mitchel tried by a packed court and transported in May under the rapidly passed Treason-Felony Act, and the editors of the *Nation, Irish Felon* and *Irish Tribune* arrested in June, the government took further decisive action against the Confederation in July, moving the suspension of habeus corpus in Ireland until March 1849 to facilitate the internment of its leaders. Crawford was again one of a handful of MPs to speak and vote against this. While he had no sympathy for the aims of conspirators, he stated that attention should be directed at the root causes of disaffection, which coercion would not touch. Starvation still ravaged parts of the country, and economic depression was universal; remedial measures alone, he insisted, could address the crisis. Internment of suspects had been tried before and had failed to quiet Ireland for long.[159] Consistently, he again spoke and voted against the extension of the suspension for a further six months when this came up in February 1849.[160]

As he had predicted, the rapid passage of the suspension bill spurred even the more reluctant members of the Confederation into attempting open rebellion out of face-saving desperation and a sense of personal honour. On 24–25 July the would-be rebels sought to raise members of Confederate Clubs and sympathetic peasants into armed action in Counties Kilkenny and Tipperary, only to face strong and effective opposition from the great majority of the Catholic clergy in the countryside. Despite occasional flashes of local enthusiasm, support rapidly drained away under the combined influences of clerical disapproval, the failure of the rebels to supply provisions or arms, and O'Brien's insistence that private property remain unmolested. The shambolic affair ended after a brief firefight with a police detachment at the Widow McCormack's farmhouse near Ballingarry and the subsequent arrest of O'Brien and most of his remaining followers by police reinforcements.[161]

Against this background of open insurgency, Crawford's stand against the suspension of habeus corpus, followed by his denunciation of Russell for failing to introduce urgently needed remedial measures, drew much opprobrium. To the *Times* he had given 'rebels and enemies a weak pretense for asserting that when rebellion broke out one more solemn appeal was made, but in vain, to the justice of the legislature'. The rebels themselves had no interest in his 'remedial measures', it asserted, while their promotion merely distracted the Irish from the moral imperative of self-help.[162] The *Londonderry Sentinel* declaimed that there was 'not a more contemptible, or as it would seem, viciously disposed member of the lower house than Mr Sharman Crawford. The most eccentric and extravagant crotchet will find him among its prosy and bewildered advocates, the most seditious factionists need not despair of his assistance'.[163] Alarmed that more conservative Protestant farmers might be scared off by Crawford's stance, the Ulster Tenant Right Association under McKnight moved to distance themselves from his rejection of coercion by suggesting that his position was mainly due to the demands of his Rochdale constituents.[164] There was a significant risk of acquiring guilt by association with the rebels, but Crawford did have some support for his stance from within the northern Presbyterians: the Comber minister Rev. John Rogers spoke out against a loyal address pressed by Henry Cooke on the Belfast Presbytery, warning against giving voluntary aid to a deceitful government and insisting on the addition of a pro-tenant right amendment.[165]

Long familiar with press criticism, Crawford ignored attacks made on him and maintained his consistency. He had for many years been personally friendly with O'Brien, and deeply regretted his resort, however reluctant it might be, to armed rebellion. It is no surprise then, that Crawford agreed to chair a public meeting in Dublin that October which resolved to petition the lord lieutenant for clemency for O'Brien, whose conviction for treason-felony carried a formal sentence of death even though the jury had recommended mercy. He then headed a deputation to the viceroy to request a stay of execution until the petition had been signed.[166] Having done this, he left the management of the campaign in the hands of the lord mayor, but continued to channel appeals for clemency to Dublin Castle after his return to Crawfordsburn.[167] He also supported protests against the packing of juries (excluding Catholics) at the state trials.[168]

O'Brien was grateful for these interventions, which led to the commutation of his sentence to transportation to Van Diemen's Land, and wrote to Crawford both to thank him and to justify his actions. He had, he observed, always sought to act honourably in what he believed the country's best interests, and was reconciled to his fate, as 'imprisonment is preferable to the freedom of a country gentleman resident in the south and west of Ireland surrounded by wretchedness which he had no power to alleviate'. He concluded with a personal tribute to Crawford, praising his recent Rochdale speech for its 'lucid and able exposition of the systematic defects observable in English government and legislation for this country'.[169] Crawford responded by reaffirming their friendship and assuring him that he believed him to have acted from patriotic motives, even if he thought his practice misguided.[170]

He subsequently spoke against the government's bill to retrospectively legalise the transportation of the state prisoners, and continued to demand humane treatment for O'Brien and the others following their removal to Van Diemen's Land.[171] His sympathy for the Confederates as idealistic political prisoners, even while he repudiated their revolutionary methods, would later pay political dividends, especially following the release of Duffy in 1849 and his re-establishment of *The Nation* later that year.[172]

In the short term, however, the polarisation over the abortive rebellion and government resort to political coercion was highly damaging to the tenant-right movement. In the southern provinces, large-scale political organisation became virtually impossible in the months following Ballingarry. In the north, the reappearance of rebellion (however abortive it turned out to be and however strongly opposed by the Catholic clergy) reinvigorated Protestant fears about political Catholicism and Ribbonism that had mellowed somewhat in the wake of Daniel O'Connell's death. The public affirmations of loyal support offered to the government by the reconstituted Orange Order, and the administration's surreptitious encouragement of this, gave a boost to an organisation that had been in the doldrums, and marginalised those within the Order who had been taking an interest in tenant-right agitation.[173] McKnight appears to have harboured hopes that the spirit of the 'Garvagh Resolutions' of July 1848 might be recovered, but with the movement as a whole falling again under the leadership of conservative landowners such as the Earl of Enniskillen, Crawford was more pessimistic:

> The old 'No Popery' cry seems to have been successfully raised by those who desire to uphold their own interests by sacrificing the interests of the people and the welfare of state [...] the Orangemen are now stimulated and caressed by those who had before deserted them. Every topic to excite man against man is now again being raised, even by those who ought to be the ministers of 'peace and good-will towards men'; and thus Orangemen are deluded into the suicidal course of becoming the forgers of their own chains.[174]

At the same time, his own long-standing animosity towards the Order had not been forgotten by its devotees; one Orange organ alleged that '[h]e probably remembers that Orangemen more than once marred the projects of his party and friends – particularly in 1798.'[175]

An upsurge of assertive sectarian incidents and demonstrations peaked with the bloody encounter between Orangemen and Ribbonmen at Dolly's Brae in south Down on 12 July 1849. This was sparked by local Orange insistence on asserting their 'loyalty' by parading from their rally at Lord Roden's Tollymore Park estate through what was recognised as a 'Catholic' district on their return to Rathfriland. What began as a fire-fight between two antagonistic armed factions (with a detachment of constabulary also acting in defence of what was a legal if highly provocative Orange parade), descended into a what appeared to be a sectarian pogrom that left, in an account published by the pro-Orange *Newry Telegraph*, at least thirty dead (all Catholics) and many wounded. The deaths in particular of several women and children, and the burning of Catholic properties and a chapel, provoked outrage against the parade organisers and pro-Orange magistrates and alarm in government circles.[176] Nor was this the only bloody confrontation that year. William's son James had been present as a magistrate on 17 March at an armed clash between Ribbonmen, Orangemen and the police at Crossgar, that had left three dead, and there were several sectarian assassinations in the area.[177] The government reacted to Dolly's Brae by dismissing the Orange leaders Roden and William and Francis Beers from the magistracy, and passing the Party Processions Act in 1850 to ban contentious parades, both of which Crawford strongly supported. He concluded that Orangeism 'must be utterly destructive to the good order of society in a mixed community of Protestants and Catholics'.[178] However, massive damage had been done to communal relations in Ulster by the religious polarisation of 1848–9.

Considering this sequence of events in retrospect, the *Banner of Ulster* was convinced that the government had exploited the overblown threat of the Irish Confederation to quash the more dangerous social movement for tenant right:

> The tenant right association was proceeding vigorously, and was fast swamping the repeal movement by absorbing it into the incomparably more rational, as well as more practical adjustment of the land-tenure question. [...] the government had no idea of carrying an effective measure of tenant right, unless its members could not possibly avoid it, and this NECESSITY would *infallibly have arisen*, if the government had not been able to divert the attention of the Orange body from the tenant right agitation to the temporary danger, which its own organs laboured so earnestly to exaggerate. [...] It was quite as much with a view to getting the Ulster 'tenant right' taken down from the Orange banners, as for any object belonging to mere loyalty, that so many country and other gentry last year enrolled themselves in the ranks of the Orange association. The latter have, beyond all doubt, been deceived and openly humbugged [...]

While this sweeping conspiracy theory owed much to radical rhetoric, it did reflect the reality of divided allegiances on the part of many rural lower-class Orangemen, and the paper left open the possibility that they could be recovered for the tenant struggle.[179] In reality, however, the perceived threat of a revived revolutionary nationalism on the model of 1798 had rallied Orangemen under their traditional landed leadership and expanded the movement's appeal among Irish Protestants, developments that were only partly offset by the fall-out over Dolly's Brae.[180]

In the meantime the Ulster Tenant Right Association appeared to have gone into suspension. McKnight later recorded his belief that there had been a state campaign to entrap its leaders by use of agents provocateurs.[181] Whether true or not, in the absence of legitimate forms of social protest, agrarian violence filled the void in the winter of 1848–9. South Antrim and adjacent parts of Down saw the outbreak of a series of incendiary attacks on the property of landlords and large farmers, which were blamed by the Conservative press on Crawford's campaign, but were due more to evictions and notices to quit served on the tenants of the extensive and highly-rented Hertford estates.[182] Agrarian unrest also flared among the Catholic small tenants of south Down, south Armagh and north Louth at the same time, with local Ribbonism appearing to offer some rudimentary organisation.[183] The continuation of such unrest into 1850 was lamented by one northern paper as marking the inroads of 'Tipperaryism' in Ulster, stirred by the 'communist' rhetoric of some clergy, although it urged the adoption of Crawford's legislative proposals as the only means of calming the situation.[184] The coercive legislation of 1847–9 had clearly not pacified Ireland, and it was at this stage unclear if a mass tenant-right movement would re-emerge to offer an alternative to localised violence and sectarian polarisation.

Forming the 'League of North and South', 1849–50

With tenant agitation temporarily repressed in the early months of 1849, Crawford focused on pressing for amendment of the Irish poor law and arguing for a more constructive response to the continuing crises of hunger and clearances in parliament and the press. Despite the adverse circumstances, he did not completely abandon his campaign for land reform, and on 22 February introduced a motion for the removal of legal obstacles to land improvement and employment. In this he rehearsed arguments that would reappear later that year in print in *Depopulation Not Necessary,* outlining a series of measures he believed essential including tenant-right legislation.[185] Supporters and opponents alike complemented him on his perseverance, but the motion was dropped after the chief secretary committed to bringing in several ameliorative bills that session.

Given the difficulties now surrounding outdoor meetings, Crawford seized on another issue as a platform for public protest at government policy. Facing strong resistance from British middle-class public opinion to any further relief expenditure for Ireland, the government had resorted to making a limited additional relief loan to the 'distressed' western poor law unions dependent on the imposition of a rate-in-aid for its repayment. Crawford attacked this in the commons as an infringement on the 1800 union, which rested on 'the principle of united responsibility'.[186] Any additional famine relief costs must in justice, he asserted, fall on the imperial exchequer and not on parts of Ireland.[187] Although he had no truck with that brand of Ulster particularism that rejected sympathy with the still famine-stricken west and its 'improvident' people, he saw the rate-in-aid issue as an opportunity to publicly criticise the Whig government, not least as public meetings in Ulster on this subject had magisterial support and hence legal cover. In March he appeared at a 'ratepayer's meeting' in Down, at which his son John acted as secretary, where he urged the people of Ireland to insist on their rights and reject unjust impositions.[188] His arguments were echoed by many in the Presbyterian clergy and tenantry, with one speaker at a meeting on Downshire's estates warning that 'the spirit that animated the Volunteers of Dungannon – still lives'.[189]

Crawford did not oppose the government's principal 'remedial' measure for 1849, the encumbered estates bill, which was intended to stimulate agricultural production by attracting entrepreneurial capitalists to purchase land from indebted Irish proprietors, but in the absence of tenant security he thought it of limited utility and subsequently criticised it for promoting evictions.[190] Later commentators were to blame the 1849 act for introducing new landowners with no knowledge of or with outright hostility towards customary tenant right, and who were ruthless in removing the 'surplus population' from their new properties.[191]

Crawford's attacks on the rate-in-aid in the commons drew the attention of the *Illustrated London News*, which devoted a pictorial 'parliamentary portrait' to him on 5 May 1849 (Figure 24). There were, it observed, 'few more frequent speakers in the house than the hon. Member for Rochdale on all questions involving considerations of civil and religious liberty, and of reform, political, financial or municipal'. His speech against the third reading of the rate-in-aid bill was, the paper went on, characteristic of him, in drawing attention in graphic terms to the continued suffering of the Mayo peasantry and upbraiding the English liberals for shirking the responsibilities of the state and failing to act to curb ejectments. However, while the paper acknowledged the moral force of his words, it also noted the stylistic flaws that limited his parliamentary success:

> Mr Sharman Crawford can scarcely be called an effective speaker, notwithstanding that his speeches are usually marked by appropriate diction and much sound common-sense. His voice is weak, making him difficult to be heard, and his efforts to overcome that defect, impart to it a strained tone, which falls painfully upon the ear; while his manner, though not lacking earnestness, is tame, and devoid of animation.[192]

This lack of oratorical skill no doubt fuelled the personal criticism of British and Irish opponents of tenant right who were quick to brand him a 'crotchet' and dismiss his projects as impracticable.

The 1849 session was particularly barren territory for land reform measures and, despite working on a draft bill to create 'asylum settlements' for evicted tenants on reclaimed lands, Crawford made no further attempt at legislation that year, concentrating instead on his writing.[193] He was ill when John O'Connell proposed his own tenant-right bill in June, and wrote to apologise for not being present to support it, even if he despaired of its success. In the end, the debate on O'Connell's bill was 'counted out', with only thirty-four MPs present in the chamber at 4 am. This was the third time that session the bill was set back by procedural delays, a too frequent fate for back-bench measures opposed by the party managers. O'Connell assured him that he would have deferred to Crawford had he intended to proceed with his own bill, but feared the predominance of landlord prejudices in the house presaged further frustration.[194] Clearly there was no chance of any progress so long as outdoor agitation on tenant-right remained inert.

As the measures of coercion began to lapse from mid-1849 the tenant movement started to re-emerge, initially in the north. The socio-economic conditions that had spurred its initial formation had, according to one correspondent of the *Londonderry Standard*, not improved. Despite a good grain harvest that year, the potato crop was again blighted and prices depressed, while farmers remained heavily burdened and vulnerable:

> Our fields are blasted again, and famine will follow in the black track, if means are not adopted to counteract the effects of this renewed devastation. The harvest the sickle is now reaping is rich and full; but what avails it? – it is forfeited before it is gathered. The rent, unabated in many cases, the whole three years of famine, must be paid. Taxes, rates, tithes, forsooth, and all such just and necessary demands must be discharged; and then where will the farmer and his family find sustenance? […] I solemnly believe that ruin is hovering over every grade of our social system if some change for good is not speedily effected.

Where, he asked, was the Ulster Tenant Defence Association at this time when it was so sorely needed?[195]

Responding to such concerns, the Coleraine Tenant Right Association reformed and held a 'densely packed' public meeting in late July, chaired by the borough's Peelite MP, John Boyd. It is frequently stated that the first Tenant-League associated body to emerge in 1849 was at Callan in Co. Kilkenny, but the Coleraine association appears to have preceded it by several months.[196] Speaking at its first meeting, Samuel Greer stressed that only the passage of genuine tenant-right legislation could prevent a repeat of the calamities of famine, and welcomed the apparent conversion of the Society for the Amendment of the Law in England to the necessity of protection of tenant property. McKnight added that he was confident that these principles were now gaining ground with English and Scottish farmers, and that he hoped the 'last remnants of the feudal code' would soon be swept away throughout the country.[197]

Greer followed up the meeting with a series of letters published in the provincial press, elaborating on the resolutions of the Coleraine association, urging its emulation in both Ireland and Britain, and singling out Crawford's approach to land reform as the soundest one.[198] O'Connell praised the series to the Repeal Association, although the *Banner* criticised

Greer's proposed scheme as inadequate in failing to prioritise a judicial system for reducing rents. This suggests a degree of personal rivalry between Greer and McKnight, who by 1849 was editing the Belfast-based Presbyterian paper, although they agreed on other points such as the necessity of sweeping away the 'gothic' laws of primogeniture and entail and the maintenance of free trade.[199] This preoccupation reflected the reality that the collapse of the value of tenant right during the deepening agricultural depression seriously reduced its effectiveness as a form of tenant security.[200] In a later letter Greer insisted that rents must indeed be cut and urged his readers to consult *Depopulation Not Necessary* for evidence of sheer scale and ruthlessness of landed clearances and the remedy for them.[201]

By the end of the year, the *Banner* was observing 'symptoms of reanimation' of the tenant-right movement across Ulster and called for it to counter the renewed protectionist agitation being got up by the landed class. In an environment of continuously falling agricultural prices, it argued that 'the only protection really wanted is a *reduction of rents* sufficiently sweeping to enable the tenant farmers to live and to have some profitable return for their own industrial labour'. Public meetings followed at Coleraine, where 'actuated by a hearty, vigorous orthodoxy [...] they have kept alive the tenant right movement', and in Down, although Crawford was prevented from speaking by recurring bouts of ill health.[202] A 'monster meeting' at Shanerod near Dromara in the latter county on 20 December heard letters read from Crawford and McKnight and speeches from a number of Presbyterian clergy, including Rev. John Rutherford, who described the tenant movement as a continuation of the anti-slavery campaign, now directed against the 'white tenant slavery of the north of Ireland'.[203] Opposition to American slavery would remain a frequent point of reference at tenant-right meetings in Ulster, usually linked by analogy with local agrarian grievances, and Crawford was likened to William Wilberforce.[204]

Attempts by the Conservative press to smear the Presbyterian clergy with the charge of 'Mitchelism' were robustly refuted in the *Banner,* which pointed to the social conditions driving the revived agitation, which were far worse than those of Mitchel's transportation.[205] 400 or 500 Presbyterian clergy were, the paper claimed, active in support of the movement and prepared to face the consequences if necessary. For many of the clergy, the campaign against the landed establishment was a natural corollary to their parallel antagonism towards the privileges and arrogance of the established church.[206]

In the south the movement was also reviving, albeit no longer with the leadership of John O'Connell, who, facing family bankruptcy, stood down as leader of the Repeal Association at the start of January 1850.[207] In the re-established *Nation,* Duffy published articles promoting a new constitutional agitation, focused on tenant right and embracing northern Protestants; in October a correspondent enthusiastically recalled 'Sharman Crawford's letter to the provincial tenant right meeting, held in Dungannon, in the summer of last year, or the manner of its reception by twenty thousand choice men of the province. In a word our association should be "racy of the soil".'[208] As in the north, clerical involvement was crucial in the development of successful local bodies, including at Callan, where a tenant protection society was formed in mid-October 1849 demanding fair rents, the recognition of tenant right, and industrial employment of the labourers.[209] The local priests Fr Thomas O'Shea and Fr Matthew O'Keefe were central to its leadership.[210] Efforts were made to ensure that the new organisation kept within the law as well as appearing 'respectable', and it became the model for others rapidly established across Leinster and Munster, although it sought a broad base of support.[211] In December O'Keefe shared a platform with Charles Kickham (who has supported the Confederates the previous year and would later play a leading role in Fenianism) at a well-attended meeting near Mullinahone, Co. Tipperary, where a new society had already been formed.[212] At Ballingarry the following February, O'Keefe urged tenants to 'repent' from offering rack-rents and urged an alliance with the British free-traders against the clearing landowners.[213]

Crawford's health had recovered sufficiently for him to attend a Down county meeting called to discuss resolutions for the restoration of protection on 9 January 1850 at Downpatrick, and to take on the landed establishment led in person by Downshire and the county MPs. In the view of the *Freeman*, his challenge produced a decisive defeat for both the economic and political reactionaries:

> The Orange leaders were there to marry Orangeism and protection, but the people were on their guard. They raised their own standard – a green placard – on which were inscribed 'moderate rents, a cheap loaf, tenant right, and no surrender.' The people, as was fit, triumphed under this standard, and the Orange faction was defeated.

Crawford's speech at the meeting was seen as central to this outcome and was loudly applauded by the farmers present: the tenants wanted, he argued, no protection but that from inordinate rents, and the protection of the tenant's property created by his own labour and money, while the labourers needed cheap food for their families. Manufacturing industry, now returning to dynamic growth in Ulster, would bring prosperity to all classes if not curbed by tariffs and if accompanied by land reform.[214] The *Whig* agreed that Crawford's triumph in carrying a pro-free trade and tenant-right amendment had at least temporarily realigned county politics along economic rather than sectarian lines at the expense of the gentry, as 'Dolly's Brae was forgotten; and the usually opposing parties were seen fraternising together, to teach poor Lord Downshire his insignificance'.[215] This public connection of tenant right to free trade offered the potential of winning over British free-trade radicals, and Crawford sent letters and pamphlets to their leaders; Bright was sympathetic, but Hume continued to regard civic equality between Catholics and Protestants as the key Irish issue, while conceding that 'Ireland must continue to suffer until the population is raised to that condition of "independent farmer", only then can there be an improvement'.[216]

Large meetings in support of tenant right and rent reductions followed at Saintfield, Newtownards and Banbridge on 15, 19 and 28 January, at which McKnight and the Presbyterian clergy took leading roles, with some escalating their rhetorical attacks on 'feudal' landlordism to an extent that concerned moderates. The *Coleraine Chronicle* expressed concern that 'communist speeches' by clergymen were leading to 'Tipperaryism in the north' but was sure that only the passage of Crawford's bill could pacify Ulster. Other meetings were held at Cork and Kilkenny in the same month.[217] While local enthusiasm for tenant right was similar to the first phase in 1847–8, central co-ordination still remained lacking. The political way forward remained unclear, and the popular press was pessimistic about parliamentary prospects of success, despite the debt British liberals owed Ireland for its resounding rejection of agricultural protection.[218]

Crawford turned again to the modality of the public letter to assert his intention to persist with legislation to legalise tenant right for 'industrial tenancies'. He recognised that agricultural depression had now made the issue of 'fair rent' central:

> The value and consequent existence of tenant-right depends on the *amount* of the rent. If rent be more than its just proportion of the produce, the tenant-right is proportionately reduced in value, and may become without any value and unsaleable. [...] This fall in prices, and the embarrassments created by the failure of the potato crop, has put the tenant in this position; and in all cases in which the rent has been adjusted at the high rates of protection prices, the tenant-right has been virtually extinguished – it is unsaleable; and thus the improving tenant has lost the whole of the security which he thought he possessed for the value of his industry.

Under these conditions, it would be pointless to pursue tenant right without some mode of judicial determination of rents linked to changing prices, an intervention which he argued there were precedents for, including that voluntarily applied on his own lands.[219]

Another bout of ill-health resulted in a delay to his arrival at Westminster until late March 1850.[220] In the meantime he was well enough to attend a tenant-right rally at Donaghadee in north Down on 20 February and address the crowd of around 1,200, assuring them that he would channel their opinions and demands to the legislature. Such public meetings were the 'safety-valves of grievances', giving the people a real alternative to self defeating agrarian crime, outbreaks of which had again racked the county that winter.[221] But they should also demonstrate to Englishmen the determination of the people to assert their just rights through 'an honest, open and decided declaration of opinion'. He proposed a deputation of tenants travel to London, where he would assist them to lobby British MPs directly, a point endorsed enthusiastically by McKnight.[222] Writing to another tenant meeting at Killinchy a few days later, he assured them he would be in his place in parliament to address the planned reintroduction of Somerville's tenant compensation bill by the government. This meeting also heard Rev. John Rogers denounce Londonderry, his agent Andrews and son Castlereagh for their rental policies and their criticisms of and threats towards the Presbyterian clergy for daring to oppose it.[223]

The proposal of a tenant deputation to London was rapidly taken up by the northern associations, with members selected by early April, including McKnight, Rogers and Bell. Samuel Ruddell of the Lurgan Tenant Right Association wrote to the southern bodies (in a letter strongly endorsed by the *Freeman's Journal*) urging them to send their own delegates to work together as a team and noted that Crawford, R. J. Tennent, and Torrens McCullagh had undertaken to make the introductions to leading figures in all parties, protectionists as well as the reformers.[224] This call for southern representation initially went unanswered except for Wilson Gray of Claremorris, Co. Mayo, who was later joined by J. F. Maguire, but the delegates soon met with reliable radical supporters such as Poulett Scrope and Bright as well as the Cork city MP William Fagan, who agreed to support the reintroduction of Crawford's bill. However, the lobby correspondent of the *Freeman* was sceptical that parliament would accept any measure including a clause to regulate rent, and thought it plausible that a heavily amended version of Somerville's bill might satisfy them, if it removed the proposed machinery and time limits for compensation and protected existing tenant-right interests. Even if unsuccessful, a full debate on the government bill might allow for the public discussion of tenant-right principles.[225] The *Freeman* concluded that a 'league between north and south' was now imminent.[226]

The decision by the Ulster tenant deputation and their parliamentary supporters to reject Somerville's bill *in toto* was met with some relief in the south, even if it meant no progress was likely that season. Hope was placed instead in the passage of the government's Irish county franchise bill, which was intended to increase the number of tenant voters, the continuing consciousness-raising work of the delegation in London, and the promotion of Crawford's bill, now presented in a 'completely remodelled and corrected' form due to his 'untiring energy'.[227] Private meetings with leading British political figures followed, including with the former premier Peel, who was politely attentive if non-committal, and Russell, who was 'frank and cordial', but warned that 'transferring the tenants into the position of proprietors, and making over to them the proprietory rights that now belonged to the landlords, was a proposition that the house of commons would scarcely entertain'.[228] After meeting Sir James Graham the deputation concluded that they were starting to make some progress in addressing the 'English' views of leading politicians and obliging them to take the Irish tenant-right issue seriously.[229] Positive coverage of their work in the London *Weekly Chronicle* was cited as a major step forward in winning hearts and minds.[230]

Writing to Duffy on his return from London, McKnight assured him that real progress had been made. Although Crawford's reworked bill was a compromise measure, he was sure it would attain their shared objectives in time:

> My own object is to have *the soil of Ireland for the Irish* – to *assure* to every man by law the fruits of his own industry, and consequently to make his *parliamentary* and *other franchises his own in fact as well as in theory*. I would not give one *traneen* for any tenant-right legalization which will not result in an independent franchise *ex vi termini*, and as for success, I simply ask myself two questions – first, is the demand *right* in itself, is it founded on *moral justice*? Secondly, is it calculated to *benefit* society as an element of sound polity, and is public opinion likely to sustain it against opposition? The second of these questions, together with its answer, is almost *necessarily* involved in the first, and, having satisfied myself on these points, I seriously commit all the rest to divine providence, because I feel assured that *as certainly as a divine power exists, so certainly will a day of deliverance come to the oppressed*[.]

McKnight was of the opinion that British political reformers and free-traders would rally to them out of self-interest so long as Irish opinion was unified and assertive on the issue. While he welcomed the adherence of the ex-O'Connellite 'Old Ireland' forces, it was in '"Young Ireland" chiefly that the men of the north, and myself especially, will repose any very large amount of implicit faith', and he proposed that he and Duffy jointly prepare the ground for a national conference in Dublin.[231]

Reviewing the situation in early May, a committee of pro-tenant right MPs at Westminster, chaired by Crawford, agreed to take advantage of the upcoming debate on Somerville's bill to push amendments such as 'might reasonably be expected to satisfy the country both north and south'. These included provision for retrospective improvements and the recognition of tenant right linked to these and of the full custom where it existed.[232] In the end, however, they were not given the chance. Later that month Russell declared that the bill would be postponed until the government had time to consider the written objections submitted to him by the tenant deputation. If this was prolonged unreasonably, the *Banner* observed, Crawford's bill – which was itself a moderate compromise that landlords would be foolish to dismiss – should be tabled to provoke the necessary debate. This was consequently introduced in June, although it never got to the stage of a second-reading debate.[233]

Rather than proceed with his own compensation bill, Somerville opted, to the fury of the tenant-righters, to give the government's endorsement to a bill 'for improving the relations of landlords and tenants' drawn up by Lords Westmeath and Lucan to criminalise the cutting of crops by tenants in the evenings. Lucan was already notorious for his ruthless clearances in Mayo, and even English reformist opinion saw his measure as adding insult to injury.[234] When it was claimed that the bill was intended simply to prevent fraud by tenants against their landlords, Crawford responded that 'it left the frauds practised by landlords unrestrained'.[235] This bill was withdrawn, but the session ended with a statement from Russell again deprecating any measure based on 'extreme views' that would transfer property from landlord to tenant.[236]

In late April 1850 the *Freeman* announced plans for a national tenant-right conference in Dublin, with invitations issued to 'the trusted men of the provinces who have up to this been conducting the agitation in their respective localities', with the aim of getting agreement on a common platform and tactics and establishing a co-ordinating body. If religious and regional differences could be overcome and agreement hammered out on a measure, it believed an all-Ireland movement could not be stopped.[237]

A provisional committee was established with three secretaries – John Gray of the *Freeman*, Sam Greer, and Frederick Lucas, a strong-minded and abrasive Catholic convert from Quakerism who had moved his clericalist journal *The Tablet* to Dublin in late 1849 – and took on itself the tasks of preparing rules and a programme for discussion for the proposed 'Tenant League'. Invitations were circulated via the *Freeman* and the *Nation*, and elicited widespread support from the provincial nationalist press and parochial Catholic clergy. Both the *Banner* and the *Londonderry Standard* indicated their support and urged northern societies to participate, although Ulster also asserted its distinctiveness by holding a provincial representative meeting in Belfast on 12 June, albeit one explicitly preparatory for the national conference.[238] Crawford wrote to Gray that he would attend the Dublin meeting if he could disengage from parliamentary business but that they should not postpone on his account, and that he would hold off proceeding with his own bill until the conference had the opportunity to discuss it.[239]

The conference was put back to 6 August, although Crawford was still unable to attend due to the pressing business of opposing the renewal of the 1847 coercive legislation in the commons.[240] This also allowed time for further mass meetings in Ireland to build up a head of steam, including at Enniscorthy in Wexford, Dundalk in Louth and Kilmood in Down.[241] The *Freeman* reported the alarm provoked in both Whig and Conservative papers in Ireland by the intensity of the campaign, and predicted that the landed interest would now be obliged to make concessions.[242] In May the Presbyterian Synod of Belfast flouted Cooke's denunciation of the 'perfect communist interpretations' of some ministers and voted in favour of supporting the political campaign.[243] This was followed in early July by the church's General Assembly agreeing by a 'sweeping majority' to a petition in favour of legalising the Ulster custom, consolidating the already extensive clerical sympathy for the movement.[244] The *Banner* lauded this as a historic moment, when the 'whole Presbyterian population of Ulster' now demonstrated its 'complete identification' with the movement.[245]

This may have been an overstatement (the wavering stance of the *Whig* indicated hesitancy at best on the part of many urban middle-class Presbyterians) but it seems clear that the great majority in the church was supportive. Speaking for the most 'advanced' section of the clergy, Rogers wrote enthusiastically to Duffy that:

> I am delighted at the prospect of a union of the friends of Ireland. Providence has at length pointed us to our great national object which is destined I doubt not to be the rallying ground of Roman Catholic and Presbyterian – and where the hereditary foe of both will be defeated once and for ever.[246]

The northerners were well represented when the tenant conference met in Dublin on 6-8 August, with ten ministers, four priests and fourteen laymen present from the province.[247] In Crawford's absence, McKnight was voted to the chair. Rev. William Dobbin of Annaclone and William Girdwood of the Lurgan Tenants Association were made joint secretaries along with Fr O'Shea of Callan. Proceedings opened with a flourish of an ecumenical symbolism rarely witnessed since the 1790s, as Rev. John Rentoul of Ballymoney observed that he, as a Presbyterian minister, had come 'from the far north to shake hands with the Roman Catholic priests from the south and west as my brothers, and to unite our hearty energies in our country's cause against oppression and wrong, having for our motto, "union nor division," for our common rights and liberties, and the future prosperity of Ireland'. Fr James Redmond of Arklow responded that he had been deeply moved by the words of the Presbyterian clergy and greeted the first he met that day as a brother in the common cause; no political and religious disunity must be allowed to intrude.

The remarkable degree of religious unity between Presbyterians and Catholics evident in summer 1850, would come under some strain as the 'papal aggression' crisis, and Catholic defensiveness in reaction to it, came to the political forefront over the following months. Radical Presbyterians, such as McKnight and the clergymen Rogers and John Coulter, had to work hard to minimise the threat of resurgent anti-Catholicism in Ulster to the League project.[248]

Although there were some disputes over precise wording, the conference quickly agreed its three principal resolutions which would form its national programme: that a fair valuation to determine rent was indispensable, that the tenant should have fixity of tenure so long as he paid the fair rent thus determined, that the tenant should be free to sell his interest in his holding for the current market value, and that 'where the rent has been fixed by valuation, no rent beyond the valued rent shall be recoverable by any process of law'. The new Tenant League would also take into consideration the condition of agricultural labourers and propose measures for their protection and advancement. A subsidiary resolution moved by Lucas seeking to determine the equitable amount of rent as the residue after the farmer's time, skill, industry, risk and capital was computed stirred more controversy as appearing to dictate too much to the valuators, but was approved in a watered-down form suggested by McKnight.[249] These resolutions went some way beyond the terms of Crawford's bill, but reflected a consensus of the movement north and south. To landed and Conservative critics this amounted to 'communism' and the confiscation of private wealth, but to supporters it was simply what was just and necessary for Ireland's regeneration.[250]

In the wake of the conference the new Tenant League established a leadership council, which took rooms in Beresford Place in Dublin and met weekly to co-ordinate the movement. Its members included Lucas and Duffy as well as the northern editors McKnight and James Godkin of the *Londonderry Standard*, but not Crawford himself. It immediately issued circulars calling for support to both the Catholic hierarchy and Presbyterian clergy, and launched an appeal to raise £10,000 through subscriptions from home and abroad to fund its work.[251] The council delegated Shea Lalor of Killarney to liaise with Crawford at Westminster on future legislation, however, with parliamentary business finally at an end, Crawford himself attended a council meeting on 13 August and agreed in principle the terms of a bill to curb evictions.[252] At this point he appeared fully in alignment with the League and its objectives, at least in public, although over the next few months signs of rifts over tactics and language would start to open up, with opponents doing their utmost to exaggerate and exploit these. McKnight contrasted Crawford's relationship with the League with John O'Connell's failure to grasp its principles and continued to defend him from critics and endeavoured to heal any rifts.[253]

To be effective the League would also need a block of MPs at Westminster prepared to support Crawford's legislative initiatives, and it undertook to support only candidates who were pledged to its principles for land reform, and who would withhold it from any ministry which would not advance them. As Whyte observes, this commitment to political 'independence' was not seen as particularly controversial at the time, although its application was later to be bitterly contested.[254] With the old Repeal party now in a state of wholesale disintegration, some nationalists saw the tenant right issue as a vehicle for rejuvenation and worked to rebuild around this issue (and the accompanying questions of religious equality and franchise reform). One anonymous commentator wrote to Duffy to outline the progress made by summer 1850 to 'unite the scattered fragments of the once powerful Irish party into a compact mass and erect upon it the foundation and of a new and firm structure'; repeal would not be wholly given up, but out of necessity subordinated while 'the country must be raised from the [...] helpless condition of a pauper and put on the strength and dignity of a man'.[255] Many MPs were however, cautious about joining the new body. Only James Fagan of Co. Wexford and William Keogh of Athlone were at its inaugural conference, and three others – Maurice Power of Cork, Ouseley Higgins of Mayo and McCullagh of Drogheda – were active in the early months. But from these limited foundations would grow the 'Independent Irish Party'. Strains between those, especially the northerners, who insisted that the League restrict itself to tenant-right issues alone and those seeing it as vehicle for other political objectives were present from the start, although kept in check until the end of 1852.[256]

At the same time as these high-political structures were being formed, the League was consolidating itself on the ground through local organisation, and many new parochial committees appeared in 1850–1. The proceedings of these were reported in the sympathetic press, but the League took the additional step in June 1851 of establishing a monthly newspaper, *The Irish Tenant League*, to transmit the ideas of the leadership to the provinces and report in detail the proceedings of the weekly public meeting in Dublin and the multiple local committees. Subscriptions from the Catholic and Presbyterian clergy were essential to support the paper as well as the wider movement (many bought multiple copies to distribute in their parishes), but sustained fund-raising was clearly a problem, and the publication appears to have folded in mid-1852.[257]

The re-emergence of the League as a mass movement inevitably alarmed landlord opinion and encouraged them to rally around Conservative leaders. An 'ex-MP' (probably Henry Lambert of Wexford) no doubt spoke for many in an 1851 pamphlet excoriating the Whig government for betraying and persecuting the landed class in Ireland and warning of the new danger from tenant agitators. Claiming himself to be an indulgent landlord, he nevertheless defended mass evictions as unavoidable and complained that the existing law permitted 'a dishonest tenant with a good attorney [to] with impunity plunder and defy his landlord'. Resistance to the tenant-right campaign was, he asserted, essential if his endangered class was to survive at all.[258] Conway Dobbs, a barrister and member of the Co. Antrim landowning family, warned the Dublin Statistical Society that tenant right was merely a premium to idle and improvident tenants, and a serious tax levied on an improving landowner seeking to consolidate his holdings. Only exclusive reliance on contractual bargains could facilitate the recovery of Ireland. Others placed their faith in the market-based vehicle of the encumbered estates act and warned that any concession on tenant-right would impede the providential reconstruction of society.[259] From such statements it is evident that the Famine had a radicalising effect on both the advocates and opponents of land reform, rendering compromise yet more unlikely.

There was evident enthusiasm locally for the parliamentary strategy articulated by Crawford and others at public rallies, but also an impatience with the slow pace of change in the context of continuing high levels of distress and social insecurity. In a number of places older modes of agrarian resistance were looked to alongside the new political strategy, with 'tenant-right' rhetoric being employed to legitimate more direct forms of action aimed at landlords, agents and their lower-class allies. This was evident on the extensive Londonderry estates in Down in 1849–50, where the agent believed there was a widespread and successful campaign of intimidation (especially in the form of incendiarism) in operation against anyone prepared to take the farm of an evicted tenant. This had a significant impact on the management and income of the estate, albeit further depressing tenant-right values, and was replicated elsewhere. In parliament the proprietor blamed the clergy's doctrines of 'communism and socialism' for stirring up such criminality. An increase in coercive measures to extract rent arrears, ordered by a frustrated Londonderry in autumn 1850, proved counterproductive and simply stirred further agitation led by the local clergy.[260]

In the distressed hill country of the Armagh-Louth-Monaghan borderlands Tenant League agitation became interconnected with older traditions of violent resistance to landlordism, although the liberal and nationalist press was at pains to refute claims of formal linkages. Attacks, in several cases fatal, on agents, bailiffs and landlords escalated in the district in 1850–2 and were explicitly connected to threats or enactment of eviction and the distraint of crops and livestock for arrears of rent. Formal League organisation in the area was hampered by difficulties in raising funds and by local disputes, which left some of the rural poor to regard direct action by secret societies as their only mode of redress. After the attempted murder of several landlords in the borderlands the Dublin Castle executive responded with a security crackdown in winter 1851–2, obliging Crawford and the League to further distance themselves from the unrest.[261]

Despite the resurgence of older forms of peasant resistance on the margins, the tenant-right movement that had emerged by 1850 was formally committed to constitutionalist action and the pursuit of change through legislation. Its northern and southern wings had distinct characteristics, but were nonetheless deeply interconnected in rhetoric, symbolism and personnel, with developments in each region echoing and stimulating further activities elsewhere. By the time of the formation of the central Tenant League in Dublin in summer 1850 this was already a national organisation, albeit one that had to manage internal tensions and pressures between its component parts. The iconic figure of Sharman Crawford was central to its national coherence, and his continuing allegiance would prove crucial to its fortunes in the following years.

7. 'The League of North and South', 1850–61

Tensions and compromises: the Tenant League, 1850–1

The newly established Tenant League faced already well-defined challenges as to how best to pursue its legislative objectives in the face of a hostile or indifferent British parliament. The *Banner of Ulster* suggested it establish a 'mission to England', with agents paving the way for 'monster meetings' in British cities, mobilising the Irish migrant population and sympathetic clergy, and hopefully also the British working classes with whom Sharman Crawford had developed a strong rapport.[1] However, with British liberal papers such as the *Daily News* still denouncing the League as an 'experiment in agricultural chartism', it appeared middle-class opinion would be hard to win over.[2] In the short term, the organisation fell back on the tried and tested mode of mass meetings in the Irish provinces, starting at Kilkenny in September, which was chaired by the future MP William Shee, and heard speeches from the northerners Rev. John Rogers and James McKnight, the latter denouncing 'landlord absolutism' for keeping 'Irishmen slaves in the land of their birth' (Figure 25).[3]

Crawford himself appeared as the principal speaker at the Meath Tenant League meeting held in the market square of Navan on 10 October, where he gave a speech that was subjected to intense press scrutiny. He made it clear that he was in alignment with the League, but also that he would remain personally independent of it. What they were jointly pursuing, he insisted, was not class war, but a campaign to acquire equitable justice for all classes on the basis of 'live and let live'. This meant not the abolition of landlordism but the removal of its monopoly status and the unjust powers over others granted by the state. Summarising his agrarian philosophy he insisted that as land was the foundation of all wealth and social order, it must therefore be treated differently from other forms of property:

> The land is the great basis of the social fabric; it supplies food for the people – it supplies clothing for the people – it supplies employment for the people – it supplies the foundation for manufacture and the foundation for commerce (hear, hear). Therefore it is essentially the foundation for every means of life which any class of the community can require (hear, hear). Then, sir, the monopoly has been created in the hands of a few. That monopoly you may suppose, was created for the interests of the state. Well then, if society deems it necessary to create that monopoly, it is equally necessary that the state should take care that that monopoly should not be applied to the disadvantage of the community for whose interest it was created (hear, and cheers).

The state already interfered where equal bargaining was impossible (for example through the usury laws, restrictions on child labour and the passenger acts to protect emigrants), and it was, he concluded, essential it do the same for Irish tenants.

The League, he observed, had proposed state interference through linking rents to a fair valuation of land and via the legalisation of tenant right. These were positions he had consistently advocated since his 1837 pamphlet, from which he quoted at length, and he reaffirmed that he would adhere to valuation to determine a fair rent as a fundamental principle. The one area where there was not complete unity of opinion lay, he admitted, in his continuing insistence that legislation must insist on the law recognising only an 'industrial occupancy' as a basis for fixity and penalising the neglectful tenant, and he urged the League to adopt this. This did not imply indifference to the situation of tenants who had been denied the opportunity to improve or who were incapable of doing so due to their poverty: so long as it was accompanied by legal curbs on ejectments, good tenants on holdings that would come under fair rents would, he was sure, quickly build up such an industrial tenant right. Cottiers, who were still being subjected to murderous evictions, would need to be protected and assisted through other means – either the sort of reclamation scheme he had advocated in *Depopulation Not Necessary*, or (less desirably) by assisted emigration. Labourers would find their wages enhanced as secure tenants employed more of them on improvement works. If these appeared 'extreme remedies' to some, the extreme evils of the situation demanded them and the League had emerged to assert public pressure for the necessary solutions. At the same time, he would remain formally independent of the League in advocating and pursuing what he thought right, while giving it his 'general support'.[4]

This semi-detached position was consistent with Crawford's insistence on maintaining his individual integrity as an elected tribune of the people in parliament. However, in excluding himself from the central council of the League he enhanced the potential for misunderstanding and division and denied himself the opportunity to shape its agenda over the coming months.

The *Times* was quick to dismiss this public appearance by the 'old and [...] somewhat crotchetty' Sharman Crawford.[5] More importantly, given its influence on northern English industrial liberalism, the *Manchester Guardian* accused him of impulsiveness and poor economic reasoning in advocating a policy that contradicted the free-trade principles of laissez-faire and smacked of French communism, a charge which led Crawford to respond by reiterating his critique of Irish landlords as a monopolistic class created and maintained by the state.[6] Demonstrating greater attention to nuance than the English papers, the *News-Letter* welcomed what it discerned as his more conciliatory tone at Navan, while the *Northern Whig* sought to raise questions about his genuine adherence to the League by parsing his speech for inconsistencies, especially on valuation and fixity of tenure.[7] McKnight in the *Banner* responded that any differences between Crawford and the League were on mere points of detail.[8] The *Whig* was not prepared to let the matter drop, commenting obsessively on every hint of dissension and stressing the 'extremism' of the League and the revolutionary background of Duffy in particular, themes also taken up by the Tory press in the north, which (true to form) equated the League with the United Irishmen.[9]

In November the *Whig* reported that Crawford had now fallen out with the League's leadership and was blocking the holding of a proposed mass meeting in Down if it did not agree resolutions based on his own bill.[10] Early in the month, a planning committee chaired by one of Crawford's tenants, James Bingham of Rademon, met in Downpatrick and invited him to speak at the rally there on 14 November, and its postponement appeared to bear out the *Whig's* claims of a schism.[11] The *Downpatrick Recorder* crowed that the movement was now at an end as it had lost its talisman who would no longer work with 'the rebels of '48 who are rebels in heart still'.[12] This obituary proved premature, although it seems evident that there were indeed significant differences of opinion in play.

A letter sent by Crawford to the organisers of the Dundalk tenant right rally in early December 1850 sought 'candidly' to explain his position. Principles, however popular and just, had to be turned into workable legislation if they were to stand any chance of successful enactment, and his own bills had set out to attain this balance. He could only support a bill proposed by the League if it met these criteria, but none had yet been proposed. When it was, a political coalition must be built reaching beyond Irish tenant farmers, as they had to 'create in its favour the moral power of the public opinion of the intelligent portion of the British community'. This was by no means a renunciation of the work of the League, as:

> I am in a position to urge on the people the necessity of a persevering and united agitation on this question; and a selection of representatives who will honestly support their just claims. No redress of old established grievances was ever carried unless by the power of the people being brought to bear, by a constitutional action, upon the government and the legislature; and by such means I trust the tenants of Ireland will ultimately obtain the redress of their grievances and the establishment of their rights.[13]

What was at issue was a contest of wills over the specific content of the League's draft legislation, not of its central purpose, but the rift was nevertheless embarrassing. Later that month he wrote in support of the postponed Down meeting, which finally assembled on 30 December at Newtownards. While he endorsed their demand that tenant right be formally recognised in legislation, he was again reserved as to his own position. His letter was nevertheless cheered, and McKnight made the best of the awkward situation, praising him at length and quoting from his Navan speech. The *Banner* editor insisted that if the League's platform now went beyond Crawford's previous bills, it did so in the knowledge that he himself was dissatisfied with these previous compromises. Attempts to open up a wedge between them were, he concluded, simply attempts by the landlord press to smear the League.[14] Nevertheless, Crawford's physical absence from a platform just a few miles from Crawfordsburn (and from a subsequent meeting at Downpatrick on 8 January 1851) gave further ammunition to that press, and the *News-Letter* summised that this accounted for the low number of attendees at both meetings.[15]

While the Tenant League continued to hold rallies in the early months of 1851, Crawford's attention was turned elsewhere, towards opposing both the 'centralisation' of Irish institutions and the government's Ecclesiastical Titles Bill. After a series of bouts of ill health he had also decided to stand down as an MP, with a formal announcement made to the electors of Rochdale in early April.[16] Nevertheless, he continued to appear in the commons when able and insisted on adding a clause drawing attention to the necessity of land law reform to H.W. Barron's motion for a debate on the state of Ireland, in an attempt to 'stir up the slumbering land question'.[17] Soon afterwards the tensions that had been brewing between him and the Tenant League came to the surface. Replying to letters from the Meath tenant right associations urging him to reconsider his intention to leave parliament and instead stand as a League candidate for that county, Crawford set out the reasons for his reluctance to do so. While he remained fully committed to tenant right, he wrote, the League's failure to endorse his definition connected to '*industrial occupation and value created by the tenant*', and adherence to the popular principle of absolute fixity of tenure for all tenants without any reference to improvements, was something he could not pledge himself to. If this was indeed the will of the people, it should be for others to take on the task of legislating for it.

For Crawford there were moral, economic and practical issues at stake: idleness should not be awarded the same privileges as industry, and his preferred labour theory of value as the basis for tenant right needed to be upheld, but also the principle of 'industrial tenant-right', which he had (he believed) worn down parliament into acknowledging, should not be overthrown in the vain pursuit of something that would be attacked as more fundamentally undermining the rights of private property.[18] His obdurate stance may also have reflected his long-standing concern for the plight of the agricultural labourer. While many in the League may have been preoccupied solely with the prospects of the tenant farmer (and the Famine had exacerbated conflict between tenants and labourers in many places), Crawford insisted that the interests of the two classes were interrelated, but only so long as the tenants were given reasons to employ labourers on improvements that would raise the living standards of all. Without this, he believed, tenant-right would amount to an exclusive class demand. Labourers continued to lack their own leadership voices in this period, but tensions between a substantial tenantry evolving towards middle-class status and the subordinated labourer class would continue to punctuate agrarian movements from the 1850s onwards.[19]

Crawford's approach had received theoretical support in April 1850 when the Catholic lawyer and professor of jurisprudence and political economy at Queen's College Galway, Denis Caulfield Heron, presented a paper on the ownership of tenant improvements to the Dublin Statistical Society. Countering the predominantly 'orthodox' liberal consensus in that society, Heron argued that the added value to the soil created through the tenant's labour belonged by natural right to the tenant, and that this entitlement was recognised in Roman civil law if not in the continuing feudal tenets underlying English common and statute law. As social progress had rendered feudal social structures redundant, land law must be reformed on more rational and utilitarian lines to promote the prosperity of the greatest number. The principles of civil law, he maintained, recognised the tenant's right to a rent abatement in case of natural catastrophe (such as had been created by the potato blight), and of the existence of a 'lien' on the land created by his improvements, which he could not in equity be deprived of except by compensation at full value. Granting tenant right on these terms, he concluded, would make them free citizens: 'Soldiers of agriculture, let them become – their labour free, and its fruits secured to them – the best guardians of public order!'[20] If Heron's position remained very much a minority one within Irish political economy, the intellectual heft he supplied was useful to Crawford's case. However, this was to some extent countered by his colleague at Galway, Crawford's former protege and now professor agriculture Thomas Skilling, who urged him to go further and grant the tenant '*a permanent right to occupation*'.[21]

Crawford may also have been conscious of the potential political advantages of being seen to curb the more utopian aspects of the League. The liberal *Irish Quarterly Review*, for example, declared itself a supporter of the extension of the Ulster custom across the island, as a 'common sense' answer to landlord abuses and neglect, but vented furiously against what it saw as the dangerous demagogic 'slangwhangers' Lucas and Duffy and their ludicrous advocacy of rent set by valuation. 'Let Sharman Crawford,' it concluded in March 1851, and

> those men who have consistently, untiringly, and against all the yelpings of faction, toiled onwards for many a weary year in the cause of the Irish farmer, suggest, or frame, the necessary law of tenant-right. [...] Let the tenant league, casting aside the fellowship of those speculating traders in politics who damage its reputation and clog its progression, give its honest, open, legal support, to the tenant-right of the tenant-farmers' old and tried champions; and then will true men throng to its standard ready to support it in all its difficulties [...][22]

Even if he was reluctant to concede to demands to drop valuation for rent, Crawford may well have recognised the importance of holding the line on 'industrial occupancy'.

Crawford's throwing down of the gauntlet to the League on this issue, after several months of silence, naturally drew public attention.[23] What followed demonstrated how important Crawford's leadership was for the movement. Fearing that it might disintegrate if its best-known advocate and exemplar of co-operative landlordism walked away, the *Freeman* urged the League council to compromise and accept his bill and Crawford to consider his apparent resolve to retire. It would be a public calamity if the movement's icon be lost to the cause: 'The sight of him suggests a thousand thoughts in palpable, practical form, favourable to the rights of the tenantry, that mere words, however striking, illustrative, or argumentative, could ever sum up'.[24] The *Dublin Evening Post* added that, by scaring away such men as Crawford, the League had damaged its credibility with many tenant farmers, and stood little chance of electoral success as a consequence.[25]

Evidently sensing that any public rift with Crawford at this time would indeed be damaging, Lucas responded quickly on behalf of the council, assuring the *Freeman* that it sought genuine co-operation with Crawford, and that it would devote its upcoming conference in Belfast on 30 April–1 May to seeking resolution of any differences with him. They had hoped to meet him in person, but as he would be detained at Westminster the League would pursue an interview as soon as possible thereafter.[26] Commentary from the provinces suggested, however, that such a reconciliation might prove problematic. Addressing the Callan Tenant Protection Society, Fr O'Shea lamented the disagreement with 'that excellent and patriotic gentleman, Mr Sharman Crawford', but insisted that it was an essential principle of the League that tenant right be based on occupancy alone and not on industrial improvement, and that the tenant should have an absolute fixity of tenure, even when the landowner offered to buy out the full value of his tenant right.[27] The criticism that 'Mr Sharman Crawford's remedy would be no remedy at all' for rack-rented tenants was taken up by the county newspaper in Kilkenny.[28]

The Belfast meeting, which was well attended by tenants from the surrounding counties, avoided such specifics, with speakers reiterating instead the differences with Crawford were solely over words not fundamentals. But the *Whig* insisted that words were serious things, and that only an unambiguous endorsement of Crawford's bill would satisfy its critics.[29]

The *News-Letter*, as well as making sectarian attacks on Catholic speakers present at the meeting, claimed Crawford's polite but firm letter explaining the reasons for his absence and refusing to pledge himself contained an attack on the 'dishonesty' of the League's leadership.[30] Nevertheless, the Belfast meeting resolved that Lucas and McKnight should go to London without delay, with a view to 'terminating, if possible, any existing differences' with Crawford. Following the recommendation of Duffy and Lucas that such an action would be essential to satisfy the northerners, the Council agreed, but added O'Shea to the deputation to give a voice to the south.[31] Lucas believed the need for resolution was urgent if the Irish MPs were to be pressurised to act that session, and reminded Duffy he should take every opportunity to keep recalcitrant members of the League on side.[32] At the same time, Lucas reprimanded Duffy for excessive caution in excusing the reluctance of MPs to adopt a clause to protect tenants from confiscation of rent arrears, a measure he noted that Crawford had already endorsed and that League members would insist upon.[33]

On 24 May the *Freeman* triumphantly announced the success of the deputation's meeting with Crawford, asserting that all differences had 'vanished' during a conference marked by mutual goodwill. A joint statement had of necessity been postponed due to Crawford's sudden return to Ireland on the death of his son Frederick, but it was certain this would soon be signed off. A minute of the meeting noted that a 'firm foundation' had been laid 'for a union between the League and Mr Crawford' and his followers.[34] The League members agreed to support Crawford's bill as a 'valuable instalment of their demands' in return for the addition of several face-saving additions, including a clause that tenants with improvements worth over a certain value should receive a lease in perpetuity at a fair rent (or a lease for a moderate length if the improvements were of lower value), and another incorporating his previously announced support for a temporary ban on evictions until a meaningful value of tenant right could be created on a holding. Lucas was sure that in giving ground to Crawford now, they would be able to persuade him to go further in future.

Although Tory papers depicted this agreement as a signal defeat for the League, the *Nation* was upbeat, flagging the 'treaty of alliance' as the foundation for a summer of agitation throughout the country.[35] Rev. David Bell assured a public meeting that any differences with 'that excellent Irishman and patriot' Crawford had been more imaginary than real and were now wholly resolved.[36] Behind the scenes, however, this rapprochement was not quite as amicable as it was reported. Crawford complained that Lucas had misrepresented to the council his reservations on certain points and resolved 'to hold no further personal communication with Mr Lucas, unless in the presence of a witness'.[37] Although papered over at the time, this was an intimation of troubles lying ahead between the two men.

The deal drew some predictable fire from hardline Connerite advocates of 'perpetuity and valuation', but seems otherwise to have been popular, especially in the north.[38] His son buried, Crawford returned to the commons and maintained a high profile as a critic of the Ecclesiastical Titles Bill and of another bill that would have removed the requirement on railway companies to pay for tenant right to occupiers in cases of compulsory purchase.[39] Although there was now insufficient time to re-introduce his tenant right bill that session, along with McCullough he sponsored a bill to give the protection of leases to tenants on encumbered estates now facing mass eviction by new purchasers; this was thrown out, but the fact it received support from only fourteen Irish MPs drew attention again to the nature of the country's representatives at a time when the government was tottering and a general election appeared likely.[40] He committed himself to bringing his own bill back before parliament in 1852.[41]

To symbolise the 'league of north and south', now reinforced by the apparent resolution of any differences with Crawford, the League planned a 'great aggregate meeting' on the banks of the River Boyne near Drogheda. Originally scheduled for 12 July 1851 as a celebration of non-sectarian unity in riposte to Orangeism, the date was put back to 14 July to accommodate the Presbyterian clergy, whose General Assembly (presided over by Dr John Coulter, an active supporter of tenant right as moderator) would only end in Belfast on the 12th. Reporting to the League Council, John Cashel Hoey, who later succeeded Duffy as editor of the *Nation,* observed that the organising committee intended to fly over the Boyne obelisk the 'union-tricolour' of the League – an adaption of T. F. Meagher's 1848 flag uniting orange and green that had been appropriated by the movement, but now with a 'Presbyterian blue' central bar replacing the original white.[42] The *Freeman* enthused that the event would transcend Ireland's divisive history and mark a new beginning:

> as the children of one common land, they shall henceforth – Northman and Southron – meet as bretheren, join as bretheren, and work as bretheren, for the redemption of that land, and the protection of all its sons, whether they rally under the banners of the orange or the green. [...] Hurrah then, for the Boyne water, Sharman Crawford, unity and tenant right!![43]

Crawford's anticipated presence at the rally would ensure it would serve as 'the first step towards victory'.[44]

The effect was somewhat spoiled by Crawford's eventual inability to attend due to the continuing press of parliamentary business, and the absence of many of the Presbyterian clergy due to the overrun of the Assembly meetings and the reluctance of many to travel on a Sunday. Letters of apology and support were read from Paul Cullen (now Archbishop of Armagh), Bishop Cantwell of Meath and the moderator Dr Coulter, and most importantly from Crawford himself, who called for public support for the reintroduction of his bill, as 'unless backed by the concentration of the opinion of the country, *on that principle,* any efforts of mine must be abortive and destitute of any useful result'. He understood that the League now endorsed his incrementalist 'step by step' approach and urged patience: 'we must act practically, or we shall get nothing.[45]

It fell to Fr James Dowling of Clonmellon, Co. Westmeath, to propose that the meeting formally approve Crawford's bill on behalf of the League, 'as an approximation of what was due to justice', which it promptly did. Representing the north at the rally, McKnight followed by proclaiming that the adherence of Crawford was a signal victory, as:

> one of the great objects which their enemies had long been striving to effect was the separation of Mr Crawford from the League. His heart, however, was sound – he was a sincere patriot in the cause of his country. His life was devoted to the emancipation of the tenant farmers, and consequently these designs had all been defeated and Mr Crawford was united with the League (loud cheers).

As the sun re-emerged at the end of a very wet day, he took confidence from the symbolism of the historic site:

He hoped the day was a prophetic omen of their future triumphs (hear, hear). The spot upon which they stood had been frequently associated with the contrivances of the policy that had kept their country in chains (hear, hear). Its name had too often been made the watchword of Irish dissension and degradation. But those days were gone, and upon that auspicious occasion they had the orange and the green waving above their heads; they had virtue and Erin on their side, and they should inevitably triumph [...][46]

Reflecting on the event, Maguire reported that, despite the weather, it had been 'one of the largest and best provincial assemblies since the days of the monster meetings', and most importantly had demonstrated that 'there was no longer even the semblance of difference between Mr Sharman Crawford and the League'.[47]

The sentiments and symbols of the Boyne meeting soon found their way into popular culture. The *Irish Tenant League* published one ballad sent to it from the north which predicted the eclipse of Orange dissensions with the rise of the tenant movement, and which the journal thought to be an 'original of the native type' as sung at country markets. The song contained hints of an underlying United Irish memory, now channelled behind the League:

> The squires and the gentry, the privileg'd few
> Who led on such capers, I'll swear it's too true;
> Yet the game they play'd off; they play'd it too long,
> Tho' our music be rusty we'll give them a song;
> We'll screw up our harp, and we'll tune up our lays,
> And pledge our best faith for more generous days;
> We'll twine up the orange, and weave it with green
> But no party colours no more will be seen.
> > Then tenant right, tenant right, on we will go,
> > Let critics or curs say this, that or no.
> The staunch hardy Scot, aye consistent and true,
> In Ulster's bleak hills, with his banner so blue,
> Has joined hand in hand for a righteous cause,
> With Erin's proud sons of the south, with applause.
> The noble descendants of Gracchi of old,
> When Rome in its splendour, the arts did unfold,
> This union so just, so hallow'd and brave,
> Will bear down our foemen, and country save.
> [...][48]

Another, highly sentimental, ballad referencing the 'voice of the Boyne' as a challenge to landlord depredation was reported to be very popular in Meath.[49]

At the next meeting of the League's council, Fr O'Shea waxed lyrically about the symbolic power of the recent meeting in attaining what the Volunteers of 1782 and O'Connell in 1843 had failed to achieve – at last the 'waters of the Boyne had washed out the stain' of Irish disunion and 'orange and green would assuredly carry the day'. Lucas chose instead to focus on the practical: his and Duffy's meetings in London had surpassed all expectations, as not only was Crawford now fully on board, but 'the most influential and independent of the Irish members' were engaged to work with him and the League to carry his bill next session. Their task now was to work to bring over additional Irish MPs through the deployment of public pressure, beginning with a conference at which the details of the bill would be formally agreed.[50]

Crawford himself summoned the Irish MPs to attend this in Dublin on 20 August.[51] Certainly there now appeared greater grounds for optimism. Frustrated that the prime minister had ruled out introducing any ministerial measure on the question next session, and confident that even the 'most thorough-going' Leaguers had now accepted the logic of Crawford's incrementalist position, even the *Whig* now believed the country would rally unanimously behind him and Russell would be obliged to give way.[52] The *Freeman* proposed that the agreed bill be made the touchstone for all 'popular' candidates standing for election, with a view to creating a 'phalanx ready and able to decide the fate of cabinets', that is, holding the parliamentary balance of power, but that the movement must also be realistic as to what was achievable rather than holding out for everything it desired.[53]

The conference met privately at the Imperial Hotel, Dublin, on 20 August 1851, and after five hours deliberation, agreed on a bill virtually identical to Crawford's proposal of 1850, with some additional clauses added to protect tenants at will from eviction in districts where the tenant-right custom did not prevail. The *Freeman* reported that 'a strong parliamentary party, and a great country party' was now assembled to support it, including at least thirteen MPs.[54] At a public meeting at the Music Hall the following day, eight MPs joined Crawford and the council of the League on the platform to seal the alliance. Following Crawford's address from the chair, William Keogh (MP for Athlone) and John Sadlier (Carlow) spoke in support, although the latter's introduction of issues relating to the Ecclesiastical Titles Bill drew rebukes from some. These two, along with George Henry Moore (Mayo), who was also present and had taken an interest in land reform since 1850 despite being a large proprietor, were leading figures in the 'Irish Brigade' (later reconstituted as the Catholic Defence Association) formed that session to oppose the titles bill and pursue other pro-Catholic policies; Crawford had worked with them on the campaign against the bill and insisted that they be brought into the movement despite Duffy's reluctance, although he insisted that religious issues should be kept separate from the tenant movement.[55] Several months later Keogh appeared to commit himself completely, telling his constituents that he would 'not support any political party which does not make it part of its political creed to do full justice to the tenant in Ireland'.[56]

Denominational unity was very much the dominant note of the Imperial Hotel meeting; Rentoul spoke for the many Presbyterian ministers present in lauding the alliance of north and south under the guidance of the movement's 'Nestor'. He thanked 'his southern fellow-countrymen, in the name of the Presbyterians, his bretheren of the north [...] for their appreciation of the virtues of Sharman Crawford', and concluded that the time for action had at last arrived.[57] For its part, the *Freeman* welcomed the adhesion of the members of the Catholic 'Irish Brigade' as likely to boost the cause in parliament, and reassured the Presbyterians that they would prove sound allies.[58] However, the *Nation* warned, presciently as it turned out, that success was assured so long as the priests and popular leaders insisted on giving the tenant question priority over all others and not allow 'religious liberty [to] be made a stalking horse for some persons to ride into parliament, if by any chance it be allowed', and the *Vindicator* insisted that any hint of religious discord must be kept off League platforms at all costs.[59] The warning was timely: almost immediately the *News-Letter* accused the League of having sold itself to 'Popery'.[60]

Despite the League's calls for unity around Crawford's bill as a necessary '*interim* measure' that it could adopt without in any way compromising its fundamental principles, there were still some rumblings in the movement over its formal adoption.[61] The *Nation* carried a letter questioning the very viability of a parliamentary strategy, given the landlord stranglehold over both the commons and the lords, and criticising Duffy for even entertaining the idea.[62] In south Leinster, the *Kilkenny Journal* kept up a regular sniping against Crawford as taking a retrogressive stance on the land question and criticised the League leadership for having conceded too much ground to him.[63] Such critiques necessitated action by the League's leaders: its official organ reprimanded the *Journal* for failing to grasp political strategy, and at Callan in September O'Shea and O'Keefe defended the compromise to the Tenant Protection Society, and brought in Shee to back them up. Drawing on Crawford's published writings, Shee assured his audience in a 'masterly speech' that the omission of the term 'perpetuity' of tenure from the bill was for sound reasons of optics, while his bill would work pragmatically to deliver this in practice.[64] No dissent was recorded at Callan; at nearby Castlecomer however, the local committee observed that the bill would deliver only one of the three key points of the League (adjudication of fair rents), but it would nevertheless do its duty in supporting it.[65]

To add ballast to its argument, the League issued an address to the people of Ireland in early October 1851. This reiterated the case that the continuing social crisis of Ireland – marked by impoverishment, evictions and mass emigration – made action urgent in the face of despair of improvement at home. The League had already, it claimed, succeeded in pressurising many landlords to abate rents, but the only real solution to the crisis was for the people to back it in agitating for Crawford's tenant-right bill.[66] The *Nation* agreed that there could be no guarantee that Crawford's bill would pass, but insisted that there could be no compromise on its principles of setting fair rents by valuation and protecting poor tenants from eviction for arrears if Ireland was escape the stifling effects of famine, free trade and mass emigration.[67] As the League for the first time now also extended its activities to the west, with meetings at Scariff, Kilrush and other places in Clare and at Ballinrobe, Co. Mayo, support for Crawford's bill spread.[68]

The relief and enthusiasm for this turn of events in Down was palpable. Addressing the baronial tenant right committee for Ards and Castlereagh at Newtownards on 30 September, Bell called on them to undertake the return of Crawford for the county at the next elections.[69] An attempt by Londonderry to bar his tenants from attending a mass meeting in the same town several weeks later ignited an already smouldering antagonism between him and the tenant movement in the county. Londonderry's public threats of eviction against tenants who defied him had already provoked angry feelings.[70] Large numbers of his tenants attended the meeting and expressed vigorous support for Crawford, despite the presence of the estate bailiffs and threats of retribution against tenants in arrears.[71] Perhaps more attuned of the shifting political winds than his irascible father, Castlereagh, as one of the sitting members for the country, now wrote to express his concurrence in 'the importance of securing a good measure of tenant-right for Ireland', and bearing testimony to 'the great and useful service personally rendered to the cause' by Crawford, a stance welcomed by the *Whig*.[72] Suggestions were made in the press that Crawford and Castlereagh might run together on a joint ticket.

In December, at a tenant-right 'soiree' held in the Presbyterian church at Annaclone, the parish priest Fr John Macken lauded the 'men of Newtownards' for putting forward 'Sharman Crawford, who should be able to command the vote of every Presbyterian, liberal Protestant, and independent Roman Catholic in the county', and welcomed the apparent adhesion of Castlereagh, whose 'accession to the ranks of the tenant-right representatives would be of inestimable advantage'. In contrast, Downshire and his 'nominee', Lord Edwin Hill, were lambasted for religious bigotry and opposing tenant right.[73] The ever-outspoken Rogers accused the landlords of what amounted to murder during the famine; their apologists stood 'over the one indiscriminate grave of 2,000,000 of their fallen countrymen, whom landlordism first robbed, then starved, and lastly, consigned to the shroudless and coffinless pit, called [...] the grave of union workhouses.' He concluded that if the people of Down failed to return their friend Crawford at the next election 'they deserve to be what their enemies have written them down, "slaves forever"'. His audience appeared to agree that it was now time for political retribution against those responsible for their miseries.[74]

While even the *Kilkenny Journal* was certain that with such support Crawford was sure of election 'in the interest of the League', it was also clear that there would be strong opposition. The Presbyterian theological rivals turned political allies Montgomery and Cooke both attended a dinner given by Downshire to his tenants at Hillsborough that month, in what was taken as electioneering in that family's interest, and the *News-Letter* urged a pan-Protestant mobilisation to oppose Crawford and the League.[75] It seemed certain to many that 1852 would be a year of decision on the tenant-right question, one way or the other.

The 1852 session

Under the Septennial Act no general election was required before summer 1854, but as the UK entered a period of acute political instability it seemed highly unlikely the current parliament would last that long. In December 1851 the foreign secretary, Lord Palmerston, was obliged to resign following his unauthorised recognition of Louis Napoleon Bonaparte's coup d'etat in France, and he subsequently allied with the opposition in seeking to bring down Russell's increasingly fragile administration. In February 1852 the government was defeated on its militia bill and Russell resigned, to be succeeded by a minority Conservative ministry headed by the 14th Earl of Derby (previously Lord Stanley), who had led the protectionist wing of that party since its split with Peel over the corn laws in 1846. The Conservatives indicated their intention of dissolving parliament but opted to delay this until the end of the session, preferring the benefits of a temporary incumbency to the risks of immediate electoral conflict with both the Whigs and the unreconciled Peelites.

The change of government put the Tenant League, along with the allied Catholic Defence Association, on to an electoral war footing, but the extension of the session also gave Crawford another, and as it transpired, final, chance to pass his landlord and tenant bill from the backbenches. To raise morale and flag the extent of popular support behind him before his return to Westminster, the League organised a public meeting and banquet at the Music Hall in Belfast on 28 January 1852, at which the old Volunteer John Sinclair took the chair.[76] The *Belfast Mercury* reported the building was packed with enthusiastic attendees from town and country, who appeared confident that even should the bill not pass that session, the League was acquiring sufficient popular momentum to ensure greater electoral success and through this potential leverage over any new and unstable administration.[77]

Crawford was acutely aware that the upsurge in agrarian violence in Armagh, Monaghan and Louth, which acquired greater intensity over the winter of 1851–2, was being used by their enemies to discredit both the tenant movement and himself personally.[78] Some Ulster landlords claimed these disturbances were the result of an extensive conspiracy against themselves and their agents, although the evidence suggests that most were localised violent reactions to threatened eviction or loss of employment and that connections to formal Ribbonism were marginal and claims of direct League participation (as opposed to looser inspiration) were spurious.[79] A select committee on Irish outrages at Westminster would be the site of sustained attempts by ministers to link such crime to the League in the following months. The *Banner* insisted that the League had never been established in the disturbed area, where the remnants of Defenderism and lawlessness had persisted for over sixty years.[80]

Crawford addressed the issue directly at the Belfast meeting: violent agrarian crime was morally reprehensible and was undermining the 'just and holy cause' of tenant right, and he would support any measure that would genuinely tend to curb it. But it was useless and hypocritical to seek to coerce such manifestations without addressing the root causes of rural misery. He would, he asserted, make no apologies for agrarian outrage, but it must be understood that it arose from the despair and degradation of the cottier system, which had rendered the labouring class acutely vulnerable to the vagaries of the potato harvest and the whims of evicting landlords. When the crop failed (as so often in recent years), 'agrarian disturbances were produced, with death and emigration from the soil' due to lack of peasant security. Crawford, and the speakers who followed, urged a mass petitioning campaign in the localities to maximise the momentum behind his bill in parliament and draw people away from such illegal activities.[81]

The *Whig* expressed relief that the meeting had responded so positively to Crawford's denunciation of crime, and now gave its cautious support for his bill, albeit alongside additional liberal measures to free landowners from the remnants of feudal constraints on their freedoms, a theme which drew on the publications of the liberal economist William Neilson Hancock, previously Whately professor of political economy at Trinity College Dublin and now a professor at the newly opened Queen's College Belfast.[82] Although still highly suspicious of the League, the paper would strongly support Crawford's forthcoming candidacy in Down.[83] R. J. Tennent agreed that getting rid of 'the old feudal and technical rubbish' in land law should be given a higher priority, although he was ready to give some support to Crawford's initiative out of personal respect for him.[84] Also responding favourably to Hancock's liberal critique of 'feudal' landlordism and the laws that upheld it (although noting he had side-stepped the crucial question of tenant-right), Patrick McMahon observed in the Catholic *Dublin Review* that no parliamentary 'club of landlords' or 'geocrats' would ever agree to a meaningful landlord-tenant bill.[85] To the *Freeman*, the Belfast meeting had proven the 'moral attachment' of the northern tenants to Crawford and the cause of constitutional agitation, and it looked forward to seeing him take his seat in future as MP for his native county.[86] For its part, the ultra-tory *Dublin Evening Mail* prophesied that in reintroducing his bill under current circumstances, Crawford and his allies had 'kindled a fire' from which 'torrents of blood' would flow.[87]

While Crawford returned to Westminster to lead the 'Irish brigade' of MPs on the land question, the League offered support in the form of a rejuvenated petitioning campaign, distributing a template to the local committees for their use.[88] An address issued in January urged the country to put its shoulder behind the parliamentary strategy, which alone offered any prospect of success on the models of the Catholic Emancipation and Anti-Corn Law League. Should Crawford's bill falter again, the movement must be ready for an all-Ireland electoral struggle to return its supporters en masse. The cost of failure would be continuing forced depopulation and sustained rural misery.[89]

These inspiring sentiments needed to be matched by political organisation. The League had suffered a string of electoral setbacks in 1851 by-elections as its candidates had lost out to better financed Whigs lacking any commitment to land reform but who had campaigned against the Ecclesiastical Titles Bill. However the League drew optimism from the success of Vincent Scully in the Co. Cork by-election of March 1852, adding to the Brigade a Catholic landowner who had published a detailed book on the land question advocating significant reforms of tenure as well as facilities for tenant purchase of their farms.[90] This was followed by a series of constituency nominations by liberal clubs and tenant associations of candidates favouring 'independent' stances and supporting tenant right.[91]

The *Banner* welcomed the Whig government's dropping of its own 'hypocritical' land measure at the start of the 1852 session and attributed this to pressure from the League.[92] The way was thus cleared for a direct assault on landlordism via Crawford's bill, which stood first in the commons order book for 10 February and which the 'Tenant Right Brigade' of MPs in the house would now ensure received a proper debate, even if it stood little chance of passing.[93] Introducing his bill to what was for once a well-attended house in what the League praised as 'one of the wisest and most temperate speeches we ever read', Crawford was again explicit in his condemnation of agrarian outrage, and insistent on the need for the state to win legitimacy for the rule of law through reform rather than resort to coercion:

> The people had not a proper respect for the law; and where that was so, there could never be peace or security for property; the most barbarous murders were committed in connexion with the occupancy of land. Yet the Irish were naturally a kindhearted people. All the evils existing at the present day in the social relations of Ireland might be traced to the want of security on the part of the tenant.[94]

The home secretary and prime minister were obliged to respond with what the *Freeman* dismissed as 'objections and sophistries [...] clumsy in the extreme' in their opposition to the bill, while speeches from Crawford, Sadlier and Keogh were praised as 'of signal ability' and Bright's apparent support for the bill was particularly welcomed as raising hopes that the 'Manchester party' would follow him.[95] A joint address issued by Crawford and Keogh then called on 'the Irish people' to support the bill's progress through further petitions and public meetings, with some early success, although the *Times* countered by warning its middle-class English readers that Crawford's 'craze' would perpetuate Irish agricultural backwardness and render landowners into mere pensioners without pensions.[96] Petitions started to arrive promptly, including one from the students of Assembly's College and

Queen's College Belfast, which caused consternation in Conservative circles and calls for the disciplining of those involved.[97]

The formation of Derby's administration on 23 February altered if it did not transform the political landscape, and the League pointed optimistically to his sponsorship of a (weak) tenant compensation bill in 1845, and more importantly the fragility of his administration and therefore its dependence on potential allies.[98] The stance adopted by the new Irish attorney-general, Napier, would be crucial, but his statements were at first 'opaque'. The *Banner* was sceptical of his good faith, suspected a ruse on Irish land reform to see the Conservatives through the coming elections, and identified his hand behind a recent book by the Dublin lawyers William Ferguson and Andrew Vance that had rejected tenant right and included 'several pages of unmeaning mis-statement and slander' against the League.[99] While the Conservatives evidently remained the party of the landed interest, this may have been somewhat unfair to Napier personally. A lawyer from a Belfast merchant background, he recognised the beneficial effects of the Ulster custom, and was planning a suite of land bills that he hoped would square the circle 'by both increasing landlords' control over their property, while at the same time recognising the interest of those tenants who had investing in improving their holdings'.[100]

When the second reading of Crawford's bill came forward on 31 March, he opened the six-hour debate by drawing attention to the 109 petitions presented in its support as evidence that 'he stood there [as ...] the messenger of a nation', but also offered to have the bill's details discussed by a select committee, alongside any government measure if one was proposed, so long as the principle of the bill was approved at this time.[101] Napier reacted by welcoming his 'candid and temperate' tone and hinted at some future concessions on tenant compensation, but insisted that he could not support parliamentary interference in the contractual relations between landlord and tenant and in customary practices where they existed, not least as these varied between districts, and insisted that the laws of property remained the basis of civilisation. The new chief secretary Lord Naas and Irish solicitor-general James Whiteside, along with Crawford's perennial nemesis Emerson Tennent, all sitting for Ulster seats, were more openly hostile and dismissive of Crawford personally as well as his bill.[102] The subsequent adjournment of the debate without a division was regarded as a triumph by Tory obstructionists, but a further slot for debate was secured by Crawford for 5 May, after 'presenting another file of petitions' to the speaker.[103] The delay seems to have caused Crawford little concern, as it kept the issue before the Irish public for a further month during what was already an extended electioneering campaign and gave time for more petitions to come in; on 13 April Crawford welcomed another from Cavan, and noted that 120,000 signatures had now been collected behind his bill.[104]

A number of Irish MPs spoke for and against the bill in the resumed second-reading debate, including Lord Claud Hamilton (MP for Tyrone and a member of the administration), who denounced it as 'dangerous and revolutionary' and repeated the hackneyed charge that the Tenant League was a new incarnation of the United Irishmen. When put to the vote the bill was lost by a margin of 110. The minority was, however, an unprecedentedly large one of fifty-seven (plus tellers), made up of forty-five Irish MPs and 14 British radicals or liberals; twenty-nine other Irish MPs were absent and a minority of thirty-one had voted against.[105] The *Banner* affirmed that '[e]very one knew, and expected, that the bill would be lost; but the country has good reason to take courage from the significant fact that nearly sixty members of the house of commons have now declared for tenant right, instead of only fourteen or fifteen, or at most twenty, as in former experiences of a like nature'.[106] Addressing his supporters in a public letter, Crawford drew a contrast between the disingenuous behaviour of the current MP for Lisburn (Emerson Tennent) and the defiance of landlordism demonstrated by the borough's voters in electing his father in 1783, and defended his bill and motives against deliberate Tory misrepresentation. Napier, he conceded, had been more polite towards him, but could not be trusted to bring forward a land bill that would protect the existing Ulster tenant right, as he had praised the work by Vance and Ferguson that explicitly ruled out any retrospective compensation for tenant improvements. Crawford urged supporters to mobilise now in the electoral struggle, especially in Ulster, which alone of the provinces had seen a large majority of its MPs vote against the bill. The stakes could not be higher:

> Th[e] customary tenant-right which I desire to render valid by law is represented by the landlords as being a *boon* and not a *right*, and thereby it creates that political serfdom which places the electors of Ulster in feudal bondage, and sustains that system of vassalage by means of which the representation of several of the finest counties of Ulster are held as heir-looms in the hands of a few high families. [...] The removal of this tenant from his occupation, which the landlord has the power to do, transfers him from his comfortable home to the poorhouse or death. Here, then, is a chain of slavery held in the landlord's hand which the tenant bears with a reluctant and degrading submission, but which he cannot break without enduring consequences too serious for the claims of public virtue to require from him. Then mark me – the great question at issue on the tenant-right bill is, whether this aristocratic dominion is to be upheld or abandoned – whether the tenant is to be a serf or a freeman.[107]

Commenting favourably on the address, the *Whig* concurred that '[i]f the recent debate does not stimulate the constituencies of Ulster to rid themselves of some of the nightmares that press on them in the shape of "Conservative" representatives, we shall be greatly disappointed'.[108] With legislation now definitively off the table, attention focused on the electoral contests across the island, and most importantly, in Down.

The government was initially optimistic about making electoral gains in Ireland given the travails of Whiggery in the wake of the Famine and Ecclesiastical Titles crisis. However the Conservatives proceeded to alienate Irish Catholic opinion through issuing a viceregal proclamation reminding them that it remained illegal for Catholics to perform their religious ceremonies in public, followed by their perceived failure to prevent an anti-Catholic pogrom in Stockport in Cheshire that was triggered by a religious procession in June.[109] These issues would stimulate electoral support for candidates associated with the Catholic Defence Association, but in the north-eastern counties were subordinated to a more class-based political confrontation over agrarian reform.

'A battle like Waterloo': The County Down Election of 1852

Two developments gave initial hope to Crawford and his supporters that the 1852 contest in Down would prove a more serious challenge than those of 1830 and 1831. The first was the enactment of the Irish Franchise Act of 1850, which went some way to addressing the problem of the highly constricted county electorates. Extensive depopulation and depressed incomes had combined to slash the size of the already small electorates during the Famine. The new legislation rationalised the contentious registration system and brought in a new qualification based on the occupation of property to a poor law valuation of £12 for counties, with some simple tax and residence criteria. The new electorate of around 135,000 in the counties and 28,000 in the boroughs was smaller than some had forecast, but was still a substantial increase on pre-Famine levels.[110] Hoppen calculates that forty-nine per cent of the new county electorate in Down was comprised of tenants with a poor-law valuation of £12 to £20, opening the right to vote to middling farmers and raising the electorate to 10,690 (the second largest of all Irish counties), although still excluding the rural majority of small farmers and agricultural labourers.[111] Although a religious breakdown of the electorate is not available, it is likely that the remaining property qualification underweighted the Presbyterians and more especially the Catholics (who accounted for 45 per cent and 32 per cent respectively of the county's population in 1861).[112] Nevertheless, the Tenant League welcomed the franchise reform as opening the way to potential political gains.[113]

The second development was an incipient civil war within the landed camp in the county. The sitting MP Lord Castlereagh's recent shift towards supporting some form of tenant-right legislation had angered his father, the elderly third Marquess of Londonderry, whose antagonism towards the assertive land-reform agitation on his own estates had hardened even while he made some concessions on rent abatements in an attempt to curb it.[114] Castlereagh's Peelite support for free trade and the Maynooth grant had also alienated many of the county gentry, who hoped that a new Protectionist administration would restore the corn laws and take a more robust anti-Catholic line, and who clearly preferred a more uncompromising Conservative candidate to rally around.[115] Considering his position untenable, Castlereagh informed his father that he would not seek re-election, a move welcomed by the *News-Letter*, which was sure that as a 'pro-Popery' candidate he would have been sure to lose.[116] He announced his retirement publicly on 24 February, although the liberal press remained hopeful he could be persuaded to reconsider and run as a popular candidate, and Castlereagh kept this option open as late as April.[117]

Londonderry responded angrily to his son's apparent abandonment of his duty in thus throwing up the 'family seat' in the commons, which he observed had cost the Stewarts £80,000.[118] Turning to his eldest nephew David Stewart Ker, himself a substantial landowner with estates at Portavo in north Down, at Montalto near Ballynahinch (Lord Moira's old estate) and around Downpatrick, and who had previously been MP for Downpatrick, Londonderry offered him the support of his interest, access to his poll-books and financial resources if Ker agreed to come in for the county on his uncle's terms. Together, he told Ker, 'we could defy Sharman Crawford, his subscriptions, and the League'.[119] What followed was hotly contested and later fought out through leaks of correspondence to the press with self-justifying annotations.[120] Londonderry believed (with some justification) that Ker had undertaken to stand as the Mount Stewart candidate, and not 'on his own bottom', but it soon became clear that Ker felt he had made no such commitment and that he was free to run as an 'independent' Conservative, and rejected all calls to stand aside.[121] Ker clearly believed the moment was opportune to break with the established aristocratic order and build his own power-base in the county.[122] By late February he had already canvassed most of the county landowners and was confident they would support his 'Protestant and Conservative principles' and unite behind him against the common threat posed by Crawford and the League.[123]

Londonderry's intense rage over what he saw as Ker's treason, and his irritation with Downshire's evident reluctance to rule out co-operation with a candidate who had acquired a substantial gentry following, led him to propose his own man to run against both Ker and if necessary Downshire's candidate (his brother Lord Edwin Hill).[124] This alarmed many in the landed interest. Londonderry's agent John Andrews thought that, while the League was weaker in the county than in 1849, without a restoration of the old junction the candidacy of a 'high protectionist Orange candidate' such as Ker would upset the equilibrium.[125] Crawford had not yet committed himself, but in response to Londonderry he made clear that he would allow his name to go forward for the county if the tenant farmers demanded it and Castlereagh was not a candidate:

> I have heard by public rumour [...] that a movement was going on among the tenant farmers with a view to returning me for the Co. of Down at the next general election. This is all I know upon the subject and all I can say to you is this – I am determined that I will not offer myself or seek a return either for the constituency I now represent, for the County Down, or for any other constituency in the United Kingdom – or enter into any contest or pay one farthing towards any contest to promote my own return, or that of any member of my family. But I do not go to the length of pledging myself to say that circumstances might not occur which would render it my duty to serve if returned. [...] This would depend upon the state of the tenant right question for the advocacy of which till it be settled I will not shrink so long as I have bodily health and strength to perform any service in the cause.[126]

His positive response to a requisition from a tenant association in Newtownards in mid-April finally confirmed his candidacy and eliminated the vain hope of some in the landed camp that a clash might be avoided.[127]

Londonderry now pressed his cousin, John Vandeleur Stewart, to stand in the family interest. Stewart, a small proprietor in Donegal, was loyal to his family's head but evidently reluctant to take on what he quickly saw was an unwinnable contest as an aristocratic 'nominee' that could damage the family's standing in the county for years to come.[128] Other proprietors urged a compromise, but Londonderry doubled down on running his candidate to maintain his family honour and committed £10,000 to support a contest.[129] Downshire's decision to ensure the election of his brother by instructing his tenants to plump for Lord Edwin, while reserving a decision on transferring surplus votes until it was clear which of the other Conservatives was stronger, further infuriated Londonderry, who ranted that 'surely the county Down gentlemen could never suppose me capable of eating dirt to such an extent as now to slink away under the base hypocrisy of a treacherous nephew and the timidity of a certain number of most kind people, who, believe me, in their wishes to save themselves from Sharman Crawford are combining for their own suicide'.[130] He persuaded himself that Downshire was intent on reasserting a Hillsborough monopoly in the county by attaching Ker 'to the Downshire chariot'.[131] Londonderry's intemperate defence of what he regarded as his aristocratic entitlement now threatened a complete breakdown of concord within the landed camp, with the magnates exchanging antagonistic letters.[132]

While he remained personally loyal, Stewart alerted his cousin to the failure of his own canvass and the real reasons why landowners were rallying to Ker, despite his moral failings: the dread of Crawford's success and with it the security of landed property. He warned Londonderry off considering any dalliance with Crawford as a means of spiting his county rivals, as this would be both personally offensive and politically disastrous for the family interest.[133] Worried that the split might damage Conservative prospects nationally, lord lieutenant Eglinton offered to arbitrate, but to no avail.[134] Attempts by Londonderry's sister and David's mother, Selina Ker to patch up family relations were equally fruitless.[135]

In the end, however, a mixture of sustained pressure and flattering inducements by a body of Tory country gentlemen marshalled by Robert Bateson and J.W. Maxwell, combined with Stewart's pessimism, induced Londonderry reluctantly to back down. Preoccupation with eliciting a form of words soothing to his pride, and insistence on promises of future support for a Mount Stewart candidate, led the peer to drag out the drama until early June.[136] At that point he finally withdrew Stewart and instructed his tenants to plump for Hill. Maxwell, on behalf of most landowners in the county, expressed relief that, even at this late stage, the most acute danger had been averted: 'Our position is bettered, and I hope will ensure our success, but Sharman is strong without money. All our efforts must be energetically directed to secure his defeat'.[137] While Stewart's withdrawal was regarded by both the League's supporters and detractors in the press as a serious setback to its hopes in Down, the battle was still far from over.[138]

Landed anxiety was enhanced by Ker's own erratic behaviour. A manifesto in March distanced himself from protectionism and hinted at some 'moderate' tenant-right measure.[139] Bateson feared that Ker was now 'in the hands of a radical clique who are favourable to Sharman' and that his supporters might give their second votes to Crawford and thus allow 'that hypocritical old sinner' to be returned.[140] Downshire himself started to express concern for his brother if Ker could not be induced to co-operate.[141] The Londonderry camp voiced some cynical satisfaction, and concluded that he and Ker would share the blame if Crawford was successful.[142] However, under sustained pressure from the county gentry, which came 'to the rescue of the Conservative candidates from themselves', and belatedly recognising the real threat posed by the League to his ambitions, Ker eventually moved to a formal coalition with the Hill interest by early July. There were some concerns that the reconciliation had come too late, but it was clear that by the hustings the Conservative civil war had been suspended and the League would face a relatively united front.[143]

The tenant-right activists approached the Down contest with optimism and high levels of commitment. They were as conscious as their landed opponents that any serious challenge would require Crawford to stand, as his personal popularity alone was likely to offset the suspicions some Protestant tenant-farmers might have of the Dublin-based League and its allies in the Catholic Defence Association.[144] Subscriptions were soon being raised from the tenants to support a Crawford campaign, while middle-class radicals were encouraged to join them through appeals to popular memory; one elector urged them to abandon idle pursuits as 'would such have been the conduct of your Volunteer and United fathers, with their motto "the people, the source of all power?"'.[145] In north Down the League had already flexed its muscles in replacing a land agent with an 'honest League man' at the previous poor law guardian elections, and was confident by February that four-fifths of the electors in the parish of Donaghadee were already pledged to Crawford. Political meetings continued throughout the spring in the county, connecting the petitioning campaign in support of

Crawford's bill to preparations for an electoral crusade behind him.[146] Presbyterian clergy, most prominently Julius McCullough of Newtownards and John Rogers, were active at these meetings, joined on occasion by Catholic clergymen and by League activists such as McKnight. The latter reiterated the case that the bill would bring social equity, and assured an enthusiastic crowd at Portaferry that if they acted unanimously it was 'impossible [...] for landlords to exterminate a whole public.[147]

Such was the level of political activity that Andrews feared that 'under the influence of excitement and agitation the tenants generally may prove much less manageable than in former times', as the tactics of 1830–1 were now redundant, and believed that the tenants had been turned by the 'quiet instigation of tenant-right committees'.[148] Andrews was certain that behind the scenes Crawford was already 'advising them by what means [...] they can contest the county at a very trifling expense, which, no doubt, under the new act will be perfectly within their power'.[149]

The introduction of Stewart into the electoral mix further antagonised the tenant movement. The radical press denounced him as a reactionary bigot, strongly opposed to tenant right and a petty tyrant on his own Donegal estate, charges which he denied as malicious.[150] The publication of Londonderry's leaked letter asserting his entitlement to a 'family seat' merely added fuel to the fire.[151] One landed supporter welcomed Stewart's strong Protestantism, but worried that the 'extension of Sharman Crawford's communist principles amongst tenant farmers in this neighbourhood' had negated his own influence over them.[152] With feeling running as high as the rhetorical register suggests, and landowners raising a 'bribery fund', plans were laid by the League for a 'defensive system' to protect tenant electors from any financial or tenurial retribution.[153] It was clear that the landed interest's resources far exceeded those of the tenant movement, which had apparently budgeted the modest sum of £800 for electoral expenses, looking to popular enthusiasm and moral force to make up what it lacked in financial clout.[154]

A tenant-right committee chaired by William Girdwood was established at the Plough Hotel in Belfast in early April to manage Crawford's campaign, supported by a finance committee including Guy Stone.[155] Girdwood warned electors against false claims by landlord candidates of support for some form of tenant right, and urged them to vote for Crawford alone.[156] At least in the northern part of the county, parochial bodies were active, with reports of parties from Newtownards daily canvassing the farmers, and relaying positive accounts to the central committee on their returns.[157] Andrews could not help expressing admiration of their achievements.[158] By late June the *Whig* expressed confidence that tenants would now stand up to any attempts at coercion from estate offices and Crawford would come top of the poll by a large majority.[159]

Returning from London during a break in the session, Crawford himself appeared at a rally at Kilkeel at the start of June attended by some 3,000, including, it was reported, a number of Orangemen. After an enthusiastic reception, he re-emphasised the benefits his bill would bring to the tenant farmers, and its interrelationship with freedom of election; the allegation of communism was, he insisted, a nonsense, as he proposed merely the securing of the 'just rights' of both tenant and landlord to that property that was rightfully theirs, and no more. But his speech also gave significant attention to the plight of poorer non-electors, recalling the sufferings of famine, which had 'carried away' one in ten of the population, a depopulation still at work through clearances and emigration. The solution to the ongoing crisis lay in securing the tenant right and fair rents that would give security to the tenant farmer at home and encourage employment of labour, but also (and equally importantly), in the defence of the free trade that would ensure cheap food for the labouring poor.[160]

This latter theme acquired some popular resonance during the campaign. Barney Hughes, the leading Catholic liberal entrepreneur of Belfast, and other bakers supplied the Crawford camp with 'outsized loaves' for public display and these were paraded through localities in the county. At Gilford:

> [a] number of electors and friends of Mr Sharman Crawford procured a large loaf, weighing about twenty pounds, and having placed it on the top of a pole proceeded through the townlands of Clare, Ballydugan, and Bleary, passing in their route by Shane-hill, and finally returned to Gilford. The assembled multitude, numbering 5,000, at the very lowest calculation, proceeded in a body through the streets of the village, cheering vociferously for Sharman Crawford, tenant right and free trade, and expressing in no measured terms their hostility to Hill, Stewart and Ker.[161]

It is difficult to assess Crawford's appeal to the non-electors, although Tory papers criticised him for attracting only the support of weavers and not substantial tenants, and it was reported that in the industrial villages of Donaghcloney and Tullylish the weavers and labourers were threatening larger tenants with dire consequences if they voted against him.[162] This area on the border of Down and Armagh had a long tradition of popular radicalism, witnessing manifestations under the label of 'Tommy Downshire's Boys' of non-sectarian collective action by small farmers and weavers to protect their economic interests from landlords, linen-masters, tithe proctors and poor-law guardians between 1829 and 1847, with some success.[163] Certainly his supporters deployed bitter memories of famine sufferings in their attacks on the landlords, albeit within a construction that equated the interests of the tenants with those of the wider rural population: Rev. John McCreedy asked at Boardmills, 'If the landlords were the real friends of the people, why were homesteads deserted and whole districts depopulated?'.[164]

Crawford himself appeared at later rallies as the poll approached, again stressing the need for political reforms such as the ballot and highlighting that his bill was the minimum land reform needed, and by no means intended as a final solution.[165] These appear to have been well attended; Stone, who praised Crawford's 'very good and moderate' speech at Newtownards, privately estimated the open-air crowd there at around 2,000.[166]

As was anticipated, the Orange Order sought to mobilise its strength against Crawford and the League. William Johnston of Ballykilbeg, emerging as the dominant personality in the movement post-1849, ensured that the subject was central at the County Grand Lodge meeting in late April and that it resolved to use 'every exertion' to return Hill and Ker.[167] Concerned by evidence that some Orange tenant farmers were being attracted to Crawford's rallies (a strategy again actively pursued by McKnight), the County Grand Master felt it necessary to write to all lodges warning them against communism and insisting on support for the Tory candidates, while its allied press claimed that McKnight had equated Orangemen with Ribbonmen.[168] Orangemen were active in canvassing for Hill and Ker and generating anti-Crawford propaganda, as well as exerting more direct forms of electoral pressure at the polls.[169]

The regional Tory press, principally the *News-Letter, Newry Telegraph* and *Downpatrick Recorder,* took up the crusade against Crawford, combining personal vituperation and overt sectarianism with attempts to undermine the unity of the tenant-right movement. A number of potential points of weakness were exploited to rally Tory support. The open electoral alliance between the League and the Catholic Defence Association clearly unsettled some of the former's northern supporters and was seized on by its enemies as evidence that the League was merely a 'popish' front and its Protestant adherents either dupes or traitors to religious truth. A correspondent in the *Telegraph* insisted that Crawford had ever been the ally of papists and 'infidel levelling democrats'.[170] Crawford was also pilloried for his overt opposition to the regium donum, against which he had again voted in 1852. To the *News-Letter* this was evidence of his antagonism towards true Presbyterian interests and perhaps also of an underlying infidelity or crypto-papism.[171] This was an issue that threw the orthodox Presbyterian *Banner* onto the defensive; it responded by representing the Tory candidates as defenders of an oppressive 'prelatical' establishment. It was clear however that the majority of Presbyterian clergy remained in the Crawford camp, despite condemnations of incendiary 'clerical agitators' and the interventions of Montgomery and Cooke on the Conservative side.[172] Indeed the radical clergy produced a pamphlet attacking both men as traitors to the tenant farmers and for seeking to 'curry favour with their task-masters' in the landed elite.[173] Allegations were made that Crawford did not fully support his own bill; these were more easily dismissed, but the liberal press felt it necessary to distance the campaign from the League, denying (rather implausibly) the northern tenant-right movement's direct connections with that body.[174]

Printed squibs and satires appear less common than in previous county elections, but were not entirely absent, with one circulated that combined alarmism about Ribbonism with recyclings of older tropes of personal mockery dating back to 1830. Parodying Moore's 'Meeting of the Waters', it had Crawford versify that:

> There is not in this world a prospect so sweet
> As the place where the Leaguers and Ribbonmen meet,
> Oh, the last crystal drop from my nose shall depart,
> Ere the days of those meetings shall fade from my heart.[175]

The Tenant League also had its own songs, which it was alleged the Ker camp was seeking to subvert by interpolating verses sympathetic to their own candidate.[176] A version of Burn's *Scots wha' hae* was recited by Crawford's supporters at Boardmills to raise morale:

> Now's the day and now's the hour,
> See the clouds of serfdom lour,
> See approach coercive power,
>   Threats and slavery.

> By ejectments, woes, and pains,
> By our desolated plains,
> By the blood of Irish veins,
>   Let's swear we shall be free.

> Lay the Derby faction low —
> Trade and tenant-right's the go —
> Every vote's a killing blow —
>   Let us do or die.[177]

Another punning ballad published under the title 'Begone Dull Ker' sought to inspire confidence in the strength of numbers and warned he would 'filch the *big loaf* away'.[178] Posters were circulated urging electors to 'Be men!! [...] Show the government you are determined to be treated no longer by the landlords like Russian serfs'.[179] Both sides thus sought to utilise elements of popular culture to propagate their political messages.

Agents, bailiffs and in some cases landlords in person toured their estates to counter the League's canvassers, reportedly issuing veiled threats against dissident tenants; Richard Blakiston-Houston confided that 'Last week I was round all my tenants, and I think I shall be able to poll almost all for Lord Edwin Hill and Ker. The five Catholics I have will not vote at all. About seven will vote for Sharman Crawford and Ker, but I think when the day comes most of the seven will be taken suddenly ill'.[180] It was alleged in the press that the agents and bailiffs on Londonderry's estates were also making intimidatory threats, perhaps without the landlord's knowledge, and that smaller landowners were also doing so more openly.[181] A pro-Crawford elector from Iveagh complained that 'no-one who has not a lease on all the Downshire estates has dared to refuse' the command to vote for 'this young nincompoop, Hill'.[182]

The *Dublin Evening Post* discerned a move by landowners to crush the 'rebellious spirit' of the tenantry through a resort to 'terrorism', although this was strenuously denied by the proprietors and their allied press.[183] The *Whig* reported that Lord Ranfurly's tenants had been warned by agents of the consequences of voting for Crawford, and Lord Annesley's agent Shaw had written to his tenants, 'On your own heads be the consequences if you spurn my advice' to vote for Ker and Hill.[184] It was later alleged by John Bright that he was aware of 'cases in which [...] tenants were visited with every description of harassing annoyance which the landlord and agent could possibly bring on them'.[185]

As Hoppen has observed, given the large number of non-contractual concessions permitted to tenants by landlords that were subject to arbitrary withdrawal, and the toleration of rent arrears through the 'hanging gale' system, voting against the proprietor's wishes could cost a tenant heavily, even if not always pursued to actual ejectment.[186] An 'Association for the Protection of the Elective Franchise' was set up by Crawford's supporters to offer financial and legal support to any electors subjected to retribution, but its resources were limited as by mid-July it had only twenty-nine subscribers, who had pledged £2000.[187] A handbill was circulated, ostensibly written by a former supporter of Crawford now critical of his 'impracticability' and association with the League, warning his voters not to be deceived by the claims of the Protection Society. Beneath a veneer of friendly advice, the warning of the consequences of defying the landlords was stark: 'Tenant farmers, do you think the Protection Society will give you either the indemnity or the cash [for arrears]? NOT THEY INDEED! Beware, then! Beware! Look in time to yourselves, your wives and children (Figure 26).'[188]

Neither the Protective Association nor Girdwood's committee could compete with the 'enormous sum' expended by the landed camp, which Andrews estimated at seven to eight thousand pounds each by Hill and Ker.[189] Hill's camp had quickly re-employed the election agents and canvassers released on Stewart's withdrawal at considerable expense and deployed this personnel both before and during the polling.[190] Observers believed this counter-campaign was having a toll on likely voters, and that 'the supporters of Mr Sharman Crawford are somewhat less confident of their ability to cope with the formidable organisation of the Orange and Protestant party on behalf of Lord E. Hill and Mr Ker', and that, as Andrews came to think by early July, there would be 'a shrinking and falling back, and that he will be left in the lurch as he was in 1831'.[191] Crawford's committee privately acknowledged on 16 July that there was 'no certainty of success', but decided they must press on with the nomination and poll.[192] The stage was now set for an electoral contest that the *Newry Telegraph* proclaimed would be politically decisive: 'a battle like Waterloo'.[193]

Despite growing tensions, the Down campaign had been relatively peaceful, but this was not to last. On 3 July the local magistrates banned a tenant-right meeting at Waringstown after some 10,000 people had reportedly assembled, on the grounds that it would be the site of violent clashes between opposing parties. The claim was rejected as fictitious by the radical press, which countered that the Tory magistrates had been alarmed by the number of Orangemen attracted to the meeting in support of Crawford.[194] A few days later Crawford's platform at Dromara was physically attacked by a drunken crowd of 'bludgeon men', forcing the sudden cancellation of another rally to avoid a full-scale riot. Girdwood linked the mob to the Tory candidates and alleged Ker's gamekeeper had been directly involved in organising it.[195] The near coincidence of the election with the 'marching season' further raised the temperature and may have drawn many Orangemen back to their traditional political loyalties. In Newtownards, an illegal Orange march by around a thousand on the 12th was followed by a sectarian riot, with the tearing down of an arch erected by Catholic 'Greensmen' accompanied by cries of 'to h— with Sharman Crawford and the Pope'.[196] There were also riots in Belfast (where the Conservative candidates had already triumphed at the polls) and it appears that revived Orange activity in other parts of the county was provoking a counter-reaction from the Ribbon lodges, which had been quiet in the preceding months, and which the *News-Letter* now charged with acts of political terrorism and intimidation in support of Crawford.[197]

Open conflict spilled out at the county nomination day on 19 July at Downpatrick, with mobs from each side violently engaged in a 'sanguinary encounter'. Newspaper accounts are partisan and conflicting, but it appears that there was an intense and violent struggle for physical control of the court house, initially occupied (with what appeared to be magisterial connivance) by a Tory crowd led by the butcher Tommy Hughes, 'so notorious in electioneering and party conflicts in Downpatrick', who were then ejected with much force by a larger pro-Crawford mob, many drawn from the Dromara district and seeking revenge for the attack there. An Orange counter-assault saw the smashing of the court-house windows by a volley of stones and the flooring by a missile of the former Presbyterian moderator Rev. John Coulter, who was present to nominate Crawford. The crowd within voiced exuberant enthusiasm for the candidate, as '[f]oremost among the "boys" was a young fellow who supported a placard upon a pole, and a remarkably overgrown loaf surmounted with a bouquet of roses. On the placard were the words "Crawford, and the big loaf – tenant-right and no surrender"'.

At the same time the resort to violence and disruption of proceedings was an embarrassment and forced the tenant-right leadership (including Girdwood and Crawford's sons) to remonstrate with their supporters for the restoration of order and allow 'fair play'. Although there was evident support for the declaration of one pro-Crawford rioter that 'the peasant and the peer are equal here today', after an adjournment proceedings were allowed to continue and the three candidates finally nominated.[198] However, despite the deployment of the military to keep order, rioting broke out again later in the day as the crowds dispersed, in what the *Banner* interpreted as an attempt by Ker and Hill to use mercenary elements to provoke a 'war of classes'.[199]

This affray was soon overshadowed by the yet more extensive violence and open intimidation displayed on the polling days of 22–23 July. For the first time the county was divided into four polling districts, centred on the towns of Newtownards, Hillsborough, Downpatrick and Newry. It was soon evident that each would see a struggle for control of the polls and hence the ability to vote, with the outcome determined by the relative strength of local factions and the deployment of police and military forces. At Newtownards, where the Crawford camp was strongest and thoroughly organised, the appearance of what Andrews described as 'a large Hill and Ker bludgeon mob' was insufficient to prevent heavy polling with police and military protection, with over three-quarters of the registered electors having voted by the afternoon of the first day, leaving Crawford over 400 votes ahead in the district (Figure 27).[200] Nevertheless, the actions of the anti-Crawford crowd, described variously as comprising a 'low episcopalian mob from Belfast', as employees of Ker brought across the lough by boat to disrupt the election, and as local Orangemen, drew widespread anger. An attack on Crawford's committee rooms, and on a Presbyterian minister, only seen off following the brandishing of a borrowed pistol by the reverend gentleman, added to the sense of outrage.[201] Several members of the 'bludgeon mob' were later found guilty of riot and assault at the next assizes, despite having denied shouting 'to h__l with Sharman Crawford and the *big* loaf'.[202]

In Hillsborough and Downpatrick the anti-Crawford mobs had the upper hand from the start of polling, with the alleged connivance of magistrates drawn from the Hill and Ker estates respectively, and reports that they were 'treated' at the Tory candidates' expense. The *Banner* stated that 'terrorism and mob-outrage' had been evident in the county town, with between twelve and fourteen 'nearly murdered by the gentry's paid assassins' (later reports gave two killed), and with Crawford voters, distinguishable by their display of white ribbons, subjected to assault and intimidation at polling booths, making it virtually impossible for many of them to cast their votes, A crowd of some 5,000 of his supporters from the heavily Catholic Castlewellan and Loughinisland districts had to be dissuaded from attempting to enter the town.[203] Even those voters who made it through the fracas to the booths could find themselves frustrated by the absence of unbiased officials:

> at one of the polling places no less than a hundred and ten electors, who came in to vote for Sharman Crawford, resisting all landlord influence, and defying all landlord intimidation, were unable to record their votes at all, owing to the want or proper agents or assistants to bring them up to the booths, from any approach to which they were deterred by the savage threats of the infuriated mobs in the interests of the Tories, who would allow no voter to approach unless accompanied by someone known to them to be in the interest of Lord Edwin Hill or Mr Ker. So complete was the organization on that side, that in so many of the booths there were half a

dozen professional agents, poll-clerks, tally clerks, and 'whippers in,' to the *one* competent or authorized person in the interest of Mr Crawford. Hence it is easy to understand the result.[204]

The *News-Letter* responded with claims that 'the approaches to Hillsborough were infested by League desperadoes' who had attacked convoys of cars bringing Hill and Ker voters to the poll, and it seems unquestionable that such counter-violence was manifest, even if it seems on a much smaller scale and to much less effect than in the polling towns.[205] Both appear to have been undersupplied with official forces: ninety-one soldiers and forty-five constables were deployed at Downpatrick, ninety-eight and fifty respectively at Hillsborough – both significantly fewer than at Newtownards and Newry and a fraction of the manpower available during the earlier borough elections at Downpatrick and Newry – and they evidently struggled to maintain public order.[206] Girdwood was certain that the military at Downpatrick had acted in a discriminatory fashion against Crawford voters.[207]

At Newry, where Crawford had been expected to prevail in a district with a significant number of Catholic electors, violence was also witnessed. According to the *News-Letter*:

> A short time before the opening of the booths, a body of men, not fewer in number than 800, advanced into the town by the north road, with several priests at their head. Every one of them was armed with a strong bludgeon, no doubt with the intention of re-enacting the drama performed on Monday at Downpatrick. On their arriving opposite to the court-house, they apparently purposed to take possession of the booths, and were rushing up, with cheers for 'Sheerman', when under the orders of Mr Warburton, RM, a troop of horse charged into their midst, whilst the constabulary, a large body of whom were drawn up around the court-house, dashed in and disarmed every one of the League bravoes of their bludgeons; and upon searching them […] pistols and abundant ammunition, with bayonets and other deadly weapons, were found secreted upon the persons of many, who were immediately handcuffed and taken into custody. The polling then proceeded peaceably for the first hour, and, in consequence of the League party having gained and kept possession of the booths, the voting was in favour of Mr Crawford, who, at two o'clock, was some forty ahead. In the mean time, the excellent resident magistrate issued [a] notice, which seemed to produce a sensible effect upon the League rabble.[208]

With order restored by the RM with threats of mass transportation, it was reported that large batches of tenant voters were now brought to the booths to vote as directed by their land agents, and in the end Crawford was outvoted here, as in Hillsborough and Downpatrick.[209] Overall it was estimated that at least 2,000 registered county voters did not cast their ballots, and strongly implied in the press that these were mostly Crawford supporters frightened off by intimidation or by threatened sanctions.[210] Of those who did vote, the surviving poll books for certain districts indicate that some seventy-three per cent of Presbyterians voted for the Tory ticket (only slightly behind the figure for Anglicans but well in advance of that for Catholics), indicating the failure of the majority of pro-Crawford Presbyterian clergy to retain control of their flocks in the face of landed pressure and violence, and the counter-appeals to pan-Protestant unity voiced by Cooke and his allies.[211] However, Crawford's clear victory in the heavily Presbyterian Newtownards district (covering the baronies of Upper and Lower Ards and Lower Castlereagh) would have somewhat offset this figure for county as a whole had it been included.

In these circumstances, the electoral outcome was predictable. Despite winning by around two to one in the Newtownards district, the Crawford voters were overwhelmed in the other three districts and he ended with 3,133 votes, to Ker's 4,117 and Hill's 4,654.[212] An analysis by Girdwood indicated that an unusually high proportion of voters, some 2,500, had plumped for Crawford, as opposed to only 670 for other candidates, indicating an acute degree of partisan polarisation.[213]

The *News-Letter* triumphantly proclaimed the victory of loyalism, as 'the vast bulk of the electors preserved themselves untainted by the Popish 'tang', and the socialist fever'.[214] The *Newry Telegraph* 'thank[ed] GOD that in this Thermopylae, the County of Down, "The Protestant Boys HAVE CARRIED THE DAY."'[215] The formal announcement of victory and Ker's speech was cheered by an Orange mob led by Tommy Hughes in Downpatrick, who was reported to have shouted 'who fears to speak of '98?'.[216] The liberal *Belfast Mercury* blamed the excesses of League agitators for provoking a counter-productive proprietarian reaction and hence denying Crawford the seat, while also asserting that it had not 'the slightest doubt [...] that if the electors were to give their votes according to their feelings, Mr Crawford would head the poll, at a long interval'.[217] To the *Vindicator* the outcome reflected mobilised sectarianism: 'Religious feeling has done more for Hill and Ker than landlord intimidation in many districts. That blind Orange rancour which has so often interfered, and by exciting vile passions, resuscitated old prejudices, and erecting class against class, has turned the people from the contemplation of their true interests, to indulge in party hatred, has contributed its portion to Mr Crawford's defeat.'[218]

Crawford's own interpretation for the defeat came in an address 'to the friends of tenant right' published on 27 July. The exertion of aristocratic power in the county had, he wrote, left 'the chains of feudal despotism still clank[ing] around' the electors' necks. A landlord league had stifled the free voice of the people through 'the reckless application of coercion, intimidation, and unlawful violence in every possible form'. With some honourable exceptions (such as Dufferin), the proprietors had acted illegally, unconstitutionally and immorally, compelling their tenantry to act against their own interests and consciences, as well as:

> Stimulating the worst passions of infuriated mobs, collected together from distant parts to serve their purposes, and to coerce and intimidate by the terror of the bludgeon those whose principle of honour and virtue were proof against their threats and their promises; and by the collection of these riotous mobs, provoking in some cases a defensive retaliation, impossible to be repressed on the other side by those desirous to protect life and preserve order. When the minds of the lower classes are thus corrupted and depraved by such conduct, emanating from their superiors in rank and authority, who ought to set before them examples of virtue and order, on those men who so act will justly rest the responsibility for the crimes of the people.

Crawford went on to praise the 'noble band' of voters who had defied such intimidation while expressing sympathy with those who had lacked the courage or opportunity to resist such odds. The underlying problem lay, he concluded, with the despotic power in the landlords' hands to annihilate the value of a farmer's tenant right if they so chose, unless and until this was accorded legal protection, but he urged his supporters not to despair, for victory would ultimately be theirs.[219]

If there was any question as to whether Crawford would slip quietly into political retirement, it was dispelled by his decision to follow up the address by appearing at a League dinner at Newtownards on 30 August. Despite attempts by Stone and his own sons to dissuade him from participating in an event which would be regarded as further provocation by the landed interest, Crawford persevered, ignoring warnings from Londonderry that to proceed might lead to 'riot, confusion and bloodshed' as well as punishment of those tenants who might attend.[220] A threatened legal suit against him by the Down proprietors stiffened his resolve, but he denied that any personal disrespect to Londonderry was intended in holding the meeting at a polling town where the bulk of his supporters had voted.[221] In the end the dinner proceeded without disturbance and was attended by upwards of 700 people beneath banners celebrating 'The 3,155 honourable and independent electors of the County Down. – Union is strength. – Perseverance'. It was attended by national leaders of the Tenant League, a number of liberal Belfast industrial and civic figures and a delegation from Rochdale, headed by Livsey (with letters of apology read from Cobden and Bright). Numerous speakers, including Crawford himself, claimed a moral victory which had been denied to the people by 'feudal power'. In response to the testimonial, Crawford attributed his political values to his father and urged others to take forward the campaigns to which he had devoted his political life and which alone would bring social peace and justice for tenant and landlord alike. He affirmed he would stand over the assertions made in his address concerning the 'tyrannical thraldom' imposed on electors by a portion of the aristocracy, which was both immoral and unconstitutional. He added that, while prepared to acknowledge any landowner who had refrained from undue influence, he would not retract his charges against them as a group and was prepared to present evidence in court that would vindicate him.[222]

Downshire was certain that Crawford had been backed by 'the Chartist League in Manchester' and that his ruin must be pursued in the interests of maintaining property rights:

> He distinctly charges our party with having gained the election by intimidation and those who signed that document with carrying the bludgeon war out, and reserving to him and his party all the [...] self denial that does not belong even to their nature. No man ever did sit down to write or did write so cool and deliberate a lie as he did on that occasion, and he must take the consequences [...]. And as for kicking a man when down, I never did it, but if that is the true version of it, the sooner we begin the better! I will not for one attempt to dissuade one person from carrying out his action. His is an impudent and barefaced, though underhand, mode of bringing the north, the Tories, and property into disrepute [...] This old man, blundering as he is, is deeper than we give him credit for, and though he is beaten he must be silenced from lying, and his teeth drawn, and the way to do it is to prove him as he is a liar, or to make him confess it.[223]

However it was a group of eleven smaller county proprietors, led by Bateson and Maxwell, who drew up and proceeded with the legal action on the grounds that Crawford's comments amounted to slanderous personal accusations against them as individuals.[224] Londonderry and some other proprietors thought this was counter-productive and unlikely to succeed, and Maxwell himself had to admit that if there were landlords who had acted 'imprudently' they would need to be kept out of the witness box.[225] Deferential tenant loyalty to free-spending, paternalistic landowners (including both Ker and Downshire) was undoubtedly a factor in the election, but the risks of drawing judicial attention to the wide range of less savoury methods of electoral control were high.[226] Seeing the action as a distraction, and wary of subjecting vulnerable tenant witnesses to cross-examination in court, Crawford agreed with his son James a form of words that affirmed that his charges were against the system of landlord intimidation in general rather than individually against the complainants.[227] After several months this action was called off when the landlords accepted this 'explanation', without the further retraction and apology demanded, albeit at significant expense to Crawford in legal fees, and with both sides claiming vindication.[228]

A petition against the return of Ker and Hill was lodged by the merchant James Boyle of Rostrevor on grounds of 'gross, extensive, systematic, and open and notorious bribery, treating and corruption', but was withdrawn, allegedly due to lack of interest by the Whig party's political agent in pursuing it in parliament.[229] With the cost of election petition trials for counties running at an average of £2,500, this was beyond the already overstretched resources of Crawfordsburn and its allies.[230] Retribution against tenant electors who had voted for Crawford appears to have been real enough, and on the Londonderry estate 'very considerable terror' was imposed by the imposition of ejectments and processes for arrears on those had defied the proprietor's instructions. Seventy tenants who were in arrears were ordered to pay in full within two months, or face distresses or ejectments.[231] On his relative Alexander Stewart's property, reports of punishment of Crawford plumpers through the withdrawal of a fifteen per cent rent abatement led the *Londonderry Standard* to ask, 'Do they want to drive the people of this province into an agrarian insurrection?'[232] In March 1853 John Malcom of Corcraney wrote to the *Whig* to state that he had been evicted and denied the right to sell his tenant right by Downshire's agent because he had 'exercised the elective franchise according to the dictates of my conscience, and gave a *plumper* for the honest, upright and independent tenant-right candidate William Sharman Crawford'. Malcom claimed he had been thrown into arrears by the destructive effects of the famine and that the full arrears had been demanded for payment while Conservative voters were permitted to continue holding over, although his claim was denied by Downshire's agent, who dismissed him as a drunkard who had allowed his holding to deteriorate.[233]

For many supporters of Crawford, the 1852 contest was remembered as a heroic defeat, and recollections of it were long treasured. As late as 1900 a ballad composed shortly after the poll was still circulating, and was published as a reminder that Crawford's campaign had been a popular crusade and remained relevant half a century on:

> Before the election the county together
> Resolved for their rights to firmly stand;
> And all pull together like brother and brother,
> Against landlord oppression, the curse of the land.
>
> And elect Sharman Crawford, the pride of the nation,
> Who laboured for years in his country's cause,
> To gain for the farmer his emancipation
> From rack-renting tyrants, dictation and laws.
>
> Then in a short time we will have an election,
> So still to your principles firm remain
> And the boys of Dromara are ready for action,
> And sweep out the courthouse for Crawford again.[234]

As well see, such intense memories which would give rise to a more successful political challenge to landlordism in the county in 1874.

Disintegration and division, 1852–5

Sharman Crawford's defeat in Down was mirrored by that of tenant-right candidates right across the northern province. In Antrim T. H. Jones, belatedly acknowledging the electoral power of the O'Neill and Hertford landed interests, which were actively supported by Henry Cooke, withdrew before the poll.[235] In Tyrone, where Crawford's son William junior had declined to stand, H. B. Higgins' loss was attributed to the stirring of 'no-Popery' sentiment by the sitting Tory MPs, while in Donegal widespread intimidation was blamed for the League's failure.[236] Greer's challenge in Co. Londonderry also fell short, although he was praised for coming only 400 votes behind in a poll of 3,500, thereby ending the era of unchallenged aristocratic nomination.[237] John Gray was defeated in Monaghan, despite Crawford's personal endorsement, due to 'landlord intimidation' of voters and reportedly also to Presbyterian defections.[238] This left only the liberal Presbyterian linen manufacturer William Kirk at Newry as a potential supporter of Crawford's bill elected for an Ulster constituency, although he was reluctant to act with the 'Independents'.[239]

It was small consolation that a number of northern Tory candidates had felt obliged to make some form of commitment to tenant compensation on the hustings to counter the League.[240] McKnight in the *Banner* sought to put the best face on a bad situation in response to implied criticism from the southern nationalist press. The elections were, he asserted, 'a bold, constitutional insurrection of the democratic masses for their own class emancipation'.[241] Nevertheless, it had clearly been demonstrated that the landed proprietors of Ulster, who had weathered the storms of the Famine much better than their southern counterparts, remained a formidable political obstacle to radical success.

This series of setbacks shifted the balance of power within the Tenant League away from the northerners, as the movement had at the same time achieved an impressive number of successes in the south, including the election of Duffy at New Ross, Maguire at Dungarvan and Lucas in Meath. There were growing suspicions about the motives of the latter, who Crawford (and the CDA leadership) had criticised for running as a 'Catholic' candidate against two pledged supporters of tenant right and displacing the Protestant 'independent' MP Henry Grattan junior, but McKnight was still close to Duffy and believed they could together steer the movement forward on non-sectarian, 'Young Ireland', principles.[242]

The marginalisation of the north was not at first fully evident. Crawford retained great personal respect within the movement, and was invited to take the chair of the Tenant League conference which assembled in Dublin in September, and a consolatory dinner was held in his honour.[243] In what was intended as a celebration of his political career, he was lauded by League speakers and in letters read from three Catholic archbishops. In response he again highlighted the personal inspiration of the 'Volunteers of '82', who were represented at the dinner by the venerable John Sinclair, who had joined the movement as a youth of sixteen and was believed to be its last surviving member. Crawford drew attention to his consistency in seeking to end the depopulation of Ireland through measures of social justice, and reversed Tory slanders by depicting himself as the true social conservative, while accusing the landlords of self-destructive 'communism' in pursuing the arbitrary confiscation of the property of others. He placed his faith in the League to pursue the campaign through popular mobilisation in the spirit of non-sectarian unity.[244]

The conference on 8–9 September, attended by the impressive number of forty-one Irish MPs, determined the movement's post-election strategy. After some restiveness on the part of the MPs led by Moore, it reaffirmed that the 'Independents' would remain aloof from any Whig or Tory government that did not make tenant-right legislation on the principles of Crawford's bill a cabinet matter, that they would act as a separate party at Westminster, and that the re-introduction of Crawford's 1852 bill would now be entrusted to William Shee as the new MP for Co. Kilkenny. The campaign would continue to be supported through fund-raising and petitioning meetings in the counties.[245] A few days later Crawford again refuted claims in the hostile *Belfast Mercury* that he was not fully in support of his bill, explaining its evolution and the necessity of adding the 'temporary' clauses to protect small tenants against eviction for famine arrears while they built up their tenant right value. The bill was intended for all of Ireland and not just Ulster, and had the force of national public opinion behind it.[246] At the same time, he continued to insist that it was compatible with free trade as it did not dictate (even if it did incentivise) the adoption of a judicial fair rent, and that this interference was justified on utilitarian grounds.[247] His stance, and that of the League, continued to command significant grass-roots support in Down, perhaps enhanced by the bitterness generated by the electoral contest: popular meetings at Killinchy and Boardmills in October resolved to reignite their agitation behind the bill.[248] Rogers and like-minded Presbyterian clergy remained defiant supporters of the tenant cause in the north, despite their electoral defeat.[249]

This optimistic (if perhaps superficial) unity within the movement held until towards the end of the year, when the focus of attention shifted back to Westminster as a new session opened. The 'Independent Party' at least nominally held the balance of power between the British parties.[250] On behalf of the Derby government Napier brought forward his delayed tenant compensation bill in mid-November along with three other land reform measures to give landlords greater powers over their estates, shortly before Shee reintroduced what remained universally termed 'Sharman Crawford's bill' in the commons.[251] Shee attributed Napier's concession of the principle of retrospective compensation to Crawford's sustained advocacy, while at the same time rejecting the government's bill as inadequate. He paid credit to the self-sacrificing example of his predecessor, who had sought to prevent famine through stimulating agricultural production.[252] Shee's tactic in late 1852 was to get Crawford's and Napier's bills referred together to a select committee, where further evidence might be heard in a less partisan setting, and potentially a measure agreed 'with the best features of each adopted'. Rather to the surprise and irritation of many Irish Conservatives and despite the thundering of the *Times*, the home secretary conceded this point and the bill, for the first time, passed formally through a second reading, to the delight of the pro-League press.[253] Duffy observed that the administration had offered enough concessions for the Independents to induce them to shore it up.[254]

Speaking at a dinner in Derry held in honour of Greer, Crawford endorsed Shee's tactics, as he was certain that any direct comparison with Napier's overly complex compensation bill would highlight the superiority of his own in ensuring a full and fair return of the money and labour laid out by tenants on agricultural improvement.[255] Following up in a public letter on New Year's Day he paid tribute to the distance Napier had travelled, while at the same time criticising his bill as continuing to embody the feudal principle inherent in the idea of 'exhaustion' over time of the value of a tenant's improvements and threatening to undermine the Ulster custom. However, he advised that a degree of pragmatism was now necessary: the movement should not try to hold out for every detail of his own bill, but focus on lobbying for what was achievable through the select committee, so long as this protected a permanent tenant right in actuality, if not necessarily under that name. He thought that the protective clauses added in 1851 remained necessary, but might now best be introduced as a separate bill rather than allowing them to drag down the tenant right bill to another defeat.[256]

This shift towards compromising on what he regarded as details reflected his reading of the limits that agitation had reached in 1852, but would antagonise others in the movement for whom the bill was less a practical object in itself than the shibboleth on which the Independent Party had been forged. For Lucas and Duffy the bill was more a means to the end of re-establishing an independent nationalist (and for Lucas, a Catholic) party, and legislative achievement appeared a secondary consideration. From this point their paths increasingly diverged.

If the referral of the bills to the select committee had been intended as a government manoeuvre to prolong the life of the Derby administration by neutralising temporarily the opposition of the Independent Party, it was quickly undermined by the prime minister's intemperate dismissal of the very principle of tenant right several days later in response to attacks on it by Lord Roden. Derby sweepingly assured Irish landed Conservatives (no doubt much to their relief) that 'he thought that the principle on which the tenant-right bill was framed was entirely subversive of all rights of property' and it should never be passed.[257] This statement of veto appeared to undermine Napier and shut the door on both bills.[258] Derby's speech greatly antagonised the Independent Party MPs and thereby presaged the return of the Conservatives to the opposition benches, as the government was shortly afterwards defeated on its budget bill when they voted against it along with the opposition, and he resigned on 17 December 1852.[259]

The formation of a new administration, a coalition of Whigs and Peelites under the premiership of the Earl of Aberdeen, appeared to open opportunities for the tenant-righters; the new prime minister and his chancellor of the exchequer William Gladstone had earned a degree of respect in Ireland for opposing the 1851 Ecclesiastical Titles Bill and were untainted by Russell's deadly policy failures during the Famine. But the change of government instigated a crisis in the Independent Party that tore its already fragile unity wide apart. At the end of December two of its MPs, John Sadlier and William Keogh, defected to the new administration, the former being rewarded with a junior lordship of the treasury, the latter with the office of solicitor-general for Ireland. A third Catholic MP, Anthony O'Flaherty of Galway, was rumoured to have been offered the under secretaryship, and while this did not proceed, he defended Sadlier and Keogh's actions and argued their appointments symbolised the desire of Aberdeen's government to be seen as open to Irish reforms.[260] Several other MPs, including Sadlier's brother James and his cousins Vincent and Frances Scully, were understood to be supportive of their defection. But for many in the Irish Party this was an unpardonable betrayal – both men had been founders of the Catholic Defence Association and had taken the pledge to remain independent from

British parties in 1852 – and Lucas excoriated them in print for breaking these bonds and moved quickly to have the League endorse this condemnation.[261]

Crawford's initial public response was more ambivalent, stressing the necessity of the unity of the 'Irish Brigade' and continued public mobilisation behind it, while at the same time observing that 'we cannot doubt that such acceptance of office by them is accompanied by an expected power to advance this particular question to which they are so strongly pledged'.[262] He wrote to Sadlier to clarify his position: 'Whilst I declare that the mere fact of having accepted office in this newly-arranged government is no ground for impeaching those who gave the pledge at the conference as traitors, I hold that they are on trial before their country and that by their future conduct in office they ought to be judged, and either honoured or degraded as they shall prove themselves true or faithless servants in their country's cause'.[263] This evident reluctance to burn bridges with men who might act as a fifth column within the new administration was to pit him against Lucas and Duffy, although he retained the support of McKnight and the *Banner* and also that of some newspapers in the south.[264] In effect, Crawford was taking a calculated gamble that Sadlier and Keogh were indeed 'honest friends of a just settlement' and would work to promote this from within the administration: this turned out to be an error of judgment, especially once the extent of Sadlier's personal financial corruption was exposed, although this was not known about in early 1853.[265] Keogh, on the other hand, has been defended as a consistent Catholic liberal unionist (he had originally been elected as a Peelite in 1847), who was far from alone in regarding 'independent opposition' as a tactical ploy that should be set aside now that a government he deemed sympathetic to Catholic and agrarian grievances had been formed.[266] There is little evidence, however, that either sought to negotiate any firm commitments on tenant right (or other reforms) before taking office.[267]

Crawford and McKnight were joined by others in urging the Irish Party to give the new administration the benefit of the doubt. The radical Christian socialist Lord Goderich, who had struck up a rapport with Duffy in 1852 and discussed with him establishing a new British 'People's Party' which would ally with the Irish, now told him that the new government offered the only hope to get through a new reform bill and thereby attain a meaningful tenant right measure.[268] Duffy, however, opted to reject this advice and follow Lucas in insisting on an uncompromising adherence to strict 'independence'.[269]

The appointments of Sadlier and Keogh triggered by-elections under the place acts in Carlow and Athlone, which focused the Independent Party and Tenant League's attention. The decision of the League leadership to take revenge on Sadlier by actively supporting his 'Orange' opponent John Alexander created a deep schism, and drew fire from moderate Catholics including some clergy, who found a voice in the recently founded *Telegraph* (which was edited by William Bernard MacCabe and funded by Sadlier) in opposition to the Dublin 'press-gang' of the *Tablet*, *Nation* and *Freeman's Journal*.[270] Lucas' declared sympathy for Conservative politics further stoked fears of a conspiracy. With Sadlier now citing Crawford in his defence, it was inevitable that these divisions would escalate.[271] The *Nation* declared that Crawford's recent behaviour on the defections must rule him out of (as had recently been mooted) being put forward at a by-election due in Galway borough:

His late attempts [...] to prop up by his authority the place-taking policy of the pledge-breakers would bar his efforts in the west. No one doubts his goodness of heart, and his benevolence as a landlord; but he does not seem to be made of the sterling metal required by the bold policy of the present day.[272]

By the start of February 1853, the alliance was rapidly disintegrating as the *Nation* launched attacks on McKnight and the Presbyterian ministers Rogers and Bell for refusing to accept the official line of the League Council and allegedly plotting with Sadlier. The *Banner* insisted on due process before any condemnation of the defectors, bitterly denounced any 'Orange' electoral alliances, and alleged that the personal spite of the 'Dublin cabal' lay behind the attacks on the northern Leaguers.[273] McKnight claimed the new administration was 'prepared to fairly and honestly take up the question' and deserved a fair trial; liberal administrations, the *Banner* elaborated, should always be regarded as potential allies by Irish reformers until proven otherwise. McKnight had long harboured concerns about what he regarded as the anti-Protestant authoritarianism of Lucas and the *Tablet*, which was stifling 'liberal Catholicism' and offering ammunition to ultra-Protestants.[274] It was now clear to him that Lucas really intended 'to have an *ecclesiastical* brigade, under tenant-right pretences' and break faith with the northerners, and that Duffy had abandoned his 'Young Ireland' ideals in allying with him.[275] Despite some divisions over the policy within the southern Catholic community, the split was thus taking on a markedly confessional hue.

Against this backdrop Shee and Crawford continued to make practical preparations for the upcoming select committee, with the latter urging a deputation from the Ulster tenant associations travel to London to represent the farmers.[276] This deputation met with the chief secretary, the Peelite Sir John Young, in March, and reported positively.[277] Crawford himself arrived in London in May to add his voice to theirs and speak to Graham and the prime minister.[278] Shee had sought to keep clear of the party split, but remained personally close to Crawford and agreed in thinking it worthwhile to lobby Aberdeen directly.[279] The membership of the select committee gave grounds for initial optimism, with a majority of its Irish members 'known as warm partizans of Mr Sharman Crawford's land "craez"', while the English members included Bright. The *News-Letter* was certain the government had sold out Irish property in making the selection of a majority 'infected with the communist virus', but the tenant deputation led by McKnight and Rogers warned of the determination of the Irish Conservatives on the committee to maintain landed privileges, the manoeuvring of Napier, and the uncertainty of government policy, and hence the need for continuing popular pressure.[280] Reports received before the Easter recess suggested that the committee had accepted the principle of Crawford's arguments about tenant property, although the devil would lie in the details yet to be agreed.[281]

Crawford believed that there was sufficient good faith on display to maintain his line of allowing the government a 'fair trial'. He wrote to Francis Scully to support him in the face of hostile resolutions passed against him and his fellow Tipperary MP James Sadlier (brother of the defector) at a meeting of the Catholic clergy of Cashel. Shee's parliamentary tactics were, he held, consistent with the resolutions of the 1852 conference, and it would be premature to denounce the administration before the select committee reported and it responded. Indeed, political tactics favoured demonstrating to Aberdeen the importance of Irish votes rather than slavishly following the Conservatives in opposition. Scully was thus right to follow Crawford's own precedent in sitting 'on one of the benches below the middle gangway, on the government side' to demonstrate his conditional support. Crawford's principal concern was with the corporate character of the clergy's action, as they should never 'assume political authority, in any form, *as a separate body*'. This was a fine line to tread given the support the tenant-right movement had received from the Presbyterian General Assembly, but the Cashel resolutions would, he argued, prove counter-productive to genuine Catholic interests.[282]

However, the Shee-Crawford strategy was already starting to unravel. In early May 1853 the only cabinet member on the select committee, Palmerston, made the 'extraordinary, and in many respects, inexplicable statement' that he saw no necessity for any legislation on the Irish land question. This undoubtedly reflected his own personal doctrine as an Irish landowner of uncompromising laissez-faire convictions, who had opposed all previous legislative initiatives and insisted on preserving the power to evict at will to 'improve' his Co. Sligo possessions.[283] However, he had kept these opinions private in the committee until this point, and the *Banner* speculated hopefully that this shift reflected his own political calculations and a backlash against 'Ultramontane' provocation from Lucas rather than official government policy.[284] But it was clear that Palmerston had wider support within the Whig party on this head: the former Irish law officer William Tighe Hamilton went into print to criticise Napier's bills as poorly drafted and to insist on a return to solely voluntarist principles in landlord-tenant relations.[285]

Worse was to follow. On 7 May the *Morning Advertiser* reported that Crawford's 'communistic land scheme' had been given its death-blow, strangled by a majority of seventeen to eight in the select committee.[286] Shee then withdrew the bill from consideration in protest. The *Banner* hoped that Crawford's arrival in London might yet turn things around and extract some concessions from the government, but this was accompanied by a 'parliamentary explosion' from Duffy and the Independent MPs excoriating the administration and its Irish converts, making this less likely.[287] This very public defeat provoked a letter from one of the 'Cashel priests' Crawford had previously criticised, questioning his judgment and adherence to the true cause of the tenant farmer.[288]

Sensing that his long campaign for tenant right legislation now faced a final defeat and conscious of the incipient collapse of the League as a unified force, Crawford now urged his supporters to push for the compromise of accepting a heavily amended version of Napier's bill, which it appeared the government might yet support, as a 'tolerable installment of industrial justice'.[289] With McKnight and Rogers he returned to Westminster to lobby MPs on inserting the strongest possible retrospective compensation clauses into that bill.[290] In mid-July Crawford wrote to McKnight expressing some satisfaction with substantive concessions made by Napier in amendments to his bill, and concluded that, although still restricted to compensation for buildings and not for reclamation of the soil, the bill, 'though imperfect, contains an acknowledgment of great and just principles, and even if passed in its present form would establish a basis on which future amendments could be claimed for the extension of its principles to all such matters as the just security of tenants' property would require'.[291] The *Whig* subsequently praised Keogh as solicitor-general for facilitating the progress of the amended bill in what was a crowded legislative session, and Young for adding a late amendment to permit compensation for reclaimed waste land. It singled out Kirk, Scully and Bright in the commons for their constructive support, while still lamenting the absence of 'six representatives from Ulster with *half* the ability and the *whole* of the honesty of honest Sharman Crawford'.[292]

Napier himself wrote privately to Crawford expressing satisfaction that they had at last reached a constructive agreement and that a measure which combined their joint desire to solve the problem would pass the commons, and hopefully also the lords. He saluted Crawford's 'honesty of [...] purpose to secure the fruit of their industry, in a spirit of justice', and agreed that the 'decent farmer class are the strength of our population and ought to be dealt with liberally and equitably'.[293]

This compromise 1853 measure was however to fall at the last hurdle. Despite support from the Duke of Newcastle as the government spokesman in the lords, the bill was strongly opposed in a motion pressed by the 'bitter bad landlord' and former Whig cabinet member Lord Clanricarde, and shelved for reconsideration by another select committee.[294] Newcastle, who under his previous title of Lord Lincoln had moved the 1846 Irish land bill, wrote personally to Crawford to reassure him that the government had avoided the 'very mischievous effect' of a defeat because it still intended to press for a settlement in a future session. [295] The potentially propitious moment had passed, however, and it would be 1870 before any legislation sympathetic to tenant claims would finally reach the statute book.

This setback was followed by another frenzy of bloodletting within the tenant movement. At a conference in September, Crawford again urged the pragmatic course that while they would still campaign for full recognition of tenant right, they must be prepared to take the best bill they could get through parliament in the first instance, especially now that both houses appeared to have accepted the principle of retrospective compensation.[296] Shee agreed that the amended government measure would give them about two-thirds of what they had demanded and should thus not be repudiated as an achievable step.[297] The meeting broke up in disorder, however, as McKnight and Lucas issued allegations of falsehood and double dealing against each other in heated exchanges.[298]

The League convened another conference in October that saw this escalate further, and the northerners level charges that the leadership 'clique' was pursuing agitation for their own self-interested motives and 'sectarianising the movement', and in turn being threatened with expulsion.[299] Venting his fury with McKnight in the press, Lucas also turned on Crawford, who had upheld the former's charges against Lucas of seeking to subvert the passage of the amended Napier bill that session in collusion with the chief secretary, and who publicised his distrust of Lucas' honesty going back to 1851, when he had resolved never to meet Lucas without the presence of a witness.[300] In a lengthy letter in the *Tablet*, Lucas accused him of having drawn and wielded his 'stiletto, manufactured in 1851'; the truth was that:

> having plotted with [McKnight] the perpetration of a gross and outrageous calumny, and finding him not reputable enough to get credit for the falsehood, you step forward to shield him as you best may, and lend you strength to his arm to drive the poisoned weapon home. [...] to violate every instinct of honour, in order to help your friend or confederate to rob the character of another man is not generally deemed permissible. [...] I know that in this dispute with you and Dr McKnight I have great odds to encounter; because, among you all, you have such a faculty of perverting fact and inventing conversations that, if the power of truth were not great, a plain man in the world would have no chance with such cunning artists.[301]

Although Lucas was publicly supported by Duffy in the *Nation*, for many in the movement this full-blooded attack on 'the father of tenant right' was a step too far.[302] Shee traced the collapse of subscriptions to the *Tablet* to Lucas' intemperance, and moderate papers such as the Cork *Southern Reporter, Newry Examiner* and *Londonderry Journal* joined the *Banner* and *Whig* in defending Crawford's integrity and pragmatism.[303]

Any remaining cohesion within the League was now collapsing, but Shee persisted with sending to Crawford in November his amended version of Napier's bill, incorporating what he believed to be the essential principles of the 1852 bill and asking for his support if its terms went far enough to safeguard the Ulster tenant right in practice.[304] McKnight thought this was now unavoidable, as it 'were a senseless, as well as a suicidal, apostasy, to neglect an almighty reform movement at the very hour of its final triumph, if only ordinary diligence shall be applied to its realisation'.[305] Crawford himself issued an address adding his support, reflecting on his eighteen years of agitation and drawing a line in the sand between what was now potentially attainable, what remained desirable, and what had previously been demanded, such as the temporary ban on all evictions, but which was clearly now unobtainable and no longer essential as Ireland was recovering from Famine and agricultural depression and evictions rapidly declining in number.[306] He now favoured, he wrote to Shee, in addition to the 'universal' compensation bill, a separate bill for Ulster to protect the payment for 'goodwill' in tenant-right payments, although he doubted this would succeed given the hostility of the province's MPs.[307] Shee's most prominent clerical ally, Fr James Redmond of Arklow, agreed fully with Crawford as the 'father of tenant right [...] a man of unstained honour, of inviolate truth and unquestionable patriotism', that with national recovery the circumstances had changed and an effective compromise was still in sight.[308] The anti-Lucas papers and Crawford personally protested that the Dublin press 'cabal' had suppressed his and Shee's public correspondence, although Gray responded that 'if Mr Sharman Crawford chooses to write pamphlets and call them letters, he must consent to submit to the hard necessity of having them omitted or inserted according to the inexorable law applicable to all – space'.[309]

By late 1853 the tenant right movement was also evaporating on the ground, as public meetings were becoming thinly attended.[310] The open civil war between its leaders, loudly commented upon by the Tory press, had taken its toll. But so too had the developing agricultural recovery, which was especially marked in Leinster and Ulster, and which saw farmers' profits rise with a run of good harvests from 1852 and the value of tenant-right recover and eventually surpass previous levels. With some notorious exceptions on the western seaboard, the number of evictions declined significantly, from nearly 20,000 families in 1850 to some 8,600 in 1852 and just over 2,100 in 1854 (and not again exceeding this figure before 1881).[311] At the same time, landowners on the whole did not pursue rent increases commensurate with the rise in prices, at least in the more commercialised regions, reducing the real burden of rent to most tenants.

The threat of war provoked by Russian military intervention in the Danubian principalities in 1853, followed in March 1854 by the formal British declaration of hostilities against Russia in what became known as the Crimean War, further boosted farming profits due to large military orders for beef, pork and horses and the disruption of grain and flaxseed imports from the Russian empire. Although Belfast's linen industry was badly disrupted by the shortage of the latter, farmers throughout the country benefitted from sustained high food and flax prices during and for some time after the war and tillage made some (temporary) recovery from the Famine slump, creating more demand for agricultural labour and higher wages.[312]

None of this dissuaded Crawford from the desirability of attaining land reform, as he restated at a dinner given in honour of the Newry MP William Kirk and the end of 1853, but he was fully aware of the growing weakness of the movement, and anxious to promote what seemed the still achievable goal of attaining an amended form of Napier's bill in 1854.[313] However hopes of a success were fading. The Aberdeen government was preoccupied with the 'Eastern question' and then with managing an escalating series of military and supply disasters in the east, while the landed interest was preparing to push back against any significant concessions. Having come under pressure from Irish proprietors such as Lord Donoughmore, Napier now produced a pamphlet and letters distancing himself from the 1853 compromises he had previously agreed.[314] Meanwhile, the *Irish Quarterly Review* highlighted what it took to be the Achilles heel of the tenant movement – its apparent lack of concern for the interests of the labouring classes in its pursuit of the narrow 'class interest' of the farmers.[315] Edward Bullen, secretary of the Royal Agricultural Society of Ireland, criticised Crawford for promoting the incomprehensible and intolerable doctrine of 'joint ownership' between landlord and tenant, warned bourgeois readers that the principle if accepted could open industrial profits up to claims from their employees.[316] Simultaneously with this landed counter-offensive, Crawford continued to be denounced by League voices of betraying the principle of independent opposition and being seduced by a 'knot of canny northerns' to seek a deal for Ulster only and abandon the rest of the country to its fate.[317]

In an exchange of public letters, Crawford remonstrated with Napier on his return to a more hardline stance that the bill which had gone to the lords had been 'anomalous and unsafe' and that it should not be carried forward.[318] Newcastle was also now backing away, complaining that, while 'I must confess my astonishment at the course taken by Mr. Napier', all he could do was to seek to refer the bills to a select committee: 'My time is now so entirely absorbed by the preparations for war in addition to the ordinary colonial business of my department that I fear these bills can hardly fail to suffer by being in my hands'.[319] It was now inevitable that the lords select committee would now throw out the tenant-right bill in its previously amended form, leading the *Banner* to denounce Napier as a 'Protestant Jesuit'.[320]

Sensing that the only chance of movement now lay with a revived grass-roots campaign behind Shee's bill, and that this could only be done in the north by making a clean break with the League, Crawford spoke at a rally at Draperstown, Co. Londonderry, in March 1854, announcing his personal renunciation of the Dublin organisation and its strategy:

> the Tenant League seemed an Irish emanation of the Carlton Club; and he could not identify himself with a body whose members were the enemies of all reform – the enemies of the rights of the people – the enemies of every measure of popular right. He felt bound to express himself thus strongly, because he saw recently an address urging the friends of the tenant-right to pay their contributions to the League. He would advise them to keep their money amongst themselves, to put it into the hands of safe men, and to use it when wanted for useful purposes. [...] He was not the man to make himself the slave to any government; but, at the same time, he never would permit himself to enter into an organization against a government, so long as

that government evinced an inclination to do rightly and honestly to the people (Cheers). He then inculcated the quelling of religious dissension, and the union of creeds in working out that common good.[321]

The declaration seems to have had the desired effect in Ulster, motivating McKnight and the Presbyterian clergy and bringing larger numbers to the following rallies.[322] The Ulster Tenant Right Association was re-launched in Derry with the aim of restoring the spirit of the original movement of 1847. Warning that they would seek the 'whole hog' of his 1852 bill if a just compromise was rejected by the lords, Crawford sought to turn the outbreak of war into a reason for the government to grant their demands, as without concessions, emigration would continue to drain 'the bone and sinew of the people', to Britain's detriment.[323]

Crawford's demarche inevitably divided opinion. To the sympathetic *Weekly Telegraph*, his speeches had reignited the northern movement and ended the apathy brought on by the 1852 defeats, and some southern provincial papers reacted positively to his condemnation of continuing mass emigration.[324] To League loyalists, on the other hand, it was simply further evidence of his political treachery, and it gave rise to the emergence of a hostile body in Belfast led by Lucas' ally James McConvery, which claimed that Crawford and Shee had abandoned the cause of the tenantry.[325] In any case, Shee's bill again went nowhere that session, with the government washing its hands of any meaningful land legislation for Ireland.[326] Both Conservative and League opponents berated Crawford and Shee, with some justification, for placing any reliance on the goodwill of the Aberdeen coalition.[327] Already deeply frustrated with the lack of public support for the bill, Shee responded by refusing to attend the League conference that autumn so long as it indulged in 'insult and menace' and later dissociating himself from it completely, while his Catholic clerical allies accused the League council of suppressing all dissent from the Lucas-Duffy line.[328]

All was not well within the rump League camp either. The Independent Party suffered from a further series of defections by MPs anxious to secure patronage or genuinely persuaded of the benefits of liberal government.[329] Of the party's leaders, Duffy had been suffering from recurrent illness and was becoming increasingly pessimistic about the Irish political situation and the chances of attaining any form of land reform. The idea of a 'league of north and south' had been a natural extension of his non-sectarian Young Ireland ideals, and the Independent Party had at first appeared to offer the possibility of a coherent nationalist movement united around land reform to replace the collapsed and divided movements of 1847–8. However, he could not countenance the defections and found himself increasingly dependent on Lucas, whose 'theocratic' tendencies conflicted with some of his own aspirations, but on whose bid for clerical leadership he now also depended. In the course of 1855 Duffy took the decision to abandon Irish politics as hopeless, give up his New Ross seat and emigrate to the colony of Victoria in pursuit of a fresh political start. McKnight, writing in the *Londonderry Standard*, expressed sympathy for him and laid the blame for his departure and the failure of the League on the 'Saxon adventurer' Lucas.[330]

At the same time, Lucas' campaign to politicise the Catholic clergy under his own direction had antagonised Archbishop Paul Cullen, who took steps to curb Lucas' associates, including the Callan priests, in 1854, and to exercise his extensive influence in Rome to elicit a papal condemnation of overt clerical involvement in Irish politics. Cullen was also bitterly hostile towards Duffy as a quondam revolutionary tainted by the European anti-clericalism of 1848 and saw him as an 'Irish Mazzini'. Attempts to resist Cullen's agenda preoccupied Lucas for much of 1854–5, leading to embittered and exhausting confrontations with the archbishop and his allies, a failed appeal to Rome, and ultimately the terminal breakdown of Lucas's health.[331] He was to die of cardiac failure in October 1855, leaving leadership of what remained of the movement to Moore. By that point little except the name was left of both the Tenant League and the Independent Party, and the optimism of 1850–2 lay in ruins.

The end of tenant right? 1855–61

It would have been out of character for Crawford to abandon the cause that he had devoted his political life to, even if, as he admitted, there appeared by 1855 to be an 'apathetic silence' in the country on the subject. In an address at the start of that year he denounced the 'unconstitutional and demagogic' policy of the 'remnant of that Tenant League' and called for a return to the popular enthusiasm and the religious unity of 1852, along with the pragmatic building of alliances that had more chance of success than any absolutist 'independent opposition'.[332] McKnight, now back at the helm of the *Londonderry Standard*, observed that the 'Dublin Cabal have now virtually finished their career' and called on local societies, north and south, to forward 'balefuls of petitions' in support of Shee's reintroduced bill.[333] Despite some successful rallies, however, the revival proved disappointing, with the *Banner* complaining about tenant farmers who would mutter against landlords at their own firesides, but fail to manifest this feeling through public action.[334]

Crawford retained admirers in the south and was proposed by Fr O'Regan of Kanturk for one of the Co. Cork seats. The idea gained the endorsement of the *Southern Reporter* and *Limerick Examiner*, and the liberal candidate Rickard Deasy was ready to give way to him, but the move was vetoed by vocal opposition from the Lucasite clergy in the county and Crawford's insistence that he would stand only if the tenants were unanimous for him.[335] Deasy, who took the seat by default, went on to be solicitor-general and attorney-general for Ireland in the second Palmerston administration of 1859–65, and co-sponsored the laissez-faire Irish land measures passed in 1860, the antithesis of the League's objectives.

Crawford was part of an Ulster delegation in April 1855 to meet the new lord lieutenant the Earl of Carlisle (whom Crawford had previously known as chief secretary as Lord Morpeth). Although Carlisle appeared personally sympathetic, the prospects for government support were very limited with the intransigent Palmerston now prime minister (a post he would hold for most of the following decade) and the more congenial Peelites in opposition after the collapse of the Aberdeen coalition in February.[336] Shee's bill was again emasculated by a series of hostile amendments, with the *Nation* observing that Palmerston, the 'deadliest enemy of tenant right', had eventually given it the coup de grace through his deprecation of any interference with landlord-tenant contracts.[337] Seemingly undeterred, Crawford yet again called for a united outdoors campaign against feudalism. Despite some backsliding, a majority of Irish MPs still supported the bill, and must now, he argued, vote together against the government's money bills (in an echo of his previous strategy of 1844) to get it to come to terms. This was, he asserted, the true and constitutional meaning of 'independent opposition', and it was the responsibility of electors to ensure their representatives acted according to the popular will.[338] He found time also to answer laissez-faire attacks on tenant-right agitation, and allegations in the *Belfast Mercury* that all its agitators were self-interested hacks. While the campaign was not dependent on him, and 'although advancing years may impair my usefulness, I am still able to do some service in the cause, and ready to stand forward side by side with the tenant farmers in the peaceful struggle for their rights'.[339]

Writing to the electors of Meath at the by-election caused by Lucas' death, Crawford avoided mentioning his former antagonist by name, but stressed that dissension within the leadership had been the principal cause the of the movement's malaise. He remained optimistic not just about a fair tenant-right measure, but other necessary social reforms. Conscious of criticisms that the League that had neglected the labourers, he drew specific attention to the need for legislation to improve their livelihoods beyond the provision of cottages, which he saw as an integral part of the wider 'tenant question':

> I do not wish to see the man who *labours* on the soil expelled from the *occupation* of the soil. The condition of the labourer never can be raised until he has the power to acquire an interest in the soil, and has that object to aspire to as a stimulus to industry and economy. So long as the labourer has no other recourse to look forward to for the wants of sickness or old age but the poor-house, and to become the recipient of pauper taxation, he never can attain the elevation of mind which is the only true source of improvement in his moral or social condition. I conceive there are means of facilitating the establishment of small tenements in localities, which, under proper regulations, would promote the labourer's prosperity, and in connection with education would ensure improved cultivation, and secure the landlords full rent. The labourer – the working man – is the source of all national prosperity, and yet there is no class of the community whose interests are so little cared for by the laws and institutions of the United Kingdom.[340]

He continued to regard his 1849 tract *Depopulation Not Necessary* as relevant on this matter, and sent copies to Belfast newspapers.[341] Crawford was himself scouted as a potential candidate for Meath, but as previously with Cork, residual hostility from Lucasites rendered this a non-starter.[342]

Despite his efforts by 1856 it appeared that the tenant right movement was moribund. Shee declined to reintroduce his bill that year given the government's now overt opposition, and an alternative moved by Moore was soon unceremoniously withdrawn. The *Times* thundered on the presumed demise of the 'tenant-right delusion' that what Ireland needed was the free sale of property through the Encumbered Estates Court, unimpeded by any restrictions not sanctioned by liberal political economy.[343] This claim appears to have provoked Crawford, who had been relatively quiet during the session, into returning to the public press. Although the acute levels of clearances seen in the Famine had now dissipated, he warned both that such conditions might return in the future, and that there was a specific problem of 'clearances for improvement' precisely on those properties bought by speculators under the Encumbered Estates Court. This might be summarily addressed by giving the courts powers to halt evictions until a tenant's claims for compensation for improvements made to their holdings had been equitably resolved.[344] A subsequent letter criticised the rump Tenant League for failing to speak out for the small farmers and cottiers thus impacted by the drive to clear land for large grazing farms to satisfy British demand for beef: 'It is the fashionable doctrine to call this improvement; but the extermination of human beings, and the substitution of brute animals for the human race on the soil of Ireland, is not an improvement grateful to my mind'. He continued to adhere to the view that for those without any meaningful tenant right, a scheme of 'home colonisation' at state expense, creating small tenancies on waste lands, was desirable. The Tenant League, he concluded, had made the fatal error of abandoning the model of the Anti-Corn Law League with its focus on a single achievable end and openness to different political positions, and should no longer delude the people with false hopes.[345]

Crawford's letters on this subject clearly struck a nerve. The *Freeman's Journal* endorsed his attack on clearances and urged Irish MPs to rally around him and McCullagh, to promote legislation to curb evictions. The paper's comments suggested some disillusionment with the League, and its editor John Gray was soon to leave it with some acrimony.[346] The *Tablet*, now owned and edited by John Edward Wallis, also offered an olive branch, urging the League to invite Crawford to its next convention, as his 'indiscretions and weaknesses should not outweigh a long life of public services, or, at least, of laborious public efforts'.[347] This was all rather too late, and was anyway strongly resisted by the most obdurate and bitter voices of 'independent opposition'.[348] Nevertheless, Crawford persisted; writing to the League he complained of Moore's disparagement of him, but urged it to replace the now unattainable 1852 bill with one enacting tenant right in the 'simplest practical form', along with separate legislation to assist the emigration of evicted tenants (at the landlord's expense) if home colonisation could not be achieved. Crawford's addition that 'there were individual members elected in 1852 who deserve the highest reprobation' may have been intended as a belated distancing from Sadlier, whose suicide in February 1856 had been followed by revelations of his criminal financial speculations.[349]

The need for at least a semblance of unity was increased when Palmerston called a snap general election for April 1857 with the aim of vindicating his aggressive foreign policy after censure in the commons. Crawford, now in his seventy-sixth year, decided not to seek nomination again, despite suggestions by Smith O'Brien (now returned from his Tasmanian exile) that the Independent Party should have found a seat for him.[350] Tenant-right enthusiasm was not entirely dead in the north: Greer stood again for Co. Londonderry with Crawford's active support and backing from the Presbyterian clergy, and pulled off an unlikely victory.[351] Hoping that some of the northern borough constituencies might also be vulnerable, Crawford – as so often in his career – appealed to a sense of radical history against the prevailing malaise, reminding his readers of Lisburn's struggle against 'aristocratic domination' in 1783 and of the need to rediscover that spirit.[352]

Such calls had limited impact with Ireland approaching the peak of its post-Famine agricultural recovery, and, with the exception of Greer's narrow win and the return of Kirk in Newry (largely with Catholic support), the tenant-right movement again foundered in Ulster. Elsewhere the Independent Party also did poorly in the face of internal division and Cullen's continuing antagonism, with Moore losing his Mayo seat and Shee being defeated in Kilkenny. In Down, in an ironic reverse of the 1852 contest, David Ker now stood as a Palmerstonian Liberal-Conservative in opposition to a more orthodox Conservative front of Lord Edwin Hill and William Forde. Taking revenge for Ker's insubordination of 1852, Downshire and his allies mobilised their interests against him; unenthusiastic support from Crawford and the tenant-right movement, to whom Ker now appealed for endorsement, and backing from the newly succeeded fourth Marquess of Londonderry, were insufficient to save Ker from a decisive defeat.[353] The *News-Letter* crowed that the 'poor old disappointed and mortified gentleman of Crawfordsburn [had sought] to awaken the dormant spirit of the Tenant League communists and revolutionists of 1852' in vain.[354] The *Banner* also treated it as a repeat of that highly charged contest, with 'the tenants [...] sent to the poll like so many African negroes to a sale at New Orleans' in the absence of the electoral freedom that would have allowed Crawford and Ker to be returned.[355] In truth, however, there was little evidence of the excitement and optimism of 1852, and Crawford concluded that only the secret ballot would free tenants to vote freely and honestly in their own interest and to ask them to risk everything again for such little hope of success was folly. As a free trader and having declared himself in support of some measure to uphold the Ulster custom, Ker was preferable to the Tories, but only just.[356]

The 1857 defeats were the final blow for the remnants of the Tenant League, which collapsed into embittered factions engaged in internecine warfare.[357] The League staggered on into 1858 under the nominal leadership of J. F. Maguire, but with minimal support and abandoning any commitment to retrospective compensation.[358] Crawford proposed it be superseded with a new organisation under untainted leadership, but the conditions were not conducive to any revived 'league of north and south', and a separate Ulster Association was reformed in Belfast with Crawford as president.[359] This aimed to pursue the 'special claims' of Ulster in terms of seeking legalisation of the custom, while also aiming for an Ireland-wide retrospective compensation bill and the secret ballot, the latter a potential ground for fraternal collaboration with British reformers.[360] However, as both the Conservative and laissez-faire liberal Ulster press asserted, many farmers were now wary of risking their revived tenant-right values and landlord goodwill given that Palmerston was resolutely against legislation, rendering success as far away as ever.[361] The return of Derby with another minority Conservative administration in February 1858 made little difference despite initial optimism in 'Independent' ranks, as neither Greer's nor Maguire's rival tenant-right motions that year made any progress and the Conservatives failed to produce their own land bill.[362] The Ulster Association survived into 1859 under Greer's leadership, but was unable to prevent his defeat at the general election of that year.[363]

With legislation checked in parliament apparently indefinitely, Crawford turned to highlighting specific incidents of tenant oppression by landlords, initially the evictions of numerous tenants without compensation by Lord Leitrim around Milford in Donegal and by Colonel Arthur Lewis in Monaghan in 1857–8.[364] Crawford initiated a subscription for one of Lewis's tenants, John Byrne, allegedly ejected because of his religious beliefs, which drew ecstatic praise from Catholic journals such as Denis Holland's *Ulsterman*.[365] In April 1858 he extended his campaign to the distressed peasantry of the impoverished Donegal districts of Gweedore and Cloughaneely, rejecting the denials of any crisis made by the clerk of the Dunfanaghy board of guardians and endorsing the claims issued by the local Catholic clergy and by Holland in his articles on the 'Donegal sheep war'. Crawford now revived his criticisms of the effects of the Gregory clause on poor occupying tenants and repeated the clergy's criticisms of increased rents, the cancellation of traditional commonage rights following the creation of commercial sheep-runs, the imposition of a levy for additional policing as a collective punishment for resistance, and the absence of improvement due to insecurity.[366] His protest was cited in the commons by the Clonmel

MP John Bagwell in support of his case for a formal investigation, and Crawford and his son James later gave evidence to a select committee based on observations made during their journey of three days to the area, in which they had visited the peasants in their cabins and observed their living and working conditions. He was confident there was no surplus of population in western Donegal, but that the people could only thrive if permitted larger allotments that they could reclaim with secure tenancy on affordable rents. As in 1849, 'home colonisation' remained his favoured solution to the social crisis of the west that was continuing to produce 'extermination'.[367] The reformist Irish press expressed outrage when the committee reported favourably to the local landlords and ignored the 'disinterested' evidence of the Crawfords, while the pro-landlord prints accused them of being the gullible victims of frauds perpetrated by agitating priests.[368]

Refusing to accept the official line that benevolent landlordism was transforming the west, Crawford prophesied in a letter to the *Times* that so long as the wretchedness and injustice he had witnessed in Donegal persisted, the flame of violent agrarian grievance associated with 'Ribandism', which had again made a bloody appearance that year, would never be extinguished. What he had seen around Gweedore had simply confirmed everything he had argued and campaigned for over the previous quarter century, as it was 'a true sample of the general landlord system which has existed over the west and the south of Ireland'. Without alleviation such conditions were likely to bring the return of famine in time. The delinquency lay equally with the proprietors and with the state, which had denied the necessary reforms for years in the face of overwhelming evidence and grudging admission of the principle of intervention, and which turned repeatedly to coercion when justice was required.[369] He remained more than prepared to denounce those proprietors who routinely demanded such tyrannical measures to protect themselves from the consequences of 'exterminating' improvement, writing to Downshire in 1859 that '[i]f you wish to "improve" estates by "expelling from the soil the bone and sinew of the country" all your coercion and oppression will only render life and property every day less secure'.[370]

Crawford thus ended his lifelong campaign for land reform in Ireland without success, but with a reassertion of defiance and calls for the public to adhere to the model of attaining legislative change through peaceful mass agitation. Characteristically of the man, he seemed to revel in opprobrium heaped upon him so long as this drew attention to his arguments. As throughout his career, he warned those frustrated by inertia away from the superficial attractions of revolutionary conspiracy (by then taking the form of the new Fenian movement), which he believed must always prove counterproductive.[371]

The 1859 general election would prove the nadir of the tenant-right movement, with the Independent Party disappearing completely and both Greer and Kirk losing their seats in an Ulster where Presbyterians had their minds on more spiritual concerns in that year of evangelical revival. Crawford himself was approached to stand in both Co. Kilkenny and Drogheda, and he appears to have seriously considered the latter offer, which might allow him a last opportunity to pursue land reform, but the incumbent James McCann changed his mind about retiring and the opportunity passed.[372]

Ignoring his numerous critics, he continued to write public letters to the end of his life excoriating landlord malpractice, including that of the Tory leader Derby, who had threatened mass evictions on his Doon, Co. Limerick, estate as a collective punishment following a murder there. Crawford urged the revival of tenant-right agitation and criticising the Palmerstonian adherence to laissez-faire in agrarian relations that allowed such abuses to go unchecked.[373] This 1859 letter was praised by the French liberal Catholic economist Adolphe Perraud and reprinted for a French audience as the epitome of the Irish land question.[374] Crawford's last public address on the subject, to the Westmeath Farmer's Club at Mullingar, was to attack the Irish chief secretary Edward Cardwell's 1860 land improvement measure as an 'enabling bill for landlords', as it excluded retrospective improvements and facilitated landlord undertakings. He took no pleasure, he concluded, in the lauded 'improvement' of Ireland since 1847 which had been brought about by means of death, extermination and emigration.[375] A follow-up letter critically dissected it and Deasy's land tenure act, which sought to place landlord-tenant relations solely on terms of legal contract, and reminded the tenants that they needed only to find their moral courage to take electoral action in pursuit of their just rights.[376] He also persisted in advocating the interests of the labourers as well as the tenant farmers, in 1861 contrasting the better condition of French labourers with access to small plots with those of Ireland and Britain.[377]

Shortly before his death he was confronted by another notorious incident that appeared to confirm the arguments about predatory landlordism he had articulated for decades. In April 1861 forty-four families were evicted at Derryveagh by John George Adair, who had assembled a large estate in the highlands of Donegal from purchases made in the Landed Estates Court. Like Derby, Adair had used the legal powers available to him to impose a collective punishment of ejectment on a community for their alleged complicity in the murder the previous year of one of the Scottish shepherds he had introduced to manage his commercial sheep-runs. Crawford's old friend O'Brien wrote to him expressing outrage and urging him to act.[378] Crawford's response indicated a degree of personal exhaustion verging on despair. While he approved of O'Brien's plan to stir up poor law boards to protest, and suggested he reuse of his arguments in his letter written on the Derby evictions to 'that worthless and now extinct body termed the Irish Tenant League', he thought little could be done about Adair: 'I must confess that I have been so long urging upon the mind of Ireland the question of the land, without the least effect, that I feel discouraged from any further attempt on the subject; anything I say falls as a dead letter upon the public mind […]'.[379]

Only after his death later in 1861 would the tide gradually start to turn, with the rise of a more sympathetic historicist economics, the emergence of a more open-minded British Liberal party leadership after 1865 and the revival of agrarian agitation. It was left to his children James and Mabel to play some part in this new politics, but his contribution would not be forgotten. Despite the ignominious collapse of the 'league of north and south', the ideal of constitutionalist land agitation persisted and remained associated in the public mind with the legacy of the 'father of tenant right'.

8. Family, reform and religion, 1844–61

The Sharman Crawfords of Crawfordsburn

As we have seen, William Sharman Crawford sought to involve his large family, and especially his older sons, in his political campaigns from the 1830s, and encouraged them to emulate his combination of popular political reformism and co-operative landlordism.[1] However the anomalies of the household's position in being at once the leading embodiment of radical liberalism in Down while remaining a part of the county's constellation of landed estates created strains that became increasingly evident towards the later years of William's life. His children each came to adopt their own political and social positions and reacted to the changing circumstances of their times in different ways. While it appears that all remained respectful towards their father's politics during his lifetime and adhered to a generally liberal political stance, this was embraced with varying degrees of interest, enthusiasm and commitment. Several found William's personal abstemiousness conflicted with their own material aspirations. The subsequent public careers of the two children closest to his radical vision, James and Mabel, will be dealt with in more detail in the next chapter: they ensured that what might be termed 'Sharman Crawfordism' in Ulster survived its titular founder, at least for another generation. The present chapter will focus on the family dynamics in the later years of William's life and consider his final contributions to debates on democratic reform, empire and religion up to his death in 1861.

The Sharman Crawfords had eleven children born between 1808 and 1827 who survived to adulthood. The family was rocked by a series of deaths in 1844–51, beginning with William's wife Mabel Frideswid, after a lengthy and debilitating illness, in December 1844. She was soon followed by her eldest daughter Maria just three months later at her home, Oldbridge House in Meath, due to complications following childbirth.[2] May 1851 saw the death from a sudden onset of 'inflammation' of Frederick, who had been born in 1814 and was the couple's fourth surviving son. Aged thirty-six, he had already established a public profile for relief work during the Famine and as a political aide to his father. The *Freeman's Journal* noted his demise had 'suddenly removed, from a scene of great usefulness, one of the most benevolent men that ever graced society'.[3] Mabel's illness and death in particular appears to have spurred William into writing his incomplete 'retrospective memorandum' in 1844 and he subsequently revised his financial arrangements to ensure for the future of his remaining children.[4]

The most difficult family relationship was between William and John, the heir to the estates. In 1835–6 they had still been close and William had confided regularly to his son his political hopes and strategies. He had funded John's 'grand tour' in North America as an educational exercise, while encouraging him to be economical 'as much as consistent with the proper expenditure of a gentleman where you are known'.[5] Some of this appears to have rubbed off, as John confided to his mother that in New York '[t]here is as much aristocratic feeling and nonsense as with us and it is the less excusable'.[6] Nevertheless, it appears that John reacted against what he saw as the democratic excesses of American politics and began to question the extent of his father's radicalism. His sister Maria observed to him that:

> You acknowledge your politics are a little changed and if a visit to America would have the same effect on Papa and Charley [their brother Charles, born 1816] I would not be sorry that they took an excursion; many things sound very well in theory that will not be found to answer well or cannot be carried into practice and I dare say you have found that the case in America – but enough of politics which I hate [...][7]

On his return John appears to have taken a less prominent role in supporting William's political activities than his brothers and followed instead the more conventional path of the heir apparent to a liberal landowner. He was active in local government and on regional and national agricultural societies, becoming a magistrate in 1837, high sheriff of Down in 1839 and in 1852 joining the newly established Royal North Down Rifles Militia as a part-time major.[8] However, he also suffered from recurring bouts of ill health (perhaps related to an episode in 1839 when he was rescued from drowning by his brother Arthur and several boatmen) and for unknown reasons he never married.[9] He appears to have aspired to better relations with his peers in the county gentry, appealing (unsuccessfully) to his father to call off the post-1852 election political dinner, and riding regularly with the Down hunt.[10] By the later 1850s his relationship with his father appears to have broken down, with communications being made via his brother James as an intermediary.

John was closest to his brother Arthur (born 1811), who was educated at Trinity College Dublin and King's Inns and was called to the Irish bar in 1834 (Figure 28). Arthur initially undertook legal practice but his fortune was made by marrying in 1846 his cousin Louisa Alicia, daughter of the highly successful brewer William Crawford of the Beamish and Crawford Brewery in Cork city. After his marriage a wealthy man independently of the family landholdings, he invested in the Belfast Banking Company, becoming a director in 1861 and later chairing its board of superintendence.[11] Arthur's lifestyle appears to have changed to reflect his enhanced income; in 1855 a 'Mr Sharman Crawford' was reported as having laid out 1,800 guineas on a racehorse for the Derby, an expensive sporting luxury his father would not have indulged, but which presaged Arthur's family's later preoccupation with even more costly elite sports.[12] However, like his childless elder brother (to whom he in turn became heir apparent), Arthur remained within the Liberal political camp, and was central to the formation of the Ulster Reform Club in Belfast in 1864, even if his liberalism was of a decidedly moderate orientation that sought to maintain the rights and privileges of professional and commercial wealth. Retaining a sense of public service typical of the family, he served as a commissioner into the Irish endowed schools in 1855–8.

As we have already seen, the third son James was mentored by his father to undertake the principal management of the estates (except for Stalleen, which fell to Arthur). This appears to have been intended as a temporary arrangement, but James adapted well to the role of agent and became his father's closest confidante on agrarian and political matters by the 1840s. He briefly considered taking a salaried land agency post with Lord Dufferin, but, with his brothers' agreement, was able to acquire considerable independence as the resident squire at Rademon house for the period of his lifetime, acting as a magistrate from 1845 and serving on the Downpatrick board of guardians.[13] Like John, he never married. James shared his father's religious seriousness and attraction towards Presbyterianism. In 1845–6 he was a leading figure in the secession of much of the parish congregation at Kilmore in protest against the 'Tractarian' innovations of the rector Rev. John Mussen, who was backed by the high-church Bishop Mant of Down and Connor. The controversy appears to have been sparked by Mussen's refusal to continue collecting 'poor's money' (an urgent matter with the onset of famine) as well as concerns over his adoption of high-church ritualism. A locally printed tract issued by the protesters recalled the intense personal antagonisms this generated in 1846:

> Nearly the whole of the congregation went to church on the Sunday, as agreed on, when Mr Mussen took the opportunity of preaching a most violent sermon against them, – so much so, that a number of them were very near leaving the church during its delivery – but immediately after it was finished, they rose and left before the reading of the prayer for the church militant [...][14]

Whereas similar attempts to impose liturgical innovations by members of Mant's clergy in Antrim and Down were abandoned after congregational revolts in 1845–6, at Kilmore it led to James and many others joining the orthodox Presbyterian congregation at Crossgar.[15] This conversion, alongside his popularity with the tenantry, would help lay the foundations for his subsequent political career in the 1870s.[16]

Of the younger sons, Charles had acted as his father's political secretary in the 1830s and seems to have fully embraced his radicalism (to the extent of mocking his brother John as a 'great Tory').[17] Although also admitted to the Irish bar in 1839, Charles' career would take a different turn into public service. Influenced by his father's advocacy of a humane poor law, he was drawn towards engagement with the new system, first acting as a returning officer for elections in the South Dublin and other unions, before being appointed to an assistant commissionership in early 1847.[18] Although the appointment inevitably drew accusations that his father had sought a patronage appointment for his son, this seems unlikely as he was openly critical of the government at the time and took little interest in the pursuit of patronage that occupied so much of the energies of many of his fellow MPs.[19]

An assistant commissionership was no sinecure, and Charles took on this post at the worst possible moment, as the already stressed and underfunded system slid into the abyss under the sheer weight of famine destitution. He appears to have done whatever he could in the circumstances to uphold the legal entitlements of the poor (limited as these were) in the unions he was responsible for against systematic local abuse and neglect. This was not, as one writer dubiously claimed, as cushy 'job' for the son of a prominent political figure, and it involved regular translation from district to district as circumstances demanded.[20] He criticised and recommended the suspension of those boards of guardians who demonstrated incompetence and allowed their workhouses to become dangerously overcrowded, but had no power to compel bankrupt unions to open auxiliary accommodation.[21]

In the wake of the Famine, Charles was often called upon to resolve heated disputes over religious provision and alleged proselytism in the workhouses, which he appeared to deal with even-handedly and effectively, although there were complaints from some guardians when he removed the master of Coleraine workhouse for staging a 'party demonstration' of children on the 12th of July.[22] More typical was the commendation of the South Dublin guardians of his 'uniform attention to the interests of the union, and for the clear and satisfactory expositions he has always given on all matters of doubt or difficulty, as likewise for the just and impartial manner in which he has conducted every investigation referred to him at the instance of the board'.[23] By 1860 he was one of only two inspectors in the 'senior class', earning a salary of £700, but the strain was proving too much and he retired that year on grounds of ill health, returning to legal practice in the capital.[24] He was an active member of the Social and Statistical Inquiry Society of Ireland, and, in recognition of his expertise, was appointed a commissioner of inquiry into Irish poor law reform in 1877–9.[25]

The youngest sons William junior (born 1823) and Henry (born 1825) both had successful business careers. By 1846 William had a general stores premises near Donegall Quay in Belfast, but soon moved into partnership as an agent for the Royal Exchange Insurance Company. This proved profitable, and by 1862 he was a director of the Northern Banking Company (a rival to his brother Arthur's Belfast Bank).[26] He married Emily Macaulay of Larne in 1854.[27] He was considered as a potential tenant-right candidate for Tyrone in 1852, but opted to restrict himself to municipal politics in Belfast.[28] Defeated for the Dock Ward as a liberal candidate in 1855, he was nevertheless elected later that year as an assessor for the Smithfield Ward, and was associated with the radical Protestant lawyer John Rea in moving the 'chancery suit' against the closed and corrupt Tory town council that year.[29] Rea complained that his plan to run William junior as the liberal parliamentary candidate for Belfast in 1857 and pay his election expenses had been blocked by the mayor, who had also misused his power to permit Crawford to be attacked by a mob at the hustings.[30] Despite his reported popularity 'with all classes' and active involvement with the town's Working Men's Institute, William may have become frustrated with the growing conservatism of Belfast political life (and possibly also by Rea's defection to support the 'independent' Orange candidate William Johnston in 1868), and relocated to Dublin around 1869.[31] Although he retained connections in Belfast his career now lay elsewhere.[32] He died at Oporto in Portugal in 1879, where he had been managing the port wine export business he had purchased with his partner George Reid from the long-established Van Zeller family.[33]

Henry followed a similar pathway: he also established himself as a businessman and shipping agent in Belfast in the 1850s, becoming agent for several insurance companies in collaboration with his brother.[34] He represented the family's long-standing interest in railway development as a director of the Belfast and County Down Railway, whose line crossed the Crawfordsburn demesne on a new viaduct in 1863.[35] Henry followed his brother John as a part-time officer in the North Down Militia, and married Ellen, the daughter of James Goddard of Belfast in 1862.[36] By 1865, however, he had moved to Dublin and become established there in the wine trade, in which he became extremely successful.[37] His family remained involved in the company after his death in 1905; Sharman Crawford and Co. was specialising in fortified wines and operating from Abbey Street in Dublin as late as 1926 having survived the loss of its premises during the Easter Rising a decade earlier.[38]

Sharman Crawford's three younger daughters, Arminella, known in the family as 'Ella' (born 1818), Mabel (born 1820) and Eleanor (born 1827) lived with him at Crawfordsburn until his death in 1861. All were constrained by the conventional gender expectations placed upon women of their class in the period, and of the three it was Mabel alone who would find ways of asserting her voice in the public sphere and vigorously challenging those restrictions. Her public career will be considered in the following chapter. References to the sisters are relatively sparse in the 1840s–50s, although as we have seen they were active in charitable activity during and in the aftermath of the Famine. They were involved with the Belfast Ladies Association for the Relief of Connaught, which was praised by the visiting American philanthropist Asenath Nicholson for its non-denominational character and focus on assisting women and children through both direct aid and supporting training in useful skills.[39] Some of these charitable engagements had an evangelical orientation, such as when the 'Misses Sharman Crawford' were recorded as vice-patronesses for bazaars in aid of the Connaught Industrial and Scriptural Schools associated with the leading Presbyterian Rev. John Edgar.[40] Given Mabel's later articulated distaste for proselytism, this may have reflected more Ella's personal inclinations along with a desire to do good works through the town's existing charitable bodies.[41] Ella also sought to promote the development of Irish women's manufactures, making a collection of 'fancy work' samples to be sent out for display at a new repository at Madras patronised by the Belfast-born colonial governor Sir Henry Pottinger.[42]

Most strikingly, the 'Misses Crawford [of] Crawfordsburn' were in 1846 vice-presidents of the Belfast Ladies' Anti-Slavery Association. This body had been set up in the wake of Frederick Douglass' first visit to Belfast in 1845 in part through the initiative of the Quaker Maria Webb and Mary Ann McCracken, who were also on its committee. In September 1846 it issued an address to the ladies of Ulster, reminding them that many of the three million enslaved Americans were descendants of those dragged from their homes in Africa by British subjects under British laws, and that it remained their moral duty to protest against the continuing existence of the institution in the Americas. The address made an explicit connection between evangelical philanthropy and the anti-slavery cause, but also offered a detailed analysis of the two wings of the abolitionist movement in America, and declared it would support both despite expressing stronger sympathy for the more advanced wing led by William Lloyd Garrison. Aware that the calls for Irish famine relief had a priority on donations, it asked ladies instead to send hand-made items for sale at abolitionist bazaars, to spread the message through their networks and families, and to help prepare emigrants 'to withstand the corrupting exhalations from the slave states that have filled even the northern with prejudices against the negro and his abolition friends'.[43] Mary Ann McCracken was reported to have frequently distributed such tracts to emigrants. The committee was active as least until 1855, although public enthusiasm had waned.[44]

Despite their father's reputation for asceticism, all three sisters seem to have attended, with their brothers, the balls and other social functions normal for people of their social rank, at Cheltenham and Dublin as well as in Belfast and the county's big houses.[45] Mabel and Eleanor were both 'presented' at a viceregal drawing room in 1849, with the social correspondents commenting at length on the sisters' dresses.[46] Following her mother's death, Ella appears to have to some extent acted as a political hostess at Crawfordsburn. She and her sisters attended a reception for the visiting lord lieutenant at nearby Clandeboye in 1855.[47] Ella died unmarried at Crawfordsburn in 1865, where she had continued to live with her brother John following her father's death and after her sisters had departed.[48] The youngest daughter, Eleanor, married in 1863 her cousin Thomas Douglas Crawford, son of the wealthy wine merchant James Crawford of Bloomfield.

Setting up and securing so many children on career and marriage pathways was expensive, and clearly created some anxiety for the aging William Sharman Crawford. At the time of Arthur's marriage in 1846 he had drawn up charges on his estates, amounting to £4,000 for each of his children; these were payable on his death, but could be accessed earlier, as when he advanced William junior £1,000 from his entitlement in 1848, presumably to assist the formation of his Belfast business concerns. By 1857 both William junior and Henry had already received half their entitlement.[49] An amendment to his will in 1854 clarified these arrangements following Frederick's death. His decision in the 1840s to peg his estate rentals below any increase in the prices of agricultural produce was becoming more difficult to maintain as prices soared in the mid to late 1850s. In early 1856 he again informed his tenants of his reluctance to increase rents, despite his 'just claims' to do so following sustained price rises, because of the failure to attain legislation that would ensure their security.[50] Explaining the continuation of this policy in a public letter a year later, he stated that what he could do regarding the latter was curbed by the entailed state of much of his lands (specifically the Upper Iveagh townlands).[51]

William's personal dress style, which was deeply intertwined with his 'popular' political persona, continued to stress frugality and economy. The former editor of *Northern Whig* wrote after his death of his 'seedy-looking' appearance and lack of interest in fine clothing or fashion:

> This old gentleman dressed shabbily enough in black seedy broad-cloth, 'a world too wide', and clumsily fashioned by the village tailor. His boots were broad enough in all conscience to keep from pinching his corns. His hat looked as if it had (as it may have been) bought at one of those houses in Holywell or Wych street, London, where they dress up old mixed-up 'tiles' and sell them as new for a small consideration. And his hands were covered by black cotton gloves at least a full inch too long in the fingers.

He added that '[w]hen his sons were boys, his habit was to buy a small bale of broadcloth, hand it over to the village tailor aforesaid, and have himself and the youngsters measured and clad in it'.[52] Such penny-pinching was perhaps understandably resented by some of his offspring and his seemingly obdurate adherence to keeping low rents was increasingly regarded as a check on their status aspirations to gentility.

William's generosity towards his tenants had previously provoked a dispute with Arthur over the Meath estate in 1851, which had led to the father formally relinquishing management of Stalleen to his son. William wrote sharply:

> Now do not suppose I do this from any angry feeling I do it entirely from a sense of what is just to you, and what is consistent with my own position. It would be unpardonable of me, when I have settled the property on you to do anything injurious to you or which you would suppose to be injurious [...] my anxious desire is that my memory should suffer no depreciation in the feelings of my family who come after me; as they would do if they could think that to serve a whim of my own, I had sacrificed their permanent interests.[53]

The priorities of family expectations and tenant-right practice were thus coming into conflict with each other. Given the depressed income from the estates, Crawford had been obliged to borrow to meet advances on his family commitments, but was adamant that he would not saddle his land with any mortgages (although he had previously lent money to others on the security of land). He was equally opposed to selling off any portions of the old Sharman estate to raise funds. The issue now was how to increase rents without reneging on his life-long commitments to tenant right, especially with respect to his own tenants.[54]

In early 1857, William discussed with James a possible solution to this financial and political dilemma. In the absence of a tenant compensation act and with what now appeared to be a permanent elevation of agricultural prices, he proposed that the rents now be revised in return for an enhancement of tenant security. This might be done by offering his tenants leases in perpetuity in return for 'fining down' the rent — that is, the payment of up-front sums in return for low and secure long-term payments. If successful, this would produce the cash necessary to meet his family settlements, while at the same time securing the tenants from any threatened losses following a change of ownership or sale of portions of the estate. Tenants would not be obliged to 'fine down', but if they chose not to they would take on themselves the future risk for the security of their tenant right and would remain tenants at will at higher rents. William was sure that this solution would benefit both the family and the tenants, but was acutely aware that, on his entailed (pre-1827) lands, he lacked the power to grant such perpetual leases without the formal approval of his heir.[55] The problem, he confided to James, was the breakdown in John's health (there is an implication of mental health concerns) and his poor relations with his father, which he feared would produce a veto if the matter was pushed to a decision:

> My impression is that John's opinions are not moulded in the same cast that mine are, upon the land question – or in fact upon any question – small or large – his action with me is rather the result of respect and dutiful submission, than an impression of my views being right – I think he looks upon them as (in parliamentary language) <u>crotchets</u> which may be forgiven, but not approved, and his personal attachment and kindly feeling (of both which there is not a doubt) prevents him <u>manifesting</u> any contrary views to mine. The case however is different, when a matter affecting his future property is under discussion, and I should apprehend produces a want of confidence in any arrangement I might propose. I can not urge my views, even if he were in health. If I did, it would either produce a disagreement or an unwilling submission which I could not accept. But then on the other hand – what is <u>my</u> position? Here I am one of that unfortunate class – the <u>nominal</u> owner of landed property. The <u>apparently</u> responsible owner – without the slightest power to do any act in its arrangement. My son has no power any more than myself during my life but he can <u>withhold the power</u> from me – both of us certainly can do nothing. Here I am come to the time of life, which would render me desirous to settle these matters. Then you can conceive the humiliation which I would feel in asking leave of my son to do any thing I might wish to do on the estates – I can not descend to that – so I see no alternative but that matters must work on as chance may have it during my lifetime.

This highly personal letter ended with a lament that his own advanced age was in part responsible for curbing the life chances of his younger children.[56]

Later in the year he hoped that John's improving health might facilitate an open discussion of the question, but was also mulling dividing up the Crawfordsburn demesne for building plots and moving the family home to Rademon as an alternative.[57] Although negotiations with John now appeared a possibility, he still feared the worst, suspecting that his son's concerns arose from a sense of landed amour-propre: 'aristocratical dignity might be lowered by it – true enough it would – but a certain rental without the possibility of drawback or without trouble would be the greatest possible blessing in my mind'. Creating perpetual tenancies would deprive the landlord of 'territorial power', and there was still strong social prejudice against breaking this mode of elite control over the land and its occupants, despite his own life-long aspiration to do just that. He asked James to retain a copy of his own statements on the matter that might (if necessary) be released to his tenants after his death to assure them that he had acted in good faith with them and had respected the 'holy responsibility' of collaborative landlordism.[58]

As anticipated, John – strongly supported by Arthur – opposed their father's plan, on the grounds that the tenants had not improved sufficiently and hence did not deserve the boon proposed. John and Arthur may have been influenced in their opposition by the experience of the nearby Donegall estate; its heavily indebted proprietor had issued large numbers of perpetual leases at low rents in return for up-front fines from 1822, but this had not saved his successor from having to sell Belfast and its environs under the Encumbered Estates Court at a considerable loss on its paper value in the 1850s.[59] To William their argument missed the point that the security given by perpetual leases at affordable rents would guarantee the family's income. He was willing to discuss a compromise of offering the perpetuities first to the larger, more active tenants, in the hope that once established, the policy would stimulate industry and eventually be extended; he still felt it 'a duty to induce my successor to join me' in fulfilling his promise to place his tenants in a more independent position.[60] However, blocked by his son's obduracy, he was obliged to abandon the scheme in 1858.[61]

Worn down by family resistance, and now in his eighty-first year, William felt it necessary to formally cede all remaining control over the estates to John in early 1861.[62] John would proceed to raise rents (albeit consensually given the surge in prices at the time) after 1865, and would also sell off a chunk of the estate at Ballyvarnet near Bangor for building lots in 1877.[63] Although there were important continuities in the management of the estates after 1861, not least due to James's continuing role as the practical manager of the business, his father's more radical vision for the future was not realised, and under his successors the distinctiveness of Crawfordsburn's land management practice began to fade.

Empire, armies and reform

While William Sharman Crawford's radical reformism was principally concerned with domestic affairs, he also had a long record of criticising what he saw as the aggressive expansion of the British empire overseas and the social conventions and militarism at home that made this possible. This was evident in his attendance at the inaugural Universal Peace Convention, an international event held at Joseph Sturge's prompting in London in 1843, where he moved a resolution that 'the recent wars in China, Afghanistan, and now on the Ameers of Scinde, are […] gross violations of all equitable Christian principles, and directly calculated to prejudice the reception of evangelical truth in heathen nations, as well as to deprecate the character and influence of the British people throughout the whole civilized world'.[64] He had already spoken out against the first Opium War against Qing China (1839–42), and in 1844 protested in parliament 'against the bloody, unjust, and unnecessary wars that had taken place in India' and was in a small minority of eleven who voted against celebrating the achievements of Sir Charles Napier, who had just conquered the province of Scinde (modern Sindh) for the empire.[65] All of these stances reflected his adherence to the brand of anti-war 'moral radicalism' associated with Sturge in the 1840s, and to which Crawford remained attached to the end of his life.[66]

This did not mean that he opposed the existence of the empire in its entirety or Ireland's place within it – both of which he accepted as established facts. As we have seen with regard to his plan for a federal constitution in 1843–4, he saw in the example of the newly established constitution of Canada in 1840 a model for Ireland's future relationship with Britain and its possessions (just as Isaac Butt was to do again following the further extension of Canadian autonomy with the British North America Act of 1867). This led some Repealers to criticise him for seeking to 'render perpetual' Ireland's 'colonial condition and character', but as with many Irish liberals Crawford believed a reformed empire, moving towards greater colonial autonomy and renouncing militarism, was a more achievable ambition than forcible separation from a geopolitical entity then at its global apogee.[67]

For Crawford, the point where domestic reform and overseas aggression intersected lay in the existence of a large standing army in the UK (supplemented by the East India Company's own extensive armed forces in the east up to 1858). A critique of military expenditure had been central to his assertive if unsuccessful 1840s campaigns against the annual supply vote. He calculated the 'home' military forces in 1844 at around 88,000 (including the paramilitary Irish Constabulary), and argued such an establishment was both unnecessary and unconstitutional. The real reason for such an enormous garrison was not the defence of the realm, but to secure the elites against any threat from the working class in Britain and the people of Ireland, whose just rights they continued to deny. The inequitable taxation regime ensured that it was the poor and not the rich who bore the costs of this bloated military deadweight.[68] This line of argument was predictably unpopular in parliament, but reflected a voluntaristic approach to national defence that looked back to the citizen-soldier volunteering of his father's era now revivified through his engagement with Sturge's promotion and Cobden's endorsement of an international peace movement.[69] This position had some popular support: a branch of the peace society was established in Rochdale in 1846 and sent him a petition signed by 1,483 inhabitants protesting against the enlistment system and sending soldiers overseas.[70]

It is hardly surprising that, in conformity with these long-held principles, Crawford opted to back his allies Cobden and Bright in publicly criticising Britain's participation in the Crimean War in 1854–6. In the context of the patriotic war fervour rampant in both Britain and Ireland this was not a popular option; as Cobden wrote to him, 'when all classes from the Queen to the beggar join more or less in hallooing on this war it may well stagger one's convictions to find himself almost alone in opposition to it. Hence the pleasure I find in discovering that I have your concurrence and sympathy'. They were in agreement that such jingoist excitements were mere distractions diverting 'the attention of the public from domestic reforms and thus throw[ing] a veil over every deformity of our social system'.[71]

Although now retired from parliament, Crawford was prepared to voice his opinions on the matter in the public arena, especially as the war ground towards a stalemate. He took advantage of a presentation made to him for his services to the borough of Rochdale in October 1855 to express his scepticism of the administration's claims:

The country was now engaged in war. Was it carried on for any purpose connected with the right interests of the people? Was it to establish the liberty of Europe? He hoped it was; but he warned the people of England to take care that they were not deceived. He warned them to take care that they were not spending their money and blood for a useless purpose.[72]

The Palmerstonian press condemned him for failing to grasp the war's 'noble causes' and making such a speech in time of conflict, while reserving its full fire for the larger target of Bright, who had also made an anti-war speech at the same reception.[73] Crawford responded by questioning the government's claim to be acting to 'sustain popular rights, and to restore obliterated nationalities in Europe', when its objectives were tied up with secret diplomacy, unchecked by any democratic oversight. A war allegedly for the 'liberties of the world' was being pursued through alliances with despotic foreign powers such as the Prussians and Austrians.[74] Even Crawford's loyal supporters in the *Banner of Ulster* clearly had some concerns about his stance, while it chose to contrast his quiet questioning with what it depicted as the brawling demagoguery of Bright.[75] In a follow-up letter, Crawford acknowledged that the war was popular, but repeated his suspicion of Palmerston's bona fides.[76] This was a difficult position to hold given widespread Irish enthusiasm for the conflict, although some were to echo in private his rejection of the militarism it spurred.[77] At the same time Crawford was not unsympathetic to the well-publicised plight of the poorly-supplied ordinary British soldiers overseas and their families at home, and indeed he and his family contributed generously to the Patriotic Fund established in 1854 to aid widows and orphans of soldiers and sailors killed in the war.[78]

He responded similarly to the Indian rebellion of 1857, subscribing to the fund set up to assist Europeans injured, bereaved or forced into flight by the revolt, while at the same time criticising the oppression and misrule that had driven the Indians to acts of desperation.[79] In a private sermon, read to his household on the fast day instituted by the state to pray for deliverance from the rebellion on 7 October, he declaimed:

> We confess before thee that we are guilty as a nation in various ways but more especially in the treatment of the people of our Indian territory who have been for a long series of years subjected to our dominion. We confess that our rule has not been for the good of the people, nor for the praise or honor of thy holy name and we must fear that we must further confess that it has been used for the sordid object of the extortion of wealth by the oppression of tyrant power: – that for this unholy purpose we have used our armies to depose sovereigns and to annex territory to our dominions, without the sanction of the will of the people subjected to our rule. That we have thus levied tribute and taxes for the support of our government, whilst at the same time, we have permitted our servants placed in India for the discharge of civil and military duties to obtain by unjust extortion the means of personal aggrandizement and wealth. That even when other means failed, torture has been used by our servants to exact unhallowed revenue for the maintaining of our despotism: – that in pursuance of this guilty object the interests of the people of that country have been committed to the management of a commercial company, whose sole object was to seek by that connection the improvement of their trading interests, on the prosperity of which their very existence depended: – that treaties and engagements have been violated and the settlement of property according to the laws of India has been unscrupulously set aside.

If divine providence had, as some held, given Britain influence over India to disseminate religious truth, this had been squandered by the materialist pursuit of wealth and power, which had 'brought into contempt that holy religion of which it should have been our object to extend the benefits as well by example as instruction'. While Crawford was prepared to pray for the relief of those Europeans who had settled there, and the success of any armies dispatched to protect them so long as these did not pursue vengeance, his underlying view was that in the absence of consent, only Indian independence would free Britain from the moral contagion that had brought disaster down upon it. 'O Lord', he concluded, 'teach our governing powers that no nation has a right to assume or hold by force of arms usurped dominion over any other nation [...]'. Britain's colonial crimes, immoral resort to offensive war and political depravity at home had, he believed, denied it any entitlement to rule others.[80] Such an interpretation was very much at odds with the general tenor of public fast day sermons in Britain, which combined calls for moral rearmament at home and the governance of India with a discursive justification of British colonial mission.[81]

A public statement he made some weeks later at a county meeting in support of the relief fund was more circumspect. He could not deny, he said, the truth of the accounts of many atrocities against British residents carried out by the rebellious sepoys, or the need for punishment of such crimes. Nevertheless, they must remember that the people of India (most of whom were not involved in any violence) were hostile to British domination for good reasons, having been subjected to the rapacity of the East India Company for generations, which had been unchecked and empowered by British governments. If Britain was to retain control in India, a complete revision of its administration, making it responsible to its people and governing in their interests and according to the true precepts of Christianity, was now essential, and there must be no retribution against the general population.[82] The following year he wrote to the non-electors of Rochdale to congratulate them on local protests against continuing abuses in India, and to praise Bright (now MP for Birmingham) on his principled stand against the matter being turned into a party-political football.[83]

Having taken this stance, it should come as no surprise that he was dismayed by the decision of his grandson, Fitzherbert Coddington, to accept a commission in the East India Company's army in 1857. He wrote to his father Henry 'in sorrow' over what appeared to him a demonstrably immoral decision, as in the wake of the rebellion, the true extent of the 'wicked administration of the affairs of India' by the Company had been revealed, not least by Sir Charles Napier's own reports. As the revolt had been sparked by a criminal system of government, any campaign to repress it, in which his grandson seemed so anxious to participate, could be neither just nor honourable.[84]

Crawford clearly endorsed the view that maintaining such injustice would provoke future unrest in the sub-continent, even if he never developed a full-blown critique of British colonialism there. While his support for the Indian relief funds marked him out from the most extreme strands of Irish nationalism voicing support for the rebels, his attacks on British misrule in India placed him in alignment with the 'advanced' position voiced by the *Nation* and at odds with the growing popular imperialism evident in the north and reinforced by episodes such as the 'martyrdom' of the Ulsterman Brigadier John Nicholson (a hyper-violent instigator of collective punishment of 'disloyal' natives) at the siege of Delhi.[85]

It is evident that Crawford placed some importance in retaining his connections with Rochdale, and especially with his old friend Thomas Livsey, appearing there in October 1855 wearing his election cockade of 1841 to receive a testimonial from the civic authorities.

This was not simply a matter of nostalgia, as he wrote later to Livsey that he placed great hopes in a revival there of the campaign for franchise reform that had been largely dormant since the late 1840s.[86] He remained a member of the Ballot Society, speaking in support of the secret ballot (and observing it had already been adopted in some of the Australian colonies such as Victoria) and of franchise extension, both in London and to 'large and enthusiastic' meetings in Rochdale in 1857–8.[87] Radical hopes were restored by Bright's commitment to introduce a parliamentary reform bill in the 1859 session; Sturge and Crawford lobbied him to include manhood suffrage (at the age of twenty-five) in it to 'unite all true reformers'.[88] In this they were unsuccessful – Bright opted for a ratepayer franchise in boroughs and a £10 rental franchise in counties – but he did include the ballot and a major redistribution of seats, and consulted Crawford on the Irish elements of the latter.[89] The inclusion of the ballot was enough to retain his support for it as an incremental measure, especially as it appeared that the Whig-liberal leaders Palmerston and Russell (then rivals in opposition) might take a more 'advanced' bill seriously as a means to unite the party behind their personal leadership, at a time when the Conservatives were contemplating a much more muted measure. Crawford spoke in support of Bright's bill at a rally at the Dublin Rotunda on St Patrick's Day 1859.[90]

This return to the public arena by the elderly Crawford sparked contemptuous hostility in some circles. To the *Belfast Mercury* he embodied the fruitless agitational politics of the past in an age of Victorian material progress and in Ulster of evangelical reawakening that year:

> He appears to have taken 'no note of time.' He thinks the world still wags in the senseless way it did when O'Connell ridiculed him as 'Sharman in the white waistcoat!' His ambition was ever to be a demagogue without possessing the qualifications for the distasteful office [...] yet would not bear the expense and other attendant ills. But private ambition is one thing, and public career another – combine both, however, and let us soberly ask, what is there in Mr Sharman Crawford's combined career that entitles him, this year of grace, 1859, to come forward and sound the tocsin for a renewed agitation? Why should he now cry out – 'Agitate, agitate, agitate?' What has he been doing during the matured years of his life? Has he been exempt 'from the toil of dropping buckets into empty wells, and growing old in drawing nothing up!' Has not this been truthfully his vocation, and why should we now follow him as a prophet and a guide?[91]

Shrugging off such jibes, Crawford reissued his 1843 speech on the moral and political necessity of 'complete suffrage' as *The Non-Elector's Plea for the Suffrage: Addressed to the Non-electors of Rochdale*. An afterward joked that, unlike some, there was no danger of him drifting rightwards into Toryism as he grew older, and reasserted that he remained certain that the 'old body of the constitution' needed the invigoration of 'the infusion of new blood of working classes', as the only way by which the stability and prosperity of British empire could be secured.[92]

He celebrated Cobden's return for the borough in the general election of that year, reaffirming the dictum that neither he nor the people sought revolution, but rather the restoration to the people of their own constitution.[93] Although the 1859 reform bill was frustrated by parliamentary manoeuvring, it is evident that Crawford was still held in high esteem in Lancashire, and among the next generation of franchise reform activists nationally, and he was invited to join the Parliamentary Reform Committee in London later that year.[94]

His membership of this was not passive; he warned them that any bill that did not remove property qualifications, stamp out electoral corruption and treating, and provide the safety of the secret ballot would be useless. Experience had shown that '[t]o extend the franchise in Ireland is utterly worthless unless some freedom of election is granted'.[95] His intervention seems to have had effect, as the committee resolved that any acceptable bill must include 'a large extension of the suffrage; an equitable re-distribution of seats; assimilation of the electoral laws of England, Scotland and Ireland; a repeal of the Septennial Act; and vote by ballot.'[96] He continued to liaise with old radicals such as John Bowring (who praised him as the 'most incorruptible of public men') and Cobden.[97]

A few months before his death, he was still to be found, to the disgust of those who had hoped the reform movement finally dead, on a platform, chairing by invitation a meeting in the Belfast Corn Exchange. A hostile reporter noted:

> His speech, addressed to an audience of working men, nearly akin to a mob assembly, with his usual judgment, was crammed with quotations from Blackstone and pamphlets on political economy! It being deplorably dry, the crowd relieved themselves by shouts of an indescribable character. Eventually, amid much tumult, four 'indignation' resolutions were put from the chair, and declared to be passed, with astonishing power of lung. The reformers were indignant with everybody, and everything, and closed their proceedings in a blaze of righteous fury.[98]

But where his enemies simply saw a 'veteran in the ranks of failure' posturing before a mob, he regarded himself as consistently adhering to the principles that had first impelled him into political life in 1829 – challenging the 'oligarchy of the landed and moneyed aristocracy', and the class legislation it pursued, for as long and insistently as this was necessary. There was still hope, he concluded, that Belfast could throw off the curse of sectarian conflict (so painfully witnessed in the bloody and sustained riots of 1857) and return to the forefront of radical reformism it had occupied in his father's time. Aware he was himself both a connection to and also a relic of that past, he urged his audience to find new leaders from the town to take forward the struggle for class justice.[99]

In this final public speech he returned again to the evils of the standing army and the extension of foreign possessions by war as means of creating patronage jobs for the upper classes, at the expense of the taxes of the unenfranchised poor. Militarism, especially when related to imperialism, continued to preoccupy him in these latter years, and he penned a series of 'Questions to a Soldier' in 1860 (which it appears went unpublished). His concern here was with the potential conflict between conscience, informed by religious sensibility, and the slavish subservience of the soldier to the orders of the state. While he accepted the possibility of a just war, in his experience most of those recently pursued by Britain had not met this criterion and hence had placed soldiers in moral jeopardy. Colonial wars posed this issue of the use of violence to expropriate indigenous peoples most starkly:

> As for example refer to the wars in India undertaken by the East India Company – which service was particularly sought for, in consequence of the higher pay and emoluments welded to it. Were not these wars generally for the purposes of aggression on the natives of the country – were such wars justifiable according to the precepts of the blessed founder of Christianity? Again take the present war in New Zealand – a war to take possession of the lands from the poor native inhabitants against their will. Is this a justifiable war according to Christian principle – and yet here the hired soldier becomes the agent of the state without any discretion

of his own – committing practically murder and robbery and devastation, although all the time professing the religion and service of Jesus Christ.[100]

The second Opium War (1856–60) also attracted his condemnation, as 'clearly a war of vengeance for a former defeat of the British forces by a people acting in their own defence against an unlawful aggression made for the sole object of British aggrandisement. If such an attempt had been made by China towards England, would it not have been held as affording the ground for justifiable resistance[?]'.[101]

Boarding schools for boys, which were growing in popularity among the Victorian elite, including the Ulster gentry although not as yet the Belfast middle classes, also drew his fire.[102] These institutions, far removed from the beneficial influence of family values and genuine religion, were, he believed, perpetrating precisely that moral dissipation that made more likely such political evils as '[u]ndertaking unjustifiable wars, and diffusing all the dreadful evils of death and plunder through peaceful communities'. In these schools 'boys learn it is no sin to sell themselves to the state to be the instruments of all such works'.[103] His own children would be educated at home before in some cases proceeding to university so as to spare them from such dangers.

For Crawford, self-defence was one of the few acceptable justifications for war, but how should a society defend itself without the corrupting influence of a standing army? His answer looked back to the tradition he had inherited from his father. In 1859, in response to a war-scare with France, the government had called on local authorities in Great Britain to promote the formation of volunteer military units to act as a part-time national defence force in case of invasion. The call met with an enthusiastic reaction, especially from middle-class rifle clubs, and the bodies raised would go on to form the basis of the later Territorial Army. The idea of voluntary service was one close to Crawford's heart, but he was angered by the deliberate and 'degrading' exclusion of Ireland from the new volunteer movement, and he penned a long letter on the subject, initially addressed to Palmerston but later redirected to the secretary of the Irish Rifle Association and published as a short pamphlet. The reason given for this sidelining of Ireland, he noted with disgust, was the 'Orange aggression' — specifically, the shooting of Catholics following an illegal Orange parade at Derrymacash, Co. Armagh, in July 1860 – which were being used as an excuse to refuse extension of the volunteer movement.[104]

His reaction was to offer a historical sketch of the Irish Volunteers of 1778–93 as a justification of Ireland's entitlement to participation in the new movement.[105] The Volunteers had, he maintained, not only deterred foreign intervention and maintained order, but acted as a transformative force in Irish politics by devoting 'themselves, by the moral power of constitutional agitation, to the redress of the enormous grievances then inflicted on Ireland by British rule'. In rejecting the revolutionary infiltration and foreign entanglements of the United Irishmen they had demonstrated their underlying loyalty, while continuing to demand popular reforms of a corrupt system; but the government's suppression of the Volunteers in 1793 had removed this moderating force and propelled Ireland towards the disaster of the 'bloody civil war' of 1798. The consequence had been a forced and imperfect union: as 'the seditious proceedings of the United Irishmen and the rebellion of 1798 afforded the opportunity – and Ireland suffered (what I now must call) the irremediable misfortune of the total extinction of her local legislature – without obtaining even then or since the compensation of an intimate incorporation with England on provisions of equality and justice'. The expediency of his argument led Crawford to also defend the record of the Yeomanry, at least from 1803, and to play up their role in national defence and down their sectarianism, but his principal focus was on the older Volunteer movement. He concluded that admission of Irishmen to the new defensive body, albeit under requirements of good behaviour, could again have a transformative effect of rebuilding local pride and patriotism, and overcoming partisan passions and crime.

However by 1860, with sectarian animosities rampant in Ulster and the emergence of Fenianism, Crawford's backward-looking appeal to an idealised past appeared a forlorn hope, and he admitted as such privately, lamenting that after fifty-nine years the union remained nominal and British government uninterested in solving its problems.[106] Both the unionist and nationalist press praised his writing on the Volunteers as history, and the *Whig* lauded him as the 'patriarch of patriotism', but most could see only a very limited application of his history to the troubled present.[107]

Religion and conversion to Unitarianism

Throughout most of his life William Sharman Crawford had adhered to a sincere, if highly unorthodox, Anglicanism. He had been a church warden during his youth in Moira and Waringstown, although over time he became less directly involved with parochial affairs.[108] His Protestantism was of an ecumenical cast, open to engagement with a range of doctrinal positions and tolerant of Catholicism while at the same time persuaded of the moral and spiritual superiority of reformed Christianity. However, relations with clergy of his own church had been strained by the increasingly strident hostility towards any form of religious establishment he had embraced by the 1830s and his insistence on the strict separation of church and state. For him, religion was a serious but personal matter, which should inform the moral conscience and action of public figures but which was at risk of corruption from any privileges or endowments which must render the church subservient to the state or from doctrines which undermined the primacy of moral social action. Consequently, his politics had been shaped by a campaigns for religious freedom, from Catholic emancipation in 1829 through sustained drives for the abolition of tithes and church rates (and more problematically for his Presbyterian and Catholic allies, also for the removal of the regium donum and the Maynooth grant).[109]

In the mid-1840s he had endorsed the Anti-State Church Association (later renamed the Liberation Society), and by the 1850s he was an open supporter of the case for disestablishing the Anglican church in Ireland, and he wrote in support of his Rochdale successor Edward Miall's parliamentary motion for this in 1856.[110] By 1859 he was also ready to support Miall's call for English disestablishment, warning that 'Parliament is the pope of the established church', and musing that it retained its position solely from its association with aristocratic pretensions and social fashionability.[111]

His adherence to strict voluntarism in both countries intensified rather than softened over time. This could occasionally provoke unease among some of his supporters, as for example, when he led the Newtownards board of guardians in opposing any funding from the rates for the provision of a Catholic altar and vestments, which was requested by the Catholic workhouse chaplain in 1859. When the poor law commissioners upheld the chaplain's claim, Crawford and the board took them to court and won. He insisted that his stance had in no way arisen from anti-Catholic bigotry, but from the principle of the strict separation of church and state, which should be maintained in all public institutions, including the workhouses.[112]

In the years following his forced retirement from parliament in 1852, he continued to support the churches of different denominations, although he had no longer a direct political interest in doing so. This frequently took the form of participating in fundraising for the erection or repair of new buildings or providing retirement testimonials to clergy, and included the orthodox Presbyterian congregations of Ballygilbert, Second Bangor and Ballycopeland, the remonstrant (non-subscribing) Presbyterians of York Street in Belfast, where he laid the foundation stone of a new church in 1855, and the Methodist New Connection in Bangor.[113] He was present at the consecration of the new Catholic church in Bangor in 1851 and made a financial contribution.[114] Absent from these press reports is any mention of William attending services of the established church, apart from funerals to the graveyard of the parish church at Kilmore, where the family had inherited a burial vault from the Crawfords in 1827, although presumably he continued to attend divine service in the Bangor area until the later 1850s (Figure 31).[115]

As we have seen, James Sharman Crawford left Kilmore parish church with many other congregants to join the Presbyterians in 1846 following a dispute over ritualism. His father however, despite his open rift with his own denomination, remained formally an Anglican for some years thereafter. However, his papers indicate a crisis of faith in his final years, which would lead to his formal adoption of Unitarianism and membership of the non-subscribing Presbyterian congregation of Holywood by the time of his death. By June 1855 he had read the Holywood minister Rev. Charles McAlister's 'remarkable sermon' on unitarianism and noted his agreement with its argument that the Trinity was unscriptural and the Athanasian creed (which formed part of Anglican doctrine and liturgy) both unreasonable in its assertions and uncharitable towards those of other denominations. He commented that he now found Anglican beliefs both irrational and insufficiently reformed, and the requirement to repeat the Athanasian Creed in particular could not be reconciled to his conscience.[116] Over the following years he collected and carefully annotated a number of printed sermons by other unitarian clergymen, singling out those by the Belfast ministers Rev. John Scott Porter and Rev. William Bruce (son of his father's friend of the same name), praising the latter for combatting 'the blind submission to human creeds and doctrines without exercising the powers of the mind to determine whether agreeable to scripture or not'.[117]

Spurred by the new requirement to enter religious affiliation in the Irish census return, and perhaps sensing that death was approaching, in early 1861 he prepared several personal statements for the benefit of his family, insisting they '[o]bserve I die holding the professions of faith hereunto annexed; a member of Mr. McAlister's congregation in Holywood' and setting out in some detail his reasons for leaving the established church.[118] These memoranda, along with several sermons he prepared at the time to read to his household, distilled the thinking he had previously expressed in his marginalia – that the creeds espoused by the established church were unscriptural and that he could not in conscience subscribe to them, and that it was an 'aristocratical church' more concerned with social prestige and state control than religious truth. To remain within it would have been not only hypocritical but have placed his soul in peril. He appears to have become a regular attender at the Holywood non-subscribing church, an imposing neo-classical edifice designed by Charles Lanyon and opened in 1849, in which McAlister ministered for over sixty years. Crawford left written abstracts of sermons preached there, the final one written cogently just three weeks before his death.[119]

At the same time, he made it clear that he could not accept the orthodox Presbyterian church's Calvinist doctrines, for the 'Westminster Confession proclaims that God has through all eternity decreed that some will be saved and some damned without any agency to the individual – is it to be believed that this is the true doctrine of our blessed saviour Jesus Christ?'. Too many, he lamented, remained dutiful members of the churches they were born into without reflecting critically on their professions and beliefs. True Christianity must combine the use of God-given rationality with adherence to the teachings of Christ himself, which were 'such a benevolent system, as must command the admiration of all mankind and exhibit in the strongest possible manner the divine origins of the doctrines which he taught and the love of the Almighty God towards his creatures. Then I would say what is the responsibility of any man who attempts to make salvation depend upon incomprehensible dogmas of faith?'.[120] The Calvinist doctrine of predestination he found to be unscriptural, cruel and likely to incline people towards an antinomian disregard for their own sins and for the moral social action enjoined by Christ's teaching. In contrast, '[t]he Unitarian church is based on the principle that the greatest means of acceptance with the Almighty is the fulfilment of the moral duties as commanded by our saviour and carrying out the objects of the Christian dispensation in love to God and love to man. That man is not by nature corrupt as he emanates from the creative hands of God, but becomes corrupt by his own evil use of power and qualifications conferred on him by the creator.' The true Christianity it taught urged people to step away from the emotional safety net of assurance through faith to engage with a social gospel that addressed the relationships between people, including, he noted, those between landlords and tenants and in political participation.[121]

In his 1861 religious profession he returned to his long-standing preoccupation with the morally debilitating consequences of state religion, particular in relation to militarism and its legitimation of state violence and aggressive imperialism. He wrote:

> When the conduct of men is scrutinized even of men bearing the reputation of the highest degree of respect for religious ordinances, how great are the inconsistencies we witness. How can such men professionally sell themselves to the state to be murderers of their fellow creatures, without regard to the conformity of this act with the will of God. Every man who adopts the army as a profession does this [...] How can governments carry fire and sword against unoffending communities for the purpose of enlarging dominions or acquiring improved commercial profits (as the British government are doing at this moment in China – and have done for centuries past in India) – How can religious parents deliberately educate their sons to enter into this profession[?][122]

He addressed this theme in a sermon read to his household, which may have created certain tensions within the family, with two of his resident sons serving as officers in the Irish militia in the 1850s.[123]

A final memorandum of 1861 entitled 'My faith' attempted to summarise the outcome of his spiritual reflections, and point to the adoption of a liberal and rational mode of Christianity:

> I believe the holy scriptures of the old and new testament as declaring the will of God and the rules of faith and duty; and as containing all knowledge necessary for salvation, but not at the same time subscribing to the doctrine that every portion of the said scriptures historical and doctrinal are subject to an inspiration from God almighty. [...] I believe that God in his mercy will accept my imperfect services, and will pardon my sins – through the means of the scheme of redemption of which our blessed Redeemer was the instrument, and that Jesus Christ still continues to mediate on behalf of the human race with the great and merciful God.

In the case of any apparent anomalies within scripture, he noted, Christ's own teachings must be given precedence, and 'no doctrine should be accepted which is contrary to the practice and mercy of God', or in contradiction to God-given human reason. He was aware, given the contemporary development of biblical criticism, that the text of the bible was the product of many translations, some of which may have involved errors of misconstructions of the original. The Old Testament, in particular, should thus be understood in its historical context and not treated as literally true, as it was 'adapted to the knowledge and habits of the generations of men at the day in which they were written and especially with regard to the phenomena of nature, and not as stating real facts of these phenomena'. Some critical reflection was required, as the 'prophetic portions of the Old Testament are declared by the writers of them to be the word of God – but it does not follow, that we are bound to admit the same authority as to every other portion of the various sayings and records of the New Testament'.[124]

Crawford's faith, then was one of a liberal Christianity closely aligned to enlightened rationality, informed by an awareness of developments in biblical criticism of his own times. The great evangelical revival in Ulster of 1859 and its emotional excesses left him largely unmoved, and he posed sceptical questions to the orthodox Presbyterian clergy about how they could reconcile their faith in predestination with endorsement of such individual charismatic manifestations.[125] His belief in a practical Christianity was, nonetheless, deeply and sincerely held and it had, at least in part, motivated his long political career and consoled him that he had pursued the path of righteousness despite every setback. He concluded that 'every man is responsible according to his means of knowledge and intellect, as well as the temporal means of life which the Almighty has conferred upon him to do the utmost good in his power to his fellow man'.[126]

Death and commemoration

William Sharman Crawford died on 17 October 1861 at Crawfordsburn, some six weeks after his eighty-first birthday. His death had come suddenly, as he had chaired the Newtownards board of guardians two days previously as normal, afflicted by nothing worse than a cold. He may then have suffered a stroke which had rendered him 'speechless' on the 16th, and, it was reported, his end came without indication of much suffering and with his children present at his bedside: a classic Victorian 'good death'.[127] He was buried four days later in the family mausoleum at Kilmore, following a service led by the Unitarian

Rev. Charles McAlister, who spoke of his 'blessed and peaceful end to an honoured and useful life'. Although the interment was intended to be private, 'a very great assembly from Belfast and various parts of the counties Down and Antrim' followed the hearse from Rademon, and Livsey was present to convey the respects of the borough of Rochdale. Large numbers of the tenants attended, in the words of the *Northern Whig*, to express 'both in looks and words their heartfelt regret for the good old man, good landlord, and good friend whom they had lost'.[128] Sharman Crawford's funeral was inevitably a political event.

His public profile ensured that numerous papers, in Britain as well as Ireland, carried death notices or longer obituaries. While most were either positive or neutral, some writers continued to believe it necessary to attack his ideas and principles in death as they had in life. One of the most prominent of these critical assessments came in the free-trade liberal *Belfast Mercury*. His candidacy for Belfast in 1832, the writer asserted, had been a 'fatal mistake', leading to the infusion of the poison of party politics into Belfast life and setting back the cause of liberalism for decades. He should never have ventured on the contest for Down in 1852, when men's minds were driven to 'insanity' by the tenant-right campaign, and his charges against the squirearchy of electoral abuses had only led to a humiliating apology. His vanity and the adulation paid to him had 'obscured his mental vision', with the consequence of his being 'hoodwinked' by disreputable parties such as the Donegal priests in 1859 and Daniel O'Connell decades before. While his adherence to the principles of liberty were sincere, his views on the land question 'were most confused, and, as far as they were intelligible, most revolutionary'. Despite his proposed 'socialist' solution, his own practice as a landlord, the writer averred with some venom, had been to deny his own tenants adequate security. His political career, in all its 'dogged determination', was thus a warning to sensible men of what to avoid.[129]

The *News-Letter* thought Crawford's policies mischievous precisely because he had held them so honestly and consistently, and hence misled others. But unlike its Palmerstonian rival it was ready to admit his personal generosity as a landowner and devotion to local administration and improvement, and thus avoid speaking too much ill of the dead.[130] The ultra-Protestant *Warder* was less forgiving, dismissing him as 'somewhat self-willed and narrow-minded', he had 'spent his life dipping buckets into empty wells', and had 'laboured in vain, and leaves no public monument behind him'.[131] In contrast the Dublin *Daily Express* praised his virtues and political talents, recalling in particular his defiance of O'Connell, while at the same time continuing to regard his tenant-right proposals as 'utopian'.[132]

As might be expected, the more liberal northern papers were more effusive about Crawford's life and legacies. The *Northern Whig*, putting aside the inconsistency of its support for him, perceived that his sudden death had 'awakened universal regret' in Belfast. Following his father's patriotic and reformist example, he had devoted his life to contesting the 'unlimited monarchy' of landlordism and the evils of the system it had created, and had, 'by his fearless agitation of the great question [...] brought public opinion to bear on it to an extent previously unknown'. If his campaign for legislation had not yet succeeded, he had by popularising the issue induced many proprietors to adopt a more liberal system of land-letting; throughout his life and despite all setbacks he had been consistent and 'his love of popular rights never abated'. His memory would remain honoured not only by the tenant farmers but by all friends who shared his reforming values.[133] To the *Banner of*

Ulster his death had left a political blank that could not easily be filled; both his example as a landlord, his writings and his political practice were exemplary manifestations of social justice.[134] His old ally James McKnight penned a long tribute in the *Londonderry Standard* to the 'father of tenant right', which also drew an explicit connection between his virtues and those of his father's generation in contrast to the decadence of the present:

> William Sharman Crawford belonged, in reality, to the patriotic school of the last century, exhibiting a clearness, manliness, enlargement, and moral nobility of purpose, immeasurably superior to that grovelling retrocession, for which so many among the descendants of the great men who, in this country, adorned the last age, are now chiefly distinguished in society. Irish patriotism, in the age alluded to, was eminently characterized by its Roman virtues, disdaining even the appearance of selfishness, combining the loftiest political morality with comprehensive liberalism in every branch of statesmanship, and casting over its policy the illustration of a calm, though really enthusiastic, integrity.

The corrupt and self-interested politicians of modern times had failed to understand him and mocked his 'crotchets' and 'annual crazes', but he had remained unshakable in pursuing the right and just course, and even the local 'feudal Tory' press had failed to find a valid criticism of him of and his principles on his death. Skating around defeats such as the 1852 election, he directed attention to Crawford's continuing engagement with public affairs, noting he had written a long letter on grand jury reform a few weeks prior to his death.[135]

Reflecting his stature as a political actor of national standing in Ireland, the Dublin liberal and nationalist press also printed celebratory obituaries. To the *Evening News* he was a 'true, honest, benevolent old man', and 'in him the Irish tenant has lost a great, a faithful, and an earnest friend'.[136] The *Dublin Evening Post* agreed that he was the 'one of the purest and most single-hearted of public men', and quoted the *Whig's* tribute at length.[137] Even John Gray's *Freeman*, with which he had often crossed swords, praised him as 'almost the last of the race of great men', loyally devoted to the rights of the Irish people, while the *Nation* (now owned and edited by A. M. Sullivan) buried any recollection of animosity in a long and lyrical encomium. Crawford had been, it claimed, one of Ireland's national heroes, who 'gather round them the history of the land in their time, and become a part of it'. If he had failed in his campaign to bring justice to the tenant, the fault lay elsewhere, for he had rendered achievable through his sustained efforts what had once seemed merely visionary. Although, it admitted, he was never an advanced nationalist, he had been 'filled with the leaven of national views' and embodied the spirit of his father's Volunteers.[138]

In Britain the *Times* offered a neutral assessment of Crawford's life, acknowledging his personal benevolence and the veneration in which he was held by the tenants, and recalling his courage in standing up to O'Connell and in proposing the alternative of federalism, while at the same time noting his repeated failure to attain his land bill. It quoted both the *Freeman's* and *Evening News'* positive accounts.[139] As was common, a number of British papers reprinted the *Times'* notice, although some drew directly on the longer *Northern Whig* obituary.[140] Not surprisingly, the Rochdale press was more fulsome, praising him as a 'friend of the people'; on the mayor's instructions, a muffled peal of bells had been sounded in the town 'as a public expression of regret and concern at the mournful event, as so far as possible to do honour to departed worth'.[141] Cobden and Bright's organ *The Morning Star* enthused on his work for the universal suffrage and free-trade campaigns, noting the failure of the former marked 'one of the saddest but most instructive chapters in our national biography', but that Crawford's 'brave, indomitable, unwearied devotion' to democratic reform deserved commemoration.[142]

Preparations for more formal memorialisation soon followed. In Belfast, an engraved and autographed commemorative portrait was produced, which had been drawn by the American artist Napoleon Sarony (later more famous as a celebrity photographer) from a portrait photograph recently in the town taken by his brother Oliver. The print was also sold in Rochdale.[143] The *Banner* observed that, although not originally created as a form of memorialisation, the printing of the image so soon after Crawford's death would allow 'the many thousand friends, supporters and admirers of the departed gentleman [to] shortly have an opportunity of furnishing themselves with an artistic remembrance on one who, amongst friends of the people was [...] "the best of the good"'.[144] It seems probable that the photograph on which it was based is the one now held by the Ulster Museum in the undated Coey Album of cartes-de-visites, and a version of the engraving was re-issued by Gilmour & Dean of Glasgow in 1882 as a supplement to the short-lived Liberal paper the *Belfast Weekly Post* (Figures 29 and 30).[145] In 1879 the National Gallery of Ireland purchased a copy of Thomas Goff Lupton's mezzotint of Knight's 1843 oil portrait of Sharman Crawford, which it put on public display in its new portrait gallery.[146] Another, posthumous, portrait appears to have been painted by F. A. Piccione, a member of an emigre family from the Austrian-controlled territories in northern Italy and who also created the altarpiece for St Malachy's church in Belfast; it was publicly displayed as part of the Belfast Working Men's Industrial Exhibition at the Ulster Hall in 1876, but now appears to be lost.[147]

Large memorials to public figures were still relatively uncommon in Ulster in this period. The bronze figure of the recently deceased Earl of Belfast, son of the third marquess of Donegall and popular for his philanthropic endeavours, was funded by public subscription and erected in College Square in 1855 as Belfast's first free-standing statue.[148] Co. Down contained several monuments to military figures: a granite obelisk was unveiled at Rostrevor in 1826 to the memory of General Robert Ross (the uncle of David Ross MP), who had died following his assault on Washington DC in 1814, and a memorial pillar and statue of the imperial soldier General Robert 'Rollo' Gillespie was erected in 1845 in the village square of Comber, paid for by the Masonic Order of which he had been a member. A similar memorial to the third Marquess of Downshire had been put up on an elevated site outside Hillsborough at the estate's expense in 1848. The builder, James Archer, had designed a monument in the same style to the Earl of Caledon in Tyrone several years before.[149]

Crawford himself had supported the commissioning and erection of a prominent memorial to his old political rival the third Marquess of Londonderry, perhaps at the prompting of his son, with whom he had been reconciled in 1852 and who had hosted a dinner in his honour at Newtownards in 1854.[150] At the end of October 1856 Crawford chaired a meeting in Belfast that selected Lanyon and Lynn's design for a watch tower built of local basalt in the Scottish baronial style to sit atop Scrabo Hill near Newtownards. Although an appeal was made to the tenantry, it appears the bulk of the expense (which rose to £2,300) was met by a smaller number of subscribers, headed by the French emperor

Louis Napoleon.[151] As chair of the building committee, Crawford presided over the laying of the foundation stone at Scrabo in February 1857.[152] The *Whig* commented positively on the non-partisan nature of this event, and treated it as the just commemoration of a patriotic and improving landlord.[153] Perhaps attracted to this style of monument, Crawford had also subscribed to and promoted the building of a baronial-style memorial tower to the medieval patriot William Wallace near Stirling in Scotland, although this project was not completed until 1869.[154]

The initiative to create a memorial to Crawford himself appears to come from his own tenants, and the *Whig* reported they had already appointed collectors for this purpose by the start of February 1862, and urged the wider public to become involved in this tribute.[155] The *Londonderry Standard* added that 'it must not be a merely local affair on the part of Mr Crawford's tenantry. Ireland owes a debt of ineffaceable gratitude to Mr Sharman Crawford, and the intended monument ought to be taken up at once as a national obligation'.[156] Shortly after, the Belfast Parliamentary Reform Association, chaired by John Scott of May Street Foundry, resolved to establish a Sharman Crawford Association to disseminate his writings and speeches on democratic reform and raise money from working men and middle-class supporters both for the memorial and the relief of destitution in the town.[157]

The Sharman Crawford Association appears to have been short lived, but the committee to raise funds for a memorial continued its work under the chairmanship of Dr Hans Harper of Killyleagh, and extended its reach to 'all friends and public admirers'. High profile subscriptions were received from Lords Dufferin and Londonderry and James McCann MP, but most came from tenant farmers. By May 1862 over £630 had been collected.[158] The eventual cost was to be £1,400, raising which may have delayed construction by some time in a period of agricultural recession.[159] However by March the following year Lanyon and Lynn had been appointed architects and an elevation on the Rademon demesne selected as the site, perhaps reflecting James' greater enthusiasm for the project than his brother John at Crawfordsburn.[160] Taking the form of an obelisk modelled on the much larger Wellington Monument in Dublin's Phoenix Park (itself finally completed after lengthy delays in 1861), and placed on a stepped plinth, it was to be constructed of sandstone brought from the family's own quarry at Sheephouse in Meath, which began to arrive by boat in summer 1863 (Figure 32).[161] A striking bronze medallion portrait of Crawford with female supporters representing Hibernia and Agriculture was commissioned from the architect's brother Samuel Ferris Lynn and cast in London, and shipped via Belfast at the family's expense in May 1865 and inserted into the face of the obelisk (Figure 33).[162] An adjacent text panel sought to distil its subject's virtues:

> This monument has been erected by a grateful and attached tenantry, and other friends, in memory of one who, during a long life, was ever a most kind and considerate landlord, the friend of the poor, and the universal advocate of tenant right, and of every measure calculated to promote civil and religious liberty.

It is unclear when the memorial was completed as no unveiling ceremony is recorded in the press, and it has tended over time (and especially after James Sharman Crawford's death in 1878) to be overlooked as lying on private land rather than on a more publicly accessible site. Dissatisfaction with access to the Rademon monument appears to have stimulated a campaign for a more prominent memorial some years later. In 1872 the *Newry Reporter* expressed support for a new one at Crawfordsburn, as well as the republication of his letters and speeches, although neither project came to fruition.[163] Another proposal was aired in 1876 for a statue to him in Down to counter the recently unveiled Cooke memorial in Belfast (which took the site previously occupied by the Earl of Belfast and was associated with the Orange Order), but nothing came of this either.[164] In the end, it would not be through memorials, but in his surviving writings, and through the actions of his children, that Crawford's legacy would be sustained. If his hopes for a radical dynasty, expressed in Rochdale in 1855, that 'his son, and his son's son, and their posterity, as long as his name was known among them, might be stimulated to follow in a course which had earned for him so honourable a distinction', proved to be too sanguine, his children James and Mabel in particular were to make significant contributions to the Ulster radical tradition.[165]

9. Legacies and succession: the Sharman Crawfords after 1861

The shade of Sharman Crawford and Irish land reform, 1861–70

There were some signs that the balance of political opinion on Irish land reform was already starting to turn when William Sharman Crawford died in 1861. It soon became clear that the contractually-based 'solution' to landlord-tenant relations embodied in the Cardwell-Deasy reforms of 1860 had little impact on either stimulating landed investment or curbing tenant agitation and unrest. As the Irish agricultural economy lurched into deep recession in 1859–63, with renewed potato blight threatening (if not in the end delivering) a return of famine conditions, the optimism associated with the farming boom of the mid 1850s quickly faded. Economic distress fuelled another surge of mass emigration, and a new and more potent revolutionary nationalist movement, the Irish Republican Brotherhood (IRB), sought from 1858 to make use of agrarian discontent to recruit farmers' sons and labourers into its secretive 'circles'. Even when a run of good harvests and improving prices from 1864 restored some of the lost gains to farmers, conspiratorial agitation had established itself and was now supported by well-financed diasporic bodies such as the Fenian Brotherhood and subsequently its offshoot Clan na Gael. Although the majority of the Catholic clergy and more substantial farmers were hostile to Fenianism, the fear of a return to bad times stimulated moderate tenants to seek self-protection in collective action, and non-revolutionary nationalists to search for alternatives to the appeal of Fenianism.

The 1859–63 crisis also had an impact on economic thought in Ireland. Previously optimistic about the 'liberating' impact of the Famine and Encumbered Estates Act on the Irish economy, the Dublin Statistical Society saw impassioned debates follow the unexpected return of distress. In 1862 Denis Caulfield Heron, previously professor of political economy at Queen's College Galway, attacked the dominant narrative of progress and claimed that in the absence of effective tenant security Ireland had not seen any real improvement since the disaster of the Famine. Free-trade liberals such as W. N. Hancock and Mountifort Longfield were loath to abandon their position that the 'defeudalisation' of land law since 1849 had brought about agricultural transformation but were ultimately forced to concede ground. By the mid-1860s Hancock was questioning his previous assumption that the laissez-faire principles behind the Cardwell-Deasy acts would strengthen rather than undermine what he saw as the valuable customary form of tenant right and was starting to take an interest in the ancient Irish Brehon laws. A more fully-developed historicist economics was taking shape during the decade, most evidently in the work of C. E. Cliffe Leslie, which questioned the universalism previously characteristic of liberal political economy and propounded that societies at different stages of historical development needed economic strategies specific to their individual circumstances. When applied to Ireland, this thinking tended to legitimise the recognition of customary practices and the adoption of land legislation deemed appropriate to Ireland alone. Refracted through economists such as J. S. Mill and J. E. Cairnes, this approach was having an impact on Liberal party doctrine by the end of the decade.[1]

The renewed economic crisis also drew some observers to re-read Crawford. Criticising lord lieutenant Carlisle's complacent assertion in 1862 that Ireland was a country naturally suited to producing 'flocks and herds' on large grassland farms, the *Northern Whig* directed its readers' attention to *Depopulation Not Necessary*. Drawing on heterodox economists, it observed, Crawford had demonstrated the greater productivity of small tillage farms, and this had not changed in the meantime.[2] An 1864 pamphlet by a landed author, warning of the negative economic consequences of the continuing flight of small farmers and the necessity of the Ulster custom as the only way of retaining them and ensuring essential investment in improvements, provoked the *Standard* to observe that this simply vindicated Crawford. Its editorialist concluded that 'History is already beginning to record its justifying verdict on the labours of the original "tenant-right agitators;" and British statesmanship is destined, ere long, to follow in the wake of history'.[3] The *Standard* also drew confidence from Mountifort Longfield's recent presidential address to the Dublin Statistical Society, which appeared belatedly to commit that body to support the principle of tenant right.[4] Welcome support for the cause came also from the *Economist*, previously a bastion of laissez-faire fundamentalism, which now quoted Mill and Thornton approvingly on the need to maintain the security of Irish small farmers. The *Standard* observed that its columnist, realising at last the truth of Crawford's utilitarian arguments:

> declares that the Irish doctrine of 'tenant-right', which has been sometimes haughtily repudiated as 'half-Maori, and half-Hindoo,' is no absurdity, but on the contrary, a dictate of the common sense of mankind, as well as of sound philosophy in its application to the occupancy of land. Ribbonism, Fenianism, and other agrarian combinations the writer justly regards as social excrescences necessarily growing out of Irish land-grievance, and he accordingly advocates an equitable, courageous system of remedial legislation as the only effectual cure for the evils complained of.[5]

From 1864 John Francis Maguire, now the Liberal MP for Dungarvan sought to revive the defunct land agitation along Tenant League lines, but the *Standard's* negative commentary demonstrated that northern bitterness over the splits of the 1850s persisted.[6] Despite this, some southern supporters were also prepared to give Crawford his due as the late 'father' of the movement.[7] Maguire's 1865 motion for a new tenant-right measure was seconded by W. E. Forster, the radical Liberal MP for Bradford and future Gladstonian Irish chief secretary, who warned of the alienation of Irish emigrants and the Irish diaspora by heartless British policies – the government must not, he concluded 'shut the door of hope to the poor and uneducated peasantry of that unhappy country'. Crawford's bills were recalled by others as serious attempts to solve a continuing problem.[8]

The appointment of a commons committee of inquiry into the issue suggested that at least some of the interests previously hostile to tenant-right legislation were now softening in response to the changing intellectual and political context. Although evidently still reluctant, the elderly Palmerston now admitted the desirability of encouraging tenant improvement by granting security of return, a concession that led the *Banner of Ulster* to wish Crawford still lived to hear the prime minister 'admitting the very spirit of the Ulster tenant right question'.[9] Dufferin was praised for making a 'tenant-right speech' to his tenants at Clandeboye, and although he preferred independent valuation of improvements to the unregulated free sale of goodwill, it was hoped he would express his support for legislative intervention to Maguire's committee.[10] However the committee was suffocated before parliament was dissolved for the general election of July 1865.[11] During the election Irish land issues played only a subordinate role, although Greer, who had granted his own tenants in Co. Londonderry perpetual tenancies at low rents (as Crawford had planned to do on his estates in 1856–8), ran again unsuccessfully for the county on a Crawfordian platform.[12]

The politics of Irish land were to be transformed by the escalation of activity provoking a 'Fenian scare' in 1865–9, the struggles for leadership and redefinition of the Liberal party following Palmerston's death in October 1865, and the revival of partisan polarisation associated with the formation of another minority Conservative government in 1866–8, led initially by Derby and then by the more politically opportunistic Benjamin Disraeli. McKnight welcomed Palmerston's death as removing a great obstacle to reform, but lamented the absence of a 'second Sharman Crawford' to lead the tenant movement.[13]

The short-lived Liberal administration of Earl Russell introduced in 1866 an Irish tenant compensation bill (albeit without a retrospective clause) that was rejected out of hand by the leading Irish Conservative Lord Naas as overturning the 'correct' doctrine embodied in the contractualist 1860 legislation, but which was supported, despite its limitations, by Mill, then serving a brief term as MP for Westminster. Mill insisted along historicist lines that Ireland must be governed according to Irish exigencies and not English routine. He was now convinced, he told the commons, that Ireland urgently required the legal recognition of the tenant-right custom as it existed, although he doubted that anything stronger could be carried. But if 'Ireland is ever to prosper with peasant farming, fixity of tenure is an indispensable condition'.[14] Chichester Fortescue's 1866 bill, which retained substantial powers to the landlord, failed to generate much support in Ireland as it fell far short of Crawford's 1852 measure, and was lost on the collapse of Russell's government. Nevertheless, the Liberals had rediscovered an openness to Irish land reform that extended even to the party's patriarch Russell himself, who, while not abandoning the principle of maintaining the rights of property, now believed legislation to penalise arbitrary evictions was necessary to ensure its duties were enforced.[15] Land reform was taken up as party policy by their new leader in opposition, William Ewart Gladstone, who declared his support for agrarian reform as a mode of undermining support for revolution in the aftermath of the Fenian Clerkenwell explosion in December 1867. Once in office he was pressed by John Bright into embracing such legislation, despite the caution of the landed Whigs.[16]

Isaac Butt, who had lost his Youghal seat in 1865, made his first major contribution to the land question in 1866 with the publication of *Land Tenure in Ireland: A Plea for the Celtic Race*. In this he revived the argument for 'fixity of tenure at a fair rent', demanding legislation that would make all existing tenants 'perpetual lessees' paying a head-rent determined by valuation for a term of sixty years. Only such a radical step, he asserted, could hope to check the threats posed by the continuing high levels of emigration and the rise of Fenianism.[17] Butt's 'revolutionary' proposals looked back to the Connerism that had influenced Tenant League policy before the compromise with Crawford in 1851; they were, he asserted, essential if Ireland's social disintegration was to be checked. Critics pointed out that Butt's scheme was unlikely to end emigration and that it fell far short of the forcible confiscation and redistribution of land demanded by the Fenians themselves, but it nevertheless helped place 'tenant right' back onto the remedial agenda for Ireland.[18]

Gladstone's commitment to disestablishing the Church of Ireland as a measure of Irish 'pacification' had a polarising effect on elections in Ulster in 1868 and tended to overshadow his less clear undertaking to pursue a more extensive Irish land reform bill. However, the land issue did also appear on the hustings. The extension of the Irish borough franchise in 1868, bringing some categories of working-class voters into the urban electorates, created opportunities for the Liberals in the three largest towns in the province where Presbyterian-Catholic voting coalitions could be constructed. Richard Dowse won a comfortable victory in Londonderry city, relying predominantly on Catholic votes to succeed where Greer had failed in 1860 and 1865, before going on to be solicitor-general and later attorney-general for Ireland in 1870–2, in which capacity he supported ably Gladstone's Irish land bill. William Kirk, who had endorsed Crawford's bill in 1852, was returned for Newry with strong Catholic support after a nine-year absence from parliament. Belfast, however, was the most interesting contest. The Presbyterian landowner and urban developer Thomas McClure was the first Liberal elected for the town since 1847, and it was noted that his views on land reform were 'founded on those held by Sharman Crawford'.[19] He was joined by the 'independent' Orange Conservative William Johnston of Ballykilbeg, an antagonist of Crawford in 1852, but who now ran against the 'official' Conservative establishment that had dominated Belfast politics for decades (represented as candidates in 1868 by the architect Charles Lanyon and the textile magnate John Mulholland), and who also endorsed tenant right to 'give fair play to the industrious tenant' along with other 'popular' policies.[20]

By the following year even the *Times* was now admitting that a substantive measure of Irish land reform was urgently required. Noting that the question had been before the public for a generation since Crawford introduced his 1835 bill and the Devon Commission had reported in 1845 (but ignoring its own previous resistance), the paper now urged observers to study foreign land systems as models for Ireland and advocated the adoption of a moderate measure such as Fortescue's bill.[21] The *Daily News* added that 'the stage of blank apathy and contented ignorance which defeated the well-meaning attempts of Mr Sharman Crawford to remedy the evils which he attacked, is a quarter of a century behind us'.[22] In fact Fenian positions on the land question were more varied than the *Times* editorial suggested; while Lalorite rhetoric was indeed widely voiced by some Fenians, Rev. David Bell, who had worked with Crawford in the Tenant League era, was now among the movement's numbers, and Charles Kickham of Tipperary, probably the most prominent agrarian Fenian in the 1860s, was still prepared to cite Crawford approvingly.[23]

The return of agricultural prosperity after the crisis of the early 1860s saw farmers' incomes rise in proportion to their participation in the highly lucrative cattle and livestock-product export trade. Tenant-right values now soared to unprecedented levels in Ulster, possibly to a value of £35–40 million by 1874. However, this very surge created new anxieties in an environment where many landlords continued to seek the custom's curtailment as an impediment to rent-maximisation and consolidation. Setting upper limits to rates of payment was becoming more common. While it was widely acknowledged that evictions had become infrequent and most landowners now received comparatively more 'moderate' rents, the exceptional cases of arbitrary eviction and rackrenting, and increased use of notices to quit to extract payments, often by new proprietors who had bought portions under the Encumbered Estates Act, served as reminders of the continuing insecurity of the tenants, especially should another economic recession arrive. Such practices tended to undermine already strained relationships of mutual trust in the countryside.[24] Tenant fears, along with expectations raised by political developments at Westminster, spurred the revival of the moribund tenant-right movement in the north towards the end of the decade.

At a mass meeting of the Route Tenant Defence Association in Ballymoney in November 1869, the veteran McKnight reminded his audience that what they were demanding – legalisation of the 'Ulster custom of tenant right' – had been defined many years before by Crawford. Compensation for improvements was but one part of the aggregate of tenant right and would not be accepted by them as a stand-alone measure, he continued; only formal recognition of joint-ownership between landlord and tenant would now suffice both for Ulster and the other provinces.[25] A commentator added that McKnight's reward for a lifetime of struggle appeared near at hand, and regretted that Crawford 'who fought the battle for popular rights, and died encased in armour' was not alive to witness it.[26] Further meetings endorsing the principles of Crawford's bill followed in Donegal, Londonderry and Tyrone, while at a meeting in Newtownards the following March he was lauded as the 'Moses of his time'.[27]

Southern commentators were generally less reverential towards Crawford and recalled the limitations of his bills of the 1850s, but in some places his memory was also a touchstone of the revived 1869–70 agitation. At the bitterly contested hustings for the Tipperary by-election of November 1869, it was a spokesman for the imprisoned Fenian Jeremiah O'Donovan Rossa who observed that passage of either Crawford's or Napier's bills of 1852 would have kept 'one and a half millions of the Irish race in their own country', while simultaneously denouncing those who had broken the unity of the 'independent party' and stating that only permanent tenancy at a judicially fixed rent would now suffice.[28] Despite his insistence that he had been a consistent supporter of substantive land reform and a critic of laissez-faire, the Liberal candidate Denis Heron lost the election, but then won a narrow victory over Kickham the following year after Rossa was disqualified as a felon.

Despite differences between the northern and southern agitations, a number of Ulster representatives were present at a national land conference convened in Dublin in February 1870 (following an earlier provincial conference in Belfast) to lobby the government. Unable to be there due to illness, McKnight wrote to pledge his support and observed that northerners would regard the attainment of Ulster tenant right as defined by the preamble of Crawford's 1850 bill as the minimum they would accept, while now also looking towards the ultimate aim of tenant purchase of their farms under terms recently set out by Bright.[29]

It is unclear how familiar Gladstone himself was with Crawford's ideas and principles. In his diary he notes reading Crawford's 1837 pamphlet on the subject, although the entry is for 29 June 1870, by which time the land bill had already gone to the house of lords.[30] In introducing the bill in February, he had mentioned Crawford's persistence in pressing the matter in parliament, but had not elaborated on this.[31] Under the influence of the Scottish colonial administrator George Campbell his preference had been for a measure based solely on the 'customary' phenomenon of Ulster tenant-right that would have partially sidestepped the contractualist demands of the '3Fs', but resistance from the cabinet Whigs led to this being watered down and a cumbersome system of 'compensation for disturbance' being offered beyond Ulster. Although passed into law, the 1870 measure was too compromised to attain the closure of the land question desired by the prime minister.[32]

Defending the bill in the lords, Lord Granville was rather more effusive about Crawford's legacy, noting that, after starting with the moderate demand for compensation for improvements thirty-five years before, as 'the subject grew in his hands [...] the scope and strength of the bills increased'.[33] The English lord chancellor, Lord Hatherly, regretted that he had voted against Crawford's bills was an MP, but had the consolation that, while 'I failed in my duty in regard to the Irish tenantry, I rejoice that now, at the latter end of my life, I have had an opportunity of doing this justice to the Irish people'.[34] Others with long memories were not so sentimental. Crawford's old ally Poulett Scrope (who had stepped down as an MP in 1867) was concerned that the concessions offered in the bill would be pared away, and urged the inclusion of clauses to establish a standard of rent that would guide the decisions of a new land court, and to encourage the reclamation of waste lands.[35] Neither of these were taken up although attempts by Conservatives in the lords to 'mutilate' the bill through the introduction of hostile amendments were curbed by the efforts of the Irish lord chancellor Thomas O'Hagan combined with the restraint of Disraeli as opposition leader.[36] O'Hagan, who had known him well, later defended the bill as attaining more than had ever been possible in Sharman Crawford's day.[37]

Despite widespread support for the principle of Gladstone's land bill in Ulster, there was from the start some concern about the imprecision of its terms. McKnight warned the government in March 1870 that its failure to define the 'Ulster custom' in the bill might thwart its enactment and conjectured that this may have arisen from attempts by recalcitrants within the administration to undermine Gladstone's reforming zeal. The defence that the custom was highly variable in its essence was refuted by McKnight, who put this down to the frustration strategies adopted by estate managers: a precise and usable definition could be found both in Crawford's 1850 bill and the report of the Devon Commission and should be incorporated into the measure. McKnight was ignored, and his prophetic warning that a botched bill would 'fill Ulster with consternation and discontent [and] would multiply litigation and chronic warfare between landlords and tenants', appeared to be borne out.[38] However the full working out of these issues was yet to come. In 1870 the act was welcomed as an 'instalment of fair play' and treated as a vindication of Crawford's campaigning by pro-tenant voices in Ulster.[39]

James Sharman Crawford and County Down politics, 1861–85

As we have seen, James was the son politically and socially closest to his father's ideals (Figure 35). Although authority over the Down estates ultimately lay with his brother John as the succeeding heir in 1861, in practice James appears to have been given a fairly free hand in management, retained his own household at Rademon with an income from the estate revenues.[40] In accordance with John's preferences, the rents were increased after 1865, although James was at pains to explain that this had been done only in line with the poor-law valuation and with delays and exceptions to allow tenants sufficient time to adjust, and in a period of renewed high prices. He clearly retained his personal popularity with the estate's tenantry and was assured that his management conformed with tenant-right expectations.[41]

Initially his public activity was constrained to his home district in east Down; he remained a very active member of the Downpatrick board of guardians and chaired baronial presentment sessions as a member of the county grand jury.[42] As a magistrate he intervened successfully to argue for clemency in the case of Robert Moffat, an elderly tenant holding land on both the Rademon and nearby Killinchy estates, who in 1856 was tried for killing his eldest son in a drunken dispute.[43] In 1869 he joined the board of governors of the new Down Lunatic Asylum in the county town.[44] Although a member of several agricultural societies, as well as taking an interest in the 1867 national meeting of the Social Science Congress in Belfast, James's wider networks were principally Presbyterian.[45] He retained the zeal of the convert, playing an active role in the affairs of local congregations and the Sunday schools movement, and also in more extended Presbyterian initiatives to address its national funding in the wake of the abolition of the regium donum in 1869. By 1874 he had been ordained as a ruling elder on the kirk session at Crossgar, entitling him to be elected to sit on the church's ruling body, the general assembly.[46] The cultivation of these connections would prove politically beneficial to him as demand for Presbyterian political representation grew and denominational grievances over practical exclusion from local government, the magistracy and government appointments continued to fester.

James's standing in the county was enhanced by reports of the philanthropic work he undertook. Some of this was through direct assistance, as he 'went about doing good, his medicine and his money alike were freely distributed amongst the sick and the poor of his locality, irrespective of sect or creed'.[47] He intervened on occasions to seek the termination of what he saw as excessive punishments of 'fallen' women in the workhouse, and argued against the abusive system of 'hiring out' children as easily-exploitable labourers.[48] Although politically opposed to him, the *Downpatrick Recorder* could not help but praise his efforts as a *'model guardian'*: 'Workhouse children are prisoners – not criminals; and men like Mr Crawford, who spend time, health, and money in exertions for their welfare are entitled to the thanks of the whole community for their services'.[49] From 1870 he and several other guardians sponsored an annual summer excursion for the workhouse children, along with some of the elderly inmates, from Downpatrick to the Rademon estate. It was reported at the time that Downpatrick was the only union in Ireland which permitted such outings, although others followed suit.[50] The annual event involved some public spectacle, as the children marched through the town behind a brass band, bearing 'flags with appropriate mottoes', before boarding the train to Crossgar. At Rademon the children were fed and encouraged to play games, they were given toys and books as prizes, and there was music and dancing. The Sharman Crawford monument served as a centrepiece for the entertainments. In 1872 the clerk of the union spoke to thank their host:

> They had stood that day at the foot of a monument erected to the memory of one of the greatest and most enlightened patriots Ireland had produced. (Cheers.) He saw inscribed upon it the statement that William Sharman Crawford was not merely a consistent politician, but that he was the friend of the poor. He did not know how far it might be true that philanthropy, like genius, was oftentimes hereditary; but this he could say that the son of that great man was

not behind the father in deeds of kindness and benevolence. (Cheers.) Mr James Sharman Crawford was known for his active efforts on behalf of the poor in every part of the county. He was esteemed as a practical philanthropist, a useful country gentleman, and a sincere and unaffected Christian.[51]

A number of inmates from the county asylum also attended these excursions.[52] By 1874 the annual procession through the town, led in person that year by James (by now an MP), had reportedly become a popular event with the town's inhabitants, who turned out in the streets to cheer the parade, with some then accompanying the children, patients and their carers onwards to Rademon.[53] If life in the Victorian workhouse and asylum remained mostly bleak for their inmates, James' initiatives no doubt not only brought some welcome relief, and also did much to humanise them in the eyes of the local population. Writing with some sentimentality, the local paper observed that the children's mothers were assembled at the workhouse gates to witness the return procession, and 'the eyes of many of the women glistened with delight as they recognized the smiling happy faces of the children, who seemed quite proud at the thought of the fine show they were making in all their bravery of brilliant flags and lively music'.[54] More hard-headedly, James believed such demonstrations were also important to 'raise the character of the workhouse in the estimation of the ratepayers' who witnessed them.[55] Visits to the estate were not restricted to workhouse children; in 1876 and 1877 he hosted some 700 children of the Mountpottinger Presbyterian Sunday School, from a newly developed working-class district of east Belfast that served the burgeoning shipyards. Once at Rademon, it was recorded, the school's flute band processed around the Sharman Crawford monument, playing the 'Dead March' in tribute to the departed patriarch.[56]

With the exception of Greer's short-lived breakthrough in Co. Londonderry in 1857–9, land reform had been largely sidelined in Liberal politics in Ulster while the party concentrated on the concerns of the urban middle class. However, there was evidence of a gradual recovery in tenant-right activity from 1867, even if the continued absence of the secret ballot still hampered it in the counties. In November 1869 the Route Tenant Defence Association was established at Ballymoney in north Antrim and quickly emerged as a leading radical voice in the province; it was emulated by other bodies such as the Down Farmers' Union in 1872.[57]

Gladstone's 1870 land act had sought to enact the substance of William Sharman Crawford's demands for legal recognition of Ulster tenant right, but limited this to the areas where it was already in existence, while creating a flawed mechanism for compensation for disturbance in other parts of the island. Although welcomed as symbolically important, dissatisfaction escalated as the act was tested in the courts in the succeeding years. The legislation had failed to define the Ulster custom, leaving the courts open to accepting longstanding infringements as established practice, while the mechanisms for claiming compensation were cumbersome and expensive and it offered no regulation of rent increases.[58] Initial criticisms of the measure's shortcomings on hustings and in parliament were voiced by the 'independent' Orange-Conservatives William Johnston (MP for Belfast from 1868) and J. W. Ellison Macartney, who narrowly lost a by-election in Tyrone in 1873 before topping the poll there in 1874 with widespread support from tenant farmers.[59]

It was this controversy that thrust James into the realm of active politics. Tenant organisation in the county was shaken out of complacency by an adverse judicial decision in 1872 on a case involving a claim for leasehold tenant right.[60] The newly-founded Down Farmers' Union called on him to preside at a meeting in December to consider the recent decisions of the land tribunals interpreting the act and give voice to the disillusionment these spurred. His candidacy for the county was now proposed to rally support for amendments connected with his iconic name.[61] Although Tories were confident that Down and Antrim were 'sterling strongholds of Ulster Conservatism', the secret ballot act of 1872 at last appeared to open opportunities for a renewed challenge.[62] In early 1873 the *Newry Reporter* observed that the land act had not been 'what its originators intended' and that growing popular dissatisfaction was now manifest in the tenant-right societies. It hoped James would now 'champion the cause his honoured father had so much at hear[t]'.[63] Momentum was building behind a Sharman Crawford revival, with the Down Farmer's Union expanding its local branch network and getting tenant voters registered.[64]

Much ink was spilled over William's legacy. While moderates tended to support the *Northern Whig's* view that Gladstone's 1870 act had exceeded Crawford's proposals and should not be upset, the revived tenant-right movement asserted that this was not the case. The *Coleraine Chronicle*, for example, supported the Route Association's 'Ballymoney Programme', which proposed the extension of Crawford's 1852 bill to all of Ireland, and observed that, unlike the flawed 1870 act, it had defined the Ulster custom succinctly and accurately.[65] In January 1874 James chaired a national tenant-right conference in Belfast to plan for the forthcoming general election and which had significant southern representation. The venerable McKnight again took the lead in elucidating the nature of the Ulster custom and the need for amending legislation.[66] The joint secretaries to the conference were S. C. McElroy of the Route Association and editor of the *Ballymoney Free Press*, and – reflecting the aspiration to revive the all-Ireland spirit of 1850 – the Co. Dublin farmer and home-ruler Andrew Kettle, who would later play a central role in the Land League agitation, and the debates focused on the attainment of fixity of tenure and fair rents.[67] Introduced by the Presbyterian moderator as an honourable successor to his 'visionary' father, James addressed the conference on its second day; denying personal ambition he declared himself moved by the calls from the tenantry for new legislation to address the specific failures of the 1870 act and truly embody his father's principles. His hope was that the conference would not stimulate any class warfare, but instead establish the spirit of social co-operation required for a 'final and satisfactory settlement' of the land question. Looking beyond the particularist issue the legal definition of the Ulster custom, he welcomed representatives from the south and west, who had made a persuasive case for its extension to the whole island, and he expressed 'great hopes that co-operation of north and south will tend to a fuller understanding of each other, and we will find that we have no separate interests, and that we will all join in the same ardent desires for the welfare of our common country'.[68] As he would discover in the following years, the realities of the fissiparous relationship between the northern and southern movements, now heightened by the explosive issue of home rule, rendered maintaining this idealised unity as difficult in practice as it had been in the 1850s.

The dissolution of parliament was announced a few days later and it was confirmed that James would stand for Down with the endorsement of all the Liberal party factions.[69]

With the public support of his brother John he issued his address at an 'enthusiastic' public meeting on 30 January. He linked his campaign explicitly with that of his father; his own aim would be to 'assist the tenant farmers to bring their ancient tenant-right custom into the position it should be', while at the same time maintaining support for Gladstone, who had demonstrated his genuine commitment to the cause of reform.[70] A veteran of 1852 enthused that 'with the name of Crawford emblazoned on the flag of freedom, it would be an everlasting disgrace if it should not wave in victory', adding that voting was at last now a matter solely between the elector and his conscience.[71] Another placard proclaimed to the electors 'You are perfectly free!! Vote for Crawford the son of the first professor of the first tenant right bill'.[72]

The sitting Conservatives, Lord Edwin Hill-Trevor and Colonel William Forde, appear to have taken an overly complacent view of proceedings; there was some attempt to stir up sectarian antagonisms and to mobilise the Orange Order behind the Tories, but in the short campaign (polling was on 9 February 1874) the reformers demonstrated greater activity and energy, and had significant Catholic as well as liberal Presbyterian support and clerical backing.[73] Aware of growing social unrest, Conservative candidates across the province now felt it necessary also to make some avowal, however half-hearted, of support for land reform, along with seeking to cast doubt on whether the ballot would truly be secret.[74] This led the Crawford campaign, which was effectively co-ordinated by the solicitor Charles Brett in Belfast through a network of enthusiastic local agents, to issue a number of placards and instructions to canvassers painstakingly explaining the operation of the secret ballot and reassuring voters that it was indeed secure and that attempts at intimidation would be legally resisted.[75] Nevertheless, there was reportedly some confusion over the new voting system. It was later recalled that:

> [o]ne man when asked to go to the box exclaimed 'A'll gang into nae box; A'm voting for Crawford, an A dinna care a damn wha kens it.' Another, leaving the box and opening his paper in the middle of the room, displayed a huge cross he had made opposite the name of Hill-Trevor, and challenged everyone present with the query, 'Is thon a' richt noo, mester'?[76]

When the votes were counted, James had come second for the two-seat constituency with 4,814 votes, around 200 behind Hill-Trevor and 131 ahead of Forde, thereby overcoming, in the view of the *Newry Reporter,* 'the odious and tyrannical coalition of landlords' and avenging his father's 1852 defeat. Unquestionably the secret ballot had made the breakthrough possible, as James himself acknowledged, although the small margin of victory indicated that Conservatism also had a marked popular base in the county and that deference to the 'great families' remained strong for many at a time of general agricultural prosperity.[77] Sectarianism had also been mobilised: one supporter observed from Banbridge that 'the Orange element has been imported and the town and neighbourhood resounds with the music of fife and drum', while a rumour was being circulated that Crawford was a 'papist'. His placards were also systematically torn down in some districts 'as fast as the[y] were put up', allegedly by 'Orange ruffs', and replaced with 'no surrender ones'.[78] Nearly 4,000 of Crawford's votes were 'plumpers', as before indicating a high level of partisan polarisation.[79] Violence was much less in evidence than twenty-two years before, but was still a factor, and mounted police were deployed in Downpatrick after an attack on

Crawford's victory parade.[80] Fighting was also expected at Dromara as it was reported that Forde was bringing Orange bands there on election day.[81] Although 'Orange' districts such as Dromore were reported to be dejected by what Conservatives regarded as a humiliating defeat, there was 'rejoicing' with illuminations and parades at Crawfordsburn and Bangor, and in the predominantly Presbyterian Newtownards polling district, which had reportedly backed Crawford by a factor of ten to one, an even greater ratio than for his father in 1852.[82]

Crawford's success was part of wider pattern of a Liberal surge across the province, facilitated by active financial and canvassing support from the tenant-right associations, many of the Catholic and Presbyterian clergy, and the newly founded Ulster Liberal Society in Belfast. Both Co. Londonderry seats were taken with large majorities along with the boroughs of Coleraine, Newry and Dungannon, and with very close contests in Counties Antrim and Donegal. This hardly compensated for the loss of McClure's seat in Belfast, the near-annihilation of the Liberals in the other provinces by Isaac Butt's new Home Rule party and the defeat of Gladstone's exhausted and fractious ministry by Disraeli's resurgent Conservatives in Great Britain, but it appeared to presage a new dawn for Ulster Liberalism.[83] The new electoral coalition would, however, soon come under strain, not least from the divisive issue of the national question – in the new session the five Ulster Liberal MPs, led by Prof. Richard Smyth, immediately took a stance by refusing to support a motion for Irish home rule, drawing fire from nationalist papers claiming that William Sharman Crawford had himself favoured repeal.[84] Most northern Presbyterians supported the MPs' stance, although a few – such as the Belfast evangelical Rev. Isaac Nelson – had come to see the Home Rule party rather than the Liberals as embodying the true inheritance of the tenant-right movement and Presbyterian radicalism, and espoused ideas of 'federalist' autonomy for Ireland.[85]

Early in the 1875 session James Sharman Crawford indicated he would introduce a bill to 'ensure the full tenant-right custom in Ulster', including unfettered freedom of sale, the assumption that every holding in Ulster was subject to tenant-right unless the landlord could prove otherwise and the inclusion of leaseholders in its terms. However he and his colleagues absented themselves from a national land conference in Dublin in January, which was chaired by the Belfast merchant W. D. Henderson and included northern as well as southern delegates.[86] This raised fears that the Ulster Liberal MPs would now pursue a narrowly sectional strategy in open conflict with the Home Rulers, who were coalescing around Isaac Butt's proposals to extend tenant-right across the island.[87] This concern was evident at the Antrim land conference in April, which criticised Crawford for being too narrow in his ambition and for pressing ahead with his bill without national co-ordination.[88] Butt himself sought a compromise, announcing in May that he had agreed with Crawford that the latter would support Butt's amendment to extend the Ulster custom nationally, and swinging his party behind the Down MP's bill.[89] Crawford stated that 'He and those who acted with him were not forgetful of other parts of Ireland', while stating that including the other provinces posed certain practical problems.[90]

Despite its moderation, Crawford's 1875 bill was lost by a factor of two to one and the Liberal leader Lord Hartington was evidently unenthusiastic, although tenant-righters took comfort both from his admission that some amendment of the 1870 act was necessary, and from the large number of Liberal backbenchers who had voted with Crawford.[91] The

Free Press welcomed it as a step towards legally defining tenant right, while observing that if applied to Ulster it could not long be resisted for all of Ireland, while farmers societies elsewhere criticised Butt for failing to move his own bill that year and warned of Ulster 'going at alone'. Stung by such criticisms, by September the *Free Press* was also criticising any Ulster-first approach.[92] Nevertheless, the popularity of the 1875 bill in Ulster embarrassed the province's Conservative MPs and clearly rattled the administration, which considered creating a royal commission into the land question to shelve the matter for at least two years and hopefully give the Conservatives time to prepare for what would otherwise would not be 'a very pleasant' election.[93]

While many Ulster tenant societies rallied to the slogan of 'Sharman Crawford's bill and no surrender', their eyes were also fixed on the restoration of a Gladstone government which they believed would respond more positively to popular demands. But with Gladstone temporarily out of political leadership, the Conservatives holding a firm majority at Westminster, and Ulster 'Constitutionalists' countering with their own, weaker, tenant-right proposals, Crawford saw his mission as keeping the matter before the commons and the public, following his father in playing a political 'long game'. This involved holding a regular series of public meetings, addressed by speakers such as Smyth and the solicitor Hans McMordie, and chaired by Crawford.[94] An attempt by a county landlord to prove hypocrisy in James's own land management practice fell flat and further enhanced his reputation, although his support for the Tory government's 1875 coercion act (a step his father would never have endorsed) damaged him with Catholic voters.[95]

In the 1876 session he reintroduced his bill, now 'acting in perfect union' with Butt, who had also revived his own land bill. They agreed that if both were defeated a royal commission of inquiry would be sought instead.[96] In this spirit of co-operation James wrote a letter of support to a conference summoned by the newly formed Central Tenants Defence Association in Dublin to promote Butt's bill.[97] His own bill was delayed until June and then adjourned indefinitely after a debate, although the *Whig* observed that he had spoken more fluently than before and that his allusions to continuity with his father's campaigns had been well received on the Liberal benches.[98]

However, controversy erupted when the Ulster Liberals divided over Butt's bill when it finally came forward the following month.[99] Crawford's silent vote against it drew the fury of the nationalist *Ulster Examiner,* the mouthpiece of Bishop Dorrian of Down and Connor, which accused him of betrayal and hypocrisy: his actions had alienated the other provinces and broken the contract on which the renewed national movement had been formed. It followed, to the paper, that northern Catholic support should be withdrawn from Crawford and any other Liberals who sided with him.[100] Allegations that he 'was simply trying to clothe himself in the cloak of his father, which was yards too big for him, and that he was thus amusing his constituency, who were content with any kind of a representative so long as he bore the popular patronymic' were damaging, and northern representatives were thrown on the defensive at the national land conference that October.[101] It fell to McElroy to rescue some common ground by praising Butt's invaluable services and pointing out that Smyth and several other Liberals (if not Crawford) had supported his bill.[102]

The point at issue between Crawford and Butt was essentially that which had divided his father from the Connerites in 1850–1 – Butt's bill included a demand for 'absolute' fixity of tenure whereas James followed his father in regarding this as unattainable in legislation and instead opting for a form of 'practical' fixity. Nevertheless, he seems to have belatedly recognised the tactical error of his vote and at the start of the next year wrote to Butt offering an explanation 'for the sake of avoiding disunion' and followed this up with a public speech aimed at re-establishing concord.[103] With Butt's authority within his party now starting to publicly slip away, however, this olive branch came too late. Nevertheless, Crawford amended the 1877 version of his bill explicitly to extend the Ulster custom over all of Ireland, although in the commons ballot for backbench bills it was again held up until the end of the session.[104] The Ballymoney paper observed that, while not of the most advanced school, his 1877 bill was greatly improved and would prove of value to all.[105] This did not prevent the bill from being denounced by Ulster Tories as simply a more indirect mode of attaining the 'communistic' objectives of the more radical reformers.[106] Crawford avoided his previous mistake and voted for Butt's renewed bill that year, and hopes revived (for some at least) that Presbyterians and Catholics might again be re-united over land reform.[107]

If the Ulster Liberals' strategy had been to re-engage Gladstone with the priority of land reform, there is some evidence they were succeeding by 1877. Gladstone had returned to the leadership of the Liberal party following his campaign for an investigation into the 'Bulgarian atrocities' carried out by Ottoman imperial forces in the Balkans in 1876–7 (a campaign Crawford supported), and his attention was now again drawn to Ireland.[108] With his brother John, James Sharman Crawford sought to lure Gladstone to Ulster and to stay at Crawfordsburn. While unsuccessful, when the 'Grand Old Man' came to Ireland on a private visit in October 1877, staying at Kilruddery House near Bray, James and a delegation from the Down Farmers' Association met him and they engaged in 'animated conversation' for three quarters of an hour, thanking him for the 1870 act but drawing attention to its 'mutilations' and the need for remedies.[109] Gladstone appeared attentive, and promised a future visit to the north (although this never transpired).[110]

The Gladstone visit boosted the confidence of the Ulster tenant-right movement, and a series of meetings urged Crawford to reintroduce his bill.[111] Indeed, the second reading of his bill in January 1878 received the closest vote yet, being defeated by only eighty-five to sixty-six (even with most of the Home Rulers absent).[112] The Route Association believed success could not now be far away, and Crawford himself wrote to the *Times* in answer to its attacks, insisting his bill was not confiscatory, but would ensure the value of the property created by the tenantry to themselves by enforcing and amplifying the 'wise and statesmanlike settlement made in 1870'.[113] This spirit of assertive optimism can also be seen in a popular pamphlet by an anonymous 'Antrim tenant-farmer', probably published in 1877, which also sought to depict the demands of the Ulster movement as seeking to perfect the 1870 act, which had given the tenant farmer dignity and respect from his landlord (Figure 34). *The Annals of Ulster Tenant-Right* featured an imaginary dialogue between the secretaries of the rival 'Ulster Tenant-Right League' and 'Ulster Constitutional Association', over the course of which a third, neutral, participant, becomes convinced of the rightness of the tenants' cause, especially once the 'Constitutionalist' is obliged to fall back on pro-Orange and anti-democratic arguments. The tenant-right spokesman insisted that the 1870 act had begun to extinguish 'those unhealthy poisons which infected the good relations that should have existed between the landlord and the respectable portion of their tenantry', while the ballot act had freed them from estate office persecution. For these reasons, 'the name of William Ewart Gladstone, coupled with that of Sharman Crawford, will always hold a favoured place in the esteem and affections of the tenant-farmers of Ulster', and the Ulster Liberals would see through, with Gladstone, the amendments necessary to complete the reform.[114]

However the Ulster tenant movement received a severe setback on 24 April 1878 with the unexpected and sudden death after a short illness of James Sharman Crawford at the age of sixty-five. Although mocked by some in London for his unsophisticated oratory, he had been widely admired in Ulster for his personal merits and commitment to the reform movement, as well as for continuing to embody his father's radical political tradition. The *Whig* commented on his 'singularly amiable and genial disposition, [and] what might be considered most engaging simplicity of character, which impressed itself on all who came within his personal influence', while to the *Newry Reporter* he was 'a prince among men' and a true patriot.[115] The *Ballymena Advertiser* noted that 'for a lifetime his walk and conversation have been before the public, and have proved him a true-hearted, good man'.[116]

The Presbyterian clergy officiating at his funeral at Kilmore stressed his self-sacrificing contributions to the church's work and moral leadership regarding the poor, but it was left to the *Freeman's Journal* to sum up his political contribution. Although never a nationalist and often at odds with the Home Rule party leadership, he had served his country well:

> The house of commons will miss the kindly face of Mr Sharman Crawford, and Ireland could have better spared many another Ulster man than the unobtrusive but vigilant member for Down. Mr Crawford was regarded with the utmost dislike by the Ulster Tory landlords. It was not that Mr Crawford personally gave them offence, for he was one of the meekest of men – unless, indeed, when tenant-right was endangered, and then he became as vigorous almost as Mr O'Donnell; but they recognized in him the representative of an enemy they dreaded – the growing liberalism and independence of the farmer under the influence of education and the ballot.[117]

The *Free Press* reported sorrow at his death in the Route, but was sure his measure would ultimately triumph, as it had now been adopted by the Liberal party.[118]

It is difficult to say how James Sharman Crawford would have reacted to the outbreak of the Land War in the year following his death. His agrarian objectives in the 1870s had been relatively moderate and appeared more so in the context of the Land League's escalated demands from 1879, although it is possible that the onset of a deep agricultural depression with its associated distress and sharp rise in evictions might have had a radicalising effect on him as it had his father in the 1840s, and it is significant that his brother John adopted a more 'advanced' public position in 1880 (despite evidence of private reservations). However the overt nationalism of the Land League, involving as it did an alliance between more strident Home Rulers looking to Charles Stewart Parnell for leadership, and 'Ribbon-Fenian' activists inspired by Michael Davitt, who was now calling for land nationalisation and redistribution, would have posed him serious challenges, especially following the restoration of a Gladstone government in 1880. Even McElroy and the Route Association strongly resisted what they regarded as the 'revolutionary' Land League, and effectively curbed its attempt to agitate the Ballymoney district in 1880–2.[119]

Stung by the unexpected defeat of 1874, the Down Conservatives had reorganised and in 1878 found a candidate with some heft in Charles, Viscount Castlereagh, heir to the Londonderry marquessate and a future lord lieutenant and cabinet minister. Castlereagh's campaign loudly proclaimed his adherence to some form of tenant-right and played up Liberal weakness in the face of the growing home rule threat to the union and sharp divisions between Catholics and Presbyterians over education questions. The Liberals quickly nominated William Drennan Andrews, grandson of the United Irish founder and son of the former Londonderry agent John Andrews of Comber. Andrews was a rising legal star and a queen's counsel, but did not share James Sharman Crawford's county-wide standing and long engagement with agrarian politics. One Tory paper noted he also lacked the 'talismanic influence' of the Sharman Crawford name, and that his adherence to unitarianism had curbed enthusiasm for him among the orthodox Presbyterian clergy.[120] Another major problem for the Liberals was the overt hostility of the *Ulster Examiner*, which had restated its criticism of Crawford's moderation and particularism in its obituary, and urged Down Catholics to look instead to a Home Ruler.[121] No nationalist stood in 1878, but with Castlereagh tactically making vague hints about Conservative sympathy for self-government and on Catholic education (while at the same time looking to Orange support), the Catholic vote was split more than previously.[122] With 'all the machinery of the rent offices' mobilised behind him, and some £14,000 laid out from the family's funds, Castlereagh pulled off an impressive win, taking 6076 votes to Andrews' 4701 to regain the 'family seat' lost in 1852.[123]

This was, however, not the end of the Sharman Crawford electoral involvement with the county. Taking note of the failure of 1878, the Liberals turned again to a member of the family at the general election of 1880, in the hope that this legacy would carry them over the line. John lacked his brother's high public profile, but was nonetheless a lifelong Liberal and still seen as an indulgent landlord and friend of tenant right (Figure 36). The *Belfast Morning News*, a Catholic paper owned by the Gray family, came out strongly in support of him, more as his father's son that for his own merits, as '[t]he name of Crawford is one to conjure with in the Yorkshire of Ireland [... and] associated for long years with the struggle for the emancipation of the agricultural classes'.[124] For his part, John now combined appeals to his father's legacy with support for the '3Fs' and land transfer:

> I cannot, as the son of William Sharman Crawford, refuse to stand by the people in the coming contest. My father fought the battle of tenant right and independence when the farmers had few friends to plead their cause. My brother did his duty when the occasion demanded. Today I am ready to renew the struggle in the hope of securing the tenant-right custom in its integrity for the farmers of all Ireland. I shall therefore vote for any measure that gives them FREE SALE, FAIR RENTS and PERMANENCE of POSSESSION. But I regard the creation and development of a peasant proprietorship as the safest and best remedy for many of the evils under which the people of this country suffer.[125]

Crucially, it was reported that the Ulster Home Government Association (the northern wing of the Home Rule movement) had endorsed him, although this opened him up to additional Tory attacks that, like his father, he was no supporter of the union.[126] Responding to the charge, the *Whig* sketched a family history over three generations that, in its view, had embraced popular patriotism without adherence to Irish nationalism:

'[t]he lord of Derrynane always looked upon the chief of Crawfordsburn as a rival who would not be permitted anywhere near his throne'. The 'heroic' spirit of 1852 was again evoked. Hostile attempts were made by other papers to draw a distinction between James' liberal land management and his brother's more conservative approach, but relations on his estates were said to be good despite the agricultural crisis and growing demands for rent abatements, and these fell flat.[127] In desperation Castlereagh's camp turned to insinuating that the ballot was not in fact secret, thereby raising a renewed threat of retribution against disloyal tenants on the large estates.[128] It is difficult to know precisely what impact this had, but the 1880 election turned out to be extremely close. Despite being a rather undynamic candidate and lacking effective county-wide organisation, John fell just twenty votes behind Castlereagh, the second-ranked Conservative candidate, making Down one of the most marginal constituencies in the UK that year. With 5,579 votes John had attained more supporters than his brother in 1874, but still narrowly lost the contest. A legal challenge was mounted citing undue landlord influence and intimidation but was rejected in the courts.[129] The land agitation had a mixed effect on the elections in Ulster that year, with renewed tenant-farmer anger over self-interested landlord behaviour and threatened evictions counterweighted by growing Protestant fears that the Land League was a front for nationalist and Catholic political objectives and too extreme in its demands for the overthrow of landlordism. Liberal gains in the northern counties (albeit not in Down and Antrim despite high hopes in both) were offset by losses in all but one of their borough seats.[130]

By 1880 it was clear that the name of Sharman Crawford was still a potent, if declining, asset in electoral politics. While William's memory was still frequently evoked at tenant-right meetings, his surviving sons elicited diminishing enthusiasm. As the Land War continued, there were increasing tensions on the family's estates, and due to John's illness it was the more acerbic Arthur who now clashed with the tenants, reverting to a more conventional landlord stance. In January 1881 those on the upland townland of Dunbeg complained that the run of bad seasons, combined with competition from America and the high cost of labour were forcing many into debt and penury and called for a twenty-five per cent cut in rents.[131] Arthur refused to consider a request to reduce the rents of the leasehold tenants at neighbouring Drumgiven, telling them that they had received their leases on good terms and to review them now would be unfair to the tenants at will.[132]

The Stalleen tenants also petitioned for a twenty per cent reduction 'pending the settlement of the land question' in 1881, using the memory of William Sharman Crawford to advance their case. Unmoved by this, Arthur commented unsympathetically that, while he desired to walk in his father's footsteps, the appeal was unreasonable; they were already underrented given the rise in prices since his father's time and he lamented that 'the more one does for people the more they expect'. He added that given existing charges such a reduction would cut his income by forty per cent and might force him to sell up. He and his relative and agent D. L. Coddington of Oldbridge House were convinced the Land League was behind these demands.[133] The Meath tenants repeated their appeal in 1887, complaining that the continuing agricultural depression had reduced prices by forty per cent and exhausted their savings; they calling for a twenty-five per cent rent reduction, but again Coddington assured him they were exaggerating and had been put up to it by an agitating priest, and agreed with Arthur that the most that could be conceded was to continue the temporary fifteen per cent abatement allowed the previous year, with further aid to deserving individuals.[134] In 1882 Arthur also initially rejected any rent reduction to a Rademon tenant who had formally appealed to the Land Commission established to review rents under Gladstone's 1881 Irish Land Act, telling him to sell his tenant-right and take a smaller holding, although he changed his mind after meeting the tenant and striking a bargain.[135] The Banbridge tenants again memorialised him for a reduction of their rents in 1885.[136] The patina of Sharman Crawford landlordism was thus evidently wearing thin as the conflicted decade of the 1880s progressed.

This seems to have posed no obstacle, following John's death in June 1884, to Arthur being proposed by the Ulster Liberal Association as their candidate for a Co. Down by-election that November, which was necessary due to Castlereagh's succession as sixth Marquess of Londonderry. Arthur's Conservative opponent would be Richard Ker, son of William's rival in 1852 and ally in 1857 and now head of that major landowning family. Even more than in 1880, Arthur, whose principal concerns lay in the Belfast business world, was dependent on the family name rather than his own personal appeal. When evidence came to light of previous sweeping dismissal of the aspirations of western smallholders ('He was not in favour of granting peasant proprietorship to those people in the west of Ireland that they heard so much about, and who were living in places that were not fit for swine'), his chances of holding the Catholic and nationalist vote, already strained by its poor relations with the Gladstone administration and the expansion of the Irish National League into Ulster, evaporated.[137] Arthur lost to Ker by nearly 400 votes in a reduced turnout, reportedly to both Conservative and nationalist rejoicing.[138] The defeat marked, as Thompson has observed, a milestone in the process of irreversible Liberal decline in the province after its brief flourish in the years up to 1880.[139]

Despite the success in the north of Gladstone's second Irish Land Act of 1881 in satisfying the desires of the more substantial tenant farmers through granting the 'three Fs' and judicial rent reductions demanded by the Ulster tenant-right lobby, the press concluded that the Liberals had squandered their advantage and had failed to address the continuing difficulties of the smaller landholders.[140] Increasingly tenants complained that the scale of reductions failed to take into account the higher valuation of land in Ulster due to tenant improvements and that the process of determining judicial rents was too slow, being held up further by landlord appeals.[141] To the *Coleraine Chronicle* in 1884 the 'old wine' of county leadership had deteriorated and Liberals needed to reflect dissatisfaction with the new act.[142]

There was some discussion of Arthur standing for the new single-member constituency of East Down created under the Redistribution of Seats Act in 1885, but in the end he opted not to run.[143] After more than half a century Sharman Crawford involvement in county politics under radical and Liberal colours had run its course. When the family's political aspirations were revived a decade and a half later, their political orientation would be very different.

Mabel Sharman Crawford and the rights of women, 1852–1912

By some way the most radical and visionary of William Sharman Crawford's children was his third daughter Mabel, who was to combine her father's concerns for economic justice and full democracy with a pioneering and committed feminism. Born in Dublin in 1820 and named for her mother, Mabel lived mostly at Crawfordsburn from 1827 until her father's death in 1861 and subsequently in Dublin and London and remained single until her death in 1912. Her early life is relatively obscure prior to the publication of her first works in the 1850s, but it appears that, along with her sisters, she became involved in philanthropic and anti-slavery activities in Belfast in the 1840s, and it is very likely that she was also engaged with the political affairs that dominated the life of the household.

Although a committed democrat, William had followed the Chartist strategy of restricting his demands for universal suffrage to men only, at least in the first instance. Nevertheless, there was widespread female participation in the movement (including in Rochdale), even if it did not develop a distinct and sustained women's suffrage platform.[144] In 1842 the *Times* explicitly accused Crawford and his allies of hypocrisy on this head:

> We are sick of these deceivers of the people. Were they consistent with themselves, they must at least give the franchise to women; for women have property and personal rights as well as men, are taxed as well as men, and must obey the laws as well as men, or like men, be punished for breaking them. Many most highly educated persons are women; women write about political economy, and vote at the India-house; and a queen sits upon the throne.[145]

The intention here was not seriously to promote female enfranchisement but to undermine the case for democratic reform by connecting it to what the paper's male readers would regard as an absurd proposal. By 1844, however, Crawford was prepared to admit the principle that women could, under certain conditions, be included in the franchise, although at the time this was still regarded as politically impractical.[146] For his daughter's generation, such hesitations were no longer tolerable, and became even less so as the male franchise was widened in the UK in 1867 and 1884.

Although Mabel's early life in some ways conformed to the patriarchal gender conventions of the day for women of her class, she appears to have become conscious of wider political developments and to have begun to question the multiple constraints placed upon women.[147] Her father certainly had female supporters who were politically engaged, such as Sophia Stuart of Crevevagh House in Tyrone, who wrote to him in 1852 that 'I believe gentlemen in general imagine we poor ladies have nothing to say on such things. In this however I beg leave most humbly to differ from them, as I think it is only right to know at least a little of everything that goes on'.[148] It is likely that Mabel also became aware about this time of the development of the growing movement for women's political rights across the Atlantic, as the *Belfast Mercury* – a paper taken at Crawfordsburn – reported on the Women's Rights Convention at Westchester, New York, in 1852. The paper's commentary may have been sarcastic, but was still likely to have made an impression on its readers:

> we are told that as many as five hundred ladies are occasionally to be seen and heard in solemn convention, asserting their rights in terms of bold and eloquent earnestness which could not be surpassed by a League meeting in England, or a tenant-right demonstration in this country.[149]

She may also have been aware of the writing of the pioneering American female journalist Grace Greenwood, who visited Belfast in September 1852 and wrote approvingly of 'that generous-souled man and honest politician, Sharman Crawford', who had, she noted, recently been defeated by means of intimidation and bribery.[150]

Mabel's first public articulation of her own voice came in the relatively conventional form of a novel, *Fanny Denison,* which she published in London under her own name in autumn 1852.[151] The *Globe* noted that it had attracted public curiosity as 'the first work of the daughter of an eminent public character', but praised it as a 'powerful story' about the varying fortunes of the protegee of a rich lady, whose self-denial placed her in 'the most trying positions', requiring her to demonstrate moral fortitude. It was, the reviewer concluded, a novel of the best class.[152] Mabel published a second novel in 1864, *The Wilmot Family,* also directed primarily at an English audience.[153] It was reviewed as a 'good wholesome novel' and 'simply and well written, although not free from the occasional femininity of style'.[154] It was a tale of an honest Yorkshire yeoman farming family nearly corrupted by their unexpected attainment of riches from a bequest, and the 'social shams' to which they were then subjected. This askance view of gentry pretensions and the delusions of pursuing riches certainly reflected the moral worldview of the Crawfordsburn household. Other reviews found it morally excellent but lacking in sensation or excitement and unsubtle in its treatment of an unoriginal theme.[155] Mabel's principal talents lay elsewhere than in fiction and she soon turned to other and less well trodden pathways.

The first of these was travel writing, where she showed herself more adventurous and ready to engage more directly in political and economic controversies. In 1856–7 she spent ten months travelling with an unnamed female companion in the Grand Duchy of Tuscany and neighbouring Italian states. She published her account of the visit as *Life in Tuscany* in April 1859. The book appeared on the cusp of the Italian Risorgimento and drew considerable attention in the UK, but her principal concern had not been to comment on contemporary Italian nationalist politics but rather to 'throw a light upon the character, condition, and ideas of the people of that land'.[156] She appears to have self-consciously modelled her text on two earlier books on Italian journeys by Irish women, Lady Morgan and the Belfast-based writer Mrs T. Mitchell, and like them used the text to draw comparisons and comments on Irish social life as well as describing what she saw.[157] Her own book is lucid, fluently written, and closely observed. Writing principally for a British audience, she adopted a self-consciously 'English' persona, but her preoccupations and concerns nevertheless betrayed an Irish sensibility which combined her formative Ulster-radical family background with her own developing feminist voice.[158]

As a traveller, she preferred to visit 'thoroughly Italian' locales, lodging with peasant households to immerse herself in local customs and manners, displaying greatest interest in the domestic lives and economies of these 'contadini' families. Although she also included picturesque description and personal reminiscences, her use of the ethnographic and familial registers in establishing the tone of her book may have been a strategy for differentiating it from other rival texts, as well as reflecting the agrarian interests she had inherited from her father. She demonstrated an awareness of the political economy as well as the landscape and social conditions and conventions of the districts she surveyed. Viewing the densely populated Apennine valleys above Lucca, she observed the growing trend towards seasonal and longer-term labour migration, and drew comparisons with socio-economic conditions in pre-Famine Ireland: 'What the potato was to the Irish peasant a few years ago, the chestnut is to the dwellers amidst these hills at the present day;

and, like the former article of food, should the latter be annihilated by some fell disease, the dread Irish tragedy of 1846 would be re-enacted on a similar scale amongst these Apennine glens'.[159]

At the heart of *Life in Tuscany* are two chapters where the author engaged in extensive social commentary. In 'The peasant', she drew a fundamental contrast between the inherent fertility and productivity of the Tuscan soil and the impoverished living and moral conditions of the peasantry despite their industriousness. To explain this anomaly, she drew attention to the pernicious effects of the sharecropping (mezzadria) system, which imposed backbreaking labour on men and women alike, but under contracts which reserved the bulk of the most valuable produce and profit to the landlord, leaving the peasant family with a life of social despair.[160] If many tiny farms were indeed too miniscule to support a family in comfort, many other small farms were rendered unprofitable by the exactions of the landlord or his fattore or steward, to which were added the harsh levels of taxation levied on the land, alongside conscription, to pay for the military infrastructure of the Tuscan state.[161]

To make a bad situation worse, the arrival of vine disease had further depressed living conditions; given that 'with not less fondness than the Irishman clings to the potato, does the Tuscan peasant to his vine', the consequences of this blight were similarly disastrous.[162] Crawford's sympathy with these hospitable but downtrodden people is evident in her direct quotations of the complaints of peasant women: 'We live like the beasts […] to work hard, and to fare badly, is our lot from childhood to the grave'.[163] She sought thereby to capture a reality of the effect on families of declining living standards, brought on by the destruction of traditional land rights, escalating debts and growing population leading to sporadic famines, which were often ignored by foreign commentators and by local elites.[164] The chapter finishes with an expressed hope that radical political change would lead to the restoration of a 'free peasantry', and bring with it a profound improvement in the material, moral and domestic conditions of the rural population.[165]

If this chapter most closely mirrored her father's preoccupations and theories – indeed she 'affectionately dedicated' her book to him – her chapter on 'Society' pointed forwards to her own evolution as a feminist. Reflecting on her interactions with the middle-class women of Florence, she expressed forthright criticism of their gender subordination, which she contrasted to the greater freedom available to 'English' ladies such as herself, and noting with some irony the way in which her 'most commonplace exploits [had] been magnified into heroic actions' by her Italian peers.[166] The long reign of despotic government had, she believed, distorted the public character and morals of all in the Grand Duchy, but it was the particular plight of women that drew her attention, and the place of the dominant orientalising 'social code' in entrenching this and undermining proper family life.[167] The acute lack of personal freedom and proper education accorded to Italian women had robbed them of self-respect and moral value, she concluded, creating a self-perpetuating pattern of subordination to men and infantilisation of their minds. This was no natural condition, but the 'artificial product' of social conditioning and the absence of education for girls to develop their intellectual faculties. The only solution to this baneful state of affairs was to change the social code to elevate the condition of girls and women; an object which, she argued, Italian patriots should embrace as their duty.[168]

Convinced that these social codes and economic structures, associated more with civil despotism than Catholicism, were at the root of Tuscany's and by extension Italy's woes, Crawford chose not to demonise the religion of the majority in a manner common to British travel writers. Like her father a sincere, if unorthodox, Anglican, she found much to fault in Catholicism, especially in the 'useless' institutions of contemplative monasticism. At the same time, she evinced respect for what she regarded as the deep and genuine faith of the ordinary people and praised religious orders active in charitable endeavours.[169] If, as Jennifer O'Brien has observed, Irish society became bitterly polarised in mid-century over the threat Italian nationalism was deemed to pose to the temporal power of the papacy Mabel appears to have struggled to avoid taking religious sides, reflecting a family tradition of subordinating religious difference to social concerns.[170]

Life in Tuscany received mixed reviews, including a decidedly misogynist one in a Birmingham paper which mocked her for parroting her father's agrarian nostrums and for her prim moralising.[171] Her book attracted more positive notice elsewhere, and extracts were published in a number of regional British and Irish newspapers.[172] In Paris, *Le revue des deux mondes* carried a lengthy review that engaged with her treatment of Tuscan women, but criticised her for taking too 'English' a view of Italian life.[173]

She was sufficiently emboldened by this reaction to leave Ireland again in 1859 for a more ambitious journey to French-occupied Algeria, the fruits of which she would publish several years later. Over a number of months she, with one or two female companions, travelled through the interior as far as the edge of the Sahara, staying with both Arab and colonist families and occasionally 'roughing it', and conversing with a range of people in French and rudimentary Arabic (Figure 37). The preface to her 1863 book *Through Algeria* contained an impassioned 'plea for lady tourists', written in refutation of the male critics who had ridiculed the idea of unescorted women travellers abroad. Her strongly-argued defence of 'feminine liberty of action' did not, she asserted, require the overthrow of the culture of female domesticity, but rather an acknowledgment of the right of those unmarried women of means, such as herself, who chose to transcend it and travel for instruction and enjoyment. She was prepared to face down misogynistic mockery to assert her rights:

> The butt of wit and witling, the satirist's staple theme, the 'unprotected' lady looms large before the popular gaze as a synonym for that ideal gorgon, the 'strong-minded woman;' from whose wooden face, hard features, harsh voice, blunt manners, and fiercely independent bearing, society shrinks in horror. To be confronted with such a fancy portrait of myself, is, in truth, no pleasant thought; but as every innovation must have its victims, I accept my menaced fate, cheered by the conviction that my immolation will prove of benefit to that class of tourists which, in these pages, I represent.[174]

Through Algeria shared the same close attention to local customs and conditions but lacked the empathetic sympathies of its predecessor. Shocked at what she regarded as the barbarity and superstition of north African native life, Crawford fell back on orientalist tropes and ethnic stereotyping to make sense of what she encountered. Thus, Algerian Arabs were indolent and unclean and Jews untrustworthy, and Islamic treatment of women (who were 'degraded into a toy or slave') she found appalling. She drew an exception for the Kabyle people of indigenous Berber descent of the Atlas mountains, who had bravely resisted the

French until 1857 and demonstrated enterprise and intelligence, and who treated women with greater respect and equality than other natives.[175] Although aware of the violence and early failures of French colonialism, she nevertheless endorsed the colonial project in north Africa, predicting a future where, as in British Australasia and Canada, the settlers would eventually displace the natives demographically and economically and thereby advance human civilisation.[176] These were not controversial views among the Victorian middle classes, although somewhat at odds with her father's more overtly critical views of empire and they pose problems for modern readers. A sympathetic review in *Duffy's Hibernian Magazine* in 1863 of the French orientalist Eugène Fromentin's Algerian travelogues may also have come from her pen; although anonymous, the text suggests an affinity with the places mentioned and highlights Fromentin's attention to ethnography and the place of women.[177]

Mabel's volume was generally well reviewed with some expressing sympathy for her 'plea' for women travellers, although the *Dublin Evening Mail* grumbled that it was likely to prejudice (male) readers against what was otherwise a fine travelogue.[178] Mabel's later opinions on empire appear to have been broadly Gladstonian, insisting that it serve a moral purpose of social improvement to be justified. She visited British-controlled Egypt in 1894, requesting an interview with the Khedive's mother, who was an important public figure in that society. She lamented that '[a]s far as I have been able to judge, European influences have not modified in any degree the dreary lives in any class of the women of Cairo'.[179] In 1895 she supported a debating motion that civilisation was impossible under Muslim rule on the grounds that 'Women must be FREE before freedom could exist among us, or true civilization', and that personal experience of Islamic societies had demonstrated to her that religious-based oppression must everywhere be challenged.[180]

Returning to Ireland, Mabel inherited the significant sum of £4,000 on her father's death in 1861 and appears to have determined to use this in a way that would honour his memory and ideals. After investigating a number of alternatives in the western counties, in 1869 she purchased through the landed estates court a small property on which to carry out her experiment. The principal source for her initiative, a short article she wrote for the *Contemporary Review* in 1887, does not specify the exact location except to offer the fictional name 'Donaleague', presumably to keep away overly intrusive journalists. In fact the property she had purchased was a lot of 135 acres at Shanacoole on the bankrupt Bayley estate in west Waterford, which was 'sold to Mr A. Tidsell, in trust for Miss Mabel Crawford' for £1,030 on 20 April 1869.[181] Six tenants were listed on the rental, one a large leaseholder, the others on smallholdings with yearly tenancies; the whole paid a gross rent of £66 of which £48 would be net to the new owner.[182]

She had, she recalled, to work hard to dispel her tenants' fears that she was just another despotic 'land-shark' like so many purchasers. Consequently, she sought to put into practice her father's agrarian theory and principles, along with her own vision of the social responsibility incumbent on a female landowner. Writing nearly twenty years later, she explicitly rejected the anti-Catholic and racial prejudices typical of what she termed the 'gloomy political creed of Orange Ulster' which attributed social backwardness and grievance-mongering to Catholicism, and credited her freedom from such misconceptions to the inheritance she derived from her father, who had 'a very different belief [... and] who, year after year, vainly tried to arouse the attention of legislature to the crime-provoking injustice of the laws to which the tenant-farmer was subject'.[183] The history of the Hearts of Oak and Hearts of Steel of eighteenth-century Ulster proved, she observed, that Protestants could be goaded into agrarian outrage by landlord oppression and unjust laws just as much as Catholics. Her experience had demonstrated the possibility of landlord-tenant co-operation for mutual benefit, when the landowner voluntarily surrendered some of his or her legal entitlements. She had adopted in full the Ulster custom of tenurial relations on her land, but also employed her own experience of observing during her travels the skills and practices of peasantries in France, Italy and Belgium. She praised the educational efforts of the Catholic clergy but she also distributed books to the neighbouring tenant and labourer families and urged the diffusion of practical agricultural education at state expense to raise productivity and thereby increase the demand for labour and curb emigration.

To humanise her account and generate the empathy of the reader, Mabel provided affectionate pen-portraits of her small tenant families, highlighting their endeavours to improve themselves if given the opportunity, while also acknowledging the linguistic barriers to communicating with all:

> Of all my tenants, Phil Tiernan was in every respect the best, and he solely owes the prosperity he now enjoys to years of hard and unremitting toil on an (originally) eight-acre farm adjoining my wild garden. At the time when […] he entered on the occupation of the farm, his three boys were in their early childhood, and even when they had arrived at an age to give some small help in agricultural work, he kept them at school, resolved that they would have the advantages he had never enjoyed; for Phil did not know how to read or write, and he had only a very imperfect knowledge of English. With his tidy, industrious, Irish-speaking wife I could not interchange a word. […] Extending from year to year the boundaries of his tiny farm by continuous reclamation, he points with well-justified pride to the great mounds of stones that strikingly attest the severity of the toil by which the reclamation has been effected.

Mabel assisted the family with a loan to replace their cow and found both the rent and loan repaid without complaint, and noted that Phil greatly improved his holding through adding outbuildings and giving employment to others. Much, however, was due to the agreement of a 'fair' rent, as, 'for all Phil's goodness, honesty and industry, if he had had the crushing rents to pay exacted from the lately-evicted tenants of Bodyke, he could not have prospered'.[184] Her empathetic narrative was generally well received in the British and Irish press, with one English paper describing the article as 'worth tons of theoretical essays'.[185] The *Freeman* praised her exceptional practice and attributed this to the doctrines she had learnt from her father, 'whose name is still remembered with gratitude'.[186]

While she believed her small agrarian experiment fully successful, she insisted that she had not been so naïve as to believe that most Irish proprietors would follow her example of partnership with their tenants. During the Land War in 1880 she wrote to the *Times* asserting that in Ireland the averred rights of property had no moral force and advocating stronger land legislation to protect small tenants from the threat of eviction and unfair rent increases – proposals that would later be enacted in substance in Gladstone's 1881 Land Act. Desperation to protect their family homesteads and livelihoods was what had driven some to violent agitation and more to give their silent support to such actions.[187] Her letter drew rebuttals from defenders of conventional landlordism including Lords Lifford and Cloncurry, both of whom assumed the author of the correspondence to be a man.[188] Her letter (and response to Lifford) attracted wider press attention and polarised opinion along partisan lines, with the *Belfast Morning News* asserting that they had demonstrated 'the masterly position she has been assigned as an authority upon the Irish land question', but the *Whig* fearing that only the report of the land commission would dissipate the ignorance and prejudice with which she had been met.[189] Looking beyond the tenants, Mabel also took a close interest in the living conditions of the agricultural labourers, and in 1879 gave a paper to the Social Science Congress in Manchester proposing legislation to oblige landowners in both Ireland and Britain to repair or replace labourers' cottages or forfeit all claim to rent; it was a 'humiliating fact', she stated, that 160,000 families were still living in one-room hovels in Ireland and it was now time for the state to intervene.[190]

From her 1887 account it appears the upheavals of the Land War (1879–82) and subsequent Plan of Campaign (1886–90) had left her small Waterford estate untroubled and her personal popularity undiminished: 'the warm Irish greeting I so often heard, "Ge naydian tholet agus ge me fa de wahe too" (God bless you, and long life to you), was uttered with a heartiness which showed that it was a genuine expression of friendliness and goodwill'.[191] While there may have been some paternalist wishful thinking here, her sentiments were genuine, and she also remained ready to engage in serious public controversy on the subject. In 1888 she disputed the issue in the economics section of the British Association for the Advancement of Science meeting at Bath.[192] Gladstone himself read her tract in 1889, although he did not record his opinions on it in his diary.[193] Anxious to solidify her achievements, in 1880 Mabel granted her tenants a lease for ever on their lands, essentially giving them security of tenure no matter who owned the estate, an act praised at the time as setting a 'noble example' and embodying her father's aspirations of the 1850s.[194] She then took advantage of the land purchase clauses in the 1885 Ashbourne Land Act to offer their plots to her tenants as owners, and was advanced £820 for this purpose by 1889, making hers the first Sharman Crawford lands to pass to occupier ownership.[195]

From the later 1860s Mabel became increasingly involved in campaigns to advance women's rights, including but not limited to the demand for the parliamentary vote. In 1868 she joined a Belfast committee to advocate for George Shaw-Lefevre's Married Women's Property Bill, which would grant at least a modicum of legal and financial autonomy to married women when it passed in 1870. The committee brought her into contact with Isabella Tod, already the leading feminist activist in the north of Ireland, who established the North of Ireland Women's Suffrage Society in 1871, and with whom Mabel would work closely up to 1886.[196] By 1869 she appears to have become resident in Dublin and involved in feminist networks there as well as maintaining her links to the north. Always a strong believer in the value of girls' education, she was a supporter of the Queen's Institute in the city, established in 1861 to offer opportunities for female technical and later artistic education.[197] She also contributed generously to the scholarships and prizes fund of the Belfast Ladies' Institute, founded in 1867 to advance access to third level education for women.[198] In 1878 she formed part of a northern delegation, with Tod and the pioneering educationalist Margaret Byers, to lobby for the inclusion of girls schools in the Irish Intermediate Education Bill which was then proceeding – a campaign which was to prove successful and stimulate demands for female access to university education.[199] She later wrote a memorial on behalf of the Society for School and University Education of Women in Ireland for presentation to the chancellor of the new Royal University, pointing out that 'A fair proportion of the endowment funds might be equitably given to girls, in order that the facilities for their education might be increased'.[200] She continued to pursue these objectives, along with advocating more practical and technical education at primary level, over the following years.[201]

The terms of the second reform act of 1867 continued to exclude women from the franchise, spurring a renewed campaign for their inclusion. In that year Millicent Fawcett took a leading role in forming the London National Society for Women's Suffrage, and sister bodies followed in provincial cities. By 1870 a Dublin committee had been established in the wake of a popular lecture given by Fawcett in the city, including Mabel along with Annie Robertson and Barbara Collett.[202] Mabel was (with Lady Wilde and James Haughton) re-elected to the committee in 1871 and represented the Dublin committee at national conferences.[203] However, she does not appear to have been directly involved with the Dublin Women's Suffrage Association, which emerged in 1876 under the leadership of Anna Haslem to replace the older committee. This does not seem to have been the result of any lapse of interest on Mabel's part – she remained a subscriber to the Manchester National Society for Women's Suffrage and in 1877 was with Tod at a London meeting in support of Jacob Bright's bill to enfranchise female ratepayers – but perhaps to her preoccupation with the management of her landed property in these years.[204] She was back in Dublin 1878 for a meeting of the British Association for the Advancement of Science and shared a suffragist platform with the Haslems on that occasion.[205] Her brother James, now MP for Down, was also a supporter of the women's suffrage movement; he attended a meeting of the London Society in 1874, spoke with Tod at a franchise rally in Glasgow in 1876, and voted for the abortive suffrage bills of the 1870s.[206] Tod would later lament his death, noting he had 'rendered invaluable service to our cause, and has left a blank not soon to be filled up'.[207] While the relationship between Mabel and her family is unclear after 1861, she at least shared some political common ground with James, and they were both present at the 1876 meeting of the British Association in Glasgow and both signed the 1877 Irish petition for female enfranchisement.[208]

From the early 1870s Mabel appears to have spent more time in London and to have become involved with the franchise and related campaigns there, while maintaining her Irish links.[209] Although not one of the leading speakers of the movement, she took the platform at a Dublin rally of the Womens' Suffrage Association in 1881 to make the case that 'it would be solid and substantial gain for the entire community if women were permitted to exert influence upon the legislature by a vote at the election of its members'.[210] Perhaps her principal contribution to the campaign was to act as editor, on behalf of the Central Committee of the National Society for Women's Suffrage, of an 1879 publication putting women's views on the question before the public. Published as *Opinions of Women on Women's Suffrage,* this sought to collate the views of some one hundred women engaged in non-political activities in public service, the arts, sciences, professions and philanthropy, with extracts from the writings of recently deceased women in public life such as Harriet Martineau. In her personal statement, Crawford drew on her experience of 'oriental' travel:

> 'If a husband provides his wife with a due supply of food and clothing, she should never go outside the door.' said an Egyptian dragoman. 'Would you like a perpetual indoor life?' I asked. 'Certainly not, but I am a man,' was the conclusive answer. In England, where women

have an admitted right to the enjoyment of personal liberty, the majority of Englishmen at the present day reason in dragoman fashion. They have yet to learn that, if the physical health of women is admittedly impaired by confinement within a limited space, her mental health also suffers through legislative disabilities; and that it is as unfair to deprive her, on the grounds of sex, of political liberty, as in the oriental mode, to shut her up within four walls. At the present day the Turkish empire is crumbling into ruins through the consistently enforced rule of the exclusively domestic sphere of woman, whilst society in England is vivified by a general infringement of this principle. The feminine philanthropist – designer and director of some beneficent public work – is essentially a politician; and, happily for the poor and friendless, this feminine poacher on masculine preserves is an ordinary feature of English life, in town and country. To say that a woman is unfit to vote in a land where a woman rules, is like saying that to pull an oar requires more intelligence than to steer.[211]

Extracts from the pamphlet were read in parliament, but for all the intensity of the arguments made, it remained a minority concern attracting the support of only a handful of MPs.[212] It would take a new generation prepared to adopt more assertive tactics, and the social change facilitated by the widening of female education that Crawford, Tod and Byers had pursued in Ireland, eventually to transform it into a mass movement.

Despite the setbacks encountered by the suffrage movement in these years, Mabel demonstrated the same degree of obstinate persistence in pursuing her political objectives as had her father. In 1884 she was part of a group which unsuccessfully lobbied Gladstone to include female heads of households in the third reform bill then in preparation.[213] In addition to pursuing enfranchisement she was also involved in campaigns to legally curb the working hours of young women in drapery establishments, and in the London Female Protection Society, which sought to protect vulnerable young Irish migrants from the lures of false 'employment registries' which were implicitly fronts for prostitution.[214] By 1885 she was persuaded that her efforts to alert Irish opinion to this danger, through letters to the provincial papers and the Catholic bishops, had made some impact, but still urged legislation to halt the 'hideous traffic' through targetting the organisers of such vice and not the victims.[215] She was active in the National Vigilance Association that emerged to campaign for this end under the leadership of W. T. Stead, the editor of the *Pall Mall Gazette,* with whom she became friendly.[216] At the same time, she strongly believed that the problem needed also to be addressed from the other side too, with Irish girls requiring training in useful skills that would help them find well-paid and useful employments overseas.[217]

Gladstone's adoption of a home rule policy for Ireland in early 1886 deeply divided the women's suffrage movement as well as the Liberal Party and tenant-right movement. The impact on Liberalism in Ulster was particularly destructive – ultimately forcing the Liberal Unionists who now rejected his leadership into what became the fatal embrace of the larger Conservative party, and leaving the minority who retained allegiance to Gladstone exposed to allegations that they were the disloyal catspaws of an aggressive Catholic nationalism. This was a polarisation that William had sought to avoid so far as possible in his lifetime, but the Liberal-Nationalist alliance of 1886 seemed to leave little if any room for political manoeuvre for those concerned that the primacy of the 'national question' would crowd out all other reformist politics. James had sought to follow his father's agrarianist pathway while an MP in the 1870s but felt obliged to vote against Butt's home rule motions and, with all but a handful of his fellow Presbyterians hostile to Irish self-government, would have found it very difficult to adhere to Gladstone had he lived beyond 1878. Nevertheless, his former colleague Thomas Dickson, Liberal MP for Dungannon and then Tyrone, did remain loyal, arguing that a Tory-dominated government would never grant full justice to tenant farmers.[218] This was, however, a minority view among Protestant Liberal agrarian reformers, most of whom looked now to the 'rising star' of radical Liberal Unionism, T. W. Russell, to deliver their objectives through an alliance with Joseph Chamberlain and the anti-Gladstonian British radicals who had followed him out of the Liberal party, and with those Conservatives who might favour a 'constructive unionist' policy to 'kill home rule with kindness'.[219]

William's second son Arthur was by now head of the family and owner of Crawfordsburn. Given his closeness to Belfast's commercial and industrial elite as a director of the Belfast Bank, and his generally more conservative outlook, Arthur had no hesitation in committing himself to Liberal Unionism and was a leading figure in the convention establishing that party in Belfast in March 1886. He remained president of the Ulster Reform Club and was regarded as a 'valued friend' of Isabella Tod's Womens Liberal Unionist Association, which she set up in 1888.[220]

His sister Mabel took a diametrically opposed view, even though this meant breaking not only with Arthur but with her long-standing feminist allies Tod and Byers, who both joined the Liberal Unionists on the grounds that an Irish home-rule parliament would set back the attainment of women's rights in the UK and throughout the empire.[221] This issue came to a head at a meeting of the National Political Union in Kensington in June 1886, where Tod and Fawcett clashed with Michael Davitt, who pointed out Tod's inconsistency in claiming proud descent from the Volunteers and United Irishmen while baulking at a constitutional measure much milder than the 'constitution of 1782'. When her turn to speak came, Mabel sided with Davitt and:

> in a telling speech, supported the claims of the Irish people to national autonomy. As a Protestant who had been seventeen years among the Catholics of the south of Ireland, she could bear testimony to their freedom from religious bigotry, which she regretted to say could not be said of the Protestants of her own province of Ulster.[222]

The *Freeman* claimed her father William and his federalist project as the progenitors of the modern Protestant Home Rule Association in Ulster, and his daughter's adherence appeared to give some credence to this contested assertion.[223] The argument was reinforced by Gladstone himself, who cited in the commons the repeated frustration of Crawford's tenant-right measures as evidence of the 'selfish interests of the British parliament' and the need for Irish legislative autonomy.[224] Mabel herself appeared to endorse the claim, reminding the Liberal-Unionist *Northern Whig* that her father had 'lived and died a true patriot in the full sense of the word'.[225]

Now fully committed to the campaign for home rule, Mabel spoke at meetings in London on behalf of the Women's Liberal Federation to urge opposition to the propaganda work of the Tory Primrose League.[226] This was the context in which her 1887 article on landownership appeared, although her work cannot be simply dismissed as propaganda. She was a member of the ladies' branch of the English Home Rule Union, using its platforms to draw attention to the evils of evictions in Ireland, and supported the deployment of 'Home Rule vans' throughout the country to raise consciousness through distributing publications and hosting lantern slide lectures highlighting evictions and the government's resort to coercion.[227] Although she may not have been the London-based 'Belfast Liberal' who wrote to the *Northern Whig* in later 1890 to argue that Liberal Unionists should denounce the unremitting coercion applied by Lord Salisbury's ministry and place their trust in the anti-Parnellite Irish leaders Justin McCarthy and John Dillon, she would no doubt have agreed with the case made that:

> Ulstermen [should] ask themselves which side at such a juncture the friends of the farmers of Ireland like Sharman Crawford and Professor Smyth in the old days would have taken. Justin McCarthy and the Radicals of England want no miserable war of class against class or race against race: no separation from England, but only peace to get along with their country's business.[228]

In 1892 she sent to Gladstone a copy of the her father's 1833 pamphlet *Suggestions with Reference to the Necessity of Constituting a National Body to Manage the Local Interests and Local Taxation of Ireland*, which had been reissued that year by the Liberal candidate for North Antrim William Dodd, to remind voters that the 'father of tenant right' was also a convinced federalist.[229] No doubt she endorsed the *Freeman's* view that he was 'a great Protestant Home Ruler' and hoped Gladstone would agree.[230] At least some Liberal Unionists, such as the radical Presbyterian minister J. B. Armour, declared themselves convinced by Dodd's invocation of the memory of Sharman Crawford and went over to the Liberals, although not enough to swing the election in the north-Antrim heartland of the Route Tenant Right Association. Dickson also fell short in South Tyrone, fighting as a Liberal on a home rule and land reform ticket that also evoked the Sharman Crawford name.[231]

This engagement with home rule brought Mabel into contact with a range of other 'patriotic' Irish societies both in Dublin and London which intersected with her interests. In 1890 she joined the provisional committee of the Irish Industrial League, a non-partisan body established to promote the revival of national industries and the replacement of foreign imports by local products.[232] In 1892 she also became a member of the Irish Literary Society in London, which had the elderly Charles Gavan Duffy (now returned from Australia via retirement in Nice) as its president, and who called for a cultural awakening similar to that of Young Ireland in the 1840s. The society attracted members from a range of political positions including prominent writers such as Douglas Hyde, W. B. Yeats and Oscar Wilde.[233] She was certainly not overawed by such august literary figures, for example upbraiding George Bernard Shaw to his face in a different venue in 1894 when he asserted 'men's intellectual superiority' over women.[234]

Her first concern remained the rights of women. She remained prominent on suffrage platforms through the 1890s as a member of the National Society for Women's Suffrage and the Women's Liberal Federation, enduring the continuing setbacks to the campaign.[235] She wrote angrily in 1890 about the confinement of women visitors to the house of commons behind a metal grille, placing them in her view in a kind of political 'Purdah' cognate to that of oriental women.[236] This symbolic subordination was a continuing source of resentment, and the grille would become the subject of a suffragette attack in 1908. Other Victorian gender conventions also drew her ire, and she was involved in the Rational Dress Society which aimed to replace the 'fantastic creations of Paris fashions' with clothing that would facilitate women's natural movement and working life, such as knickerbockers and dresses with pockets.[237] Throughout the ages, she argued in an article for the journal *Women's World*, then edited by Oscar Wilde, challenges to prevailing orthodoxies by women had provoked 'social scares', and the same was true in reaction to the 'revolt of women' in the Victorian age. But while many women were content with the domestic sphere, others would continue to struggle for the freedoms that would allow them to realise their potential; these 'exceptional women, to whom nursery cares and household duties are distasteful, ought to have as free an outlet for the satisfaction of their individual tastes, as is the case with men whom nature prompts to enter on some career outside ordinary masculine vocations'.[238]

Mabel's last significant foray into print came in 1893, when she took up the issue of domestic abuse of wives in an article for the *Westminster Review*. It was a scandal, she wrote, that neither law nor public opinion offered any meaningful defence to married women from violence or abuse carried out in the home, and even domestic murder met with lenient punishments. An attempt to improve the situation by an 1878 law had failed as it had left to the discretion of judges the imposition of maintenance orders to support 'battered' wives and their children, thus deterring women from going to court out of fear of penury and retribution. Her carefully researched piece cited numerous cases of judicial failings leading to injury and death, all of which derived from the immoral doctrine of wives' legal subordination to husbands, and which proved the necessity of more effective legislation and its implementation.[239] She continued to pursue the case for reform of the criminal law relating to women through correspondence in the following years, suggesting the use of the lash on the most brutal men, but prioritising the need for financial protection for abused women through separation orders.[240]

While she kept politically active throughout her seventies, and regularly spoke at London debating and intellectual societies such as the Pioneer Club, by the end of the century she was beginning to slip out of the public arena. She was however still a member of the executive committee in 1901 of the amalgamated Central Society for Women's Suffrage in England and wrote to Dufferin that year to urge his vote for Lord Aberdeen's amendment to permit women to sit as councillors in the local government of London.[241] Illness may have hampered her continuing activity thereafter. Mabel died at her home in Kensington on 14 February 1912, six years before the attainment of the first tranche of women's enfranchisement in the UK.[242] A staunch believer that education was essential to women's liberation, she left a large bequest of £2,000 to endow a scholarship at the London School of Medicine for Women, which was awarded annually in her name.[243] Although largely ignored by obituarists, the *Irish Book-Lover* identified her in 1912 as the 'last surviving child of William Sharman-Crawford "the father of Irish tenant-right"', and as the author of *Life in Tuscany*.[244] She was unquestionably and self-consciously her father's daughter in her radical commitment to social and political reform, but the obituarist missed the extent to which she had taken that legacy in new and dynamic directions and made her own important contribution to the campaign for women's rights in her later life.

The end of Crawfordsburn radicalism, 1891–1934

William Sharman Crawford had struggled to keep the antithetical forces of radicalism and gentry status in balance within his family, but his elder sons John and Arthur opted both for a more conventional relationship with their tenants and a moderate form of liberalism that for Arthur transitioned easily into Liberal Unionism from 1886. In the succeeding generation the balance would break down completely and Crawfordsburn become associated with a very different political colouration, which would find itself in conflict with new iterations of both rural and urban radicalism and in turn ally itself with populist sectarianism.

This did not at first appear inevitable. Arthur and his wife Louisa's eldest son William Henry (born 1847) survived childhood and in 1870 was given a partnership on his mother's family's thriving brewing business in Cork, succeeding his cousin William Horatio Crawford to joint directorship on the latter's death in 1888.[245] In 1880 William Henry spoke at a rally in support of his uncle John's Liberal candidacy for Down.[246] However he died suddenly in December 1889, reportedly of typhoid fever, and without leaving any male children.[247] As Arthur's second son had already died in 1862, this left his third son unexpectedly as the new heir to Crawfordsburn. Robert Gordon Sharman-Crawford, who was born in 1853 (and who came to adopt the double-barrelled version of the surname, by then increasingly fashionable in gentry circles), had opted for a military career, despite his late grandfather's intense dislike of professional soldiering, first in the North Down Militia and subsequently with the regular army as a lieutenant and then captain in the 15th Hussars and later the 16th Lancers.[248] As such he acquired significant imperial experience; his unit was stationed in India until 1881 and he travelled to Australia and New Zealand when he took leave in 1877.[249] By 1884 he was in Ireland, where his troops undertook coercive policing duties in the wake of the Land War.[250]

Following his elder brother's death, Robert Gordon resigned from the army and returned to Crawfordsburn in 1890, soon being made a magistrate and adopting the lifestyle of a country gentleman.[251] He inherited the estates on his father's death in September 1891, and also stepped into his places as an ex-officio guardian (and later chair) of the Newtownards union and as member of the superintendence board of the Belfast Bank. Reluctant to abandon completely his previous career, he rejoined the militia, was promoted to lieutenant-colonel in 1898 and retired in 1903 with permission to retain his then rank of full colonel.[252] As befitted his place as a significant landowner, he was appointed high sheriff for the county in 1894–5 and participated, as was expected of him, in the usual range of agricultural societies and committees.[253] Meanwhile in 1890 his younger brother Arthur Frederick took over the joint management of Beamish and Crawford and established his family residence at Lota Lodge in Glanmire.[254] He held twenty-eight per cent of the shares in the company following its incorporation in 1895, with his elder brother holding another twenty-two per cent as a sleeping partner and receiving a substantial annual income from the concern that largely insulated him from anxiety over the future of his landed holdings.[255] Arthur Frederick thus became a leading business figure in Cork city, gifting the site for and equipping its new technical institute (opened in 1912 on what was renamed Sharman Crawford Street to honour his philanthropy) and continuing the Crawford family's patronage of the city's art gallery and its associated school.[256]

As a landowner, Robert Gordon Sharman-Crawford appeared careful not to upset the generally good relations with his tenantry retained by his uncles and father, unlike Lord Dufferin, whose infringements on the Ulster custom caused unrest on the neighbouring estate in 1898.[257] Nevertheless, he had no direct experience of his grandfather's agrarianism, had a preference for lofty paternalism, and instinctively gravitated towards a 'landlord' position in the continuing disputes over land, attending meetings of the Irish Landowners' Convention in Dublin in the 1890s. It was implausible that he could (should he have wanted to) take on the mantle of a political 'tenant-righter'.[258] Perhaps indicative of his different attitude towards property was his decision to close the Crawfordsburn demesne to the public, allowing only occasional access to invited groups.[259] His grandfather's policy of open access, aligned with his 'popular' political persona, had occasionally given rise to problems, as when unruly or on occasion drunk and violent visitors had taken advantage. An incident of 'gross misconduct' (involving a stabbing) in 1857 had led to a temporary suspension of free access, although this appears to have been soon lifted and public access was retained under John.[260] Arthur re-opened the grounds to the public in 1886 after a temporary closure to install electric light to illuminate both the house and glen. Given the proximity to Belfast, the *News-Letter* thought it would be an absolute calamity if access was barred, but this appears to have been what happened in the 1890s, with the demesne becoming a private space.[261] This became a political issue in 1900 when an opponent remarked that 'the gates of Crawfordsburn were now opened, but Colonel Crawford had for years shut those gates against the public, closing against them the beauties of nature'. In 1901 he was again upbraided for refusing to open the estate to an excursion of the Belfast workhouse children.[262] Hints were also dropped in the heat of an electoral contest that he had appealed against decisions of the land court to reduce his rents, and that he was not universally popular with his tenants.[263]

Robert Gordon inherited his father's Liberal Unionist political orientation and was invited as such to participate in the organising committee of the Ulster Unionist Convention of 1892, which was summoned to demonstrate united resistance to an anticipated second Home Rule bill.[264] He followed the Duke of Abercorn and Earl Erne as a platform speaker at the event held in Belfast's Botanic Gardens, indicating the prominent place members of the landed elite retained within the movement.[265] Not all unionists were happy with the convention, however, and the *Ballymoney Free Press* dismissed it as a body dominated by Conservatives and landlords with only a few real Liberal Unionists involved.[266] It's not clear whether it considered Sharman-Crawford as one of the true or feigned Liberal Unionists, but he would soon be placed by others into the latter category. At this time, however, his wife Annie (who was English by birth) also became politically involved, attending a Liberal Unionist 'at home' organised by Tod in 1894 and subsequently joining Unionist women's bodies.[267] Around the same time, Robert Gordon joined the committee of the Ulster Loyal and Patriotic Union, then led by Lord Ranfurly and William Young, through which he became familiar with the leadership group of the Ulster Unionist movement.[268]

Over time the distinction between Liberal Unionists and Conservatives began to break down and different fractures within unionism became more evident. These came to the surface in North Down in 1898, at a time when fears of home rule were receding following the final retirement of Gladstone in 1894 and the return to power of a Conservative-Unionist government the following year. The constituency had been held by the Conservative landowner and Orangeman Thomas Waring since its creation in 1885. On Waring's death in 1898 Robert Gordon was discussed as a possible replacement, but at this time he declined to stand.[269] The candidate who emerged from the constituency's landed elite was John Blakiston-Houston, a landowner and vice-lord lieutenant for the county, but it became clear that he would not be unopposed. The Scottish Conservative and former London county councillor Thomas Lorimer Corbett issued a challenge, taking a stance that was more populist and anti-Catholic than the 'county' Unionist candidate, and garnering significant Presbyterian support. Corbett was defeated at the by-election by a narrow majority, but the deep divisions and underlying class and religious antagonisms within unionism in the district had been revealed (not least by the electoral rioting that followed in Newtownards) and could not be easily resolved.[270]

To the disappointment of the *Free Press* no explicit 'tenant-right' challenge to the landed candidate in North Down had come forward, as 'there is surely something better for Ulster Liberal Unionists to do than hew wood and draw water for territorial Unionism'.[271] 1892 had been a low point for agrarian radicalism in the north: T. W. Russell was criticised for leaning too close to the Unionist leadership and in Tyrone 'the old Sharman Crawford tenant-righters are opposed to him for his deliberate betrayal of the small farmers'. But from the mid-1890s he began to transition his brand of unionism in a more anti-Conservative agrarianist direction as frustration with the slowness of land purchase grew.[272] Although a parliamentary under-secretary in Salisbury's administration from 1895, Russell continued to proclaim his allegiance to the land reform movement, telling his supporters in 1896 that it was '[b]y the constitutional labours of men like Sharman Crawford, Dr McKnight, Richard Smyth, Hugh Law and Isaac Butt – aye, and shame be it said that it should have required it – by the unconstitutional work of the Land League, this horrid system has been all but brought to the ground'.[273] Corbett, who was something of a political opportunist, kept a formal distance from Russell, but had clearly observed his developing insurgency closely and learned the lesson of the utility of intra-unionist class as well as denominational politics. He would try his luck again two years later.

One reason why Sharman-Crawford may not have proceeded with his own candidacy in 1898 was his preoccupation with a major sporting endeavour that year. Both he and his brothers had long taken an interest in the expensive pursuit of competitive yachting, and he had become vice-commodore of the Royal Ulster Yacht Club. Sharman-Crawford had reportedly been part of a syndicate which had in 1897 planned to build a yacht to challenge for the Americas Cup, but by the following year he had instead come to play a part in the wealthy tea magnate Sir Thomas Lipton's better financed bid.[274] Indeed, it was Robert Gordon who travelled to America in 1898 to formally present Lipton's challenge to the New York Yacht Club and agree the terms on which Lipton's boat the 'Shamrock' would compete against them.[275] Although the 'Shamrock' was defeated in 1899, the race made Sharman-Crawford's name in elite yachting circles, and he was involved in a similar capacity in Lipton's unsuccessful challenges in 1901, 1903, 1920 and 1930, which in total would cost over a million pounds.[276] The connection with Lipton would also prove politically useful, and Sharman-Crawford introduced him to the future prime minister of Northern Ireland, James Craig, aboard his yacht in 1902.[277]

In 1897 Sharman-Crawford had joked that his yachting activities would not impede his duties as chair of the Newtownards board of guardians.[278] He seems to have extended the same paternalistic attitude towards local government more generally as this was reformed under the 1898 Local Government Act. In 1899 he stood in the Killyleagh district for the new Down County Council, assuring the voters that he would be apolitical in his interests and concerned primarily with the improvement and defence of the interests of agriculture, while at the same time being careful to pay fealty to the still potent local memory of his grandfather and uncle James.[279] Once elected he became a fixture on the new council, rising to be vice-chair by 1902 and promoting agricultural interests, which he interpreted in a mostly technocratic fashion.[280] In a similar spirit he would represent Ulster on the Irish Council of Agriculture from 1900.[281]

His local government success may have given him a taste for elections, and he was now happy to have his name put forward, following a memorial and deputation from the 'leading Conservatives of North Down', for that constituency at the general election of 1900. Blakiston-Houston had stepped down and Corbett had again put himself forward with strong backing from the newly-formed Presbyterian Unionist Voters' Association, to the horror of the 'county' establishment.[282] They clearly hoped that the Sharman Crawford name was still 'one to conjure with', although now ironically it would go forward in opposition to a Presbyterian insurgency against Anglican landed control of the constituency.[283] In addition to attacking the landed interest as crypto-nationalists, Corbett was aware that he needed to separate the Sharman-Crawford running against him from the memory of the radical contestants of 1852, 1874 and 1880, and stressed in his speeches that Robert Gordon was simply the catspaw of a landed clique who were opposed to any further land reforms leading to transfer of ownership or concessions to the working man.[284] While the local paper rejected this claim and respected Sharman-Crawford's personal honour, it nevertheless agreed that on the land question 'he [Sharman-Crawford] has forsaken the banner of his forefathers. We do not blame him for doing so. Every man has a right to his own convictions'.[285] Despite his assertions that he too was in favour of a generous land purchase scheme and that he was fully in support of the government's expansionist imperial policy (in what was referred to as the 'Khaki election' during the ongoing Second Anglo-Boer War), the sustained aggression of Corbett's campaign and mobilisation of populist Presbyterian and temperance feeling placed Robert Gordon on the back foot, a position from which he failed to recover.[286]

Both candidates felt obliged to present their cases before the recently-formed Ulster Tenant Defence Association, whose chairman prefaced his remarks by recalling the Down election of 1852 and declared the body's objective was to supersede the '3Fs' with 'FPP' – fair price purchase for the tenant. The colonel thought his answers to their queries, in which he announced himself in favour of a measure for compulsory purchase (albeit at the higher value), sufficiently popular to have them published in an election flyer. They were accompanied by an endorsement by the Liberal Unionist Thomas Andrews of Comber, who recalled the candidate's grandfather as one 'who lit the fiery cross of tenant-right in County Down […] which has since been embodied in the law of the land', and praised the colonel as upholder of the family tradition.[287] Such 'trimming' on land reform by established Unionist candidates was common in that and subsequent years in response to the revived agrarian movement.[288] However in North Down the Association refused to declare for either candidate, leaving the advantage with Corbett, who highlighted his opponent's membership of the Landlord Convention and claimed he was 'biased by all training and surroundings in favour of class privilege and self-interest'.[289] Even the *Northern Whig* abandoned Crawfordsburn, answering the question 'is it the Sharman Crawfords or the County Down landlords who have changed?' with the observation that he was in open alliance with the successors of those men whose conduct his grandfather had so vigorously condemned.[290]

The result was a humiliation, with Corbett triumphing by a majority of 1,263 votes in a poll of 7,796. It was celebrated as 'a rare union of Orangemen and radicals' and welcomed by some Presbyterian spokesmen as having finally broken the back of landlordism in the county.[291] This was an overstatement, but it was certainly a high-profile upset of what would later be termed 'big house unionism', and a severe setback also for Robert Gordon's political ambitions. If he was to succeed in future, greater unionist political discipline behind its 'natural leaders' and a campaign that appeared to transcend class and denominational issues would be required. Corbett, who supported Russell's 1901 motion for compulsory purchase but otherwise proved less radical in parliament than some of his followers had hoped, appeared to agree. He accepted Sharman-Crawford's conciliatory 1904 proposal for a unified North Down Unionist Association to help see off any threat arising from disunion by choosing agreed candidates in future. This body endorsed Corbett in 1906, but the colonel would retain a prominent role in it through to his death.

Sharman-Crawford was active in the committee that met in Belfast at the end of 1904 to establish the new Ulster Unionist Council (UUC) as a single governing body for the party that would focus on resisting all attempts to revive home rule as well as combatting internal disunity.[292] One development which made this necessary was the escalating threat posed by Russell's campaign to reignite the radical agrarian tradition within Ulster Protestant politics. By 1900 he was pursuing the specific measure of compulsory land purchase to oblige recalcitrant landowners to sell to their tenants on more favourable terms. Russell (himself the grandson of an evicted Scottish crofter) finally broke with the Liberal Unionist leadership in the wake of the 1900 election, rejecting their claim that the current government had attained William Sharman Crawford's aims.[293]

Despite the overt political realignment of 1886, Presbyterian resentments at continuing Anglican supremacy in Ulster society and the Irish administration had evidently not disappeared and fuelled Russell's insurgency in a much more overt manner than was manifest in Corbett's opportunistic campaigns of 1898 and 1900.[294] Russell launched his campaign at the radical town of Ballymoney in November 1900, and opened the door for collaboration with the nationalist United Irish League led by William O'Brien. Endorsed by the Ulster Tenant Defence Association, he then established his own organisation, the Ulster Farmers' and Labourers' Union and Compulsory Sale Association in 1901.[295] He now made an explicit bid for the mantle of William Sharman Crawford and the Tenant League, praising Crawford's pioneering efforts for land reform in his book *Ireland and the Empire*, in his platform oratory and in parliament.[296] He told his supporters at Garvagh that 'if anything taking place there moved the spheres above, Sharman Crawford's spirit must look down on these meetings with supreme satisfaction'.[297] This demarche brought down on Russell and his allies the fury of both Ulster Unionist MPs led by Colonel Edward Saunderson and the British government, but, as the *Irish News* observed, the name of Sharman Crawford was still one to inspire many in Ulster: 'Mr Crawford lived down Orange abuse; Mr Russell will survive the colonel's fire and fury'.[298]

The Russellites now proceeded to contest by-elections under their own banner, threatening to unite the Presbyterian and Catholic tenant farmer vote behind their popular agrarian demands. The first challenge came in East Down in early 1902, one that Russell proclaimed would be the greatest contest in Ireland for a generation. The Presbyterian solicitor James Wood came forward as the Russellite challenger, while Sharman-Crawford wisely declined an invitation to face him, despite holding a council seat in the district.[299] The *Whig* denounced Wood as a traitor to Liberal Unionism, and alleged that he had accused William Sharman Crawford and James McKnight of having betrayed the Tenant League in 1853.[300] The *Irish News* responded to this attempt to ignite a history war by pointing out that Crawford had been constrained by the landlord intimidation of the 1850s and that his bill could not be taken as the unchanging axiom of tenant demands, and it printed the claim of the Kennaught Farmer's and Labourer's Association that had he still been alive Sharman Crawford would be 'found this day in his native place of East Down on the platform with Russell and Wood, and holding out a welcoming hand to Redmond too, in order to bring peace and prosperity to the land he loved'.[301] Wood himself was reported to have claimed that the 'mantle of Sharman Crawford' had fallen on himself, to the mockery of his Conservative opponents.[302] However, the official Unionist candidate Robert Wallace, also a colonel in the militia (and on active service in South Africa at the time) shared many of the unpopular characteristics of his North Down counterpart in 1900. The appeal to patriotic imperialism fell flat despite the denunciations of the Russellites by Sir Edward Carson, and in less florid terms by Colonel Sharman-Crawford himself, and Wood carried the seat at the polls.[303]

The Russellites came up short in South Antrim the following year, where the Unionist candidate was Charles Craig of the Belfast Presbyterian industrial family. But again they posed a serious challenge and Russell had deployed deep agrarian memory in support of his candidate Samuel Keightley: 'If the farmers were about to take possession of their land, they had to thank the men who followed Sharman Crawford and were bludgeoned at the poll'.[304] Charles's brother James Craig lost to a Russellite (with strong nationalist support) in the North Fermanagh by-election in March 1903, and the insurgency continued. The political pressure generated by these contests, alongside a vigorous agitation in the south and west by the UIL, pushed the chief secretary George Wyndham into agreeing to a land conference that in turn produced a new land bill. The Wyndham Act of 1903, as it became known, strongly encouraged land transfer by making large amounts of Treasury funding available at favourable rates for purchase loans, as well as offering generous premiums to encourage landlords to sell. It stopped short of Russell's demand for compulsory purchase powers, but did something to dent the popularity of his campaign, as more substantial tenants were quick to take advantage of the act and many landowners were by now inclined to sell up if the price was right.[305] The Russellites' electoral gains (including East Down) were lost in the subsequent general election of 1906 with only Russell and R. G. Glendinning in North Antrim being successful. Nevertheless, despite the opportunity the 1903 Act gave the party to reassert its claims to be that of cross-class 'consensus' within the Protestant community, the Unionist leadership remained anxious about the potential for dissension on economic and social questions.

Sharman-Crawford demonstrated a readiness to co-operate with the 1903 land act by opening negotiations with his Rademon tenants regarding purchase of their farms in January 1904, although at a Crossgar meeting they resolved not to accept his offer.[306] The huge cost of construction of his new mansion at Crawfordsburn (at up to £20,000), which he began that year, may have been a factor in his initially setting too high a price.[307] By spring 1905, however, an agreement had been struck with the Banbridge estate tenants.[308] Wood sought to make political capital out of the stalled negotiations at Rademon, accusing Sharman-

Crawford of breaking his word and hence proving the necessity of legal compulsion of sales.[309] By 1908 the sale of the Upper Iveagh lands was complete, but those elsewhere in the county were still delayed, giving Woods further ammunition at the January 1910 election in East Down. The Rademon holdings appear not to have changed hands until after the Northern Ireland compulsory purchase act of 1925.[310] The sale of the Meath estate at Stalleen was however completed by the beginning of 1914.[311]

In addition to the Russellite threat, the Ulster Unionist leadership was alarmed in 1904–5 by the 'devolution scheme' mooted within Arthur Balfour's government as an attempt to undermine home rule through conceding a weaker form of Irish self-government. The backlash against this brought down Wyndham and under-secretary Sir Anthony MacDonnell, but not before the UUC had been formed to assert unity in the face of perceived betrayal by the British government as well as from its internal enemies in Ulster. Russell had hoped that a just solution to the land question would end the demand for home rule, but when this failed to transpire after 1903 he shifted his ground towards accepting what he had previously opposed. Although re-elected as an independent Unionist in South Tyrone in 1906, he rejoined the Liberals the following year. In the highly polarised 'Home Rule' election of January 1910 he lost the seat, only to take North Tyrone (with nationalist support) at a 1911 by-election. But as the Home Rule party gained ground under John Redmond, older enmities within Unionism were (at least temporarily) suppressed and radicalism again relegated to the margins. Wood stood again in East Down as a Liberal in January 1910, retaining a significant forty-three per cent of the vote against James Craig, but his successor slipped back in the December 1910 election which was fully dominated by the constitutional question. Despite efforts of Russell and his allies, the implementation of the 1903 land act (supplemented by a Liberal measure to promote sales in 1909), took the sting out of agrarian radicalism for many northern Presbyterians. An attempt by the Presbyterian nationalist antiquarian Francis Joseph Bigger to stimulate agrarianist memory through his 1910 book *The Ulster Land War of 1770,* an enthusiastic if rather disorganised account of the Protestant Steelboys and their antecedents, failed to find its intended audience.[312]

However the fading of Russellism did not immediately benefit Sharman-Crawford's political ambitions. In North Down, the still-popular Corbett had seen off a Russellite 'radical' in 1906 now with the full support of the 'county' establishment, and as the incumbent he was returned unopposed in January 1910.[313] Yet despite the public reconciliation, when Corbett died later that year it was to the prominent Scottish Presbyterian William Mitchell-Thomson that the district Unionist Association turned, as Sharman-Crawford still appeared hesitant to risk another candidacy in the predominantly Presbyterian constituency despite the more propitious circumstances.[314]

Sharman-Crawford was finally able to attain his ambition of election to parliament in 1914. In part this was due to his cultivation of a range of elements within the unionist coalition. The colonel had been a member of the UUC since its inception and friendly with the increasingly influential Craig brothers. Perhaps due to his association with the Belfast Bank, he was appointed treasurer of the UUC in 1912, a post he would continue to hold until his death in 1934.[315] Although he was not yet an Orangeman, he now also patronised that organisation, speaking at the re-opening of the Newtownards Orange Hall in 1910 and assisting with the purchase of banners and regalia.[316] However, most important in his political rehabilitation was his personal relationship with Carson, who became leader of the Ulster Unionist Party (UUP) in 1910. After the death of his first wife in 1913, Carson became engaged to and married the following year Ruby Frewen, a Yorkshirewoman twenty-seven years his junior, whose father had been the commander of Sharman-Crawford's cavalry regiment and with whom he had remained on good terms.[317] As family friends the Carsons would be frequent house-guests at Crawfordsburn over the following years, unquestionably enhancing Robert Gordon's standing in Unionist eyes, and he privately advised Carson on the opinions of the Ulster leadership on sensitive matters (Figure 39).[318]

In 1911 Sharman-Crawford was present at the joint meeting of the Unionist Associations and Clubs and the Orange Order at which Carson announced the formation of a provisional government for Ulster should the proposed third Home Rule Bill proceed.[319] Partition was now on the agenda, even if Carson personally continued to regard Ulster resistance principally as a means of blocking home rule for the whole island. Speaking in Bangor soon after, Sharman-Crawford echoed the increasingly militant rhetoric of the movement, warning that any who did not join the Orange Order or the Unionist Clubs would be regarded as opponents who would need watching. While they were not insurrectionists, he continued, the clubs would engage in drilling, and he was sure the British army would never fire on them if they acted in defence of Ulster.[320] From this it was a small step to armed parading, and in April 1912 the colonel was at the head of a demonstration of an estimated twenty thousand Orangemen and clubmen in the town.[321] On 15 December he and Colonel Wallace were reportedly members of a delegation that overcome Carson's reservations on raising an armed resistance force, and shortly after he was ready to announce at a Bangor rally that a new and 'more forward' organisation was being planned to demonstrate its hostility to home rule. Timothy Bowman credits him at this meeting with the first public use of the term 'Ulster Volunteer Force' (UVF) anywhere in the province.[322] A few days later he wrote to Carson on behalf of the Irish Unionist Alliance warning that as the Home Rule Bill was now certain to pass and Conservative support was slipping in England, 'non-peaceful' resistance must be anticipated in the future.[323] His support for the policy of resorting to 'all means necessary' to defeat the 'home rule conspiracy' made him an active participant in the formation of the paramilitary UVF over the course of 1913, and his previous military rank and training entitled him to a prominent position within it.[324]

By July 1913 Sharman-Crawford had enrolled 2,500 men into his North Down UVF Regiment. They were paraded for inspection by Carson himself at Six Road Ends near Bangor on 24 July when news arrived that the colonel's only son Terence, who had followed his father into military service, had been killed in a motorcycling accident. Despite this family tragedy, Sharman-Crawford insisted that the review proceed as planned, and was rewarded for his dedication to the cause by appointment to the advisory board of the UVF and to the small standing committee established to plan a provisional government for Ulster.[325] He would also take responsibility for managing the UVF's finances, expending over £89,000 by May 1915 (not including the £60,000 set aside for illegal arms purchases in a fund directly controlled by James Craig), and for raising pledges for an 'Indemnity Fund' to give financial support to the families of casualties should the force be mobilised.[326] Undoubtedly the death of his only son generated significant local sympathy for the colonel and his wife, not least after newsreel of the funeral was projected for public consumption at the new Bangor Picture House.[327]

Perhaps inevitably, Sharman-Crawford's prominent role within the UVF invited some parallels with his great-grandfather's activity in the late eighteenth century. The 'Volunteer portrait' of Colonel William Sharman was hung prominently in the new Crawfordsburn House. Praising the UVF on the occasion of their review by Carson at Balmoral in September 1913, the *Belfast Telegraph* historicised the movement as part of a long tradition of Ulster self-defence bodies mobilised to maintain their 'religion and liberties' and drew attention to the Crawfordsburn portrait as a link between past and present. The paper claimed that, like the Volunteers, they 'are compelled to unite for self-defence, not against a foreign foe, but in order to retain their rights and liberties in the empire to which they rightfully belong, and whose protection they are naturally entitled to claim'.[328] This simplified history chose to suppress the role of the Volunteers in extracting a form of Irish self-government well in advance of the limited federalist autonomy offered by the third Home Rule Bill, and the association of Sharman with the more radical campaigns for Catholic and democratic political rights against both the British administration and the Irish Protestant establishment. Nevertheless, like many other from the gentry class, Sharman-Crawford appears to have taken immense pride in their new volunteer movement; in collaboration with Lady Londonderry he designed a new flag for the North Down Regiment that year.[329]

His close connection with Carson and prominence within both the UUC and UVF leadership made Sharman-Crawford appear a plausible candidate for the predominantly Protestant working-class seat of East Belfast when a vacancy arose there at the height of the 'Ulster crisis' in March 1914.[330] Nominated unanimously by the Unionist Association with the support of the District Master of the Orange Order (who bore the unlikely name of John Hume), the colonel drew attention to his close friendship with Carson, whom he pledged to follow loyally in parliament. At the same time, he was 'prepared to lead his regiment of Volunteers against any combination that would attempt to drive them from under the union jack', as any effort to impose home rule would mean, in the words of Randolph Churchill in 1886, that 'Ulster will fight'. Such militant rhetoric played well in the constituency amid the political excitements of the moment, and he was elected unopposed. Some vague references were made in the campaign to the name of Sharman Crawford being 'associated with many great battles fought in the interests of the people', but these were not specified; however, in a belated echo of his aunt's politics (and perhaps reflecting also his wife's political involvement) the colonel declared himself in favour of votes for women.[331]

Sharman-Crawford never had to face the dilemma of seeing through the UVF's threat of armed rebellion against the government and was quick to declare his support for the British war effort when hostilities with the Central Powers broke out in August 1914. Addressing the North Down UVF in September he urged them to enlist in what he promised would be a separate Ulster division of the British army, offering to lead them himself if 1,000 volunteered, although in December of that year he and his UVF regiment were still carrying out manoeuvres in the Holywood hills prior to another inspection by Carson at Crawfordsburn.[332] However, as the war continued, Sharman-Crawford did eventually follow a number of his Volunteers into the 36th (Ulster) Division. As he was now in his sixties and too old for active service, he was given command of the 3rd reserve battalion, the 18th Royal Irish Rifles, which would remain in Down as a recruitment and training unit.[333] Joint recruitment events would bring him into an uneasy co-operation with his former antagonist Redmond, but Sharman-Crawford's militant unionism had not been abandoned but redirected under the exigencies of international war.[334] He was outraged by the Easter Rising in 1916 and attended the subsequent commission of inquiry as an observer, but was sure (and in the end proven correct) that a united Ulster Unionism would reap dividends from the widening fissures the rebellion produced within Irish nationalism.[335]

Apart from a brief visit to France in early 1916, Sharman-Crawford spent the war on the home front, suffering injury only when he lost part of a finger in a gun-testing exercise in London.[336] This permitted him to continue to attend parliament, where he was a loyal if undistinguished member of the UUP. His interventions were restricted mostly to two areas – the first being agriculture, where he was at last able to find some common ground with Russell on the need to increase home production as joint members of the Council of Agriculture.[337] The second was conscription, on which the colonel became one of the loudest voices calling for extension of national registration and then full conscription to Ireland, a move resisted by the British government until late in the war (and then announced with disastrous political consequences in spring 1918).[338] He was one of the twenty Unionist representatives appointed to the Irish Convention in 1917–18, where he combined a robust defence of the principle of partition and advocacy of the idea of 'home rule all round'.[339] He confided to Lady Londonderry that he thought nothing good would come out of the Convention, which proved to be the case given the growing polarisation and the electoral rise of Sinn Féin from 1917.[340]

Yet despite this political and military service to unionism, as a landed gentleman Sharman-Crawford was still a poor fit for a seat in an industrial city, and when his East Belfast district was divided into three in the 1918 redistribution he was passed over in each of the new constituencies at a time when the party felt obliged (at least temporarily) to cede some ground to labour-unionist representation.[341] He was also again rejected by the North Down Unionists for a vacancy in that seat, losing in a ballot to the Presbyterian lawyer T. W. Brown. This demonstrated, as one newspaper observed, the limitations of authority of the Unionist 'old guard', as 'Colonel Sharman-Crawford, one of Sir Edward Carson's right-hand men, finds himself out in the cold'.[342] The specific vehicle for the Presbyterian campaign in North Down in 1918 was the temperance cause, and on this he was particularly weak, as 'a director of a trust which owns scores of public houses across Ulster' and hence allegedly an advocate of 'Rum Rule'.[343] The connection with Beamish and Crawford had been financially beneficial for the family at a time of falling income from land, but by 1918–19 this had become something of a political albatross.[344] This further humiliation appears to have had an impact on Robert Gordon's health, which led him to take a three-months' vacation in the West Indies in early 1920.[345]

However, as in 1914 another political crisis proceeded to pull the disparate Ulster Unionist movement together and restore something of its leadership's challenged authority and with it Sharman-Crawford's political fortunes. Throughout 1920 the Irish War of Independence was escalating in intensity as the Irish Republican Army (IRA) increased its attacks on crown forces and Ulster Unionists rallied behind the party leadership in its insistence on the implementation of that year's Government of Ireland Act, which formally created a parliament and executive for the six north-eastern counties as 'Northern Ireland'. Chairing meetings of the UUC in May-June 1920 addressing partition, Sharman-

Crawford declared himself totally unsympathetic to the case made by the Unionists of the three 'outer Ulster' counties that its endorsement of a six-county Northern Ireland amounted to a betrayal of the 1912 Ulster Covenant, and he was supportive of Sir James Stronge's argument that changed political circumstances had now rendered the Covenant redundant.[346] Tempers frayed so badly over this 'sell-out' that Sharman-Crawford felt obliged to lead a rendition of 'God save the King' immediately after the UUC vote to quell dissent.[347] He also contributed to the establishment of the new state as chair of the Ulster Association of County Councils, and was rewarded with a CBE.[348] In July 1921 he succeeded without contest James Craig (now prime minister of Northern Ireland) in the seat of Mid Down, serving as a stop-gap representative at Westminster before that seat was abolished in 1922.[349]

As part of the establishment of devolved governance, in 1922 the representation of Northern Ireland at Westminster was cut from thirty to thirteen seats, with only two left in Down. Although the county was now safe territory for Ulster Unionists, it appears that Sharman-Crawford was again passed over for nomination in favour of middle-class Presbyterian professionals.[350] Of greater concern to the new administration was the implementation of proportional representation for elections to the new Northern Ireland parliament, a system that the colonel warned would require absolute party unity behind its approved candidates if UUP control of the new state was not to be undermined.[351] Continuing in his role as UUC treasurer, he identified the Labour Party, which now had significant urban working-class Protestant as well as Catholic support, as a real threat to the party, which it would require effective electoral expenditure to counter.[352]

However, he was spared having to take his own chances in this new political system through his appointment in June 1921 as one of the inaugural senators of the new northern state.[353] The senate, an upper chamber of twenty-six members, was chosen by the lower house and had no nationalist representation until 1929. In practice its role was ornamental rather than practical, but it gave a political berth to many of the old titled families of the province, along with 'loyal' country gentlemen such as Sharman-Crawford. The senate's opening was followed by a celebratory dinner at Crawfordsburn, attended by the prime minister's wife Lady Craig.[354] The colonel remained an active member until his death in 1934, contributing to debates on subjects of particular interest to him, including the final land purchase measure for Northern Ireland in 1925, agriculture and rural development.

Robert Gordon Sharman-Crawford thus ended his career as a pillar of the new UUP establishment in the devolved administration of Northern Ireland. He survived the Irish revolutionary decade with his interests largely intact, despite an attempted arson attack on Rademon House in June 1922 by IRA insurgents. In fact, as much damage seems to have been done by the defending force of B-Special Constables, who were accused of staging a 'bogus attack', with several allegedly breaking into the house cellar to make themselves drunk with the colonel's stock of (presumably Cork-produced) porter. In a strange echo of the Moira Yeomanry mutiny of 1808, in response to disciplinary action the Crossgar B-Special unit refused to take orders from RUC officers or patrol the Rademon demesne and had to be suspended for a time.[355] The same year the colonel's name was found on a 'hit-list' recovered from a raid on Belfast's Falls Road with the comment 'to be shot at sight'. It transpired that the writers, who were not 'local men', had confused him with Colonel Frederick ('Fred') Crawford, who had organised the UVF's Larne gun-running in 1914, took an active role in Protestant paramilitarism after 1918 and now commanded the south Belfast B-Specials. Unlike many others, both Crawfords survived the early 1920s 'Troubles' unscathed, and Fred wrote in 1933 to congratulate Robert Gordon on his eightieth birthday, reminding him of their friendship and joint service to the 'old brigade' of Unionism since the early 1890s and reflecting on 'a very useful [life] to your country and dear old Ulster and fellow men generally'.[356]

In 1921 Sharman-Crawford finally abandoned any semblance of Liberal Unionism on belatedly joining the Orange Order, now virtually a requirement for every UUP politician. Any reasons he may previously have held for hesitating, he now stated, had now disappeared; he told the Down bretheren assembled at Craigavad on 12th July 1921 that 'He thought that when King William had landed just opposite there he must have turned his eyes towards that hill, and no doubt he was looking down on them and wishing them God-speed that day'.[357] He was now a 'loyalist' defender of 'Ulster's freedom' as guaranteed by partition and Unionist self-government, and believed that Northern Ireland had no real friends in the UK parliament except a few die-hards; its future would depend on the firm leadership of Craig and the party, and a readiness to crack down hard on any internal or external threats.[358] There is no record of him questioning the political subordination or exclusion of the substantial and unreconciled Catholic minority of Northern Ireland, who were the principal victims of this new dispensation and who suffered disproportionately from the intense communal violence of 1920–22 and the subsequent discrimination and retention by the state of coercive capacity under the Special Powers Acts.

Despite his strong support for partition, the colonel was still prepared to remind his supporters that they also remained Irishmen and should seek to pursue the restoration of peace in the south while upholding the integrity of the northern state. No doubt he was influenced in this by the fact that his brother remained a member of the Protestant business community in Cork throughout this period, where his interests had diversified from brewing to wartime munitions and later also tanning.[359] Arthur Frederick had been a leading light in Cork Unionism, as a member of the city grand jury from 1892 and deputy lieutenant for the county in 1918; in 1917 had proposed (to Sinn Féin jeers) that trust be placed in the deliberations of the Irish Convention, on which his brother then sat, and in 1918 he took the unpopular line of supporting conscription.[360] Fears for his and his associates personal safety led to the stockpiling of arms and ammunition in the offices of Beamish and Crawford in 1921, for which he and his chief accountant were briefly detained by the police.[361] However, he weathered the storm, and with his fellow director Richard Henrik Beamish came to adopt a pragmatic stance on Irish independence and support for the 1921 Treaty. In 1922 he was proposed by the Cork Chamber of Commerce for membership of the senate of the new Irish Free State, although he was not elected.[362] Despite the new nationalist dispensation, he and his family remained resident in the city and active in its business, philanthropic and sporting life until his death in 1943, when he was succeeded as a director of the company by his son Gerald and daughter Aileen.

Thus little if any of the radical legacy of William Sharman Crawford survived within the family by the 1920s. Colonel Sharman-Crawford was prepared to recall his grandfather publicly in a senate speech in 1921 supporting the completion of land purchase, but only to defend the historical record of landlords in what amounted to an inversion of the actual politics of tenant-right:

[He was] the descendant of one who was in his day the originator of what was known as the Ulster custom. The Ulster custom was of course at first very successful, but afterwards it required the amendments which the land acts had provided. There were good landlords and bad landlords, and there were good tenants and bad tenants, He had talked to a good many tenants lately who were still holding, and they all assured him that they would sooner go back to what were called the bad days, because rent at the present time was only a minor question as compared with the burden of rates and taxes. The farmers of Ireland had to thank two landlords for practically initiating the movement of which now nearly 75 per cent were receiving the benefit – one, of course [...] was his grandfather, and the other was the grandfather of the speaker [Dufferin], who introduced an Irish land bill as far back as 1853, so that, after all, landlords did their duty in that respect.[363]

Never the most self-aware of political figures, there is no evidence that he gave much thought to just how far Crawfordsburn's politics had shifted to the right during his tenure.

Long distressed by the untimely death of his own son, in his later years Sharman-Crawford was attracted to spiritualism, which experienced a popular boom in the post-Great War years. Introducing a lecture at the Ulster Hall by Shaw Desmond in 1933 he stated that he frequently spoke to his son the through spiritualist communications.[364] On his own death from pneumonia, contracted on a visit to New York in 1934, some attempts were made (by a nationalist spokesman) to connect him to his grandfather as the bearer of 'a name long cherished and still honoured in the cottages of Ulster in connection of the courageous championship of the cause of tenant right'.[365] Beyond a shared commitment to promoting agriculture and participation in local government, these were, however, decidedly strained at best.[366]

The death of Robert Gordon Sharman-Crawford marked the end of the male line of the family at Crawfordsburn. His only daughter Helen Mary had married Captain Hugh Carver in 1910 and spent most of the rest of her life in Cheshire. Unlike her extremist cousin Irene, who joined the Chelsea branch of the British Union of Fascists and wrote articles for *The Blackshirt* in 1934–5, Helen took no active interest in politics, and is remembered most for having an ornamental rose named in her honour.[367] Her son Robert Hugh Carver, who served as an Royal Air Force corporal during the Second World War, inherited when he came of age in 1941 and subsequently took the name Sharman-Crawford, but faced with the burden of death duties and taxes opted to sell Crawfordsburn in 1947.[368]

In the meantime, the house and demesne had been leased to William Stewart, the Ulster Unionist MP for South Belfast since 1929. Stewart issued a challenge to mainstream unionism in 1938 through his launch of the more economically-liberal Ulster Progressive Unionist Association, but no members of his party were returned to the Stormont parliament in the general election of that year. He fell from grace when his company was charged with defrauding the War Office on a number of contracts in 1944 and he was fined £10,000 before dying in 1946.[369]

The contents of the house, including the furniture, books and art accumulated by the family over several centuries, were auctioned off over five days in April 1947, raising some £20,000. Most of these were scattered to different collections, but the Robinson and Knight portraits of Colonel William Sharman and William Sharman Crawford, along with several other items such as the Moira Volunteers gorget, made their way to the Belfast Museum and Art Gallery (later the Ulster Museum).[370] A UVF flag (probably that designed by Robert Gordon for the North Down Regiment) was presented in his memory to St John's

Church, Helen's Bay, while the bugle of the Fartullagh Volunteers (a memento of Colonel Sharman's era) was bought by UUP headquarters.[371] The family papers later came to the Public Record Office of Northern Ireland via the family's solicitors in Belfast. The house and 152 acres of the demesne were purchased by the government to establish a Tuberculosis hospital for children and convalescents. The hospital was opened by the minister Dame Dehra Parker in 1950, who observed that it was once 'the seat of a family that had served Northern Ireland well, and the building was now going to carry on those traditions of service'.[372] With incidence of TB declining under National Health Service, it was replaced by a geriatric hospital after 1959 which was eventually closed and the building sold to developers for conversion to luxury apartments in 1990.[373] Much of the Crawfordsburn demesne parkland and seashore was re-opened to the public as a local-authority country park in 1969, once again giving access to the site to the people of North Down and Belfast, as had been the case in William Sharman Crawford's day. However little recollection of the landscape's connection with the Sharman Crawfords (or, beyond the park's name, of the Crawfords who preceded them) remains visible today.[374]

Conclusion

As this study has demonstrated, the political life and legacy of William Sharman Crawford cannot be understood in isolation from the radical dynasty that he was born into and sought to sustain into the next generation. If in this he was only partially successful, the Sharman Crawford political tradition of radicalism was nevertheless carried forward to the early 1880s in county politics by several of his sons, and in a more innovative and progressive way to the end of the century by his daughter Mabel, as an advocate of women's rights. Still, there was an inherent paradox in a democratic reformer seeking to ensure his political legacy through the conventions of familial inheritance. The early nineteenth-century model of the 'gentlemanly radical', while successful in providing some legitimacy for popular reformist leaders at the time, was inherently unstable and proved not to be easily transferrable across generations. As we have seen, the gravitational pull of a gentry lifestyle, the experience of military service, and the ideological appeals of imperialism, British nationalism and 'big house' paternalism, combined to invert the politics of Crawfordsburn by the end of the nineteenth century. Although Sharman Crawford's grandson Robert Gordon affected to see no contradiction between his conservative Unionist politics and those of his ancestors, his relationship with the descendants of the Co. Down electoral insurgents of 1831, 1852, 1874 and 1880 was strained at best and the memory of his grandfather was deployed against him politically on a number of occasions.

There was nothing predetermined about the political trajectory of the family. The social and political antecedents of William Sharman of Moira were located firmly within the conservative milieu of the Anglican minor gentry of the eighteenth century, and he benefitted in his early life from family and state patronage, conformity to the religious establishment and a 'good marriage' within the landed order. His social position entitled him, as with many others of his class, to adopt a leading role locally in the 'patriotic' self-defence and reform movement that emerged in Ireland after 1778, which initially appeared compatible with officeholding. What distinguished him was the unusual extent to which he was prepared to follow the logic of extra-parliamentary reform agitation in the era of the American and French revolutions towards a radical political position by the mid-1780s, even as most other prominent landowners (including his erstwhile mentor Lord Moira and the Volunteer commander Lord Charlemont) backed away from the developing democratic and pro-Catholic turn within Volunteering in Ulster. Sharman became an active player in the reformist campaign, with resonance well beyond his own base in the Lagan Valley. If his uninspiring tenure as patriot MP for Lisburn revealed his lack of formal oratorical skills (something of a family trait) and perhaps also the personal ambition required for national leadership, he was nevertheless highly regarded as an incorruptible pillar of Volunteering virtue, and perceived by both the conservative county elite and the Dublin establishment as a political threat.

Sharman's pathway to radicalism was personal and reflected both reading in enlightenment political commentary and a desire to align himself with a popular reformist mass movement as a mode of refashioning social bonds that had been strained to breaking by both class conflict and religious antagonisms. This rendered him ready and willing to serve symbolically at the head of Belfast's celebration of the French Revolution in 1791, although he was not part of the ultra-radical network of younger Presbyterians coalescing then into the United Irish brotherhood. As a liberal constitutionalist rejecting republicanism, he did not follow these Volunteering colleagues into the conspiratorial revolutionary movement which would culminate in the bloody defeat of 1798. If state repression from 1793 flagged the ineffectiveness of both the 'outdoors' reform movement and its Whig-patriot allies, Sharman's decision not to be drawn into the counter-revolutionary forces of the Yeomanry and Orangeism meant that his posthumous reputation would survive the cataclysm of the rebellion untainted, and his memory and that of the Volunteers would serve as a rallying-point for the radicalism that was gradually reconstructed in the north after 1803.

It fell to his son William to seek to revivify the non-revolutionary radical tradition his father had embodied, a path he would follow self-consciously. However, both the absence of propitious circumstances and his limited means impeded the start of his political career until he was in middle age. The combination of his inheritance of the Crawford lands and name in 1827 with the mobilisation of liberal Protestant support for Catholic emancipation in 1828–9 gave him both the ability and motivation to take an active role in reformist politics. From 1830 until his death in 1861 he acquired and retained a high degree of prominence in a series of widening concentric circles – initially in his home county of Down and the burgeoning industrial town of Belfast, and by 1833 beyond to Dublin and national politics via election for Dundalk to the Westminster Parliament, and later to Rochdale and the British democratic mass platform of the 1840s.

What did radicalism signify for Sharman Crawford? From his father he derived a constitutional reformism that combined a Whiggish concern for 'rebalancing' the Irish and British constitutions through 'restoring' popular representation via free elections to the commons, with elements of radical enlightenment political thought filtered through the British reformers' contributions to the 1783 Dungannon Convention deliberations. But whereas his father had been drawn both to the ideal of the 'people in arms' as a mode of extracting concessions from an entrenched establishment, the experience of the bloody catastrophe of 1798 appeared to close off this avenue for change for the younger William. The rise of O'Connell's (mostly) non-violent mass agitation in the 1820s appeared to offer an alternative road map and given his inheritance he was drawn towards its demands for Catholic emancipation and broader political reforms. By the 1830s he had self-identified with radicalism, which he understood as 'the striking at the root of our evils and of the abuses of the state – I mean the taking out the canker at the root, and to give the whole tree new vigour and life', and over the course of the decade came to embrace full democracy.[1]

Crawford was, however, no nationalist. Like his father a self-conscious Irish patriot with a strong sense of national identity and a marked preference for some mode of Irish self-government, his approach to the 'national question' was always pragmatic. While he regarded the 1800 Act of Union as a deeply flawed source of dangerous instability and poor governance, he could not but be conscious of the growing acceptance of its economic benefits among his fellow Ulster liberals and found their concerns about Catholic majoritarianism enhanced by his own bruising encounters with O'Connell's ego and the Repeal party machine from the mid-1830s. At the same time, he felt no attraction to the imperially-inflected British nationalism that increasingly combined with virulent anti-Catholicism in popular conservative unionism, and actively criticised British colonialist aggression and the domestic culture of militarism that supported it.

His proposed solution to this dilemma was federalism – a project he shared with some other contemporary authors such as Thaddeus O'Malley but one with which he became particularly strongly associated in the public debates of the 1830s–40s. Under the long shadow of 1798 Crawford regarded a federal relationship with Britain as the only workable compromise that could satisfy Irish aspirations to national self-government with the geopolitical realities of British imperial power, ensure continuing participation in the commercial advantages of the UK's free-trade area, and address the fears of Irish Protestants over their future in a democratised Catholic-dominated Irish society. Despite O'Connell's political flirtation with the idea in 1844, federalism fell between the poles of Irish nationalist and British colonial intransigence and Crawford failed to persuade northern liberals of its desirability. When revived as 'home rule' after his death in the 1870s–80s, it divided his children, with his sons coming to adhere to a liberal unionist position they now deemed essential for electoral success in Ulster, while his daughter (by 1886 in exile in London) claimed him as a prototype home-ruler.

For William Sharman, popular political reformism, preferably marshalled through the associational bonds of Volunteering, was an end in itself. The 'patriot' social agenda was vague beyond reducing the burdens on 'the people' of unjust taxation and the 'old corruption' of placemen and sinecurists. His son's social agenda evolved over time, in large part through engagement with the social forces politicised by the campaigns for democratic reforms, beginning with his failed electoral campaigns in 1831–2. Initially prepared to accept some enhanced form of the Whig legislative proposals underlying the Reform Acts of 1832, he subsequently came to reject these as grossly inadequate, and by 1838 was ready to sign up to the fully democratic demands of the People's Charter and remained strongly attached to these (even if on occasion he was at times prepared to make some tactical concessions on household suffrage or triennial parliaments). His pragmatic strategy of seeking to build a wider cross-class alliance behind the democratic agenda – first in Belfast with the Ulster Constitutional Association in 1840–1 and subsequently with Joseph Sturge in the Complete Suffrage Union of 1842–4 – drew the fury of Chartist purists, but his integrity was rarely questioned and he maintained with Thomas Livsey a progressive alliance in his adopted political home of Rochdale throughout the 1840s and was ultimately reconciled with the Chartist leader Feargus O'Connor.

The frustrated outcomes of these initiatives demonstrated both the strength of the established political order and the wariness of bourgeois reformers in parliament and the country, but his sincere adherence to democracy (evident in continuing advocacy through to his death) cannot be questioned. Constitutionalism required a focus on parliament as a representative institution and source of legislative change, and pending its democratisation it was, he believed, essential that it be used as a sounding board for demanding essential reforms, as 'it would be impossible to rouse public opinion upon any subject, unless the people saw there were men in the house ready to support their rights by advocating their measures, and carrying them to the test of a division'.[2] If this meant being labelled a 'crotchet' to be constantly politically denigrated by the political establishment, this was a price worth paying for the opportunity to wear down resistance over time through sheer legislative persistence.

Crawford shared with his newfound allies John Bright and Richard Cobden a strong attachment to the liberal doctrines of free trade and the destruction of 'monopolies' as drivers of economic development and social transformation. However, campaigning amongst the working-class non-electors first of Belfast and subsequently of Rochdale made him acutely aware of the immense social costs of industrialisation and the realities of class conflict and left him open to popular demands for state intervention for the redress of popular grievances. At one end the fiscal demand for a reduction of indirect taxation on consumption (and its concomitant of cutting 'wasteful' state expenditure) lay within the liberal mainstream, and in industrial relations disputes he saw himself (and was regarded as such by the representatives of the Belfast weavers for example) as an honest broker seeking to reach reasonable compromises between capital and labour. But he also enthusiastically advocated a generous compulsory poor law in Ireland, based on the principle of outdoor relief for most applicants, and was a strong supporter of the campaign in Rochdale to subvert the implementation of the 'less eligibility' dogma of the new English poor law of 1834. If the state in both countries had a role in delivering the welfare entitlements deemed legitimate by the mass of the population, he also became convinced that it had an obligation to regulate labour conditions, and unlike Bright and Cobden he was an outspoken supporter of Ashley and Fielden's measures for restricting working hours for all and protecting vulnerable groups in the workforce.

The social intervention most associated with his name was, however, the campaign for the legal enactment of tenant right in Ireland. As we have seen, his thinking on this was shaped by his own agrarian practice of collaborative landlordism, which involved full recognition of customary forms, active partnership with tenant farmers, and a conscious decision to set 'equitable' rents that were below market rates and determined through flexible mechanisms. To some extent this approach to landlordism was derived from the practice inherited from both his father and the Crawford family, but he went well beyond this to embrace the role of tribune of the tenant class, devoting much of his life to promoting state intervention to ensure tenurial security, which he consistently argued would not disadvantage non-profiteering landowners. Despite denunciations of 'communism' (a charge made popular on the right by the Paris événements of 1848) his vision was one of radical liberalism rather than socialism, as he insisted he was merely seeking to protect the tenant's custom-based capital from confiscation, or to allow him to safely accumulate it from his own agricultural efforts.

At the same time (and unlike some other leaders of the tenant movement) he was also acutely aware of the crisis facing the landless or land-poor agricultural labourers, whose very existence was thrown into question by the sustained potato failures from 1845. Granting tenant security was seen as part of the solution as this would boost labour demand, but Crawford also insisted also on effective famine-relief measures in the short term and major public works of reclamation creating secure small farms for labouring families as a longer-term solution. The efficacy of this proposal can be questioned (especially given his ideological hostility to the alternative of mass assisted emigration) but stands in sharp contrast to the laissez-faire dogmatism and reluctance to mobilise relief or reconstruction resources that defined British government policy in the later, deadly, stages of the Great Famine, and which he attacked relentlessly in parliament and press.

As with much of his other campaigning, Crawford approached land reform with a mixture of focus on what he regarded as achievable outcomes and pragmatism with respect to the means of attaining this. While always more than ready to chart his own path in politics (and believing he owed responsibility only to his constituents and not to a party) he was conscious that a landlord-dominated parliament would only concede meaningful reform in response to a combination of sustained persuasion and pressure from without. The latter was limited before the 1840s, but gathered pace as tenant right was incorporated into the Repeal mass platform in 1843 and Ulster farmers reacted with hostility to the perceived threat to their provincial custom in the Devon Commission report of 1845. As the Famine radicalised tenant farmers (especially those in the north and east more at risk of dispossession and bankruptcy than of starvation) and their clerical interlocutors, Crawford's moment appeared to have finally arrived. Nevertheless, he was always tentative in his relationship with what became the Tenant League in 1850, preferring to maintain his autonomy and requiring significant concessions from its southern leadership on his favoured principle of 'industrial tenant right' in 1851. His alliance with the radical Presbyterian James McKnight was crucial in fully integrating him into the Ulster mass movement and paving the way for the set-piece confrontation of the Down election of 1852, during which Crawford came closest to endorsing an outright class struggle against his fellow members of the landowning gentry. Although the Tenant League rapidly disintegrated in the following years, Crawford remained a loyal adherent of the principles of tenant right, even if his proposals remained unrealised until the decades after his death.

If much of what informed Crawford's politics was derived from what he regarded as common-sense principles of the public good, supported by (but not dependent on) the heterodox economic ideas of commentators such as George Poulett Scrope, John Stuart Mill and W. T. Thornton, and owing something to Benthamite rationalism, he was at the same time deeply moralistic in his radicalism. This was most evident in his emotive attachment to religious voluntarism, a position that would ultimately lead to support for disestablishment across the UK and a personal conversion to Unitarianism. His radicalism was tempered by pragmatism on a number of heads, but not on the question of religious freedom, and it was over his intransigence on the immediate and total abolition of Irish tithes that he split acrimoniously with O'Connell in 1836–7. Sincere in his religious convictions, he was never an evangelical (and ignored the Ulster revival of 1859) but found common ground with many nonconformists who were in his staunch opposition to chattel slavery and developed a political bond with the moral radical Joseph Sturge, and was able to articulate the case for tenant right in a moral frame of reference that spoke to the Ulster Presbyterian clergy in particular. His son James, a convert to orthodox Presbyterianism from 1846, would inherit this understanding, and succeed where his father had failed twice, in riding a wave of Presbyterian insurgency (allied with Catholic support) to win in Co. Down as a Gladstonian Liberal in 1874.

The nineteenth century was on the whole a difficult environment for Ulster radicalism. The state, whether managed by Tory/Conservative or Whig/Liberal administrations, was preoccupied with maintaining political and social control by whatever means necessary and tended to make concessions only belatedly and under extreme pressure. Gladstone was a partial exception, but the botched nature of the 1870 Land Act and extraction of the 1881 Act as a consequence of the Land War ensured his government received limited credit for finally delivering what the Tenant League had demanded in the early 1850s. Irish nationalism, whether constitutionalist or revolutionary, attracted the energy and idealism of many convinced that the transformation of Irish society required the restoration of full self-government or the total severance of the colonial relationship. In this context, radical liberalism in Ulster was always prone to being squeezed between the antithetical forces of a nationalism that attracted few Protestant converts and a popular conservatism that found its most overt manifestation in Orangeism. As Belfast liberalism atrophied from the 1830s the radical tradition was rallied in the countryside through campaigns for land reform which had the potential to mobilise large numbers across sectarian divides. Crawford was central to this politics of popular reform in the 1840s–50s and its echoes continued to resonate through to the campaigns of his son James in the 1870s and of T. W. Russell (who in turn claimed his mantle) in the early twentieth century. However, as Hall concludes, for all the energy exerted by its exponents, Ulster liberalism was fatally undermined by the intensification of communal identities that tended to squeeze out this common public sphere, and the collapse of any residual confidence in the British constitutional tradition to deliver meaningful reform on the part of the Catholic majority on the island.[3]

In the absence of extensive 'ego-documents', it is more difficult to offer a conclusive understanding of William Sharman Crawford the man. However, approaching his death, he summed up the 'principles of action' that had determined his public life:

> 1st. A determination to do that which I believed to be right, founded on my own judgment on all matters of <u>principle.</u>

> 2nd. That every man is responsible according to his means of knowledge and intellect, as well as the temporal means of life which the almighty has conferred upon him, to do the utmost good in his power to his fellow man.

> 3rd. That in conformity to the two previous principles it is a crime to make any profession, political or religious, contrary to the real convictions of mind and conscience, or to make any professions without due consideration of their truth.[4]

In a modern era in which such an avowal of idealism tends to face not only dismissal but often outright mockery, Crawford's ethical political vision might appear hopelessly anachronistic if not potentially hypocritical. We are more than aware now of how the grossest of social and gender inequalities, the resort to violent repression of dissent, and national and racial subordination of peoples within the British empire were justified and rationalised in Victorian moralising rhetoric. Yet Crawford chose rather to expose these rather than adopt them in pursuit of personal gain.

Like most of his contemporaries, Crawford had his own blind spots and lacked perfect consistency in his thought and practice. Charles Gavan Duffy recalled him as being 'proud, punctilious and angular, unlikely to forget past affronts, and more solicitous to be conspicuously right than to be successful'.[5] Even more sympathetic commentators such as Denis Holland noted his lack of a sense of humour and a 'cold, shy and reserved' manner that obscured an inner warmth of character.[6] Nevertheless, his personal sincerity and obstinate insistence on pursuing what he regarded to be right were acknowledged even by his political opponents. Duffy thought Crawford's table-talk was 'a good deal too like a professor for a dinner table. He does not talk, he harangues. It is fine, however, to note the genuine sympathy of this big proprietor with the working farmer'.[7] There was a 'driven' character to his politics that reflected a preoccupation not to squander the ideological inheritance derived from his father, combined with a personal ethic that drew equally on enlightenment liberal idealism and a faith centred on the 'social gospel' and the pursuit of religious freedom. If he and other members of his family lacked the ambition, ruthlessness and personal charisma required for front-rank political careers, they nevertheless dedicated themselves to being gadflies for radical change, and not without some success.

Could 'Sharman Crawfordism' survive the man himself? Although his vision of a radical dynasty was at best only partly successful, it is clear that his children James and Mabel self-consciously sought to maintain and further develop his political ideals after his death, with electoral vindication on James's part in 1874 and the adoption of a transformative feminist agenda within the radical-liberal tradition by Mabel, although she felt it necessary to relocate to London to allow this free rein. The family inheritance became inverted in the next generation, as the conservative heir to the estates, Robert Gordon Sharman-Crawford, was politically checked in 1900 by a populist candidate utilising the Presbyterian and tenant-right cards against him. Nevertheless, the conservative unionist project of which Robert Gordon was an active proponent was ultimately to succeed, with Russellite agrarian radicalism marginalised, the northern labour movement deeply divided and the Ulster Unionist movement able to capitalise on its nationalist opponents' missteps and the support of its British Conservative allies.

The new Northern Ireland state of 1921 was intentionally a 'cold house' for liberalism, its political culture grounded on the maintenance of communitarian majoritarianism and the hegemonic place of the UUP reinforced by the abolition of proportional representation by 1929 and the gerrymandering of local government boundaries. What is remarkable is the survival of any radical-liberal politics at all under such adverse circumstances. Nevertheless, echoes of Sharman Crawfordite politics might still be discerned. In 1956 Rev. Albert McElroy, a Unitarian minister at Newtownards and former Northern Ireland Labour Party activist, re-established the Ulster Liberal Party (and later its journal, *Northern Radical*) as a self-conscious attempt to revive a form of non-sectarian reformist politics rooted in a historical tradition.[8] Although they struggled electorally, the Ulster Liberals succeeded in returning the Catholic lawyer Sheelagh Murnaghan as Stormont MP for Queen's University in 1961; she used her eight year tenure to promote the abolition of capital punishment, advancing the rights of women and minorities (including Travellers) and human rights bills for Northern Ireland.[9] These attempts to reform the state foundered in the face of Unionist obduracy and the Liberals went on to support the Northern Ireland Civil Rights Movement, only to be swept away amid the polarisation surrounding the collapse of the state into vicious civil conflict from 1969. However a strand of liberalism followed former party executive member Oliver Napier via the New Ulster Movement into the cross-community Alliance Party in 1970, retaining an underlying commitment to non-violent reformism and civil rights without a nationalist orientation.[10] It is not unreasonably to see Sharman Crawford as a distant ancestor of these political developments.

Although a man of his own times, his political and social principles remain relevant. The objects he pursued in the face of considerable opposition, including democratic rights and political transparency, humane welfare entitlements and social protections, abandonment of regressive taxation and the end of proprietorial and ecclesiastical privileges, shared education and the separation of church and state, are those associated with the emergence and maintenance of modern liberal-democratic societies. His attempts to find a pragmatic settlement to the Irish constitutional question that respected different communal and national identities and fears, combining representative government for Ireland with a recognition of the existing geopolitical realities in the form of a radical federalism, continues to have evident resonances in contemporary Northern Ireland and beyond. Sharman Crawford's was a radical political life worthy of modern attention.

Notes

NOTES TO INTRODUCTION

1. William Sharman Crawford, *Depopulation Not Necessary: An Appeal to the British Members of the Imperial Parliament Against the Extermination of the Irish People* (2nd edn, London, 1850), p. 9, p. 31.
2. John Mitchel, *The Last Conquest of Ireland (Perhaps)* (Glasgow, [1861]), p. 219.
3. *Nonconformist*, 23 Oct. 1861.
4. Fergus Whelan, *May Tyrants Tremble: The Life of William Drennan, 1754–1820* (Dublin, 2020), James Smyth, *Henry Joy McCracken* (Dublin, 2020), Kenneth Dawson, *The Belfast Jacobin: Samuel Neilson and the United Irishmen* (Dublin, 2017), Mary McNeill, *The Life and Times of Mary Ann McCracken, 1770-1866* (rev. edn, Dublin, 2019). See also 'Mary Ann McCracken Foundation', http://belfastcharitablesociety.com/mary-ann-mccracken-foundation/ (acc. 12 June 2020).
5. Marianne Elliott, *Wolfe Tone: Prophet of Irish Independence* (London, 1989), James Quinn, *Soul on Fire: A Life of Thomas Russell* (Dublin, 2001), Patrick M. Geoghegan, *Robert Emmet: A Life* (Dublin, 2002).
6. Danny Mansergh, *Grattan's Failure: Parliamentary Opposition and The People in Ireland 1779–1800* (Dublin, 2005), James Kelly, *Henry Flood: Patriots and Politics in Eighteenth-Century Ireland* (Dublin, 1998).
7. Jonathan Jeffrey Wright, *The 'Natural Leaders' and Their World: Politics, Culture and Society in Belfast, c. 1801-32* (Liverpool, 2012); John Bew, *The Glory of Being Britons: Civic Unionism in Nineteenth-Century Belfast* (Dublin, 2008), Gerald R. Hall, *Ulster Liberalism 1778–1876* (Dublin, 2011). See also Alice Johnson, *Middle-class life in Victorian Belfast* (Liverpool, 2020).
8. Roger Courtney, *Dissenting Voices: Rediscovering the Irish Progressive Presbyterian Tradition* (Belfast, 2013).
9. Julie Nelson, '"Violently democratic and anti-Conservative": an analysis of Presbyterian "radicalism" in Ulster, c.1800–52' (Ph.D. dissertation, University of Durham, 2005).
10. James Quinn, *John Mitchel* (Dublin, 2008), Helen F. Mulvey, *Thomas Davis and Ireland: A Biographical Study* (Washington, 2003), David A. Wilson, *Thomas D'Arcy McGee* (2 vols, Montreal and Kingston, 2008–11). Charles Gavan Duffy, however, lacks a full modern biography.
11. Emmet O'Connor and John Cunningham (eds), *Studies in Irish Radical Leadership: Lives on the Left* (Manchester, 2016), Brian Casey (ed.), *Defying the Law of the Land: Agrarian Radicals in Irish History* (Dublin, 2013).
12. James Epstein, *The Lion of Freedom: Feargus O'Connor and the Chartist Movement, 1832–1842* (London, 1982), Paul A. Pickering, *Feargus O'Connor: A Political Life* (Monmouth, 2008), Robert Sloan, *William Smith O'Brien and the Young Ireland Rebellion of 1848* (Dublin, 2000).
13. R. F. Foster, *Charles Stewart Parnell: The Man and his Family* (Hassocks, 1976), Dana Hearne (ed.), *Anna Parnell, The Tale of a Great Sham* (Dublin, 2020).
14. Simon James Morgan, *Celebrities, Heroes and Champions: Popular Politicians in the Age of Reform, 1810–67* (Manchester, 2021).
15. Brian A. Kennedy, 'Sharman Crawford, 1780–1861: a political biography' (D.Litt. dissertation, Queen's University Belfast, 1953); 'Sharman Crawford on the repeal question', *Irish Historical Studies (IHS)*, 6 (1948–9), pp 270–73; 'Sharman Crawford's federal scheme for Ireland', in H. A. Crone, T. W. Moody and D. B. Quinn (eds), *Essays in British and Irish History in Honour of J. E. Todd* (London, 1949), pp 235–54; 'Sharman Crawford on Ulster tenant right', *IHS*, 13:51 (1963), pp 246–53.
16. James Quinn, 'Crawford, William Sharman', *Dictionary of Irish Biography (DIB)* (Cambridge, 2009), Sidney Lee revised by Alan O'Day, 'Crawford, William Sharman (1781–1861), politician and landlord in Ireland', *Oxford Dictionary of National Biography (ODNB)* (Oxford, 2004).
17. There is an entry on Col. William Sharman by James Quinn in *DIB* and a brief note on James Sharman Crawford in his father's entry in the same publication, but nothing on Mabel Sharman Crawford. For the first published commentary on her writing, see Peter Gray, 'Mabel Sharman

Crawford's *Life in Tuscany*: Ulster radicalism in a hot climate', in M. Corporaal and C. Morin (eds), *Traveling Irishness in the Long Nineteenth Century* (London, 2017), pp 35–50.

18. The Sharman Crawford papers are held by the Public Record Office of Northern Ireland under the classmark D856 and comprise some 2,500 items. For more information, see http://www.rascal. ac.uk/index.php/institutions/public-record-office-northern-ireland-proni/sharman-crawford-papers (acc. 12 June 2020).

19. *Londonderry Standard (LS)*, 24 Oct. 1861.

NOTES TO CHAPTER I

1. William's mother appears not to have played a prominent role in his later life, but wrote to express her 'overwhelming joy' on his marriage in 1772, Elizabeth to William Sharman (WS), n.d. [1772], Public Record Office of Northern Ireland (PRONI), D856/FA/36. He had a younger brother named Richard and three sisters who have mostly disappeared from the historical record.

2. George Dames Burtchaell (ed.), *Alumni Dublinenses: A Register of the Students, Graduates, Professors, and Provosts of Trinity College, in the University of Dublin 1593–1860* (London, 1924), p. 744.

3. Sharman voted with the government in 1753–4, Anon., *Thoughts on Some Late Removals in Ireland, in a Letter to the Rt. Hon. the Earl of Kildare* (London, 1754).

4. David Whamond Donaldson, 'Britain and Menorca in the eighteenth century' (PhD dissertation, Open University, 1994), pp 133–42; For his defence of Kane's administration, see Sharman to Henry Finch (July 1738), in W. A. Shaw (ed.), *Calendar of Treasury Books and Papers, Vol. 3, 1735–1738* (London, 1900), p. 496.

5. 'Extracts from letters written by the late Chas. H. O'Neill, to *Belfast Daily Mercury*, copied by James O'Laverty', PRONI, D856/F/60; Title deeds to Banbridge estate (1745), ibid., LR1/472/1/A/14. For Kane's will, which left his personal estate to Sharman, see The National Archives (TNA), PROB11/683/109.

6. Captain Sharman was a subscriber to (amongst other texts) Richard Barton's *Lectures in Natural Philosophy … Upon the Petrifications, Gems, Crystals and Sanative Quality of Lough Neagh in Ireland* (Dublin, [1751]), and Anon, *A Continuation of the Proceedings of the Incorporated Society in Dublin, for Promoting English Protestant Schools in Ireland* (Dublin, 1738).

7. *Belfast News-Letter (BNL)*, 22 Feb. 1803.

8. E. Joyce Best, *The Huguenots of Lisburn: The Story of the Lost Colony* (Lisburn, 1997); W. H. Crawford, *The Impact of the Domestic Linen Industry in Ulster* (Belfast, 2005), pp 7–22.

9. Conrad Gill, *The Rise of the Irish Linen Industry* (Oxford, 1925), pp 108–16; Harry Gribbon, 'The Irish Linen Board, 1711–1828', in M. Cohen (ed.), *The Warp of Ulster's Past* (Basingstoke, 1997), pp 83–5.

10. *BNL*, 19 May 1758, 5 Feb. 1762; *Hibernian Journal (HJ)*, 28 Aug. 1784; Crawford, *Domestic Linen Industry*, pp 113, 144–5.

11. William Sharman (sen.) to WS, 30 Oct., 13 Nov. 1773, PRONI, D856/FA/25, 27.

12. Copy of the notice of the marriage of Wm. Sharman, Lisburn and Miss Arminolla [sic] Willson, Purdysburn, taken from the 'Belfast News-Letter' (5 Jan. 1773), PRONI, D856/F/7; William Sharman (sen.) to WS, 20 Jan., 1 Feb. 1773, PRONI, D856/FA/19, 21.

13. *Westminster Magazine*, July 1773, p. 386.

14. Arminella Willson to WS, 28 Sept. 1772, PRONI, D856/FA/15.

15. Jonathan Jeffrey Wright (ed.), *An Ulster Slave-Owner in the Revolutionary Atlantic: The Life and Letters of John Black* (Dublin, 2019), pp 20–2.

16. WS, Notebook, PRONI, D856/F/10. William had two other married sisters and a brother, Richard, Pedigree of Crawford of Crawfordsburn, National Library of Ireland (NLI), Genealogical Office (GO) Ms 182, p. 304.

17. *Saunder's News-Letter (SNL)*, 3 Feb. 1777; Sharman's bond on Lord Moira, 1 May 1779, PRONI, D856/F/1. Sharman was later obliged to seek a judgment for repayment of the debt in instalments between 1788 and 1804, S. Fowler to John Sharman Crawford (SC), 17 May 1870, ibid., D856/F/71.

18. Walter Harris, *The Antient and Present State of the County of Down* (Dublin, 1744), p. 103.

19. Anon. (ed.) *Parliamentary Gazetteer of Ireland* (3 vols, 1846), II, p. 782.

20. William Wilde (ed.), *Memoir of Gabriel Beranger, and His Labours in the Cause of Irish Art and Antiquities, from 1760 to 1780* (Dublin, 1880), p. 164.

21. *Belfast Evening Post (BEP)*, 23 Oct. 1786.

22. Anon., *Letters by a Farmer* (Belfast, [1787]), p. 30.

23. *Northern Star (NS)*, 9 June 1792.

24. A Patrick Brontey was also a tenant at nearby Lacken townland in 1841. Memo on Leckan rents, 13 Jan. 1841, PRONI, D856/B/6/1.

25. Correspondence re will of Catherine Bronte relating to Leckan, Co. Down, Jan. 1859–Apr. 1862, PRONI, D856/B/6/19; *General Valuation of Ratable Property in Ireland. Union of Banbridge* (Dublin, 1863), p. 100.

26. Angus MacKay, 'A crop of Bronte myths', *Westminster Review*, 144 (July 1895), pp 424–37.

27. William Hincks, 'Plate, taken on the spot in the County of Downe, representing spinning, reeling with the clock reel, and boiling the yarn' (1783), NMNI, BELUM.P411.1936.

28. It was recalled in 1875 that the eviction without compensation of a number of tenants who had refused a significant rent rise in 1783 led to outbreaks of arson and to some of those evicted and their sons later joining the United Irishmen and fighting at Ballynahinch, *Weekly Press*, 9 Apr. 1875.

29. Rosemary Richey, 'Rawdon, John', in *DIB*.

30. *Belfast Mercury (BM)*, 24 Aug. 1784.

31. In 1776 the parish of Moira was estimated as 34 per cent Anglican, 34 per cent Presbyterian and 32 per cent Catholic, Kerby Miller and Liam Kennedy, 'Irish migration and demography, 1659–1831', in K. Miller et al (eds), *Irish Immigrants in the Land of Canaan: Letters and Memoirs from Colonial and Revolutionary America, 1675–1815* (Oxford, 2003), p. 664.

32. John O'Donovan to Thomas Larcom, 27 Mar. 1834, Ordnance Survey (OS) Letters, Royal Irish Academy (RIA), 14C 13/8.

33. Philip Luckombe, *A Tour Through Ireland* (Dublin, 1780), p. 312.

34. William Sharman (sen.) to WS, 27 Apr. 1773, PRONI, D856/FA/23.

35. James S. Donnelly, 'Hearts of Oak, Hearts of Steel', *Studia Hibernica*, 21 (1981), pp 7–73.

36. Lady Moira to Townsend, 12 Mar. 1772, PRONI, D4009/2.

37. Lady Moira to Townsend, 14 Mar. 1772, PRONI, D4009/3.

38. Extract of a letter from a lady in the north, to a gentleman in Dublin, dated Mar. 23, *Finn's Leinster Journal (FLJ)*, 1 Apr. 1772.

39. John Moore to Arthur Annesley, 29 Apr. 1775, in W. H. Crawford (ed.), *Letters from an Ulster Land Agent, 1774–85* (Belfast, 1976), p. 4.

40. Donnelly, 'Hearts of Oak', pp 62–73.

41. James McKnight, *The Ulster Tenant's Claim of Right* (Dublin, 1848), pp 39–40.

42. Lord Moira to Francis Coutts, 10 June 1794, PRONI, D892/I/3.

43. *FLJ*, 19 Mar. 1774.

44. [Andrew Craig], 'Autobiographical sketch of Andrew Craig 1754–1833. Presbyterian minister of Lisburn (continued)', *Ulster Journal of Archaeology (UJA)*, 2nd ser., 14:2/3 (1908), pp 51–5.

45. James Kelly, 'The politics of Volunteering', *Irish Sword*, 22: 88 (2000), pp 139–56.

46. T. G. F. Patterson, 'The Volunteer companies of Ulster, 1778–93', *Irish Sword*, 7 (1965–6), pp 108–9.

47. Ibid., p. 208.

48. John Moore to Arthur Annesley, 14 Aug. 1780, in Crawford (ed.), *Letters*, p. 27.

49. *BNL*, 20 Apr., *Dublin Evening Press (DEPr)*, 7 July 1781, John Slade to Lord Hillsborough, 2 Aug. 1779, PRONI, D607/B/102.

50. [Craig], 'Autobiographical sketch', pp 51–5. Craig remained close to the Sharmans after his transfer to Lisburn in 1782; he married Arminella's sister Margaret and was left 100 guineas and a copy of Col. Sharman's portrait in Arminella's will in 1808.

51. Michael O'Connor, '"Ears stunned with the din of arms": Belfast, Volunteer sermons and James Magee, 1779–1781', *Eighteenth-Century Ireland*, 26 (2011), pp 51–79.

52. Patterson, 'Volunteers', pp 205–6.

53. *BNL*, 22 Feb. 1803.

54. F. J. Bigger, 'The National Volunteers of Ireland (continued)', *UJA*, 2nd ser., 15:4 (1909), pp 141–8; Richey, 'Rawdon, John', *DIB*.

55. *BM*, 20 Apr. 1784. Foster was the conservative speaker of the Irish parliament.

56. *BEP,* 7 Dec. 1786.

57. *Dublin Journal (DJ),* 9 Apr. 1782.

58. Thomas MacNevin, *History of the Volunteers of 1782* (4th edn, Dublin, 1845), pp 156–60.

59. Crawford, *Domestic Linen Industry,* pp 113–15.

60. Anon., *An Historical Account of the Late Election of Knights of the Shire for the County of Down* ([Dublin], 1784), pp 37–9.

61. Ibid., pp 109–12, 117–21.

62. *BM,* 19 Sept. 1783. For the context, see Peter Jupp, 'County Down elections, 1783–1831', *IHS,* 18:70 (1972), pp 177–206.

63. *BM,* 20, 23 Apr., 4 May 1784; Patterson, 'Volunteers', p. 206.

64. Padhraig Higgins, *A Nation of Politicians: Gender, Patriotism, and Political Culture in Late Eighteenth-Century Ireland* (Madison, 2010), pp 138–9.

65. Anon, *Historical Account,* pp 126–7.

66. J. R. R. Adams, 'Reading societies in Ulster', *Ulster Folklife,* 26 (1980), pp 55–64.

67. An 1820 survey found that of the population of 12,026, 53 per cent were members of the established church, 27 per cent Presbyterians and 18 per cent Catholics, 'An account of a parochial visitation of Lisburn parish, commencing 13 November 1820', PRONI DIO/1/19/75.

68. *DEP,* 9 Dec. 1779; ibid., 6 Apr. 1780.

69. *DEP,* 19 Sept. 1780.

70. Earl of Hertford, *A Letter to the Belfast First Company of Volunteers* (Belfast, 1782).

71. F. J. Bigger, 'The National Volunteers of Ireland, 1782', *UJA,* 15:4 (1909), pp 144–5; *DEP,* 21 Nov. 1782.

72. Bigger, 'National Volunteers'.

73. *SNL,* 8 Aug., *DJ,* 8 Aug. 1782.

74. Kenneth Dawson, 'A house divided: The Belfast Charitable Society in the age of revolution', in O. Purdue (ed.), *The First Great Charity of This Town: Belfast Charitable Society and its Role in the Developing City* (Dublin, 2022), pp 41–2.

75. Peter Smyth, '"Our cloud-cap't grenadiers": the Volunteers as a military force', *Irish Sword,* 13 (1977–9), pp 185–207; James Kelly, 'Select documents XLIII: a secret return of the Volunteers of Ireland in 1784', *IHS,* 26:103 (1989), p. 270.

76. *BNL,* 1 Mar. 1782.

77. Anon., *Concise Compendium of Military Manoeuvres, Represented by Accurate Engravings [...] Particularly Addressed to the Irish Volunteers* (Dublin, 1781).

78. Kelly, 'Select documents XLIII', p. 292; Charles Topham Bowden, *A Tour Through Ireland* (Dublin, 1791), p. 238.

79. *NS,* 7 July 1792.

80. The tune proved enduring and was played at a political meeting presided over by his son William in 1840, *Northern Whig (NW),* 3 Oct. 1840.

81. *Public Advertiser,* 2 Nov. 1787.

82. Anon., 'Additions to Irish Volunteer and Yeomanry relics', *Belfast Municipal Museum and Art Gallery Bulletin,* 1:1 (1949), pp 7–10.

83. *BM,* 16 July 1784.

84. *BM,* 15 Oct. 1784.

85. Pádraig Ó Snodaigh, 'Some military and police aspects of the Irish Volunteers', *Irish Sword,* 13 (1977–9), pp 217–29; the Belfast radical Samuel Neilson fully endorsed the need for the Volunteers to preserve order, as 'every workman [should] have a full and adequate reward for his labour, but let the result be settled by *contract* not by *violence*', *NS,* 9 June 1792.

86. Higgins, *Nation of Politicians,* pp 203–10. For Sharman's refusal of such a commission, see *BM,* 20 Apr. 1784.

87. James Kelly, 'Parliamentary reform in Irish politics: 1760–90', in D. Dickson et al. (eds), *The United Irishmen: Republicanism, Radicalism and Rebellion* (Dublin, 1993), p. 80.

88. *DEP,* 8 July 1783.

89. *DEP,* 8 July 1783.

90. Charlemont letter, 24 July 1783, in *The Manuscripts and Correspondence of James, First Earl of Charlemont* (2 vols, London, 1891), I, 9, pp 113–14.

91. Ibid., pp 114–15; Danny Mansergh, *Grattan's Failure: Parliamentary Opposition and The People in Ireland 1779–1800* (Dublin, 2005), pp 84–7.

92. William Sharman 'To the Volunteers of Ulster', 19 July 1783, in *Letter from the Committee of the Volunteers of Ulster to the Duke of Richmond* (n.p., 1783).

93. Anon. (ed.) *A Collection of the Letters Which Have Been Addressed to the Volunteers of Ireland on the Subject of a Parliamentary Reform* (London, 1783).

94. Martha McTier to William Drennan, Sept. 1783, in D. A. Chart (ed.), *The Drennan Letters* (Belfast, 1931), pp 17–18. Wyvill was chair of the Yorkshire Association for reform, 1779–83; the third Duke of Richmond was a supporter of American independence, concessions to Ireland and extensive parliamentary reform.

95. WS to Jebb, 11 Oct. 1783, in *Collection of the Letters*, pp 108–11. For Sharman's attempts to reconcile these opinions, see Draft memorandum re Irish Volunteers, n.d. (1783), PRONI, D856/D/4.

96. 'Heads of a plan of a parliamentary reform, proposed by the Ulster committee of correspondence to the provincial assembly of Volunteers, and by them referred to the grand national convention', in *Collection of the Letters*, pp 111–14. Radicalised by the American Revolution, Cartwright had argued from 1776 for manhood suffrage, annual elections, the secret ballot, equal electoral districts, abolition of property qualifications and the payment of MPs – elements later incorporated into the *People's Charter* in 1838, see Rory T. Cornish, 'Cartwright, John', in *ODNB*.

97. Higgins, *Nation of Politicians*, pp 199–200.

98. Kelly, 'Politics of Volunteering', pp 151–2.

99. *SNL,* 15 Sept. 1783; Anon., *The History of the Proceedings and Debates of the Volunteer Delegates of Ireland, on the Subject of a Parliamentary Reform* (Dublin, [1784]), pp 6–15.

100. MacNevin, *Volunteers,* pp 197–8; Kelly, 'Parliamentary reform', pp 81–3.

101. Mansergh, *Grattan's Failure,* pp 92–7.

102. *Volunteers Journal (VJ),* 1 Dec. 1783.

103. E. M. Johnston-Liik, *MPs in Dublin: Companion to History of the Irish Parliament 1692–1800* (Belfast, 2006), p. 223.

104. *BM,* 8 Aug. 1783. Todd Jones was the son of an Anglican landowner and doctor at Corry's Glen, Co. Down, Patrick Rogers, 'A Protestant pioneer of Catholic emancipation', *Lisburn Historical Society Journal,* 9 (1995).

105. Thomas Ward to Lord Hertford, 12 June 1783, *NW,* 1 Mar. 1888. Ward was captain of one of the town's Volunteer units.

106. *SNL,* 18 Aug. 1783.

107. *BM,* 19 Aug. 1783, *DEP,* 10 Jan. 1784; *NW,* 1 Mar. 1888.

108. Anon. (ed.), *Votes of the House of Commons, in the First Session of the Fourth Parliament of Ireland* (Dublin, 1783–4), pp 150, 327, 335, 393, 535, 538; *The Parliamentary Register: or, History of the Proceedings and Debates of the House of Commons of Ireland, Vol. 2* (Dublin, 1784), p. 322; *BM*, 27 Apr. 1784. In 1788 he and others were again detained for refusing to pay the fine for non-attendance, *Times,* 15 Mar. 1788.

109. *BM,* 9 Mar. 1784.

110. *Walker's Hibernian Magazine,* Jan. 1786, pp 41–2.

111. *HJ,* 23, 27, 30 Aug.; *VJ,* 1 Oct. 1784.

112. *BM,* 24 Aug., 7 Dec. 1784.

113. [John Robert Scott], *A Review of the Principal Characters of the Irish House of Commons* (Dublin, 1789), pp 52–3; see also *FLJ,* 9 Aug. 1788.

114. WS to the electors of Lisburn, *VJ,* 9 Feb. 1784.

115. Hillsborough to Northington, 1783, PRONI, T755/1, pp 345–6.

116. WS memorandum – critique of Irish trade policy and export orientation, c. 1783, PRONI, D856/D/2, p. 2; Higgins, *Nation of Politicians,* pp 223–33.

117. Norman Vance, 'Volunteer thought: William Crawford of Strabane', in D. G. Boyce and V. Geoghegan (eds), *Political Discourse in Seventeenth and Eighteenth-Century Ireland* (Basingstoke, 2001), pp 257–69.

118. WS memorandum on the economic position of Ireland (n.d.), PRONI, 856/D/2, p. 1.

119. John Robert Scott, *Parliamentary Representation: Being a Political and Critical Review of All the Counties, Cities, and Boroughs of the Kingdom of Ireland* (Dublin, 1790), pp 5–6.

120. MacNevin, *Volunteers,* p. 210.

121. Higgins, *Nation of Politicians,* pp 213–14.

122. Moore to Annesley, 3 May, 10 Nov. 1783, in Crawford (ed.), *Letters,* pp 42–4.

123. *BNL,* 20 Jan. 1784.

124. Moore to Annesley, 28 Feb. 1784, in Crawford (ed.), *Letters,* pp 48, 71–2.

125. *SNL,* 24 Sept., *Freeman's Journal (FJ),* 7 Aug., 23 Oct.; *HJ,* 20 Aug., 29 Oct., *BM,* 29 Oct., 2 Nov. 1784; Mansergh, *Grattan's Failure,* pp 99–100, Kelly, 'Parliamentary reform', pp 86–6.

126. *BM,* 12 Nov. 1784.

127. Whelan, *May Tyrants Tremble,* pp 41–5.

128. William Todd Jones, *A Letter to the Electors of the Borough of Lisburn* (Dublin, [1784]), pp 54–5; Higgins, *Nation of Politicians,* pp 219–20.

129. Whelan, *May Tyrants Tremble,* pp 44–5, 51–2.

130. WS, Draft address of the assembly of delegates for promoting a parliamentary reform, n.d. (1784), PRONI, D/856/D/4/B.

131. WS, 'An abstract on the difficulties of all reformers in religion, the sciences and politics', n.d. (1784), PRONI, D856/D/4/A.

132. *DEP,* 5 Feb.; *BM,* 26 Apr. 1785.

133. 'Verses by a northern member of congress', *FJ,* 12 Feb. 1785.

134. *FJ,* 7 May 1785.

135. Kelly, 'Select documents XLIII', pp 268–92.

136. MacNevin, *Volunteers,* pp 211–12.

137. *BM,* 29 Apr., 17 May 1785.

138. *BM,* 8 Apr. 1785. The paper was published in 1783–6 by John Tisdall, later the first printer of the *Northern Star* in 1792.

139. *FLJ,* 2 Feb. 1789.

140. P. D. H. Smyth, 'The Volunteers and parliament, 1779–84', in T. Bartlett and D. Hayton (eds), *Penal Era and Golden Age: Essays in Irish History 1690–1800* (Belfast, 1979), pp 113–36.

141. *DEP,* 7 May 1785, *BNL,* 13 May 1785.

142. Drennan to McTier, 20 May 1785, Jean Agnew (ed.), *Drennan-McTier Letters* (3 vols, Dublin, 1998–9), I, p. 209.

143. Draft Resolutions of a club', n.d. PRONI, D856/D/1, p. 35; *Morning Herald,* 10 Mar. 1786; James Kelly, 'Elite political clubs 1770–1800', in J. Kelly and M. J. Powell (eds), *Clubs and Societies in Eighteenth-Century Ireland* (Dublin, 2010), pp 277–8.

144. *BNL,* 20 June 1788. He was involved in a number of other societies, some cultural such as the 'Sons of Handel' and others philanthropic, such as the Abecedarian Society, which assisted 'distressed school masters and mistresses', *DEP,* 17 May 1789, 27 May 1790.

145. *VJ,* 22 Oct. 1784.

146. For women's participation in Volunteering, see Higgins, *Nation of Politicians,* pp 178–201.

147. John Martin Robinson, *Temples of Delight: Stowe Landscape Gardens* (London, 1990), p. 102.

148. Pamela Scott, '"Temple of Liberty": building a capitol for a new nation', *Library of Congress Information Bulletin,* 20 Mar. 1995, https://www.loc.gov/loc/lcib/9506/capitol.html (acc. 23/12/20).

149. *BM,* 19 Oct. 1784.

150. [Anon.], Ode for the birthday of Master John Hill Sharman, 12 of August 1791, PRONI, D856/F/3.

151. *BM,* 7 Sept. 1784.

152. *BNL,* 29 Apr. 1785; *SNL* 21 July 1785, 17 July, 19 Oct. 1786, 17 July 1787.

153. *Times,* 23 July 1787. This was, however, a marked reduction on the 3,300 who had participated in the 1785 Belfast review, *SNL,* 21 July 1785.

154. *BNL,* 13 Sept. 1785.

155. WS 'To the officers of the different Volunteer corps reviewed at Dromore on 2nd Sept., 1789', *BNL,* 2 Oct. 1789.

156. Address to William Sharman, reviewing general, Ibid.

157. *DEP,* 12 Aug., 2 Sept. 1790; *BM,* 12 Aug. 1789.

158. *FLJ,* 29 Sept. 1789; 'Address from a forty-shilling freeholder of Ballynahinch to the real, honest, independent freeholders of the county of Down who love honour and honesty', 15 May 1790, PRONI, T3367/3/17.

159. Thomas Atkinson, 'Ode sacred to the patriotic virtues of Col. Sharman', in *Hibernian Eclogues* (Dublin, 1791).

160. Mansergh, *Grattan's Failure*, pp 117–18.

161. Elliott, *Wolfe Tone* (London, 1989), p. 114.

162. 'Declaration of the Volunteers and inhabitants of the large town and neighbourhood of Belfast, on the subject of the French Revolution' (14 July), *BNL*, 15 July 1791.

163. WS to Joy, 5 Sept. 1791, in Bigger, 'William Sharman', pp 4–5.

164. *FLJ*, 24 July 1791.

165. Ibid. For support in Belfast for Polish constitutionalism, see 'Polish Revolution', in [William Bruce and Henry Joy, eds], *Belfast Politics: or, a Collection of the Debates, Resolutions, and Other Proceedings of That Town* (Belfast, 1794), pp 47–8.

166. Nini Rodgers, *Equiano and Anti-Slavery in Eighteenth-Century Belfast* (Belfast, 2000); Krysta Beggs-McCormick, '"Methinks I see grim Slavery's Gorgon form": abolitionism in Belfast, 1775–1865' (PhD dissertation, Ulster University, 2018), pp 43–8.

167. Nancy Curtin, *The United Irishmen: Popular Politics in Ulster and Dublin 1791–1798* (Oxford, 1994), pp 43–4.

168. *NS*, 20 June 1792.

169. *BNL*, 10 July 1792; *Belfast Politics*, p. 52.

170. Martha McTier to Drennan, 8 Nov. 1792, [Nov. 1792], Agnew (ed.), *Drennan-McTier Letters*, I, 423, 430; Anon., *An Account of the Belfast Review and Celebration of the French Revolution*. (Edinburgh, 1792), p. 15.

171. Whelan, *May Tyrants Tremble*, pp 96–100. This vote endorsed that of a previous Belfast town meeting in January, *NS*, 31 Jan. 1792.

172. Eamon O'Flaherty, 'The Catholic Convention and Anglo-Irish politics, 1791–3', *Archivium Hibernicum*, 40 (1985), pp 14–34; Curtin, *United Irishmen*, pp 44–5.

173. *NS*, 28 July 1792.

174. Ibid., 18 July 1792.

175. T. W. Tone diary, 14 Aug. 1792, in R. B. McDowell, T. W. Moody, and C. J. Woods (eds), *The Writings of Theobald Wolfe Tone 1763–98, Vol. 1* (Oxford, 1998), p. 244.

176. The raising of these corps was promoted with sectarian intent by Lord Annesley, but most Volunteers in south Down adhered to equal treatment of Catholics, Mansergh, *Grattan's Failure*, pp 143–5.

177. *NS*, 26 Sept. 1792.

178. Ibid.

179. [Bruce and Joy], *Belfast Politics*, p. 85.

180. *NS*, 15, 26 Dec. 1792.

181. *BNL*, 18 Jan. 1793.

182. Todd Jones to the editor, *NS*, 9 Feb. 1793.

183. Martha McTier to Drennan, n.d. (Jan. 1793), 8 Feb. 1793, Agnew, *Drennan-McTier Letters*, I, 467, 487.

184. *BNL*, 5 Feb. 1793.

185. *NS*, 16 Feb. 1793.

186. *NS*, 20 Feb., *Morning Chronicle (MC)*, 23, 28 Feb. 1793; Elliott, *Wolfe Tone*, pp 205–6.

187. *FLJ*, 23 Feb., *BNL*, 22 Feb. 1793.

188. *FJ*, 20 Feb. 1793.

189. *NS*, 20 Feb. 1793.

190. Sharman to Neilson, 28 Aug. 1790, PRONI, D856/D/5.

191. Kenneth L. Dawson, *The Belfast Jacobin: Samuel Neilson and the United Irishmen* (Newbridge, 2017), pp 15–18. Neilson's father had been the Presbyterian minister at Ballyroney and the family held land at Ballybrick, a townland mostly owned by Sharman, ibid., pp 1–2.

192. Whelan, *May Tyrants Tremble*, p. 67.

193. Samuel McTier to Drennan, 9 July 1791, Agnew, *Drennan-McTier letters*, I, 363; A.T.Q. Stewart, *A Deeper Silence: The Hidden Origins of the United Irishmen* (Belfast, 1998), pp 158–9.

194. Tone, diary entries for 17–18 Aug. 1792, McDowell et al (eds), *Writings of Wolfe Tone, Vol. 1*, 249–50, See also Tone's letter to the *BNL*, 23 Aug. 1792, in ibid., pp 252–3.

195. Todd Jones joined the Dublin Society in Nov. 1791. Rewarded by the Catholic Committee for his services in 1793, he subsequently dropped out of public life, Rogers, 'A Protestant pioneer of Catholic emancipation'.

196. Mansergh, *Grattan's Failure,* pp 128–30; Curtin, *United Irishmen,* pp 24–7.

197. *Belfast Politics,* pp 122–35; Thomas Bartlett, 'Ireland during the revolutionary and Napoleonic wars', in J. Kelly (ed.), *The Cambridge History of Ireland, III, 1730–1880* (Cambridge, 2018), pp 85–6.

198. Martha McTier to Drennan, Mar. 1793, 1 Apr. 1793, Agnew, *Drennan-McTier Letters,* I, pp 502–3, 509.

199. [Anon.], *Authentic Copies of a Declaration of the Rights of Englishmen; A Bill for a Reform in Parliament: and a Letter to Lieut. Col. Sharman, by His Grace the Duke of Richmond* (London, 1794); Joseph Gurney, *The Trial of Thomas Hardy for High Treason* (London, 1795); Curtin, *United Irishmen,* pp 59–61; Kelly, 'Parliamentary reform', p. 87.

200. Allan Blackstock, *An Ascendancy Army: The Irish Yeomanry, 1796–1834* (Dublin, 1998).

201. *Belfast Politics,* pp 141–304.

202. The Lisburn Volunteers paraded to the town's mass house in 1792, where they had listened to the priest's 'sensible and polite discourse', *DEP,* 4 Dec. 1792.

203. Anonymous letter to the lord lieutenant and the lords and commons of Ireland, 5 Feb. 1795, PRONI, D207/5/61.

204. Thomas Lane to Downshire, 24 May 1796, PRONI, D607/D/62.

205. Lane to Downshire, 26 May 1796, PRONI D607/D/63, 19 June 1796, D607/D/73.

206. *BNL,* 24 Apr. 1796; *NS,* 2 May 1796.

207. Lane to Downshire, 19 June 1796, PRONI, D607/D/73.

208. D. McMullan to Downshire, 13 Sept. 1796, PRONI, D607/D/163.

209. *BNL,* 2 Dec. In contrast, a public meeting at Ballynahinch in October, over which Moira presided, accompanied statements of loyalty to the crown with support for freedom of religious conscience for all, advocacy for the end of parliamentary abuses, and mutual self-defence against outrages arising from 'religious zeal', *BNL,* 28 Oct. 1796.

210. Between 1776 and 1831 the Presbyterian share of Moira parish fell from an estimated 34 per cent to 19 per cent while the Anglican share grew from 34 per cent to 53.5 per cent, Miller and Kennedy, 'Irish migration and demography', p. 664.

211. Gillian O'Brien, '"Spirit, Impartiality and Independence": *The Northern Star,* 1792–1797', *Eighteenth-Century Ireland,* 13 (1998), pp 20–2.

212. John Stevenson (ed.), *A Frenchman's Walk Through Ireland, 1796–7, Translated from the French of de Latocnaye* (Belfast, 1917), pp 250–5.

213. Cecil Kilpatrick (ed.), *The Formation of the Orange Order 1795–1798: The Edited Papers of Colonel William Blacker and Colonel Robert H. Wallace* (Belfast, 1994), pp 104–5.

214. *BNL,* 9 Apr. 1798.

215. One prominent casualty of the battle was Viscount O'Neill, formerly Patriot MP for the county and a colonel of the Volunteers, and a friend of Sharman's.

216. *FLJ,* 23 June 1798.

217. Guy Beiner, *Forgetful Remembrance: Social Forgetting and Vernacular Historiography of a Rebellion in Ulster* (Oxford, 2018), p. 52. The drum was purchased in 1912 by Col. Sharman's great-grandson Robert Gordon Sharman-Crawford, and kept in his house at Crawfordsburn until the contents were auctioned in 1947, *Belfast Telegraph (BT),* 14 Apr. 1947.

218. T. G. F. Paterson, 'Lisburn and neighbourhood in 1798', *UJA.* 3rd ser., 1 (1938), pp 194–5.

219. *FLJ,* 23 June 1798.

220. Patterson, 'Lisburn'; George Stephenson to Downshire, 17 June 1798, PRONI, D607/F/251.

221. A. T. Q. Stewart, *The Summer Soldiers: The 1798 Rebellion in Antrim and Down* (Belfast, 1995), p. 233.

222. *Statesman,* 7 June 1844.

223. Jupp, 'Down elections, 1783–1831', p. 199.

224. 'Journey to Moira Castle, in 1799', in William Wilde (ed.), *Memoir of Gabriel Beranger, and his Labours in the Cause of Irish Art and Antiquities, From 1760 to 1780* (Dublin, 1880), p. 164.

225. William Sharman, 'On William Sharman junior dancing a hornpipe at a ball, 1799', PRONI, D856/F/3.

226. Thomas Robinson, painting of Colonel William Sharman, 1798, NMNI, BELUM.U141.

227. John Hewitt, 'Thomas Robinson: portrait of Colonel William Sharman and letter to Thomas Stott', *Belfast Municipal Museum and Art Gallery Bulletin*, 1:1 (1949), pp 1–7; Eileen Black, 'Volunteer portraits in the Ulster Museum, Belfast', *Irish Sword*, 13 (1977–9), pp 181–3.
228. George Barnes, *The Rights of the Imperial Crown of Ireland Asserted and Maintained, Against Edward Cooke, Esq.* (Dublin, 1799), p. 7; Crawford to unknown, [1799], PRONI, D856/D/6.
229. *BNL*, 28 Jan. 1803.
230. *BNL*, 22 Feb., 4 Mar. 1803. For the identification of 'Hafiz' as Stott, see Hewitt, 'Thomas Robinson'.
231. *NW,* 10 Jan. 1860. See also *NW,* 1 Mar. 1888.
232. *FJ*, 29 Apr. 1837.
233. *The Witness*, repr. in *Ballymena Advertiser*, 24 Mar. 1877.
234. [John Wolcot], 'Pitt and his statue', *The Works of Peter Pindar, Esq.* (4 vols, London, 1816), IV, pp 223–4.
235. Higgins, *Nation of Politicians*, p. 238.
236. Hall, *Ulster Liberalism*, pp 20–1; Stephen Small, *Political Thought in Ireland, 1776–1798* (Oxford, 2002).

NOTES TO CHAPTER 2

1. William Sharman's year of birth is given by some sources (including the *Oxford Dictionary of National Biography*) as 1781, however his 'Retrospective memorandum' of 1844 and the age of death given on his funerary monument at Kilmore confirm the year of 1780. Kennedy, who had access in 1953 to the family bible with birth dates inscribed, agrees this dating, 'Sharman Crawford', pp 1–2.
2. William Sharman Crawford (WSC), 'Retrospective memorandum' [c.1844], PRONI, D856/D/1.
3. Kennedy suggests he attended Rev. Charles Moore's school in 1790, 'Sharman Crawford', p. 4.
4. WSC, 'Retrospective memorandum'. William Sharman senior subscribed to the publication of Irish scholarly texts, including Francis Dobbs' *Universal History* (8 vols, Dublin, 1787–1800), and Rev James Gordon's *Terraquea; or, a New System of Geography and Modern History* (4 vols, Dublin, [1794–8]).
5. W. D. Morrow, who had viewed the library in 1947, in *Belfast Telegraph (BT)*, 10 Sept. 1977.
6. See for example, WS, 'For the birthday of Master William Sharman, 3rd of September 1791, composed in the course of the preceding night', 'On William Sharman junior dancing a hornpipe at a ball, 1799', PRONI, D856/F/3.
7. Miscellaneous personal papers and memoranda, c.1780–5, PRONI, D856/F/4.
8. Charles Topham Bowden, *A Tour Through Ireland* (Dublin, 1791), p. 238.
9. Peter Harbison, 'Gabriel Beranger (c.1729–1817) in County Down', *Ulster Journal of Archaeology (UJA)*, 3rd ser., 64 (2005), pp 154–9. 'Collection of drawings, of the principal antique buildings of Ireland designed on the spot & collected by Gabriel Beranger', Royal Irish Academy (RIA) 3C 30.
10. William Sharman (WS) to Samuel Neilson, 28 Aug. 1790, PRONI, D856/D/5; 'Song, composed by Mrs Willson', PRONI, D856/F/3.
11. *Belfast Commercial Chronicle (BCC)*, 18 May 1808.
12. WSC, 'Retrospective memorandum'; C. J. Woods, 'Joy, Henry, jnr', *DIB*.
13. [Kate Newmann], 'James McDonnell (1763–1845), in *Dictionary of Ulster Biography*, http://www.newulsterbiography.co.uk/index.php/home/viewPerson/973 (accessed 3 Oct. 2019); Allan Blackstock, *Double Traitors? The Belfast Volunteers and Yeomen, 1778–1828* (Belfast, 2000).
14. Anon., *Crawfordsburn House, Crawfordsburn, Co. Down: Important Sale by Auction* (Belfast, 1947), p. 50.
15. *BNL*, 28 Mar. 1800.
16. *BNL*, 30 July 1803.
17. Allan Blackstock, 'A forgotten army: the Irish Yeomanry', *History Ireland* 4:4 (1996), pp 28–33.
18. WSC, 'Retrospective memorandum'; E.B. Littlehales to Sharman, 28 Apr. 1804, PRONI, D856/D/7.
19. *Crawfordsburn House*, p. 26.
20. Evidence of WSC to *Select Committee on Orange Lodges, Associations or Societies in Ireland. Report, Minutes of Evidence, Appendix*, HC1835 (377), XV, pp 300–1. Crawford's interlocutors asserted that

the corps was also an Orange lodge, no. 554, but he denied knowing this was the case, or that the corps had ever marched in a 12 July parade, ibid., pp 396–7.

21. William's resignation did not prevent his younger brother, John Hill, serving as an officer in the same unit in 1809, *FJ*, 31 Jan. 1809.

22. Allan Blackstock, *An Ascendancy Army: The Irish Yeomanry, 1796–1834* (Dublin, 1998), pp 194–5, 256–7.

23. WSC, 'Retrospective memorandum'.

24. See WSC, *A Review of Circumstances Connected with the Past and Present State of the Protestant and Catholic Interests in Ireland* (Dublin and Belfast, 1833).

25. WSC to Richardson (30 Oct.), *BNL*, 9 Nov. 1860.

26. C. J. Woods, 'Historical revision: was O'Connell a United Irishman?' *Irish Historical Studies (IHS)*, 35:138 (2006), pp 172–83.

27. WSC, 'Retrospective memorandum', PRONI, D856/D/1. Guy Beiner inaccurately treats Sharman Crawford's statement as embodying 'loyalism' in his otherwise excellent *Forgetful Remembrance*, pp 55–6.

28. Trevor McCavery, '"As a plague of locusts come in Egypt": rebel motivation in north Down', in T. Bartlett et al (eds), *1798: A Bicentenary Perspective* (Dublin, 2003), pp 212–25.

29. John Sharman Crawford (SC) to WSC, 9 Nov. 1835, PRONI, D856/D/42. Sampson, an Anglican lawyer from Londonderry, had been a Volunteer officer from 1782. Bryson survived penal enlistment to the British army and escaped to New York in 1799, Peter Gilmore et al, *Exiles of '98: Ulster Presbyterians and the United States* (Belfast, 2018), pp 153, 196–7; David A. Wilson, *United Irishmen, United States: Immigrant Radicals in the Early Republic* (Ithaca, 1998), pp 164–5.

30. Petition of the Radical Association of Barnsley, with covering letter by WSC, Aug. 1836, TNA, HO 17/105/96; Paul A. Pickering, *Feargus O'Connor: A Political Life* (Monmouth, 2008), pp 5–21.

31. *Belfast Protestant Journal (BPJ)*, 1 Dec. 1849; 'Autobiography of James Hope', in R. R. Madden, *The United Irishmen: Their Lives and Times*, 3rd ser. (3 vols, Dublin, 1846), I, pp 286–92.

32. Anon., *Narrative of the Proceedings of the Contested Election for the County of Down in the Year 1830* (Belfast, 1830), pp 96–7.

33. Thomas MacNevin, *The History of the Volunteers of 1782* (Dublin, 1845).

34. William Sharman, 'On William Sharman Junior dancing a hornpipe at a ball, 1799', PRONI, D856/F/3.

35. John Crawford to unknown, n.d. [c.1799], PRONI, D856/D/6.

36. *Irishman*, 17 May 1822.

37. Martha McTier to Drennan, 3 Jan. 1784, Agnew, *Drennan-McTier Letters*, I, p. 149.

38. Birth notice for a son born to Mrs Sharman, *BNL*, 30 Jan. 1807; *Journal of the Association for the Preservation of the Memorials of the Dead in Ireland*, IV (1900), p 218.

39. Mabel F. Sharman to John Crawford, 23 Feb. 1817, PRONI, D856/F/30.

40. Mabel F. SC to John SC, 10 Nov., 3 Dec. 1835, 10 Mar. 1836, PRONI, D856/D/41, 43, 46. She was a patroness of the national Anti-Corn Law League bazaar in 1842, *Nonconformist*, 26 Jan. 1842.

41. Letters from Arminella to William Sharman, n.d. [c. 1805–8], PRONI, D856/F/24.

42. Margaret to Mary Craig, n.d. [c.1805], PRONI, T2757/1/7; A[ndrew] to Margaret Craig, n.d., PRONI, T1475/2/k; *BCC*, 9 Mar. 1808.

43. The castle had already been demolished by 1814, when a traveller described the town of Moira as being in a ruinous state, E. G. A., 'Sketches from a tourist's note-book', *Belfast Monthly Magazine*, 12:68 (31 Mar. 1814), p. 192.

44. Edward Dupre Atkinson, *An Ulster Parish: Being a History of Donaghcloney (Waringstown)* (Dublin, 1898), p. 87.

45. A. Atkinson, *Ireland Exhibited to England in a Political and Moral Survey of Her Population, and in a Statistical and Scenographic Tour of Certain Districts* (2 vols, London, 1823), I, 217, WSC memoranda, n.d., PRONI, D856/A/6/12.

46. *Select Committee on Orange Lodges*, p. 300; Letters from Lord O'Neill to Sharman, Dec. 1820–June 1821, PRONI, D856/F/32; Sharman to John Adams, Feb. 1826, ibid., D856/B/6/4.

47. *Newry Telegraph (NT)*, 3 Apr. 1845.

48. WSC to Robert Martin (24 Feb.), *Northern Whig (NW)*, 6 Apr. 1835.

49. 'Crawford, Arthur Johnston', in D. R. Fisher (ed.) *The History of Parliament: The House of Commons 1820–1832* (London, 2009) (*HOP 1820-32*).

50. Arthur J. Crawford to Lady Londonderry, 26 Nov. 1812; Lord Londonderry to A. J. Crawford, n.d. [1812], PRONI, D856/F/25-27; *Banner of Ulster (BOU),* 19 Oct. 1861.

51. WSC to Maria Crawford, 22 Feb. 1827, PRONI D856/A/6/4.

52. Copy of royal license to William Sharman of Stalleen in Co. Meath to bear the name of Crawford in addition and quarter those arms, 14 Mar. 1827; Copy of grant of arms to William Sharman of Stalleen, Co. Meath on his assuming under Royal License and in conformity with the will of John Crawford, late of Crawfordsburn, Co. Down, the name and arms of Sharman Crawford, 12 July 1827, NLI, GO Ms 151, pp 32 and 50–1; Ms 107, pp 9–10.

53. One of these resident tutors was George Hill, subsequently a non-subscribing Presbyterian minister and the librarian of Queen's College Belfast, 1850–80, *Coleraine Constitution,* 14 Feb. 1885.

54. [Robin Masefield], *Twixt Bay and Burn: A History of Helen's Bay and Crawfordsburn* (n.p., 2011), p. 11. The Crawfords were originally Presbyterians, with James Crawford serving as an elder of First Bangor congregation in 1765, ibid., p. 12.

55. Photograph of Crawfordsburn House, PRONI, D2460, 'Watering places in the north of Ireland', *Belfast Weekly News,* 19 June 1875.

56. Fred Heatley and Hugh Dixon (eds), *Belfast Scenery in Thirty Views, 1832. Drawn by Joseph Molloy and Engraved by E. K. Proctor, London* (Belfast, 1983).

57. While the parish of Killyleagh was similar to the Crawfordsburn holdings in being predominantly Presbyterian, Kilmore had a small Catholic majority, and Magherahamlet a ratio of 48 per cent Presbyterian, 38 per cent Catholic and 14 per cent Anglican in 1861, *Census of Ireland for the Year 1861, Part IV,* HC 1863 [3204-III], LX, pp 426, 435–6.

58. U. H. Hussey de Burgh, *An Alphabetical List of the Owners of Estates of 500 Acres or £500 Valuation and Upwards, in Ireland* (Dublin, 1878), pp 105–6. For the Sheephouse quarry, which provided much of the stone for building in Drogheda, see Samuel Lewis, *A Topographical Dictionary of Ireland* (London, 1837), I, p. 481, James SC to Arthur SC, 4 Mar. 1850, PRONI, D856/C/6/12.

59. De Burgh, *Owners of Estates,* pp 105–6. There had been no major changes in the size of the Sharman Crawford estates since 1827.

60. *BNL,* 12 Oct. 1813.

61. *NW,* 23 May 1831; WSC to Joseph Stevenson, 8 June 1835, PRONI, SCH524/7B/29/27.

62. *FJ,* 13 Oct. 1803, *BNL,* 23 Apr. 1805; *BCC,* 23 May 1812.; see Jupp, 'County Down elections', 186.

63. *Belfast Monthly Magazine,* 9 (July 1812), pp 80–1.

64. *Morning Register (MR),* 9 May 1829.

65. Kennedy, 'Sharman Crawford', p. 21.

66. County Down commission of the peace for William Sharman, 28 Dec. 1808, PRONI, D856/F/23.

67. *BNL,* 12 July, 1 Nov. 1808. See also ibid., 9 Apr. 1819. The incident was notable for its non-sectarian character, echoing the Oakboy and Steelboy protests of the 1760s-70s, see Allan Blackstock, 'Tommy Downshire's Boys: popular protest, social change and political manipulation in Mid-Ulster 1829–1847', *Past and Present,* 196 (2007), p. 133.

68. *BCC,* 18 Nov. 1811.

69. Maj. Thomas D'Arcy to Sir Francis Leveson Gower, 12 Jan. 1830, National Archives of Ireland (NAI), CSO/RP/OR/1830/183.

70. *DEP,* 17 July; *BNL,* 30 Aug. 1830; WSC evidence to *Select Committee on Orange Lodges,* pp 301–12; *NW,* 13 Feb. 1832.

71. WSC to Sir William Gossett, 3 Mar. 1831, NAI, CSO/RP/OR/1831/217.

72. *NW,* 13 Feb. 1832, William Frederick Ebhardt to Gosset, 14 May 1833, NAI, CSO/RP/1833/2305.

73. O'Donovan to Thomas Larcom, 5 Apr. 1834, OS Letters, RIA, 14/C/13/14.

74. O'Donovan to Larcom, 19 Apr. 1834, OS Letters, RIA, 14/C/13/20.

75. WSC, 'Retrospective memorandum', PRONI, D856/D/1.

76. Suzanne T. Kingon, 'Ulster opposition to Catholic emancipation, 1828–9', *IHS,* 34:134 (2004), pp 137–55.

77. WSC to editor, 23 May; Mr Willson's statement, 23 May, *BCC,* 24 May 1828; Jonathan Wright, *The 'Natural Leaders' and Their World: Politics, Culture and Society in Belfast, c.1801–32* (Liverpool, 2012), pp 124–6.

78. *BNL,* 28 May 1828; Kennedy, 'Sharman Crawford', pp 12–18.

79. Fergus O'Ferrall, *Catholic Emancipation: Daniel O'Connell and the Birth of Irish Democracy* (Dublin, 1985), pp 210–11, 235–6.

80. *BCC.*, 24 Jan. 1829. Newport was MP for the city of Waterford 1803–32 and briefly chancellor of the Irish exchequer in 1806–7.

81. *NW*, 26 Feb. 1829.

82. WSC to Rev. Edward Groves and N. P. O'Gorman, 27 Apr., *MR*, 29 Apr. 1829.

83. Jupp, 'County Down elections'.

84. Lists of freeholders, Co. Down, 1830, PRONI, T761/19.

85. Forde to J. W. Maxwell, 6 June 1826, PRONI, D3244/G/1/36.

86. 'Forde, Matthew (1785–1837)', *HOP 1820–32*.

87. Meeting of the freeholders of Down, 19 May, *NW*, 20 May; ibid., 20 Sept. 1830.

88. *FJ*, 8 Aug. 1830.

89. Anon., *Narrative … of the Contested Election for the County of Down in 1830* (Belfast, 1830), p. 96.

90. W. E. Reilly to Downshire, 30 Aug. 1829, W. A. Maguire (ed.), *Letters of a Great Irish Landlord: A Selection from the Estate Correspondence of the Third Marquess of Downshire, 1809–45* (Belfast, 1974), pp 148–9.

91. WSC to the freeholders of Down, July 1830, PRONI, D856/D11.

92. William Sharman to General Stewart, 25 July 1805, PRONI, D3030/N/18.

93. Address by a farmer of Killinchy to freeholders of Down, 20 July 1805, PRONI, D856/D/8.

94. Anon., *County of Down Election, 1805* (London, 1805), pp 78–80.

95. WSC to the freeholders of Down, July 1830, PRONI, D856/D11.

96. WSC to the tenants on his estates in the barony of Upper Iveagh, 19 July, *Dublin Mercantile Advertiser*, 9 Aug. 1830.

97. *BNL*, 10 Aug. 1830.

98. Cassidy was an ultra-Tory controversialist, agent and close associate of Lord Londonderry; his letters were first published in the *News-Letter*.

99. *Narrative*, pp 46–7, 69–72.

100. 'An elector to the editor of the News-Letter', ibid., pp 25–9.

101. C. J. McClure, 'Aspects of County Down elections, 1820-31', (MA dissertation, QUB, 1986), pp 20–2, Kingon, 'Ulster Protestant politics', pp 112–13; O'Donovan to Larcom, 30 Mar. 1834, OS Letters, RIA, 14C 13/10.

102. McClure, 'Aspects', pp 47–8.

103. *NW*, 22 July 1830.

104. *FJ*, 8 Aug. 1830

105. *Narrative*, pp 77–156. The club later blamed violence on the arrival of 'an organized mob of several hundred men' from the Downshire estates, marshalled and plied with whiskey by their bailiffs, *DEP*, 28 Sept. 1830.

106. Jupp, 'County Down elections', pp 195–6; McClure, 'Aspects of Down elections', p. 54.

107. *NW*, 19 July, 9, 23 Sept. 1830.

108. *Narrative*, the caricature is pasted into the front matter, the 'explanation' is at p. 160.

109. Anon., *Belfast Election: A Collection of Squibs and Songs Issued Prior to the Contest for the Representation of the Borough* (Belfast, 1832), p. 36.

110. [Denis Holland], 'William Sharman Crawford', *Irish Emerald*, 25 Sept. 1869.

111. *DEP*, 28 Sept. 1830.

112. *Narrative*, p. 159; *BNL*, 21 Sept. 1830.

113. O'Connell to Cloncurry, *NW*, 24 Jan. 1831.

114. *BNL*, 4 Jan. 1831.

115. WSC to N. C. Whyte, 8 Jan. 1831, PRONI, D2918/8/54.

116. WSC to Whyte, [8 Jan, 1831], Draft petition, PRONI, D2918/8/55, 56; *BNL*, 25 Jan., *NW*, 21 Mar. 1831.

117. *NW*, 31 Mar. 1831, Kingon, 'Ulster Protestant politics', p. 204.

118. *FJ*, 4 May 1831.

119. Wright, *Natural Leaders*, pp 128–9.

120. *NW*, 24 Jan., 21 Mar. 1831.

121. WSC to Castlereagh (20 Jan.), *BCC*, 21 Jan. 1837.

122. *DEP*, 5 May 1831.

123. *BNL,* 13 May 1831.

124. Hall to [Nugent], 4 May 1831, PRONI, D552/A/6/6/44.

125. Price to Nugent, 27 Apr. 1831, ibid., D552/A/6/6/39.

126. H.W. Bowden to Nugent, 29 Apr. 1831, ibid., D552/A/6/6/41; [Henry Lanktree, ed.], *The Down Squib-Book: Containing an Impartial Account of the Contested Election for the County of Down, in May 1831* (Belfast, 1831), p. 4.

127. Castlereagh to the freeholders of Down, in ibid., pp 7–8.

128. 'Destruction of £10 freeholders!' in ibid., pp 10–11; Castlereagh to the freeholders of Down, 7 May, in ibid., pp 12–13.

129. Kingon, 'Ulster Protestant politics', pp 137–9.

130. *NW,* 5 Jan. 1832.

131. O'Connell to Cloncurry, in *NW,* 24 Jan., *NW,* 30 Mar., 12 May 1831.

132. 'Paddy Blake's Echo', *Down Squib-Book,* p. 56.

133. Election poster issued by the Belfast Committee, 3 May 1831, PRONI, D1748/G/780/3.

134. Election posters issued by the Belfast Committee, 4 May 1831 and n.d., PRONI, D1748/780/1-2.

135. *Down Squib-Book,* p. 40.

136. Ibid, pp 45–53. Cross was master of the Lancastrian Poor School in Belfast and cashier of the town's savings bank, see Joseph Lancaster, *Epitome of Some of the Chief Events and Transactions in the Life of Joseph Lancaster* (New Haven, 1833), p. 18.

137. *Down Squib-Book,* p. 43.

138. Ibid., pp 56–7. Red and black lists of voters had been used by the 'popular' Stewart and Ward campaign in Down in 1790, see Jupp, 'County Down elections', p. 195.

139. *Down Squib-Book,* pp 63–4.

140. 'The beggar's petition', ibid., pp 64–5.

141. Expense account of WSC, in the contested Co. Down election of 1831, PRONI, D856/D/12; Jupp, 'County Down elections', p. 185.

142. K.Theodore Hoppen, *Elections, Politics and Society in Ireland, 1832–85* (Oxford, 1984), pp 74–85.

143. *Down Squib-Book,* pp 69–71.

144. WSC to the independent freeholders of Down (21 May), *BNL,* 24 May 1831.

145. *BNL,* 24, 27 May, *BCC,* 4 June, WSC to Andrew Nugent, 2 June 1831, PRONI D552/A/6/6/48; One of Crawford's sons had met with Nugent's tenants at Portaferry on 6 May, draft letter by Andrew Nugent [May 1831], D552/A/6/6/45.

146. 'Lord Castlereagh', *BNL,* 31 May 1831.

147. Frank Thompson, *The End of Liberal Ulster: Land Agitation and Land Reform 1868–86* (Belfast, 2001), pp 11–14.

148. Jupp, 'County Down elections', pp 197–8.

149. *Down Squib-Book,* pp 61–4; *NW,* 7 June 1832.

150. *NW,* 21 Apr. 1831.

151. *NW,* 26 May 1831.

152. WSC to Dufferin, in *NW,* 1 Mar. 1832, Dufferin to WSC, 13 May 1831, PRONI, D1071/B/C/21.

153. Kingon, 'Ulster Protestant politics', pp 248–9.

154. *NW,* 16 May 1831.

155. *NW,* 26 May 1831.

156. O'Connell to Duncannon, 24 Apr. 1831, M. R. O'Connell (ed.), *Correspondence of Daniel O'Connell* (8 vols, Blackrock, 1972–80), IV, p. 303; WSC to P. M. Murphy, *DEP,* 22 Jan. 1831; *Down Squib-Book,* p. 38.

157. *MR,* 27 Oct. 1831.

158. *MR,* 25 Nov.; Edward Dwyer to WSC, 25 Nov. 1831, PRONI D856/D/16.

159. William Fagan, *The Life and Times of Daniel O'Connell* (2 vols, Cork, 1847–8), II, p. 114, p. 157.

160. *NW,* 17 May 1832.

161. *NW,* 24 May, 23 Aug. 1832.

162. Wright, *Natural Leaders,* pp 46–7, 130–5.

163. Son of the tobacco merchant William Emerson, he had married Letitia, daughter of William Tennent and inherited his lands and property after adopting his surname in 1832, Jessica March, Lawrence William White, 'Tennent, Sir James Emerson', in *DIB.*

164. J. E. Tennent to the editor, 28 Aug., *NW,* 30 Aug.; *BNL,* 7 Sept. 1832; Requisition to J. Emerson Tennent, esq., 8 Sept. [1832], PRONI, D2922/C/2/1.

165. *BNL,* 14 Sept. 1832. For McKnight's moderate conservative politics at the time, see Andrew R. Holmes, 'Union and Presbyterian Ulster Scots: William McComb, Thomas McKnight, and *The Repealer Repulsed*', in G. Carruthers and C. Kidd (eds), *Literature and Unions: Scottish Texts, British Contexts* (Oxford, 2018), pp 165–91.

166. McKnight to Miss Barber, 30 Mar. 1826, 20 Mar. 1828, in Anon. (ed.), *Extracts from Original Letters of James McKnight* (Belfast, 1916), pp 2–3.

167. *BNL,* 29 Apr. 1831.

168. McKnight to Miss Barber, 1 Jan. 1833, *Extracts from Original Letters,* pp 8–9.

169. WSC to James Stevenson Blackwood, 24 Dec. 1832, PRONI, D1748/G/130/4.

170. WSC to E. Getty, [Sept. 1832], PRONI, D608/10; WSC to Grimshaw, 12 Oct., PRONI, D395/9A; *BNL,* 28 Aug. 1832.

171. *BNL,* 7 Sept. 1832.

172. Anon., *Belfast Election,* p. 37.

173. *NW,* 27 Aug.; WSC to John Edgar, 21, 24 Oct., *NW,* 19 Nov. 1832

174. *NW,* 13 Sept. 1832

175. *BNL,* 28 Aug. 1832.

176. 'Orange Institution', *BCC,* 24 Nov. 1832.

177. *Belfast Election,* pp 14–15.

178. Ibid., pp 22–3. A 'braw biggin' is a fine building.

179. 'Song', ibid., pp 27–9.

180. Catherine Hurst, *Religion, Politics and Violence in Nineteenth-Century Belfast: The Pound and Sandy Row* (Dublin, 2002), pp 22–33.

181. *NW,* 10 Sept. 1832.

182. WSC to E. Getty, 29 Aug. 1832, PRONI, D608/11.

183. WSC to electors of Belfast, 17 Sept., *BNL,* 18 Sept.; Grimshaw to Templemore, 3 Sept., Templemore to Grimshaw, 9 Sept. 1832, PRONI, D608/13-14.

184. Edward Getty to R. J. Tennent, 2 Nov. 1832, PRONI, D1748/G/130/1.

185. WSC to electors of Belfast, 6 Nov., *NW,* 12 Nov. 1832; 'Memorial signed by nine inhabitants of the borough of Belfast, to Edward Smith Stanley, claiming that they have been denied the right to vote under the new Reform Act despite being partners in substantial mercantile businesses and commercial premises in the city', 15 Oct. 1832, NAI, CSO/RP/1832/5223.

186. Kingon, 'Ulster Protestant politics', pp 207–8.

187. *NW,* 29 Nov. 1832.

188. Thomas McManus to Grimshaw, 6 Sept. 1832, PRONI, D608/15.

189. *Belfast Election,* pp 20–1.

190. 'Jemme Tempo's address', 'Lord Arthur is a candidate for far-famed Belfast', ibid., pp 39–41, 53–8; 'Song', n.d. (1832) PRONI, D2930/8/43.

191. 'In North-Street my father once dwelt', n.d. (1832), PRONI, D2930/8/45.

192. WSC to R. McDowell and E. Getty, n.d. [Dec. 1832], PRONI, D608/17.

193. R. J. Tennent to WSC, 26 Dec. 1832, PRONI, D1748/G/130/5.

194. WSC to electors of Belfast, 8 Dec., *BCC,* 10 Dec. 1832

195. *NW,* 6 Dec. 1832.

196. 'XYZ', 10 Dec. 1832, PRONI, D608/16.

197. 'The destruction of the "naturals"', *Belfast Election,* pp 47–8. Dominic Bryan and S. J. Connolly, *Civic Identity and Public Space: Belfast Since 1780* (Manchester, 2019), p. 75.

198. Stephen May to Lord O'Neill, 26 Dec. 1832, NAI, CSO/RP/1832/6370.

199. Hoppen, *Elections,* pp 44, 55–6. The largest occupational imbalance was among 'gentlemen', who voted nearly two to one in favour of Chichester and Emerson Tennent.

200. Patrick Cunningham to R. J. Tennent, 3 Apr. 1834, PRONI, D1748/G/135/1.

201. Hoppen, *Elections,* p. 70. In 1835 a petition was signed by 282 Belfast Catholics stating that they had been required to take 'insulting' oaths before being admitted as electors, *NW,* 29 June, *BCC,* 2 Sept. 1835; Ian Budge and Cornelius O'Leary, *Belfast Approach to Crisis: a Study of Belfast Politics 1613–1970* (London, 1973), p. 32.

202. *NW,* 20 Sept. 1832.

203. Hall, *Ulster Liberalism*, pp 88–92.
204. Anon., *Electors of the Borough of Belfast Registered at the Special Sessions under the Reform Act; Distinguishing how Each of Them Voted at the First Election* (Belfast, 1833).
205. Bryan and Connolly, *Civic Identity*, pp 53–6; Kingon, 'Ulster Protestant politics', p. 278.
206. Bryan and Connolly, *Civic Identity*, pp 57–9.
207. Hoppen, *Elections*, pp 5–10.
208. James Stevenson Blackwood to WSC, 22 Dec., WSC to Blackwood, 24 Dec., Tennent to WSC, 26 Dec. 1832 PRONI, D1748/G/130/2, 4, 5.
209. WSC to J. Lamb, 24. Dec., WSC to Tennent, 29 Dec. 1832, PRONI, D1748/G/130/3, 6.
210. Printed squib: 'Third edition of a parody on "C—ke he hath a cunning eye"' (n.d. [1832]), PRONI D913/8.
211. *BCC*, 3 Apr. 1833; *NW,* 9 Nov. 1837. See also Beggs-McCormick, 'Methinks I see', pp 108–12.
212. John to Mabel SC, 28 Apr. 1836, PRONI, D856/D/18.
213. Legacies of British Slave-ownership, 'Henry Barry Coddington', https://www.ucl.ac.uk/lbs/person/view/-1408596435 (acc. 16 June 2020).
214. *BCC*, 14 Apr., *NW,* 27 Apr. 1838; *Sheffield Independent*, 24 June 1843.
215. Nini Rodgers, *Ireland, Slavery and Anti-Slavery, 1612–1865* (Basingstoke, 2007), pp 279–86.
216. *NW,* 8 Jan. 1846.
217. Daniel Ritchie, '"The stone in the sling": Frederick Douglass and Belfast abolitionism', *American Nineteenth-Century History*, 18:3 (2017), 245–72; Beggs-McCormick, 'Methinks I see', pp 125–34.
218. *The Anti-Slavery Reporter*, 1:6 (1 June 1846), 91; Alex Tyrell, *Joseph Sturge and the Moral Radical Party in Early Victorian Britain* (Bromley, 1987), pp 46–118.
219. *North Star,* 5 May 1848.
220. WSC, *A Review of Circumstances Connected with the Past and Present State of the Protestant and Catholic Interests in Ireland* (Dublin and Belfast, 1833), pp 47–8. For his attendance at the Kildare Place Society in 1830, see J. M. Reilly to Dufferin, 4 Mar. 1832, PRONI, D1071/B/C/21.
221. Kingon, 'Ulster Protestant politics', pp 148–51.
222. Circulars relative to Wm. S. Crawford, Lord Dufferin and people of parish of Bangor (Feb. 1832), PRONI, D856/D/18/1.
223. *NW,* 27 Feb. 1832.
224. WSC, *Letter to Lord Dufferin and Claneboy* (Belfast, 1832), PRONI, D856/D/18/3A; this was also published in *NW,* 1 Mar. 1832.
225. Grey to WSC, 6 Mar., Ruthven to WSC, 13 Apr. 1832, PRONI, D856/19/2, 20.
226. Anon., *The Bangor Rout: Ane New Ballad, to the Tune of 'Chevy Chase'* (n.p., 1832)., PRONI, D856/18/2.
227. 'A Protestant of Bangor' to the editor, *Morning Post (MPo)*, 15 Mar. 1832.
228. Dufferin to WSC, 5 Mar., WSC to Dufferin, 7, 10 Mar. 1832, PRONI, D1071/B/C/21.
229. Lewis, *Topographical Dictionary*, I, 183; Angelique Day and Patrick McWilliams (eds), *Ordnance Survey Memoirs of Ireland, Vol 7. Parishes of County Down, II, 1832–4, 1837* (Belfast, 1991), p. 25.
230. *NW,* 20 Sept. 1832.
231. *Hansard's Parliamentary Debates, 3rd series (Hans 3)*, 68: 717–18 (7 Apr. 1843).
232. Ibid., 81: 1371 (30 June 1845), *NW,* 12 Jan. 1860.
233. *Unitarian Chronicle,* Dec. 1832.
234. *BNL,* 6 Sept. 1833.
235. WSC to Chalmers, Sept. 1833, PRONI, D856/G/1; Thomas Chalmers, 'The effect of man's wrath in the agitation of religious controversies: a sermon preached at the opening of the new Presbyterian chapel in Belfast, on Sabbath, September 23, 1827', in Chalmers, *Sermons Preached on Public Occasions* (Glasgow, n.d.), pp 161–92.
236. *NW,* 23 Aug. 1842.
237. *Sun,* 2 May 1844.
238. WSC to the editor, *Newry Examiner (NE)*, 8 Mar. 1842.
239. *NW,* 22 Aug. 1844, Julie Nelson, '"Violently democratic and anti-Conservative": an analysis of Presbyterian "radicalism" in Ulster, c.1800–52'. Ph.D. dissertation, University of Durham, 2005, pp 71–4.
240. *NW,* 24 June 1841
241. *NW,* 20 Dec. 1832.

1. The full title, *A Review of Circumstances Connected with the Past and Present State of the Protestant and Catholic Interests in Ireland, Also, of the Principal Arguments For and Against the Legislative Union, Particularly as Connected with Those Interests; and Suggestions with Reference to the Necessity of Constituting a National Body to Manage the Local Interests and Local Taxation of Ireland, in Connection with the Imperial Parliament* (Dublin and Belfast, 1833) suggested a process of working through ideas on paper.
2. Ibid., p. 10.
3. Ibid., pp 21–2. Although he admitted that the franchise was based on property, he argued that as MPs represented all in their constituencies, not just voters, population should be the basis for the allocation of seats, ibid., pp 24–5.
4. Crawford may have had in mind here events such as the 'Carrickshock incident' in Kilkenny in December 1831, when a clash between tithe collectors and their military escort and local resisters led to seventeen deaths, see Gary Owens, 'The Carrickshock incident, 1831: social memory and an Irish cause célèbre', *Cultural and Social History*, 1 (2004), pp 36–64.
5. WSC, *Review of Circumstances*, p. 26.
6. Ibid., p. 40.
7. *NW,* 14 Feb. 1833.
8. *FJ,* 13 Mar. 1833.
9. *FJ,* 26 Sept. 1833.
10. Ibid., 10 Oct. 1833; WSC, *The Expediency and Necessity of a Local Legislative Body in Ireland, Supported by a Reference to Facts and Principles* (Newry, 1833).
11. Ibid., pp 3–4, [Thomas Spring Rice], 'Ireland', *Edinburgh Review,* 57 (1833), pp 248–79.
12. WSC, *Expediency and Necessity*, p. 13.
13. Ibid., p.27.
14. Ibid., p. 39.
15. Ibid., pp 40–1.
16. Ibid., pp 48–9.
17. [Thaddeus O'Malley], *The Federalist, or a Series of Papers Showing How to Repeal the Union so as to Avoid a Violent Crisis, and, at the Same Time, Secure and Reconcile All Interests* (Dublin, 1831). It appears only the first three out of a projected seven parts were published, Fergus A. D'Arcy, 'Religion, radicalism and rebellion in nineteenth-century Ireland: the case of Thaddeus O'Malley', in J. Devlin and R. Fanning (eds), *Religion and Rebellion* (Dublin, 1997), pp 97–105.
18. WSC, *Expediency and Necessity*, p. 59. His attacks on the Whig ministry drew a response from the chief secretary, who denied Crawford's claim that 'the ears of England should ever be closed to the cries of a starving Irish peasantry', *Hans 3,* 22: 1358 (24 Apr. 1834: Littleton).
19. WSC, *Expediency and Necessity*, pp 72–3.
20. *FJ,* 28 Dec. 1833.
21. *NW,* 13 Jan. 1834.
22. *NW,* 20 Jan. 1834.
23. *NW,* 27 Jan., 3 Feb. 1834. Like the *Newry Examiner (NE)*, the *Northern Herald* (1833–6) was owned by Charles Teeling, see *Newry Telegraph (NT)*, 22 Jan. 1834. The *Herald* was edited by Thomas O'Hagan in 1834–5 and gave his first journalistic appointment to Charles Gavan Duffy.
24. Daniel O'Connell (DOC) to P. V. FitzPatrick, 20 Sept. 1833, in W. J. Fitzpatrick (ed.), *Correspondence of Daniel O'Connell the Liberator* (2 vols, London, 1888), I, pp 389–90.
25. 'Mr O'Connell's second letter', *BCC,* 19 Oct. 1833.
26. *Pilot,* 14 Jan. 1834.
27. *Hans 3,* 21: 421 (17 Feb. 1834).
28. WSC to DOC, 20 Jan., *BCC,* 27 Jan. 1834; *Weekly Register (WR),* 25 Jan. 1834.
29. *Pilot,* 11 Apr. 1834.
30. R. L. Sheil to WSC, 2 May 1834, PRONI, D856/D/21.
31. Oliver MacDonagh, *The Emancipist: Daniel O'Connell, 1830–47* (London, 1989), pp 100–1.
32. WSC to DOC, *Pilot,* 2 June 1834. The regium donum dated to 1672 as a royal payment, but from 1804 was paid out of a parliamentary grant; by 1836 the fund was valued at £25,400 per annum, meeting around half the salary costs of the Presbyterian clergy, see George Mathews, *An Account of the Regium Donum Issued to the Presbyterian Church of Ireland* (Dublin, 1836).

33. Nelson, 'Violently democratic', pp 21–31.
34. WSC to DOC, *MR*, 21 Oct. 1834.
35. DOC to WSC, 17 Sept. 1834, PRONI, D856/D/22.
36. DOC to WSC, *Pilot*, 1 Oct. 1834.
37. *NE*, 29 Mar. 1834, DOC to FitzPatrick, 10 May 1834, Fitzpatrick (ed.), *Correspondence*, I, pp 435–6.
38. Philip Salmon, 'Dundalk', in *HOP 1820–32*. By January 1835 the number of registered voters had fallen to 290, WSC to John SC, 1 Jan. 1835, PRONI, D856/D/24.
39. John Morgan to DOC, 23 Nov. 1834, O'Connell, *Correspondence*, V, p. 206.
40. *Pilot*, 5 Jan. 1835.
41. WSC to John SC, 1 Jan. 1835, PRONI, D856/D/24.
42. *NE*, 3 Jan., *Pilot*, 7 Jan. 1835.
43. *NW*, 1, 8 Dec. 1834, MacDonagh, *Emancipist*, pp 116–19.
44. *NE*, 14 Jan. 1835.
45. *NE*, 17 Jan. 1835.
46. *NE*, 14 Feb. 1835.
47. *NW*, 22 Jan. 1835.
48. WSC to unknown, 26 Jan. 1835, NLI, MS 49,491/1/403.
49. WSC to John SC, [Mar.], [10 Mar. 1835], PRONI, D856/D/25, 26/1.
50. MacDonagh, *Emancipist*, pp 120–2.
51. *DEP*, 14 Mar. 1835
52. WSC to Tennent, 24 Feb., 11 Mar., 5 Apr. 1836, PRONI, D1748/G/130/8, 9, 11.
53. Tennent to editor of Ulster Times (draft), 12 Jan. 1837, PRONI, D1748/G/689/1.
54. WSC to the editor, *Pilot*, 7 Aug. 1835. *Hansard* indexes sixteen contributions to debate in 1835, nineteen in 1836 and fourteen in 1837, excluding petition presentations.
55. [James Grant], *Random Recollections of the House of Commons, From the Year 1830 to the close of 1835, Including Personal Sketches of the Leading Members of All Parties* (London, 1836), pp 325–6.
56. *NW*, 30 Mar. 1835. Crawford now again enjoyed the enthusiastic support of the *Northern Whig*, 2 Apr., 8 June, 10 Sept. 1835.
57. Pickering, *Feargus O'Connor*, pp 60–1.
58. *Hans 3*, 27: 800–1 (3 Apr. 1835).
59. WSC to John SC, 21 Mar. 1835, PRONI, D856/D/28.
60. WSC to John SC, 27 Mar. 1835, PRONI, D856/D/29.
61. WSC to John SC, 27 June, PRONI, D856/D/32. When Mulgrave and his wife visited Down later that year, the Sharman Crawfords were treated as intimates, Mabel SC to John SC, 10 Nov., PRONI, D856/D/41, *NW*, 26 Oct. 1835.
62. WSC to John SC, 14 July 1835, PRONI D856/D/34.
63. *NE*, 20 June, 16 Dec. 1835; *MR*, 5 Sept. 1836.
64. *Morning Chronicle* (*MC*), 13 June 1835.
65. WSC to John SC, 9 July 1835, PRONI, D856/D/33. He was a member of the Irish railways committee that urged the government to promote construction in 1838, and in 1852 he was one of first to travel across the new Craigmore viaduct on the Portadown-Drogheda line, *First Report and Proceedings of the General Railway Committee* (Dublin, 1838), *Times*, 9 Nov. 1838, *FJ*, 17 May 1852.
66. MacDonagh, *Emancipist*, pp 129–30.
67. Kingon, 'Ulster Protestant politics', pp 172–81.
68. WSC to Nugent, 23, 24 Oct., PRONI, D552/A/6/6/55, 57; *BNL*, 7 Nov. 1834.
69. *DEP*, 1 Nov. 1834.
70. WSC to Nicholas Whyte, 19 July 1836, PRONI, D2918/8/77.
71. *Hans 3*, 28: 593–5 (10 June 1835). For the widespread Presbyterian opposition to Cooke's 1834 initiative, see Nelson, 'Violently democratic', pp 111–15.
72. *NW*, 27 July 1835, 29 Feb. 1836.
73. Meade to Hillsborough, 15 Aug. 1836, PRONI, D671/C/12/591.
74. Hillsborough to Peel, 15 Jan. 1837, PRONI, D671/C/12/666.
75. WSC evidence to *Select Committee on Orange Lodges*, p. 312.
76. WSC to John SC, 31 July 1835, PRONI, D856/D/36.

77. *NW,* 10 Aug. 1835; Kevin Haddick-Flynn, *Orangeism: A Historical Profile* (Kibworth Beauchamp, 2019), pp 208–15.

78. *Hans 3*, 30: 72–8 (4 Aug.); 266–310 (11 Aug. 1835).

79. Ibid., 31: 833–5 (2 Feb. 1836).

80. WSC to Tennent, 24 Feb. 1836, PRONI, D1748/G/130/8.

81. Mabel SC to John SC, 10 Mar. 1836, PRONI, D856/D/46.

82. Haddick-Flynn, *Orangeism*, pp 215–16; Daragh Curran, *The Rise and Fall of the Orange Order During the Famine Years* (Dublin, 2020), pp 74–82.

83. *Hans 3*, 29: cols 218–20 (2 July 1835); *Bill for the Amendment of the Law of Landlord and Tenant in Ireland*, HC 1835 (402), III.299.

84. WSC to John SC, 31 July 1835, PRONI, D856/D/36.

85. WSC to John SC, 14 July 1835, PRONI, D856/D/34.

86. *Hans 3*, 30: 410–11 (12 Aug. 1835).

87. WSC to John SC, 5 Aug., PRONI, D856/D/38; *Pilot*, 7 Aug. 1835. The *Pilot* was owned and edited from 1827 by Richard Barrett, previously a reactionary Protestant and a convert to O'Connellism, who became notorious for his 'reckless' and extreme antagonism towards O'Connell's opponents, James Quinn, 'Barrett, Richard', *DIB*.

88. WSC, *Observations on the Irish Tithe Bill Passed in the House of Commons in the Last Session of the Imperial Parliament, Submitted for the Consideration of the Electors of Dundalk* (Dundalk, 1835), pp 8–9.

89. Ibid., pp 11–19.

90. [William Tait], 'William Sharman Crawford, esq., upon the Irish tithes bill', *Tait's Edinburgh Magazine*, 6 (Dec. 1835), pp 822–3.

91. WSC to O'Connell, *BCC,* 19 Dec. 1835

92. WSC to John SC, 31 Dec. 1835, PRONI, D856/D/44.

93. *MR*, 18 Jan. 1836.

94. WSC to John SC, 5 Apr. 1836, PRONI, D856/D/47.

95. WSC to John SC, 26 May 1836, PRONI, D856/D/50/1.

96. *Hans 3*, 34: 1135–44 (1 July 1836).

97. Ibid., 34: 520–38 (14 June), WSC to the liberal constituents of Dundalk (5 July), *NW,* 11 July 1836.

98. WSC to Scrope (20 Dec.), *NW,* 26 Dec. 1833, [G. P. Scrope], 'Poor-law for Ireland', *Quarterly Review*, 44 (Feb. 1831), pp 511–54.

99. For the background, see Peter Gray, *The Making of the Irish Poor Law, 1815–43* (Manchester, 2009), Chapters 3–4.

100. *Evening Chronicle (EC)*, 7 July 1835. For Tocqueville's visit to Newport, see Emmet Larkin (ed.), *Alexis de Tocqueville's Journey in Ireland, July–August 1835* (New York, 1990).

101. *Hans 3*, 29: 691–3 (17 July 1835).

102. Ibid., 1107–11 (27 July 1835).

103. Morpeth to Mulgrave, 17 July 1835, Normanby Papers, Mulgrave Castle, M/465; Gray, *Poor Law,* pp 154–5.

104. *Observer*, 28 June 1835.

105. *Hans 3*, 29: 333 (8 July 1835); Gray, *Poor Law,* p. 83, p. 155.

106. WSC to John SC, 9 July 1835, PRONI, D856/D/33.

107. WSC to John SC, [1 Aug. 1835], PRONI, D856/D/37. Crawford followed through on his threat to vote against the coercion bill along with Smith O'Brien, *Hans 3*, 30: 476–8 (13 Aug. 1835).

108. *DEP,* 3 Dec. 1835.

109. WSC to Howell, *MR*, 13 Apr. 1836.

110. DOC to FitzPatrick, 1 Apr. 1836, O'Connell, *Correspondence,* V, pp 365–6.

111. *Hans 3*, 33: 604–6 (4 May 1836).

112. WSC to John SC, [26 May 1836], PRONI, D856/50/1.

113. Gray, *Poor Law,* pp 87–91.

114. *Times,* 4 May 1835, 28 Sept. 1836, *Spectator*, 30 Jan. 1836.

115. DOC to FitzPatrick, 1 Apr., O'Connell, *Correspondence,* V, 365–6; *FJ,* 1 Oct. 1836.

116. *Times,* 17 Nov. 1836.

117. WSC to Whyte, 8 July 1837, PRONI, D2918/8/82.

118. *Hans 3*, 38: 360–83 (28 Apr. 1837).

119. Ibid., 383–402.

120. Ibid., 1165–9 (2 June 1837).
121. Feargus O'Connor, *A Series of Letters …to Daniel O'Connell* (London, 1836); Pickering, *O'Connor*, pp 70–1.
122. MacDonagh, *Emancipist*, p. 153.
123. *Times*, 2 Aug. 1836.
124. *NE*, 21 Dec. 1836. Crawford compiled detailed notebooks on American and other relief systems, WSC to John SC, 31 Dec. 1835, PRONI, D856/D/44; Notebook and memoranda of WSC, 1835–46, ibid., D856/D/23.
125. *NE*, 21 Dec. 1836.
126. *London Mercury*, 8 Jan. 1837.
127. *FJ*, 6, 13 Jan. 1837.
128. Gray, *Poor Law*, pp 237–40.
129. For concern about a 'sub-movement' led by Sheil, see Lawless to WSC, *FJ*, 2 Jan. 1837.
130. *FJ*, 5, 6 Apr. 1837.
131. *Hans 3*, 38: 383–8 (28 Apr. 1837).
132. *FJ*, 9 Sept., 1 Nov. 1837, 26 Jan. 1838.
133. Gray, *Poor Law*, pp 195–214, 253–80.
134. 'To the friends of "real justice" to Ireland', *BNL*, 13, 16, 20 Feb.; WSC to DOC, *FJ*, 27 Apr. 1838.
135. *Times*, 3 Mar. 1838.
136. WSC to the editor (13 June), *DEP*, 14 June, WSC to O'Connell, *Times*, 7 Aug. 1838.
137. WSC to Crean, Letter II (12 Sept.), *BNL*, 18 Sept. 1840.
138. *Dublin Monitor (DM)*, 13 Apr. 1841.
139. *Report from the Select Committee of the House of Lords on the Laws Relating to the Relief of the Destitute Poor, and into the Operation of the Medical Charities in Ireland*, HC1846 (694), IX, 387–405 (17 Mar. 1846).
140. WSC to DOC, *MR*, 28 July 1836.
141. WSC to Mr French, *DEP*, 20 July 1836.
142. WSC to liberal constituency of Dundalk, *MR*, 25 Aug.; idem., *Pilot*, 5 Sept. 1836.
143. WSC to liberal constituency of Dundalk, *Times*, 21 Sept. 1836.
144. *MR*, 7, 28 July 1836; *Pilot*, 27 July 1836.
145. *BCC*, 10 Aug., *MR*, 3 Oct. 1836.
146. DOC to WSC, *Times*, 6 Oct. 1836.
147. WSC to DOC, *Pilot*, 7 Oct. 1836.
148. Cloncurry to WSC, *DEP*, 11 Oct. 1836.
149. WSC to Cloncurry, *DEP*, 15 Oct. 1836.
150. *Pilot*, 28 Oct. 1836.
151. *NW*, 19 Nov. 1836.
152. *Scotsman*, 30 Nov. 1836.
153. *MR*, 25 Nov. 1836.
154. *The Age*, 2 Oct. 1836; *The Satirist*, 11 Sept., 5 Feb. 1837.
155. [John Doyle], 'HB Sketches No. 458, "A Scene from Hudibras"' (1 Dec. 1836). Hogarth's print series for *Hudibras* was republished in London in 1822.
156. *Morning Post (MPo)*, 11 Feb. 1837; *Kerry Evening Post*, 14 Dec.; see also *Warder*, 17 Dec. 1836.
157. *FJ*, 3 Jan. 1837.
158. Lawless shared Crawford's historical interest in the Volunteers as a manifestation of radical non-denominational collaboration, see his *The Belfast Politics Enlarged; Being a Compendium of the Political History of Ireland for the Last Forty Years* (Belfast, 1818).
159. *NW*, 7 Jan. 1837.
160. *WTS*, 15 Jan. 1837.
161. *FJ*, 14 Jan. 1837.
162. DOC to WSC, 17 Jan., PRONI, D856/D/53; published in *Pilot*, 18 Jan. 1837.
163. *FJ*, 20 Jan. 1837
164. *FJ*, 20 Jan. 1837.
165. *Pilot*, 20 Jan. 1837.
166. *Pilot*, 27 Jan. 1837.

167. Mulgrave to Morpeth, 27 Jan. 1837, Castle Howard, N. Yorkshire, Castle Howard Papers, J/19/1/14 f.4.

168. Repr. In *DEPa*, 26 Jan. 1837. The *Newry Telegraph* was controlled by the strongly anti-Catholic Henderson family, who would also later take over the *Belfast-News Letter* beginning with James Alexander Henderson's appointment as joint editor in 1845.

169. Guy Stone's diary, 17 Jan. 1837, PRONI, D826/2/1.

170. *NE,* 1 Oct. 1836.

171. Ibid., 5 Oct. 1836.

172. *MR,* 28 Jan. 1837.

173. *FJ,* 30 Jan., *Pilot,* 30 Jan. 1837.

174. WSC to electors of Dundalk (25 Jan.), *NW,* 28 Jan. 1837.

175. *NW,* 31 Jan. 1837.

176. WSC to M. Staunton (30 Jan.), *MR,* 1 Feb. 1837.

177. *NE,* 8 Feb. 1837.

178. *NW,* 30 Mar.; *Hans 3,* 38: 463 (3 May); *FJ,* 5 May 1837.

179. *Hans 3,* 38: 652–6 (5 May 1837).

180. [John Doyle], 'HB's Sketches No. 466, "Another Scene from Hudibras"' (10 Feb. 1837).

181. WSC to John SC, 8 May 1837, PRONI, D856/D/54.

182. *FJ,* 9 May 1837.

183. WSC to agent on Rademon estate (24 May), *BNL,* 2 June 1837.

184. *FJ,* 7 June 1837.

185. MacHale to DOC, 4 June 1837, O'Connell, *Correspondence,* VI, p. 46.

186. DOC to FitzPatrick, 9 June 1837, Fitzpatrick, *Correspondence,* II, pp 95–6.

187. *Hans 3,* 38: 1370 (9 June); *MR,* 10 June, *Pilot,* 12 June 1837.

188. *MR,* 13 June 1837.

189. WSC to John SC, 13 June 1837, PRONI, D856/D/55. The adherence of several Connacht MPs may have been related to the growing impatience of Archbishop John MacHale with O'Connell's concessions, see MacDonagh, *Emancipist,* pp 158–9.

190. *NW,* 27 June 1837.

191. Ruthven to the editor, *Times,* 26 Aug. 1837.

192. WSC to the secretary of the Dundalk Reform Registry (29 June), *FJ,* 3 July 1837.

193. WSC to DOC (22 Aug.), *FJ,* 26 Aug., *Pilot,* 1 Sept. 1837. Crawford's criticism of O'Connell did not render him a republican; he was later involved in the civic reception of Victoria and Albert when they visited Belfast in 1849, *NW,* 7, 11 Aug. 1849.

194. Mulgrave to Russell, 8 Sept. 1837, Russell Papers, TNA, PRO30/22/2F fols 60–5.

195. WSC to DOC, Letter III (7 Sept.), *FJ,* 11 Sept. 1837.

196. WSC to DOC, Letter IV (12 Sept.), *MR,* 15 Sept. 1837

197. *FJ,* 26 Aug., 2 Sept.; *MR,* 31 Aug. 1837

198. *MR,* 6 Sept., *FJ,* 5, 13 Sept. 1837.

199. *Pilot,* 13 Sept. 1837.

200. *London Mercury,* 3, 10, 17 Sept. 1837.

201. DOC to the People of Ireland (2 Sept.), *MR,* 7 Sept. 1837.

202. *Pilot,* 25 Sept., 4 Oct, 15 Nov.; *FJ,* 26 Oct. 1837.

203. *MR,* 7 Nov.; DOC to WSC (18 Nov.), *BNL,* 24 Nov. 1837.

204. WSC to DOC (9 Nov.), *NW,* 11 Nov. 1837.

205. DOC to WSC (18 Nov.), *BNL,* 24 Nov. 1837.

206. WSC to DOC (23 Nov.), *NE,* 25 Nov. 1837.

207. *Londonderry Standard (LS),* 13 Sept.; *NW,* 3 Oct. 1837. For his appeal to radical Presbyterian memory, see WSC to the friends of religious liberty in Ulster (16 June), *NW,* 18 June 1838.

208. Fagan, *O'Connell,* II, 598–9, 646.

209. WSC to editor of Wexford Independent (30 Nov.), *MR,* 8 Dec. 1837, and see below, Chapter 5.

210. WSC to DOC (24 Apr.), *BCC,* 30 Apr.; WSC to DOC (5 May), *MR,* 9 May 1838.

211. *Journal des débats,* 17 Nov. 1837, 16 Oct. 1838.

212. WSC to Hughes (22 May), *FJ,* 26 May 1838.

213. WSC to DOC (2 Aug.), *Times,* 7 Aug. 1838.

214. *NW,* 21 Aug. 1838. O'Connell's reference to the significance of Crawford's white waistcoat is obscure, but may refer to the uniform of the Loyal Lambeth Association, a radical armed group affiliated to the London Corresponding Society, revealed in the treason trial of Thomas Hardy in 1794, see John Barrell, *Imagining the King's Death: Figurative Treason, Fantasies of Regicide, 1793–6* (Oxford, 2000), pp 220–1.

215. *Pilot,* 20 Aug. 1838.

216. *Spectator,* 25 Aug. 1838.

217. *Northern Liberator,* 25 Aug. 1838.

218. WSC, 'Observations on Irish policy, addressed to British reformers', *Tait's Edinburgh Magazine,* 5: 57 (Sept. 1838), pp 552–4.

219. *BNL,* 11 Sept. 1838.

220. WSC, 'Observations on the present position of the cause of religious liberty' (6 Oct.), *MR,* 11 Oct. 1838.

221. DOC to FitzPatrick, 23 Oct. 1838, in Fitzpatrick (ed.), *Correspondence,* II, 154.

222. WSC, 'Observations on the present position of the cause of religious liberty', Letter II (10 Oct.), *FJ,* 13 Oct. 1838.

223. *MR,* 15 Oct. 1838.

224. *FJ,* 17, 22 Oct., *Pilot,* 24 Oct. 1838. O'Hagan was later a Liberal MP and Gladstone's Irish lord chancellor in 1868–74 and 1880–1.

225. Steele to the 'Men of Ireland', 11 Oct., repr. in *Boston Pilot,* 24 Nov. 1838.

226. *FJ,* 20, 25 Oct. 1838.

227. *Times,* 27 Nov.

228. *Dublin Monitor,* 8 Dec. 1838. The paper was owned and edited by James Charles Coffey and described itself as being 'conducted on principles of the most uncompromising liberalism'.

229. WSC to the Friends of religious liberty in Ulster (1 Dec.), *NW,* 4 Dec. 1838.

230. *LS,* 29 Aug. 1838.

231. *LS,* 5 Dec. 1838.

232. WSC, *A Defence of the Small Farmers of Ireland* (Dublin, 1839).

233. WSC to the editor (18 Mar.), *NW,* 19 Mar. 1839.

234. WSC to editor of Anti-Corn Law League Circular, 4 Nov. 1839, Manchester Archives, Anti-Corn Law League papers, Letterbook 1838–40, GB127.BR MS f337.2.A1, Vol. 2, p. 282.

235. *Manchester Times (MT),* 14 Jan.; *Manchester Guardian (MG),* 15 Jan. 1840.

236. *DM,* 21 Mar. 1840.

237. *NW,* 5 Feb., *BNL,* 12 Apr. 1839.

238. *Times,* 27 Sept. 1839.

239. *FJ,* 18 Apr. 1839. Mulgrave had been promoted to Marquess of Normanby in June 1838.

240. *NW,* 18 Apr., *DM,* 20 Apr. 1839.

241. *Champion,* 28 Apr., *Northern Liberator,* 4 May 1839.

242. WSC to Ralph Walsh (14 Oct.), *Pilot,* 16 Oct. 1839.

243. DOC to the TPU (18 Oct.), *Pilot,* 21 Oct. 1839.

244. *LS,* 13 Nov., *MR,* 21 Nov.; *NW,* 23 Nov. 1839.

245. MacDonagh, *Emancipist,* pp 185–7.

246. *DM,* 18 Apr. 1840.

247. *NW,* 23 Nov. 1839.

248. *NW,* 9, 11 Jan. 1840. The declaration was signed by numerous Presbyterian and Catholic clergy (including two bishops) and a scattering of Anglicans.

249. *NW,* 18 July 1840.

250. *Nonconformist,* 22 Sept. 1841. For the context, see Christopher Ridgway (ed.), *The Morpeth Roll: Ireland Identified in 1841* (Dublin, 2013).

251. He argued that Irish reformers should refrain from toasting 'the English portion of the administration' on St Patrick's Day, WSC to R. J. Tennent, 13 Mar. 1841, PRONI, D1748/G/130/21.

252. *BNL,* 14 Jan. 1840.

253. Ross was a former military officer and a proprietor at Rostrevor.

254. WSC to the friends of liberty in Ulster (27 Apr.), *FJ,* 30 Apr. 1840.

255. *BNL,* 1 May 1840.

256. WSC to Emerson Tennent (6 May), *NW,* 7 May 1840.

257. *NW,* 25 June 1840.
258. *Morning Advertiser (MA),* 22 June 1840.
259. *BNL,* 2 Oct. 1840.
260. *NW,* 30 June 1840.
261. *NW,* 21, 23, 25 July 1840.
262. WSC and Ross to the Friends of Liberty in Ulster (21 July), *DEP,* 23 July 1840., *FJ,* 1 Aug., *NW,* 15 Aug. While the *Vindicator* would come out against the UCA, the *Newry Examiner* endorsed it on 26 Aug. 1840.
263. Ross to R. J. Tennent, 12 Oct. 1840, PRONI, D1748/G/577/2.
264. *NW,* 15 Aug. 1840.
265. *DM,* 22 Aug. 1840.
266. *NW,* 20 Aug., *MR,* 1, 10, 15 Sept., *BNL,* 1 Sept. 1840; WSC to Crean (7 Sept.), *DM,* 8 Sept. 1840.
267. WSC to Crean, Letter II (12 Sept.), *BNL,* 18 Sept. 1840.
268. O'Connell's 1841 visit to Belfast was satirised in [William McComb and James McKnight], *The Repealer Repulsed! A Correct Narrative of the Rise and Progress of the Repeal Invasion of Ulster: Dr Cooke's Challenge and Mr. O'Connell's Declinature, Tactics, and Flight.* (Belfast, 1841).
269. *NW,* 27 Aug. 1840.
270. *BNL,* 2 Oct. 1840.
271. *BNL,* 6 Oct. 1840.
272. *NW,* 12 Dec. 1840.
273. UCA circular, 3 Dec., PRONI, D1748/G/130/19; WSC to editor (13 Dec.), *NW,* 15 Dec. 1840.
274. *NW,* 17 Dec. 1840.
275. *DM,* 19 Dec. 1840.
276. Ibid.
277. WSC to the editor (23 Dec.), *NW,* 24 Dec. 1840.
278. WSC to Samuel Smiles (2 Dec.), *Leeds Times,* 26 Dec. 1840.
279. Ross to J. G. Mitchell (24 Dec. 1840), *BNL,* 26 Jan. 1841.
280. J. G. Kohl, *Travels in Ireland* (London, 1844), p. 338.
281. Belfast *Vindicator (BV),* 26, 30 Dec. 1840.
282. *DM,* 22 Dec., John O'Connell to WSC, 26 Dec. 1840, PRONI, D856/D/58.
283. WSC to Belfast O'Connell Committee, 7 Jan., RIA, Gavan Duffy Bequest Box 1, 12/P/15/1; published in *MR,* 11 Jan. 1841.
284. In issuing his challenge to O'Connell to personally debate with him, Cooke drew attention to the humiliation of Crawford in Dublin: 'I, by God's help, will attempt to prevent you; and that, Mr O'Connell, not in your favourite style of "*Sharman my jewelling,*" but in calm, deliberate and logical argument', Cooke to O'Connell (5 Jan.), *BNL,* 8 Jan. 1841.
285. Hirst, *Religion, Politics and Violence,* pp 49–51.
286. Andrew R. Holmes, 'Union and Presbyterian Ulster Scots: William McComb, Thomas McKnight, and *The Repealer Repulsed*', in G. Carruthers and C. Kidd (eds), *Literature and Unions: Scottish Texts, British Contexts* (Oxford, 2018), pp 165–91.
287. WSC to John O'Connell (8 Jan.), *DM,* 9 Jan. 1841.
288. *DEP,* 19 Jan, 1841.
289. *BCC,* 20 Jan. 1841.
290. *NW,* 2 Feb. 1841.
291. *NT,* 9 Feb.; *NW,* 11 Feb. 1841.
292. UCA circular, 19 Feb., PRONI, D1748/G/130/20; *NW,* 25 Feb. 1841.
293. Hall, *Ulster Liberalism,* p. 95.
294. Crawford later confided to R. J. Tennent that Ross had alienated both himself as the house by 'over speechifying and underwork', Tennent to Eliza Tennent, 22 Nov. 1847, PRONI, D1748/H/46/133.
295. WSC to R. J. Tennent, 13 Mar., PRONI, T1748/G/130/21; *NW,* 3 June, WSC to the editor of the Vindicator (21 Oct.), *NT,* 28 Oct. 1841.

NOTES TO CHAPTER 4

1. William Lovett, *The Life and Struggles of William Lovett, in the Pursuit of Bread, Knowledge and Freedom* (London, 1876), pp 111–12.
2. Ibid., pp 112–13.
3. London Working Men's Association (LWMA), *The People's Charter;With the Address to the Radical Reformers of Great Britain and Ireland* (London, 1848 edn), p. 7. Emphasis in original.
4. Ibid., p. 5, p. 9.
5. Pickering, *O'Connor*, pp 74–5.
6. *People's Charter*, p. 4.
7. Malcolm Chase, *Chartism,A New History* (Manchester, 2007), pp 11–19. By April 1839 it claimed a readership of over 400,000, Pickering, *O'Connor*, p. 76.
8. MacDonagh, *Emancipist*, pp 163–8.
9. John Temple, *What is Property?* (London, n.d. [c.1836]).
10. *Times*, 3 Aug. 1837.
11. WSC to editor of True Sun, *FJ*, 14 Aug. 1837.
12. *Leeds Times (LT)*, 19 Aug., 2 Sept. 1837.
13. WSC toWilliam Cook (10 Oct.), *Northern Liberator (NL)*, 21 Oct. 1837.
14. Address toWSC (16 Oct.), *London Dispatch*, 22 Oct. 1837.
15. WSC to John Fraser (10 Nov.), *FJ*, 28 Dec. 1837.
16. *MA*, 11 Jan.; *Northern Star (NS)*, 13 Jan. 1838.
17. *NS*, 13 Jan. 1838.
18. *NW,* 20 Jan. 1838.
19. *NS,* 20 Jan. 1838.
20. *WR*, 13 Jan., *Pilot*, 17 Jan., *MR*, 24 Jan. 1838.
21. *Manchester Courier (MCo)*, 9 June 1838.
22. *BNL,* 9 June 1838;WSC to Lovett (13 Sept.), *MR*, 24 Sept. 1838.
23. *NS*, 29 Sept. 1838.
24. WSC to Lovett (27 Nov.), *Era*, 9 Dec. 1838.
25. *NS*, 10 Nov. 1838.
26. TheWorking Men's Association to the Irish People, *MR*, 18 Dec. 1838.
27. 'A Vision of Britain Through Time: Rochdale District' http://www.visionofbritain.org.uk/unit/10076780 (accessed 12 Nov. 2019). Figures are for the modern boundaries of Rochdale district. The parliamentary borough proper had a population of around 34,000 in 1841 and 41,500 in 1851, John Garrard, *Leadership and Power inVictorian Industrial Towns, 1830–80* (Manchester, 1983), p. 8.
28. Patrick Joyce, *Work, Society and Politics: The Culture of the Factory in Late Victorian England* (Brighton, 1980), Garrard, *Leadership and Power*, p. 10.
29. Franklin Howorth, *Reflections on the Distress of the Poor. An Address Occasioned by the Late Riots in the Manufacturing Districts and the Fatal Affray at Rochdale* (Rochdale, 1829).
30. Taylor represented the town in the national Chartist convention in 1839 and on the National Charter Association in 1840, Chase, *Chartism*, p. 162, Garrard, *Leadership and Power*, pp 127–9.
31. William Robertson, *The Social and Political History of Rochdale* (Rochdale, [1889]), pp 10–16; *LT,* 15 Dec. 1838.
32. Clement Royd to Lord John Russell, 24, 29 Dec. 1838, Chadwick to Russell, 16 Mar. 1839,TNA, HO 40/37/18, 21, 141; M. R. Lahee, *Life and Times of the Late Alderman T. Livsey* (Manchester, [1865]), pp 26–31.
33. Robertson, *Rochdale*, pp 19–21.
34. Ibid., p. 190.
35. MilesTaylor, 'Bright, John (1811–1889), politician', *ODNB*.
36. R. Barry O'Brien, *John Bright* (London [1910]), p. 68.
37. Garrard, *Leadership and Power*, pp 110–11.
38. Of the nonconformists, the Methodist Association (at 29 per cent in 1851) was the largest and most influential, containing many members of the town's middle-class elite. Eithne Nightingale, *The Religious and Political Crisis of Rochdale Parish 1825–1877* (Rochdale, 1993), p. i, Garrard, *Leadership and Power*, pp 10–11.
39. Henry Fishwick, *History of the Parish of Rochdale* (Rochdale, 1889), pp 243–6.

40. Robertson, *Rochdale*, p. 18; Fishwick, *Rochdale*, p. 246; Garrard, *Leadership and Power*, pp 116–17, 130. A number of women ratepayers were active in these meetings, see Lahee, *Livsey*, pp 45–7.

41. John Edward Nassau Molesworth, *Remarks on Church Rates and the Rochdale Contest* (Rochdale, 1841), p. 36.

42. Nightingale, *Religious and Political Crisis*, pp 6–15.

43. *MG*, 28 Oct. 1840.

44. Robertson, *Rochdale*, pp 321–2.

45. WSC to James Aytoun (1 June), *NW*, 15 June 1839.

46. *NS*, 27 June, *Blackburn Standard (BS)*, 1 July 1840.

47. *MCo*, 25 July, *BS*, 29 July 1840.

48. *NS*, 1 Aug. 1840.

49. *FJ*, 3 Aug. 1840.

50. Copy of Requisition to WSC, 26 Nov., PRONI, D856/D/57; *LT*, 3 Oct. 1840.

51. *Leeds Mercury (LM)*, 3 Oct.; WSC to Smiles (26 Oct.), *LT*, 31 Oct. 1840.

52. Pickering, *O'Connor*, pp 90–101.

53. *NS*, 17 Oct. 1840.

54. *NS*, 24 Oct. 1840.

55. *LT*, 28 Nov.

56. *NS*, 5 Dec. 1840.

57. *NS*, 9 Jan. A further warning was published on 20 Feb. 1841.

58. Chase, *Chartism*, pp 172–5.

59. *Times*, 23 Jan. 1841.

60. L. Pitkethly to the editor (26 Jan.), *NS*, 6 Feb. 1841.

61. Matthew Roberts, 'Daniel O'Connell, Repeal, and Chartism in the age of Atlantic revolutions', *Journal of Modern History*, 90:1 (2018), pp 1–39.

62. *NS*, 30 Jan. 1841.

63. WSC to an elector of Rochdale, *LT*, 1 May 1841.

64. WSC to editor of *NW* (8 Feb.), *BV*, 13 Feb. 1841.

65. WSC to the electors and inhabitants of Rochdale (7 June), *NS*, 19 June 1841.

66. *Yorkshire Gazette*, 6 Feb. 1841.

67. *MG*, 2 June 1841; Robertson, *Rochdale*, pp 325–7.

68. *MCo*, 12 June 1841.

69. *MCo*, 26 June 1841.

70. Frank Neal, 'Manchester origins of the English Orange Order', *Manchester Region History Review*, 4:2 (1990–1), pp 12–24.

71. Dorothy Thompson, 'Ireland and the Irish in English radicalism before 1850', in J. Epstein and D. Thompson (eds), *The Chartist Experience: Studies in Working-Class Radicalism and Culture, 1830–60* (London, 1982), pp 120–51.

72. Fishwick, *Rochdale*, p. 269.

73. Robertson, *Rochdale*, p. 327.

74. *MG*, 10 June, WSC, Copy of address to the borough of Rochdale, 7 June 1841, PRONI, D856/D/62.

75. WSC to the electors and inhabitants of Rochdale (7 June), *NS*, 19 June 1841.

76. *NS*, 12 June 1841.

77. *EC*, 28 June 1841.

78. *MC*, 1 July, *MCo*, 3 July 1841.

79. Robertson, *Rochdale*, pp 335–9.

80. *MCo*, 17 July 1841.

81. *MG*, 3 July 1841. The cockade is preserved at PRONI, D856/D/61.

82. *Manchester Times (MT)*, 3 July 1841; Phillips to Rochdale magistrates, 3 July 1841, TNA, HO 41/16/179.

83. *Bolton Chronicle (BC)*, 3 July 1841.

84. Printed circular of Benjamin Heape, Rochdale (Returning Officer), *A Copy of the Poll of the Electors of the Borough of Rochdale on 1st July 1841 on Which Occasion Wm. S. Crawford was Returned by a Majority of 64* (Rochdale, [1841]), PRONI, D856/D/63.

85. *NS*, 24 July 1841.

86. *MG*, 30 Mar., *Hans 3*, 62: 703 (18 Apr. 1842).

87. *Economist,* 16 Sept. 1843.

88. John Evans, *Lancashire Authors and Orators* (London, 1850), pp 76–7.

89. Henry Crone to Emerson Tennent (20 July), *NW,* 25 July; Crone to DOC, 20 July 1839, O'Connell (ed.), *Correspondence,* VI, pp 261–2.

90. *NW,* 7, 12 Aug. 1841.

91. *BV,* 27 Apr. 1844, *DM,* 6 May, *BOU,* 10 May 1844.

92. *BNL,* 25 Oct. 1852; Alice Johnston, '"Some hidden purpose"? Class conflict and co-operation in Belfast's Working Men's Institute and Temperance Hall 1865–1900', *Social History,* 42:3 (2017), pp 399–419.

93. *MG,* 18 Aug. 1841.

94. *FJ,* 27 Aug. 1841.

95. George Holyoake, *The History of the Rochdale Pioneers, 1844–1892* (3rd edn, London, 1900), pp 67, 170–1; Lahee, *Livsey,* pp 131–5.

96. *Hans 3,* 59: 232–3 (25 Aug. 1841).

97. Ibid., 457–63 (28 Aug. 1841).

98. *Nonconformist,* 1 Sept. 1841; Cobden to Frederick Cobden, [28] Aug., Cobden to C. P. Villers, 13 Sept. 1841, Anthony Howe (ed.), *The Letters of Richard Cobden, Vol. 1, 1815-47* (Oxford, 2007), pp 231, 235–6.

99. Cobden to Watkin, 9 Oct. 1841, Howe, *Letters of Cobden,* I, pp 237–8.

100. *NS,* 4 Sept. 1841.

101. TNA, CO/904/8, fol. 375 (13 Oct. 1841). O'Higgins was the son of a Catholic small farmer from Co. Down and admirer of Cobbett. He joined the Dublin Charter Association in 1839 before serving as president of the IUSA 1841–8, see Bridget Houricane, 'O'Higgins, Patrick', *DIB.*

102. [Patrick O'Higgins], 'Landlords and tenants: tyrants turning tenants out' (Oct. 1845), repr. in *United Irishman (UI),* 4 Mar. 1848.

103. *Hans 3,* 59: 634–40 (20 Sept.).

104. *FJ,* 7 Oct., *Times,* 5 Oct. 1841.

105. *Hans 3,* 59: 925–36 (28 Sept. 1841).

106. Ibid., 64: 94–111, 611–12 (17, 24 June), 65: 325–7, 496–8, 605–12 (19, 22, 25 July 1842).

107. Cobden to J. Sturge, 30 Mar. 1839, Howe, *Letters of Cobden,* I, pp 160–1.

108. *LT,* 27 Nov. 1841, Tyrell, *Sturge,* pp 119–21.

109. D. W. Bebbington, 'Miall, Edward (1809–1881)', *ODNB*; Anon., *The Rise and Progress of the Complete Suffrage Movement, Reprinted from the Eclectic Review* (London, 1843), pp 11–13; *Nonconformist,* 24 Nov. 1841.

110. *Nonconformist,* 12 Jan. 1842.

111. *MT,* 18 Dec. 1841; Tyrell, *Sturge,* pp 122–3.

112. *NS,* 19 Feb. 1842.

113. *MT,* 5 Mar. 1842. For Collins and Vincent, see Chase, *Chartism,* pp 194–5.

114. Chase, *Chartism,* p. 195.

115. *The Struggle,* 10 (1842). John Pearce (ed.), *The Life and Teachings of Joseph Livesey* (London, 1885), p. xlvii.

116. Joseph Sturge circular, 'Complete Suffrage', 17 Feb. 1842, in Collections dealing with political societies, 18th and 19th Centuries. Vol. III, British Library (BL), Add Ms 27,810, fol. 87.

117. John Belchem, *Popular Radicalism in Nineteenth-Century Britain* (Basingstoke, 1996), pp 83–5.

118. FOC to Irishmen of Glasgow, *NS,* 20 Nov. 1841.

119. FOC to the working classes, and none other, *NS,* 18 Dec. 1841.

120. *NS,* 19 Mar. 1842.

121. *MA,* 6 Apr. 1842.

122. *Rise and Progress of the Complete Suffrage Movement,* pp 15–18.

123. Anon, *Minutes of the Proceedings at the Conference of Representatives, of the Middle and Working Classes of Great Britain: Held at [...] Birmingham, April 5th, 1842, and Three Following Days* (Birmingham, 1842), pp 17–20.

124. Circular by Sturge, 11 Apr. 1842, in Collections dealing with political societies, BL, Add Ms 27,810, fol. 202.

125. In February, Livsey had made a 'very animated speech' at a mass meeting against the new sliding scale and an effigy Peel was burned at Rochdale, *MG,* 16 Feb. 1842.

126. *NS,* 16 Apr. 1842.

127. *Mr O'Brien's Vindication of his Conduct at the Late Birmingham Conference* (n.p., 1842), cited in Chase, *Chartism,* p. 200.

128. While popular with Irish Chartists, the inclusion of repeal was opposed by Lovett and leading Scottish Chartists, see Christine Kinealy, '"Brethren in bondage": Chartists, O'Connellites, Young Irelanders and the 1848 uprising', in D. Ó Drisceoil, and F. Lane (eds), *Politics and the Irish Working Class, 1830–1945* (Basingstoke, 2005), p. 89.

129. *NS,* 23 Apr. 1842.

130. *Hans 3,* 62: 907–21 (21 Apr.); *Nonconformist,* 27 Apr. 1842.

131. The *Freeman's Journal* (25 Apr. 1842) complained that 39 Irish 'Liberals' were absent without excuse at the division.

132. *MC,* 22 Apr. 1842.

133. *Times,* 23 Apr. 1842.

134. *DM,* 25 Apr., *NW,* 26 Apr. 1842.

135. *Hans 3,* 62: 1373–81 (2 May), 63: 13–88 (3 May 1842); Thompson, 'Ireland and the Irish', p. 134.

136. Chase, *Chartism,* pp 204–6.

137. *NS,* 21 May 1842.

138. Chase, *Chartism,* pp 208–9, *Hans 3,* 65: 861–3 (29 July 1842).

139. WSC to Sturge (17 May), *MT,* 28 May; *Hans 3,* 63: 986–9 (30 May 1842).

140. WSC to Sturge (31 May), *Nonconformist,* 8 June 1842.

141. Tyrell, *Sturge,* p. 126.

142. Chase, *Chartism,* pp 212–27.

143. Tyrell, *Sturge,* pp 128–9.

144. *Leicester Chronicle,* 4 June, *MT,* 6 Aug., *MCo,* 6 Aug., *NS,* 13, 27 Aug. 1842; Robertson, *Rochdale,* pp 21–3. For O'Brien's relationship with Crawford, see Michael J. Turner, 'Ireland and Irishness in the political thought of Bronterre O'Brien', *IHS,* 39:153 (2014), pp 40–57.

145. *Scotsman,* 1 Oct. 1842.

146. *Nonconformist,* 5 Oct. 1842.

147. Collins to Sturge (5 Oct.), *Nonconformist,* 12 Oct. 1842.

148. Hume to WSC, 19 Sept. 1842, PRONI, D856/D/62.

149. *NS,* 15 Oct. 1842.

150. *Nonconformist,* 19 Oct. 1842.

151. Anon, *Memoir of the Chartist Agitation in Dundee* (Dundee, 1889), pp 66–70.

152. WSC, *A Defence of the Rights of the Working Classes* (London, 1843), pp 19–24.

153. Ibid., pp 37–40.

154. WSC to Sturge (24 Dec.), *Times,* 29 Dec. 1842.

155. *Times,* 29 Dec. 1842, 2 Jan. 1843; Chase, *Chartism,* pp 226–9.

156. *MG,* 28 Jan., *NS,* 28 Jan. 1843.

157. *MT,* 24 June 1843.

158. Chase, *Chartism,* pp 236–40.

159. *LT,* 22 Apr., *Bradford Observer (BO),* 27 Apr., *NS,* 29 Apr. 1843.

160. *Times,* 28 June 1843.

161. William Cooper to unknown, 27 Jan. 1843, TNA, HO, O.S.433

162. *Hans 3,* 67: 1080–2 (17 Mar.), *LT,* 18 Mar.; WSC to Sturge (18 Mar), *BO,* 6 Apr. 1843.

163. *Hans 3,* 68: 531–8 (6 Apr.); *MC,* 6 Apr. 1843. For the wider context, see Peter Gray, '"Shovelling out your paupers": The British state and Irish Famine migration, 1846–50', in *Patterns of Prejudice,* 33 (1999), pp 47–65.

164. *LT,* 22 Apr., *NS,* 13 May 1843.

165. *Hans 3,* 69: 500–8 (18 May 1843).

166. Ibid., 69: 513–14, 521–3, 528–9 (18 May); WSC to the editor (19 May), *MC,* 20 May, Cobden to Sturge, *MT,* 27 May 1843.

167. *Hans 3,* 70: 157–9 (20 June 1843).

168. *NS,* 10 June, *Albion,* 1 May 1843.

169. *NS,* 5 Aug. 1843.

170. Cobden to Sturge, 28 Mar. 1843, Howe, *Letters of Cobden,* I, p. 318.

171. Tyrell, *Sturge*, pp 146–7.
172. WSC to Sturge (21 Sept.), *Times* 27 Sept. 1843.
173. WSC to Sturge (1 Dec.), *Cork Examiner (CE)*, 11 Dec. 1843.
174. *NS*, 28 Oct. 1843. O'Connell approved the strategy in an open letter to Sturge, *Times*, 31 Jan. 1844, although he had taken little interest in his previous overtures, Sturge to DOC, 16 Dec. 1841, O'Connell, *Correspondence*, VII, p. 128.
175. *BO*, 30 Nov. 1843; *MCo*, 21 Jan. 1844.
176. *CE*, 4 Dec., *MA*, 8 Dec. 1843.
177. WSC to Sturge (21 Nov.), *CE*, 1 Dec. 1843.
178. *Spectator*, 23 Dec., *NS*, 23 Dec. 1843, 27 Jan. 1844, *LT*, 27 Jan., *Nonconformist*, 3 Jan. 1844.
179. *MG*, 31 Jan. 1844.
180. *Hans 3*, 72: 79–139 (1 Feb. 1844). Cobden privately dismissed the new Sturge-Crawford project as surpassing his comprehension, Cobden to C. P. Villiers, [28 Jan. 1844], Howe, *Letters of Cobden*, I, pp 351–2.
181. *Economist*, 3 Feb. 1844.
182. *LT*, 3 Feb. 1844.
183. *BO*, 6 Feb. 1844.
184. *NS*, 10 Feb. 1844.
185. *Hans 3*, 72: 296–303 (6 Feb. 1844).
186. *Times*, 8 Feb., *MPo*, 9 Feb., *Scotsman*, 10 Feb. 1844.
187. *Nonconformist*, 24 Jan. 1844.
188. *LT*, 17 Feb., *BO*, 22 Feb., *Hans 3*, 72: 484 (10 Feb. 1844).
189. *Nonconformist*, 14 Feb. 1844.
190. *MG*, 24 Feb. 1844.
191. *MG*, 28 Feb., *NS*, 16 Mar. 1844. 'Shoy-hoy' was an obsolete term for scarecrow, originally used by William Cobbett to mock his political enemies.
192. *BO*, 29 Feb., *LT*, 2 Mar., *NS*, 2, 9 Mar., *Nonconformist*, 7 Feb. 1844.
193. WSC to the unenfranchised people of Great Britain and Ireland (9 Mar.), *NS*, 16 Mar. 1844.
194. *Nonconformist*, 6 Mar., *NS*, 16, 30 Mar. 1844.
195. *Spectator*, 6 Apr., *NT*, 4 Apr. 1844.
196. The statement on women is missing from the *Hansard* account (74: 1170–4, 14 May), but was included in the *Freeman's Journal* report of his speech (16 May 1844). Sturge also privately conceded that women should have the vote 'under some circumstances', Tyrell, *Sturge*, p. 108.
197. WSC to Sturge (17 May), *BO*, 30 May 1844.
198. *Hans 3*, 80: 894–6 (26 May 1845). His amendment was defeated by 253 to 33 votes.
199. Henry Richard, *Memoirs of Joseph Sturge* (London, 1864), pp 319–20.
200. *Nonconformist*, 11 Dec. 1844.
201. Portrait of William Sharman Crawford (1843) by John Prescott Knight, NMNI, BELUM U.4501.
202. Evans, *Lancashire Authors*, pp 76–80.
203. *NW*, 7 Sept. 1844.
204. Engraving with autograph of William Sharman Crawford (after T. G. Lupton), n.d., PRONI, T1129/411.
205. MacDonagh, *Emancipist*, p. 210.
206. Ibid., pp 220–1, 226–7.
207. WSC 'Observations addressed to the Repealers of Ireland' (14, 16, 25 Oct.), *Times*, 18, 22, 29 Oct., *Spectator*, 23 Oct.; Steele to DOC, 21, 23 Oct. 1841, O'Connell, *Correspondence*, VII, pp 122–4.
208. W. H. Dyott to the editor (16 Feb.), *FJ*, 22 Feb.; Patrick O'Higgins to Bishop Blake (6 Feb.), *NS*, 4 Mar. 1843.
209. *FJ*, 10 Apr.; *Hans 3*, 69: 1010–15 (29 May), *NW*, 6 June 1843.
210. John Lennon, 'The Repeal Grania-Uaile', in *The 'Irish Repealer's Mountain Harp,' of the Triumphant Year of 1843* (Dublin, 1843), pp 14–15.
211. *FJ*, 27 July 1843.
212. *Hans 3*, 69: 1010–15 (29 May), 70: 1359–60 (27 July 1843).
213. *NW*, 22 July 1843.
214. WSC to the editor of the Dublin Monitor (22 July), *FJ*, 27 July 1843.
215. DOC to WSC (28 July), *Nation*, 29 July 1843.

216. *Nation,* 5 Aug. 1843.

217. Davis to Smith O'Brien, n.d., NLI, Ms 432/887; C. G. Duffy, *Thomas Davis: The Memoirs of an Irish Patriot, 1840–46* (London, 1890), pp 249–50, 262–3.

218. WSC to DOC (1 Aug.), *FJ,* 7 Aug. 1843.

219. *NW,* 19 Oct. 1843

220. *Hans 3,* 72: 160–2 (2 Feb.), 73: 420–1 (29 Feb. 1844).

221. *CE,* 9 Aug. 1843.

222. Ross to editor of Vindicator (6 Nov.), *FJ,* 9 Nov.; Caulfeild to WSC (9 Dec.), *DM,* 27 Dec. 1843.

223. O'Malley to the editor, *FJ,* 7 Dec. 1843.

224. Miles Gerald Keon, *The Irish Revolution, or What can the Repealers do? And What Shall be the New Constitution?* (Dublin, 1843), pp 14–18.

225. *DM,* 30 Oct., *NW,* 12 Dec. 1843.

226. MacDonagh, *Emancipist,* pp 241–2.

227. *DM,* 8 Dec. 1843.

228. WSC, draft speech on federalism, n.d. [1843], PRONI, D856/D/77.

229. WSC, 'Federalism: observations addressed to the friends of political liberty in Ireland' (6 Jan.), *BNL,* 12 Jan. 1844.

230. *BNL,* 12, 26 Jan. 1844.

231. For its visual representation, see Peter Gray, '"Hints and hits": Irish caricature and the trial of Daniel O'Connell, 1843–4', *History Ireland,* 12:4 (2004), pp 45–51.

232. WSC to J. L. Arabin and J. O'Hea (16 Sept.), *DM,* 20 Sept. 1844.

233. *Times,* 23 Sept. 1844, John Grey V. Porter, *Agricultural and Political Irish Questions Calmly Discussed* (London, 1843). Porter was heir to the Belleisle estate in Fermanagh, Desmond McCabe, Sylvie Kleinman, 'Porter, John Grey Vesey', *DIB.*

234. John Grey V. Porter, *Ireland: The Union of 1801, 41 Geo. III., Cap. 47, (all on one side), Does and Always Will Draw Away from Ireland Her Men of Skill, … A Federal (the only Fair) Union Between Great Britain and Ireland Inevitable* (London, 1844). The pamphlet, which drew heavily on Crawford's 1833–4 publications but lacked their intellectual rigour, was pilloried in *NW,* 3 Oct. 1844.

235. J. Morgan O'Connell to DOC, 13 Sept., O'Connell, *Correspondence,* VII, pp 268–9.

236. [John Wilson Croker], 'Repeal agitation', *Quarterly Review,* 75 (Dec. 1844), pp 222–92.

237. DOC to Smith O'Brien, 1 Oct. 1844, in O'Connell, *Correspondence,* VII, p. 272.

238. *FJ,* 27 Sept., 17 Oct. 1844.

239. The list, prepared by W. E. Hudson, listed leading Catholic Whigs such as Thomas Wyse and the O'Conor Don, as well as future administrators William Somerville and Torrens McCullagh, Duffy, *Davis,* pp 256–7.

240. Robert Sloan, *William Smith O'Brien and the Young Ireland Rebellion of 1848* (Dublin, 2000), p. 118.

241. DOC to Ray (2 Oct.), *Tablet,* 19 Oct. 1844.

242. DOC to FitzPatrick, 8 Oct. 1844, O'Connell, *Correspondence,* VII, p. 275.

243. DOC to Ray (12 Oct.), *FJ,* 15 Oct. 1844.

244. DOC to FitzPatrick, 12 Oct., DOC to Maurice O'Connell, 17 Oct. 1844, O'Connell, *Correspondence,* VII, p. 276, p. 279.

245. Murphy had been a treasurer of the O'Connell testimonial fund in 1829 and aide to Lord Edward Fitzgerald in 1798, see Woods, 'Was O'Connell a United Irishman?', p. 182.

246. DOC to Smith O'Brien, 21 Oct., O'Connell, *Correspondence,* VII, pp 280–1. See also FitzPatrick to DOC, 26 Oct. 1844, ibid., p. 283.

247. 'The Irish provincial press on the federal movement', *DEP,* 22 Oct. 1844.

248. Duffy to DOC (11 Oct.), *CE,* 21 Oct. 1844.

249. C. G. Duffy, *Young Ireland: A Fragment of Irish History 1840–50* (London, 1880), pp 578–84; Richard Davis, *The Young Ireland Movement* (Dublin, 1987), pp 60–6.

250. W. J. O'Neill Daunt, *Letters … in Answer to Wm Sharman Crawford, Esq., on the Repeal of the Union* (Dublin, 1843); MacDonagh, *Emancipist,* pp 256–7.

251. DOC to FitzPatrick, 31 Oct., 2 Nov. 1844, O'Connell, *Correspondence,* VII, pp 288–9, 290–1.

252. DOC to O'Neill Daunt, 27 Oct. 1844, ibid., p. 283.

253. FitzPatrick to DOC, [c.4 Nov. 1844], ibid., p. 291; *NW,* 5 Nov. 1844. Crawford's reluctance to give ground on his position unless persuasive rebuttals were presented is suggested in WSC, Memorandum on his differences with other federalists [1844], PRONI, D856/D/79.

254. Ross to Davis, n.d. (Oct. 1844), Duffy, *Davis,* p. 250.

255. Ross to Davis, n.d. (Oct./Nov. 1844), ibid.

256. *NW,* 12, 13, 16, 19 Nov. 1844.

257. WSC, 'Local legislation for Ireland' (7 Nov.), *NW,* 12 Nov. 1844.

258. WSC to O'Brien. 18 Nov. 1844, cited in Duffy, *Young Ireland,* p. 595.

259. For his notes on American and Norwegian modes of governance, see WSC, Notebook and memoranda, 1835–1846, PRONI, D856/D/23.

260. WSC, Heads for the constitution of an Irish parliament, [1844], PRONI, D856/D/70; WSC, Memoranda containing heads of a bill for a federal union between Gt. Britain and Ireland formed on the model of the 1840 Canada Union Act [1844], D856/D/71; WSC, Heads of a plan for the imperial representation of Ireland under a federal system, [1844], D856/D/72.

261. *Nonconformist,* 5 Oct. 1842.

262. WSC, Heads of a plan [1844], PRONI, D856/D/72.

263. WSC, Notes for a speech on federalism [Nov. 1844], PRONI, D856/D/73.

264. WSC 'On local legislation for Ireland', III (11 Nov.), *NW,* 16 Nov. 1844.

265. WSC, 'Local legislation for Ireland', IV (12 Nov.), *NW,* 19 Nov. 1844.

266. DOC to Ray (8 Nov.), *NW,* 14 Nov. 1844.

267. [W. Nassau Senior], 'Ireland', *Edinburgh Review,* 79 (Jan. 1844), 259–61; Russell to Leinster, 13 Sept. 1844, Russell Papers, TNA, PRO30/22/4, Kevin B. Nowlan, *The Politics of Repeal: A Study in the Relations between Great Britain and Ireland, 1841–50* (London, 1965), pp 73–4.

268. *MC,* 12 Nov. 1844.

269. Francis Wyse, *Federalism. Its Inapplicability to the Wants and Necessities of the Country; Its Assumed Impracticability Considered* (Dublin, 1844).

270. *BOU,* 15 Nov. 1844.

271. *NW,* 14 Nov. 1844.

272. *Nation,* 2, 9 Nov. 1844.

273. Duffy, *Young Ireland,* p. 594.

274. *DM,* 18 Nov. 1844.

275. *CE,* 20 Nov. 1844.

276. *FJ,* 27 Nov. 1844.

277. *NW,* 30 Nov.; Davis to O'Brien [Nov. 1844], cited in Duffy, *Young Ireland,* pp 615–16.

278. Duffy, *Young Ireland,* pp 600–1.

279. Davis to Tennent, 4 June 1845, PRONI, D1748/G/141/4.

280. Nowlan, *Politics of Repeal,* pp 60–1, 71–2.

281. HB (John Doyle), 'HB Sketches No. 822. Dropping it like a Red-Hot Poker!' (London, 1844).

282. *MPo,* 21 Jan. 1845.

283. *DM,* 20 Nov. 1844. Duffy claimed to have tried, without success, to assist the federalists in establishing their own paper in 1844, *Young Ireland,* p. 579.

284. *Spectator,* 1 Nov., *Nonconformist,* 13, 20 Nov., *NS,* 16 Nov., 7 Dec. 1844.

285. *NW,* 19 Nov. 1844.

286. Cited in Duffy, *Young Ireland,* p. 589; Nowlan, *Politics of Repeal,* pp 76–7.

287. WSC to Smith O'Brien, 8 Sept. 1847, in Brian Kennedy (ed.), 'Select document: Sharman Crawford on repeal, 1847', *IHS,* 6:24 (1947), pp 270–3.

288. *NW,* 16, 20 Nov. 1847; Kennedy, 'Sharman Crawford', p. 321a.

289. WSC to Maginn (9 May 1848), *Irishman,* 11 July 1874.

290. Petition of the Lurgan Tenant Right Association, and response from WSC (28 Apr.), *Pilot,* 1 May 1848.

291. *Pilot,* 10 May, *FJ,* 11 May 1848.

292. *Pilot,* 14 July, *BNL,* 21 Jul, *Belfast Protestant Journal (BPJ),* 22 July 1848.

293. Curran, *Rise and Fall of the Orange Order,* pp 150–3.

294. WSC to J. W. Beck (15 July), *BNL,* 21 July 1848.

295. W. J. O'Neill Daunt, *Ireland and her Agitators* (new edn, Dublin, 1867), p. 169.

296. Frank Wright, *Two Lands on One Soil: Ulster Politics Before Home Rule* (Dublin, 1996), pp 141–50.

297. *First General Report of the Society for Promoting Annual Sessions of the Imperial Parliament in Dublin for the Transaction of Irish Business* (Dublin, 1848).

298. *DEP,* 16 Sept., 21 Nov., *NW,* 21 Sept. 1848.

299. *FJ,* 18 Nov., *DEP,* 19 Dec. 1848, WSC to Lord Massereene (5 Feb.), *NW,* 15 Feb. 1851, Massereene to WSC, *CE,* 11 May 1855.

300. WSC to secretary of Anti-Centralization Association (22 Jan.), *DEPa,* 25 Jan., *FJ,* 28 Jan. 1851. For the context, see Peter Gray, "'Ireland's last fetter struck off": the lord lieutenancy debate 1800-67', in T. McDonough (ed.), *Was Ireland a Colony?* (Dublin, 2005), pp 87–101.

301. WSC to Massereene (12 May), *BN,* 18 May 1855.

302. Kennedy, 'Sharman Crawford's federal scheme for Ireland', pp 235–54.

303. John Kendle, *Ireland and the Federal Solution: The Debate over the United Kingdom Constitution, 1870–1921* (Kingston and Montreal, 1989), pp 8–31; Colin W. Reid, "'An experiment in constructive unionism": Isaac Butt, Home Rule and federalist political thought during the 1870s', *English Historical Review,* 129:537 (2014), pp 332–61.

304. *Irishman,* 11 July 1874.

305. *MT,* 27 May 1843.

306. J. E. N. Molesworth, *The Rochdale Magistracy. Copy of a Letter Extracted from the 'Manchester Courier', January 8th, 1842, from the Rev. J.E.N. Molesworth, D.D. Vicar of Rochdale, to Clement Royds, Esq. Senior Magistrate* (Rochdale, 1842).

307. *FJ,* 14 Mar. 1844. He presented a Rochdale petition against capital punishment in 1846, *MA,* 20 June 1846.

308. *FJ,* 16 Mar., *NT,* 16 Mar., *Warder,* 23 Mar. 1844.

309. *Times,* 1 May 1844.

310. *MCo,* 30 June 1847.

311. *Hans 3,* 79: 939–41 (18 Apr.), 80: 186–8 (5 May 1845), 82: 1236, 1260–1 (30 July 1845).

312. *FJ,* 8 May, *LT,* 10 May, 7 June 1845.

313. *MG,* 3 Dec. 1845.

314. WSC to Livsey (14 Dec.), *MT,* 21 Dec. 1850.

315. *MG,* 4 Mar., *BNL,* 7 Mar. 1851.

316. *Hans 3,* 117: 1022–59 (20 June 1851).

317. [J. E. N. Molesworth], *Correspondence Between Wm Sharman Crawford, Esq., MP for Rochdale, and Rev. Dr Molesworth, Vicar of the Same, on the Papal Aggression, and on the Spiritual Liberties and Temporal Rights of the Established Church* (London, 1851).

318. *MCo,* 15 Mar. 1851.

319. *MG,* 1 May 1844.

320. *MC,* 4 May 1844.

321. *Hans 3,* 83: 416 (29 Jan. 1846).

322. *BV,* 22 Apr. 1846.

323. *Hans 3,* 86: 516–20 (13 May 1846).

324. *NS,* 6 Feb., *Hans 3,* 90: 135–6 (17 Feb. 1847).

325. For Ross's opposition, see Wright, *Two Lands,* pp 106–7.

326. *Pilot* (Rochdale), 3, 13 Mar. 1847, p. 17.

327. *Hans 3,* 91: 1124 (21 Apr. 1847), 111: 845, 1234–6 (6, 14 June 1850), *ES,* 9 Aug. 1849.

328. *Hans 3,* 66: 1239–43 (23 Feb. 1843), 76: 366–9 (4 July 1844); Graham to WSC, 25 Mar. 1844, PRONI, D856/D/67. *Hans 3,* 81: 408–12, 1448–51 (12 June, 3 July 1845).

329. Graham to WSC, 23 Oct., PRONI, D856/D/69, *LT,* 26 Oct. 1844.

330. *MCo,* 2 Nov. Livsey was supported by a petition signed by over 11,000 ratepayers, *Times,* 11 Nov. 1844.

331. *MCo,* 23 Nov. 1844; *EM,* 13 Jan. 1845.

332. *Hans 3,* 77: 216–18, 78: 694–708 (7 Feb., 11 Mar. 1845).

333. Garrard, *Leadership and Power,* pp 150–1.

334. Ibid., p. 152–3, *MG,* 3 Dec. 1845.

335. *Times,* 26 Apr., *MCo,* 28 Apr. 1847.

336. *MG,* 25 Sept., 2 Oct. 1847. Although absent from the Rochdale inquiry, Crawford was acutely aware of the anger such cases provoked in Ireland; the death in Newtownards workhouse that month

of a seasonal labourer 'returned' from Scotland in a state of fever drew attention in the press, see *DEP,* 9 Sept. 1847.

337. *FJ,* 8 Nov. 1847.

338. *English Gentleman,* 31 May 1845.

339. *NS,* 19 Sept. 1846.

340. *MT,* 10 July 1846.

341. *NS,* 18 Feb. 1846.

342. Holyoake had sought to appropriate Crawford's small-farm plan as part of a co-operative alternative to what he saw as the self-defeating operation of trade unions, G. J. Holyoake, *The Advantages and Disadvantages of Trade Unions* (Sheffield, [1841]).

343. Pickering, *O'Connor,* pp 105–9, 121.

344. Ibid., pp 124–6.

345. Chase, *Chartism,* pp 247–61, 277–9.

346. Feargus O'Connor, *A Practical Work on the Management of Small Farms* (5th edn, Manchester, 1847), pp 117–20.

347. *NS,* 19 Feb., 17 June 1848.

348. Chase, *Chartism,* pp 327–9.

349. *NS* 5, 12 Aug., 11 Nov. 1848, 22 Dec. 1849.

350. WSC to the secretary of the Rochdale Freehold Land Society, *MT,* 5 Feb. 1851.

351. Pickering, *O'Connor,* pp 143–7.

352. *NS,* 19, 26 Apr. 1851.

353. Ibid., 4 Jan. 1851.

354. *MT,* 10 July 1847.

355. Chase, *Chartism,* pp 280–5.

356. *Pilot,* 7, 14 July 1847, p. 50.

357. *LM,* 29 May 1847.

358. *MT,* 25 June, *MG,* 24 July, WSC's reply to the requisition of the electors of Rochdale, 24 July 1847, PRONI, D856/D/90.

359. *MCo,* 31 July 1847.

360. *Observer,* 9 Apr., *ES,* 10 Apr., *Hans 3,* 98: cols 119–20 (10 Apr. 1848).

361. [R. J. Richardson], *New Movement: Household Suffrage, Triennial Parliaments, Vote by Ballot, No Property Qualification, and Equal Electoral Districts* (Manchester, 1848).

362. *Hans 3,* 106: 1287–8 (3 July 1849).

363. Kinealy, 'Brethren in bondage', pp 94–103.

364. *UI,* 4 Mar. 1848; John Belchem, '1848: Feargus O'Connor and the collapse of the mass platform', in Epstein and Thompson (eds), *Chartist Experience,* pp 269–310.

365. Ibid.

366. *NS,* 6 May 1848, 5 May 1849.

367. Handbill 'The reform meeting held at the public hall, Rochdale' (1848), Local Studies Centre, Touchstones Rochdale, website, https://www.link4life.org/discover/local-history-online/riots-radicalism/chartists/reform-meeting-rhym (acc. 12 Mar. 2016).

368. *MC,* 25 May 1848; Anon., *Plan of Organization of the People's League* (London, 1848).

369. *Hans 3,* 116: 943 (14 May 1851).

370. Pickering, *O'Connor,* pp 151–4.

371. *FJ,* 21 Nov. 1848, *MCo,* 14 Feb. 1849. In 1849 he supported a bill for triennial parliaments, while voicing his preference for annual elections, *Hans 3,* 105: 869–70 (22 May 1849).

372. *NS,* 20 Apr. 1850; *MG,* 5 May, 6 Dec. 1851.

373. WSC to secretary of Lancashire Public Schools Association, 26 Jan., 7 Mar. 1849, Manchester Archives, LPSA papers, M136/2/3/726, 728.

374. *Leader,* 13 Dec. 1851.

375. *Daily News (DN),* 5 Oct. 1855, *Rochdale Observer (RO),* 1 Aug. 1857, 8 May 1858.

376. *RO,* 18 May, 18, 25 June, 20 Aug. 1859, WSC, *The Non-Elector's Plea for the Suffrage: Addressed to the Non-Electors of Rochdale ... Containing an Abstract of his Speech of 1843, in Moving the Reform Bill of the Complete Suffrage Association* (Rochdale, [1859]).

NOTES TO CHAPTER 5

1. WSC to Mrs Crawford, 22 Feb. 1827, PRONI, D856/A/5/4.

2. Johnstone, a Presbyterian elder, was appointed in 1816 and remained in post for over 30 years, *DR,* 16 May 1846, *BOU,* 19 Jan. 1864; for Bellew, see *BCC,* 5 Oct. 1839.

3. Arminella SC to John SC, Feb. 1836, PRONI, D856/F/45.

4. Address to WSC, from the tenantry on his Redemon [sic] estate (14 Feb.), WSC to Robert Martin (24 Feb.), *NW,* 6 Apr. 1835.

5. WSC to Rademon tenants (2 Jan.); Resolution of Rademon tenants (10 Jan.), *BNL,* 17 Jan. 1843.

6. *NW,* 13 Apr. 1835.

7. *BNL,* 12 Feb. 1828, 27 Feb. 1829, 14 Aug. 1832.

8. *BCC,* 30 Jan. 1841.

9. WSC to Andrews, *NW,* 12 Apr. 1860.

10. *Report of Her Majesty's Commissioners of Enquiry into the State of the Law and Practice in Respect to the Occupation of Land in Ireland (Devon Commission), Minutes of Evidence, Part I,* HC1845 [605-6] XIX, p. 196 (WSC, 11 Jan. 1844); WSC to Rademon tenants (2 Jan.), *BNL,* 17 Jan. 1843.

11. *BNL,* 1 Dec. 1837; for an example of a three-life lease granted in 1798 by Arthur Johnston, see Lease for three lives of James Bingham, 7 Nov. 1798, PRONI, D556/64; P. Roebuck, 'Rent movement, proprietorial incomes and agricultural development, 1730–1830', in Roebuck (ed.), *Plantation to Partition* (Belfast, 1981), pp 84–5.

12. *NW,* 27 Sept. 1859.

13. *Devon Commission, Part I,* p. 196. In Co. Down the 'Scotch' or 'Cunningham' acre was generally used, an intermediate measure between the larger Irish and the statute acre, and amounting to 1.29 statute acres in area.

14. 'Corporation of Killileagh', *NW,* 27 May 1833.

15. *Poor Inquiry Commission, First Report, Appendix (F),* HC1836 [38], XXXII, p. 314.

16. W. A. Maguire, *The Downshire Estates in Ireland 1801–1845* (Oxford, 1972), p. 39.

17. WSC to John Revans (Dec. 1833), *Poor Inquiry Commission, First Report, Appendix (C), Part II,* HC1836 [35], XXX, pp 30c–31c.

18. WSC to Daniel Cavit, 23 Mar. 1838, PRONI, D856/B/6/1. 'Mere cottiers' were excluded from this arrangement, with Crawford planning to examine their situation personally at his next visit.

19. *Griffiths Valuation,* Lackan, parish of Drumballyroney.

20. Fr John S. Keenan to WSC, 25 June 1838, PRONI, D856/B/6/1.

21. *NW,* 22 June 1839. For Crawford's praise of Fr Keenan as a pastor to his flock, see WSC to Keenan (21 Sept.), *DM,* 30 Sept. 1844.

22. Memo on Lacken tenants who did not pay, June 1844, PRONI, D856/B/6/1.

23. *Devon Commission, Minutes of Evidence, Part I,* HC1845 [605-6] XIX, p. 197 (11 Jan. 1844).

24. Timothy W. Guinnane and Ronald I. Miller, 'Bonds without bondsmen: tenant-right in nineteenth-century Ireland', *Journal of Economic History,* 56:1 (1996), p. 120; Maguire, *Downshire Estates,* pp 138–47.

25. Jonathan Binns, *The Miseries and Beauties of Ireland* (2 vols, London, 1837), I, pp 59–60, 84–5.

26. William Barron to WSC, 5 Mar. 1849, PRONI, D856/C/6/8.

27. Thompson, *End of Liberal Ulster,* pp 35–8.

28. Mabel SC to John SC, 10 Nov. 1835, PRONI, D856/D/41.

29. Mabel SC to John SC, 3 Dec. 1835, PRONI, D856/D/43.

30. WSC to John SC, 5 June 1835, PRONI, D856/D/30, *NW,* 13 Sept. 1845, *BOU,* 10 Sept. 1859.

31. *NW,* 12 Nov. 1842; *Coleraine Chronicle (CC),* 22 Apr. 1848, *NT,* 7 Oct. 1854.

32. *BCC,* 25 Nov. 1854.

33. *FJ,* 13 May 1829.

34. *First Report of the Royal Agricultural Improvement Society of Ireland* (Dublin, 1841).

35. Thomas Campbell Foster, *Letters on the Condition of the People of Ireland* (London, 1846), pp 234–7.

36. *MR,* 20 Feb. 1841, *Belfast Mercury (BM),* 2 Sept. 1854.

37. James Mitchell, 'Thomas Skilling (1793–1865) Professor of Agriculture Queen's College, Galway: part 1: his career to 1849', *Journal of the Galway Archaeological and Historical Society,* 57 (2005), pp 65–89; Crawford was acquainted with Wallscourt, who sought to replicate the Ralahine

experiment in co-operation on his own estates, R. J. Tennent to Eliza Tennent, 16 Mar. 1848, PRONI, D1748/H/56/149.

38. *BNL,* 16 Aug. 1844.

39. *NW,* 3 Aug. 1841, *BNL,* 12 Aug. 1842.

40. *Poor Inquiry Commission, First Report, Supplement to Appendix (D),* HC1836 [36], XXXI, p. 220.

41. *FJ,* 29 Sept. 1851.

42. *Poor Inquiry Commission, First Report, Appendix (F),* HC1836 [38], XXXII, pp 126–8.

43. WSC to the tenantry of the Rademon estate (17 Aug.), *NW,* 20 Aug. 1842.

44. WSC, Draft for a private agreement between landlord and tenant re compensation for improvements in the case of the eviction of tenants holding from year to year, or at will or by determinable tenure, n.d. (1846), PRONI, D856/D/86.

45. WSC to the tenants on his estates, 25 Dec. 1846, PRONI, D856/D/85.

46. Peel to WSC, 16 Jan. 1847, PRONI, D856/D/87.

47. WSC to his tenants (12 Dec. 1846), *BCC,* 13 Jan. 1847.

48. Guinnane and Miller, 'Bonds without bondsmen', pp 113–42.

49. Arthur SC to Thomas Barron, 11 Jan. 1850, PRONI, D856/C/6/8. Two other families were also assisted to emigrate from Stalleen, Arthur SC to WSC, (Jan. 1850), ibid. D856/C/6/10.

50. Some complainants on the Banbridge estate blamed James for failing to comply with his father's previous valuations for rent, see letters of John McMahon, Joseph McKibbin, Archibald Dickson and Elizabeth Corbett, 12–15 Jan. 1850, PRONI, D856/B/6/12.

51. WSC to James SC (Dec. 1849), PRONI, D856/A/6/10.

52. Printed circular: To the tenants on Mr Sharman Crawford's estates in the county of Down, 28 Dec. 1849, PRONI, D856/A/6/9.

53. WSC, Agreement with Co. Down tenants, 28 Dec. 1849, PRONI, D856/A/6/9.

54. *BOU,* 1, 8 Jan., *FJ,* 3 Jan. 1850.

55. WSC to James SC, 4 Jan. 1850, PRONI, D856/A/6/10.

56. Address to WSC (4 Apr.), *NW,* 9 Apr. 1850.

57. *BOU,* 9 Apr. 1850.

58. Rev. William Dobbin to the editor, *BOU,* 26 Feb. 1850.

59. *DEP,* 16 Mar. 1850.

60. John Lamb, 'Notes on the state of the country, no. 35', *NW,* 18 July 1850.

61. *NW,* 19 Jan. 1856.

62. WSC circular, 1 Jan., repr. in *BOU,* 20 Jan. 1852.

63. WSC, 'Sample notice to the tenants of the Crawford estate who are in arrears', 15 Mar. 1852, PRONI, D856/A/6/13.

64. *Ulster Gazette,* 17 Jan., *NW,* 15 Jan. 1852.

65. *LS,* 28 Feb., *Dundalk Democrat,* 26 Jan., *BNL,* 3 Mar. 1856.

66. Hoppen, *Elections,* pp 112–13.

67. See for example the praise of the 'Times commissioner' Thomas Campbell Foster, who visited Crawfordsburn in 1846, *Letters,* p. 580.

68. *Cork Constitution (CCo),* 4 Mar. 1851.

69. In 1876 Arthur's eldest son William Henry was listed as resident at Lakelands, Cork, and as holding 189 acres in the county, Hussey de Burgh, *Owners of Estates.*

70. *NW,* 2 Apr. 1835.

71. *NW,* 18 May 1835.

72. *Hans 3,* 29: 218–20 (2 July 1835).

73. *A Bill for the Amendment of the Law of Landlord and Tenant in Ireland,* HC1835 (402), III, p. 229.

74. WSC to John SC, 31 July 1835, PRONI, D856/D/36.

75. *Hans 3,* 29: 218–20 (2 July); *Times,* quoted in *NW,* 6 Aug. 1835.

76. Kingon, 'Ulster Protestant politics', pp 20–2.

77. *Evening Standard (ES),* 12 Sept. 1835.

78. *BNL,* 11 Aug. 1835.

79. James McKnight, 'The Ulster tenant-right custom: its origins, essence and legalized development', *Ulster Examiner,* 21 Jan. 1874; Thompson, *End of Liberal Ulster,* p. 40.

80. *Devon Commission, Part I,* pp 270–5.

81. WSC to the editor (26 Jan.), *NW,* 28 Jan. 1836.

82. *NW,* 22 Oct. 1835.

83. Guy Stone's diary, 17 Nov. 1835, PRONI, D826/2/1, Tennent to Stone, 7 Jan. 1835, PRONI, D1748/G/635.

84. *Connaught Telegraph,* 2, 9 Dec. 1835, see also MacHale to Russell, 26 July 1835, *The Letters of the Most Reverend John MacHale* (Dublin, 1847), p. 366.

85. WSC to Dr Mullen (14 May), *NW,* 30 May 1836.

86. *NW,* 3 Mar. 1836.

87. *A Bill for the Amendment of the Law of Landlord and Tenant in Ireland,* HC1836 (142) IV, p. 303; *Hans 3,* 32: 183–7 (10 Mar. 1836).

88. *Hans 3,* 32: 187–9 (10 Mar. 1836).

89. *MA,* 16 Mar. 1836.

90. *MR,* 11 Apr. 1836.

91. *DEP,* 16 Apr. 1836.

92. *NW,* 22, 24 Dec., Guy Stone's diary, 22 Dec. 1836, PRONI, D826/2/1.

93. WSC to Robert Dixon (12 July), *MR,* 22 July 1837.

94. Anon., *Our Natural Rights: A Pamphlet for the People. By One of Themselves. Dedicated to William Sharman Crawford* (Belfast, 1836).

95. WSC, *Observations on the Necessity of an Amendment in the Laws of Landlord and Tenant, in Conjunction with a Total Repeal of the Duties on Foreign Corn* (Belfast, 1837).

96. *NW,* 21, 23 Nov. 1837.

97. WSC, *Observations,* p. 7.

98. Ibid., pp 27–32.

99. Ibid., p. 43.

100. Ibid., p. 48.

101. WSC to the editor of the *Wexford Independent* (30 Nov.), *MR,* 8 Dec. 1837.

102. *WI,* 23 Dec. 1837.

103. *FJ,* 23 Sept. 1839; WSC, *A Defence of the Small Farmers of Ireland* (Dublin, 1839).

104. *Southern Australian,* 30 Apr. 1840.

105. Gray, *Making of the Irish Poor Law,* pp 48–9, 127, 269.

106. G. Poulett Scrope, *Plan of a Poor-Law for Ireland, with a Review of the Arguments For and Against it* (London, 1834), John Revans, *Evils of the State of Ireland: Their Causes and Remedy–a Poor Law* (London, 1837), Thaddeus O'Malley, *An Idea of a Poor Law for Ireland.* (London, 1837).

107. Peter Gray, 'Nassau Senior, the *Edinburgh Review,* and Ireland 1843–1849', in T. Foley and S. Ryder (eds), *Ideology and Ireland in the Nineteenth Century* (Dublin, 1998), pp 130–42.

108. WSC, *Defence,* pp 25–6.

109. Ibid., pp 82–5. For his critique of the conacre system of the letting of half-acre plots of manured potato grounds to labourers at extortionate rents, see *Hans 3.,* 78: 317–18 (4 Mar. 1845).

110. WSC, *Defence,* pp 79–81.

111. Ibid., p. 93.

112. James McKnight, *The Ulster Tenant's Claim of Right, or Land Ownership a State Trust* (Dublin, 1848).

113. Thompson, *End of Liberal Ulster,* p. 38; Martin W. Dowling, *Tenant Right and Agrarian Society in Ulster, 1600–1850* (Dublin, 1998).

114. Torrens to WSC (5 Oct.), *NW,* 19 Oct., Cloncurry to the editor of the *DEP* (16 Oct.), *NW,* 19 Oct. 1839.

115. *MC* quoted in *NW,* 12 Oct. 1839.

116. WSC, 'Retrospective memorandum' [c.1844], PRONI, D868/D/1.

117. *MR,* 17 Apr. 1841.

118. *BV,* 3 Apr. 1841.

119. WSC to Ray (4 Apr.), *DEPa,* 6 Apr. 1841.

120. *FJ,* 2 Feb. 1842.

121. WSC, 'Address to the tenantry of Ireland' (20 Jan.), *FJ,* 26 Jan. The *Cork Examiner* (28 Jan.) thought the bill 'tolerably fair', but not radical enough to meet fully the agrarian crisis, *FJ,* 2 Feb. 1842.

122. Anon., *Cases of Tenant Eviction: From 1840 to 1846, Extracted from the Public Journals* (n.p., n.d.); Peter Gray, *Famine, Land and Politics: British Government and Irish Society 1843–50* (Dublin, 1999), pp 43–49.

123. For Conner's position, see his *The True Political Economy of Ireland: Or Rack-Rent, the One Great Cause of her Evils, with its Remedy* (Dublin, 1835), and R. D. Collison Black, *Economic Thought and the Irish Question, 1817–70* (Cambridge, 1960), pp 24–6.

124. *Nation,* 15 Apr. 1843.

125. *Nation,* 10 June, 19 Aug. 1843.

126. *FJ,* 10 Apr. 1843.

127. Conner to WSC, *FJ,* 29 Jan. 1842.

128. Conner to WSC, *MR,* 11 Feb., *FJ,* 24 Feb. 1842.

129. Conner was a Protestant small landowner in Kildare and Queen's County, a stump orator and previously a supporter of the evangelical 'second Reformation', Patrick Maume, 'Conner, William', *DIB.*

130. WSC, 'Observations addressed to the English people, and more especially to English Members of Parliament, on the state of Ireland' (7 June), *FJ,* 14 June 1843.

131. *Hans 3,* 70: 943–4 (11 July 1843)

132. Ibid., 630–77 (4 July 1843).

133. *BNL,* 9 June, *DEM,* 2 Aug. 1843.

134. *Hans 3,* 70: 15–16 (16 June), 71: 412–18 (9 Aug. 1843). WSC to Peel, 8 July, 5 Aug. 1843, BL, Peel Papers, Add. MS 40,531, fols. 14–15, 18–19; *Bill to Amend the Law of Landlord and Tenant in Ireland,* HC1843 (490), III, p. 233.

135. *FJ,* 10 Aug. 1843.

136. *Hans 3,* 71: 418–20 (9 Aug. 1843).

137. Gray, *Famine, Land and Politics,* pp 54–8.

138. *Devon Commission, Part 1,* pp 191–9, 208–13 (11–12 Jan. 1844).

139. Ibid., pp 14–18, 69–71.

140. Downshire to W. E. Reilly, [6 Oct. 1839], in Maguire, *Letters of a Great Irish Landlord,* p. 153; Maguire, *Downshire Estates,* pp 146–7.

141. *NW,* 12 Apr. For the protest meetings, *NW,* 5 Apr., *BOU,* 11 Apr. 1845.

142. W. Neilson Hancock, *The Tenant-Right of Ulster Considered Economically* (Dublin, 1845), pp 51–4.

143. WSC to editor of *BOU* (29 Mar.), *BV,* 2 Apr., *BOU,* 11 Apr. 1845.

144. *MC,* 11 June 1845.

145. *BOU,* 17 June, *FJ,* 1 July 1845.

146. *BV,* 22 Mar. 1845.

147. Peel to WSC, 9 July 1845, PRONI, D856/D/81; *Bill to Provide Compensation for Tenants in Ireland who Have Made, or Shall Hereafter Make Improvements on the Premises in the Occupation of such Tenants,* HC1845 (578), VI. p. 177.

148. *FJ,* 14 Apr., *BV,* 9 Aug., 'Meeting of tenants at Killyleagh', *BNL,* 25 July 1845.

149. WSC to editor of *LS, Times,* 24 Nov. 1845.

150. Brian Walker, 'Politicians, elections and catastrophe: the general election of 1847', *Irish Political Studies,* 22:1 (2007), pp 1–34.

151. S. J. Connolly, The great famine and Irish politics', in Cathal Póirtéir, ed., *The Great Irish Famine* (Cork, 1995), pp 34–49.

152. See for example WSC to O'Brien, 11 Apr. 1846, NLI, MS 436/1545.

153. *Spectator,* 20 Feb. 1847.

154. *FJ,* 23 Apr. 1847.

155. WSC to E. S. Monck, W. Mansell, R. Burke and C. M. O'Loghlin (9 Jan.), *NW,* 16 Jan. 1847.

156. Stone to Relief Commissioners, 17 Feb., NAI, RLFC/3/2/8/4; Newtownards Board of Guardians (BOG) minutes, 3 Mar. 1847, PRONI, BG25/A/1, p. 158.

157. *DR,* 17 Oct. 1846.

158. *DR,* 26 Sept., 14 Nov. 1846, 20 Feb. 1847; *BCC,* 11 Jan., 29 Mar. 1847; *NE,* 3 July 1847; Manager's notebook of James SC, 1846–50, PRONI, D856/C/6/7.

159. Charles had previously acted as returning officer for elections of guardians in several unions, see *FJ,* 4 Apr. 1845, *NE,* 25 July 1846, *MG,* 6 Feb. 1847.

160. *BCC,* 12 Dec. 1846, *BOU,* 18 July 1848, *NW,* 19 Dec. 1850. The Ladies Association was also instrumental in establishing an Industrial School in 1847, in the direction of which Mary Ann McCracken played a leading role, Mary O'Neill, *The Life and Times of Mary Ann McCracken 1770–1866* (new edn, Newbridge, 2019), pp 280–1.

161. WSC to his tenants, *BCC*, 13 Jan. 1847.

162. *BV,* 24 Feb. 1847.

163. *Poor Inquiry Commission, First Report, Appendix (F),* HC1836 [38], XXXII, pp 31–2, 74–5; see also Binns, *Miseries and Beauties,* I, pp 38–56.

164. *Hans 3,* 83: 162–3 (23 Jan. 1846).

165. Ibid., 420 (29 Jan.), 727–9 (11 Feb. 1846).

166. *Hans 3,* 86: 446–9 (12 May 1846).

167. *NT,* 27 Jan. 1846.

168. Newtownards BOG minutes, 19 Aug. 1846, PRONI, BG25/A/1, p. 63.

169. James Grant, 'The Great Famine in County Down', in L. Proudfoot (ed.), *Down History and Society* (Dublin, 1997), pp 353–82. All of Crawford's Upper Iveagh holdings fell in the Banbridge union; the Rademon estate townlands were in Downpatrick union.

170. George Robinson, secretary, forwarding certified statement by James Acheson, member of BOG, Banbridge Union, 9 Feb. 1847, Famine Commission Papers, NAI, RLFC/3/2/8/41.

171. Rev. J. R. Moore to unknown, 26 Apr. 1847, 'Letter book for Earl Annesley's affairs' (1846–51), PRONI, D1854/6/3.

172. Downpatrick Union was issuing 2,899 daily rations (and selling 978 at cost price) at the same time, although Newtownards opted out of the government scheme and relied on its own resources, *Fifth, Sixth, and Seventh Reports of the Relief Commissioners, Constituted under the Act 10th Vic., Cap. 7,* HC1847–8 (876), XXIX, pp 7–8.

173. *Census of Ireland for the Year 1861, Part I, Vol. III,* HC1863 [3204], LV, pp 167–77.

174. Cited in *NW,* 10 Nov. 1846.

175. Unknown to Arthur SC, 14 July 1850, PRONI, D856/C/6/9. The outcomes for these cottiers is unclear, although the estate records express concern at the fate of one orphan girl, left destitute by the death of her relatives, who was sent to the workhouse.

176. *Census of Ireland for the Year 1861, Part I, Vol. I,* HC1863 [3204], LIV, p. 195.

177. Andrews to Londonderry, 18 Jan., 5 Feb. 1847, Durham County Record Office (DCRO), D/Lo/C/512(5)(9).

178. For the promotion of consolidation on his Magherafelt estate, which was more badly affected by famine, see A. Spotswood to Londonderry, 19 Apr. 1847, DCRO, D/Lo/C/519(6)(i).

179. *LS,* 29 Jan., *BOU,* 16 Feb. 1847.

180. Newtownards BOG minutes, 23 Dec. 1846, 17 Feb. 1847. PRONI, BG25/A/1, pp 119–21, 149.

181. Newtownards BOG minutes, 21 July 1847, PRONI, BG25/A/1, pp 236–7.

182. Wright, *Two Lands on One Soil,* pp 115–16.

183. *Hans 3,* 89: 195–8 (20 Jan. 1847), see also WSC testimony in *Report from the Select Committee of the House of Lords on the Laws Relating to the Relief of the Destitute Poor,* HC1846 (694), XI, pp 387–406 (17 Mar. 1846).

184. Newtownards BOG minutes, 21, 28 July, 1 Sept. 1847, PRONI, BG25/A/1, pp 238–9, 241, 265–9.

185. *BCC,* 25 Oct., 10 Nov. 1847.

186. Newtownards BOG minutes, 8, 29 Sept. 1847, PRONI, BG25/A/1, pp 272, 281–3.

187. Trevor McCavery, *Newtown: A History of Newtownards* (Belfast, 2013), pp 122–5.

188. Newtownards BOG minutes, 1 Dec. 1847, PRONI, BG25/A/1, pp 328–31.

189. Ibid., 5 Jan., 5 Apr. 1848, p. 349, p. 396.

190. *Return of the Expenditure of Poor Rates in Each Union in Ireland, for the Year Ended 29th September 1849; and of the Number of Persons Relieved in and out of the Workhouse in Each Union During the Same Period,* HC1850 (313), L, p. 3.

191. *DR,* 16 Oct. 1847, Banbridge BOG Minute Book, PRONI, BG/6/A/7 (27 Nov., 18 Dec. 1847, 8 Jan. 1848).

192. *NW,* 4 Nov. 1845.

193. *BNL,* 25 Dec. 1846; *NW,* 26 Dec. 1846; *FJ,* 8 Jan. 1847.

194. *Hans 3,* 83: 657–61 (10 Feb. 1846).

195. Ibid., 84: 1229 (19 Mar. 1846).

196. WSC to Lord Lincoln, 5 June 1846, Nottingham University Archives, Newcastle Papers, Ne C 9542/1–2.

197. *Hans 3,* 87: 818–23 (22 June 1846).

198. WSC to Russell (7 Dec.), *Times*, 14 Dec. 1846; see also William Smith O'Brien, *Reproductive Employment: A Series of Letters to the Landed Proprietors of Ireland* (Dublin, 1847).

199. *Times*, 14 Dec. 1846.

200. *DN*, 15 Dec. 1846.

201. *Hans 3*, 90: 448–9 (24 Feb. 1847).

202. *FJ*, 3 Apr. 1847.

203. *Hans 3*, 90: 544–8, 1064 (26 Feb., 8 Mar. 1847). His stance on income tax provoked claims that he favoured his Rochdale constituents over Irish interests, but he was persuaded that direct taxation was more equitable, *Londonderry Sentinel (LSe)*, 25 Mar. 1848, *Nonconformist*, 14 Jan. 1857.

204. WSC to the editor, *Times*, 7 Apr. 1847; *Hans 3*, 91: 217, 355–8 (19, 23 Mar. 1847).

205. *Hans 3*, 91: 575–610, 903-4 (29 Mar., 16 Apr. 1847).

206. Ibid., 97: 338 (9 Mar. 1848), *MA*, 6 July 1849.

207. *Hans 3*, 88: 772–8 (17 Aug. 1846: Russell).

208. *Hans 3*, 100: 925–37 (28 July 1848). Crawford was echoed by the radical MP for Middlesex Ralph Bernal Osborne, although he rejected Crawford's case for small farms, *Speech of Ralph Osborne, Esq., MP, on Mr Sharman Crawford's Motion 'On the Distracted State of Ireland': July 28, 1848* (London, 1848).

209. C. E. Trevelyan, *The Irish Crisis* (London, 1848).

210. WSC to James Hawkins et al, 23 June, *FJ*, 29 June 1848.

211. WSC to Westmeath, 9 Jan., *FJ*, 13 Jan., *NW*, 13 Mar. 1849; Isaac Butt, *The Rate-in-Aid: A Letter to the Rt Hon. the Earl of Roden* (Dublin, 1849).

212. *Hans 3*, 103: 49–51 (1 Mar.), 104: 249–52, 990–1 (3, 30 Apr. 1849).

213. Ibid., 105: 161, 331–4 (9, 11 May 1849); *Bill to Promote Employment of Labour in Ireland*, HC1849 (205), II, p. 487.

214. *Hans 3*, 107: 82 (9 July 1849).

215. For the 'discriminating rate' proposal, see *FJ*, 23 Jan. 1849.

216. WSC, *Depopulation Not Necessary: An Appeal to the British Members of the Imperial Parliament Against the Extermination of the Irish People* (London, 1849), p. 9.

217. Ibid., p. 7.

218. Ibid., pp 10–11. McKnight, *Ulster Tenant's Claim*.

219. *Depopulation*, p. 15, p. 24.

220. Trevor McCavery, 'The famine in county Down', in C. Kinealy and T. Parkhill, eds, *The Famine in Ulster* (Belfast, 1997), p. 117.

221. *Depopulation*, pp 5–6.

222. Ibid., p. 7.

223. *Depopulation*, pp 37–40. Paul Strzelecki, 'To the subscribers of the fund raised in June 1849, for the relief of distress in Ireland', 3 Oct. 1849, TNA, Treasury Papers, T64/366A.

224. *Fourth Report from the Select Committee of the House of Lords Appointed to Inquire into the Operation of the Irish Poor Law, and the Expediency of Making Any Amendment in its Enactments*, HC1849 (365) XVI, 862 (Strzelecki).

225. *Depopulation*, p. 12.

226. Ibid., pp 17–24. The texts referred to are: John Stuart Mill, *Principles of Political Economy: With Some of Their Applications to Social Philosophy* (2 vols, London, 1848), W. T. Thornton, *A Plea for Peasant Proprietors, With the Outline of a Plan for Their Establishment in Ireland* (London, 1848), Samuel Laing, *Notes of a Traveller on the Social and Political State of France, Prussia, Switzerland, Italy, and Other Parts of Europe* (London, 1842) and Charles Le Quesne, *Ireland and the Channel Islands, or, a Remedy for Ireland* (London, 1848).

227. *Hans 3*, 82: 15–18 (3 July 1845).

228. *Depopulation*, p. 41.

229. A combination of the collapse of the government's proposed Quebec-Halifax railway scheme and economic depression in the Australian colonies, which Crawford was aware of via contacts in New South Wales, had dampened enthusiasm overseas for 'colonisation'. For the former see Peter Gray, '"Shovelling out your paupers": the British state and Irish Famine migration, 1846–50', *Patterns of Prejudice*, 33 (1999), pp 47–65; for the latter, Francis March to WSC, 12 Jan. 1848, PRONI, D856/D/92.

230. *Hans 3*, 85: 1206–7 (28 Apr. 1846).

231. George Poulett Scrope, *How is Ireland to be Governed? A Question Addressed to the New Administration of Lord Melbourne in 1834, With a Postscript in Which the Same Question is Addressed to the Administration of Sir Robert Peel in 1846* (2nd edn, London, 1846), pp 46–61.

232. *Hans 3*, 97: 1356–69 (6 Apr. 1848).

233. John Stuart Mill, Letters in *MC*, 10, 13, 14 Oct. 1846, in A. P. And J. M. Robson (eds), *The Collected Works of John Stuart Mill, Vol. 24: Newspaper Writings, January 1835–June 1847* (Toronto and London, 1986), pp 889–98.

234. Gray, *Famine, Land and Politics*, pp 151–63.

235. *Depopulation*, p. 31.

236. Ibid., pp 16, 32–3.

237. For the development of peasant proprietarian ideas in British political economy, see Clive Dewey, 'The rehabilitation of the peasant proprietor in nineteenth-century economic thought', *History of Political Economy*, 6 (1974), pp 17–47, David E. Martin, 'The rehabilitation of the peasant proprietor in nineteenth-century economic thought: a comment', ibid., 8 (1976), pp 297–302, Bruce L. Kinzer, 'J.S. Mill on Irish land: a reassessment', *Historical Journal*, 27 (1984), pp 111–27.

238. *Depopulation*, p. 17.

239. *DR*, 5 Jan. 1850.

240. WSC to unknown, 12 Nov. 1849, NLI, Ms 49,491/1/400.

241. Graham to WSC, 18 Nov., Peel to WSC, 9 Dec. 1849, Wood to WSC, 4 Jan., Russell to WSC, 5 Jan., Grey to WSC, 9 Jan., Clarendon to WSC, 12 Jan. 1850, PRONI, D856/D/97, 99, 102, 103, 105, 106.

242. Cobden to WSC, 17 Jan. 1850, PRONI, D856/D/108.

243. *FJ*, 23, 29 Nov., *Nation*, 1 Dec., *NW*, 8 Nov., *DR*, 17 Nov., *LM*, 24 Nov., *NS*, 29 Dec. 1849.

244. In late 1848 the Irish viceroy Clarendon criticised those in Whitehall 'who sit coolly watching and applauding what they call "the operation of natural causes"', Gray, *Famine, Land and Politics*, p. 312.

245. *Depopulation*, pp 15–16.

NOTES TO CHAPTER 6

1. *Hans 3*, 87: 291 (11 June 1846).

2. WSC, 'To the occupying tenants of Ulster' (8 July), *NW*, 9 July 1846.

3. *Times*, 15 July 1846.

4. *BNL*, 21 July 1846. He later repeated his call for full compensation for retrospective improvements in F. Blakely, *Letters on the Relation between Landlord and Tenant* (Belfast, 1851).

5. 'Marcus', 'To the people of Tipperary: the tenant right of Ulster', repr. *Kilkenny Journal (KJ)*, 8 Aug. 1846.

6. *KJ*, 8 Aug., *TV*, 12 Aug. 1846. The Galician peasant revolt against a Polish noble elite left at least a thousand dead and was a contested issue in Polish memory, see Thomas W. Simons, 'The peasant revolt of 1846 in Galicia: recent Polish historiography', *Slavic Review*, 30:4 (1971), pp 795–817.

7. WSC, 'To the occupying tenants of Ulster, II', 7 Aug., *FJ*, 15 Aug. 1846.

8. WSC, 'To the occupying tenants of Ulster, IV', 29 Sept., *NW*, 1 Oct. 1846.

9. WSC, 'To the occupying tenants of Ulster, II', 7 Aug., *FJ*, 15 Aug. 1846.

10. WSC, 'To the occupying tenants of Ulster, III', 8 Sept., *FJ*, 12 Sept. 1846.

11. WSC, 'To the occupying tenants of Ulster, IV', 29 Sept., *NW*, 1 Oct. See also *NW*, 17 Sept. 1846.

12. *LS*, 18 Sept. 1846.

13. *CE*, 30 Sept. 1846.

14. *Pilot*, 11 Dec. 1846.

15. Smith O'Brien, 'Letter II–tenure', *FJ*, 30 Nov., *Times*, 30 Nov. 1846.

16. *Hans 3*, 91: 186 (18 Mar. 1847).

17. Maguire, a Catholic barrister, founded the *Cork Examiner* in 1841 and was MP for Dungarvan 1852–65 and for Cork city 1865–72.

18. The original proposal was in the *Mark Lane Express* in June, see *CE*, 3 July and *KJ*, 8 July, and Trenwith's letters in *CE*, 30 Nov., 7, 21 Dec. 1846.

19. 'To the tenant farmers of Ireland', 31 Dec. 1846, *CE*, 4 Jan. 1847.

20. [William H. Trenwith], *The Case of the Tenant Farmers: As Illustrated in a Series of Letters*

Originally Published in the Cork Examiner; By 'a Tenant Farmer' and Leading to a Proposition for the Formation of a Tenant League (Cork, 1846), p. 4.

21. *CE*, 11, 15 Jan. 1847.
22. *CE*, 27 Jan., 12 Feb.
23. *CE*, 30 Apr. 1847.
24. *CE*, 27 Jan. 1847.
25. *CE*, 5, 8, 10 Feb. 1847.
26. *FJ*, 2 Feb.; see also *NE*, 17 Feb. 1847.
27. *Nation*, 6 Feb. 1847.
28. *Nation*, 20 Mar. 1847.
29. *Hans 3*, 89: 1157–70 (11 Feb. 1847).
30. Londonderry to WSC, 14 Feb. 1847, PRONI, D856/D/88.
31. *LS*, 19 Feb. 1847.
32. *BNL*, 23 Mar. 1847.
33. WSC to Nicholas Markey, 6 Feb., *Pilot*, 19 Feb. 1847.
34. WSC to the editor, 23 Feb., *LS*, 26 Feb. 1847.
35. Ibid., 26 Feb. 1847.
36. *KJ*, 13 Feb. 1847.
37. *CE*, 26 Feb. 1847.
38. *CE*, 17 Feb. 1847.
39. *CE*, 22 Feb., 12, 26 Mar. 1847.
40. Trenwith to Murphy, 6 Mar., *CE*, 24 Mar. 1847.
41. *CE*, 9 Apr. 1847.
42. *WI*, 13 Mar. 1847.
43. *NW*, 4 Mar. 1847.
44. *BOU*, 8 Sept. 1846.
45. *Nonconformist*, 30 Dec. 1846.
46. W. T. Latimer, 'James McKnight, LL.D.' in *Ulster Biographies, Chiefly Relating to the Rebellion of 1798* (Belfast, 1897), p. 97.
47. *FJ*, 23 Mar. 1847.
48. *Coleraine Chronicle (CC)*, repr. in *FJ*, 23 Mar. 1847.
49. *LS*, 9, 16 Apr., *CE*, 14, 21 Apr. 1847.
50. *LS*, 16 Apr., *Nation*, 17 Apr. 1847.
51. A. R. Holmes, 'Covenanter politics: evangelicalism, political liberalism and Ulster Presbyterians, 1798–1914', *English Historical Review*, 125:513 (2010), pp 340–69.
52. Ibid., p. 353; James McKnight, *A Catechism of Tenant-Right; Being at Attempt to Set Forth and Defend the Rights of Tenant Farmers, Point Out Some of the Grievances Under Which They Labour, with Remedies for Their Removal* (2nd edn, Belfast, 1850), p. 7.
53. Ibid., p. 2, p. 21.
54. Maginn to Trenwith, 4 May, *CE*, 12 May 1847. Maginn was himself the son of a Tyrone farmer, had served as a priest in Donegal before becoming administrator of Derry in 1845. He died of typhus fever in 1849.
55. *FJ*, 29 May 1847.
56. *Hans 3*, 90: 502 (25 Feb. 1847). *Bill to Secure the Rights of Occupying Tenants in Ireland, and Thereby to Promote the Improvement of the Soil and the Employment of the Labouring Classes.* HC 1847 (127), IV, p. 85.
57. Russell to WSC, 26 Apr. 1847, PRONI, D856/D/89.
58. *Hans 3*, 92: 54–7 (28 Apr.), *FJ*, 1 May 1847.
59. *FJ*, 11 June 1847.
60. *Hans 3*, 93: 630–45 (16 June 1847). For Scrope's support of his tenant-right proposals, see *How is Ireland to be Governed?*, p. 61.
61. *CE*, 21 June 1847.
62. WSC to Trenwith, *CE*, 25 June 1847.
63. *CE*, 23, 28 June 1847.
64. *CE*, 30 July, 11, 13 Aug. 1847.
65. WSC 'to the occupying tenants of Ireland', 16 July, *DEP*, 22 July 1847.

66. *LS*, 25 June 1847.
67. *Armagh Guardian (AG)*, 6 July 1847.
68. *DEP*, 27 July, *FJ*, 30 July, *CE*, 2 Aug. 1847.
69. *Times*, 4 Aug., 7 Aug, 4 Sept., Somerville to Clarendon, 13 Sept. 1847, Bodleian Library, Oxford, Clarendon Papers, bundle 79.
70. Jacqueline Hill, 'The 1847 general election in Dublin city', in A. Blackstock and E. Magennis (eds), *Politics and Political Culture in Britain and Ireland, 1750–1850* (Belfast, 2007), pp 41–64.
71. Nelson, 'Violently democratic', p. 310.
72. *NW*, 12 Aug. 1847.
73. *DR*, 14 Aug. 1847.
74. William Conner, *Two Letters to the Editor of The Times on the Rackrent Oppression of Ireland, its Source – its Evils – and its Remedy – in Reply to the Times Commissioner* (Dublin, 1846).
75. *CE*, 5 Apr. See also *TV*, 6 Oct. 1847.
76. *LS*, 25 June 1847.
77. *Nation*, 31 July 1847.
78. James Bruce, *Ireland's Hope: The 'Peculiar Theories' of James Fintan Lalor* (Wilmington, 2020).
79. *Nation*, 24 Apr. 1847; Marta Ramon (ed.), *'The Faith of a Felon' and Other Writings by James Fintan Lalor* (Dublin, 2012), p. 31.
80. 'Mr Lalor's letter to the editor of the Irish Felon', *Irish Felon*, 24 June 1848.
81. James Quinn, *John Mitchel* (Dublin, 2008), pp 16–23.
82. Ibid., pp 24–6.
83. *DEP*, 22 July 1847.
84. *CE*, 13 Sept. 1847.
85. Lalor to the people of Tipperary, *CE*, 13 Sept. 1847.
86. *CE*, 17 Sept. 1847
87. *DEP*, repr. *CE*, 27 Sept. 1847.
88. *CE*, 20 Sept. 1847.
89. *CE*, 24, 27, *TV*, 2 Oct. 1847.
90. *Southern Reporter (SR)*, 25 Sept. 1847.
91. *MPo*, 30 Sept. 1847.
92. WSC to the editor, Evening Mail, repr. *BCC*, 25 Sept. 1847.
93. WSC to Ryan, 20 Sept., *CE*, 4 Oct. 1847.
94. *CE*, 8 Oct. 1847.
95. *CE*, 20 Oct. 1847.
96. *CE*, 22 Oct., 3 Nov. *TV*, 27 Oct. 1847.
97. *WI*, 6 Nov. 1847. He had sounded out the idea of 'tenant right' as a flat payment to outgoing occupiers (including sub-tenants), in 'Ireland and her present necessities', *Tait's Edinburgh Magazine*, 14 (Jan. 1847), pp 39–44.
98. *CE*, 11 Oct. 1847; Irish Prison Registers 1790-1924 1/8/10, Cork City Gaol Convicted Prisoners 1848-50 (18 Jan. 1848).
99. *CE*, 20 Nov. 1850.
100. *CE*, 4 Oct., *LS*, 8 Oct. 1847.
101. *FJ*, 30 Oct., Maginn to McKnight, 27 Oct. 1847, in Thomas D'Arcy McGee, *A Life of the Rt. Rev. Edward Maginn, Coadjutor Bishop of Derry* (New York, 1857), pp 219–20.
102. *FJ*, 1 Nov., *CE*, 3 Nov., *NT*, 30 Oct., *BPJ*, 6 Nov. The *News-Letter* drew a contrast between Crawford and the 'extreme' doctrines of Mitchel and concluded it disagreed with him only on points of detail, *BNL*, 12 Nov. 1847.
103. Robert Young, *The Political Remembrancer* (Londonderry, 1854), pp 72–3.
104. McKnight to Duffy, 14 Oct. 1847, PRONI, T1143/1. To demonstrate his sympathy for Duffy's cultural nationalism, he signed his letter Séumas Macneactáin. For his linguistic interests see Fionntán De Brún, *Revivalism and Modern Irish Literature* (Cork, 2019), pp 73–4.
105. Nowlan, *Politics of Repeal*, pp 152–3.
106. *FJ*, 8 Nov. 1847.
107. *FJ*, 10 Nov. 1847.
108. *FJ*, 10 Nov., *Globe*, 11 Nov., *CE*, 12 Nov., *Times*, 15 Nov., *Western Star*, 4 Dec. 1847; William Fagan, *The Life and Times of Daniel O'Connell* (2 vols, Cork, 1847–8), II, p. 580, p. 598.

109. *FJ*, 12 Nov. 1847.
110. Nowlan, *Politics of Repeal*, pp 155–7.
111. *FJ*, 18 Nov, *CE*, 15 Nov. 1847.
112. *Hans 3*, 95: 114–21, 128–9 (23 Nov.: Hall, Maher); Clarendon to Palmerston, 21 Nov. 1847, Palmerston (Broadlands) Papers, Hartley Library, University of Southampton, GC/CL/480.
113. *Pilot*, 22 Nov. 1847.
114. *CE*, 30 Nov. 1847.
115. *CE*, 8 Dec. 1847.
116. O'Connell to the editors of the provincial press, 12 Nov., *CE*, 17 Nov. 1847.
117. *FJ*, 2 Dec., WSC to the editor (15 Dec.), *FJ*, 17 Dec. 1847.
118. *Hans 3*, 95: 125–8 (23 Nov. 1847).
119. Ibid., 912–14, 921–3 (9 Dec.). Out of parliament, the Chartist Julian Harney praised Crawford's exposure of Irish landlords as 'enemies of the rights of labour, and robbers of the property of their tenants', *NS*, 18 Dec. 1847.
120. *FJ*, 31 Dec. 1847.
121. D. S. Johnson, 'The trials of Sam Gray: Monaghan politics and nineteenth-century Irish criminal procedure', *Irish Jurist*, 20:1 (1985), pp 109–34.
122. *BV*, 1 Jan. 1848. Bell was later forced out of his pulpit for his political activities and after 1863 was involved in the IRB, see Thomas Bell, 'The Reverend David Bell', *Clogher Record*, 6:2 (1967), pp 253–76.
123. WSC to Hughes, 26 Dec. 1847, *BV*, 1 Jan. 1848.
124. *Pilot*, 12 Jan. 1848.
125. *Pilot*, 31 Jan. 1848.
126. Bell to Duffy, 29 Aug. 1850, NLI, Ms 5757, ff. 305–8.
127. *NE*, 15 Jan. 1848.
128. *FJ*, 19 Jan. 1848.
129. WSC to editor of *NW*, 17 Jan., *Nation*, 22 Jan. 1848.
130. *FJ*, 29 Jan. 1848.
131. *FJ*, 2 Feb., *Times*, 5 Feb., *DR*, 5 Feb. 1848.
132. *United Irishman (UI)*, 12 Feb. 1848.
133. *UI*, 25 Feb. 1848.
134. *UI*, 18 Mar. Nevertheless, the pro-landlord *Dublin Evening Mail* insisted that Crawford was an egotistical cats-paw in the hands of Mitchel and Conner, who sought a 'revolution in disguise' through the tenant-right movement, *DEM*, 31 Mar. 1848.
135. Duffy diary entry (n.d., 1848), in C. G. Duffy, *My Life in Two Hemispheres* (2 vols, London, 1898), I, pp 314–15.
136. *Hans 3*, 96: 680–5 (15 Feb. 1848).
137. *FJ*, 18 Feb. 1848.
138. *BOU*, 18 Feb. 1848; Nelson, 'Violently democratic', pp 152–3.
139. WSC to the tenant farmers of Ireland, but more particularly of Ulster, 28 Feb., *LS*, 3 Mar. 1848.
140. *Hans 3*, 97: 311–12 (7 Mar. 1848).
141. Ibid., 863–7 (22 Mar. 1848).
142. Ibid., 872–7.
143. *Hans 3*, 97: 1004–14 (24 Mar.), *FJ*, 25 Mar., 3 May 1848.
144. WSC to McKnight, 25 Mar., *NW*, 28 Mar. 1848.
145. *BOU*, 5 May 1848. Mill was later persuaded by Duffy to offer some low-key support to the Tenant League, Mill to Duffy, n.d. [1850], 17 June 1851, NLI, MS 5757, ff. 265–6, 343–5.
146. *NW*, 28 Mar. 1848.
147. Joseph Napier, *The Speech of Joseph Napier, Esq. on Mr Trelawny's Amendment to Mr S. Crawford's Motion for the Second Reading of the Outgoing Tenants (Ireland) Bill. In the House of Commons, Wednesday, April 5th, 1848* (London, 1848).
148. [Samuel O'Sullivan], 'Tenant-right', *Dublin University Magazine*, 31:184 (Apr. 1848), pp 498–512.
149. *UI*, 8 Apr. 1848.
150. WSC to McKnight, 17 Apr., *MC*, 25 Apr. 1848.
151. *NE*, 3 May 1848.

152. *LS,* 12 May 1848.
153. WSC to McKnight, 22 May, *BOU,* 26 May 1848.
154. *NE,* 27 May 1848. Curran, *Rise and Fall,* pp 124–5.
155. *BOU,* 2 June, *Hans 3,* 99: 974–6 (21 June 1848).
156. Curran, *Rise and Fall,* pp 125–7.
157. *Boston Pilot,* 8 Apr. 1848.
158. *Hans 3,* 98: 119–20 (10 Apr. 1848)
159. *Hans 3,* 100: 725–7 (22 July 1848).
160. Ibid., 102: 368, 511–12, 894–6 (6, 9, 19 Feb. 1849).
161. Sloan, *William Smith O'Brien,* pp 238–90.
162. *Times,* 29 July 1848.
163. *LSe,* 29 July See also *DR,* 28 July 1848.
164. *LS,* 4 Aug. 1848.
165. Nelson, 'Violently democratic' p. 88.
166. *FJ,* 13 Oct. 1848.
167. *DEM,* 16 Oct., C. Connellan to WSC, 17, 22 Oct. 1848, PRONI, D856/D/93, 94.
168. *FJ,* 9 Dec. 1848.
169. Smith O'Brien to WSC, 7 Dec. 1848, PRONI, D856/D/95.
170. WSC to O'Brien, [1848], in Kennedy, 'Sharman Crawford', pp 343–4.
171. *Hans 3,* 106: 825–6 (25 June 1849), *NS,* 27 July 1850.
172. *FJ,* 5 Apr. 1849.
173. Curran, *Rise and Fall,* pp 127–9.
174. *BNL* 21 July 1848. For McKnight, see *BOU,* 31 Dec. 1850.
175. *BPJ,* 1 Dec. 1849.
176. Haddick-Flynn, *Orangeism,* pp 226–9, Sean Farrell, *Rituals and Riots: Sectarian Violence and Political Culture in Ulster, 1784–1886* (Lexington, 2000), pp 1–4; *NT,* 14, 17 July, *NE,* 18 July 1849.
177. *NS,* 24 Mar. 1849.
178. WSC to F. Forde (30 Oct.), *FJ,* 2 Nov., *NT,* 6 Nov. 1849.
179. *BOU,* 26 Oct. 1849.
180. Curran, *Rise and Fall,* pp 172–4.
181. *LS,* 25 June 1870.
182. *DEP,* 4 Jan. 1849. See also *BOU,* 4 Jan. 1850.
183. Kerron Ó Luain, 'The Ribbon societies of Counties Louth and Armagh, 1848–1864', *Seanchas Ard Mhacha,* 25:1 (2014), pp 115–41.
184. *CC,* 23 Feb. 1850.
185. *Hans 3,* 102: 1133–6, 1147 (22 Feb. 1849).
186. *Hans 3,* 103: 49–52 (1 Mar.), see also ibid., 104: 249–52 (3 Apr. 1849).
187. Ibid., 990–1 (30 Apr. 1849)
188. *NE,* 17 Mar. 1849.
189. *Times,* 5 Mar. 1849.
190. *Hans 3,* 113: 702–4 (2 Aug. 1850).
191. James Godkin, *The Land-War in Ireland* (London, 1870), p. 326; Michael Davitt, *The Fall of Feudalism in Ireland* (London, 1904), pp 67–8.
192. *Illustrated London News (ILN),* 5 May 1849.
193. Draft bill to provide for poor tenants on eviction, PRONI, D856/D/100.
194. WSC to John O'Connell, John O'Connell to WSC, *FJ,* 14 June 1849.
195. *LS,* 4 Oct. 1849.
196. For this claim, reflecting a general tendency to downplay the movement in the north, see Davitt, *Fall of Feudalism,* p. 68; J. H. Whyte, *The Independent Irish Party 1850–9* (Oxford, 1958), pp 5–6.
197. *CC,* 4 Aug. 1849.
198. Greer to the tenant farmers of Great Britain and Ireland, Letter 1, 30 Aug., *CE,* 5 Sept., Letter 2, 6 Sept., *WI,* 12 Sept. 1849.
199. *BV,* 13 Oct., *BOU,* 7, 14 Dec. 1849, 4 Jan. 1850. McKnight was succeeded at the *Standard* by James Godkin, a former Congregationalist minister and committed tenant-righter, who was instrumental in setting up a tenant defence association at Strabane, *Nation,* 20 Apr. 1850.
200. An Ulster tenant farmer to the editor, *CE,* 30 Nov., 10 Dec. 1849.

201. Greer, Letter 12, *CE*, 22 Nov. 1849.

202. *BOU*, 18 Dec. 1849.

203. *BOU*, 21 Dec., *Nation*, 29 Dec. 1849.

204. *BOU*, 1 Mar. 1850. See for example Rev. Alexander Goudy's parallels drawn at a rally in Derry between the anti-slavery message of *Uncle Tom's Cabin* and the plight of the oppressed 'freemen' of Ireland, *NW*, 9 Dec. 1852.

205. *BOU*, 28 Dec. 1849.

206. Nelson, 'Violently democratic', pp 136–8.

207. *BOU*, 4 Jan. 1850.

208. 'M' to the editor, *Nation*, 6 Oct. 1849. The phrase had first appeared in the prospectus to the *Nation* in October 1842.

209. *FJ*, 18 Oct., *TV*, 31 Oct. 1849.

210. C. J. Woods, 'O'Shea, Thomas', in *DIB*.

211. *FJ*, 16 Nov. 1849; Whyte, *Independent Irish Party*, p. 6.

212. *TFP*, 19 Dec., *Nation*, 29 Dec., *TV*, 14 Nov. 1849.

213. *Nation*, 9 Feb. 1850.

214. *FJ*, 11 Jan. 1850.

215. *NW*, 12 Jan. 1850

216. Hume to WSC, 10 July 1850, PRONI D856/D/109.

217. *BNL*, 23 Jan., *FJ*, 23, 31 Jan., *CE*, 16 Jan., *NW*, 18 June, *CC*, 23 Feb. 1850, Nelson, 'Violently democratic', pp 163–9.

218. *FJ*, 26 Jan., *BOU*, 5 Feb. 1850.

219. WSC, 'A plea for tenant right', 12 Feb., *NW*, 14 Feb., *Nation*, 23 Mar. 1850.

220. *FJ*, 18 Feb. 1850.

221. There had been a series of arson attacks, rent protests and shooting at an agent on the Ker estate near Killinchy in February 1850 leading to a heavy police presence, see Peter Carr, *Portavo: An Irish Townland and its Peoples, Part 2* (Belfast, 2005), p. 384, p. 651.

222. *BOU*, 22 Feb. 1850.

223. *BOU*, 1 Mar. 1850. John Rogers was minister of 2nd Comber from 1839 and later professor of sacred rhetoric at Assembly's College and moderator of the General Assembly in 1863 and 1865. He has been central to the tenant campaign on the Londonderry estate for several years, see Nelson, 'Violently democratic', p. 156.

224. *FJ*, 11 Apr. 1850.

225. *FJ*, 18, 20 Apr. 1850.

226. *FJ*, 24 Apr. 1850.

227. *FJ*, 25 Apr. 1850.

228. *FJ*, 26 Apr., 3 May, *BOU*, 30 Apr. 1850.

229. *FJ*, 6 May 1850.

230. *FJ*, 16 May 1850.

231. McKnight to Duffy, 13 May 1850, PRONI, T1143/2.

232. *FJ*, 8 May 1850.

233. *BOU*, 21 May, 4 June, *FJ*, 22 May 1850. WSC to the tenant deputation, 10 June, *BOU*, 13 June 1850.

234. *FJ*, citing *DN*, 19 July 1850.

235. *Hans 3*, 113: 595, 602 (31 July), 896, 902–3 (8 Aug. 1850).

236. *FJ*, 7 Aug. 1850.

237. *FJ*, 26 Apr. 1850.

238. *BOU*, 21 May, 14 June *DEP*, 28 May, *LJ*, 10 July 1850.

239. *Nation*, 10 May, *FJ*, 15 May 1850.

240. WSC to Gray, 3 Aug., *CE*, 9 Aug., *Hans 3*, 113: 702–3 (2 Aug.), 881–2 (6 Aug.), 939–40 (8 Aug.), 973 (9 Aug. 1850).

241. *Nation*, 15 June, *NE*, 27 July, *BOU*, 30 July 1850.

242. *FJ*, 19 June 1850.

243. Holmes, 'Covenanter politics', p. 354.

244. *FJ*, 5 July 1850.

245. *BOU*, 5 July 1850.

246. Rogers to Duffy, 19 July 1850, PRONI, T1143/13.

247. Whyte, *Independent Irish Party,* p. 12.

248. Nelson, 'Violently democratic', pp 244–8.

249. *NW,* 8 Aug., *CE,* 9 Aug. 1850.

250. *FJ,* 24 Aug., *BOU,* 27 Aug. 1850.

251. The League's meetings were also covered by the Irish-American press. D'Arcy McGee remitted small sums from Boston, although American support seems overall to have been limited, *Boston Pilot,* 31 Oct. 1850, *Nation,* 26 Apr. 1851.

252. *DEP,* 17 Aug. 1850.

253. McKnight to John O'Connell, 1 Oct., *FJ,* 4 Oct. 1850.

254. Whyte, *Independent Irish Party,* pp 12–13.

255. Anon to Duffy, 21 July [1850], NLI, Ms 5757, fols 281–95.

256. Rodgers to the editor, *BOU,* 14 Oct. 1853.

257. *Irish Tenant League (ITL),* July 1851, pp 17–19.

258. [H. Lambert], *A Memoir of Ireland in 1850. By an Ex-MP,* (Dublin, 1851), pp 80–1. Similar arguments were made in [Henry Grant], *Ireland's Hour* (London, 1850).

259. Conway E. Dobbs, *Some Observations on the Tenant-Right of Ulster: A Paper Read Before the Dublin Statistical Society* (Dublin, 1849); Anon., *Observations on the People, the Land, and the Law, in 1851* (Dublin, 1851).

260. *Hans 3,* 108: 755–8, 109: 221–33 (14 Feb. 1 Mar. 1850); Anne Casement, 'The tenant-right agitation of 1849–50: crisis and confrontation on the Londonderry estates in Co. Down', in L. Rees, C. Reilly and A. Tindley (eds), *The Land Agent, 1700–1920* (Edinburgh, 2018), pp 133–52.

261. Kerron Ó Luain, '"Craven subserviency had vanished. Bitter hostility had arrived": agrarian violence and the Tenant League on the Ulster borderlands, 1849–52', *IHS,* 43:163 (2019), pp 27–54.

NOTES TO CHAPTER 7

1. *Nation,* 7 Sept. 1850.

2. *DN,* 10 Oct. 1850.

3. *CE,* 30 Sept. 1850.

4. *FJ,* 11 Oct. 1850.

5. *Times,* 12 Oct. 1850.

6. *MG,* 26 Oct., WSC to the editor, *MG,* 2 Nov., *NW,* 14 Nov. 1850.

7. *BNL,* 15 Oct., *NW,* 15 Oct. 1850.

8. *BOU,* 15 Oct. 1850.

9. *NW,* 29 Oct., *DR,* 19 Oct., 9 Nov. 1850.

10. *NW,* 9 Nov. 1850.

11. *Nation,* 9 Nov., *NW (citing DR),* 12 Nov., *NT,* 12 Nov. 1850.

12. *DR,* 16 Nov. 1850.

13. WSC to James O'Hanlon and Samuel Bradford, 3 Dec., *FJ,* 6 Dec. 1850.

14. *BOU,* 31 Dec. 1850.

15. *BNL,* 1 Jan. 1851.

16. *MG,* 5 Apr. 1851.

17. *Hans 3,* 115: 1291–2 (8 Apr.), *DEM,* 11 Apr. 1851. Barron was MP for Waterford city.

18. R. J. Kelly and T. Lynch to WSC, 29 Mar., WSC to the editor (14 Apr.), *FJ,* 22 Apr. 1851.

19. See Pádraig G. Lane, 'Perceptions of agricultural labourers after the Great Famine, 1850–1870'. *Saothar,* 19 (1994), pp 14–25.

20. D. Caulfield Heron, *Should the Tenant of Land Possess the Property in the Improvements Made by Him? A Paper Read Before the Dublin Statistical Society, on Tuesday, 23rd of April 1850* (Dublin, 1852), p. 28.

21. Skilling to WSC, *NW,* 14 Feb. 1850.

22. Anon., 'The Tenant League v. common sense', *Irish Quarterly Review,* 1, no. 1 (Mar. 1851), pp 25–45.

23. *BNL,* 25 Apr., *DR,* 26 Apr., *BM,* 26 Apr. 1851.

24. *FJ,* 22 Apr. 1851.

25. *DEP,* 24 Apr. 1851.
26. Lucas to the editor (22 Apr.), *FJ,* 24 Apr. 1851.
27. *Nation,* 26 Apr. 1851.
28. *KJ,* 14 May 1851.
29. *NW,* 1 May 1851.
30. *BNL,* 2 May 1851.
31. *FJ,* 3 May, *Nation,* 10 May 1851.
32. Lucas to Duffy, n.d. [May 1851], NLI, Ms 5757, ff. 257–9.
33. Lucas to Duffy, n.d. [1851], NLI, Ms 5757, ff. 321–32.
34. *FJ,* 24 May 1851.
35. *DR,* 31 May, *Nation,* 7 June 1851.
36. *ITL,* 17 June 1851.
37. WSC to McKnight, *Times,* 17 Oct. 1853.
38. Secretary of the Glen and Donoughmore Valuation and Perpetuity Association to the editor (10 June), *Nation,* 21 June 1851.
39. *Hans 3,* 117: 1022–3, 1117 (20, 23 June), *FJ,* 20 June 1851.
40. *FJ,* 28 June, *Hans 3,* 117: 1237–8 (25 June 1851); *Bill to Encourage and Facilitate the Granting of Leases on Incumbered Estates in Ireland,* HC1851 (109), III.563.
41. *Hans 3,* 118: 348 (8 July), Lucas to the editor, *FJ,* 3 July, *Nation,* 12 July 1851.
42. *Nation,* 5 July, *FJ,* 15 July 1851; C.G. Duffy, *The League of North and South* (London, 1886), p. 78, p. 89. A similar flag appeared at a League meeting at Ballybay, (*Nation,* 5 Oct. 1850), and may also have drawn on older agrarian traditions – a 'common and tri-coloured flag' had been flown by the 'Tommy Downshire's Boys' in west Down in 1830, see Blackstock, 'Tommy Downshire's Boys, p. 142.
43. *FJ,* 11 July 1851.
44. *Evening Freeman (EF),* 12 July 1851.
45. WSC to A. Keappock, 11 July, *FJ,* 15 July 1851.
46. *FJ,* 16 July 1851.
47. *CE,* 18 July 1851.
48. 'The Tenant League', *ITL,* Oct. 1851, p. 71.
49. 'The farmer's hope', *ITL,* Nov. 1851, p. 86.
50. *FJ,* 17 July 1851.
51. *FJ,* 6, 15 Aug. 1851.
52. *NW,* 19 July 1851. The *News-Letter* agreed that the 'impracticables' of the League had been 'knocked under' by Crawford, 22 Aug. 1851.
53. *FJ,* 9 Aug. 1851.
54. *FJ,* 21 Aug. 1851.
55. WSC to J. Sadlier, G. O. Higgins and J. Burke, 3 Sept., *FJ,* 4 Sept. 1851; Moore was regarded as a moderate land reformer with views similar to the northern liberals, D. O. Maddyn to G. H. Moore, n.d. (1850), in Maurice G. Moore, *An Irish Gentleman: George Henry Moore* (London, 1913), pp 199–200; Whyte, *Independent Irish Party,* pp 31–2.
56. *FJ,* 30 Oct. 1851.
57. *FJ,* 22 Aug. 1851.
58. Ibid.
59. *BV,* cited in *Nation,* 23 Aug. 1851.
60. *BNL,* 25 Aug. 1851.
61. *ITL,* Sept. 1851, pp 33–4.
62. 'South Saxon' to the editor (25 Aug.), *Nation,* 30 Aug. 1851.
63. *KJ,* 24 Sept., 22 Oct., 26 Nov. 1851.
64. *ITL,* Nov. 1851, p. 68, *Nation,* 20 Sept., *FJ,* 22 Sept. 1851.
65. *Nation,* 27 Sept. 1851.
66. *FJ,* 6 Oct. 1851.
67. *Nation,* 8 Nov. 1851.
68. *ITL,* Nov. 1851, p. 65, Dec. 1851, 90-2, *FJ,* 13 Jan. 1852.
69. *BNL,* 3 Oct. 1851.
70. *ITL,* Oct. 1851, pp 67–8.
71. R. Kelly to Londonderry, 21 Oct. 1851, DCRO, D/Lo/C/164.

72. *NW,* 23 Oct. 1851, *Hans 3,* 108: 1022–3 (18 Feb. 1850).

73. *BM,* 11 Dec. 1851.

74. John Rogers, *The Speech of the Rev. John Rogers, Comber, at the Tenant Right Soiree, Anaghlone, on the 9th December Last, in Reply to the Attack of the Rev. Drs Cooke and Montgomery, at the Hillsborough Dinner, on the Tenant Farmers of Ireland* (Belfast, 1851), pp 10–11.

75. *BNL,* 17 Dec., *KJ,* 24 Dec. 1851.

76. McKnight to R. J. Tennent, 26 Jan. 1852, PRONI, D1748/G/415. Sinclair had been chair of Crawford's election committee in 1831.

77. *BM,* 29 Jan. 1852.

78. *CE,* 7 Jan. 1852.

79. David Ker to Richard Ker, 24 Jan. 1852, PRONI, D2651/5/8; Ó Luain, 'Ribbon Societies', pp 115–41.

80. *BOU,* 23 Jan. 1852.

81. *BM,* 29 Jan. 1852.

82. *NW,* 29 Jan. 1852; W. Neilson Hancock, *Impediments to the Prosperity of Ireland* (London, 1850).

83. *NW,* 15 Apr. 1852.

84. Tennent to McKnight, 26 Jan. 1852 (draft), PRONI, D1748/G/415/1B.

85. [Patrick McMahon], 'Prosperity of Ireland', *Dublin Review,* 28 (June 1850), 399–420, p. 407.

86. *EF,* 3 Feb. 1852.

87. *DEM,* 13 Feb. 1852.

88. *ITL,* Jan. 1852, p. 99.

89. Council of the Irish Tenant League to the people of Ireland, (28. Jan) *ITL,* Jan. 1852, p. 105.

90. Vincent Scully, *The Irish Land Question, With Practical Plans for an Improved Land Tenure, and a New Land System* (Dublin, 1851).

91. Whyte, *Independent Irish Party,* pp 50–3.

92. *BOU,* 6 Feb. 1852.

93. *BOU,* 10 Feb. 1852.

94. *Hans 3,* 119: 333–40 (10 Feb.), *ITL,* Feb. 1852, p. 114.

95. *EF,* 12 Feb., *BOU,* 13 Feb. Visiting Belfast later that year, Bright indicated in a speech that must have disappointed Crawford that he favoured only a partial version of the bill, limiting compensation to past improvements no more than twenty years old, and only in places where the Ulster custom prevailed, *NW,* 5 Oct. 1852.

96. 'Address to the People of Ireland' (12 Feb.), *Nation,* 14 Feb., *Times,* 12 Feb. 1852.

97. *FJ,* 18 Feb., *BOU,* 20 Feb., *BNL,* 27 Feb. 1852.

98. *ITL,* Feb. 1852, p. 116.

99. *BOU,* 16 Mar., *ITL,* Apr. 1852, p. 130; William Dwyer Ferguson and Andrew Vance, *The Tenure and Improvement of Land in Ireland Considered with Reference to the Relation of Landlord and Tenant, and Tenant-Right* (Dublin, 1851).

100. Andrew Shields, 'Joseph Napier and the Irish land bills of 1852', *Australasian Journal of Irish Studies,* 9 (2009), p. 38.

101. *Hans 3,* 120: 439–44; *Bill to Provide for the Better Securing and Regulating the Custom of 'Tenant Right' as Practised in the Province of Ulster, and to Secure Compensation to Improving Tenants Who May Not Make Claim Under the Said Custom, and to Limit the Power of Eviction in Certain Cases,* HC1852 (47) IV, p. 369.

102. *Hans 3,* 120: 444–52 (31 Mar. 1852).

103. *DEM,* 2 Apr., *NW,* 3 Apr., *BOU,* 6 Apr., *ITL,* Apr. 1852, p. 132.

104. WSC to Reddy (13 Apr.), *FJ,* 22 Apr. 1852.

105. *Hans 3,* 121: 266–99. However, only three of its Irish supporters were Ulster MPs, and all three – Castlereagh, Rawdon and Tennent – would resign or lose their seats in 1852.

106. *BOU,* 11 May 1852.

107. WSC, 'Observations addressed to the occupying tenants of Ireland, and more particularly to the tenants and electors of Ulster' (10 May), *NW,* 13 May 1852.

108. *NW,* 13 May 1852.

109. Whyte, *Independent Irish Party,* pp 57–62.

110. Hoppen, *Elections,* pp 17–18.

111. Ibid., pp, 28, 105, 157; *Abstract of the Number of Electors on the Register of 1852-53 in Each County, City and Borough in Ireland,* HC 1852–53 (957), LXXXIII.413, p. 2.

112. *Census of Ireland for the Year 1861, Part IV, Vol. II,* HC 1863 [3204-III], LX.1, p. 440.

113. *Nation,* 7 Feb. 1852.

114. *NW,* 3 Jan. 1852.

115. J. V. Stewart to Londonderry, 6 Feb. 1852, DCRO, D/Lo/C/166/168.

116. Castlereagh to Londonderry, 6 Feb., DCRO, D/Lo/C/166/1; *BNL,* 18 Feb. 1852.

117. Castlereagh to the gentlemen, clergy, freeholders and electors of Down [21 Feb.], *NW,* 24 Feb.; *BOU,* 27 Feb.; W. B. Price to J. W. Maxwell, 15 Apr. 1852, PRONI, D3244/G/1/159.

118. Londonderry to Blandford, 6 Feb. 1852, DCRO, D/Lo/C/166/2.

119. Londonderry to David Ker, 7 Feb., DCRO, D/Lo/C/1666/136.

120. Ker to Londonderry, 16 Apr., DCRO, D/Lo/C/166/154; *NW,* 15 May 1852.

121. Ker to Londonderry, 10 Feb., DCRO, D/Lo/C/166/137; J.W. Maxwell to Ker, 13 Feb. 1852, PRONI, D3244/G/1/121; Ker to Maxwell, 16 Mar. 1852, ibid., D2223/21/7.

122. Carr, *Portavo, Part 2,* pp 342–9, 380–2.

123. Ker to Stewart, 24 Feb., DCRO, D/Lo/C/520/1/iii; Ker to Londonderry, 3 Mar., Ibid., D/Lo/C/166/142.

124. Londonderry to Ker, 6 Mar., DCRO, D/Lo/C/166/143; to Downshire, 7, 11 Mar., ibid., D/Lo/C/166/9, 10; Downshire to Andrews, 8 Mar. 1852, ibid, D/Lo/C/166/11.

125. Andrews to Londonderry, 7 Feb. 1852, DCRO, D/Lo/C/166/23.

126. WSC to Londonderry, 9 Feb. 1852, DCRO, D/Lo/C/166/7.

127. *BOU,* 13 Apr. 1852; Cassidy to Londonderry, DCRO, D/Lo/C/166/61.

128. Stewart to Londonderry, 13 Mar. 1852, DCRO, D/Lo/C/520/i/iv.

129. Clanwilliam to Londonderry, 11, 12 Mar., DCRO, D/Lo/C/ 166/12, 13, Maxwell to Londonderry, 28 Mar., Londonderry to Maxwell, 30 Mar., PRONI, D3244/G/1/135, 136; Bateson to Londonderry, 3 Apr., DCRO, D/Lo/C/166/34; Downshire to Maxwell, 7 Apr. 1852, PRONI, D3244/G/1/156.

130. Downshire to Londonderry, 10 Apr., Londonderry to Downshire, 13 Apr. 1852, DCRO, D/Lo/C/166/52, 49.

131. Londonderry to Cassidy, 19 Apr. 1852, DCRO, D/Lo/C/166/82; Downshire to Maxwell, 20 Apr. 1852, PRONI, D3244/G/1/150.

132. Downshire to Londonderry, 20, 21 Apr. 1852, DCRO, D/Lo/C/166/85, 62.

133. Stewart to Londonderry, 25, 26 Apr. 1852, DCRO, D/Lo/C/166/176–7.

134. Bateson to Maxwell, 7, 11 May, PRONI, D3244/G/1/165, 167, Eglinton to Londonderry, 7, 17 May, Londonderry to Eglinton, 8 May 1852, DCRO, D/Lo/C/166/99, 74, 100.

135. Selina Ker to Londonderry, 11 May, Londonderry to Selina Ker, 11 May, DCRO, D/Lo/C/166/91, 96.

136. Downshire to Maxwell, [17 May], Bateson to Maxwell, 19, 20, 31 May, PRONI, D3244/G/1/176, 178, 179, 211; Stewart to Londonderry, 28, 29 May, DCRO, D/Lo/C/520/i/viii, x; Stewart to Maxwell, 1 June 1852, PRONI, D3244/G/1/215.

137. Maxwell to Stewart, 4 June 1852, PRONI, D3244/G/1/219.

138. Guy Stone diary, 4 June, PRONI D1447/2/1, *BOU,* 8 June, *NT,* 10 June 1852.

139. *BOU,* 26 Mar. 1852.

140. Bateson to Maxwell, 5 June 1852, PRONI, D3244/G/1/219, 220.

141. Downshire to Maxwell, 10 June 1852, PRONI, D3244/G/1/224.

142. Andrews to Londonderry, 20 June 1852, DCRO, D/Lo/C/158/202.

143. Andrews to Londonderry, 9, 17 July 1852, ibid., D/Lo/C/158/204, 206, *BOU,* 6 July 1852.

144. Andrews to Londonderry, 7 Feb. 1852, DCRO, D/Lo/C/166/23.

145. Londonderry to WSC, 9 Feb. DCRO, D/Lo/C/166/8; A County Down elector to the editor [17 Mar.], *NW,* 20 Mar. 1852.

146. *NW,* 4, 6, 9, 16 Mar., *BOU,* 10 Feb., 13 Mar. 1852.

147. *NW,* 20 Mar. 1852.

148. Andrews to Londonderry, 11, 13 Mar. 1852, DCRO, D/Lo/C/166/25, 26.

149. Andrews to Londonderry, 29 Mar. 1852, DCRO, D/Lo/C/166/29.

150. *NW,* 30 Mar., *BOU,* 2, 27 Apr. 1852.

151. *BOU,* 14 May 1852.

152. James Gordon to Londonderry, 3 Apr. 1852, DRCO, D/Lo/C/166/42.

153. *BOU,* 16, 20 Apr. 1852.
154. Cassidy to Londonderry, 21 Apr., DCRO, D/Lo/C/166/63. The landed interest hired all the professional electoral agents in the county to deny them to the Crawford camp, Cassidy to Londonderry, 22 Apr. 1852, ibid., D/Lo/C/166/64.
155. Guy Stone diary, 6, 8, 9 Apr. 1852, PRONI, D1447/2/1.
156. Girdwood to the independent electors of Down [20 Apr.], *NW,* 22 Apr., *BOU,* 23 Apr.; John H. Quinn, David Sinclair, Guy Stone, Circular letter calling for subscriptions to aid the cause of electoral representation of Co. Down, 30 Apr. 1852, PRONI, D1613/15.
157. Guy Stone diary, 30 Apr., 6, 7, 21 May, PRONI, D1447/2/1. J. K. Powell to Londonderry, 3, 10 May, DCRO, D/Lo/C/166/94, 95; *NW,* 22 May 1852.
158. Andrews to Stewart, 7 June 1852, DCRO, D/Lo/C/158/201.
159. *NW,* 24 June 1852.
160. *NW,* 5 June 1852.
161. Ibid., *BV,* 27 July 1852.
162. *BNL,* 26 May, *NT,* 6 July 1852.
163. Blackstock, 'Tommy Downshire's Boys', pp 125–72.
164. *BOU,* 2 July 1852.
165. *NT,* 24 June, *BNL,* 28 June, *NW,* 29 June, 1 July 1852.
166. Guy Stone diary, 26 June 1852, PRONI, D1447/2/1.
167. William Johnston to Maxwell, 3, 30 Apr., PRONI, D3244/G/1/149, 164; *BNL,* 30 Apr. 1852.
168. *DR,* 3, 10 July, *BOU,* 18 June 1852.
169. 'An independent elector of the Ards' to the editor, *BOU,* 27 July 1852.
170. *BNL,* 12 May 1852.
171. *BNL,* 12 May, 14 June, 19 July, *NT,* 1 July, *DR,* 12 June 1852.
172. *BNL,* 7, 16 July 1852.
173. Anon., *The 'Juvenile' Presbyterian Ministers, Being a Letter Addressed to the Editor of 'The Northern Whig', in Reply to a Speech, Delivered at the County Antrim Election, by the Rev. Dr Cooke* (Belfast, 1852).
174. *BNL,* 17 May; *BOU,* 8 June, *NT,* 10 June 1852.
175. Anon., 'The Meeting of the Leaguers' [1852], PRONI, D3244/G/1/212.
176. *BOU,* 4 June 1852.
177. *NT,* 3 July 1852.
178. *BOU,* 6 July 1852.
179. Poster, n.d., PRONI, T3317/1A.
180. Blakiston-Houston to Maxwell, 24 May 1852, PRONI, D3244/G/1/199.
181. *NW,* 19, 22 June 1852.
182. *Nation,* 22 May 1852.
183. *DEP,* 26 June 1852.
184. *NW,* 22 July 1852.
185. *Hans 3,* 128: 219–23 (14 June 1853: Bright).
186. Hoppen, *Elections,* p. 149.
187. *BOU,* 29 June, *BNL,* 19 July, *NW,* 10 July 1852.
188. Handbill, 'Tenant-right and free trade. County of Down election' [1852] in Crossle family scrapbook, PRONI, T1689/2/66.
189. Andrews to Londonderry, 19 July 1852, DCRO, D/Lo/C/158/205.
190. See correspondence of Thomas Crozier relating to the 1852 election in PRONI, D1252/24/5.
191. *MC,* 17 July 1852; Andrews to Londonderry, 9 July 1852, DCRO, D/Lo/C/158/204.
192. Guy Stone diary, 16 July 1852, PRONI, D1447/2/1.
193. *NT,* 27 Apr. 1852.
194. *BNL,* 5 July, *NW,* 6 July, *BOU,* 6 July, *NE,* 7 July 1852.
195. *BOU,* 10 July, *BM,* 10 July 1852.
196. *BOU,* 13 July, *DR,* 17 July 1852.
197. *BNL,* 14, 19 July; Eglinton to Londonderry, 25 Apr. 1852, DCRO, D/Lo/C/166/67.
198. The most detailed account was in the *Belfast Mercury,* 20 July 1852.
199. Ibid., 22 July, *BOU,* 20 July 1852.
200. Andrews to Londonderry, 22 July, DCRO, D/Lo/C/158/207, Guy Stone diary, 22 July 1852, PRONI, D1447/2/1.

201. *NW,* 22 July, *BOU,* 23 July 1852.
202. *DR,* 4 Mar. 1853.
203. *BOU,* 23 July, *NW,* 24 July, *NE,* 28 July 1852.
204. *NE,* 28 July 1852.
205. *BNL,* 23 July Claims of pro-active League violence or Ribbon involvement were strenuously denied in *BOU,* 30 July 1852.
206. *A Return of the Number of Troops, Constabulary, and Police at Each Polling Place in Ireland, During the Days of Polling at the Last General Election,* HC1852–53 (325), XCIV.699, pp 2, 5–6.
207. *FJ,* 10 Aug. 1852.
208. *BNL,* 23 July 1852.
209. *NW,* 24 July 1852. Newry was more typical of electoral violence elsewhere in Ireland, where anti-Conservative mobs were active in a number of constituencies, Whyte, *Independent Irish Party,* pp 68–71.
210. Ibid.
211. Poll books for Lower Iveagh, Upper Castlereagh and Newry baronies, in PRONI, D671/O/2/5-8, cited in Hoppen, *Elections,* p. 164.
212. *BNL,* 26 July An estate survey listed 313 who had plumped for Crawford, compared with 197 voting for Hill and 75 for Ker, 'List of the tenants on the Londonderry estates who plumped for W.S. Crawford at the late election for the county', DCRO, D/Lo/C/164, Andrews to Londonderry, 29 July 1852, ibid., D/Lo/C/158/211.
213. *BOU,* 10 Aug. 1852.
214. *BNL,* 26 July 1852.
215. *NT,* 24 July 1852.
216. *NW,* 27 July, *BOU,* 30 July 1852.
217. *BM,* 22, 24 July 1852.
218. *BV,* 24 July 1852.
219. WSC, 'Observations addressed to the friends of tenant right in Ireland, but especially to the tenant right electors of the county of Down' [26 July], *BOU,* 27 July 1852.
220. Guy Stone diary, 10, 13, 20 Aug., PRONI, D1447/2/1, Londonderry to Stone, 19 Aug., DCRO, D/Lo/C/166/117, Stone to Londonderry, 20, 21 Aug., ibid., D/Lo/C/166, 121; Londonderry to WSC, 21, 23 Aug. 1852, ibid., D/Lo/C/166/122, 116.
221. Stone to Londonderry, 23 Aug., WSC to Londonderry, 23. 25 Aug. 1852, ibid., D/Lo/C/166/113, 120, 109.
222. *BOU,* 31 Aug. 1852.
223. Downshire to Londonderry, 22 Aug., DCRO, D/Lo/C/166/115. A letter from Crawford stating that the legal action would oblige him to raise issues relating to Hill in court produced an infuriated dismissal, WSC to Downshire, 11 Oct., Downshire to WSC, 12 Oct. 1852, PRONI D856/D/116.
224. Accounts for defendants costs in the several threatened libel suits which arose from Crawford's letter to the 'Northern Whig' on July 27th 1852, PRONI, D856/D/111.
225. Londonderry to Downshire, 24 Aug., Maxwell to Londonderry, 25 Aug., Gordon to Londonderry, 27 Aug. 1852, DCRO, D/Lo/C/166/108, 107, 111.
226. For the election on the Ker estates, see Carr, *Portavo,* pp 386–95.
227. WSC to James SC, 22 Oct., PRONI, D856/D/112.
228. *BOU,* 16, 19 Nov., *DR,* 20 Nov. Crawford declined to comply with the humiliating admission of fault drafted on behalf of the landlords by the notorious Tory political fixer John Bates, cf. 'Draft letters of apology proposed by Mr Bates to be written by Wm. S. Crawford to Bateson and others', PRONI, D856/D/113, with WSC to Bates, 13 Nov., in *BNL,* 17 Nov. 1852.
229. Carr, *Portavo,* p. 394; *FJ,* 1 Mar. 1853.
230. Thompson, *End of Liberal Ulster,* p. 14.
231. Kelly to Londonderry, 19 Dec. 1852, DCRO, D/LO/C/161; McCavery, *Newtown,* pp 138–9.
232. *LS,* 16 Dec., *FJ,* 31 Dec. 1852.
233. John Malcom to the editor (30 Mar.), Fitzherbert Filgate to the editor (4 Apr.), *NW,* 2, 5 Apr. 1853.
234. *Ballymoney Free Press (BFP),* 16 Aug. 1900.
235. *BNL,* 23 July, *BOU,* 30 July 1852.
236. *MA,* 25 May, *BOU,* 30 July 1852.

237. *BM*, 22 July 1852.
238. *FJ*, 26 July 1852.
239. WSC to Gray (9 July), *CE*, 19 July, *FJ*, 10 Aug., *BOU*, 17 Aug. Kirk approved of the principle of the bill, but as a free trader was opposed to any attempt to regulate rent by law, Kirk to WSC, 24 Sept., *FJ*, 15 Oct. 1852.
240. Shields, 'Joseph Napier and the Irish land bills of 1852', p. 41.
241. *BOU*, 3 Aug. 1852.
242. WSC to Mullan (6 July), in *DEP*, 8 July, McKnight to Duffy, 16 July, PRONI, T1143/5, *Tablet*, 12 June 1852.
243. WSC to T. Kennedy et al (4 Aug.), *BOU*, 10 Aug. 1852.
244. *CE*, 13 Sept. 1852.
245. *BOU*, 10, 14 Sept. 1852.
246. WSC to the editor of the *BM*, *FJ*, 23 Sept., *BOU*, 24 Sept. 1852
247. WSC to the editor (18 Oct.), *BOU*, 19 Oct. 1852.
248. *BOU*, 26 Oct. 1852.
249. Nelson, 'Violently democratic', pp 345–8.
250. Whyte, *Independent Irish Party*, p. 93.
251. *BOU*, 16 Nov.; *Hans 3*, 123: 305–48 (22 Nov. 1852).
252. Ibid.., 1089–1123 (7 Dec. 1852).
253. Ibid., cols 1138–44, *FJ*, 9 Dec., *BOU*, 10, 14 Dec., *Times*, 9 Dec. 1852.
254. Duffy, *League of North and South*, p. 233.
255. *NW*, 9 Dec. 1852.
256. WSC 'To the tenant farmers of County Down' (1 Jan.), *NW*, 4 Jan. 1853.
257. *Hans 3*, 123: 1206–13 (10 Dec. 1852).
258. Shields, 'Joseph Napier and the Irish land bills of 1852', pp 42–3.
259. *FJ*, 13 Dec., *Nation*, 25 Dec. 1852; Duffy, *League of North and South*, pp 232–5.
260. *BOU*, 15 Feb. 1853.
261. Lucas to Keogh (30 Dec. 1852), *FJ*, 3 Jan. 1853.
262. WSC 'To the tenant farmers of County Down' (1 Jan.), *NW*, 4 Jan. 1853.
263. WSC to Sadlier (8 Jan.), *MC*, 12 Jan. 1853.
264. *BOU*, 11 Jan., *Limerick Examiner (LE)*, 9 Feb. 1853.
265. WSC to the editor, *DEP* (16 Jan.), *CE*, 19 Jan. 1853.
266. Richard A. Keogh, '"Nothing is so bad for the Irish as Ireland alone": William Keogh and Catholic loyalty', *IHS*, 38:150 (2012), pp 230–48.
267. Whyte, *Independent Irish Party*, pp 97–107.
268. Goderich to Duffy, 6 Sept., 24 Dec. 1852, 10 Jan. 1853, PRONI, T1143/7, 9, 10. Goderich was an MP 1852–9 before going to the lords as 2nd Earl of Ripon, see Anthony F. Denholm, 'Robinson, George Frederick Samuel, first marquess of Ripon', *ODNB*.
269. Goderich to Duffy, 12 Feb. 1853, PRONI, T1143/11.
270. *Weekly Telegraph (WT)*, 29 Jan. 1853.
271. *BOU*, 18 Jan. Sadlier lost his seat and was later returned for Sligo borough, while Keogh saw off a Whig challenger at Athlone with Catholic clerical support, Unknown to Duffy, 5 Feb., NLI, Ms 5757, ff. 393–4, *BOU*, 26 Apr. 1853.
272. *FJ*, 29 Jan., *MA*, 4 Jan. 1853.
273. *BOU*, 1, 8 Feb. 1853.
274. McKnight to Duffy, 5 Sept. 1851, PRONI, T1143/4. For an example of attacks on Lucas for promoting 'bible-burning' see *NT*, 18 Mar. 1852.
275. *BOU*, 4 Feb., 5 Apr. 1853.
276. WSC to McKnight, 3 Feb., *BOU*, 4 Feb. 1853.
277. *BOU*, 15 Mar. 1853.
278. *BOU*, 17 May; Graham to WSC, 4 June, Aberdeen to WSC, 5 July 1853, PRONI, D856/D/118, 119.
279. Shee to Aberdeen, Apr. 1853, in William Shee, *Papers, Letters, and Speeches in the House of Commons, on the Irish Land Question* (London, 1863), pp 34–43.
280. *CE*, 23 Feb., *BNL*, 23 Feb., *BOU*, 22 Mar. 1853.
281. *BOU*, 25 Mar. 1853.

282. WSC to Scully (25 Apr.), *CE*, 6 May 1853.

283. Gray, *Famine, Land and Politics*, pp 53–4, 185–9, 192.

284. *BOU*, 6 May 1853.

285. William Tighe Hamilton, *The Land Bills of the Late Government Considered with Reference to Sounder Legislation for England and Ireland* (Dublin, 1853).

286. *MA*, 7 May, *BNL*, 9 May 1853.

287. *BOU*, 10, 17 May 1853.

288. Dr Thornside to the editor of the *Tablet*, *CE*, 18 May 1853.

289. WSC to McKnight (16 June), *BOU*, 17 June; WSC to the Tenant Right Associations of Ulster (20 June), *BOU*, 21 June 1853.

290. *NW*, 5 July 1853.

291. WSC to McKnight (15 July), *NW*, 19 July 1853.

292. *NW*, 30 July 1853.

293. Napier to WSC, 2 Aug. 1853, PRONI, D856/D/120.

294. *Hans 3*, 129: 1500–35 (9 Aug.), *BOU*, 12 Aug., *LE.*, 13 Aug. 1853.

295. Newcastle to WSC, 24 Aug. 1853, PRONI, D856/D/121.

296. *NW*, 8 Sept. 1853.

297. Shee to Gray, 17 Sept., in Shee, *Papers*, pp, 44–51.

298. *NW*, 8 Sept. 1853.

299. *BOU*, 11 Oct. 1853.

300. WSC to McKnight, *Times*, 17 Oct. 1853.

301. Lucas to WSC (18 Oct.), *Times*, 24 Oct. 1853.

302. *Nation*, 29 Oct. 1853.

303. Shee, *Papers*, p. 51; *BOU*, 25 Oct. 4 Nov., *NW*, 27 Oct., 5 Nov., *SR*, 15, 22 Nov., *DJ*, 23 Nov. 1853, *NE*, 4 Jan. 1854.

304. Shee to WSC, 17 Nov. 1853, in Shee, *Papers*, pp 52–8.

305. *BOU*, 18 Nov. 1853

306. WSC, Address to the tenant farmers and people of Ireland, *BM*, 23 Nov. 1853.

307. WSC to Shee, 26 Nov. 1853, in Shee, *Papers*, pp 239–41.

308. Redmond to the editor, *DEP* (23 Nov.), *SR*, 29 Nov. 1853.

309. *WT*, 10 Dec., *NW*, 10 Dec, *FJ*, 13 Dec. 1853.

310. *NT*, 29 Dec. 1853, *BNL*, 13 Jan. 1854.

311. *Returns by Provinces and Counties, of Cases of Evictions Which Have Come to the Knowledge of the Constabulary in Each of the Years From 1849 to 1880*, HC1881 (185), LXXVII, p. 725.

312. Paul Huddie, *The Crimean War and Irish Society* (Liverpool, 2015), pp 155–74.

313. *BOU*, 31 Dec. 1853.

314. *DEM*, 2 Jan., *BNL*, 4 Jan. 1854.

315. Anon., 'Irish land question', *Irish Quarterly Review*, 4:13 (Jan. 1851), pp 103–41.

316. Edward Bullen, *Modern Views on the Relations Between Landlord and Tenant, Tenant Right, and Compensation for Improvements* (London, 1853).

317. *KJ*, 18 Jan. 1854.

318. WSC to Napier (15 Feb.), *BOU*, 24 Feb., Napier to WSC, 18 Feb. 1854, PRONI, D856/D/122.

319. Newcastle to WSC, 27 Feb. 1854, PRONI, D856/D/123.

320. *BOU*, 18 Apr. 1854.

321. *BNL*, 6 Mar. 1854.

322. *NW*, 9 Mar., *NE*, 15 Mar. 1854.

323. *BOU*, 1, 4 Apr. 1854.

324. *WT*, 8 Apr., *LE*, 12 Apr. 1854.

325. *Nation*, 29 Apr.; Shee to McConvery, 5 June 1854, in Shee, *Papers*, pp 80–9; *Ulsterman*, 14 Apr. 1855.

326. *DEP*, 1 July, *LE*, 15 July.

327. *BCC*, 18 July, *Nation*, 27 July 1854.

328. *SR*, 1 June, Shee to Secretary of Tenant League, 19 Sept., *Papers*, pp 242–4, Redmond to Secretary of Tenant League (19 Sept.), *MC*, 21 Sept. 1854.

329. Whyte, *Independent Irish Party*, pp 144–8.

330. *LS*, 2 Aug. 1855.

331. Lucas to his wife, 27 Jan., 24 Feb. 1855, NLI Ms 5758, fols. 116, 124; Patrick Maume, 'Lucas, Frederick', *DIB*.

332. WSC, 'To the occupying tenants and people of Ireland' (1 Jan.), *LS*, 11 Jan. 1855.

333. *LS*, 11, 18 Jan. 1855.

334. *BOU*, 24 Mar. 1855.

335. O'Regan to WSC, *DEP*, 3 Feb., *LE*., 10 Feb., 4 Apr., 11 Apr. *SR*, 7, 10 Apr. 1855.

336. *DEP*, 28 Apr. There is evidence of some personal regard between the two men, as expressed at a dinner hosted during the lord lieutenant's visit to Newtownards, *BM*, 21 Nov. 1855.

337. *Nation*, 28 July, *Hans 3*, 139: 1338–48 (24 July 1855).

338. WSC to the editor (22 Aug.), *WT*, 25 Aug. 1855.

339. WSC to the editor (25 Aug.), *BM*, 28 Aug. 1855.

340. WSC, Observations addressed [...] more particularly to the electors of Meath (29 Oct.), *FJ*, 2 Nov. 1855.

341. *Belfast Mercantile Advertiser*, 1 Apr. 1856.

342. *Tablet*, 10 Nov., *NE*, 17 Oct. 1855.

343. Repr. in *BNL*, 14 July 1856.

344. WSC to the editor, *DEP*. 6 Sept. 1856.

345. WSC to the editor of the *FJ* (13 Oct.), *NW*, 21 Oct. 1856.

346. *FJ*, 1 Nov., *LS*, 6 Nov. 1856.

347. *Tablet*, 29 Nov. 1856.

348. *Tuam Herald*, repr. in *Dundalk Democrat*, 10 Jan. 1857.

349. WSC to the Tenant League (23 Jan.), *NW*, 29 Jan. 1857.

350. *NE*, 21 Mar. 1857.

351. WSC to Friends of Counsellor Greer (28 Feb.), *LS*, 5 Mar. 1857.

352. WSC, Observations addressed to the electors of Ireland (17 Mar.), *DEP*, 19 Mar. 1857.

353. WSC to William Wallace, n.d. [Mar.], Ker draft memo, n.d. [Mar.], Ker to WSC, n.d. [Mar.], PRONI, D2223/21/9; *DEP*, 28 Mar., WSC address to the electors of Down, *BM*, 3 Apr. 1857.

354. *BNL*, 6 Apr. 1857.

355. *BOU*, 14 Apr. 1857.

356. WSC to the editor of the *DN*, *BNL*, 25 Apr.; handbill, 'The advice of William Sharman Crawford, esq., to the electors of Down', n.d. (1857), PRONI, D2223/21/9.

357. *LS*, 7 May, 30 July 1857.

358. *LS*, 26 Aug. 1858.

359. WSC to the editor (11 May), *DEP*, 12 May, *Ulsterman*, 18 May, *LS*, 21 May 1857.

360. SC to occupying tenants of Ireland (12 June), *AG*, 19 June, *LS*, 25 June 1857.

361. *DR*, 13 June, *BM*, 27 June, *LS*, 15 Oct. 1857.

362. *Hans 3*, 149: 1046–59 (22 Apr.), *NW*, 10 May 1858; Whyte, *Independent Irish Party*, pp 151–3.

363. *LS*, 30 Dec. 1858, *BM*, 11 Jan., *DJ*, 18 May 1859.

364. *LSe*, 15 Jan. 1858.

365. *Ulsterman*, 27 Jan, *DEP*, 2 Feb. 1858. Lewis's reputation was a harsh evicting landlord was maintained in the local folklore tradition, see Duchas, The Schools' Collection, Volume 0932, p. 443, https://www.duchas.ie/en/cbes/4742044/4730577 (rev. 25 July 2022).

366. WSC to the editor, *DEP*, *NW*, 12 Apr., *Nation*, 1 May 1858. Holland's account was republished as *The Landlord in Donegal: Pictures from the Wilds* (Belfast, [1858]).

367. *Hans 3*, 149: 1527–49 (14 Apr.), *Report from the Select Committee on Destitution (Gweedore and Cloughaneely)*, HC1857–8 (412), XIII.89, pp 181–8 (18 June).

368. *DEP*, 15 July, *Ulsterman*, 12, 16 July, *Nation* 28 Aug., *BM*, 6 July, *BNL*, 6 July 1858.

369. WSC to the editor, *Times*, (11 Dec.), 14 Dec. 1858.

370. WSC to Downshire (draft), 1 Feb. 1859, PRONI, D856/D/140.

371. WSC, Address to the people of Ireland (5 Jan.), *FJ*, 8 Jan. 1859, *BNL*, 17 Dec. 1858.

372. *ES*, 8 Apr., *FJ*, 23 Apr., WSC to Wogan (17 Apr.), *NW*, 25 Apr. 1859.

373. WSC to Derby (13 Nov.), *NW*, 18 Nov. 1859, WSC to Greer (3 Jan.), *BNL*, 10 Jan., WSC to William Levinge (10 Jan.), *Newry Herald*, 19 Jan. 1860.

374. Perraud toured Ireland in 1860 and published his book after Crawford's death, an event he described as universally regretted by his fellow citizens, *Etudes sur l'Irlande contemporain* (2 vols, Paris, 1862), I, pp 220, 385–6, 436–8.

375. *Belfast Morning News (BMN)*, 30 Apr., Cardwell to WSC, 23 Oct. 1860, PRONI, D856/D/148.

376. WSC, Observations on the land acts addressed to the farmers of Ireland (18 Oct.), *NW,* 19 Oct. 1860.

377. WSC to the editor of the Agricultural Review, *Wexford People*, 6 Apr. 1861.

378. Smith O'Brien to WSC, 14 Apr. 1861, NLI, Ms 447/3229.

379. WSC to Smith O'Brien, 27 Apr. 1861, NLI, Ms 447/3232.

NOTES TO CHAPTER 8

1. As early as 1836 his three eldest sons spoke from the platform of a tenant-right meeting at Newtownards, Guy Stone diary, 22 Dec. 1836, PRONI, D826/2/1.

2. *NT,* 3 Apr. 1845.

3. *FJ,* 21 May 1851.

4. WSC, 'Retrospective memorandum', PRONI, D856/D/1.

5. WSC to John SC, 6 Oct. 1835, PRONI, D856/F/44.

6. John SC to Mabel SC, 9 Nov. 1835, PRONI, D856/D/42.

7. Maria Coddington to John SC, 24 Feb. 1836, PRONI, D856/D/45.

8. *BNL,* 15 June 1852; he retired on health grounds three years later, *DR,* 21 July 1855.

9. *NW,* 26 Sept. 1839.

10. *BCC,* 14 Nov. 1853.

11. *BOU,* 20 June 1861.

12. *Era,* 18 Nov. 1855. William had been an opponent of the suspension of parliamentary business for 'Derby Day', see *Hans 3*, 121: 1168–72 (25 May 1852).

13. John SC to Dufferin, 30 Mar. 1853, PRONI, D1071/H/B/C/673.

14. Anon., *Anti-Tractarian Proceedings of the Protestant Parishioners of Kilmore, Relative to the Innovations Introduced by the Rev. Mr Mussen; Including the Correspondence with the Bishop etc.* (Downpatrick, [1846]); *DR,* 17 Oct. 1846.

15. *BNL,* 16 Jan. 1849. For the context, see Sean Farrell, 'Building opposition: the Mant controversy and the Church of Ireland in early Victorian Belfast', *IHS*, 39:154 (2014), pp 230–49, esp. p. 247.

16. He was presented with a silver tea-service by the Down tenants in 1850 as a tribute to the 'integrity and kindness' of his estate management, *NW,* 6 Aug. 1850.

17. Mabel F. SC to John SC, 3 Dec. 1835, Ella SC to John SC, 1 Feb., 14 June 1836, Charles SC to John SC, n.d. [1837], PRONI, D856/D/43, 45, 46, 56.

18. *FJ,* 4 Apr. 1845, *NE,* 25 July 1846, *MG,* 6 Feb. 1847.

19. For the pursuit of patronage, see Whyte, *Independent Irish Party*, pp 45–7.

20. *FJ,* 1 Apr. 1847.

21. Charles SC to Poor Law Commissioners (PLC), 2 Nov., Captain Gordon to PLC, 11 Nov. 1847, *Papers Relating to Proceedings for the Relief of the Distress, and State of the Unions and Workhouses, in Ireland. Fourth Series*, HC1847–8 [896], LIV.29, p. 190, p. 208.

22. *BOU,* 18 Oct. 1853.

23. *Warder,* 7 Apr. 1855. See also *Evening News (EN)*, 21 May 1859.

24. *Saunder's News-Letter (SNL)*, 10 Jan. 1860.

25. *DEM,* 20 Dec. 1865, 25 July 1871, 12 Dec. 1877, *FJ,* 19 June 1849, 17 Feb. 1879.

26. *BCC,* 4 Mar. 1846; *Henderson's Belfast Directory and Northern Repository* (Belfast, 1852), p. 186; *BNL,* 26 Sept. 1862.

27. *BM,* 28 June 1854.

28. *MA,* 25 June 1852.

29. *NW,* 28 Aug. 1855, 7 Mar. 1857, *NW,* 11 Sept., *BM,* 15 Oct. 1855.

30. *BNL,* 4 Apr. 1857.

31. *BNL,* 9 Oct. 1867, *BWN,* 14 Oct. 1871.

32. *Belfast Telegraph (BT)*, 18 May 1872.

33. Charles Sellers, *Oporto, Old and New, Being a Historical Record of the Port Wine Trade* (London, 1899), p. 245.

34. *The Belfast and Province of Ulster Directory 1863–1864* (Belfast, 1863), p. 481.

35. *DR*, 2 Sept. 1854, *NT*, 19 Nov. 1857. His father had invested in this company, and in the Atlantic Royal Mail Steam Navigation Company, see receipts for shares in latter (1859-60), PRONI, D856/F/65.
36. *BCC*, 2 Mar. 1855, *DR*, 24 Jan. 1857, *BNL*, 31 Oct. 1862.
37. *Thom's Irish Almanac for 1866* (Dublin, 1866), p. 1677.
38. *BWN*, 23 Nov. 1905, *Irish Independent (II)*, 26 Jan. 1906, *Evening Herald*, 24 Dec. 1926.
39. *BCC*, 12 Dec. 1846, *BOU*, 18 July 1848, *NW*, 19 Dec. 1850, Asenath Nicholson, *Annals of the Famine in Ireland, in 1847, 1848 and 1849* (New York, 1851), pp 46–8.
40. *BOU*, 10 Dec. 1853, *BM*, 3 Apr. 1855.
41. For her later views on proselytism, see Mabel SC, *The Irish Question: Experiences of an Irish Landowner* (London, 1888), p. 16.
42. *BM*, 23 Sept. 1851.
43. *Address from the Committee of the Belfast Ladies' Anti-Slavery Association to the Ladies of Ulster*, (1846).
44. H. Hincks to Maria Weston, 13 July 1855, ibid. https://www.digitalcommonwealth.org/search/commonwealth:cv43ps161 (Acc. 23 Dec. 2021); McNeill, *Mary Ann McCracken*, p. 295; Beggs-McCormick. 'Methinks I see', pp 149–57.
45. Ella SC to John SC, 1 Feb. 1836, PRONI, D856/F/45; *DEM*, 19 Feb. 1849, *BNL*, 22 Dec. 1851, *BCC*, 3 Dec. 1853, *NW*, 31 Dec. 1859.
46. *DEM*, 26, 29 Jan. 1849.
47. *BOU*, 6 Nov. 1855.
48. *LS*, 21 June 1865.
49. WSC to William SC junior, 31 Jan. 1848, Mr Russell to WSC, 10 May 1854, PRONI, D856/A/6/15–16; WSC memo, n.d. [1857], ibid., D856/D/127.
50. WSC draft circular to Co. Down tenants, 1 Jan. 1856, PRONI, D856/A/6/14.
51. WSC to his tenants (1 Jan.), *DEP*, 22 Jan. 1856.
52. [Denis Holland], 'William Sharman Crawford', *Irish Emerald*, 25 Sept. 1869.
53. WSC to Arthur SC, 5, 10 Nov. 1851, PRONI, D856/C/6/9.
54. WSC to James SC. 8 Feb. 1857, PRONI, D856/D/126. He had in 1832 lent £1,500 to Robert Waddell on the mortgage of his land in Co. Down, PRONI, D959/15/1/5A.
55. WSC to James SC, [7 Feb. 1857], PRONI, D856/D/126. He calculated £26,236 could be raised by fines, well exceeding the £21,500 due from the Down estates for the family settlements and other debts, WSC memo [Nov. 1857], ibid., D856/D/129.
56. WSC to James SC. 8 Feb. 1857, PRONI, D856/D/126.
57. WSC to James SC, 8 Nov. 1857, ibid.
58. WSC to James SC, 9 Nov. 1857, n.d. [1857], ibid., WSC memo, n.d. [1857], D856/D/130.
59. W. A. Maguire, 'Lord Donegall and the sale of Belfast: a case history from the Encumbered Estates Court', *Economic History Review*, 29:4 (1976), pp 570–84.
60. WSC memo, n.d. [1857], D856/D/132.
61. WSC memo, n.d. [1858], D856/D/133.
62. WSC to James SC, 26 Jan. 1861, PRONI, D856/D/126.
63. *BNL*, 29 Sept. 1877.
64. *LM*, 1 July 1843
65. *Hans 3*, 64: 1368–9 (11 July 1842), 72: 573–4 (12 Feb. 1844).
66. Tyrell, *Sturge*, pp 143–4.
67. Fr James Hughes to Repeal Association, *FJ*, 6 Dec. 1844.
68. *Hans 3*, 73: 544–6 (4 Mar. 1844). See also ibid., 96: 998 (21 Feb. 1848).
69. Tyrell, *Sturge*, pp 164–9.
70. *Nonconformist*, 2 June 1847.
71. Cobden to WSC, 27 Jan. 1855, PRONI, D856/D/125.
72. *DN*, 5 Oct. 1855.
73. *DN*, 8 Oct. 1855.
74. WSC to the editor (10 Oct.), *DN*, 15 Oct. 1855.
75. *BOU*, 11 Oct. 1855.
76. WSC to the editor of *DN* (10 Oct.), *BNL*, 17 Oct. 1855. He noted that the liberties of Poland and Hungary remained suppressed by Britain's allies.
77. See for example Elizabeth Grant, quoted in Huddie, *Crimean War*, pp 64–5.

78. *BNL,* 1 Dec., *SNL,* 28 Dec. 1854.

79. *BM,* 6 Nov. 1857.

80. Prayer of Wm. S. Crawford for the fast day, 7 Oct. 1857, PRONI, D856/G/5.

81. Don Randall, 'Autumn 1857: the making of the Indian "Mutiny"', *Victorian Literature and Culture,* 31:1 (2003), pp 3–17.

82. *NT,* 1 Dec. 1857.

83. *Rochdale Observer (RO),* 29 May 1858.

84. WSC to Henry Coddington, 23 Aug. 1857, PRONI, T2519/12/10.

85. Jill C. Bender, *The 1857 Indian Uprising and the British Empire* (Cambridge, 2016), pp 59–65; Michael Silvestri, *Ireland and India: Nationalism, Empire and Memory* (London, 2009), pp 113–38.

86. WSC to Livsey (24 Dec.), *RO,* 27 Dec. 1856. He was presented with a silver candelabrum, which Livsey assured him had been paid for in part by the pence of the poor and labouring men of Rochdale, *Nonconformist,* 10 Oct. 1855.

87. *DN,* 30 June, *MPo,* 31 July, *RO,* 1 Aug. 1857, 8 May 1858.

88. Sturge to WSC, 15 Nov. 1858, PRONI, D856/D/138.

89. Bright to WSC, 9 Jan. 1859, PRONI, D856/D/139, Miles Taylor, 'Bright, John', *ODNB.*

90. *LS,* 24 Feb., *Nation,* 19 Mar. 1859.

91. *BM,* 19 Mar. 1859.

92. *RO,* 28 May 1859; WSC, *The Non-Elector's Plea for the Suffrage: Addressed to the Non-Electors of Rochdale [...] Containing an Abstract of His Speech of 1843, in Moving the Reform Bill of the Complete Suffrage Association* (Rochdale, 1859).

93. *RO,* 20 Aug. 1859.

94. Edward S. Pryce, Circular of the Parliamentary Reform Committee, 26 Nov. 1859, PRONI, D856/D/141.

95. WSC to Pryce, 3 Dec. 1859, PRONI, D856/D/142.

96. Pryce, Circular of Parliamentary Reform Committee, 7 Dec. 1859, PRONI, D856/D/143.

97. Bowring to WSC, 21 Oct., PRONI, D856/D/147; *DN,* 10 Oct. 1860, Cobden to WSC, 29 June 1861, PRONI D856/D/149.

98. *DEPa,* 24 Apr. 1861.

99. *NW,* 18 Apr. 1861.

100. WSC memo, 'Questions to a soldier', n.d. [c.1860], PRONI, D856/G/11. Crawford was referring to the First Taranaki War of 1860–1, which was the consequence of settler land-hunger and saw use of armed force by the colonial authorities against Maori resistance, See James Belich, *The New Zealand Wars and the Victorian Interpretation of Racial Conflict* (Auckland, 1986).

101. WSC, 'Notes for a sermon on faith and good works', n.d. (1859/60), PRONI, D856/G/14.

102. Alice Johnson, *Middle-Class Life in Victorian Belfast* (Liverpool, 2020), pp 26–7.

103. WSC memo, 'Education of boys at large boarding schools', n.d. (c.1860), PRONI, D856/G/12.

104. Neil Maddox, '"A melancholy record": the story of the nineteenth-century Irish Party Processions Act', *Irish Jurist,* 39 (2004), pp 242–73.

105. WSC, Draft letter on the Volunteer movement, n.d. [c.1860], PRONI, D856/D/146. A version was published by the Council of the Royal Irish Rifle Volunteers as *Irish Volunteers, Past and Present* (Dublin, 1860), and in *BNL,* 9 Nov. 1860.

106. WSC to J. T. Lube, 25 Nov. 1860, NLI, Ms 49,491/1/401.

107. *BNL,* 9 Nov., *EN,* 12 Nov., *NW,* 14 Nov. 1860.

108. Kennedy, 'Sharman Crawford', p. 6.

109. WSC to G. H. Moore, 18 Oct., *BM,* 26 Oct. 1852.

110. *ES,* 1 May 1844; WSC to Miall (2 June), *FJ,* 7 July 1856.

111. WSC, comments on Mr Miall's speech in the *DEP* (25 Nov. 1859), PRONI, D856/G/6.

112. *NW,* 5, 9 Oct. 1859, 31 Jan., 2 Feb. 1860.

113. *BM,* 16 Feb., *LS,* 13 Sept. 1855, *BNL,* 3 Aug., *BOU,* 16 Aug. 1859, *BCC,* 21 June 1855.

114. *FJ,* 17 Sept. 1851.

115. The old parish church of Kilmore, attended by the family while staying at Rademon, was deconsecrated in 1967 and rebuilt at the Ulster Folk Museum, Cultra, in 1976.

116. WSC notes (22 June 1855) on Charles James McAlester, *The Trinity and The Athanasian Creed: A Sermon Preached in the Meeting-House of the First Presbyterian Congregation, Holywood, on Sunday, 20th August, 1854* (Belfast, 1854), PRONI, D856/G/4.

117. Printed copies of sermons with annotations by WSC, including Rev. J. Porter, *What is Protestantism? A Discourse Preached on Sunday, December 26, 1858, in the Second Presbyterian Church, Belfast* (Belfast, 1859) and William Bruce, *On the Right and Exercise of Private Judgment: A Sermon on Acts IV, 19.20, Preached on Sunday, July 8, 1860* (Belfast, 1860), PRONI, D856/G/3.

118. WSC, Profession of religious belief, 4 Jan. 1861, PRONI, D856/G/15.

119. D856/G/16-17. McAlister's wife Rachel was the daughter of Rev. Andrew Craig of Moira, who had initiated Crawford's father into the Volunteers in 1781.

120. WSC, Profession of religious belief, D856/G/15.

121. WSC, Memo on the causes of the decline in the numerical strength of the Unitarian church, n.d. (c.1861), PRONI, D856/G/13.

122. PRONI, D856/G/15.

123. WSC, 'Notes for a sermon', D856/G/14.

124. WSC, Memoranda on 'My faith', 'General observations' and 'My principles of action', n.d. [c.1861] PRONI, D856/G/8.

125. WSC, Memo: Observations on 'the revivals' and the Westminster Confession, n.d. (1859–60) PRONI, D856/G/8A.

126. WSC, Memoranda on 'My Faith', 'General Observations' and 'My Principles of Action', n.d. [c.1861] PRONI D856/G/8.

127. *Belfast Daily News (BDN)*, 18 Oct., *NW*, 18 Oct. 1861.

128. *NW,* 22 Oct. 1861.

129. *BM*, 18 Oct. 1861.

130. *BNL*, 18 Oct. The paper was also happy to publish extracts from more sympathetic obituaries in radical papers, ibid., 19 Oct. 1861.

131. *Warder,* 19 Oct. 1861.

132. *Daily Express,* 19 Oct. 1861.

133. *NW,* 18 Oct. 1861.

134. *BOU,* 19 Oct. 1861.

135. *LS,* 24 Oct. 1861.

136. *EN,* 18 Oct. 1861.

137. *DEP,* 19 Oct. 1861.

138. *Nation,* 26 Oct. 1861.

139. *Times,* 19 Oct. 1861.

140. For the former, see *Sun,* 19 Oct., for the latter, *MT,* 26 Oct. 1861.

141. *RO,* 26 Oct. 1861.

142. Cited in *Nonconformist,* 23 Oct. 1861.

143. *BMN,* 28 Oct., *RO,* 16 Nov. 1861.

144. *BOU,* 26 Oct. 1861.

145. Carte-de-visite portrait photograph of WSC, n.d. [c.1860–1], Coey Album, NMNI, BELUM. Y39038.163; 'The late Mr Wm Sharman Crawford, MP. Presented gratis with "The Belfast Weekly Post". 23rd Sept. 1882', PRONI, T1129/412.

146. National Gallery of Ireland website http://onlinecollection.nationalgallery.ie/objects/360/william-sharman-crawford-mp-17811861-irish-radical-and?ctx=1a36468c-ee41-41f8-994b-e650253fcc50&idx=0 (acc. 13 July 2021).

147. *BNL,* 24 May 1876, C.E.B. Brett, *Buildings of Belfast 1700–1914* (London, 1967), p. 23.

148. Brett, *Buildings of Belfast,* pp 47–8.

149. *BNL,* 24 Oct. 1848.

150. McCavery, *Newtown,* p. 142.

151. *BNL,* 3 Nov. 1856, C. E. B. Brett, *Buildings of North County Down* (Belfast, 2002), pp 270–2.

152. *BM,* 2 Mar. 1857.

153. *NW,* 5 Mar. 1857.

154. *Stirling Observer,* 21 Aug. 1856.

155. *NW,* 1 Feb. 1862.

156. *LS,* 6 Feb. 1862.

157. *BOU,* 13, 15 Feb., 1. 13 Mar. 1862.

158. *BNL,* 17 Mar., *NW,* 28 Mar., *BOU,* 24 May 1862.

159. *BNL,* 15 Oct. 1870.

160. *NW,* 24 Mar. 1863.

161. *NW,* 15 July 1863. The Wellington monument, designed by Sir Robert Smirke, was begun in 1817 but was long uncompleted due to shortage of funds.

162. S. F. Lynn to John SC, 11 May 1865, PRONI, D856/A/5/6.

163. *Newry Reporter,* 20 July 1872.

164. *NW,* 12 Jan. 1876.

165. *Nonconformist,* 10 Oct. 1855.

NOTES TO CHAPTER 9

1. Peter Gray, 'The making of mid-Victorian Ireland? Political economy and the memory of the Great Famine, 1847–80', in P. Gray (ed.), *Victoria's Ireland? Irishness and Britishness 1837–1901* (Dublin, 2004), pp 151–66; Dewey, 'The rehabilitation of the peasant proprietor', pp 17–47.

2. *NW,* 28 Apr. 1862.

3. Anon., *The English Press on the Irish Question, with an Irishman's View of it, by Philo-Celt* (Dublin, 1864), reviewed in *LS,* 22 Oct. 1864.

4. *LS,* 30 Nov. 1864.

5. *LS,* 18, 28 Oct. 1865.

6. *LS,* 7 Jan. 1865.

7. See William O'Neill Daunt's speech reported in *FJ,* 30 Dec. 1864.

8. *Hans 3,* 178: 570–627 (31 Mar. 1865: Maguire, Forster, McMahon).

9. *BOU,* 11 Apr. 1865.

10. *LS,* 29 Apr. 1865.

11. *LS,* 28 June 1865, [J. A. Dease]. 'Tenant compensation in Ireland', *Edinburgh Review,* 125 (Jan. 1867), pp 187–218.

12. *LS,* 28 June 1865.

13. *LS,* 3 Jan. 1866.

14. *Hans 3,* 183: 1087–97 (17 May 1866).

15. John Earl Russell, *A Letter to the Right Hon. Chichester Fortescue, MP, on the State of Ireland* (3rd edn, London, 1868), pp 27–34.

16. H. C. G. Matthew, *Gladstone 1809–1874* (Oxford, 1986), pp 192–5.

17. Isaac Butt, *Land Tenure in Ireland: A Plea for the Celtic Race* (Dublin, 1866).

18. [Dease], 'Tenant compensation', pp 206–10.

19. *LS,* 31 Oct. 1868. McClure lost the seat in 1874, but was elected at a by-election for Co. Londonderry in 1878.

20. Thompson, *End of Liberal Ulster,* pp 64–5.

21. *Times,* repr. in *BNL,* 20 May 1869. In 1858 the paper had stated bluntly that 'what Pat does with his blunderbuss, Mr Crawford proposes to do with his long letters', *Irishman,* 18 Dec. 1858.

22. *DN* repr. in *EF,* 23 Oct. 1869.

23. Charles J. Kickham, 'Ireland's cause' (4 June), *Irishman,* 12 June 1869.

24. Thompson, *End of Liberal Ulster,* pp 38–50.

25. *BNL,* 25 Nov. 1869

26. *Newry Reporter,* 27 Nov. 1869.

27. *LS,* 8 Jan., *FJ,* 22 Jan., *BNL,* 8 Mar. 1870.

28. *Nation,* 27 Nov. 1869.

29. McKnight to R. McDonnell (1 Feb.), *FJ,* 4 Feb. 1870.

30. H. C. G. Matthew (ed.), *The Gladstone Diaries, Vol. 7, January 1869–June 1871* (Oxford, 1982).

31. *Hans 3,* 199: 334 (15 Feb. 1870).

32. Matthew, *Gladstone,* pp 194–7.

33. *Hans 3,* 202: 6–7 (14 June 1870).

34. Ibid., 202: 376–7 (17 June). As William Wood he was solicitor general in 1851–2. McKnight welcomed this 'posthumous testimonial [...] to the enlightened-far-seeing statesmanship of Mr Sharman Crawford', *LS,* 25 June 1870.

35. *BNL,* 26 Apr. 1870.

36. *LS,* 25 June; [J.C. Hoey]. 'The land bill and the lords', *Dublin Review,* 15:29 (July 1870), pp 178–85.

37. *BMN*, 18 Nov. 1870.
38. McKnight to the editor (9 Mar.), *Times*, 11 Mar. 1870.
39. *BMN*, 9 Dec. 1870, *Weekly Press (WP)*, 23 Jan. 1874.
40. Receipt from James SC to John SC for £525 due to him from the estates (April/May 1862), PRONI, D856/D/132; *BT*, 19 Oct. 1877.
41. James SC to G. Brush, 13, 17 Nov., *NW*, 4 Dec. 1875.
42. *DR*, 16 May 1863, 14 Dec. 1867, 30 May 1868.
43. Crawford appears to have been instrumental in having the sentence of 15 years for manslaughter reduced to four, and Moffat was eventually released after serving two, *BOU*, 13 May, 11 Sept., *Ulsterman*, 21 July 1856. Thanks to Peter Donnelly for this reference.
44. *DR*, 10 Apr. 1869.
45. *BMN*, 13 June 1864, *Times*, 20 Sept. 1867.
46. *DR*, 8 Aug. 1863, *BNL*, 31 Aug. 1865, *Scotsman*, 1 Oct. 1869, *DR*, 18 Oct. 1873, *Newtownards Chronicle (NC)*, 31 Oct. 1874.
47. *NW*, 7 Sept. 1891.
48. *DR*, 19 July 1862, *Ulster Examiner (UE)*, 29 Aug. 1871.
49. *DR*, 29 July 1871.
50. *DR*, 6, 20 Aug. 1870. By 1875 the practice of annual excursions had also been adopted by the Armagh union, and by 1877 in Belfast, *UE*, 9 Aug. 1875, 12 Jul 1877.
51. *DR*, 24 Aug. 1872.
52. *UE*, 23 Aug. 1873.
53. *DR*, 22 Aug. 1874.
54. *DR*, 20 Aug. 1870.
55. *DR*, 5 Aug. 1871.
56. *NW*, 15 Aug. 1876, *BNL*, 7 Aug. 1877.
57. Brian M. Walker, 'The land question and elections in Ulster, 1868-86', in S. Clark and J. S. Donnelly (eds), *Irish Peasants: Violence and Political Unrest 1780–1914* (Dublin, 1983), pp 233–9.
58. Alexander R. Dinnen, *Ulster Tenant Right. Mr Jas. Sharman Crawford's Amendment Bill, and 'No Surrender'* (Belfast, 1876), pp 3–5.
59. Ibid., Paul Bew and Frank Wright, 'The agrarian opposition in Ulster politics, 1848-87', in Clark and Donnelly (ed.), *Irish Peasants*, pp 200–5.
60. Thompson, *End of Liberal Ulster*, pp 110–11.
61. *UE*, 30 Dec. 1872.
62. *BT*, 8 May 1872; Thompson, *End of Liberal Ulster*, pp 116–18.
63. *NR*, 1 Feb. 1873.
64. Thompson, *End of Liberal Ulster*, pp 156–7.
65. *CC*, 1, 8 Mar. 1873.
66. *CC*, 17 Jan. 1874.
67. *UE*, 21, 22 Jan. 1874.
68. *NW*, 22 Jan. 1874.
69. *FJ*, 26 Jan., *UE*, 29 Jan. *NW*, 30 Jan. 1874.
70. Undated memo [1874] in PRONI, D1905/2/17A/5.
71. *NW*, 31 Jan. 1874.
72. Draft placard, n.d. [1874], in PRONI, D1905/2/17A/5.
73. *BT*, 21 Jan., *BNL*, 3 Feb *UE*, 4, 7 Feb., *NW*, 9 Feb. 1874.
74. Thompson, *End of Liberal Ulster*, pp 151–2.
75. See correspondence in L'Estrange and Brett papers, PRONI, D1905/2/17A/5.
76. 'Fifty years ago in Down', *NW*, 10 Aug. 1923.
77. *NR*, 10 Feb., James SC to the electors to Down (10 Feb.), *BT*, 11 Feb. 1874.
78. James McWilliam to C. H. Brett, 4 Feb., Thomas Carey to Brett, 5 Feb., James Nelson to Brett, 5 Feb., J. S. Conner to Brett, 4 Feb. 1874, PRONI, D1905/2/17A/5.
79. *NW*, 29 Apr. 1878.
80. *BNL*, 10 Feb. 1874.
81. John Kerrey to Brett, 5 Feb. 1874, PRONI, D1905/2/17A/5.
82. *BNL*, 11 Feb., *NC*, 14 Feb. 1874.
83. Walker, 'Land question', pp 239–43.

84. *CC*, 28 Mar., *BNL*, 6 July. *Irishman*, 11 July 1874; David Thornley, *Isaac Butt and Home Rule* (London, 1964), pp 231–2.

85. Daniel Ritchie, *Isaac Nelson; Radical Abolitionist, Evangelical Presbyterian and Irish Nationalist* (Liverpool, 2018), pp 188–91, 242–3.

86. Thornley, *Butt*, pp 248–50; Thompson, *End of Liberal Ulster*, pp 157–8.

87. Ibid., pp 259–60, *FJ*, 10 Feb. 1875.

88. *WP*, 16 Apr., 28 May 1875.

89. *Irish Times (IT)*, 24 May, *FJ*, 2 June 1875.

90. *Hans 3*, 224: 1295–8 (2 June 1875).

91. *IT*, 3 June, *Weekly FJ*, 5 June 1875.

92. *Ballymoney Free Press (BFP)*, 5 Aug., 16 Sept., *FJ*, 30 Aug., *WP*, 11 June 1875.

93. Hicks Beach to Abercorn, 26 May 1875, PRONI, D623/A/316/19.

94. Dinnen, *Ulster Tenant-Right*, *NW*, 8 Nov., 18, 29 Dec. 1875, 1 Jan. 1876.

95. *Ulster Examiner (UE)*, 4 Dec., *WP*, 14 May 1875.

96. *NW*, 1 Feb., *FJ*, 10 Feb. 1876.

97. *FJ*, 15 Mar. 1876.

98. *Hans 3*, 230: 224–6 (21 June), *NW*, 24 June 1876.

99. *NW*, 3 July 1876.

100. *UE*, 7, 12 July 1876, Thompson, *End of Liberal Ulster*, p. 141.

101. *UE*, 27 Oct. 1876.

102. *NW*, 27 Oct. 1876.

103. *UE*, 11, 27 Jan. 1877.

104. *BFP*, 15 Feb. 1877.

105. *BFP*, 3 Mar 1877.

106. 'Ulster Scot's letters to the loyalists of Ulster', *BWN*, 28 Apr. 1877.

107. *FJ*, 22 Mar., *UE*, 31 Mar. 1877.

108. *IT*, 19 May 1877.

109. Gladstone to James SC, 18 Oct., *Glasgow Herald*, 24 Oct, *BT*, 23 Oct. 1877.

110. Gladstone to James SC, 7 Nov., PRONI, D856/D/151, *NW*, 7 Nov. 1877.

111. *NW*, 17 Jan. 1878.

112. *Hans 3*, 237: 491–507 (25 Jan.), *BNL*, 29 Jan. 1878.

113. James SC to editor, *Times*, 6 Mar. 1878.

114. Anon., *The Annals of Ulster Tenant-Right, By an Antrim Tenant-Farmer* (n.p., n.d. [Belfast, c.1877]).

115. *NW*, 29 Apr., *NR*, 4 May 1878.

116. *Ballymena Advertiser*, 11 May 1878.

117. *FJ*, 30 Apr. 1878.

118. *BFP*, 2 May 1878.

119. J. R. B. McMinn, 'The Land League in north Antrim, 1880–2', *The Glynnes*, 11 (1983), pp 35–40.

120. *Coleraine Constitution*, 18 May. Both John and Charles Sharman Crawford were rumoured to be alternative candidates, but neither came forward that year, *BT*, 2, 3 May, *NR*, 2 May 1878.

121. *UE*, 30 Apr. 1878.

122. *Nation*, 2 Apr. 1880.

123. *LJ*, 20 May, *Weekly FJ*, 25 May 1878; Thompson, *End of Liberal Ulster*, p. 14.

124. *BMN*, 16 Mar. 1880.

125. John SC, Address (15 Mar.), *BNL*, 17 Mar. 1880.

126. *BNL*, 19 Mar. 1880. John was also mocked for remaining unmarried, with an underlying hint of homophobia.

127. *UE*, 23 Mar., *BNL*, 31 Mar. 1880.

128. *BMN*, 6 Apr. 1880.

129. *BMN*, 4 May, 30 June 1880.

130. Thompson, *End of Liberal Ulster*, pp 188–95.

131. William Davidson to John SC, 15 Jan. 1881, PRONI, D856/A/6/30.

132. Draft reply of Arthur SC to Drumgiven tenants, 1881, ibid., 31.

133. Copy of memorial by 28 tenants to Arthur SC (Jan. 1881) and reply to same, 5 Feb. 1881, PRONI, D856/C/6/30, Correspondence of D. L. Coddington and A. S. Crawford, Jan. 1881, ibid, 31.

134. Memorial of Stalleen tenants to Arthur SC, 21 Jan. 1887 and his draft reply (Jan. 1887), Coddington to Arthur SC, 27 Jan. 1887, PRONI, D856/C/6/34-35.

135. Arthur SC to Samuel Stewart, 2 Jan., Arthur SC to W. Davidson, 15 Feb. 1882, PRONI, D856/A/6/35-36.

136. *Newtownards Chronicle (NC)*, 19 Dec. 1885.

137. *Belfast Weekly Telegraph (BWT)*, 22, 29 Nov. 1884.

138. *FJ*, 29 Nov. 1884, *BNL*, 1 Dec. 1884.

139. Thompson, *End of Liberal Ulster*, p. 291.

140. Ibid., pp 238–47.

141. Ibid., pp 266–9.

142. *CC*, 6 Dec. 1884.

143. *LJ*, 23 Nov. 1885.

144. David Jones, 'Women and Chartism', *History*, 68:222 (1983), pp 1–21.

145. *Times*, 23 Apr. 1842.

146. *FJ*, 16 May 1844.

147. *DEM*, 26 Jan. 1849.

148. Sophia Stuart to WSC, Apr. 1852, PRONI, D856/D/110.

149. *BM*, 1 July 1852.

150. 'Greenwood leaves from over the sea, No. 16', *National Era*, 21 Oct. 1852. 'Grace Greenwood' was the pen name of Sara Jane Lippincott, who became well known for her advocacy of the abolition of slavery and of women's rights.

151. Mabel SC, *Fanny Denison* (London, 1852).

152. *Globe*, 27 Sept. See also *MPo*, 29 Oct. 1852

153. Mabel SC, *The Wilmot Family* (3 vols, London, 1864).

154. *Examiner*, 15 Oct. 1864.

155. *London Review*, 5 Nov. 1864, p. 515, *Scotsman*, 21 Dec. 1864. Dickens had addressed similar themes in his *Little Dorrit* of 1855–7.

156. Mabel SC, *Life in Tuscany* (London, 1859), p. vii.

157. Lady Morgan, *Italy* (London, 1821), Mrs T. Mitchell, *Gleanings from Travels in England, Ireland and Through Italy, or Comparative View of Society at Home and Abroad* (2 vols, Belfast, n.d.).

158. For a fuller account, see Peter Gray, 'Mabel Sharman Crawford's *Life in Tuscany*: Ulster radicalism in a hot climate', in M. Corporaal and C. Morin (eds), *Travelling Irishness in the Long Nineteenth Century* (London, 2017), pp 35–50.

159. *Life in Tuscany*, pp 64–5.

160. She admitted to having an 'insular prejudice' in preferring potatoes to this diet of black bread, kidney beans, and maize porridge, ibid., p. 160.

161. Ibid., p. 165.

162. Ibid., p. 169.

163. Ibid., p. 166.

164. On the decline of peasant living conditions, see Lucy Riall, *Risorgimento: The History of Italy from Napoleon to Nation State* (Basingstoke, 2009) pp 85–91.

165. *Life in Tuscany*, pp 187–8.

166. Ibid., pp 134–5.

167. Ibid., p. 122.

168. Ibid., pp 147–8.

169. Ibid., pp 280–98.

170. Jennifer O'Brien, 'Irish public opinion and the Risorgimento, 1859-60', in C. Barr, M. Finelli and A. O'Connor (eds), *Nation/Nazione: Irish Nationalism and the Italian Risorgimento* (Dublin, 2014), pp 110–32.

171. *Birmingham Journal*, 16 Apr., *Leeds Times*, 30 Apr. 1859.

172. *Western Daily Press*, 18 Apr., *WI*, 20 Apr., *Hull Packet*, 29 Apr. The book was also published in the United States, *New York Tribune*, 29 Sept. 1859.

173. P. Brisset, 'La vie et les femmes en Toscane', *Revue des deux mondes*, 23 (Sept. 1859), pp 523–68.

174. Mabel SC, *Through Algeria* (London, 1863), pp ix–xv.

175. Ibid., pp 10, 20–5, 53–7, 239–42, 360–2.

176. Ibid., pp 157–8, 354–60.

177. Anon., 'In Algeria with a poet', *Duffy's Hibernian Magazine*, 3 (Jan. 1863), pp 44–53.

178. *John Bull*, 20 Dec. 1862, *DEM*, 16 Jan., *BNL*, 29 Jan., *Scotsman*, 27 Apr., *Globe*, 18 June 1863.

179. Mabel SC to Lord Dufferin, 18 Jan., 7 Feb. 1894, PRONI, D1071/H/B/C/688/1–2.

180. Meeting of Pioneer Club, *Shafts*, July 1895, pp 50–1.

181. *Waterford Standard*, 7, 24 Apr. 1869. Mabel SC, 'Experiences of an Irish landowner', *Contemporary Review*, 52 (Aug. 1887), pp 263–74.

182. NAI, Landed Estates Court Rentals: County of Waterford.

183. Mabel SC, *The Irish Question: Experiences of an Irish Landowner* (London, 1888), pp 3–4. The pamphlet was republished from the *Contemporary Review* by the Irish Press Agency, established by the Home Rule MP J. J. Clancy to promote the party's views in Great Britain.

184. *Experiences*, pp 11–12. The contested evictions of 28 tenant families at Bodyke, Co. Clare, in June 1887 had become a national scandal.

185. *Birmingham Daily Post*, 3 Aug. See also *Globe*, 3 Aug., *NW*, 6 Aug. 1887.

186. *FJ*, 10 Aug. 1887.

187. M. Sharman Crawford, 'The land agitation in Ireland', *Times*, 15 Sept. 1880.

188. *Times*, 18, 20 Sept. 1880.

189. M. Sharman Crawford to the editor (18 Sept.), *Times*, 20 Sept., *BMN*, 21 Sept., *NW*, 17, 2 Sept. 1880.

190. *Times*, 3 Oct., *Englishwomen's Review (ER)*, 78, 15 Oct. 1879, p. 440.

191. *Experiences*, p. 17.

192. *Scotsman*, 12 Sept. 1888.

193. H. C. G. Matthew (ed.), *The Gladstone Diaries: With Cabinet Minutes and Prime-Ministerial Correspondence. Vol. 12 1887–1891* (Oxford, 1994) (12 Jan. 1889).

194. *ER*, 15 Sept. 1880, p. 419.

195. *BNL*, 20 Apr. 1889.

196. *Atlas*, 29 Nov. 1868; Linde Lunney and Georgina Clinton, 'Tod, Isabella Maria Susan', *DIB*.

197. *DEM*, 5 May 1869, *FJ*, 24 Dec. 1872, 17 Dec. 1874.

198. *BNL*, 29 Nov. 1877.

199. In 1879 she read Tod's statement on access to higher education for women in Ireland to a special meeting of the Ladies Institute in London, which resolved to promote further legislation, *NW*, 18 July 1879, *Times*, 15 June 1880.

200. *ER*, 15 July 1880, pp 303–7.

201. *BNL*, 12 July 1882, *ER*, 15 July 1885, p. 306, Mabel SC to the editor, *NW*, 10 Sept. 1886.

202. *FJ*, 19 Apr. 1870, *ER*, Jan. 1871, p. 128; Marie O'Neill, 'The Dublin Women's Suffrage Association and its successors', *Dublin Historical Record*, 38:4 (1985), pp 126–40.

203. *Women's Suffrage Journal*, 1 June, *FJ*, 24 July 1871.

204. *NW*, 6 June 1877.

205. *NW*, 15 Aug., *DEM*, 21 Aug. 1878.

206. *BNL*, 13 July 1874, *NW*, 18 Jan., *NW*, 12 Sept. 1876. A broader alliance between the women's suffrage and tenant-right movements in Ulster is suggested by the *Weekly Press*, 12 Feb. 1875.

207. *NW*, 12 Feb. 1879.

208. *BNL*, 13 Sept. 1876, *Women's Suffrage*, 1 Apr. 1878. She was an associate member, and he a full member of the Association and on the committee for its economic science and statistics section.

209. *MPo*, 24 May 1878. The 1871 census records her as an 'autheress and landowner' resident in Kensington.

210. *BMN*, 6 Oct. 1881.

211. Mabel SC (ed.), *Opinions of Women on Women's Suffrage* (London, 1879), p. 18.

212. *NW*, 11 Mar. 1879.

213. *ER*, 15 May 1884, pp 218–25.

214. *Dublin Daily Express*, 10 Oct. 1881, *Sentinel*, Dec. 1881, *MCo*, 13 Nov. 1882.

215. Mabel SC, 'The import of Irish girls to London', *Pall Mall Gazette (PMG)*, 14 Aug. 1885.

216. *PMG*, 19 Mar., *ER*, 15 Apr. 1886, p. 186.

217. 'Irish Association for Promoting the Training and Employment of Women', *ER*, 15 Feb. 1887.

218. *BFP*, 6 Jan. 1887.

219. Alvin Jackson, 'Irish unionism and the Russellite threat, 1894–1906', *IHS*, 25:100 (1987), pp 376–9.

220. *FJ*, 20 Mar. 1886, *NW,* 10 July 1889, *BNL,* 3 May 1890.

221. Heloise Brown, 'An alternative imperialism: Isabella Tod, internationalist and "good Liberal Unionist"', *Gender and History,* 10:3 (1998), pp 358–80.

222. *FJ*, 7 June 1886.

223. *FJ*, 7 June 1886. A similar argument was made in the *NR,* 8 Feb. 1887.

224. *Hans 3,* 304: 1036–151 (8 Apr. 1886).

225. Mabel SC to the editor, *NW,* 10 Sept. 1886. For the contrary claim that had he been living, William Sharman Crawford would have been a Liberal Unionist, see *BWN,* 22 June 1889.

226. *DN,* 21 July 1887.

227. *Women's Gazette,* 15 Dec. 1888, 29 June 1889.

228. 'An Ulster Liberal' to the editor (18 Dec.), *NW,* 20 Dec. 1890.

229. William SC, *Suggestions with Reference to the Necessity of Constituting a National Body to Manage the Local Interests and Local Taxation of Ireland, in Connection with the Imperial Parliament. Reprinted with Preface by William Huston Dodd* (Dublin, 1892).

230. H. C. G. Matthew (ed.), *The Gladstone Diaries: With Cabinet Minutes and Prime-Ministerial Correspondence. Vol. 13 1892–1896* (Oxford, 1994), (9, 26 July 1892), *FJ,* 27 June 1892.

231. *BFP,* 30 June, *FJ,* 15 July 1892.

232. *BNL,* 1 Sept. 1890.

233. *Irish News (IN),* 27 Oct. 1893; Charles Gavan Duffy, George Sigerson and Douglas Hyde, *The Revival of Irish Literature* (London, 1894).

234. *Shafts,* July 1894.

235. *Women's Suffrage Journal,* 1 Aug. 1887, *DN,* 18 July 1888, *The Queen,* 24 May 1890, *ER,* 15 Apr. 1891, p. 102, *Women's Signal,* 2 Jan. 1896, 2 June 1898.

236. Mabel SC, '"Purdah" in the house of commons', *Women's Penny Paper,* 24 May 1890.

237. *The Queen,* 23 Apr. 1887, 27 Dec. 1890, *ER,* 15 Dec. 1889, p. 570, *PMG,* 19 Dec. 1890.

238. Mabel SC, 'Social scares', *The Woman's World* (Aug. 1888), pp 433–6. Wilde edited the magazine 1887–9 and sought to develop it as 'the first social magazine for women', Anya Clayworth, '*The Woman's World*: Oscar Wilde as editor', *Victorian Periodicals Review,* 30:2 (1997), pp 84–101.

239. Mabel SC, 'Maltreatment of wives', *Westminster Review,* 139:1 (Jan. 1893), pp 292–303.

240. *Truth,* 1 Nov. 1894, *Shafts,* Apr. 1896, p. 38, Mabel SC to the editor (23 Feb.), *Women's Signal,* 9 Mar. 1899.

241. *ER,* 15 Jan. 1901, Mabel SC to Dufferin, 20 June 1901, PRONI, D1071/H/B/C/688.

242. *NW,* 16 Feb. 1912.

243. *Scotsman,* 26 Aug. 1913, *Western Mail,* 7 Aug. 1915.

244. [D.J. O'Donoghue], 'Obituary: Mabel Sharman Crawford', *The Irish Book Lover,* 3 (Apr. 1912), p. 152.

245. Drisceoil and Ó Drisceoil, *Beamish & Crawford,* p. 121.

246. *NW,* 6 Apr. 1880.

247. *BNL,* 24 Dec. 1889.

248. *BNL,* 7 Nov. 1872.

249. *Naval and Military Gazette,* 16 May 1877.

250. *FJ,* 12 Mar. 1884.

251. *Army and Navy Gazette,* 31 May 1890, *BNL,* 25 Feb. 1891. He was particularly active with the Down staghounds, *NC,* 24 Jan. 1891.

252. *LJ,* 14 Oct., *NC,* 17 Oct. 1891, *BNL,* 22 Aug. 1894, *Army and Navy Gazette,* 3 Dec. 1898, 12 Dec. 1903.

253. *FJ,* 19 Dec. 1894.

254. *Cork Constitution,* 12 Jan. 1891.

255. Ó Drisceoil and Ó Drisceoil, *Beamish & Crawford,* pp 122–3.

256. Ibid., pp 185, 230–1, *CE,* 25 Feb., 5 Mar. 1909, 14 Dec. 1910.

257. *FJ,* 25 Mar., *North Down Herald (NDH),* 20 May 1898.

258. *BNL,* 26 Oct. 1894, 14 Apr. 1898.

259. *BNL,* 9 Apr. 1897.

260. *DR,* 20 July 1850; *BM,* 19 Aug. 1857.

261. *BNL,* 20 May 1886.

262. *NW,* 25 Sept. 1900. *IN,* 3 May 1901.

263. *NDH*, 24 Aug., *BNL*, 10 Sept., but see *IN*, 25 Sept. 1900.
264. *BNL*, 9 Apr, 4 June 1892.
265. Olwen Purdue, *The Big House in the North of Ireland* (Dublin, 2009), pp 170–2.
266. *BFP*, 12 May 1892.
267. *NW*, 10 Oct. 1894.
268. RG SC to Frederick Crawford, 15 Sept., Crawford to RG SC, 16 Nov. 1933, PRONI, D1700/5/6/19B-C; Ronald McNeill, *Ulster's Stand for the Union* (London, 1922), pp 30, 37.
269. *MCo*, 17 Aug. 1898.
270. *IN*, 2 Sept. 1898; McCavery, *Newtown*, pp 171–2.
271. *BFP*, 18 Aug. 1898.
272. *Irish Standard*, 9 July 1892; Jackson, 'Irish unionism', pp 379–88.
273. *FJ*, 11 Nov. 1896. For the continuing idealisation of McKnight and his clerical allies in Presbyterian circles, see Latimer, 'James McKnight, LL.D.', pp 93–106.
274. *PMG*, 27 Apr. 1897, *BNL*, 3 Aug. 1898, *CE*, 3 May 1871.
275. *PMG*, 27 Sept. 1898.
276. *BT*, 1 Nov. 1899, *DN*, 10 Oct. 1901, 8 Oct. 1902. H. B. Grimsditch (revised by Gareth Shaw), 'Lipton, Sir Thomas Johnstone', *ODNB*.
277. *NDH*, 19 Sept. 1902.
278. *BNL*, 5 Apr. 1897.
279. *NW*, 19, 20 Jan., *NDH*, 7 Apr. 1899.
280. *NDH*, 13 June 1902.
281. *CC*, 2 June 1900.
282. *Scotsman*, 7 Aug., *MCo*, 13 Aug. 1900.
283. *IN*, 11 Aug. 1900.
284. *NW*, 16 Aug., *NDH*, 7 Sept. 1900.
285. *NDH*, 17 Aug. 1900.
286. James Craig, then serving with the army in southern Africa, wrote to his mother expressing his hope that Sharman-Crawford had been elected, 20 Oct. 1900, PRONI, D1415/B/21.
287. 'North Down election. Candidature of Colonel Sharman-Crawford', n.d. [Sept. 1900], PRONI, T1129/386.
288. For parallel developments in Armagh, see Alvin Jackson, 'Unionist politics and Protestant society in Edwardian Ireland', *Historical Journal*, 33:4 (1990), pp 839–66.
289. *IN*, 27 Sept., *NW*, 5 Oct., *BNL*, 28 Sept. 1900.
290. *NW*, 8 Oct. 1900. The context was a more hard-line stance being taken by the government in support of landed interests, symbolised by Russell's dismissal from office in 1900, Jackson, 'Irish unionists', pp 391–2.
291. *IN*, 15 Oct., *NW*, 15 Oct., *NDH*, 19 Oct. 1900.
292. *NDH*, 28 Oct., *BNL*, 3 Dec. 1904, *IN*, 13 Feb. 1905.
293. James Laughlin, 'Russell, Sir Thomas Wallace', *DIB*; *NW*, 19 Oct. 1900.
294. See Richard McMinn, 'Presbyterianism and politics in Ulster, 1871–1906', *Studia Hibernica*, 21 (1981), pp 127–46.
295. Patrick Cosgrave, 'T. W. Russell and the compulsory land purchase campaign in Ulster, 1900–03', *IHS*, 37:146 (2010), pp 226–31.
296. T. W. Russell, *Ireland and the Empire: A Review, 1800–1900* (London, 1901), pp 34–7, 55, 148–54; *Hans 4*, 89: 744–5 (21 Feb. 1901).
297. *CC*, 6 Apr. 1901.
298. *IN*, 30 Nov. 1901.
299. *Daily Express*, 24 Jan. 1902.
300. *NW*, 20, 22 Jan. 1901.
301. *IN*, 30 Jan., 3 Feb.
302. *NW*, 4 Feb. 1902.
303. *BNL*, 31 Jan., *NDH*, 28 Feb. 1902.
304. *BNL*, 31 Jan. 1903.
305. Cosgrove, 'Russell', pp 236–40.
306. *II*, 14 Jan. 1904.
307. *CDS*, 11 Nov. 1904.

308. *NW,* 6 May 1905.
309. *BNL,* 20 Nov. 1905, 11 Jan. 1906.
310. *BNL,* 3 July 1908, *IN,* 19 Jan. 1910; EC 1947, PRONI, LR1/472; for the Rademon and Crawfordsburn sales between 1927 and 1933 under this act, see FIN/48/3/452, 910.
311. *Drogheda Independent,* 3 Jan. 1914.
312. Eoin Magennis, 'Protestant nationalism in Ulster, 1890–1910: Francis Joseph Bigger and the writing of the *Ulster Land War of 1770'*, *Seanchas Ard Mhacha,* 18:2 (2001), pp 102–16.
313. *NDS,* 16 Apr. 1909; Jackson, 'Irish unionism', p. 397.
314. *BNL,* 24 Oct. 1910.
315. *NW,* 24 Sept. 1912, *BNL,* 28 Jan. 1933.
316. *NW,* 24 Oct. 1910.
317. *BNL,* 29 Sept. 1914.
318. In late 1912 he warned Carson that they were concerned that too great a stress on tariff reform could cost the Unionists English seats and hence make home rule more likely, RG SC to Carson, 31 Dec. 1912, PRONI, D989/A/8/2/10.
319. *NW,* 26 Sept. 1911.
320. *CDS,* 20 Oct., *IN,* 23 Oct. 1911.
321. *CDS,* 12 Apr. 1912.
322. Alvin Jackson, *Sir Edward Carson* (Dublin, 1993), p. 37; *Dublin Daily Express,* 24 Dec. 1912; Timothy Bowman, '"The north began" ... but when? The formation of the Ulster Volunteer Force', *History Ireland* 21:2 (2013), p. 29.
323. RG SC to [Carson], 31 Dec. 1912, PRONI, D989/A/8/2/10.
324. *Scotsman,* 6 Mar. 1913.
325. *NW,* 25 July, 25 Sept., *BWN,* 31 July, *BNL,* 26 Aug. 1913.
326. Timothy Bowman, *Carson's Army: The Ulster Volunteer Force, 1910–22* (Manchester, 2007), pp 155–6.
327. *NDH,* 15 Aug. 1913.
328. *BT,* 25 Sept. 1913.
329. RGSC to Lady Londonderry, 22 Nov. [1913], PRONI, D2846/1/7/51.
330. *BT,* 31 May 1914.
331. *BT,* 1 Apr., *BNL,* 7 Apr. 1914, *Irish Citizen,* 6 Mar. 1915.
332. *NW,* 7 Sept., *BNL,* 28 Dec. 1914, 2 Jan. 1915.
333. *NW,* 17, 23 Apr. 1915.
334. *Dublin Evening Telegraph,* 15 Oct. 1915.
335. *PMG,* 26 Apr., *BNL,* 27 May 1916, *NW,* 27 Apr. 1917.
336. *BNL,* 30 May 1916.
337. *BNL,* 21 Aug. 1914, *Hans 5,* 68: 408–9 (18 Nov. 1914), *Birmingham Mail,* 24 Sept. 1915.
338. *Hans 5,* 73: 105–6 (5 July 1915), 77: 1221–3 (6 Jan. 1916), *BNL,* 9 Mar. 1916, *FJ,* 16 May 1918.
339. *BNL,* 15 June, *II,* 23 June, *FJ,* 28 July 1917.
340. RG SC to Lady Londonderry, 21 Aug. 1917, PRONI, D2846/1/7/50.
341. Patrick Buckland, 'The unity of Ulster Unionism, 1886–1939', *History,* 60:199 (1975), pp 214–15.
342. *Westminster Gazette,* 26 Nov. 1918.
343. *Forward,* 22 Mar. 1919.
344. *NDH,* 25 Oct. 1919.
345. *Irish Society,* 3 Jan. 1920.
346. RGSC to Hugh de Fellenberg Montgomery, 20 May, PRONI, D627/435/88, Stronge to Montgomery, 12 Mar. 1920, in Patrick Buckland (ed.), *Irish Unionism 1885–1923: A Documentary History* (Belfast, 1973), p. 417.
347. RG SC to Montgomery, 4 June 1920, PRONI, D627/435/95.
348. *BNL,* 12 July, *Irish Society,* 14 Aug. 1920.
349. *NW,* 28 June 1921.
350. *FJ,* 30 Oct. 1922.
351. *BNL,* 14 Feb., 21 May 1921.
352. Stronge to Montgomery, 8 Feb. 1919, PRONI, D627/437/55.
353. *BNL,* 13 June 1921.

354. Extract from Lady Craig's diary, 21 June 1921, in Buckland, *Irish Unionism*, p. 455.

355. *NW,* 15 June, *FJ,* 20 July 1922, 'Reports on irregularities by "B" Special Constables on duty at Rademon House, Crossgar', PRONI, HA/32/1/288.

356. Frederick Crawford, 'Diary of violence in Belfast, 1922', PRONI, D640/11/1 (22 June 1922); Frederick Crawford to RG SC, 11 Sept., 16 Nov. 1933, PRONI, D1700/5/6/19A, C.

357. *NW,* 4, 13 July 1921. This adherence appears, however, to have been mostly formal, and he reserved his enthusiasm for masonic activities, serving as provincial grand master of Down for 30 years and frequently hosting events at Crawfordsburn, *BNL,* 21 Mar. 1934.

358. *NW,* 29 Nov. 1921, 15 Apr. 1922.

359. *FJ,* 21 Oct. 1916, *General Advertiser,* 16 Apr. 1921.

360. *Cork Constitution,* 19 Mar. 1892, *NW,* 15 June 1917, Appointment of Arthur Frederick Sharman-Crawford as deputy lieutenant of County Cork, Apr. 1918, NAI, CSO/RP/1918/1849, Ó Drisceoil and Ó Drisceoil, *Beamish and Crawford,* p. 261.

361. *Westminster Gazette,* 21 Jan. 1921.

362. *DET,* 18 Nov. 1922, Ó Drisceoil and Ó Drisceoil, *Beamish and Crawford,* pp 265–8, 291–2.

363. *NDH,* 1 Oct. 1921.

364. *NW,* 29 Nov. 1933.

365. *Parliamentary Debates (Northern Ireland Senate),* 16, p. 85 (20 Mar. 1934: T. J. Campbell).

366. *BNL,* 21 Mar. 1934.

367. I. Sharman-Crawford, 'Where is the land fit for heroes?', 'If Conservatives were Fascists', *The Blackshirt,* 14 Sept. 1934, 11 Jan. 1935. Irene was the granddaughter of Henry Sharman Crawford and was born in Blackrock, Co. Dublin, before moving with her mother to London.

368. Names and arms, change of: Carver to Sharman Crawford (1942-3), TNA, HO 45/19329.

369. *BT,* 5 June 1944, *BNL,* 15 Mar. 1946.

370. A portrait bust of William Sharman Crawford by Patrick MacDowell also went to the museum, but this does not appear in the modern collection list of NMNI, Kennedy, 'Sharman Crawford', p. iv.

371. *NW,* 17 Apr., *BT,* 17 Apr., *BNL,* 19 Apr. 1947.

372. *BT,* 23 June 1947; *CDS,* 25 Mar. 1950.

373. *CDS,* 4 Oct. 1990.

374. Joe Furphy, 'Crawfordsburn Country Park history', https://www.myni.life/country-parks/crawfordsburn-country-park/50th-anniversary/crawfordsburn-country-park-history/ (accessed 21 Jan. 2021).

NOTES TO CONCLUSION

1. WSC to John Fraser (10 Nov.), *FJ,* 28 Dec. 1837.

2. *Hans 3,* 59: 925–36 (28 Sept. 1841).

3. Hall, *Ulster Liberalism,* pp 244–9.

4. WSC, Memorandum on 'My faith, general observations and my principles of action', n.d. [1861], PRONI, D856/G/8.

5. Duffy, *Young Ireland,* p. 596.

6. Denis Holland, 'William Sharman Crawford', *Irish Emerald,* 25 Sept. 1869.

7. Duffy, *My Life, II,* p. 55.

8. Patrick Maume, 'McElroy, Albert Horatio', in *DIB.*

9. Ruth Illingworth, *Sheelagh Murnaghan 1924–1993: Stormont's Only Liberal MP* (Belfast, 2019).

10. Patrick Maume, 'Napier, Oliver', in *DIB.*

BIBLIOGRAPHY

PRIMARY SOURCES

Manuscripts

Bodleian Library, Oxford
Clarendon papers

Boston Public Library (online)
Anti-slavery collection

British Library, London
Robert Peel papers

Castle Howard, North Yorkshire
Castle Howard papers

Durham County Record Office, Durham
Londonderry papers

Hartley Library, University of Southampton
Palmerston (Broadlands) papers

Manchester Archives, Manchester
Anti-Corn Law League papers
Lancashire Public Schools Association papers

Mulgrave Castle, North Yorkshire
Normanby papers

National Archives of Ireland, Dublin
Chief Secretary's Office Registered Papers
Landed Estates Court Rentals
Relief Commission Papers

National Library of Ireland, Dublin
Autograph letters collection
Charles Gavan Duffy papers
Genealogical Office Papers
William Smith O'Brien papers

Nottingham University Archives, Nottingham
Newcastle papers

Public Record Office of Northern Ireland, Belfast
Abercorn Papers, D623
Account of a parochial visitation of Lisburn parish, commencing 13 November 1820, DIO/1/19/75
Annesley papers, D1854
Banbridge Board of Guardians minute books, BG6
Castlereagh papers, D3030
Craigavon papers, D1415
Crawford papers, D1700

F.H. Crawford diary, D640
Sharman Crawford papers, D856
Crossle family papers, T1689
Downshire papers, D607, D671
Dufferin and Ava papers, D1071
Duffin papers, D395, D608
Charles Gavan Duffy correspondence, T1143
Ministry of Finance Papers, FIN
Foster-Massereene Papers, T2519
Ministry of Home Affairs papers, HA
Irish Unionist Alliance papers, D989
J.A. Irvine papers, T2757
Ker papers, D892, D2651
Land Registry papers, LR1
L'Estrange and Brett papers, D1905
Theresa, Lady Londonderry papers, D2846
Martin and Henderson papers, D2223
Miscellaneous genealogical papers, D3000
Montgomery of Blessingbourne papers, D627
Newtownards Board of Guardians minute books, BG25
Nugent papers, D552
Papers relating to estates and individuals in Cos Armagh, Tyrone and Down, D1252
Pelham papers (transcripts), T755
Perceval-Maxwell papers, D3244
Rose-Cleland papers, T761
Guy Stone diaries, D826, D1447
Stone and Stewart papers, D1613
Swanston papers, T1129
Tennent papers, D1748
Ulster Gift Fund records, D913
Ulster Unionist Council papers, D1327
Upritchard papers, T3317
Wallace estate papers, D5569
Whyte papers, D2918
Young family papers, D2930

Royal Irish Academy, Dublin
Gavan Duffy bequest
Ordnance Survey letters

The National Archives, Kew
Colonial Office papers
Home Office papers
Lord John Russell papers
Treasury papers

Online
Irish Emigration Database
Irish Prison Registers 1790-1924

Official Publications

Hansard's Parliamentary Debates, 3rd–5th series, 1835-1922
Parliamentary Debates (NI Senate), 1921-34
General Valuation of Ratable Property in Ireland.

Bill for the Amendment of the Law of Landlord and Tenant in Ireland. HC 1835 (402), III.299.

Select Committee on Orange Lodges, Associations or Societies in Ireland. Report, Minutes of Evidence, Appendix. HC 1835 (377), XV.

Bill for the Amendment of the Law of Landlord and Tenant in Ireland, HC 1836 (142), IV.303.

Royal Commission on the Condition of the Poorer Classes in Ireland, First Report. Appendix C, part II, HC 1836 [35], XXX.221.

Royal Commission on the Condition of the Poorer Classes in Ireland, First Report. Supplement to Appendix D, HC 1836 [36], XXXI.1.

Royal Commission on the Condition of the Poorer Classes in Ireland, First Report. Appendix F, HC 1836 [38], XXXII.1.

Bill to Amend the Law of Landlord and Tenant in Ireland, HC 1843 (490), III.233.

Bill to Provide Compensation for Tenants in Ireland who Have Made, or Shall Hereafter Make Improvements on the Premises in the Occupation of such Tenants, HC 1845 (578), VI.177.

Report of Her Majesty's Commissioners of Enquiry into the State of the Law and Practice in Respect to the Occupation of Land in Ireland, Minutes of Evidence, Part I, HC 1845 [605-6] XIX.

Report from the Select Committee of the House of Lords on the Laws Relating to the Relief of the Destitute Poor, and into the Operation of the Medical Charities in Ireland, HC 1846 (694).

Bill to Secure the Rights of Occupying Tenants in Ireland, and Thereby to Promote the Improvement of the Soil and the Employment of the Labouring Classes. HC 1847 (127), IV.85.

Fifth, Sixth, and Seventh Reports of the Relief Commissioners, Constituted under the Act 10th Vic., Cap. 7; and Correspondence Connected Therewith, HC 1847-8 (876), XXIX.

Papers Relating to Proceedings for the Relief of the Distress, and State of the Unions and Workhouses, in Ireland. Fourth Series, 1847, HC 1847-8 [896], LIV.29.

Bill to Promote the Employment of Labour in Ireland, HC 1849 (205), II.487.

Fourth Report from the Select Committee of the House of Lords Appointed to Inquire into the Operation of the Irish Poor Law, HC 1849 (365) XVI.543.

Bill to Provide for the Better Securing and Regulating the Custom of 'Tenant Right' as Practised in the Province of Ulster, and to Secure Compensation to Improving Tenants in Ireland who may not Make Claim Under the Said Custom, and to Limit the Power of Eviction in Certain Cases. HC 1850 (431), VIII.323.

Return of the Expenditure of Poor Rates in Each Union in Ireland, for the Year Ended 29th September 1849; and of the Number of Persons Relieved in and out of the Workhouse in Each Union During the Same Period, HC 1850 (313), L.

Bill to Provide for the Better Securing and Regulating the Custom of 'Tenant Right' as Practised in the Province of Ulster, and to Secure Compensation to Improving Tenants who may not Make Claim Under the Said Custom, and to Limit the Power of Eviction in Certain Cases, HC 1852 (47) IV, 369.

A Return of the Number of Troops, Constabulary, and Police at Each Polling Place in Ireland, During the Days of Polling at the Last General Election, HC 1852-3 (325), L, 699.

Abstract of the Number of Electors on the Register of 1852-53 in Each County, City and Borough in Ireland, HC 1852-3 (957), LXXXIII.413.

Report from the Select Committee on Destitution (Gweedore and Cloughaneely), HC 1857-8 (412), XIII.89.

Census of Ireland for the Year 1861, Part I: Showing the Area, Population, and Number of Houses by Townlands and Electoral Divisions, Volume I, Province of Leinster, HC 1863 [3204], LIV.1.

Census of Ireland for the Year 1861, Part I: Showing the Area, Population, and Number of Houses by Townlands and Electoral Divisions, Volume III, Province of Ulster, HC 1863 [3204], LV.1.

Census of Ireland for the Year 1861, Part IV: Report and Tables Relating to the Religious Professions, Education and Occupations of the People, Volume. II, HC 1863 [3204-III], LX.1.

Returns by Provinces and Counties, of Cases of Evictions Which have Come to the Knowledge of the Constabulary in Each of the Years from 1849 to 1880, HC 1881 (185), LXXVII.725.

Newspapers and Periodicals

Age
Anti-Slavery Reporter
Armagh Guardian

Atlas
Army and Navy Gazette
Ballymena Advertiser
Ballymoney Free Press
Banner of Ulster
Belfast Commercial Chronicle
Belfast Evening Post
Belfast Daily News
Belfast Mercantile Advertiser
Belfast Mercury
Belfast Monthly Magazine
Belfast Morning Chronicle
Belfast Morning News
Belfast News-Letter
Belfast Protestant Journal
Belfast Telegraph
Belfast Weekly News
Belfast Weekly Telegraph
Birmingham Daily Post
Birmingham Journal
Birmingham Mail
Blackburn Standard
Blackshirt
Bolton Chronicle
Boston Pilot
Bradford Observer
Champion
Coleraine Chronicle
Coleraine Constitution
Connaught Telegraph
Cork Constitution
Cork Examiner
County Down Spectator
Daily Express
Daily News
Downpatrick Recorder
Drogheda Independent
Drogheda Journal
Dublin Evening Mail
Dublin Evening Packet
Dublin Evening Post
Dublin Evening Press
Dublin Evening Telegraph
Dublin Mercantile Advertiser
Dublin Monitor
Dundalk Democrat
Economist
English Gentleman
Englishwomen's Review
Era
Evening Chronicle
Evening Freeman
Evening Herald
Evening Mail
Evening News
Evening Standard

Examiner
Finn's Leinster Journal
Forward
Freeman's Journal
General Advertiser
Glasgow Herald
Globe
Hibernian Journal
Hull Packet
Illustrated London News
Irish Citizen
Irish Emerald
Irish Felon
Irish Independent
Irish News
Irish Society
Irish Tenant League
Irish Times
Irishman
John Bull
Journal des débats
Journal of the Association for the Preservation of the Memorials of the Dead in Ireland
Kerry Evening Post
Kilkenny Journal
Leader
Leeds Mercury
Leeds Times
Leicester Chronicle
Limerick Examiner
Limerick Reporter
London Dispatch
London Mercury
London Review
Londonderry Journal
Londonderry Sentinel
Londonderry Standard
Manchester Courier
Manchester Guardian
Manchester Times
Morning Advertiser
Morning Chronicle
Morning Post
Morning Register
Nation
National Era
Naval and Military Gazette
Newry Examiner
Newry Herald
Newry Reporter
Newry Telegraph
Newtownards Chronicle
Nonconformist
North Down Herald
North Star
Northern Liberator
Northern Star (Belfast)

Northern Star (Leeds)
Northern Whig
Observer
Pall Mall Gazette
Pilot (Dublin)
Pilot (Rochdale)
Public Advertiser
Queen
Revue des deux mondes
Rochdale Observer
Saunder's News-Letter
Scotsman
Sentinel
Shafts
Sheffield Independent
Southern Australian
Southern Reporter
Spectator
Statesman
Stirling Observer
Struggle
Tablet
Tait's Edinburgh Magazine
Times
Tipperary Free Press
Tipperary Vindicator
Ulster Examiner
Ulster Gazette
Ulsterman
Unitarian Chronicle
United Irishman
Vindicator
Volunteers' Journal
Walker's Hibernian Magazine
Warder
Waterford Standard
Weekly Freeman
Weekly Press
Weekly Register
Weekly Telegraph
Weekly True Sun
Western Daily Press
Western Mail
Western Star
Westminster Gazette
Westminster Magazine
Wexford Independent
Wexford People
Women's Gazette
Women's Penny Paper
Women's Signal
Women's Suffrage Journal
Women's World
Yorkshire Gazette

Printed Primary Sources

Agnew, Jean, ed. *The Drennan-McTier Letters*. 3 vols. Dublin, 1998.

Anon., ed. *A Collection of the Letters Which have been Addressed to the Volunteers of Ireland on the Subject of a Parliamentary Reform*. London, 1783.

———. *A Letter to Wm. Sharman Crawford, Esq., MP, on the Condition of Ireland. With an Appendix Containing Extracts from Letters on the State of Ireland, Written Between the Years, 1829 & 1843. By TDD*. Cheltenham, 1844.

———. *An Account of the Belfast Review and Celebration of the French Revolution. In a Letter to a Friend*. Edinburgh, 1792.

———. *An Address to the Inhabitants of Rochdale and its Vicinity on the Subject of the Present Differences between the Weavers and their Employers*. Rochdale, 1829.

———. *An Historical Account of the Late Election of Knights of the Shire for the County of Down*. [Dublin], 1784.

———. *Annual Report of the Central Committee of the National Society for Women's Suffrage, Presented to the General Meeting, July 7th, 1888*. London, 1888.

———. *Authentic Copies of a Declaration of the Rights of Englishmen; A Bill for a Reform in Parliament: And a Letter to Lieut. Col. Sharman, by His Grace the Duke of Richmond*. London, 1794.

———. *Belfast and County Down Railway: Extension from Comber to Downpatrick with Branch from Saintfield to Ballynahinch: Declaration in Favour of the Above Extension*. London, 1853.

———. *Belfast Election: A Collection of Squibs and Songs Issued Prior to the Contest for the Representation of the Borough*. Belfast, 1832.

———. *Cases of Tenant Eviction, from 1840 to 1846, Extracted from the Public Journals*. n.p., 1846.

———. *Christmas Offering: Ireland's Landlord and Tenants' Rights Vindicated, Ejectment-Process Terminated, and Peace Established. By Verax*. Dublin, 1843.

———. *Concise Compendium of Military Manoeuvres, Represented by Accurate Engravings, … Particularly Addressed to the Irish Volunteers*. Dublin, 1781.

———, *County of Down Election, 1805. The Patriotic Miscellany, a Collection of all the Publications During the Late Election between the Hon. Colonel John Meade, and the Right Hon. Lord Viscount Castlereagh*. London: n.p., 1805.

———. *Crawfordsburn House, Crawfordsburn, Co. Down: Important Sale by Auction of the Contents of the Above Residence*. Belfast, 1947.

———. *Electors of the Borough of Belfast Registered at the Special Sessions under the Reform Act; Distinguishing how Each of Them Voted at the First Election*. Belfast, 1833.

———. *First General Report of the Society for Promoting Annual Sessions of the Imperial Parliament in Dublin for the Transaction of Irish Business*. Dublin, 1848.

———. 'In Algeria with a poet'. *Duffy's Hibernian Magazine* 3 (Jan. 1863): 44-53.

———. *Ireland: Observations on the People, the Land, the Law, in 1851, with Especial Reference to the Policy and Practice of the Incumbered Estates Court*. 2nd edn. Dublin, 1851.

———. *Letters by a Farmer: Originally Published in the Belfast Evening Post*. Belfast, 1787.

———. *Memoir of the Chartist Agitation in Dundee*. Dundee, 1889.

———. *Narrative of the Proceedings of the Contested Election for the County of Down in the Year 1830; With the Squibs, Placards, Songs etc etc. Also with the publications of the Down Elector and Notes and Illustrations by the Same. Published by an Eye-Witness*. Belfast, 1830.

———. *Observations on the People, the Land, and the Law, in 1851; with Especial Reference to the Policy and Practice of he Incumbered Estates Court*. Dublin, 1851.

———. *Our Natural Rights: A Pamphlet for the People. By One of Themselves. Dedicated to William Sharman Crawford*. Belfast, 1836.

———. *Parliamentary Gazetteer of Ireland*. 3 vols. Dublin, 1846.

———. *Plan of Organization of the People's League*. London, 1848.

———. 'Sketches from a tourist's note-book'. *Belfast Monthly Magazine* 12, no. 68 (31 March 1814): 191–97.

———. *The Annals of Ulster Tenant-Right, by an Antrim Tenant-Farmer*. n.p. [Belfast], 1877.

———. *The Bangor Rout: Ane New Ballad, to the Tune of 'Chevy Chase'*. n.p., 1832.

———. *The Belfast Election of 1832: Catalogue of an Exhibition Held in the Linenhall Library, Belfast, in the Summer of 1967*. Belfast, 1967.

————. *The History of the Proceedings and Debates of the Volunteer Delegates of Ireland, on the Subject of a Parliamentary Reform. Containing the Plan of Parliamentary Reform, the Names of the Delegates, and the State of Borough Representation, &c.* Dublin, 1784.

————. 'The Irish land question'. *Irish Quarterly Review* 4, no. 13 (Jan. 1854): 103–41.

————. *The 'Juvenile' Presbyterian Ministers, Being a Letter Addressed to the Editor of 'The Northern Whig', in Reply to a Speech, Delivered at the County Antrim Election, by the Rev. Dr Cooke; with an Appendix. By a Presbyterian Elector of Down.* Belfast, 1852.

————. *The Manuscripts and Correspondence of James, First Earl of Charlemont. Vol. 1. 1745–1783.* London, 1891.

————, *The Parliamentary Register: Or, History of the Proceedings and Debates of the House of Commons of Ireland.* 2 vols. Dublin, 1784.

————. 'The Tenant League v. Common Sense', *Irish Quarterly Review.* 1, no. 1 (Mar. 1851): 25–45, no. 2 (Jun. 1851): 246 –66.

————. *Thoughts on Some Late Removals in Ireland, in a Letter to the Right Honourable the Earl of Kildare. To Which is Annexed, a List of the Members who Voted For and Against the Rejected Money-Bill, and the Expulsion of the Surveyor-General.* London, 1754.

————. *Votes of the House of Commons, in the First Session of the Fourth Parliament of Ireland.* Dublin, 1783.

————. *Women's Suffrage in Ireland,* [Dublin], 1878.

Atkinson, A. *Ireland Exhibited to England in a Political and Moral Survey of her Population, and in a Statistical and Scenographic Tour of Certain Districts,.* 2 vols. London, 1823.

Atkinson, Thomas. *Hibernian Eclogues.* Dublin, 1791.

BAAS. *Dublin, 1878. British Association for the Advancement of Science. Second List of Resident and Non-Resident Members and Associates.* Dublin, 1878.

————. *Glasgow 1876. British Association for the Advancement of Science: Forty-Sixth Meeting, 1876. Journal of Sectional Proceedings, No. 3.* Glasgow, 1876.

————. *Glasgow 1876. British Association for the Advancement of Science. Supplementary List of Resident and Non-Resident Members and Associates.* Glasgow, 1876.

Barnes, George. *The Rights of the Imperial Crown of Ireland Asserted and Maintained, Against Edward Cooke, esq. Reputed Author of a Pamphlet, Entitled 'Arguments For and Against an Union, &c.'* Dublin, 1799.

Bassett, George Henry. *County Down Guide and Directory, Including the Borough of Newry, etc.* Dublin, 1886.

Bennett, William. *Narrative of a Recent Journey of Six Weeks in Ireland in Connection with the Subject of Supplying Small Seed to Some of the Remoter Districts.* London, 1847.

Binns, Jonathan. *The Miseries and Beauties of Ireland.* London, 1837.

Blakely, F. *Letters on the Relations Between Landlord and Tenant.* Belfast, 1851.

Bowden, Charles Topham. *A Tour Through Ireland.* Dublin, 1791.

[Bruce, William, and Henry Joy]. *Belfast Politics: Thoughts on the British Constitution [1794].* Edited by John Bew. Dublin, 2005.

Bruce, William, *On the Right and Exercise of Private Judgment: A Sermon on Acts IV, 19-20, Preached on Sunday, July 8, 1860.* Belfast, 1860.

Buckland, Patrick, ed. *Irish Unionism 1885-1923: A Documentary History.* Belfast, 1973.

Bullen, Edward. *Modern Views on the Relations Between Landlord and Tenant, Tenant Right, and Compensation for Improvements.* London, 1853.

Burgh, U.H. Hussey de. *The Landowners of Ireland: An Alphabetical List of the Owners of Estates of 500 Acres or £500 Valuation and Upwards, in Ireland.* Dublin, 1878.

Burtchaell, George Dames, ed. *Alumni Dublinenses: A Register of the Students, Graduates, Professors, and Provosts of Trinity College, in the University of Dublin 1593-1860.* London, 1924.

Butt, Isaac. *The Rate-in-Aid: A Letter to the Right. Hon. the Earl of Roden,* Dublin, 1849.

————. *Land Tenure in Ireland: A Plea for the Celtic Race.* Dublin, 1866.

Cahill, Daniel. *Dr Cahill on Tenant-Right; Saturday, the 17th of January, 1857.* Dublin, 1857.

Chalmers, Thomas C. *Sermons Preached on Public Occasions.* Glasgow, n.d.

Chart, D.A., ed. *The Drennan Letters.* Belfast, 1931.

[Complete Suffrage Union]. *Minutes of the Proceedings at the Conference of Representatives, of the Middle and Working Classes of Great Britain, held at the Waterloo Rooms and Afterwards at the Town Hall, Birmingham, April 5th, 1842, and Three Following Days*. Birmingham, 1842.

———. *The Rise and Progress of the Complete Suffrage Movement, Reprinted from the Eclectic Review*. London, 1843.

Conner, William. *A Letter to the Tenantry of Ireland: Containing an Exposition of the Rackrent System: And Pointing Out a Valuation and Perpetuity as its Only Effectual Remedy*. Dublin, 1850.

———. *The Axe Laid to the Root of Irish Oppression; and a Sure and Speedy Remedy, for the Evils of Ireland*. Dublin, 1851.

———. *The Catechism of Valuation and Perpetuity of Tenure*. Dublin, 1850.

———. *The True Political Economy of Ireland: Or Rack-Rent, the One Great Cause of Her Evils, with its Remedy*. Dublin, 1835.

———. *Two Letters to the Editor of The Times on the Rackrent Oppression of Ireland, its Source – its Evils – and its Remedy – in Reply to the Times Commissioner*. Dublin, 1846.

Connery, James. *An Essay on Charitable Economy, Upon the Loan Bank System, Called on the Continent 'Mont de Piété,' that is, the Mount, or Rather the Heap, for the Distribution of Charity; Being an Antidote to Counteract the Baneful Effects of Pawnbroking*. Dublin, 1836.

[Craig. Andrew], 'An autobiographical sketch of Andrew Craig, 1754–1833. Presbyterian minister of Lisburn (continued)'. *Ulster Journal of Archaeology*, 2nd ser., 14, no. 2/3 (1908): 51–5.

Crawford, Mabel Sharman. 'Experiences of an Irish landowner'. *Contemporary Review* 52 (August 1887): 263–74.

———. *Life in Tuscany*. London, 1859.

———. 'Maltreatment of wives'. *Westminster Review* 139, no. 1 (Jan. 1893): 292–303.

———. 'Social scares'. *The Woman's World* 1 (Aug. 1888): 433–6.

———. *The Irish Question: Experiences of an Irish Landowner*. London, 1888.

———. *The Wilmot Family*. 3 vols. London, 1864.

[Crawford, Mabel Sharman], ed. *Opinions of Women on Women's Suffrage*. London, 1879.

———. *Through Algeria*. London, 1863.

Crawford, W.H., ed. *Letters from an Ulster Land Agent 1774-85 (The Letter-Books of John Moore of Clough, County Down)*. Belfast, 1976.

Crawford, William Sharman. *A Defence of the Rights of the Working Classes*. London, 1843.

———. *A Defence of the Small Farmers of Ireland*. Dublin, 1839.

———. *A Review of Circumstances Connected with the Past and Present State of the Protestant and Catholic Interests in Ireland; Also, of the Principal Arguments For and Against the Legislative Union, Particularly as Connected with Those Interests; and Suggestions with Reference to the Necessity of Constituting a National Body to Manage the Local Interests and Local Taxation of Ireland, in Connection with the Imperial Parliament*. Belfast, 1833.

———. *Depopulation Not Necessary: An Appeal to the British Members of the Imperial Parliament Against the Extermination of the Irish People*. 2nd edn. London, 1850.

———. *Letter to Lord Dufferin and Claneboy*. Belfast, 1832.

———. 'Observations on Irish policy, addressed to British reformers'. *Tait's Edinburgh Magazine* 5 (1838): 552–54.

———. *Observations on the Irish Tithe Bill Passed by the House of Commons in the Last Session of the Imperial Parliament, Submitted to the Consideration of the Electors of Dundalk in Letters Addressed to William Brett, esq*. Dundalk, 1835.

———. *Observations; Shewing the Necessity of an Amendment in the Laws of Landlord and Tenant, in Conjunction with a Total Repeal of the Duties on Foreign Corn; and also Shewing the Propriety of all Classes of the People, in the United Kingdom, Joining in the Call for These Two Measures of Practical Reform*. Belfast, 1837.

———. *Royal Irish Rifle Volunteers: Irish Volunteers, Past and Present*. Dublin, 1860.

———. *Suggestions with Reference to the Necessity of Constituting a National Body to Manage the Local Interests and Local Taxation of Ireland, in Connection with the Imperial Parliament*. Dublin, 1892.

———. *The Expediency and Necessity of a Local Legislative Body in Ireland, Supported by Reference to Facts and Principles*. Newry, 1833.

————. *The Non-Elector's Plea for the Suffrage: Addressed to the Non-Electors of Rochdale ... Containing an Abstract of His Speech of 1843, in Moving the Reform Bill of the Complete Suffrage Association*. Rochdale, 1859.

[Croker, John Wilson]. 'Repeal agitation'. *Quarterly Review* 75 (Dec. 1844): 222–92.

Daunt, W.J. O'Neill. *Ireland and Her Agitators*. New edn, Dublin, 1867.

————. *Letters of W.J. O'Neill Daunt, Esq. in Answer to Wm. Sharman Crawford, Esq. on the Repeal of the Union*. Dublin, 1843.

Davitt, Michael, *The Fall of Feudalism in Ireland; or, the Story of the Land League Revolution*. London, 1904.

Day, Angelique, and Patrick McWilliams. Ed. *Ordnance Survey Memoirs of Ireland, Vol 7. Parishes of County Down, II, 1832–4, 1837. North Down and the Ards*. Belfast, 1991.

[Dease, James Arthur]. 'Tenant compensation in Ireland'. *Edinburgh Review* 125 (Jan. 1867): 187–218.

Dinnen, Alexander R. *Ulster Tenant Right. Mr Jas. Sharman Crawford's Amendment Bill, and 'No Surrender'*. Belfast, 1876.

Dobbs, Conway E. *Some Observations on the Tenant-Right of Ulster: A Paper Read Before the Dublin Statistical Society*. Dublin, 1849.

Dobbs, Francis, *Universal History, Commencing with the Creation*. 8 vols. Dublin, 1787-1800.

[Doyle, John]. *HB Sketches No. 458, 'A Scene from Hudibras'*. London, 1836.

————. *HB's Sketches No. 466, 'Another Scene from Hudibras'*. London, 1837.

————. *HB's Sketches No. 822. 'Dropping it Like a Red Hot poker!'*. London, 1844.

[Drysdale, George]. *The Irish Land Question. By G.R.* 2nd ed. London, 1869.

Duffy, Charles Gavan. *My Life in Two Hemispheres*. 2 vols. London, 1898.

————. *The League of North and South: An Episode in Irish History, 1850–54*. London, 1886.

————. *Thomas Davis: The Memoirs of an Irish Patriot, 1840–46*. London, 1890.

————. *Young Ireland: A Fragment of Irish History 1840–50*. London, 1880.

————, George Sigerson and Douglas Hyde, *The Revival of Irish Literature*. London, 1894.

Evans, John. *Lancashire Authors and Orators: A Series of Literary Sketches of Some of the Principal Authors, Divines, Members of Parliament, etc, Connected with the County of Lancaster*. London, 1850.

Fagan, William, *The Life and Times of Daniel O'Connell*. 2 vols. Cork, 1847–8.

Ferguson, William Dwyer. *Literary Appropriations and the Irish Land Bills of the Late Government*. Dublin, 1853.

Ferguson, William Dwyer, and Andrew Vance. *The Tenure and Improvement of Land in Ireland Considered with Reference to the Relation of Landlord and Tenant, and Tenant-Right*. Dublin, 1851.

Fishwick, Henry. *The History of the Parish of Rochdale*. Rochdale, 1889.

Fitzpatrick, W.J. *Correspondence of Daniel O'Connell, the Liberator*. 2 vols. London, 1888.

Foot, M.R.D., and H.C.G. Matthew, eds. *The Gladstone Diaries. Vol. 3, 1840–47*. Oxford, 1974.

Fortescue, Chichester. *Irish Land Bill: Second Reading: Speech of the Right Hon. Chichester Fortescue, MP, House of Commons, Monday, March 7th, 1870*. London, 1870.

Foster, Thomas Campbell. *Letters on the Condition of the People of Ireland*. London, 1846.

Gaskell, Ernest, ed. *Ulster Leaders: Social and Political*. London, 1920.

General Railway Committee. *General Railway Committee Appointed at a Public Meeting Held at the Commercial Buildings on Friday, the 22nd. Day of November, 1838*. Dublin, 1838.

Godkin, James. *The Land-War in Ireland: A History for the Times*. London, 1870.

Gordon, James. *Terraquea; or, a New System of Geography and Modern History. By the Rev. James Gordon, Vicar of Barragh, in Ireland*. 4 vols. Dublin, 1794.

[Grant, Henry]. *Ireland's Hour*. London, 1850.

[Grant, James]. *Random Recollections of the House of Commons, From the Year 1830 to the Close of 1835, Including Personal Sketches of the Leading Members of all Parties*. London, 1836.

Greer, Samuel M. *A Land Purchase Scheme for Ireland*. n.p., 1886.

————. *Freedom of Agriculture: Or the Necessity of Adequate Compensation for Permanent Improvements*. Dublin, 1850.

————. *On the Relation between Landlord and Tenant in Ireland: A Paper Read Before the Dublin Statistical Society, on Monday, April 18th, 1853*. Dublin, 1853.

Gurney, Joseph. *The Trial of Thomas Hardy for High Treason, at the Sessions House in the Old Bailey*. 4 vols. London, 1795.

Hamilton, William Tighe. *The Irish Land Bills of the Late Government Considered with Reference to Sounder Legislation for England and Ireland*. Dublin, 1853.

Hancock, W. Neilson. *Impediments to the Prosperity of Ireland*. London, 1850.

———. *The Tenant-Right of Ulster Considered Economically, Being an Essay Read Before the Dublin University Philosophical Society, with an Appendix Containing the Evidence of John Hancock, esq., Taken Before the Landlord and Tenant Commissioners*. Dublin, 1845.

Harris, Walter. *The Antient and Present State of the County of Down: Containing a Chorographical Description, with the Natural and Civil History of the Same*. Dublin, 1744.

Hayes, James. *Irish Waste Land Settlements Versus Emigration and Foreign Wild Land Settlements*. Dublin, 1858.

Hearne, Dana, ed. *Anna Parnell, The Tale of a Great Sham*. Dublin, 2020.

Henderson, J.A., ed. *Henderson's Belfast Directory and Northern Repository*. Belfast, 1852.

———, ed. *The Belfast and Province of Ulster Directory for 1863-64*. Belfast, 1863.

Henderson, W.D. *Lecture on the History and Origin of Ulster Tenant-Right. Delivered Before the National Reform Union, Manchester, March 20, 1877*. Manchester, 1877.

———. *Ulster Tenant-Right: An Historic and Economic Sketch … To Which is Added, a Letter to The Times, by the Right Honourable Lord Waveney*. Belfast, 1875.

Heron, D. Caulfield. 'Should the tenant of land possess the property in the improvements made by him?' *Transactions of the Dublin Statistical Society* 3 (Feb. 1851): 1–28.

Hertford, Earl of. *A Letter to the Belfast First Company of Volunteers, in the Province of Ulster*. Belfast, 1782.

[Hoey, J.C.]. 'The land bill and the lords'. *Dublin Review* 15, no. 29 (Jul. 1870): 178–85.

Holland, Denis. *The Landlord in Donegal: Pictures from the Wilds*. Belfast, 1858.

Holyoake, G. Jacob. *The Advantages and Disadvantages of Trade Unions*. Sheffield, 1841.

———. *The History of the Rochdale Pioneers, 1844–1892*. 3rd edn. London, 1900.

Hope, James, 'Autobiography of James Hope'. In *The United Irishmen: Their Lives and Times*. Ed. R.R. Madden. 3rd series. 3 vols. Dublin, 1846. I, 218–95.

Howe, Anthony, ed. *The Letters of Richard Cobden. Vol. 1, 1815–47*. Oxford, 2007.

Howorth, Franklin. *Reflections on the Distress of the Poor. An Address Occasioned by the Late Riots in the Manufacturing Districts and the Fatal Affray at Rochdale, etc*. Rochdale, 1829.

[Jeffrey, Francis, and William Bernard MacCabe]. 'Measures for Ireland'. *Dublin Review* 22, no. 43 (Mar. 1847): 230–60.

Jones, William Todd. *A Letter to the Electors of the Borough of Lisburn. By One of Their Representatives*. Dublin, 1784.

Kennedy, Brian A., ed. 'Select document: Sharman Crawford on repeal, 1847'. *Irish Historical Studies* 6, no. 24 (1947): 270–3.

Keogh, William. *Speech Delivered by William Keogh, Esq., MP, QC, at the Banquet Given to Him by his Constituents in Athlone, on the 28th of October, 1851*. Dublin, 1851.

Keon, Miles Gerald. *The Irish Revolution; or, What can the Repealers do? And What Shall be the New Constitution? Being a Refutation of the Arguments of the Rev. Dr Martyn, and of the Famous Objection of Mr Sharman Crawford: With a Word on Civil War, Conciliation, and a Third Course*. Dublin, 1843.

Kilpatrick, Cecil, ed. *The Formation of the Orange Order 1795–98: The Edited Papers of Colonel William Blacker and Colonel Robert H. Wallace*. Belfast, 1994.

Kohl, J.G. *Travels in Ireland*. London, 1844.

Lahee, M.R. *Life and Times of the Late Alderman T. Livsey*. Manchester, n.d. [1865].

Laing, Samuel. *Notes of a Traveller on the Social and Political State of France, Prussia, Switzerland, Italy, and Other Parts of Europe, During the Present Century*. London, 1842.

[Lambert, H.], *A Memoir of Ireland in 1850. By an Ex-MP*. Dublin, 1851.

Lancaster, Joseph. *Epitome of Some of the Chief Events and Transactions in the Life of Joseph Lancaster*. New Haven, 1833.

Larkin, Emmet, ed. *Alexis de Tocqueville's Journey in Ireland, July–August 1835*. New York, 1990.

Latimer, W.T. *Ulster Biographies, Chiefly Relating to the Rebellion of 1798*. Belfast, 1897.

Lawless, John. *The Belfast Politics Enlarged; Being a Compendium of the Political History of Ireland for the Last Forty Years*. Belfast, 1818.

Lennon, John, *The 'Irish Repealer's Mountain Harp,' of the Triumphant Year of 1843. Poems, Most Respectfully and Gratefully Dedicated to Daniel O'Connell, Esq., MP, the Transcendent Liberator of Ireland.* Dublin, 1843.

Le Quesne, Charles. *Ireland and the Channel Islands, or, a Remedy for Ireland.* London, 1848.

Lewis, Samuel. *A Topographical Dictionary of Ireland.* 2 vols. London, 1837.

London Society for Women's Suffrage. *Report of the Executive Committee Presented at the Annual General Meeting, November 6th, 1907.* London, 1907.

London Working Men's Association. *The People's Charter; with the Address to the Radical Reformers of Great Britain and Ireland, and a Brief Sketch of its Origin.* London, 1848.

Lovett, William. *The Life and Struggles of William Lovett, in the Pursuit of Bread, Knowledge and Freedom.* London, 1876.

Lucas, Edward. *The Life of Frederick Lucas, MP.* 2nd edn. 2 vols. London, 1887.

Luckombe, Philip. *A Tour through Ireland, Wherein the Present State of that Kingdom is Considered.* Dublin, 1780.

Lysaght, Edward. *A Consideration of the Theory that the Backward State of Agriculture in Ireland is a Consequence of the Excessive Competition for Land.* Dublin, 1851.

MacHale, John. *The Letters of the Most Reverend John MacHale, DD.* Dublin, 1847.

MacKnight, Thomas. *Ulster as It Is; or, Twenty-Eight Years' Experience as an Irish Editor.* 2 vols. London, 1896.

MacNevin, Thomas. *The History of the Volunteers of 1782.* 4th edn. Dublin, 1845.

Madden, Richard Robert. *The Connexion Between the Kingdom of Ireland and the Crown of England.* Dublin, 1845.

Maguire, W.A., ed. *Letters of a Great Irish Landlord: A Selection from the Estate Correspondence of the Third Marquess of Downshire, 1809–45.* Belfast, 1974.

Mathews, George. *An Account of the Regium Donum Issued to the Presbyterian Church of Ireland, with the Number Belonging to Each Congregation of Presbyterians, Methodists, Independents and other Dissenters.* Dublin, 1836.

Matthew, H.C.G. *The Gladstone Diaries: With Cabinet Minutes and Prime-Ministerial Correspondence. Vol. 7, January 1869–June 1871.* Oxford, 1982.

———, ed. *The Gladstone Diaries: With Cabinet Minutes and Prime-Ministerial Correspondence. Vol. 9 January 1875–December 1880.* Oxford, 1986.

———, ed. *The Gladstone Diaries: With Cabinet Minutes and Prime-Ministerial Correspondence. Vol. 12 1887–91.* Oxford, 1994.

———, ed. *The Gladstone Diaries: With Cabinet Minutes and Prime-Ministerial Correspondence. Vol. 13 1892–96.* Oxford, 1994.

McAlester, Charles James, *The Trinity and the Athanasian Creed: A Sermon Preached in the Meeting-House of the First Presbyterian Congregation, Holywood, on Sunday, 20th August, 1854.* Belfast, 1854.

McClintock, Aileen and W. R. Robertson. Eds. 'On the present condition of agriculture in the counties of Cork and Kerry, February 1867: a report by W. R. Robertson'. *Analecta Hibernica*, 40 (2007): 231–51.

[McComb, William and James McKnight]. *The Repealer Repulsed! A Correct Narrative of the Rise and Progress of the Repeal Invasion of Ulster: Dr. Cooke's Challenge and Mr. O'Connell's Declinature, Tactics, and Flight.* Belfast, 1841.

McDowell, R.B., T.W. Moody, and C.J. Woods, eds. *The Writings of Theobald Wolfe Tone 1763–98, Vol. 1: Tone's Career in Ireland to June 1795.* Oxford, 1998.

McGee, Thomas D'Arcy. *A Life of the Rt. Rev. Edward Maginn, Coadjutor Bishop of Derry: with Selections from his Correspondence.* New York, 1857.

McKnight, James. *Extracts from Original Letters of James McKnight, LL.D., Litterateur and Land Reformer, Editor of the 'Belfast News-Letter,' and 'Londonderry Standard.' Ninth annual report of the Presbyterian Historical Society of Ireland, 1915–16.* Belfast, 1916.

———. *The Ulster Tenant's Claim of Right, or Land Ownership a State Trust; the Ulster Tenant Right an Original Grant from the British Crown, and the Necessity of Extending its General Principle to the Other Provinces of Ireland Demonstrated: in a Letter to Lord John Russell.* Dublin, 1848.

[McKnight, James]. *A Catechism of Tenant-Right: Being an Attempt to Set Forth and Defend the Rights of the Tenant-Farmers, Point out Some of the Grievances Under Which They Labour, with Remedies for Their Removal. By the Secretary of a Tenant-Right Association.* 2nd edn. Belfast, 1850.

[McMahon, Patrick]. 'Prosperity of Ireland', *Dublin Review*, 28 (Jun. 1850): 399–420.

McNeill, Ronald. *Ulster's Stand for the Union*. London, 1922.

Mill, John Stuart. *Principles of Political Economy: With Some of Their Applications to Social Philosophy*. 2 vols. London, 1848.

Mitchel, John. *The Last Conquest of Ireland (Perhaps)*. Glasgow, 1861.

Mitchell, T. *Gleanings from Travels in England, Ireland and Through Italy, or Comparative View of Society at Home and Abroad*. 2 vols, Belfast, n.d.

[Molesworth, J.E.N.]. *Correspondence between Wm. Sharman Crawford, Esq., MP for Rochdale, and Rev. Dr. Molesworth, Vicar of the Same, on the Papal Aggression, and on the Spiritual Liberties and Temporal Rights of the Established Church*. London, 1851.

Molesworth, John Edward Nassau. *Remarks on Church Rates and the Rochdale Contest*. Rochdale, 1841.

———. *The Rochdale Magistracy. Copy of a Letter Extracted from the 'Manchester Courier', January 8th, 1842, from the Rev. J.E.N. Molesworth, DD, Vicar of Rochdale, to Clement Royds, Esq. Senior Magistrate*. Rochdale, 1842.

Molloy, Joseph *Belfast Scenery, in Thirty Views*. Belfast, 1832.

Moore, Maurice G. *An Irish Gentleman: George Henry Moore; His Travel, His Racing, His Politics*. London, 1913.

Morgan, Lady, *Italy*. 3 vols. Paris, 1821.

Napier, Joseph. *The Landlord and Tenant Bills: Reply of the Right Hon. Joseph Napier to the Letter of the Earl of Donoughmore on the Landlord and Tenant Bills of the Last Session*. Dublin, 1853.

———. *The Speech of Joseph Napier, Esq. on Mr. Trelawny's Amendment to Mr S. Crawford's Motion for the Second Reading of the Outgoing Tenants (Ireland) Bill. In the House of Commons, Wednesday, April 5th, 1848*. London, 1848.

National Complete Suffrage Union. *The Rise and Progress of the Complete Suffrage Movement. Reprinted from the Eclectic Review*. London, 1843.

National Society for Women's Suffrage. *Annual Reports of the Central Committee of the National Society for Women's Suffrage*. [London], 1875, 1883–7.

National Union of Women's Suffrage Societies. *Report of the Executive Committee Presented at the Annual General Meeting, November 27th, 1901*. London, 1901.

Nicholson, Asenath. *Annals of the Famine in Ireland, in 1847, 1848 and 1849*. New York, 1851.

O'Brien, R. Barry. *Parliamentary History of the Irish Land Question, From 1829 to 1869; and the Origin and Results of the Ulster Custom*. London, 1880.

O'Connell, John. *An Argument for Ireland*. Dublin, 1844.

———. 'Ireland and her present necessities'. *Tait's Edinburgh Magazine* 14 (Jan. 1847): 39–44.

———. *Letters to Friends in Connaught, Respectfully Addressed to Various Parties in That Province*. Dublin, 1843.

O'Connell, M.R., ed. *Correspondence of Daniel O'Connell*. 8 vols. Blackrock, 1972–80.

O'Connor, Feargus. *A Practical Work on the Management of Small Farms*. 5th edn. Manchester, 1847.

———. *A Series of Letters from Feargus O'Connor, Esq., Barrister at Law, to Daniel O'Connell, Containing a Review of Mr. O'Connell's Conduct during the Agitation of the Question of Catholic Emancipation*. London, 1836.

[O'Malley, Thaddeus]. *The Federalist, or a Series of Papers Showing How to Repeal the Union so as to Avoid a Violent Crisis, and, at the Same Time, Secure and Reconcile All Interests. By a Minister of Peace*. Dublin, 1831.

Osborne, Ralph. *Speech of Ralph Osborne, Esq., MP, on Mr Sharman Crawford's Motion 'On the Distracted State of Ireland': July 28, 1848*. London, 1848.

[O'Sullivan, Samuel]. 'Tenant-right'. *Dublin University Magazine* 31, no. 184 (Apr. 1848): 498–512.

Pearce, John, ed. *The Life and Teachings of Joseph Livesey, Comprising his Autobiography with an Introductory Review of His Labours as Reformer and Teacher*. London, 1885.

Perraud, Adolphe. *Études sur l'Irlande contemporain*. 2 vols, Paris, 1862.

Porter, J., *What is Protestantism? A Discourse Preached on Sunday, December 26, 1858, in the Second Presbyterian Church, Belfast*. Belfast, 1859.

Porter, John Grey V. *Agricultural and Political Irish Questions Calmly Discussed*. London, 1843.

————. *Ireland: The Union of 1801, 41 Geo. III., Cap. 47, (All On One Side), Does and Always Will Draw Away from Ireland Her Men of Skill, … A Federal (the Only Fair) Union Between Great Britain and Ireland Inevitable, … Lord John Russell and the Whigs, Better Conservatives than Sir Robert Peel and the Tories*. London, 1844.

————. *Some Calm Observations Upon Irish Affairs*. Dublin, 1844.

RAISI. *First Report of the Royal Agricultural Improvement Society of Ireland*. Dublin, 1841.

Ramon, Marta, ed. *'The Faith of a Felon' and Other Writings by James Fintan Lalor*. Dublin, 2012.

[Rice, Thomas Spring]. 'Ireland'. *Edinburgh Review* 57 (Apr. 1833): 248–79.

Richard, Henry. *Memoirs of Joseph Sturge*. London, 1864.

[Richardson, R.J.]. *New Movement: Household Suffrage, Triennial Parliaments, Vote by Ballot, No Property Qualification, and Equal Electoral Districts: Advocated in a Letter from John Bright, Esq., MP, and a Reply by R.J. Richardson*. Manchester, 1848.

Richmond and Lennox, Charles, Duke of. *A Letter of His Grace the Duke of Richmond, in Answer to the Queries Proposed by a Committee of Correspondence in Ireland, on the Subject of a Parliamentary Reform*. London, 1783.

Robertson, William. *The Social and Political History of Rochdale*. Rochdale, 1889.

Rogers, John. *The Speech of the Rev. John Rogers, Comber, at the Tenant-Right Soirée at Anaghlone, on the 9th December Last, in Reply to the Attack of the Rev. Drs. Cooke and Montgomery, at the Hillsborough Dinner, on the Tenant Farmers of Ireland, with Extracts from the Speeches of these Gentlemen. Also, Dr. Cooke's Certificate of Character to Mr James Martin; with Notes and Comments*. Belfast, 1851.

Russell, John, Earl. *A Letter to the Right Hon. Chichester Fortescue, MP, on the State of Ireland*. 3rd edn., London, 1868.

Russell, T.W. *Ireland and the Empire: A Review 1800–1900*. London, 1901.

[Scott, John Robert]. *A Review of the Principal Characters of the Irish House of Commons*. Dublin, 1789.

Scott, John Robert. *Parliamentary Representation: Being a Political and Critical Review of All the Counties, Cities, and Boroughs of the Kingdom of Ireland*. Dublin, 1790.

Scrope, George Poulett. *How is Ireland to be Governed? A Question Addressed to the New Administration of Lord Melbourne in 1834, with a Postscript in Which the Same Question is Addressed to the Administration of Sir Robert Peel in 1846*. 2nd edn. London, 1846.

[Scrope, George Poulett]. 'Poor-law for Ireland'. *Quarterly Review* 44 (Feb. 1831): 511–54.

Scully, Vincent. *Free Trade in Land Explained*. Dublin, 1854.

————. *The Irish Land Question, with Practical Plans for an Improved Land Tenure, and a New Land System*. Dublin, 1851.

[Senior, William Nassau]. 'Ireland', *Edinburgh Review* 79 (Jan. 1844): 189–266.

[Sharman, William]. *Letter from the Committee of Ulster Volunteers to the Duke of Richmond; the Duke of Richmond's Answer; Together with his Bill for a Parliamentary Reform. 1783*. [Belfast], n.p., 1783.

Shee, George. *To Sir Charles Gavan Duffy K.C.M.G: a remonstrance*. Dublin, 1886.

Shee, William. *Papers, Letters, and Speeches in the House of Commons, on the Irish Land Question*. London, 1863.

[Shee, William]. *The Tenants' Improvements Compensation (Ireland) Bill*. London, 1855.

Stevenson, John, ed. *A Frenchman's Walk Through Ireland, 1796–7, Translated from the French of de Latocnaye*. Belfast, 1917.

[Tait, William]. 'William Sharman Crawford, esq., upon the Irish tithes bill', *Tait's Edinburgh Magazine* 6 (Dec. 1835): 822–3.

Temple, John. *What is Property? Observations on Property Addressed to the King, the Lords and the Commons*. London, 1836.

Thom, A., ed. *Thom's Irish Almanac for 1866*. Dublin, 1866.

[Trenwith, William H.]. *The Case of the Tenant Farmers; as Illustrated in a Series of Letters Originally Published in the Cork Examiner; by 'A Tenant Farmer' and Leading to a Proposition for the Formation of a Tenant League*. Cork, 1846.

Trevelyan, C.E. *The Irish Crisis*. London, 1848.

Wilde, William, ed. *Memoir of Gabriel Beranger, and His Labours in the Cause of Irish Art and Antiquities, from 1760 to 1780*. Dublin, 1880.

[Wolcot, John]. *The Works of Peter Pindar, Esq. With a Copious Index: To Which is Prefixed Some Account of his Life*. 4 vols. London, 1816.

Wyse, Francis. *Federalism. Its Inapplicability to the Wants and Necessities of the Country; Its Assumed Impracticability Considered, with Remarks and Observations on the Rise and Progress of the Present Repeal Movement in Ireland.* Dublin, 1844.

————. *The Irish Tenant League: The Immoral Tendency and Entire Impracticability of its Measures Considered, in a Letter addressed to John O'Connell, Esq., MP; with Observations on the Character and Constitution of the Loyal Repeal Association of Ireland, as also on the Late Political Interference of the Catholic Priesthood.* Dublin, 1850.

SECONDARY SOURCES

Adams, J.R.R. 'Reading societies in Ulster'. *Ulster Folklife* 26 (1980): 55–64.

Ashton, Owen. 'Orators and oratory in the Chartist movement 1840-1848'. In *The Chartist Legacy*, edited by Owen Ashton, Robert Fyson, and Stephen Roberts. Rendlesham, 1999, 48–101.

Atkinson, Edward Dupré. *An Ulster Parish: Being a History of Donaghcloney, Waringstown.* Dublin, 1898.

Barrell, John. *Imagining the King's Death: Figurative Treason, Fantasies of Regicide, 1793-6.* Oxford, 2000.

Beames, Michael. 'Cottiers and conacre in Pre-Famine Ireland'. *Journal of Peasant Studies* 2, no. 3 (1975): 352–54.

Beiner, Guy. *Forgetful Remembrance: Social Forgetting and Vernacular Historiography of a Rebellion in Ulster.* Oxford, 2018.

Belchem, John, '1848: Feargus O'Connor and the collapse of the mass platform'. In *The Chartist Experience: Studies in Working-Class Radicalism and Culture, 1830-60,* ed. by J. Epstein and D. Thompson. London, 1982, pp. 269–310.

————. *Popular Radicalism in Nineteenth-Century Britain.* Basingstoke, 1996.

Belchem, John and James Epstein. 'The nineteenth-century gentleman leader revisited'. *Social History* 22, no. 2 (1997): 174–193.

Belich, James. *The New Zealand Wars and the Victorian Interpretation of Racial Conflict.* Auckland, 1986.

Bell, Jonathan, and Mervyn Watson. *A History of Irish Farming 1750–1950.* Dublin, 2008.

Bell, Thomas. 'The Reverend David Bell'. *Clogher Record* 6, no. 2 (1967): 253–76.

Bender, Jill C. *The 1857 Indian Uprising and the British Empire.* Cambridge, 2016.

Bew, John. *The Glory of Being Britons: Civic Unionism in Nineteenth-Century Belfast.* Dublin, 2008.

Bew, Paul, and Frank Wright. 'The agrarian opposition in Ulster politics, 1848–87'. In *Irish Peasants: Violence and Political Unrest 1780-1914,* ed. by S. Clark and J.S. Donnelly. Dublin, 1983, 192–229.

Bigger, Francis Joseph. 'The National Volunteers of Ireland (continued)'. *Ulster Journal of Archaeology,* 2nd ser., 15, no. 4 (1909): 141–48.

Black, Eileen. 'Volunteer portraits in the Ulster Museum, Belfast'. *Irish Sword,* 13 (1977–9): 181–4.

Black, R.D. Collison. *Economic Thought and the Irish Question, 1817–70.* Cambridge, 1960.

Blackstock, Allan. 'A forgotten army: the Irish Yeomanry'. *History Ireland* 4, no. 4 (1996).

————. *An Ascendancy Army: The Irish Yeomanry, 1796–1834.* Dublin, 1998.

————. 'Tommy Downshire's Boys: popular protest, social change and political manipulation in Mid-Ulster 1829–1847'. *Past and Present,* 196 (2007): 125–72.

Bowman, Timothy. *Carson's Army: The Ulster Volunteer Force, 1910–22.* Manchester, 2007.

————. '"The north began" ... but when? The formation of the Ulster Volunteer Force', *History Ireland* 21, no. 2 (2013): 28–31.

Brown, Heloise, 'An alternative imperialism: Isabella Tod, internationalist and "good Liberal Unionist"'. *Gender and History* 10, no. 3 (1998): 358–80.

Bruce, James. *Ireland's Hope: The 'Peculiar Theories' of James Fintan Lalor.* Wilmington, 2020.

Buckland, Patrick. 'The unity of Ulster Unionism, 1886–1939'. *History* 60 no. 199 (1975): 211–23.

Bryan, Dominic, S.J. Connolly, and John Nagle. *Civic Identity and Public Space: Belfast Since 1780.* Manchester: Manchester University Press, 2019.

Budge, Ian and Cornelius O'Leary. *Belfast Approach to Crisis: a Study of Belfast Politics 1613–1970.* London, 1973.

Bull, Philip. *Land, Politics and Nationalism: A Study of the Irish Land Question.* Dublin, 1996.

Carr, Peter. *Portavo: An Irish Townland and its Peoples, Part 2.* Belfast, 2005.

Casement, Anne. 'The tenant right agitation of 1849–50: crisis and confrontation on the Londonderry estates in County Down'. In *The Land Agent 1700–1920*, ed. by L.A. Rees, C. Reilly, and A. Tindley. Edinburgh, 2018, 133–52.

Casey, Brian (ed). *Defying the Law of the Land: Agrarian Radicals in Irish History*. Dublin, 2013.

Chase, Malcolm. *Chartism: A New History*. Manchester, 2007.

Connolly, S.J., ed. *Belfast 400: People, Place and History*. Liverpool, 2012.

Cosgrave, Patrick. 'T.W. Russell and the compulsory-land-purchase campaign in Ulster, 1900–3'. *Irish Historical Studies* 37, no. 146 (2010): 221–40.

Courtney, Roger. *Dissenting Voices: Rediscovering the Irish Progressive Presbyterian Tradition*. Belfast, 2013.

Crawford, W.H. *The Impact of the Domestic Linen Industry in Ulster*. Belfast, 2005.

Curran, Daragh. *The Rise and Fall of the Orange Order During the Famine Years: From Reformation to Dolly's Brae*. Dublin, 2020.

Curtin, Nancy. *The United Irishmen: Popular Politics in Ulster and Dublin, 1791–98*. Oxford, 1994.

D'Arcy, Fergus A. 'Federalist, social radical and anti-sectarian: Thaddeus O'Malley (1797–1877)'. In *Radical Irish Priests, 1660–1970*, ed. by G. Moran. Dublin, 1998, 91–110.

———. 'Religion, radicalism and rebellion in nineteenth-century Ireland: the case of Thaddeus O'Malley'. In *Religion and Rebellion: Historical Studies XX*, ed. by J. Devlin and R. Fanning. Dublin, 1997, 91–110.

Davis, Richard. *The Young Ireland Movement*. Dublin, 1987.

Dawson, Kenneth. *The Belfast Jacobin: Samuel Neilson and the United Irishmen*. Dublin, 2017.

———. 'A house divided: The Belfast Charitable Society in the age of revolution', in *The First Great Charity of This Town: Belfast Charitable Society and its Role in the Developing City*, ed. by O. Purdue. Dublin, 2022, 36–56.

De Brún, Fionntán, *Revivalism and Modern Irish Literature: The Anxiety of Transmission and the Dynamics of Renewal*. Cork, 2019.

Dewey, Clive. 'The rehabilitation of the peasant proprietor in nineteenth-century economic thought'. *History of Political Economy* 6 (1974): 17–47.

Donnelly, James S. 'Hearts of Oak, Hearts of Steel'. *Studia Hibernica* 21 (1981): 7–73.

Dowling, Martin W. *Tenant Right and Agrarian Society in Ulster 1600–1870*. Dublin, 1999.

Elliott, Marianne. *Wolfe Tone: Prophet of Irish Independence*. London, 1989.

Epstein, James. *The Lion of Freedom: Feargus O'Connor and the Chartist Movement, 1832–1842*. London, 1982.

Farrell, Sean. 'Building opposition: the Mant controversy and the Church of Ireland in early Victorian Belfast'. *Irish Historical Studies* 39 (2014): 230–49.

———. *Rituals and Riots: Sectarian Violence and Political Culture in Ulster, 1784–1886*. Lexington, 2000.

Foster, R.F. *Charles Stewart Parnell: The Man and his Family*. Hassocks, 1976.

Geoghegan, Patrick. *Robert Emmet: A Life*. Dublin, 2002.

Gerrard, John. *Leadership and Power in Victorian Industrial Towns, 1830-80*. Manchester, 1983.

Gill, Conrad. *The Rise of the Irish Linen Industry*. Oxford, 1925.

Gilmore, Peter, Trevor Parkhill, and William Roulston. *Exiles of '98: Ulster Presbyterians and the United States*. Belfast, 2018.

Gray, Peter. *Famine, Land and Politics: British Government and Irish Society 1843–50*. Dublin, 1999.

———. '"Hints and Hits": Irish caricature and the trial of Daniel O'Connell, 1843-4'. *History Ireland* 12, no. 4 (2004): 45–51.

———. '"Ireland's last fetter struck off": the lord lieutenancy debate 1800–67'. In *Was Ireland a Colony? Economics, Politics and Culture in Nineteenth-Century Ireland*, ed. by T. McDonough. Dublin, 2005, 87–101.

———. 'Mabel Sharman Crawford's *Life in Tuscany*: Ulster radicalism in a hot climate'. In *Traveling Irishness in the Long Nineteenth Century*, ed. by M. Corporaal and T. Morin. London, 2017, 35–50.

———. 'Nassau Senior, the *Edinburgh Review*, and Ireland 1843–1849'. In *Ideology and Ireland in the Nineteenth Century*, ed. by T. Foley and S. Ryder. Dublin, 1998, 130–42.

———. '"Shovelling out your paupers": the British state and Irish Famine migration, 1846–50'. *Patterns of Prejudice* 33 (1999): 47–65.

———. *The Making of the Irish Poor Law, 1815-43*. Manchester, 2009.

———. 'The making of mid-Victorian Ireland? Political economy and the memory of the Great Famine'. In *Victoria's Ireland? Irishness and Britishness, 1837-1901*, ed. by P. Gray. Dublin, 2004, 151–66.

———. 'William Sharman Crawford, the Famine and County Down'. In *The Great Irish Famine and Social Class: Conflicts, Responsibilities, Representations*, ed. by M. Corporaal and P. Gray. Oxford, 2019, 135–50.

Gribbon, Harry, 'The Irish Linen Board, 1711-1828'. In *The Warp of Ulster's Past*, ed. by M. Cohen. Basingstoke, 1997, 71–92.

Guinnane, Timothy W., and Ronald I. Miller. 'Bonds without bondsmen: tenant-right in nineteenth-century Ireland'. *Journal of Economic History* 56, no. 1 (1996): 113–42.

Haddick-Flynn, Kevin. *Orangeism: A Historical Profile*. Kibworth Beauchamp, 2019.

Hall, Gerald R. *Ulster Liberalism 1778–1876*. Dublin, 2011.

Harbison, Peter. 'Gabriel Beranger (c.1729–1817) in County Down'. *Ulster Journal of Archaeology* 3rd ser., 64 (2005): 154–9.

Hewitt, John. 'Thomas Robinson: portrait of Colonel William Sharman and letter to Thomas Scott'. *Belfast Museum and Art Gallery Bulletin* 1, no. 1 (1949): 1–10.

Higgins, Padhraig. *A Nation of Politicians: Gender, Patriotism and Political Culture in Late Eighteenth-Century Ireland*. Madison, 2010.

Hill, Jacqueline. 'The 1847 general election in Dublin city', in *Politics and Political Culture in Britain and Ireland, 1750-1850*, ed. by A. Blackstock and E. Magennis. Belfast, 2007, 41-64.

Hirst, Catherine. *Religion, Politics and Violence in Nineteenth-Century Belfast: The Pound and Sandy Row*. Dublin, 2002.

Holmes, Andrew R. 'Union and Presbyterian Ulster Scots: William McComb, Thomas McKnight, and *The Repealer Repulsed*'. In *Literature and Unions: Scottish Texts, British Contexts*, ed. by C. Kidd and G. Carruthers. Oxford, 2018, 165–91.

Holmes, A.R. 'Covenanter politics: evangelicalism, political liberalism and Ulster Presbyterians, 1798–1914'. *English Historical Review* 125, no. 513 (2010): 340–69.

Hoppen, K. Theodore. *Elections, Politics and Society in Ireland, 1832–1885*. Oxford, 1984.

Huddle, Paul. *The Crimean War and Irish Society*. Liverpool, 2015.

Illingworth, Ruth. *Sheelagh Murnaghan 1924–1993: Stormont's Only Liberal MP.* Belfast: Ulster Historical Foundation, 2019.

Jackson, Alvin. 'Irish unionism and the Russellite threat, 1894–1906'. *Irish Historical Studies* 25, no. 100 (1987): 376–404.

———. *Sir Edward Carson*. Dublin, 1993.

———. 'Unionist politics and Protestant society in Edwardian Ireland'. *Historical Journal* 33, no. 4 (1990): 839–66.

Johnson, Alice. *Middle-class Life in Victorian Belfast*. Liverpool, 2020.

———. '"Some hidden purpose"? Class conflict and co-operation in Belfast's Working Men's Institute and Temperance Hall 1865–1900'. *Social History* 42, no. 3 (2017): 399-419.

Johnson, D.S. 'The trials of Sam Gray: Monaghan politics and nineteenth-century Irish criminal procedure'. *Irish Jurist* 20, no. 1 (1985): 109–34.

Johnston-Liik, E.M. *MPs in Dublin: Companion to History of the Irish Parliament 1692–1800*. Belfast, 2006.

Jones, David. 'Women and Chartism'. *History* 68, no. 222 (1983): 1–21.

Joyce, Patrick. *Work, Society and Politics: The Culture of the Factory in Late Victorian England*. Brighton, 1980.

Jupp, Peter. 'County Down elections, 1783–1831'. *Irish Historical Studies* 18, no. 70 (1972): 177–206.

Kelly, James. 'Elite political clubs 1770-1800'. In *Clubs and Societies in Eighteenth-Century Ireland*, ed. by J. Kelly and M.J. Powell. Dublin, 2010, 264–89.

———. 'Parliamentary reform in Irish politics, 1760–90'. In *The United Irishmen: Republicanism, Radicalism and Rebellion*, ed. by D. Dickson, D. Keogh and K. Whelan. Dublin, 1993, 74–87.

———. 'Select documents xlii: a secret return of the Volunteers of Ireland in 1784'. *Irish Historical Studies* 26, no. 103 (1989): 268–92.

———. 'The politics of Volunteering, 1778–93'. *Irish Sword* 22, no. 88 (2000): 139–56.

Kendle, John. *Ireland and the Federal Solution: The Debate over the United Kingdom Constitution, 1870–1921*. Kingston and Montreal, 1989.

Kennedy, B.A. 'Sharman Crawford's federal scheme for Ireland'. In *Essays in British and Irish History in Honour of J.E. Todd*, ed. by H.A. Crone, T.W. Moody, and D.B. Quinn. London, 1949, 235–54.
———. 'Sharman Crawford on the repeal question'. *Irish Historical Studies*, 6 (1948–9): 270–3.
Kennedy, Brian A, ed. 'Select document: Sharman Crawford on Ulster tenant right'. *Irish Historical Studies* 13, no. 51 (1963): 246–53.
Kenny, Colum. 'Paradox or pragmatist? "honest" Tristram Kennedy (1805–85): lawyer, educationalist, land agent and member of parliament'. *Proceedings of the Royal Irish Academy* 92C, no. 1 (1992): 1–35.
Keogh, Richard A. '"Nothing is so bad for the Irish as Ireland alone": William Keogh and Catholic loyalty'. *Irish Historical Studies* 38, no. 150 (2012): 230–48.
Kinealy, Christine. '"Brethren in bondage": Chartists, O'Connellites, Young Irelanders and the 1848 uprising'. In *Politics and the Irish Working Class, 1830–1945*, ed. by D. Ó Drisceoil and F. Lane. Basingstoke, 2005, 87–112.
Kingon, Suzanne T. 'Ulster opposition to Catholic emancipation, 1828–9', *Irish Historical Studies*, 34, no. 134 (2004): 137–55.
Kinzer, Bruce L. 'J.S. Mill on Irish land: a reassessment'. *Historical Journal* 27 (1984): 111–27.
Lane, Pádraig G. 'Perceptions of agricultural labourers after the Great Famine, 1850–1870'. *Saothar* 19 (1994): 14–25.
MacDonagh, Oliver. *The Emancipist: Daniel O'Connell 1830–47*. London, 1989.
MacKay, Angus. 'A crop of Bronte myths'. *Westminster Review* 144 (July 1895): 424–37.
Maddox, Neil. '"A melancholy record": the story of the nineteenth-century Irish Party Processions Act'. *Irish Jurist* 39 (2004): 242–73.
Magennis, Eoin, 'Protestant nationalism in Ulster, 1890–1910: Francis Joseph Bigger and the writing of the *Ulster Land War of 1770*'. *Seanchas Ard Mhacha*, 18, no. 2 (2001), 102–16.
Maguire, W.A. *The Downshire Estates in Ireland 1801–45: The Management of Irish Landed Estates in the Early Nineteenth Century*. Oxford, 1972.
Maguire, W.A. 'Lord Donegall and the sale of Belfast: a case history from the Encumbered Estates Court', *Economic History Review*, 29, no. 4 (1976), 570–84.
Mansergh, Danny. *Grattan's Failure: Parliamentary Opposition and the People in Ireland 1779–1800*. Dublin, 2005.
[Masefield, Robin], *Twixt Bay and Burn: A History of Helen's Bay and Crawfordsburn*. n.p., 2011.
Martin, David E. 'The rehabilitation of the peasant proprietor in nineteenth-century economic thought: a comment'. *History of Political Economy* 8 (1976): 297–302.
Matthew, H.C.G. *Gladstone: 1809–74*. Oxford, 1986.
McCavery, Trevor. '"As a plague of locusts come in Egypt": rebel motivation in north Down'. In *1798: A Bicentenary Perspective*, ed. by T. Bartlett, D. Dickson, D. Keogh and K. Whelan. Dublin, 2003, pp. 212–25.
———. *Newtown: A History of Newtownards*. Belfast, 2013.
McMinn, J.R.B. 'The Land League in north Antrim, 1880–82', *The Glynnes* 11 (1983): 35–40.
McMinn, Richard. 'Presbyterianism and politics in Ulster, 1871–1906'. *Studia Hibernica* 21 (1981): 127–146.
McNeill, Mary. *The Life and Times of Mary Ann McCracken 1770–1866: A Belfast Panorama*. New edn. Newbridge, 2019.
Miller, Kerby, and Liam Kennedy. 'Irish migration and demography, 1659–1831'. In *Irish Immigrants in the Land of Canaan: Letters and Memoirs from Colonial and Revolutionary America, 1675–1815*. Oxford, 2003.
Mitchell, James. 'Thomas Skilling (1793–1865) professor of agriculture, Queen's College, Galway: part 1: his career to 1849'. *Journal of the Galway Archaeological and Historical Society* 57 (2005): 65–89.
Morgan, Simon James. *Celebrities, Heroes and Champions: Popular Politicians in the Age of Reform, 1810–67*. Manchester, 2021.
Mulvey, Helen F. *Thomas Davis and Ireland: A Biographical Study*. Washington, 2003.
Neal, Frank. 'Manchester origins of the English Orange Order'. *Manchester Region History Review* 4, no. 2 (January 1990): 12–24.
Nightingale, Eithne. *The Religious and Political Crisis of Rochdale Parish 1825–77*. Rochdale, 1993.

Nowlan, Kevin B. *The Politics of Repeal: A Study of the Relations between Great Britain and Ireland, 1841–50*. London, 1965.

Ó Drisceoil, Donal, and Diarmuid Ó Drisceoil. *Beamish & Crawford: The History of an Irish Brewery*. Cork, 2015.

Ó Luain, Kerron. "'Craven subserviency had vanished. Bitter hostility had arrived": agrarian violence and the Tenant League on the Ulster borderlands, 1849–52'. *Irish Historical Studies* 43, no. 163 (2019): 27–54.

———. 'The Ribbon societies of Counties Louth and Armagh, 1848–64'. *Seanchas Ard Mhacha* 25, no. 1 (2014): 115–41.

Ó Snodaigh, Pádraig. 'Some military and police aspects of the Irish Volunteers'. *Irish Sword* 13 (1977–9): 217–29.

O'Brien, Gillian. "'Spirit, Impartiality and Independence": *The Northern Star*, 1792-1797'. *Eighteenth-Century Ireland* 13 (1998): 7–23.

O'Brien, Jennifer. 'Irish public opinion and the Risorgimento, 1859–60'. In *Nation/Nazione: Irish Nationalism and the Italian Risorgimento*, ed by C. Barr, F. Finelli, and A. O'Connor. Dublin, 2014, 110–32.

O'Brien, R. Barry. *John Bright: A Monograph*. London, 1910.

O'Connor, Emmet and John Cunningham (eds). *Studies in Irish Radical Leadership: Lives on the Left*. Manchester, 2016.

O'Connor, Michael. "'Ears stunned with the din of arms": Belfast, Volunteer sermons and James Magee, 1779–81'. *Eighteenth-Century Ireland* 26 (2011): 51–79.

[O'Donoghue, D.J.], 'Obituary: Mabel Sharman Crawford', *The Irish Book Lover*, 3 (Apr. 1912), 152.

O'Ferrall, Fergus. *Catholic Emancipation: Daniel O'Connell and the Birth of Irish Democracy*. Dublin, 1985.

O'Flaherty, Eamon. 'The Catholic Convention and Anglo-Irish politics, 1791–3'. *Archivium Hibericum* 40 (1985): 14–34.

O'Neill, Marie. 'The Dublin Women's Suffrage Association and its successors'. *Dublin Historical Record* 38, no. 4 (1985): 126–40.

Owens, Gary. 'The Carrickshock incident, 1831: social memory and an Irish cause célèbre'. *Cultural and Social History* 1 (2004): 36–64.

Paterson, T.G.F. 'Lisburn and neighbourhood in 1798'. *Ulster Journal of Archaeology*, 3rd ser., 1 (1938): 194–9, 204–30.

———. 'The Volunteer companies of Ulster, 1778–93'. *Irish Sword* 7 (1965–6): 90–116.

Pickering, Paul A. *Feargus O'Connor: A Political Life*. Monmouth, 2008.

Purdue, Olwen. *The Big House in the North of Ireland: Land, Power and Social Elites, 1878–1960*. Dublin, 2009.

Quinn, James. *John Mitchel*. Dublin, 2008.

———. *Soul on Fire: A Life of Thomas Russell*. Dublin, 2001.

Randall, Don. 'Autumn 1857: the making of the Indian "Mutiny"'. *Victorian Literature and Culture* 31, no. 1 (2003): 3–17.

Reid, Colin W. "'An experiment in constructive unionism": Isaac Butt, home rule and federalist political thought during the 1870s'. *English Historical Review* 129, no. 537 (2014): 332–61.

Riall, Lucy, *Risorgimento: The History of Italy from Napoleon to Nation State*. Basingstoke, 2009.

Ridgway, Christopher. ed. *The Morpeth Roll: Ireland Identified in 1841*. Dublin, 2013.

Ritchie, Daniel. *Isaac Nelson: Radical Abolitionist, Evangelical Presbyterian and Irish Nationalist*. Liverpool, 2018.

———. "'The stone in the sling": Frederick Douglass and Belfast abolitionism'. *American Nineteenth-Century History* 18, no. 3 (2017): 245–72.

Roberts, Matthew. 'Daniel O'Connell, Repeal, and Chartism in the age of Atlantic revolutions'. *Journal of Modern History* 90, no. 1 (2018): 1–39.

Rodgers, Nini. *Equiano and Anti-Slavery in Eighteenth-Century Belfast*. Belfast, 2000.

———. 'Ireland and the black Atlantic in the eighteenth century'. *Irish Historical Studies* 32, no. 126 (2000): 174–92.

Roebuck, Peter. 'Rent movement, proprietorial incomes and agricultural development, 1730–1830'. In *Plantation to Partition: Essays in Ulster History in Honour of J.L. McCracken*. Belfast, 1981: 82–101.

Rogers, Patrick. 'A Protestant pioneer of Catholic emancipation'. *Lisburn Historical Society Journal* 9 (1995).

Rolston, Bill. 'A lying old scoundrel', *History Ireland*, 11, no. 1 (2003): 24–7.

Sellers, Charles. *Oporto, Old and New, Being a Historical Record of the Port Wine Trade*. London, 1899.

Shields, Andrew. *The Irish Conservative Party 1852–1868: Land, Politics and Religion*. Dublin, 2007.

———. 'Joseph Napier and the Irish land bills of 1852'. *Australasian Journal of Irish Studies* 9 (2009): 31–51.

Silvestri, Michael. *Ireland and India: Nationalism, Empire and Memory*. London, 2009.

Simons, Thomas W. 'The peasant revolt of 1846 in Galicia: recent Polish historiography'. *Slavic Review* 30, no. 4 (1971): 795–817.

Sloan, Robert. *William Smith O'Brien and the Young Ireland Rebellion of 1848*. Dublin, 2000.

Small, Stephen. *Political Thought in Ireland, 1776–1798*. Oxford, 2002.

Smilie, Patrick. 'A cautionary antecedent: the Belfast career of John Bruce Wallace'. In *William Walker, 1870–1918, Belfast Labour Unionist, Centenary Essays*, ed. by F. Devine and S. Byers. Dublin, 2018, 15–26.

Smyth, James. *Henry Joy McCracken*. Dublin, 2020.

Smyth, Peter. '"Our cloud-cap't grenadiers": the Volunteers as a military force'. *Irish Sword*, 13 (1977–9): 185–207.

Smyth, P.D.H. 'The Volunteers and parliament, 1779–84'. In *Penal Era and Golden Age: Essays in Irish History 1690–1800*, ed. by T. Bartlett and D. Hayton. Belfast, 1979, 113–36.

Steele, E.D. *Irish Land and British Politics: Tenant-right and Nationality, 1865–1870*. Cambridge, 1974.

Stewart, A.T.Q. *A Deeper Silence: The Hidden Origins of the United Irishmen*. Belfast, 1998.

———. *The Summer Soldiers: The 1798 Rebellion in Antrim and Down*. Belfast, 1995.

Sweeney, Frank. 'The founding of the Tenant League and the 1852 election in Wexford'. *The Past: The Organ of the Uí Cinsealaigh Historical Society* 30 (October 2009): 5–22.

Tesch, Pieter. 'Presbyterian radicalism'. In *The United Irishmen: Republicanism, Radicalism, and Rebellion*, ed. by D. Dickson et al. Dublin, 1993.

Thompson, Dorothy. 'Ireland and the Irish in English radicalism before 1850'. In *The Chartist Experience: Studies in Working-Class Radicalism and Culture 1830–60*, ed. by J. Epstein and D. Thompson. London, 1982, 120–51.

Thompson, Frank. *The End of Liberal Ulster: Land Agitation and Land Reform, 1868–1886*. Belfast, 2001.

Thornley, David. *Isaac Butt and Home Rule*. London, 1964.

Turner, Michael J. 'Ireland and Irishness in the political thought of Bronterre O'Brien'. *Irish Historical Studies* 39, no. 153 (2014): 40–57.

Tyrell, Alex. *Joseph Sturge and the Moral Radical Party in Early Victorian Britain*. London, 1987.

Vance, Norman. 'Volunteer thought: William Crawford of Strabane'. In *Political Discourse in Seventeenth and Eighteenth-Century Ireland*, ed. by D.G. Boyce. Basingstoke, 2001, 257–69.

Vaughan, W.E., *Landlords and Tenants in Mid-Victorian Ireland*. Oxford, 1994.

Walker, Brian M. 'The land question and elections in Ulster, 1868–86'. In *Irish Peasants: Violence and Political Unrest 1780–1914*, ed. by S. Clark and J.S. Donnelly. Dublin, 1983, 230–68.

———. 'Politicians, elections and catastrophe: the general election of 1847'. *Irish Political Studies* 22, no. 1 (2007): 1–34.

Whelan, Fergus. *May Tyrants Tremble: The Life of William Drennan, 1754–1820*. Dublin, 2020.

Whyte, J.H. *The Independent Irish Party 1850–9*. Oxford, 1958.

———. *The Tenant League and Irish Politics in the Eighteen-Fifties*. Dundalk, 1972.

Wilson, David A. *Thomas D'Arcy McGee*. 2 vols, Montreal and Kingston, 2008–11.

———. *United Irishmen, United States: Immigrant Radicals in the Early Republic*. Ithaca, 1998.

Woods, C.J. 'Historical revision: was O'Connell a United Irishman?' *Irish Historical Studies* 34, no. 138 (2006): 173–83.

Wright, Frank. *Two Lands on One Soil: Ulster Politics Before Home Rule*. Dublin, 1996

Wright, Jonathan Jeffrey, ed. *An Ulster Slave-Owner in the Revolutionary Atlantic: The Life and Letters of John Black*. Dublin, 2019.

———. *The 'Natural Leaders' and Their World: Politics, Culture and Society in Belfast, c. 1801–32*. Liverpool, 2012.

Reference Works

Dictionary of Irish Biography. Ed. James McGuire and James Quinn. 9 vols. Cambridge, 2009.
Dictionary of Ulster Biography. Ed. Kate Newmann. Belfast, 1993
Oxford Dictionary of National Biography. Ed. H.C.G. Matthew and Brian Harrison. 60 Vols. Oxford, 2004.
The History of Parliament: The House of Commons 1820–32. Ed. by D.R. Fisher. Cambridge, 2009.

Unpublished dissertations

Beggs-McCormick, Krysta. "'Methinks I see grim Slavery's Gorgon form": abolitionism in Belfast, 1775-1865'. Ph.D., Ulster University, 2018.
Donaldson, David Whamond. 'Britain and Menorca in the eighteenth century'. Ph.D., The Open University, 1994.
Kennedy, Brian A. 'Sharman Crawford, 1780–1861. a political biography'. D.Litt., Queen's University Belfast, 1953.
Kingon, Suzanne T. 'Ulster Protestant politics in the age of emancipation and reform, c.1825–35'. Ph.D., Queen's University Belfast, 2006.
McClure, C.J. 'Aspects of County Down elections, 1820–31'. MA, Queen's University, Belfast, 1986.
Nelson, Julie. "'Violently democratic and anti-conservative": an analysis of Presbyterian "radicalism" in Ulster, c.1800–52'. Ph.D., University of Durham, 2005.

Online Sources

A vision of Britain through time: Rochdale district: (http://www.visionofbritain.org.uk/unit/10076780)
Joe Furphy, 'Crawfordsburn Country Park history' (https://www.myni.life/country-parks/crawfordsburn-country-park/50th-anniversary/crawfordsburn-country-park-history/)
Legacies of British Slave-ownership website (https://www.ucl.ac.uk/lbs)
National Gallery of Ireland website (http://onlinecollection.nationalgallery.ie/objects/360/william-sharman-crawford-mp-17811861-irish-radical-and?ctx=1a36468c-ee41-41f8-994b-e650253fcc50&idx=0)
National Museums of Northern Ireland collections website: (https://www.nmni.com/collections/art)
QUB Centre for Community Archaeology website: (https://www.qub.ac.uk/sites/communityarchaeology/OurProjects/Communityexcavations/MoiraDemense/)

Index